FROM RAIL TO ROAD AND BACK AGAIN?

Modern Economic and Social History Series

General Editor: Derek H. Aldcroft

Titles in this series include:

The American Reaper
Harvesting Networks and Technology, 1830–1910
Gordon M. Winder

Land, Proto-Industry and Population in Catalonia, c. 1680–1829
An Alternative Transition to Capitalism?
Julie Marfany

The Making of a World Trading Power
The European Economic Community (EEC) in the GATT Kennedy Round Negotiations (1963–67)
Lucia Coppolaro

Eastern European Railways in Transition
Nineteenth to Twenty-first Centuries
Edited by Ralf Roth and Henry Jacolin

Vicarious Consumers
Trans-National Meetings between the West and East in the Mediterranean World (1730–1808)
Manuel Pérez-García

National Identity and the Agrarian Republic
The Transatlantic Commerce of Ideas between America and France (1750–1830)
Manuela Albertone

The River Pollution Dilemma in Victorian England
Nuisance Law versus Economic Efficiency
Leslie Rosenthal

British Mail Steamers to South America, 1851–1965
A History of the Royal Mail Steam Packet Company and Royal Mail Lines
Robert E. Forrester

Money Pits: British Mining Companies in the Californian and Australian Gold Rushes of the 1850s
John Woodland

From Rail to Road and Back Again?

A Century of Transport Competition and Interdependency

Edited by

RALF ROTH
Johann Wolfgang Goethe-University, Germany

COLIN DIVALL
University of York, UK

Routledge
Taylor & Francis Group
LONDON AND NEW YORK

First published in paperback 2024

First published 2015 by Ashgate Publishing

Published 2016 by Routledge
4 Park Square, Milton Park, Abingdon, Oxon OX14 4RN

and by Routledge
605 Third Avenue, New York, NY 10158

Routledge is an imprint of the Taylor & Francis Group, an informa business

Publisher's Note
The publisher has gone to great lengths to ensure the quality of this reprint but points out that some imperfections in the original copies may be apparent.

British Library Cataloguing in Publication Data
A catalogue record for this book is available from the British Library

The Library of Congress has cataloged the printed edition as follows:
From rail to road and back again? : a century of transport competition and interdependency / edited by Colin Divall and Ralf Roth.
pages cm
Includes bibliographical references and index.
ISBN 978-1-4094-4046-8 (hardcover)
1. Transportation—Great Britain—History—20th century.
2. Transportation—Europe—History—20th century. 3. Transportation—United States—History—20th century. 4. Railroads—History—20th century. 5. Motor vehicles—History—20th century. 6. Roads—History—20th century. 7. Competition—History—20th century. 8. Great Britain—Economic conditions—20th century.
9. Europe—Economic conditions—20th century. 10. United States—Economic conditions—20th century. I. Divall, Colin. II. Roth, Ralf.
HE243.F76 2015
388.09'04—dc23

2014031160

ISBN 13: 978-1-4094-4046-8 (hbk)
ISBN 13: 978-1-03-291978-2 (pbk)
ISBN 13: 978-1-315-58349-5 (ebk)

DOI: 10.4324/9781315583495

Contents

List of Figures *vii*
List of Tables *ix*
List of Abbreviations *xi*
Notes on Contributors *xv*
General Editor's Preface *xix*
Preface *xxi*

Introduction: From Rail to Road and Back Again? A Century of Transport Competition and Interdependency 1
Ralf Roth

PART I RAILS AND ROADS BETWEEN COMPETITION AND INTERDEPENDENCY

1 Rails and Roads Between Competition and Interdependency: a Long and Winding Relationship with Many Innovations That Failed 41
Ralf Roth

2 Shaping British Freight Transport in the Interwar Period: Failure of Foresight or Administration, 1919–34? 77
Roy Edwards

3 Conceiving Distribution in the United Kingdom: the (London and) North Eastern Railway's Discursive Response to Road Haulage, 1921–39 91
Colin Divall

4 Railway Containers in the United Kingdom and Europe during the 1920s and 1930s 109
Keith Harcourt

5 The Sea Container Revolution and Road-Rail Competition in Britain: a Preliminary Assessment of Freightliner 133
Terry Gourvish

6 Trucking in Germany: Rise and Restricted Growth, 1900–1938 153
Richard Vahrenkamp

7 Road-Rail Competition in France in the 1930s: from a Railway Perspective 171
Bruno Carrière

8 Containerisation in the United States During the Interwar Period 195
Albert J. Churella

PART II MOBILITY ON ROADS: AN INNOVATIVE SUCCESS STORY OF THE TWENTIETH CENTURY – BUT RAIL SURVIVED

9 Creative Destruction? A Schumpeterian View of Innovation in Car Transportation 217
Reiner Flik

10 Inventing the American Road: Innovations Shaping the American Freeway 233
Bruce E. Seely

11 The Development of the European Highway Network: a Literature Survey of Studies on Highway History in European Countries 275
Reiner Ruppmann

12 Motorways and the Modernisation of Britain's Road Network, 1937–70 315
Peter Merriman

13 The Metamorphosis of Public Transport Services in the Paris Region: the Modal and Moral Victory of 'Automobilism' in the 1920s and 1930s 339
Mathieu Flonneau

14 Rails in the Car Kingdom: Competition, Changes and Continuity in Urban Mobility – the Case of Turin, 1914–73 355
Massimo Moraglio

15 The City and the *Autobahn* 1926–56: How Frankfurt am Main Promoted Road Traffic and Realised an Old Dream 373
Reiner Ruppmann

Index *397*

List of Figures

1.1	Map of Central Europe including postal coach services around 1714	42
1.2	Land yacht made by Simon Stevin for Prince Maurice of Orange, 1649	46
1.3	Railway network of Europe 1870 and 1913	51–2
1.4	Road network of Europe: the vision of Kaftan in 1937 …	58
1.5	… and the outcome: the International E-Road Network in 1990	58
1.6	Part of the railway network and postal coach services on streets in the environment of Frankfurt around 1850	61
1.7	Coaches on rail in the planning sketch of List's national railway system for Germany	63
1.8	Freight car carried on a rail car: sketch from a memorandum for a horse railway from Dürrenberg to Leipzig, 1828	64
1.9	*Deutsche Reichsbahn* Street Roller, or *Culemeyer-Straßenroller* R40 of 1935	66
1.10	Remains of the LR 40.9S, among them the *Deutsche Bahn*'s last operable *Culemeyer Roller* (DB 80–671/ DB 67–071) at the railway museum in Darmstadt-Kranichstein	67
1.11	Rolling Road (RoLa) at the Southern ramp of the Lötschberg line, pulled by two Re 465 of the BLS *Lötschbergbahn* in Switzerland	68
1.12	Container Terminal Altenwerder (CTA) in 2004	71
3.1	By the Railway C.O.D. Service. Advertisement of British Railway Companies, 1920s	100
3.2	Use Road-Rail Containers for Every Form of Freight Traffic. Advertisement of British Railway Companies, 1920s	100
3.3	Railway Country Lorry Service. Advertisement of British Railway Companies, 1920s	101
4.1	Southern Railway container No. A337	119
4.2	A 5-ton hand crane No. 200 at Derby, 1938	122
4.3	A 75 horsepower Ford Tractor with the special conveyer trailer	126
4.4	Diagrams about the use of a conveyor trailer in loading and unloading containers	127
5.1	Freightliner train, circa 2009	137

7.1	PLM company's subcontractors waiting for engagement, 1934	174
7.2	Two views of the rail-road wagon 'Willème-Coder', 1933	183
7.3	Advertisement of the car manufacturer Laffly, 1929	184
9.1	Real US-per-capita income – log. scale, 1790–2000	218
9.2	Car density in the USA, by states (1910 and 1920)	219
9.3	Car density in Europe and overseas, 1900–1939	225
9.4	Real per capita income and car density in Western Europe and in the USA, 1900–1999	230
12.1	The 1946 'Tea Room Plan'	321
12.2	Cover of a brochure of the *Railway Conversion League*, 'No alternative!', 1965	324
15.1	Thurn und Taxis stagecoach lines junction at Frankfurt am Main, 1793	375
15.2	Frankfurt am Main railway junction, 1859–1920	376
15.3	Plan of Greater Frankfurt, 1923	378
15.4	The city expansion of Frankfurt alongside the principal streets, 1874–1925	381
15.5	Principal layout of the three-to-four lane HaFraBa highway through Germany, 1926	382
15.6	Frankfurt's depiction of its position in the European expressway system	385
15.7	Scheme for distributing *Autobahn* traffic into the streets of Frankfurt, 1937	388
15.8	The *Autobahn* gap next to Frankfurt	389
15.9	Road network for motorised traffic in the Rhein-Main region	391

List of Tables

0.1	Expansion of the railway networks in the world, 1850–1930 (in kilometres)	3
0.2	Comparison of the railway and road networks in the world in 2002 (in 1,000 kilometres)	18
1.1	Length of railways in the world, 1850 to 1930 (in kilometres)	56
5.1	Freightliners Ltd results, 1969–78	144
5.2	Freightliners Ltd results, 1979–87/88	146
5.3	Railfreight Distribution results (including Freightliner), 1988/9–95/6	148
11.1	Highways in Europe in 2009 and comparing figures	302
13.1	Number of STCRP buses in service on the surface network	344

List of Abbreviations

AA	Automobile Association
AASHO	American Association of State Highway Officials
AN	*Archives Nationales*
ANAS	Assozazione Nationale Auto Strade
ANMT	*Archives nationales du monde du travail* (National Labour Archives)
APLM	*Archives du Paris-Lyon-Méditerranée*
ARATP	Archives of the RATP
ASCT	*Archivio Storico della Città di Torino*
ATM	*Azienda Tranvie Municipali* (Municipal Tram Company)
AVUS	*Automobil-Verkehrs- und Übungsstraße* (Automobile Thoroughfare and Exercise Road)
B&O	Baltimore & Ohio Railroad
BDA	*Bund Deutscher Arbeitgeber*
BLPES	British Library of Political and Economic Science
BMO	*Bulletin Municipal Officiel*, the Official City Bulletin
BMV	*Bundesministerium für Verkehr* (Ministry of Transport in Germany)
BP	British Petroleum
BPR	American Bureau of Public Roads
BRB	British Railways Board
BRF	British Road Federation
BRISA	*Auto-estradas de Portugal S.A.*
BTC	British Transport Commission
CEMT	Conference of European Minister of Transport
CNE	*Conseil national économique* (National Economic Council)
COGSA	Carriage of Goods by Sea Act
CT	Container terminal
DAZ	*Deutsches Architekturzentrum*
DB AG	*Deutsche Bahn AG*
DIHT	Association of the Chambers of Industry and Commerce
DRG	*Deutsche Reichsbahn-Gesellschaft*
EHESS	*École des Hautes Études en Sciences Sociales*
ESCOTA	*Réseau autoroutes Estérel, Côte d'Azur, Provence et Alpes*
Est	*Compagnie des chemins de fer de l'Est*
FAK	Freight-All-Kinds
FHWA	Federal Highway Administration

FNTF	*Fédération nationale des transports français*
GAS	General Assembly of shareholders
GEZUVOR	*Gesellschaft zur Vorbereitung der Reichsautobahnen e. V.*
GTT	*Gruppo Trasporti Torinesi* (Turin Transport Group)
GV	*Grande vitesse*
HaFraBa	*Verein zur Vorbereitung der Autostraße Hansestädte – Frankfurt – Basel* (Association for the Preparation of Highways Hansecities – Frankfurt – Basel)
HML	Hagley Museum and Library, Wilmington, Del.
HWD	*Hessisches Wirtschaftsarchiv Darmstadt*
ICB	International Container Bureau
ICC	International Chamber of Commerce
ICC	Interstate Commerce Commission
IHK	*Industrie- und Handelskammer* (Chamber of Industry and Commerce
IRF	International Road Federation
ISO	International Organization for Standardization
ITE	Institution of Traffic Engineer
L&Y	Lancashire and Yorkshire Railway
l'EHESS	*L'École des hautes études en sciences sociales*
LCL	less-than-carload lot
LMR	Liverpool and Manchester Railway
LMS	London, Midland and Scottish Railway
LNER	London and North Eastern Railway
LNWR	London & North Western Railway
MD	Managing Director
Midi	*Compagnie des chemins de fer du Midi*
MP	Member of Parliament
MT	Ministry of Transport files at the TNA
NER	North Eastern Railway
NEVA	*Nederlandse Vereeniging voor Autosnelwegen*
NFC	National Freight Corporation
Nord	*Compagnie du chemin de fer du Nord*
NSDAP	*Nationalsozialistische Deutsche Arbeiter Partei*
NUR	National Union of Railwaymen
NYC	New York Central Railroad
OBK/OBR	*Oberste Bauleitung Kraftwagenbahnen/Reichsautobahnen* (Main Construction Directorate)
OCL	Overseas Containers Ltd
ORI	Office of Road Inquiry
PLM	*Compagnie des chemins de fer de Paris-Lyon-Méditerranée* (Paris-Lyon-Mediterranean railway company)
PO	*Compagnie des chemins de fer de Paris à Orléans* (Paris-Orléans Railway)

PRR	Pennsylvania Railroad
PV	*Petite vitesse*
PWA	Public Works Administration
RAC	Royal Automobile Club
RATP	*Régie autonome des transports Parisiens* (Paris Public Transport System)
RCH	Railway Clearing House
RCL	Railway Conversion League
RfD	Railfreight Distribution
RGCF	*Revue générale des chemins de fer*
RJ	Rees Jeffreys Archive
RKB	*Reichs-Kraftwagen-Betriebsverband*
RM	Reichsmark
RoLa	*Rollende Landstraße* (Rolling Road)
RoSPA	Royal Society for the Prevention of Accidents
RSAC	Royal Scottish Automobile Club
RWS	*Rijkswatertstaat*
SATAIC	*Société anonyme des transports automobiles industriels et commerciaux*
SATAL	*Société auxiliaire de transports d'Alsace et de Lorraine*
SATE	*Société auxiliaire de transports automobiles de l'Est*
SATOS	*Société auxiliaire de transports de l'Ouest and du Sud-Ouest*
SATTI	*Società Anonima Tranvie Torinesi Intercomunali* (Turin Inter-urban Tramway Society Ltd)
SGTD	*Société générale des transports départementaux*
SICON	*Società Italiana Casse Mobile*
SNCF	*Société Nationale des Chemins de fer français*
SR	Southern Railway
STAM	*Société des transports auxiliaires des chemins de fer du Midi*
STAPO	*Société de transports auxiliaires du réseau Paris-Orléans*
STARN	*Société de transports auxiliaires de la région du Nord*
STCRP	*Société des Transports en Commun de la Région Parisienne* (Public Transportation Company of the Paris Region, the private company that preceded the RATP)
StUFA	*Studiengesellschaft für Autostraßen* (Association for the Study of Automobile Roads)
T2M	International Association on the History of Transport, Traffic and Mobility
TEN-T	Trans-European Transport Network
TERN	Trans-European Road Network
TEU	Twenty-foot Equivalent Unit
TNA	The National Archives of the UK at Kew
TPLM	*Société auxiliaire de transports du réseau PLM*
TSGB	Department for Transport, Transport Statistics Great Britain

TTI	Texas Transportation Institute
UIC	*Union Internationale des Chemins de Fer* (International Union of Railways)
UK	United Kingdom
UNECE	United Nations Economic Commission for Europe
USA	United States of America
VIA GTI	*Générale de Transport and d'Industrie*
WPA	Works Progress Administration

Notes on Contributors

Bruno Carrière (1954), PhD, is Senior Researcher and Editor at the French Railway Historical Society. After his PhD, he turned to journalism and became an authority in the railway historical press. He was in charge for decades of the prominent French railway magazine *La Vie du Rail* history column and later Chief Editor of *Rail Passion* and *Historail*. He is an acknowledged specialist of the twentieth-century French railway history and sees in the interwar period, too often neglected by railway historians, the turning point for subsequent railway organisation, technology and commercial innovation. Besides numerous papers, his reference books are dedicated to the Paris circular line, *La saga de la Petite Ceinture* (Paris 1991), and *L'aventure de la Grande Ceinture* (Paris 1992).

Albert J. Churella is Associate Professor of History at Southern Polytechnic State University in Marietta, Georgia. His publications include *From Steam to Diesel: Managerial Customs and Organizational Capabilities in the Twentieth-Century American Locomotive Industry* (Princeton 1998) and *The Pennsylvania Railroad: Volume 1, Building an Empire, 1846–1917* (Philadelphia 2013), as well as articles in the *Business History Review* and *Enterprise & Society*. He is currently working on the second and final volume of the complete history of the Pennsylvania Railroad, between 1881 and 1901 the world's largest private corporation.

Colin Divall has been Professor of Railway Studies in the University of York since 1995. His main research interests are in the history of transport and mobility, the history of technology (particularly in the nineteenth and twentieth centuries) and the public histories of both of these fields. He has served as a member of the editorial boards of *Technology & Culture*, the *Journal of Transport History, TST* and the *International Journal for the History of Engineering and Technology*, and was until 2013 a Vice President of the International Association for the History of Transport, Traffic and Mobility (T^2M). He is working with Hiroki Shin on the history of the British railways' marketing of discretionary passenger travel, and is editing books on the relationship of history to transport policy, and on the cultural histories of mobilities, spaces and sociabilities.

Roy Edwards is Lecturer in Accounting. He got his PhD at the London School of Economics in 1991 and held a Diploma in Economics, University of London, 1988. His research interests are Business History, History of Management with special regard to Britain's railways prior to 1948. He has published on the history of the London Midland and Scottish Railway and is currently working on a history of the Railway Clearing House. Other research interests include the history of management information in decision-making.

Reiner Flik (1954) is Professor for National Economy and Economic History at the University of Nürtingen and Pforzheim. He is also Professor at the Humanities Department of the Catholic University of Eichstätt. He published a book about the motorisation in Germany: *Von Ford lernen? Automobilbau und Motorisierung in Deutschland bis 1933* (Cologne 2001).

Mathieu Flonneau is a Lecturer (*maître de conferences*) in Contemporary History at the Université Paris I Panthéon-Sorbonne, Department of AES and searcher at IRICE-CRHI. There he got his PhD in 2002 on a study about *The Automobile and the Conquest of Paris, 1910–1977. Urban Forms, Political Fields and Representations*. He is editor of a book series *Cultures Mobiles* which appears at Paris Descartes et Cie publisher. He is founding member and served in the Executive Committee of the International Association for the History of Traffic, Transport and Mobility (T^2M). He leads a research group P2M (*Passé Présent Mobilité*). He wrote numerous books and articles on transport and mobility, to mention only a few: together with Vincent Guigueno he edited *De l'histoire des transports à l'histoire de la mobilité?* (Presses Universitaires de Rennes 2009); *Les cultures du volant. Essai sur les mondes de l'automobilisme* (Paris 2008); and *Paris et l'automobile. Un siècle de passions* (Paris 2005).

Terry Gourvish is Director of the Business History Unit at the London School of Economics & Political Science, Chairman of the Business Archives Council and President of the Association of Business Historians. He has published widely on business and economic history, and on the railways in particular. His books include *British Railways 1948–73: A Business History* (Cambridge 1986), *British Rail 1974–97: From Integration to Privatisation* (Oxford 2002) and *Britain's Railways 1997–2005: Labour's Strategic Experiment* (Oxford 2008). He is currently writing a book on Dolphin Square.

Keith Harcourt has had a working life in education as a teacher, lecturer, examinations official and advisor and then in the newspaper industry as an Education Manager. Latterly he has worked as a Communications Consultant. He is the Academic Liaison Officer of The Historical Model Railway Society (HMRS) and a member of The Business Archives Council. The HMRS has huge archives of historical railway drawings, photographs and documents. He has represented the Society by giving papers and attending T^2M and SHOT conferences since 2005, as well as fostering the Society's relations with other learned societies, academics, business historians and industrial archaeologists by organising visits and workshops. Papers given include: 'Pre-war Technology Transfer in UK and US Railway Freight Handling' with Thomas C. Cornillie at the Fourth International Conference on the History of Transport, Traffic and

Mobility in Paris and Marne-la-Vallée, France from 28 September to 1 October 2006, 'The Little Boxes that didn't – Containerisation Practices on British and American Railroads' with Thomas C. Cornillie, *Annual Meeting of the* Society for the History of Technology (*SHOT) in* Lissabon, Portugal from 10–14 October *2008*, 'Rail Containerisation in the United Kingdom and Europe during the 1920s and 1930s' at the Seventh International Conference on the History of Transport, Traffic and Mobility (T^2M) Lucerne, Switzerland from 5–8 November, 2009 and 'Archives, Artefacts, Amateurs and Academics – Alliance or Atrophy' with Roy Edwards, at the Ninth Annual Conference of the International Association for the History of Transport, Traffic and Mobility (T^2M) in Berlin from 6–9 October 2011. Publications include 'UK Railway Containers 1923–1933', *The LMS Journal*, No. 35 November, 2011.

Peter Merriman is a Reader in Human Geography at Aberystwyth University, Wales. His research focuses on the histories and geographies of mobility and transport, theories of space, place, landscape and mobility and the cultural politics of Welsh nationalism, and he has written widely on the history of roads, motorways and driving in Britain. He is the author of *Driving Spaces: a Cultural-Historical Geography of England's M1 Motorway* (Oxford 2007) and *Mobility, Space and Culture* (London 2012), and an editor of *Geographies of Mobilities* (Farnham 2011) and the *Handbook of Mobilities* (London 2013).

Massimo Moraglio, PhD, is Marie Curie fellow at the Berlin Institute of Technology TU-Berlin, Center for Technology and Society. Beside many essays and book chapters, his publication includes the volume *Storia delle prime autostrade italiane (1922–1943). Modernizzazione, affari e propaganda* (Trauben 2007) and the bilingual book *Inventare gli spostamenti. Storia e immagini dell'autostrada Torino-Savona/Inventing Movement. History and Images of the A6 Motorway* (Allemandi 2006). Currently he is working on the light rail revival in the European context and the new use of urban public space.

Ralf Roth is Professor of History at the *Historische Seminar, Johann Wolfgang Goethe-Universität* in Frankfurt am Main, Germany. His numerous articles published in German, British and Spanish journals are focused on the social and cultural history of cities and communication networks. Among many others he had recently published together with Henry Jacolin: *Eastern European Railways in Transition, Nineteenth to Twenty-first Centuries* (Surrey 2013) and *Städte im europäischen Raum. Verkehr, Kommunikation und Urbanität im 19. und 20. Jahrhundert* (Stuttgart 2009); together with Karl Schlögel, *Neue Wege in ein neues Europa. Geschichte und Verkehr im 20. Jahrhundert* (Frankfurt am Main 2009); and a special issue of the *Zeitschrift für Weltgeschichte* on the topic *Weltverkehr und Weltgeschichte* (nr. 2, 2011) and *Transnationale Unternehmer – Globale Netzwerke und lokales Engagement* (nr. 1, 2013). He is currently publishing a book on *The City and the Railway in the World, 19th to 21st Centuries*.

Reiner Ruppmann, who also holds a doctorate in Business Administration, finished the study of ancient and modern history with a PhD about the origins of the German highway system. The study had been published under the title: *Schrittmacher des Autobahnzeitalters. Frankfurt und das Rhein-Main-Gebiet (Pacemaker of the Motorway Age – Frankfurt and the Rhein-Main-Area)* (Darmstadt 2011). At present he works as freelance historian, specialising in History of Traffic, Transport and Mobility. Most of his many publications to this subject were published in anthologies and journals.

Bruce E. Seely (1953) Dean of the College of Sciences and Arts and Professor of History and of Science Technology and Society at Michigan Technological University, Houghton, Michigan, USA. Founding co-editor of the journal *Comparative Technology Transfer and Society* (Johns Hopkins, 2001–10); *Building the America Highway System: Engineers as Policy Makers* (Philadelphia 1987); co-author with Mark Rose and Paul Barrett, *The Best Transportation System in the World: Railroads, Trucks, Airlines, and American Public Policy in the Twentieth Century* (Columbus 2006). Published articles include '"Push" and "Pull" Factors in Technology Transfer: Moving American-style Highway Engineering to Europe, 1945–1965', *Comparative Technology Transfer & Society*, 2, No. 3, December 2004, 229–46; 'Der americanishe Blick auf die deutschen Autobahnen. Deutsche und americanische Autobahnbauer 1930–1965', *Werkstatt Geschichte*, 21, December 1998, 11–28; 'Visions of American Highways, 1900–1980', in Hans-Liudger Dienel and Helmuth Trischler, eds, *Geschichte der Zukunft des Verkehrs: Verkehrskonzpete von der Frühen Neuzeit bis zum 21. Jahrhundert* (Frankfurt am Main and New York 1997), 260–79; and 'The Scientific Mystique in Engineering: Highway Research in the Bureau of Public Roads, 1918–1940', *Technology and Culture*, 25, October 1984, 798–831.

Richard Vahrenkamp had a chair on logistics at university of Kassel for 30 years. Now he is Emeritus. He worked on the history of logistics and the contribution the extension of the motorway system in Europe made to the rise of logistics. His main book is *The German Autobahn 1920–1945. Hafraba Visions and Mega Projects* (Cologne 2010).

Modern Economic and Social History Series General Editor's Preface

Economic and social history has been a flourishing subject of scholarly study during recent decades. Not only has the volume of literature increased enormously but the range of interest in time, space and subject matter has broadened considerably so that today there are many sub-branches of the subject which have developed considerable status in their own right.

One of the aims of this series is to encourage the publication of scholarly monographs on any aspect of modern economic and social history. The geographical coverage is world-wide and contributions on the non-British themes will be especially welcome. While emphasis will be placed on works embodying original research, it is also intended that the series should provide the opportunity to publish studies of a more general thematic nature which offer a reappraisal or critical analysis of major issues of debate.

Derek H. Aldcroft
University of Leicester

Preface

When we wake up in the morning, have breakfast and leave home for work, in many cases we drive a car to our office or place of work. But in many cases we alternatively walk a short distance to the next bus or train station to use public transport which can be a bus, a tram or regional train. In some cases it could also be a combination of a short ride with car to the railway station and then a commuter ride into the city were we can pursue daily affairs. This commuter traffic is only one piece of a complex puzzle of land transport with two big backbone networks: rails and roads. Their relationship changed tremendously in the nineteenth century from roads to rails and then again in the twentieth century in the opposite direction, from rails to roads. The latter one is what the book is about.

The idea of this book was first presented at the Seventh International Conference on the History of Transport, Traffic and Mobility organised by the International Association for the History of Transport, Traffic and Mobility (T^2M) in Lucerne, Switzerland in 2009. T^2M is incorporated as a non-profit, interdisciplinary educational organisation. It emerged from the shared agenda of a number of different groups who increasingly came to the conclusion that a new field of analysis and interpretation was required. Its mission is to encourage and promote an understanding of the historical interaction between transport, traffic and the mobility of people, material objects and ideas. However, the conference was an inspiring platform for the discussion of some of the articles collected in this anthology. Some other papers have been acquired specifically for this book. All papers are based on the latest research on the history of rails and roads and all papers have been extensively rewritten and enlarged for inclusion in this book.

We thank the authors who came from France, Germany, Italy, the UK and the USA for answering our questions and for the fruitful dialogues about their work. The result is an inspiring book that broadens our view of the past and deepens our understanding of how the modern transport system came to be what it is today. It gathers information from continental Europe, Britain and the United States of America. We believe that some breakthroughs in comparative social, political and railway history may result from what is still a first step in a very promising field.

We wish to thank Derek Aldcroft, general editor of Ashgate's Modern Economic and Social History series, the Ashgate publishers and Thomas Gray as a whole for their patient help. This book would not have reached its level of quality without the engaged, competent and critical proofreading of Claire Bell. We collected for this anthology some authors from non-English-speaking countries who expressed their ideas in a foreign language. We therefore thank Nathan Horowitz and Margriet Lacy for their professional editing of all these texts.

This book's publication is supported by the Erich-Becker-Foundation, an initiative of the Fraport AG in Frankfurt am Main.

Ralf Roth and Colin Divall
Sinntal, Germany and York, United Kingdom

Introduction

From Rail to Road and Back Again? A Century of Transport Competition and Interdependency

Ralf Roth

Some General Remarks about Rail and Road Networks

In recent years, much research has been done to address questions pertaining to changes in societies as a result of mass mobility and motorisation. As car production increased, the economy and social standards transformed Europe and North America into consumer societies.[1] This research has provided better insights into some of these developments. Today we know much more about car production, the technology of cars, the reasons for the use of cars, how cars affect the economy and society and so on.[2] But we know surprisingly little about one important condition of these developments in the area of mobility: the rise and expansion of the modern road network. What is our knowledge of its origins? How was it transformed from traditional roads and trails? Moreover, the road network was, and is, only one part of the complete system of land transport. Besides river

[1] On consumer society see Thorstein Veblen, *The Theory of the Leisure Class: An Economic Study of Institutions* (Mineola, NY 1994, orig. 1899), John Kenneth Galbraith, *The Affluent Society* (Boston, MA 1958), Stuart Ewen, *Channels of Desire* (University of Minnesota 1982), Wolfgang König, *Geschichte der Konsumgesellschaft* (Stuttgart 2000) and Christian Kleinschmidt, *Konsumgesellschaft: Grundkurs* (Stuttgart 2008).

[2] On car mobility and car production see Stephanie Tilly and Florian Triebel, eds, *Automobilindustrie 1945–2000. Eine Schlüsselindustrie zwischen Boom und Krise* (Munich 2013), Gert Schmidt, ed., *Automobile und Automobilismus* (Frankfurt am Main and New York 1999), Kurt Möser, *Geschichte des Autos* (Frankfurt am Main and New York 2002), Heidrun Edelmann, *Vom Luxusgegenstand zum Gebrauchsgegenstand. Die Geschichte der Verbreitung von Personenwagen in Deutschland* (Frankfurt am Main 1989), Barbara Haubner, *Nervenkitzel und Freizeitvergnügen. Automobilismus in Deutschland 1886–1914* (Göttingen 1998) and Rudolf Boch, ed., *Geschichte und Zukunft der deutschen Automobilindustrie* (Stuttgart 2001). On resistance against increasing motorisation see Christoph Maria Merki, *Der holprige Siegeszug des Automobils, 1895–1930. Zur Motorisierung des Straßenverkehrs in Frankreich, Deutschland und der Schweiz* (Vienna 2002), and Uwe Fraunholz, *Motorphobia. Anti-automobiler Protest im Kaiserreich und Weimarer Republik* (Göttingen 2002).

and canal shipping, the network of rails, which was developed as a parallel track next to traditional roads since the first three decades of the nineteenth century, existed before modern road construction started, that is, the construction of roads that could handle motorised car traffic. The existence of railways had to be taken into consideration in all decisions about large investments in road modernisation in the twentieth century.[3]

Do we know more about the development of the rail network in the world than about road construction? Quite a bit, I think. First, rail had its starting point in Europe and it is above all on the old continent that we call the nineteenth century the age of railways.[4] The Western European railway network was growing by thousands of kilometres in just a few decades. The German one, for example, was expanded from 35 to 60,000 kilometres between 1835 and 1900. These networks connected more or less all German cities.[5] But a closer look at the European network shows that it was not homogeneous. We find remarkable differences in its density. Fully developed railway networks that served all railway functions were growing only in Western and Central European countries. In contrast, railway construction started with a delay of two or three decades at the European peripheries, that is, in Southern, Northern and above all Eastern Europe. In many cases these networks did not achieve a density similar to that of railways in the middle of Europe.[6]

Only in North America do we observe a development comparable to that of Central Europe. On that continent the European dynamics were even surpassed.

---

3 Not much literature is available on the subject. For one of the most recent publications see Hans-Liudger Dienel and Hans-Ulrich Schiedt, eds, *Die moderne Straße. Planung, Bau und Verkehr vom 18. bis zum 20. Jahrhundert* (Frankfurt am Main and New York 2010).

4 See Ralf Roth, 'Die Eisenbahnen der Welt – formten sie wirklich ein world wide web?', *Zeitschrift für Weltgeschichte*, 12, 2, 2011, 77–106.

5 See Christoph Maria Merki, *Verkehrsgeschichte und Mobilität* (Stuttgart 2008), 47–8, and Jürgen Osterhammel, *Die Verwandlung der Welt. Eine Geschichte des 19. Jahrhunderts* (Munich 2009), 1020. See also Lothar Gall, 'Eisenbahnen in Deutschland: Von den Anfängen bis zum Ersten Weltkrieg', in Lothar Gall and Manfred Pohl, eds, *Die Eisenbahn in Deutschland. Von den Anfängen bis zur Gegenwart* (Munich 1999), 13–70, here 28–9, and Rainer Fremdling, *Eisenbahnen und deutsches Wirtschaftswachstum 1840–1879* (Dortmund 1975), 17–18, G. Stürmer, *Geschichte der Eisenbahnen. Entwicklung und jetzige Gestaltung sämmtlicher Eisenbahnnetze der Erde* (Bromberg 1872), 77–85, and 90–91, 137–48, 154–8, 161–2, and 171–6 and Theodor Schieder, *Staatensystem als Vormacht der Welt 1848–1918* (Frankfurt am Main 1980), 424–5. See also Harold Pollins, *Britain's Railways: An Industrial History* (Newton Abbot 1971), 89, and Philip Bagwell, *The Transport Revolution from 1770*, 2nd ed. (London 1988), 107–9. On the background see Carlo M. Cipolla, 'The Emergence of Industrial Societies', in Carlo M. Cipolla, ed., *The Fontana Economic History of Europe: The Industrial Revolution*, 6 vols (Glasgow 1975), vol. 4.2, 719–94, here 748, and Dionysius Lardner, *Railway Economy: A Treatise on the New Art of Transport, its Management, Prospects and Relations, Commercial, Financial and Social* (New York 1968), 154–5, and 409.

6 See for example Ralf Roth and Henry Jacolin, eds, *Eastern European Railways in Transition, Nineteenth to Twenty-first Centuries* (Surrey 2013).

With the opening of the line from Baltimore to Ellis Mills in 1829, the railway era even began before the construction of the Liverpool-Manchester railway. The line was part of a huge project to connect Baltimore to Ohio. From these modest beginnings a dense network soon covered the eastern states of the United States of America. This furious start had its reasons. Hence, there existed some important differences between American and European railways. Instead of governmental guarantees of the interest rate or railway construction by the state, the USA supported many railway projects by generous donations of land. Furthermore, the ongoing expansion to the West played an important role. In contrast to the European railways the American ones served the big colonisation process of an entire continent. Railways were not only involved in settlements and in the development of an urban landscape but were also used by settler groups who were recruited to cultivate the land donations. Thus, railways did not simply connect urban areas with each other but supported their foundation and developed in this way their own transport market in the Middle West and alongside the transcontinental lines. As a result of these specific circumstances the American railway network soon exceeded that of Europe by far. Within a few decades the largest share of the worldwide railway network was developed in North America.[7] The following table underscores this particular role. In the rest of the world we find only fragments of a network up to the period after Second World War,

Table 0.1 Expansion of the railway networks in the world, 1850–1930 (in kilometres)

Year	USA	Russia	Canada	India	Germany	France	UK
1850	14,500	500	100	0	2,100	900	3,900
1870	85,000	11,000	4,000	9,000	19,000	16,000	21,000
1890	335,000	31,000	23,000	27,000	43,000	33,000	28,000
1910	566,000	67,000	51,000	53,000	61,000	40,000	32,000
1930	692,000	78,000	91,000	71,000	58,000	42,000	33,000

Source: Daniel Headrick, *Tentacles of Progress* (New York 1988), 55, and John R. and William H. McNeill, *The Human Web: A Bird's-Eye View of World History* (New York and London 2003), 220.

Taking this into consideration one might question the thesis of a worldwide network of railways.[8] It is true that the lines outside the dense railway networks in Europe and North America did contribute to world trade and freight transport when they were connected with shipping lines and road transport. But nobody can deny the

7 On American railway construction see Derek Avery, *The Complete History of North American Railways* (Secaucus, NJ 1989), Ralf Roman Rossberg, *Geschichte der Eisenbahn*, sec. ed. (Frankfurt am Main 1984), 151, and Ralf Roth, *Das Jahrhundert der Eisenbahn. Die Herrschaft über Raum und Zeit 1800–1914* (Ostfildern 2005), 34–6 and 142–53.

8 On this topic see for example Osterhammel, *Verwandlung*, 1018–9.

shortcomings of the railway networks in a global perspective. Rail transport not only had difficulty bridging the gap formed by oceans and seas between Europe and the Americas, Europe and Australia, or even Europe and Africa, but they also faced great problems trying to conquer the landmasses on the way from Europe to Asia. Only in certain parts of Europe and North America did railways offer a fully developed continental service. In the rest of the world just a few main lines could be found – particular lines for speedy transports.

In light of all this, the idea that the railway had a monopoly on transportation at the end of the nineteenth and the beginning of the twentieth century can be refuted.[9] Additional arguments speak against the monopoly thesis. Even during the so-called Railway Age, most transportation took place on roads. The vehicles included carts, coaches, horsebuses and bicycles, and, indeed, at the end of the nineteenth century the first motor cars and motorbuses. The problem is that these forms of transport appeared in statistics only in exceptional cases. In fact, we have no reliable statistics on short-distance transportation within villages and cities, or between villages and cities that were not part of the rail network. In Germany, only 9,000 out of a total of 24,000 villages and cities had a railway station.[10] This means that even in a country with one of the densest railway networks in the world, 15,000 populated settlements had no connection with the railway network. Moreover, many parts of the world had, as mentioned above, no railway lines at all. In sum, railways were always far from having a transportation monopoly.

Yet, despite these facts, at the beginning of the twentieth century Europeans and North Americans believed that they lived in a century of railways, and that investments had to be made above all in the railway system. One example of this far-reaching conviction might be urban planning at the beginning of the twentieth century. Of course, in many parts of the world it focussed on electric railways, not on cars and modern roads. Visions about further development of a metropolis paint a very similar picture. In 1912 Gustav Schimpff, a transport official in Berlin, summarised the essentials of the future of urban planning and described the concept of an ideal major city including electric rail transport as a means for mass mobility.[11] He discussed the principles of a city with a diameter of 32 kilometres and an area of 870 square kilometres for no less than four million inhabitants.[12]

[9] Kolb characterised the position of the East German Reichsbahn as a *de facto* monopoly, and Schulz said the same about the West German *Bundesbahn*. See Eberhard Kolb, 'Die Reichsbahn vom Dawes-Plan bis zum Ende der Weimarer Republik', in Lothar Gall and Manfred Pohl, eds, *Die Eisenbahn in Deutschland von den Anfängen bis zur Gegenwart* (Munich 1998), 109–63, here 154–5, and Günter Schulz, 'Die Deutsche Bundesbahn 1949–1989', in ibid., 317–76, here 336.

[10] Andreas Predöhl, *Verkehrspolitik* (Göttingen 1958), 127.

[11] Gustav Schimpff, 'Wirtschaftliche Betrachtungen über Stadt- und Vorortbahnen', *Archiv für Eisenbahnwesen*, 35, 1912, 597–643, 849–73, 1167–1201 and 1456–82, and *Archiv für Eisenbahnwesen*, 36, 1913, 20–53 and 383–416, here *Archiv für Eisenbahnwesen*, 35, 1912, 597.

[12] Ibid. 598.

For this type of city Schimpff was definitely not looking for general solutions, but raised the question how daily mobility in all its facets could be organised in this virtual environment. He started with some quantitative relationships and calculated no fewer than 860 million rides per year, including a length of five billion passenger kilometres.[13] Then he derived eight different types of traffic – commuter, settlement, business, market, visits, rides for amusement and entertainment, leisure and cemetery traffic – and described the particularities, specific uses and daily course of each type. All eight courses were integrated then into a scheme of Local Composition of Traffic (*Schema der örtlichen Verkehrszusammensetzung*). At the periphery of such a city the frequency of users rapidly declined, while it increased in the ring of suburbs and achieved its maximum in the densely populated housing areas of the inner city. It then lost a bit in the core of the city, the business district.[14] Schimpff balanced the result with daily, weekly and monthly traffic variations and took this as the basis for his recommendations for the structure of an urban rail transport net. He proposed a radial system of electrified urban railways which should connect all areas at the periphery with the city centre. The number of stations should increase in the more densely populated areas of suburbs and should constitute a grid-forming net in the city centre. In his planning the net consisted of ten lines. The form of this net should guarantee a rapid shift of masses of people from the city centre to the periphery.[15] Looking at his concept one notices that a ring railway is missing which would have connected the system of radial lines, especially in the outer areas of this metropolis. This is surprising. Even if we take into consideration that New York was the model for his recommendations, Schimpff's outlook can also be seen in the context of a wider discussion about the future expansion of Germany's capital Berlin in the years before the First World War. Berlin had introduced with great success the *Stadt- und Ringbahn* (city and ring railway) as early as 1888.[16]

However, this enthusiasm for the future of electric cities based on public mass transportation facilities for passenger transport lasted only two or three decades.

---

13 See table 'Mittlere Fahrtlänge in der idealen Stadt', in ibid. 636. His model was New York. See ibid. 609. Schimpff based his arguments for New York on the study of Paul Wittig, *Die Weltstädte und der elektrische Schnellverkehr. Nach dem Vortrag im Berliner Architektenverein am 13. März 1909* (Berlin 1909), 13, and 28–30.

14 See Schimpff, ibid. 607–8, and 630. On the distribution of transport in space in Berlin see ibid. Tafel III.

15 See ibid. 607–8, 625–6, and 630.

16 On the discussion about the future of Berlin see Markus Tubbesing, 'Der Wettbewerb Groß-Berlin: Die Suche nach der Einheit im Großstadt-Chaos', in Harald Bodenschatz et al., eds, *Stadtvisionen 1910/2010* (Berlin 2010), 64–70. On the role of the urban rail system of Berlin see Ralf Roth, 'Die Eisenbahn verändert die Stadt – die Stadt verändert die Eisenbahn', in Wolfgang Kos and Günter Dinhobl, eds, *Grosser Bahnhof. Wien und die weite Welt* (Vienna 2006), 36–42, and Ralf Roth, 'Interactions between Railways and Cities in Germany – Some examples', in Ralf Roth and Marie-Noëlle Polino, eds, *The City and the Railway in Europe* (Aldershot 2003), 3–28.

In this period, the number of cars in the United States increased from 1.3 million in 1913 to 26.5 million in 1930, and in Europe from 1.1 million in 1922 to 5.1 million in 1930. Before the First World War, one out of every 81 inhabitants in the United States owned a car. Twenty years later it was one out of six. In Europe the development was less intense. Before 1914, in France one out of 437 and in Germany only one out of 1,567 citizens owned a car, whereas during the 1930s it was one per 40 in France and one out of 131 in Germany.[17] It became evident that investments in the road system could be rewarding and would significantly increase the mobility of society as a whole. In the years before the First World War and in the interwar period there was a clear shift in the transport policies of the forerunners of developed industrial societies towards greater support of motorisation and, consequently, of modern road construction. In the United States we see the first visions that are adapted to the possibilities and advantages of the automobile. Thus, the chairman of the American Automobile Association declared: 'together with the advent of cheap automobiles there will emerge suburbs with familyhouses, each on its own spacious grounds ... This will increase the joy of life immeasurably'.[18]

Interestingly, we find exactly the same visions eight decades earlier, in the 1830s, in comments on the kind of impact railways might have once they would be introduced.[19] Eighty years later the *deus ex machina* had a new name: 'motorisation'. But the impact of motor cars on cities was totally different from that of railways. Before the nineteenth century many cities developed in a grid pattern. Only streets for supplies from the hinterland had a radial form. Together with the expansion of the city there was a demand for some kind of beltway as bypass route. In the USA one famous example is Boston Route 128. This road project also showed the problematic dynamics of such beltways. As soon as construction started, wasted fallow land alongside this route became an object of interest to developers. Industrial sites or settlements sprawled, which caused new traffic problems on Boston's periphery.[20] But this was only one aspect.

17 On the increase in cars, see Anonymous, 'Motor car vehicle registration from 1895 to 1929', US Bureau of Public Roads, http://www.railsandtrails.com/AutoFacts/1930p15-100-8.jpg (last accessed 14 August 2010), and Hans-Joachim Braun and Walter Kaiser, *Energiewirtschaft, Automatisierung, Information seit 1914* (Berlin 1997), 109 and 125. See also Christoph Maria Merki, *Verkehrsgeschichte und Mobilität* (Stuttgart 2008), 54–7.

18 Quotation in Maxwell G. Lay, *Die Geschichte der Straße. Vom Trampelpfad zur Autobahn* (Frankfurt am Main and New York 1994), 251, with reference to Mark S. Foster, *From Streetcar to Superhighway: American City Planners and Urban Transportation, 1900–1940* (Philadelphia, PA 1981).

19 See Roth, *Jahrhundert*, 40–44.

20 On the background of the Boston case see Walter M. Whitehill, *Boston in the Age John F. Kennedy* (Norman, OH 1966). An analysis of 11 American cities also demonstrates that beltways or bypass roads were only one factor among many for the development of cities. See F. Mills, 'Effects of Beltways on the Location of Residences and Selected Workplaces', *Transport Research Board Records*, 8, 12, 1981, 26–33, and Lay, *Geschichte*, 253.

Because people preferred residential areas and industrial sites in short distance to railway lines and because most railway networks were constructed in a radial form, we find a lot of star-shaped cities at the end of the nineteenth century. People had to live within walking distance to reach the stations of these lines. With the introduction of the automobile such limitations disappeared, so the areas between the lines could be developed for new suburbs.[21] That trend was indeed very different from the predictions made by Schimpff and it was not always accompanied by 'immeasurably joy of life'. Instead of smaller villages around railway stations the landscape of suburbia emerged, critically described by Lewis Mumford as a 'multitude of uniform, unidentifiable houses, lined up inflexibly, at uniform distances, on uniform roads, in a treeless communal waste'.[22]

But it was not only the side-effect of suburbia that demonstrates the impact of automobiles on cities. Motorisation changed the whole structure of cities. One example of the early shift from a city dominated by rail and other public transport facilities for mass passenger transport to a typical twentieth-century motor car city is Chicago. We can see the penetration of the idea of motorisation already in the Burnham plan of 1909.[23] Despite harbours, parks, business districts and industrial sites, this blueprint anticipated the construction of a radial system of broad boulevards and one dominant main axe from east to west. Moreover, the map shows some diagonal through-roads based on Haussmann's plans for Paris in the 1860s.[24] The goal of the group of planners around Daniel Burnham was an expansion and modernisation of the city street system, not of the rail infrastructure. On the contrary, large parts of the railway infrastructure – freight and long-distance passenger transport – should be moved out of the city centre to the periphery. Also, the streetcar system should be replaced by a system of U-trains around the business district to clear street space for pedestrians and, of course, for motor cars.[25]

---

21 See Lay, *Geschichte*, 252.

22 The quotation continues: '... inhabited by people of the same class, the same income, the same age group, witnessing the same television performances, eating the same tasteless pre-fabricated foods, from the same freezers, conforming in every outward and inward respect to a common mold, manufactured in the central metropolis. Thus the ultimate effect of the suburban escape in our time is, ironically, a low-grade uniform environment from which escape is impossible', Lewis Mumford, *The City in History: Its Origins, Its Transformations, and Its Prospects* (San Diego, CA, New York and London 1989), 486.

23 See Burnham Plan of 1909, http://www.localecology.org/images/ChicagoPlan1909.jpg or http://www.chicagocarto.com/burnham/document.html (last accessed on 24 June 2013).

24 See Glenn Yago, *The Decline of Transit. Urban Transportation in German and U.S Cities, 1900–1970* (Cambridge 1984), 151.

25 See Daniel H. Burnham and Edward H. Bennett, *Plan of Chicago* (Chicago, IL 1909), 345, 41–2, and 88–90; George E. Hooker, *Through Routes for Chicago's Steam Railroads* (Chicago, IL 1914); C.E. Merriam, *Chicago: A More Intimate View of Urban Politics* (New York 1970, orig. 1929), 8; Daniel H. Burnham and Robert Kingery, *Planning the Region of Chicago* (Chicago, IL 1956), and C.W. Condit, *Chicago, 1920–1929* (Chicago, IL 1973).

The planning for U-trains soon seemed to make real progress and was a campaign topic in the city's mayoral race in 1915.[26] But protest movements rejected the project and demanded the expansion of the existing streetcar system and a more comfortable structure of public transport facilities in general. Consequently, the project of a U-train system in Chicago failed at the beginning of the twentieth century.[27] The shortcomings of public transport paved the way for a speedy motorisation in the interwar period, as Paul Barrett analysed in his study 'The Automobile and Urban Transport' 30 years ago.[28]

But the remodelling of cities was only one aspect of the impact of motorisation on society. Of greater importance is the question of what happened between cities, that is, the modernisation or shaping of traditional trade routes or national roads for long-distance transport by automobiles. Maxwell G. Lay wrote in his study on highways:

> The first thing that an observer from outer space would see regarding land transport systems of the developed world would be the network of highways. In the last 50 years (Lay's book appeared 1994; R.R.) streets have swallowed significant amounts of land and funding and have obviously been used in a very intensive way.[29]

Besides Europe, this development began in the United States. One of the precursors was the Long Island Motor Parkway. In 1906 it was built on a private estate as a race course for the Vanderbilt Challenge Cup. Initially the road consisted of a single lane, ten metres wide and ten kilometres long. Two years later the street was opened as a toll road, for the use of cars only, and was therefore extended to a length of 80 kilometres.[30] The name parkway originally referred to roads with a broad strip of grass between both lanes. Landscape architecture pioneers Frederick Olmsted and Calvert Vaux popularised this concept for the first time when they built Central Park in New York in 1859. In 1868 followed the Ocean and Eastern Parkways, two boulevards in the west-central part of the New York City borough of Brooklyn and some more in the interwar period. This was the time when Robert Moses started his career as expert on road construction and urban development. He was a member of the Long Island Parkway Commission from 1924 to 1963 and responsible for the construction of parkways. The government planned more parkways in response to demands for employment during the Great Depression. One could mention, for example, the George Washington Memorial Parkway

26 See Yago, *Decline*, 155.

27 On decline of public transportation see Mel Scott, *American City Planning Since 1890* (Berkeley, CA 1969), 108, and Yago, *Decline*, 153–4.

28 See Paul Barrett, *The Automobile and Urban Transit: The Formation of Public Policy in Chicago, 1900–1930* (Philadelphia, PA 1982).

29 Lay, *Geschichte*, 255.

30 Ibid. 256.

that runs next to the steep banks of the Potomac near Alexandria.[31] But all these parkways were not what we expect when we speak of a highway today.

A highway is characterised by dual carriage lanes for each direction and a separating security distance between the lanes of each direction. There is no direct access from neighbouring estates, only limited access from other roads, and it is free of even crossings. None of the parkways mentioned before satisfied these requirements. The first cross-free road of this type was the ten-kilometre-long *Automobil-Verkehrs- und Übungsstraße*, short AVUS (Automobile Thoroughfare and Exercise Road) close to Berlin. This experimental road, from Charlottenburg to Grunewald, was built between 1913 and 1921 by a private consortium. The *Studiengesellschaft für Autostraßen*, the StUFA (Association for the Study of Automobile Roads), used the AVUS as an experimental road to test different methods for road construction and pavements. In 1929 this association encouraged the German government to plan a national thoroughfare network with a length of 22,500 kilometres. Besides the AVUS, the first practical experience in highway building was gained between 1929 and 1932 with the construction of a 20-kilometre-long highway from Bonn to Cologne. Some years earlier, Mussolini's fascist state had started a modern road construction project, supporting Piero Puricelli's 1921 plan for a new Italian road network with money and guarantees. The first *autostrada* from Milan to Varese and to Lake Como was opened in 1925. It was a 50-kilometre-long highway with one carriage-way for each direction and uneven interchanges at crossings, but instead of a middle strip of grass the two lanes were separated by a double white line only. Similar to the Long Island Parkway, Italian *autostradas* were built as toll roads by private companies. Later on, the companies were transferred to the state-owned *Azienda Nazionale Autonoma delle Strade*.[32]

Parallel to the early projects in Europe there is the expansion of parkways in the United States. Their success and the model of the German highways built in the Nazi period led to the concept of the interstates, or freeways. While parkways primarily served leisure and tourism, the freeway was planned as a multifunctional highway. It was Edward Bassett, chair of the American National Conference on City Planning, who coined the word in 1930. Freeway meant, in opposition to toll roads, a complimentary use of the street.[33] First experiences were gained with the six-kilometre-long Pasadena Freeway in Los Angeles, which was opened in 1940. In a report in 1939 Los Angeles city officials had demanded no fewer than 1,000 kilometres of such city highways just for the larger metropolitan area. Another project was realised on the East Coast, the so-called Pennsylvania Turnpike from

---

31 See P. Patton, *Open Road* (New York 1986), and Christof Mauch and Thomas Zeller, eds, *The World beyond the Windshield. Roads and Landscapes in the United States and Europe* (Stuttgart 2008).

32 See F.W. Cron, 'The dynamics of Highway Curvature', part 5 of 'Highway Design for Motor Vehicles – a Historic Review', *Public Roads*, 39, 4, 1976, 163–71, and Lay, *Geschichte*, 257.

33 Lay, *Geschichte*, 258–9.

Harrisburg to Pittsburgh. The road was 270 kilometres long, built between 1938 and 1940 and a direct conversion of an old railway line into a modern road. For its construction many techniques used for German *Autobahnen* were adopted.[34] Last but not least, the concept became more widely known as a result of successful public relations by General Motors, which presented the impressive exhibition 'Futurama Highways and Horizons', designed by Norman Bel Geddes, at the 1939 World Fair in New York. The 'Futurama' had five million visitors.[35] Two years later, President Franklin D. Roosevelt, impressed by the German *Autobahnen*, formed the National Interregional Highway Committee, which should develop road projects for the after-war period when millions of soldiers would be discharged. In 1944 a report of the committee emphasised the construction of a National System of Interstate and Defense Highways.[36] Although this plan was not realised right after the end of war, the project did play an important role in the 1950s.[37]

Rails and Roads Between Competition and Interdependency

Right from its beginning, the modernisation of roads had consequences for all sorts of land transport. One of the first effects was that speedy long-distance and effective transport was no longer the monopoly of the railways. Transport historians have reflected on this shift and have drawn the conclusion that the period from the 1920s to the 1950s was characterised by sharp competition between rail and road – *Straße und Schiene – chemins de fer et routes*, and so on. Indeed, in the journal of the *Verein Deutscher Eisenbahnverwaltungen* (Association of German Railway Administrations) railway officials complained about increasing competition from motor cars:

> Today, the situation of public transport presents to the observer the image of a struggle of all against all, in which the governmental authorities are helpless and in which the law of the jungle is ruthlessly applied.[38]

---

34 See W.H. Shank, *Vanderbilt's Folly: A History of the Pennsylvania Turnpike*, 2nd ed. (York, PA 1973).

35 See Norman Bel Geddes, *Magic Motorways* (New York 1940), https://ia600208.us.archive.org/10/items/magicmotorways00geddrich/magicmotorways00geddrich.pdf (last accessed 1 March 2014). On the background see Peter M. Wolf, *The Future of the City: New Directions in Urban Planning* (New York 1974), 28.

36 E. Weiner, *Urban Transportation Planning in the United States: An Historical Overview*. US Department of Transportation, Department of Transport (Washington, DC 1986).

37 Lay, *Geschichte*, 259.

38 'Jedenfalls bieten die Zustände im öffentlichen Verkehr heute dem Beschauer das Bild eines Kampfes aller gegen alle, dem die staatlichen Hoheitsbehörden hilflos gegenüberstehen und in dem das Recht des Stärkeren rücksichtslos zur Anwendung kommt', *Zeitung des Vereins Deutschern Eisenbahnverwaltungen*, 71, 1930, 393.

The director of the *Deutsche Reichsbahn Gesellschaft*, that is, the German state railway, Julius Dorpmüller, calculated that the losses of railways from competition with trucks in goods transport amounted to 250 million Reichsmarks in 1930. He envisioned that further losses in the next year would increase to 500 million Reichsmarks and demanded protection from the state as well as laws for regulation of the tariff system. Moreover, he decided to take over the largest road haulage company, Schenker, which provided all transport to and from railway stations.[39] The answer of the motorcar lobby was similarly harsh and showed a willingness to fight.[40] In other European countries with state-run railways, and also in the US and the UK, with strong private railway companies, similar debates took place as our authors have analysed in detail in the first section of the book.

The book starts with a series of articles on reactions of railway companies to increasing competition from road transport, and also discusses the extent to which transport by rails depended on road transport at various times and in various places. The first article in particular, by Ralf Roth, 'Rails and Roads Between Competition and Interdependency: a Long and Winding Relationship with Many Innovations That Failed', analyses a 200-year-long relationship and the innovations that were intended to increase the connectivity between both systems. It starts with some basic reflections on the shift from road to rail transport at the beginning of the nineteenth century and examines the debate and experiments regarding mobile steam engines developed either for rails or for roads. In Germany it was for practical reasons that the decision was made to invest in a rail system on the model of the Liverpool-Manchester railway as long as it would be too costly to build adequate roads that could be used by steam mobiles. Interestingly, the road system had been estimated to be basically more flexible and, because of its structural density, more comfortable for users. The rail system was seen as the second-best solution but for technical reasons at that time unavoidable.[41] However, against the background of this reservation the renaissance of the road system at the beginning of the twentieth century appears in a new light. It could be seen as a new attempt to use the advantages of the road system, that is, with new cars and more suitable roads. The most attractive point for this renaissance was – as the discussants seven decades before had argued – a much denser network of roads. With these preliminaries Roth unfolds a fundamental debate on the relationship of

---

[39] See 'Rede Julius Dorpmüllers vom 30. Januar 1929', *Die Reichsbahn*, 5, 1929, 109–16, and Deutschen Reichsbahn-Gesellschaft, Hauptverwaltung, ed., *Reichsbahn und Kraftwagenverkehr. Denkschrift* (Berlin 1930). See also Studienausschuss 'Eisenbahn und Kraftwagen' beim Deutschen Industrie- und Handelstag, ed., *Eisenbahn und Kraftwagen.* Denkschrift March 1930 (Berlin 1930). On the background, see Kolb, 'Die Reichsbahn', 160.

[40] See Reichsverband der Automobilindustrie, ed., *Eisenbahn und Kraftwagen. Zur Denkschrift des Deutschen Industrie- und Handelstags* (Berlin 1930).

[41] See Roth, *Jahrhundert*, 29–32.

rails and roads and stresses the permeability of both systems and the infrastructural solutions for passenger and freight up to modern concepts of intermodality.

The book continues with an article by Roy Edwards, 'Shaping British Freight Transport in the Interwar Period: Failure of Foresight or Administration, 1919–34?', that explores the way in which the London and North Eastern Railway – the second largest of the British companies, and the one most badly affected by the economic depression – perceived and responded to the threat of road haulage in the surroundings of London. He discusses the consequences of railway reforms at this time, especially the Railway Act of 1921, and the regulation of price and service. Indeed, there was an intense debate inside the Ministry of Transport on how increasing motorisation would affect railway companies. But the Act did not give an answer to the question of how railways should deal with that competition. One answer might have been investments in service on roads and indeed, 'management was well aware of the advantage of using road delivery'.[42] They were not only aware of the problem, they also started experiments with road haulage within a 20-mile radius around railway stations. But governmental railway administration insisted on a strict separation of rails and road transport. So the debate between the Board of Railways, the Railway Clearing House, the administration of the Ministry of Transport, Parliament and lobby groups of traders was hindering pragmatic activities that would have put railways in a better position to stand up to the competition of road hauliers. Edwards demonstrates impressively

> … how difficult it was for the railway companies to manage in an environment where administrative process casually conducted, led to very real consequences for the conduct of business.[43]

This explains why an opportunity was missed for 'a smoother switch from a dominant but outdated rail based system, to a new road technology'.[44]

Colin Divall picks up a similar question in his contribution 'Conceiving Distribution in the United Kingdom: the (London and) North Eastern Railway's Discursive Response to Road Haulage, 1921–39', and also looks at the reaction of British railway companies when road haulage emerged. Indeed, since 1914 one could notice the arrival of large numbers of small road hauliers. He draws our attention to the discussion among four British railway companies and how they dealt with the regulations of the Railway Act of 1921. On the one hand they had been freed from state control and could independently expand their companies by reorganisation of labour to withstand the intensifying competition. This was mirrored in company magazines. 'Workers should see themselves as part of the sales initiative'.[45] On the other hand, all big four rapidly lost freight, complained

---

[42] Roy Edwards on page 85 of this volume.

[43] Roy Edwards on page 88 of this volume.

[44] Roy Edwards on page 88 of this volume.

[45] Colin Divall on page 97 of this volume.

about unfair competition and demanded eventually with less success a regulation of the prices of road haulage. After the Second World War rail distribution quickly declined from the 1950s onwards: Divall summarises: 'It is too easy to assume that the simple fact that road distribution grew rapidly in the interwar years spelt the eventual demise of a rail-based alternative'.[46] Research is needed to analyse in greater depth the options that had been laid on the table.

Keith Harcourt's article, 'Rail Containers in the United Kingdom and Europe during the 1920s and 1930s', directs us to a particular but key problem within the ongoing competition between rail and road, namely the relationship of ship, railway and road transport. In this respect he looks at technological changes in freight transport in Europe during the interwar period to make this type of transport more barrier-free and permeable. Against this background he introduces us to the origins of the container system in Europe in the 1920s. These containers were not developed for sea trade but for making rail transport more efficient. But contrary to the American container models, resistance to standardisation of containers was strong in Europe. The reason was a segmented rail transport market with many private and public railway companies. He outlines this by using the example of the situation in Great Britain and the role of private road hauliers and their increased numbers since the end of the First World War on the one hand, and the British railways that had been reorganised by the Railway Act of 1921 on the other hand. As an answer to the door-to-door service offered by road hauliers, British railway companies developed the container as a means to win back losses in good transport. In this respect British railway companies were not alone in Europe. In the 1920s containers became part of the service in Switzerland, Italy, France, the Netherlands and Germany. Harcourt gives us an overview of the development in Europe, which was characterised by competition between numerous different systems. At the end he draws the conclusion that, 'despite differing national commercial and political factors, the competition for freight business between rail and road was a significant and constant driver of innovation across the continent'.[47]

The thesis developed by Harcourt receives support in Terry Gourvish's essay 'The Sea Container Revolution and Road-Rail Competition in Britain: a Preliminary Assessment of Freightliner'. He rounds off the discussion of the British case with a topic about road-rail competition in distribution by containers in the decades after the Second World War. Of course, containers had an enormous impact on both transport systems – road and rail – because the motorway system became larger, the loading capacity of trucks increased as well and there had been a significant cut in investments in rail freight since the 1950s. In this situation it would have been best to strengthen all forms of intermodality between rail and road transport. Indeed, there were a lot of plans and some reforms in the 1960s for a reduction of barriers in the transport chain. But many initiatives met with resistance from trade unions. One example the author discusses in this respect

---

46 Colin Divall on page 106 of this volume.

47 Keith Harcourt on page 128 of this volume.

were the attempts of British Rail to start competition in the private freight-liner business. But the experiments up to 1978 had disappointing results and ultimately British Rail did not see any other solution than a total reorganisation in 1988, which was not successful either. Railfreight produced increasing losses until privatisation in 1996. Gourvish is of the opinion that the public sector of rail transport was unable to compete:

> The tentative conclusion here is that the railways' competitive advantage was limited not only by investment constraints and pricing weaknesses, but also by technical changes, such as the growing popularity of 40-foot containers, and the introduction of larger, heavier lorries in the UK. Larger containers have had a deleterious impact on the railways' route availability given the restricted loading gauge of the UK infrastructure, while making road haulage more competitive.[48]

All in all, we are well informed by the articles of Edwards, Divall, Harcourt and Gourvish about competition between rail and road caused by modernisation of roads and of transport vehicles for these roads in the United Kingdom. They provide us with a detailed description of the problems while taking into consideration many different aspects. But what was the situation in other countries? Richard Vahrenkamp presents some answers for Germany in his contribution 'Trucking in Germany: Rise and Restricted Growth, 1900–1938'. Reading this article we can compare the British case with the German one, that is, *Deutsche Reichsbahn* in the 1930s and the responses of this company to increasing competition from cars. But let us look closely at the beginning of truck services in Germany, its importance for national goods transport in the 1920s and 1930s, the competition with the *Deutsche Reichsbahn*, and the innovative logistical efforts that had been made to develop it. In fact we see, as in Britain, an increase in truck transport since the First World War. Numerous small companies were founded after demilitarisation as an unforeseen side effect of the Treaty of Versailles. But there were some barriers against a free development of road haulage. At this point Vahrenkamp presents a comparison of regulations concerning truck traffic in Europe and directs our attention to the structure of rail and road freight transport. That makes clear how and why regulation matters and how and why *Deutsche Reichsbahn* reacted to growing competition with road hauliers. Unlike the British example, the influence of *Deutsche Reichsbahn* in public debates and on the administration of the state was rather strong. Moreover, the company seized the initiative, bought, as mentioned above, one of the biggest road hauliers, Schenker, and attempted to monopolise all rail and truck service. This caused an intense public debate up to and at the beginning of the Nazi period. But then *Deutsche Reichsbahn* collided with the interests of the new regime to enforce modern highway construction. This is why *Deutsche Reichsbahn*'s attempts to monopolise road haulage were fended off in a struggle between Fritz Todt, the general inspector for highway construction, and

---

48 Terry Gourvish on page 151 of this volume.

Julius Dorpmüller, the minister of Transport and head of *Deutsche Reichsbahn*. But although Todt won this fight and the regime forced German railways to assume responsibility for the construction of the ambitious highway program, the results also included strong regulation rules, especially for long distance road haulage, that is, all transports over a distance of 50 kilometres should be done by railways. Vahrenkamp summarises:

> During the Nazi period, traffic policy was characterised by an unsystematic coexistence of interests, and a lack of strategic transportation planning. This led to late (1938) recognition of the importance of a large civilian fleet of heavy trucks for the purpose of war. The *Reichsbahn* took advantage of this situation, and was able to continue the marginalisation of long-distance haulage up to the transport bottleneck crisis of 1938.[49]

By the way, the last piece of deregulation in this affair regarded the permission granted to national bus lines for long-distance passenger transport four years ago, nearly eight decades after regulation in the Nazi period.[50]

A direct comparison with the German and, of course, the British case is Bruno Carrière's article 'Road-Rail Competition in France in the 1930s: from a Railway Perspective'. In France, too, there had been a drastic increase in competition between modern road transport and the *Société nationale des chemins de fer français* (SNCF). The development of automobiles was watched closely and, as in the UK and Germany, French railways started experiments with trucks and busses as early as 1906. At a very early stage rail authorities realised the potential of a more efficient road transport system. And in France, too, the idea arose to establish one's own road transport companies as the *Deutsche Reichsbahn* did with Schenker. But it was not only one big company but a whole series including SATOS (*Société auxiliaire de transports de l'Ouest and du Sud-Ouest*), SATE (*Société auxiliaire de transports automobiles de l'Est*), STAM (*Société de transports auxiliaires des chemins de fer du Midi*), STARN (*Société de transports auxiliaires de la région du Nord*), SATAL (*Société auxiliaire de transports d'Alsace et de Lorraine*), TPLM (*Société auxiliaire de transports du réseau PLM*) and STAPO (*Société de transports auxiliaires du réseau Paris-Orléans*). This business strategy was realised several years earlier than in Germany, between 1928 and 1931. But this was not the only instrument to fight competition from road hauliers. French railways also complained in a public debate about privileges of road hauliers in

49 Richard Vahrenkamp on page 167 of this volume.

50 See 'Bus statt Bahn', *Süddeutsche Zeitung* of 25 June 2010, http://www.sueddeutsche.de/wirtschaft/urteil-fernbus-linien-bus-statt-bahn-1.965296 (last accessed 18 February 2014). The law 'Über die Beförderung von Personen zu Lande' was published on 4 December 1934 and came into effect on 1 April 1935. It was taken over into Federal law of the Federal Republic of Germany in the beginning of the 1950s. See http://de.wikipedia.org/wiki/Personenbeförderungsgesetz_/Deutschland/ (last accessed on 18 February 2014).

taxation, because railways suffered additional costs for the expansion of the net and had to maintain unprofitable but politically desirable railway lines. However, all these efforts did not protect the SNCF from losses in freight and passenger transport. Its share in national freight transport fell from 75 to 53 per cent and for passenger transport from 88 to 72 per cent in the 1930s. This is why at the end of the decade there was only one last weapon to fight competition with bus transport and road haulage: dumping prices to win back customers.

Another contribution, by Albert J. Churella, 'Containerisation in the United States during the Interwar Period' discusses how the issue of containerisation and the road-rail question played out in the United States. This is very interesting because the story told so far is more or less a tale of ultimately failed or rather unsuccessful fights of railways against modern road transport systems. But here Churella presents the example of the Pennsylvania Railroad, which keenly used the idea of containers for a visionary triumph of logistics and intermodality including 'trucks, buses, ships, and aircraft'.[51] Like Harcourt, Churella also is of the opinion that containers are not a vision of the 1930s but of the decade before. Already in 1917 we find first attempts, and a little bit later the idea of a standardised box was picked up in the discussion about competition with cars. But there were other arguments. Some saw it as a technical solution to minimise burglary in the transport process. At first, containers were used in tests in the 1920s for mail service by the New York Railroad Company, the service then was taken over by the Pennsylvanian Railroads. But this was only the beginning. Together with a debate about low transport rates, costs of transport with and without containers, the box emerged and new types were presented in the 1930s. But the ambitious goal of intermodality was not reached. One reason was that containers of different railway companies could not be interchanged. This explains why containers did not stop the shift of high-value freight transport to the highways. It leads Churella to the following conclusion:

> Railroaders were prepared to set container rates in such a way as to seize traffic from weaker railroads, imperilling Congressional mandates to protect the railroad industry from self-destruction. … (But) in enforcing the law they limited the scope of container operations, even as they acknowledged the immense potential of container service.[52]

The railroad competition and its public debate up to the Second World War, and sometimes beyond, was only the first widely discussed effect of the restructuring of land transport in general. Its main dynamics unfolded after the Second World War with the distribution of cars and trucks and big investments in the road network to such an extent that we call it mass mobilisation.

---

51 Albert Churella on page 195 of this volume.

52 Albert Churella on page 212 of this volume.

The Modern Road: an Innovative Success Story of the Twentieth Century – But Rail Survived

The decades after the Second World War were characterised by the definitive breakthrough of mass motorisation and of modern road construction. The United States was the forerunner in this development. At the time, different lobby groups attempted to continue to build on visions for a nationwide modern road network that had been developed at the end of the war. A decade after the report of the National Interregional Highway Committee established by Roosevelt, one of his successors, Dwight D. Eisenhower, also appointed a presidential committee, chaired by General Lucius D. Clay, which should evaluate the demand for highways in the USA. Later on, Clay became, not by accident, a member of the board at General Motors. Moreover, other members of the Eisenhower administration had close ties with General Motors, for instance the secretary of Defence, Charles Wilson, and one of his advisors, Francis du Pont, who became director of the Bureau of Public Roads. The Clay Committee emphasised the construction of Interstates as a national necessity. Legislation to underscore this consisted of the Federal Aid Highway Act and the Highway Revenue Act of 1956.[53] The planning included eventually some 70,000 kilometres, which should be finished in 1972. But in the 1980s there were still some gaps waiting to be closed. Nevertheless, the construction of the Interstates was one of the biggest infrastructure projects in the world.[54]

But this was only a drop in the bucket compared to all initiatives worldwide to reconstruct and modernise the road system in order to make it accessible to cars.[55] This is why in the interwar period and in the decades after the Second World War a gigantic second transport network developed parallel to the railway network, with tremendous impacts on society. A strong shift from rail to road cannot be overlooked. A clear sign for this shift is the length of both modern transport networks. Although the railway network grew steadily, it fell far behind the road network. In 2002 there were one million kilometres of railway in the world. If this railway were evenly spread out in a grid system, the furthest one could ever be away from a railway would be 65 kilometres. Of the seven territories with the largest land areas, six also have the longest distances of railway. With all the progress the network has made it is only one-thirtieth, that is, circa 3 per cent, of

---

53 See Richard F. Weingroff, 'Federal-Aid Highway Act of 1956: Creating the Interstate System', *Public Road*, 60, 1, 1996 (online, no pagination), http://www.fhwa.dot.gov/publications/publicroads/96summer/p96su10.cfm (last accessed 28 February 2014). See also History of the Interstate Highway System, http://www.fhwa.dot.gov/interstate/finalmap.cfm (last accessed 28 February 2014).

54 Lay, *Geschichte*, 260.

55 On the example of US investments in road construction in South America see Bruce E. Seely, Der Pan American Highway – eine Straße zwischen zwei Kontinenten, *Zeitschrift für Weltgeschichte*, 12, 2, 2012, 141–74.

the modern road network. In 2002 there were 29 million kilometres of road in the world. If the network of roads were evenly spread out in a grid system, the furthest one could ever be away from a road would be 4.5 kilometres. Cities are mazes of roads, often congested with traffic. In cities most people live, work and sleep within a few metres from a road. Regionally the highest number of roads per square kilometre is found in Japan and the lowest in the Middle East, where most of the world's petroleum, the precondition for motorisation, is extracted.[56]

Table 0.2 Comparison of the railway and road networks in the world in 2002 (in 1,000 kilometres)

World area	Rail network	Road network	Relationship of rail and road
Central Africa	9	375	1:42
Southeastern Africa	39	709	1:18
Northern Africa	32	847	1:27
Southern Asia	75	3,899	1:52
Asia Pacific	65	1,788	1:28
Middle East	125	1,421	1:12
Eastern Asia	71	1,941	1:27
South America	94	2,703	1:29
Eastern Europe	109	1,900	1:17
North America	218	8,283	1:38
Western Europe	157	3,884	1:24
Japan	20	1,172	1:59
Total	1,014	28,921	1:29

Source: For the railway network see data source World Bank, *World Development Indicators* (New York 2005). Data are from 2002, 64 territories had no recorded rail system. The World Bank defines railway line as the length of the route available for service, irrespective of the number of parallel tracks. Rail Network http://www.worldmapper.org/display.php?selected=36 (last accessed 17 February 2014). For the road network see data source World Bank, *World Development Indicators* (New York 2005). Data base from 2002. Roads include motorways, highways, main/national roads, secondary/regional roads and all other roads in a territory. On statistical information see Road Network http://www.worldmapper.org/posters/worldmapper_map35_ver5.pdf (last accessed on 17 February 2014).

The expansion of the road network and questions of road mobility are the topic of another series of articles in the second part of the book, entitled 'Mobility on Roads: An Innovative Success Story of the Twentieth Century – But Rail Survived'. The first article of this series, by Reiner Flik, 'Creative Destruction? A Schumpeterian View of Innovation in Car Transportation', discusses the more general problems of motorised societies in the Western world and presents some general suggestions

[56] See http://www.worldmapper.org/posters/worldmapper_map35_ver5.pdf (last accessed on 17 February 2014).

regarding key decisions at the time of motorisation. He interprets the triumphal march of motorisation as one of the disruptive innovations which are so characteristic for industrialisation and which in the end produce long waves of increases in economic development. But before the automobile industry could have an impact that way, it had to surmount the resistance of the older transport business, that is, the railways, and some other obstacles. Flik is of the opinion that 'resistance to motor transport mainly came from social groups that were excluded from its use due to its high costs but who had to bear its social costs'.[57] However, after the Second World War we find an enormous increase in car production and an enormous distribution of automobiles. Car manufacturers were not only big job creators, they also had a lot of repercussions that transformed all Western societies as early as the 1920s. But what was the basic reason for this increase in the distribution of automobiles? The author answers this question with an interesting look at the motherland of mass motorisation, the United States. And there we find right from the start an increasing use of cars not only in urban agglomerations with a developed road infrastructure but also in rural areas and less developed road systems or roads in bad shape. This is why he draws the conclusion that car density did not depend on a developed road infrastructure. In his opinion there was only a loose relationship between cars and roads. Car density is in this respect not a consequence of a good road system but the development of road infrastructure and an increase in road density are consequences of the distribution of cars. But why did mass motorisation in the United States not begin in urban regions only? Flik answers: 'For the average farmer overseas, the motorcar was not a mere gadget for escaping the boredom of rural life, i.e., a consumer good. It was principally an investment good, which enhanced productivity and increased income'.[58]

The road system had a much less limiting effect on the distribution of cars than income and the amount of money that was left for investments in mobility. The condition of the road played a secondary role in this respect. The author concludes: 'There is evidence that income was also the main driving power of the motorisation of the Western European economies after the Second World War during the fourth Kondratiev (cycle; R.R.)'.[59]

This does not mean that road construction is a negligible factor: ultimately, mass motorisation to the extent that we experienced it in the decades after the Second World War would not have been possible without enormous investments in the modernisation of national road infrastructure in the Western world. That is the topic of the second article. From Bruce Seely we learn much about 'Inventing the American Road: Innovations Shaping the American Freeway'. He presents an inspiring overview of the modernisation of the road system in the United States. The contribution is of particular importance because it shows the American system as a model for motorisation worldwide. Seely draws our attention to the

[57] Reiner Flik on page 223 of this volume.
[58] Reiner Flik on page 227 of this volume.
[59] Reiner Flik on page 229 of this volume.

American highways, the largest public works project ever undertaken, including its core, the system of Interstate and Defense Highways. Thus, he agrees with Maxwell G. Lay, whom we have mentioned before. The starting point was the bad shape of roads that Flik mentioned. But it is a myth to think that American road improvement was simply a response to the automobile. No, the pressure for improvement started a bit earlier with the bicyclists and the lobby for railroad roads for the hinterland. Furthermore, the factors for realisation include hard technical and non-technical elements and we have to look at the organisation, the role of engineers as policymakers and, of course, the political consequences. In 1893 the Office of Road Inquiry had been founded, which undertook technical research and research for material and know-how in road construction. This task was transferred to the Bureau of Public Roads in 1916. There were a lot of public debates in Congress, which set up the State Highway Department. And last but not least the question had to be answered: who should pay? Investments in road modernisation required a lot of capital – a total of nearly 100 billion US-dollars in the decades between 1954 and 1986. This was such a large amount that the funding was split between state funds and bond financing supported by gas taxes, while some states additionally instituted a toll system. Seely argues: 'These funding mechanisms did more than allow the Interstate system of limited-access, high-speed roads to be built, both inside and outside cities'.[60] One should not forget either that beside organisation and funding, the modern road needed a series of technical innovations, such as durable pavements for different kinds of roads and mechanisation of the construction process itself. Moreover, the road foundation was at any time in a race with ever heavier trucks. However, the first parkways appeared – as mentioned – around 1907; then there was a stagnation from the 1920s to 1930s when the types of freeways and express highways were designed that resulted in the construction of the first 2,000 miles (3,218 kilometres) in the 1940s – surprisingly, during the war. In 1944 a plan foreseeing in 40,000 miles (64,360 kilometres) of highways was relegated to the after-war period. Seely comments: 'The organisational and financial innovations, the technical knowledge and construction tools, the planning surveys all came together in the 1950s in the form of the Interstate construction programme in every major city and across the landscape'.[61]

Seely mentions many additional details, such as the technical settings for more security and for minimising the death toll rate: standardisation of traffic signs, traffic lines, lightning of streets and so on. He ends by concluding: 'Like so many other large technical systems, the innovations that resulted in the American freeway have grown from slow, steady incremental activities of mundane elements much more than from the flashy, highly-publicised work labelled revolutionary'.[62]

60 Bruce Seely on page 239 of this volume.
61 Bruce Seely on page 253 of this volume.
62 Bruce Seely on page 264 of this volume.

All in all, Seely presents an impressive account of the modernisation of roads in the United States.

So far, Flik has presented several reasons for road development and Seely has shown the whole programme of the invention of new roads and its innovations, using the example of the United States. From the situation across the Atlantic we shift back to Europe and ask the question: What happened there? Unfortunately, no such article as Seely's has yet been written on the development of the European highway network and this is why Reiner Ruppmann in his contribution 'The Development of the European Highway Network: a Literature Survey of Studies on Highway History in European Countries' was forced first to clear the ground for further research. However, the outcome is more than that. It is a comparison of the different ways European countries modernised their major road system, and in many ways these infrastructure policies were different from the path the United States followed. Ruppmann divides the European countries into two groups, pioneers and followers. In the pioneer group he counts Italy, Germany and the Netherlands. Italy's highway system was marked by its private origins, which we have briefly mentioned above, and its model role for the German system. But its private lines did not generate the expected revenues, due to low traffic. In Germany the highway lobby attempted to base funding on a private-public partnership. But the targeted project of a long north-south connection sponsored by the *Verein zur Vorbereitung der Autostraße Hansestädte – Frankfurt – Basel*, or HaFraBa (Association for the Preparation of Highways Hanseatic cities – Frankfurt – Basel), failed and only during the Nazi regime highway construction became a big issue for governmental policy. Ruppmann does away with some legends about the role of Adolf Hitler in this process and reconstructs the real origins in societies such as the HaFraBa venture that presented a fully developed road project. This planning was adopted by the regime in all its details. However, the leading role of Italy and Germany in the European process of highway construction is not unknown, in contrast to that of the Netherlands. In this respect Ruppmann mentions especially the role of *Rijkswaterstaat*, which had been responsible for roads in this country since the late 1830s. Already in 1906 this institution presented proposals for roads for mass motorisation. Twenty years later some officials of *Rijkswaterstaat* established, on the model of the German HaFraBa, the *Nederlandsche Vereniging voor Autosnelwegen* (NEVA).

The group of followers consisted of Austria, France, Spain, Belgium, Great Britain, Luxembourg, Portugal and Switzerland. The heterogeneity of all these examples with a chaotic scheme of influences and repercussions – especially from the Italian and German models – mirrors a totally different picture from that of the United States, although the breakthrough of highway construction in Europe was heavily supported by the United States, a fact that Ruppmann underscores:

> Surprisingly, transport historians long overlooked the vital impact of the Marshal Plan and the activities of the American Bureau of Public Roads (BPR) on the early road construction after World War Two, as well as the importance of the

International Road Federation (IRF) in the introduction of American planning techniques and road construction machines into European highway projects.[63]

This is why both networks share some common origins, were used in the last decades in a very similar way and have a comparable function in Western societies. Against this background Ruppmann provides us with an outlook:

> The common attitude in the last two to three decades of lean production and intensifying globalisation was to put stock in the road or on ships, thus saving time and money. With mass motorisation, people have not only got used to driving between home and work, but also to use their cars for shopping, leisure time activities, weekend trips and holiday travels. … It seems almost impossible to change the current system. For the time being, highways will remain the backbone of European traffic, transport and mobility.[64]

From Ruppmann's panoramaic view of Europe we continue with a detailed analysis by Peter Merriman in his article 'Motorways and the Modernisation of Britain's Road Network, 1937–70'. He addresses the modernisation of roads in Great Britain and starts with the surprising fact that first notions of a modern road system already appeared in 1902 but the first section of a highway was not opened until 1958. What went wrong and what caused a delay of more than half a century? The beginning itself was not very different from Italy or Germany. Some key lobby groups, such as the British Road Federation (BRF) or later the Railway Conversion League (RCL), demanded a modern road system, that is, conversion from rail to road for the expansion of motorisation. As was the case in almost all Western European countries, their campaigns were strongly opposed by the railway companies. Roy Edwards, Colin Divall and Keith Harcourt have presented examples of this aspect. However, the public debate was carried into Parliament, which sent the German Road Delegation to Germany in 1937 to inspect the successfully implemented highways in situ. The account of this delegation poured oil on the fire and led to an intensification of the discussion about the effects of motorways. But before this discussion could show any practical results the Second World War broke out. This is why highway construction was postponed, as was the case in the United States, and had to wait for consideration as a topic of after-war policy. Indeed, we find several plans at the end of, and directly after, the war when British officials became informed about the German highway system by British Intelligence Service and when they studied the highways in the United States. The Tea Room Plan of 1946 is an example of this. But more than 12 years passed before the conversion plan of 1958 was taking shape. According to this plan 20,000 miles (32,180 kilometres)

---

63 Reiner Ruppmann on page 301 of this volume. See also Seely, 'Der Pan American Highway', 141–74.

64 Reiner Ruppmann on page 303 of this volume.

of railway tracks should be substituted by roads because of lower costs and more flexibility. But this plan was also debated with arguments both pro and con, and quite a few people would have preferred the electrification of railways, rather than a conversion of rail to road. However, Merriman draws the conclusion that strong railway companies and their presence in the public debate made Britain a latecomer in the field of road modernisation, which qualifies and puts in a different perspective common interpretations that view railways only as losers in the conflict with road transport.

Sometimes observers have interpreted the conflict between rail and road as an insurmountable contradiction that would end with the defeat of one of these systems. Most believed that the railway – a child of the nineteenth century – would lose, or already had lost, the contest. Indeed, present-day statistics show impressive shifts in the relationship between rail and road transport during the twentieth century. We have presented the quantitative relationship in length of both networks. Rails achieved only 3 per cent of the total net of all land transport systems. Additional arguments support the thesis that railways would vanish: from a dominant transport system for passengers and goods traffic, railways have now declined to become a niche business of the worldwide transport market. Nearly 83 per cent of personal transportation is done by automobiles and only 7.3 per cent by railways worldwide.[65] Does this mean the railway has gone from being a monopoly to near non-existence – from being a provider for all to a *quantité negligeable*?

We would argue a bit more carefully. Railways still exist and there must be some reason for this fact. Of course, there was a downward trend, but one must pay attention to several details that affect the data. First, the statistics are relative, expressing a relationship. This includes the fact that in absolute figures, rail transport has increased in most countries during the twentieth century. The background is the tremendous increase in global mobility and freight transport. This is why all transport systems: shipping, air transport, cars, and also railways, win. Second, there has been a change in the relationship between rails and roads in the most recent two decades, a slight increase in the proportion of rail transport vis-à-vis road transport. This is why some feel encouraged to speak of a 'renaissance' of railways.[66] This opinion is based on three areas of positive development in rail transport in comparison with its competitors, airplanes and automobiles: first, rail freight. We have discussed losses in the interbellum and after-war period. But in the past few decades rail freight has been regaining strength in many countries. Special

---

65 World Transport Report 2010/2011, ProgTrans AG, Basel: http://www.progtrans.com/html/wtr_2010.html (last accessed 12 August 2010). Quoted in Christoph Ruhkamp, 'Kein Auslaufmodell. Das Auto wahrt seine Dominanz im Personenverkehr fast ungeschmälert', *Frankfurter Allgemeine Zeitung* of 11 August 2010.

66 Bund Deutscher Architekten and Deutsche Bahn AG, *Renaissance der Bahnhöfe*, Katalog der Ausstellung mit gleichem Namen in Kooperation mit Meinhardt von Gerkan (Berlin 1996).

services in goods transport are flourishing, for example container transportation from harbour to hinterland, bringing national railway companies back into global transportation networks.[67] The consequences are far-reaching. Whereas in the 1990s, many transport experts would not bet a penny on the future of railways in goods transport, today many European railway companies are forming strategic alliances and taking over companies in neighbouring countries to compete more efficiently on the European goods transport market. The *Union Internationale des Chemins de Fer* (UIC) also speaks of success stories and global perspectives for rail freight.[68]

Second, high-speed trains successfully compete with airplanes for distances up to 1,000 kilometres. Railways may make further inroads into the business travel market if airlines have to raise their prices as a result of additional taxes, increase in fuel prices and political decisions to protect the environment. Growing extra time for security reason is another disadvantage of air transport.[69] Meanwhile, the high-speed rail networks are becoming denser, more transnational and more efficient. And they are not only in Europe and Japan anymore: they are spreading out to North America, Russia and China.[70] Especially the first and last ones are good examples. Plans for high-speed rail in the US, that is, with speeds over 177 kilometres per hour (110 mph), date back to the High Speed Ground Transportation Act of 1965. Various state and federal proposals have followed, with limited success. But since 1993 ambitious plans have been developed for ten rail corridors for high-speed rail in many parts of the USA, including California, the Midwest, New England, Florida, Texas, Pennsylvania and the Pacific Northwest, as well as the southwestern states. A federal initiative has provided eight billion dollars to develop high-speed rail projects and to stimulate US federal and state planners to

67 See Predöhl, *Verkehrspolitik*, 125.

68 See Ulrich Friese and Kerstin Schwenn, 'Rivalen zwischen Luft und Schiene. Die Zukunft der Mobilität. Bahn drängt nach Europa, Luftfahrt unter Kostendruck, Straßenverkehr dominant', *Frankfurter Allgemeine Zeitung* of 11 August 2010, and the SCI Verkehr GmbH, The Worldwide Market for Rail Freight Transport and its Operators: Markets – Trends – Players of 2008, http://www.sci.de/uploads/tx_edocuments/Product_information_MC_SGV_eng.pdf (last accessed on 28 February 2014). For UIC see Press Release No. 8 /2014: 4th UIC Global Rail Freight Conference – 'GRFC 2014' – organised with the Austrian Federal Railways (ÖBB) and to be held from 23–25 June 2014 in Vienna, http://www.uic.org/com/IMG/pdf/grfc_en.pdf (last accessed on 28 February 2014).

69 Rüdiger Soldt, 'Mit Tempo 300 durch die Champagne. Vom Wochenende an fahren TGV and ICE regelmäßig von Stuttgart und Frankfurt nach Paris', *Frankfurter Allgemeine Zeitung* of 8 June 2007, 'Fliegen auf der Schiene', *Frankfurter Allgemeine Zeitung* of 29 March 2008, Friese and Schwenn, 'Rivalen zwischen Luft und Schiene'.

70 On high-speed railway in Russia see Anthony Heywood, 'Back to the Future? Russia's Railway Transport and the Collapse of the Soviet Union in Historical Perspective', in Ralf Roth and Henry Jacolin, eds, *Eastern European Railways in Transition: Nineteenth to Twenty-first Centuries* (Surrey 2013), 257–86, here 277–80.

coordinate the expansion of high-speed services.[71] Other projects have followed, such as the California High-Speed Rail for a high-speed rail connection from Anaheim to San Francisco via San Jose, which should be completed in 2028, and two years ago Amtrak made a 151-billion-dollar proposal for the construction of a high-speed-capable rail line that would allow for a speed of more than 350 kilometres per hour and would cut trips between New York City and Washington, DC to only 94 minutes.[72]

And what about China? Until 1980 most trains in China were driven by steam locomotives because of cheap coal. But in the 1980s and 1990s they were replaced by electric and diesel engines. The result of this innovation was a remarkable increase in the maximum speed of express trains from 120 to 200 kilometres per hour since 1997, and some passenger trains already have reached a maximum speed of 350 kilometres per hour on certain sections of main lines.[73] Moreover, as of 2012 China has the world's longest high-speed rail network with over 10,000 kilometres of routes in service, including the world's longest line, the 2,298-kilometre Beijing-Guangzhou High-Speed Railway.[74] Since the high-speed rail service in China was introduced on 18 April 2007, daily ridership has grown from 237,000 in 2007 to 1.33 million in 2012, making the Chinese high-speed rail network the most heavily used in the world.[75]

Convincing is also the development of urban rail systems. It is a fact that rail transport increases in urban agglomerations when the capacity of the road network

---

71 See US Department of Transportation and Federal Railroad Administration, Vision for High-Speed-Rail in America, 1 April 2009, http://www.fra.dot.gov/eLib/details/L02833 (last accessed on 3 March 2014). See also Thomas J. Billitteri, 'High-Speed Trains: Does the United States need supertrains?', *CQ Researcher*, 19, 17, May 2009, http://library.cqpress.com/cqresearcher/document.php (last accessed on 28 February 2014).

72 See Alex Goldmark, 'Amtrak Updates High-Speed Rail Vision, What's Changed', *Transportation Nation* of 9 July 2012, and high-speed rail in the United States, http://en.wikipedia.org/wiki/High-speed_rail_in_the_United_States (last accessed on 1 March 2014).

73 See http://www.railcn.net/news/tiedaobu/railway-99672.html (last accessed on 10 October 2010).

74 See 'China's railways mileage tops 100,000 kilometres', *Xinhua* of 28 December 2013, and 'World's longest fast train line opens in China', *The Associated Press* of 26 December 2012, http://bigstory.ap.org/article/worlds-longest-fast-train-line-opens-china (last accessed on 17 February 2014).

75 See 'China's high-speed programme back on track', *Internatinal Railway Journal* of 10 January 2013, http://www.railjournal.com/index.php/high-speed/chinas-high-speed-programme-back-on-track.html (last accessed on 17 February 2014), 'China High Speed Train Development and Investment', *The China Perspective* of 27 December 2012, http://www.thechinaperspective.com/articles/chinahighspeedr-9905/ (last accessed on 17 February 2014), and http://whhh.fc2web.com/ktx/hikaku.html (last accessed on 17 February 2014), and http://en.wikipedia.org/wiki/High-speed_rail_in_China#cite_note-10000_km-1 (last accessed on 17 February 2014). See also 'China wird zum Exporteur von Superschnellzügen', *Frankfurter Allgemeine Zeitung* of 15 July 2010.

reaches its limits. Therefore, three articles in the second part present some initial explanations of how railways survived this gigantic shift from rail to road, using the example of three major cities in Europe: Paris, Turin and Frankfurt am Main. What were the consequences of motorisation and of the modernisation of the road network in the knots of the net, that is, the cities, and what does this mean for the rail systems? Mathieu Flonneau discusses this topic in 'The Metamorphosis of Public Transport Services in the Paris Region: the Modal and Moral Victory of "Automobilism" in the 1920s and 1930s'. He analyses the change in the Parisian ground transport system during the interwar period, when the streetcars vanished from the streets of Paris. But why, 'who killed the streetcar'?[76] One first explanation might be because of a successful intervention of the road, tire and oil lobbies. But the problem seems to be more complex. The author presents a sketch of the Paris transport system which consisted of a dozen private companies that dominated the passenger transport market at the beginning of the 1920s. An attempt was made to create a governmental department. But it was immediately confronted with the fact that there was not enough transport capacity for an increasing population. For a rapid closure of the gap the number of buses was increased and this is why 'bus traffic increased continuously'.[77] But increasing the number of buses and, of course, of cars collided immediately with the streetcar system and this situation ended up in a fight for space on Paris streets.

This was exactly the time when the French architectural and intellectual avant-garde developed revolutionary plans for fundamentally new types of cities. Well known are Le Corbusier's plans, such as the *ville contemporaine* or *plan voisine*, which demanded as a precondition for their realisation a total destruction of the old city of Paris, a reorganisation of the area with skyscrapers and wide and open public spaces between them. That would indeed have provided enough space for the flood of cars. But the inner city of Paris was not sacrificed to the new god of mobility. The officials found a less sensational victim, that is, the streetcar system. This is why the increase in capacity of motorbuses was accompanied by a parallel decline of streetcars in the mid-1930s. All in all, the bus system replaced no fewer than 110 tram lines. A similar picture could be drawn of Chicago in the 1920s, as did Paul Barret whom we have mentioned above. Flonneau's conclusion is that it was not only the lobby of the car industry but public necessities that altered transport systems inside urban areas, in the case of Paris at the expense of the traditional urban rail system above ground. The underground, that is, the *métro*, was not affected because it did not collide with the city's road system.

Massimo Moraglio shows us a totally different development, in the example of Turin in his article 'Rails in the Car Kingdom: Competition, Changes and Continuity in Urban Mobility – the Case of Turin, 1914–73'. As we have learned from Lay and Ruppmann, Italy played an important role in highway construction in Europe. There was enthusiasm indeed for automobiles in the interwar period

---

[76] Mathieu Flonneau on page 340 of this volume.

[77] Mathieu Flonneau on page 345 of this volume.

and this continued after the Second World War. But what did that mean for the Italian cities and especially for those cities which were centres of the prosperous Italian car industry like Turin? The fact that the city lived off Fiat did not mean that rails necessarily declined. The author

> … present(s) the example of Turin as a paradigmatic combination of struggle, compromise, integration, continuity and innovation between roads and rails, showing the contradictions, negotiations, limits and strengths of those transport systems and how they met the requirements of mobility.[78]

Moraglio discusses various schemes to modernise public transport in Turin. In the 1920s we find a mishmash of parallel streetcar lines of two companies and several city lines. Furthermore, we see a clear increase in the number of lines and in passenger numbers during the interwar period. This development was supported by the city government that followed a protectionistic rail policy. This is why this time can be called the golden era of trams despite the fact that the state implemented a gigantic programme of road construction in the 1930s. The same happened after the war. From the 1950s onward we find more and more public space being used for car mobility but this did not lead to a situation similar to what happened in Paris. The fact that public space for transport and mass mobility was limited encouraged the city officials to reconsider the concepts of urban mass mobility at the end of the 1950s and 1960s. The outcome was not a systematic substitution of trams by bus lines but an expansion of the trams and new plans for a U-train system in the 1970s. The city also initiated some experiments with an elevated train system, the Alweg train, at the end of the 1950s and the early 1960s.[79] However, the U-train plan failed because of the oil crisis at the beginning of the 1970s, but in the aftermath of this crisis trams enjoyed an even greater acceptance than ever before. The author explains why:

> Even when, in the 1960s, car ownership became a mass phenomenon, track-based mass transport system went on, as the tram was considered an indispensable part of the city's infrastructure. So the tram, which was seen by the Turin elite as a less efficient substitute for a local train network and a cheaper substitute for an underground, survived the entire twentieth century because it was the best available solution for workers' mass mobility in the industrial city.[80]

Something similar happened in the German city of Frankfurt am Main and, surprisingly, at a certain moment Frankfurt city officials saw Turin as a model to solve the urban congestion problem. The next parallel to Turin was Frankfurt's

---

78 Massimo Moraglio on page 356 of this volume.

79 See http://www.alweg.com/alwegcologne/alwegtorino1961.html (last accessed on 24 February 2014).

80 Massimo Moraglio on page 370 of this volume.

important role in the networks of highways and that is what the contribution by Reiner Ruppmann is about. He entitles his article 'The City and the *Autobahn* 1926–56: How Frankfurt am Main Promoted Road Traffic and Realised an Old Dream'.[81] What Fiat was for Turin, the highway juncture in the southwestern part of the city was for Frankfurt. Ruppmann focusses on the changes in the traffic system of the city of Frankfurt am Main within the last 200 years as the emphasis has gone from roads to railroads to roads again. As a result of its history Frankfurt is, more than other places in Germany, a striking example of competition between rails and roads but also, ultimately, of the productive integration of the two. What kind of impact did highways have on cities? Ruppmann answers this question with a description of the topic that covers nearly one century. After the First World War the effect of motorisation was on the political agenda of all major German cities. But increases in motorisation and especially truck traffic turned out to be a nightmare for regional and local road authorities because only a few roads were paved and the 'dust plague' became a big issue in the public debate, all of which made urban planners focus their attention right on the problems of road construction. This is why authorities studied the examples of the United States and the United Kingdom, that is, all the topics about which Bruce Seely has informed us. In the area around Frankfurt experiments took place to figure out what might be the best surface or what would be the outcome of separated streets for different users. This was the start of highway planning. Most German cities were not ready to fund long-distance motorcar roads but Frankfurt was. The leading city administration officials saw the far-reaching perspective of the automotive age as an opportunity for the future. They became seriously engaged in the HaFraBa association and attempted to establish a private-public partnership for the projects of a north-south and an east-west highway that would cross in the immediate surroundings of Frankfurt. Within only one year a planning group delivered a first draft of these routes. Then came the regime change in 1933 and city officials were drawn into the efforts of the regime to realise a highway network. This is why members of the city administration played an important role in highway planning and construction in the Rhine-Main region. But what was the outcome for Frankfurt? In the 1930s and during the war highways did not impact the city very much. The cities in the region, including Frankfurt, had severe problems with access roads as connections to the *Autobahn* because they had no money to build them. This could not be realised before the 1950s. But Ruppmann refers to later developments:

> Today mobility experts aspire to find intelligent combinations of the three types of transportation facilities and to facilitate movement from one form of transportation to another – the so-called intermodal traffic. In Frankfurt a very efficient three-modal traffic hub was implemented in 2000 when German

---

[81] The article is based on his groundbreaking study, *Schrittmacher des Autobahnzeitalters. Frankfurt und das Rhein-Main-Gebiet* (Pacemaker of the Motorway Age – Frankfurt and the Rhein-Main Area) (Darmstadt 2011).

> railways completed the new Intercity Express station next to the Frankfurt Rhein-Main Airport and near the *Frankfurter Kreuz*. The seeds of this state-of-the-art solution had been planted about 70 years earlier when construction of the *Autobahn* and the airport started in 1933.[82]

But what did this mean for the urban rail network? Did Frankfurt follow the Paris or the Turin case in taming the flood of cars inside a very densely populated city area, including a core that dates back to the Middle Ages? The answer is: Frankfurt followed the path of Turin. While the American type of individual mass transport caused a decline of public transport in urban areas, the same development led to an expansion of public transport in many European cities. The reason becomes clearer when we look a bit more closely at the Frankfurt case. The city was in some respect a forerunner of new urban rail projects beyond the streetcar in Germany. Soon after the beginning of mass mobility by automobiles in the 1950s the same problems appeared as in Chicago of the 1920s. Hans-Reiner Müller-Raemisch, responsible for urban planning and development in Frankfurt's city administration, described the situation: 'At the end of the 1950s the situation in the streets of the city became unbearable during rush hour. Congestions at all crossings, the streets were blocked and as well as busses and streetcars which should bring more people to their working places as individual cars stuck in the middle of the general traffic jam'.[83]

This happened despite the fact that long before the Second World War Frankfurt's city administration had created a dense and efficient streetcar system and that already in the 1930s plans had been developed to tunnel some lines in the densely built city centre. The plan failed because the tunnelling was seen as too costly. But when the problem of traffic jams increased, the idea reappeared and was seriously discussed again although the costs were calculated up to 20 or 30 million Deutsche Marks per kilometre. In this context the project of an elevated train system modelled after the Turin experimental train system also came up and was proposed at the end of the 1950s. The so-called *Alwegbahn* which had been realised in Turin in 1959 had some advantages; above all, lower construction costs compared to a U-train system. But the implementation of stations was not easy and at the end the street system in Frankfurt was too narrow for such a project. This is why Frankfurt decided to pursue a variation of a U-train system which was discussed in many German cities at the time as a solution to gain space in the streets for the automobile. The system was called *Unterpflasterstraßenbahn*, which, freely translated, means streetcars under the pavement. The idea was to run this system underground only in the inner city. In the outer areas the trains would be used more or less as normal streetcars but in separated lanes between the two directions of street traffic. One argument was that the old streetcar wagons could stay in use

82 Reiner Ruppmann on page 393 of this volume.

83 Hans-Reiner Müller-Raemisch, *Frankfurt am Main. Stadtentwicklung und Planungsgeschichte seit 1945* (Frankfurt am Main and New York 1998), 98.

in such a project.[84] The idea became part of the *Generalverkehrsplan* (General Transport Plan) of the city of Frankfurt in 1961, the city's parliament agreed in 1962, and construction work started with great success in the following years.[85]

But this was not the end of the story. While the U-train project was planned and realised by the city administration, the *Deutsche Bundesbahn* (Federal German Railway) was not involved. But shortly after the magistrates of Frankfurt had decided to build the U-train and while the system was under construction, the state railway also became interested in the expansion of its S-train lines in the urban area of Frankfurt and, furthermore, the state railway suddenly preferred a tunnel solution in the inner centre of the city. The result was the project of a huge tunnel from the east to the west side of the city including a tunnelling of the River Main.[86] This is why a rather small city of 600,000 inhabitants at the time ended up with two U-train systems. But with these investments in public rail transport it was possible to generate one million jobs, that is, 1.4 per inhabitant.[87] As a result of this development the city built upwards and developed a skyline that includes the greatest density of skyscrapers in Europe. Müller-Raemisch concludes:

> The economic success in the further development of the city gave proof to the construction of the U-train system. Without such efficient transport facility the attraction of many large and financially strong companies in such a small urban environment would have not been possible. Surveys approved that most of the employees working in the business and banking district made use of public transport and in this way diminished the car density.[88]

---

84 See Müller-Raemisch, *Frankfurt am Main*, 98, and U-Straßenbahn, http://de.wikipedia.org/wiki/U-Straßenenbahn#Frankfurt_am_Main (last accessed on 10 February 2014).

85 See Müller-Raemisch, *Frankfurt am Main*, 105–8.

86 See Müller-Raemisch, *Frankfurt am Main*, 105. On the further development of public rail transport in Frankfurt see Geschichtliche Entwicklung des Frankfurter Nahverkehrs, http://www.trampage.de/geschichte_p214.html (last accessed on 4 March 2014). On the history of Frankfurt's streetcars see Horst Michelke and Claude Jeanmaire, *100 Jahre Frankfurter Straßenbahnen: 1872–1899–1972* (Brugg/Switzerland 1972) and Anton Wiedenbauer and Hans-Jürgen Hoyer, *Fahrt in die Zukunft – Die Geschichte der Frankfurter Straßenbahn* (Frankfurt am Main 1968). On the Alweg train see http://de.wikipedia.org/w/index.php?title=Datei:FFM-ALWEG.png, and http://www.alweg.com/alwegcologne/alwegtorino1961.html (last accessed on 24 February 2014). On the U-train system and urban transport in general see Jens Krakies and Frank Nagel, *Stadtbahn Frankfurt am Main: Eine Dokumentation*, 2nd ed. (Frankfurt am Main 1989), Thomas Hanna-Daoud, ed., *Nahverkehr in Frankfurt. Trambahn, U-Bahn, S-Bahn, Omnibus, Eisenbahn.* Strassenbahn-Nahverkehr special. Nr. 7 (Munich 2000), and Stadt Frankfurt am Main, ed., *Gesamtverkehrsplan Frankfurt am Main, Ergebnisbericht 2004. Studie im Auftrag des Stadtplanungsamts zur zukünftigen Entwicklung Frankfurter Verkehrsnetze* (Frankfurt am Main 2004).

87 Müller-Raemisch, *Frankfurt am Main*, 105.

88 Müller-Raemisch, *Frankfurt am Main*, 102–3.

The success of Frankfurt contributed to a renaissance of S-trains in the 1970s and then continued also in the 1980s and 1990s up to the present. Meanwhile, this renaissance of rail transport in urban areas has spread across Europe. In many countries, local and regional public rail transport has increased in the last 30 years.[89] Since the start of the new millennium many cities have experienced a comeback of streetcars and trams and also of U- and S-trains. But it is not only Europe that rediscovered the efficiency of urban rail systems. Metropoles in the USA and in Asia have made large-scale investments in urban rail systems, too.[90] Remarkable is the change in the United States – the motherland of motorisation! Since the oil crisis of 1973 there has been a slow rethinking among American city planners and clear signs for a renaissance of public rail transport. Glenn Yago analysed this shift already in the 1980s and described how easily German, French, Swedish and Canadian cities were able to switch back to urban and regional rail systems in answer to increasing fuel prices.[91] In contrast, American cities had to deal with severe problems in that area because the technological knowledge had vanished together with the decline of public transport since the 1920s. The nearly total loss of know-how is surprising because the United States is the country where this technology was more or less invented or where the most important steps towards practical solutions were taken in the 1880s. One might mention the name of Frank J. Sprague, a naval officer and inventor who contributed to the development of the electric motor, electric railways and electric elevators. His contributions were especially important in promoting urban development by increasing the size cities could reasonably attain – through better transportation. He became known as the 'Father of Electric Traction'.[92] But after six or seven decades of intense motorisation the technology of urban rails had not only stagnated but had totally disappeared. For the planning of the modern streetcar or other urban rail systems in Los Angeles the authorities had to import know-how from Sweden and Western Germany. Similar problems appeared with S- or U-trains. Urban planners had rediscover technologies that were lost during motorisation.[93] But despite these technological and financial problems almost all larger cities were forced to increase systems

[89] See Massimo Moraglio, 'Light Rail Renaissance in European Cities: Urban Mobility Agenda and City Renewals', in Ralf Roth and Paul van Heesvelde, eds, *The City and the Railway in the World 19th to 21st Centuries* (Surrey 2014 [forthcoming]).

[90] On India see Anupama Mann, 'A Symbiotic Relationship: The Delhi Metro Rail and the National Capital Region', and Chigurupati Ramachandraiah, 'Urban Mega Projects and Civic Conflict – The Case of Hyderabad Metro Rail Project (India), both in Ralf Roth and Paul van Heesvelde, eds, *The City and the Railway in the World 19th to 21st Centuries* (Surrey 2014 [forthcoming]).

[91] Yago, *Decline of Transit.*

[92] See Frank J. Sprague. IEEE Global History Network. IEEE. http://www.ieeeghn.org/wiki/index.php/Frank_J._Sprague, and http://en.wikipedia.org/wiki/Frank_J._Sprague (last accessed on 28 February 2014).

[93] Yago, *Decline of Transit*, 207–10.

of public rail transport – even in Chicago, the forerunner of motorisation.[94] This demonstrates that also in times of mass motorisation there is a need for balanced public transport on rail, such as streetcars, U-, S- and regional trains.[95]

However, as the examples show, there is a clear renaissance of rail transport in urban environments on long-distance, high-speed lines and in some parts of freight transport. All in all, experts predict an increase in rail transport in the near future: in exact figures, from 7.3 to 8.3 per cent by 2025.[96] Can we therefore speak of a shift back from roads to rails at the beginning of the twenty-first century, a reversal of what happened at the beginning of the twentieth century? This is not very likely. Most transportation experts see a continuation of car mobility for the foreseeable future. But the question probably is wrong, and we ask it because we are looking too closely at the aspect of competition and underestimating the fact of the interdependence of the two networks. The facts are very clear: the rail network developed successfully as an answer to the limited capacity of road services in the nineteenth century, but it only broadened the transport market and did not generally replace road transport. The increase in the importance of road transportation in the twentieth century was the answer to the limitations of rail transport, for example its unsuitability for cargo freight or door-to-door service. But rail transport did not vanish in the twentieth century any more than road transport vanished in the nineteenth century when railways revolutionised the transportation of goods and human mobility with far-reaching consequences.[97] Obviously there is room for both kinds of transport, and it is not controversial to speak of them as interdependent. That interdependence is a major theme of the present volume, which offers 15 chapters that focus on the question of mobility on rails and roads, and on the innovations that had to be made in order to transform the two systems into modern and interconnected networks for all kinds of mobility in the twenty-first century.

References

Anonymous, 'Motor car vehicle registration from 1895 to 1929', US Bureau of Public Roads, http://www.railsandtrails.com/AutoFacts/1930p15–100–8.jpg (last accessed 14 August 2010).

Avery, Derek, *The Complete History of North American Railways* (Secaucus, NJ 1989).

Bagwell, Philip, *The Transport Revolution from 1770*, sec. ed. (London 1988).

[94] See Complete Guide to North & South American Metro rail and Light Rail Systems, including Subways, Els, Peoplemovers, Subte networks, http://www.urbanrail.net/am/america.htm (last accessed on 10 January 2014).

[95] Yago, *Decline of Transit*, 213.

[96] Ruhkamp, 'Kein Auslaufmodell'.

[97] See Predöhl, *Verkehrspolitik*, 127 and 130.

Barrett, Paul, *The Automobile and Urban Transit: The Formation of Public Policy in Chicago, 1900–1930* (Philadelphia, PA 1982).

Billitteri, Thomas J., 'High-Speed Trains: Does the United States need supertrains?', *CQ Researcher*, 19, 17, May 2009, http://library.cqpress.com/cqresearcher/document.php (last accessed on 28 February 2014).

Boch, Rudolf, ed., *Geschichte und Zukunft der deutschen Automobilindustrie* (Stuttgart 2001).

Braun, Hans-Joachim, and Kaiser, Walter, *Energiewirtschaft, Automatisierung, Information seit 1914* (Berlin 1997).

Bund Deutscher Architekten and Deutsche Bahn AG, *Renaissance der Bahnhöfe*, Katalog der Ausstellung mit gleichem Namen in Kooperation mit Meinhardt von Gerkan (Berlin 1996).

Burnham, Daniel H. and Bennett, Edward H., *Plan of Chicago* (Chicago, IL 1909).

Burnham, Daniel H. and Kingery, Robert, *Planning the Region of Chicago* (Chicago, IL 1956).

Cipolla, Carlo M., 'The Emergence of Industrial Societies', in Carlo M. Cipolla, ed., *The Fontana Economic History of Europe. The Industrial Revolution*, 6 vols (Glasgow 1975).

Condit, C.W., *Chicago, 1920–1929* (Chicago, IL 1973).

Cron, F.W., 'The dynamics of Highway Curvature', part 5 of 'Highway Design for Motor Vehicles – a Historic Review', *Public Roads*, 39, 4, 1976, 163–71.

Deutschen Reichsbahn-Gesellschaft, Hauptverwaltung, ed., *Reichsbahn und Kraftwagenverkehr. Denkschrift* (Berlin 1930).

Dienel, Hans-Liudger and Schiedt, Hans-Ulrich, eds, *Die moderne Straße. Planung, Bau und Verkehr vom 18. bis zum 20. Jahrhundert* (Frankfurt am Main and New York 2010).

Dorpmüller, Julius, 'Rede Julius Dorpmüllers vom 30. Januar 1929', *Die Reichsbahn*, 5, 1929, 109–16.

Edelmann, Heidrun, *Vom Luxusgegenstand zum Gebrauchsgegenstand. Die Geschichte der Verbreitung von Personenwagen in Deutschland* (Frankfurt am Main 1989).

Ewen, Stuart, *Channels of Desire* (University of Minnesota 1982).

Foster, Mark S., *From Streetcar to Superhighway: American City Planners and Urban Transportation, 1900–1940* (Philadelphia, PA 1981).

Fraunholz, Uwe, *Motorphobia. Anti-automobiler Protest im Kaiserreich und Weimarer Republik* (Göttingen 2002).

Fremdling, Rainer, *Eisenbahnen und deutsches Wirtschaftswachstum 1840–1879* (Dortmund 1975).

Galbraith, John Kenneth, *The Affluent Society* (Boston, MA 1958).

Gall, Lothar, 'Eisenbahnen in Deutschland: Von den Anfängen bis zum Ersten Weltkrieg', in Lothar Gall and Manfred Pohl, eds, *Die Eisenbahn in Deutschland. Von den Anfängen bis zur Gegenwart* (Munich 1998), 13–70.

Geddes, Norman Bel, *Magic Motorways* (New York 1940), https://ia600208.us.archive.org/10/items/magicmotorways00geddrich/magicmotorways00geddrich.pdf (last accessed 1 March 2014).
Goldmark, Alex, 'Amtrak Updates High-Speed Rail Vision, What's Changed', *Transportation Nation* of 9 July 2012.
Hanna-Daoud, Thomas, ed., *Nahverkehr in Frankfurt. Trambahn, U-Bahn, S-Bahn, Omnibus, Eisenbahn*. Strassenbahn-Nahverkehr special. Nr. 7 (Munich 2000).
Haubner, Barbara, *Nervenkitzel und Freizeitvergnügen. Automobilismus in Deutschland 1886–1914* (Göttingen 1998).
Headrick, Daniel, *Tentacles of Progress* (New York 1988).
Heywood, Anthony, 'Back to the Future? Russia's Railway Transport and the Collapse of the Soviet Union in Historical Perspective', in Ralf Roth and Henry Jacolin, eds, *Eastern European Railways in Transition: Nineteenth to Twenty-first Centuries* (Surrey 2013), 257–86.
Hooker, George E., *Through Routes for Chicago's Steam Railroads* (Chicago, IL 1914).
Kleinschmidt, Christian, *Konsumgesellschaft: Grundkurs* (Stuttgart 2008).
Kolb, Eberhard, 'Die Reichsbahn vom Dawes-Plan bis zum Ende der Weimarer Republik', in Lothar Gall and Manfred Pohl, eds, *Die Eisenbahn in Deutschland von den Anfängen bis zur Gegenwart* (Munich 1998), 109–63.
König, Wolfgang, *Geschichte der Konsumgesellschaft* (Stuttgart 2000).
Krakies, Jens and Nagel, Frank, *Stadtbahn Frankfurt am Main: Eine Dokumentation*, sec. ed. (Frankfurt am Main 1989).
Lardner, Dionysius, *Railway Economy. A Treatise on the New Art of Transport, its Management, Prospects and Relations, Commercial, Financial and Social* (New York 1968).
Lay, Maxwell G., *Die Geschichte der Straße. Vom Trampelpfad zur Autobahn* (Frankfurt am Main and New York 1994).
Mann, Anupama, 'A Symbiotic Relationship: The Delhi Metro Rail and the National Capital Region', in Ralf Roth and Paul van Heesvelde, eds, *The City and the Railway in the World 19th to 21st Centuries* (Surrey 2015, forthcoming).
Mauch, Christof and Zeller, Thomas, eds, *The World beyond the Windshield. Roads and Landscapes in the United States and Europe* (Stuttgart 2008).
McNeill, John R. and William, H., *The Human Web. A Bird's-Eye View of World History* (New York and London 2003).
Merki, Christoph Maria, *Verkehrsgeschichte und Mobilität* (Stuttgart 2008).
Merki, Christoph Maria, *Der holprige Siegeszug des Automobils, 1895–1930. Zur Motorisierung des Straßenverkehrs in Frankreich, Deutschland und der Schweiz* (Vienna 2002).
Merriam, C.E., *Chicago: A More Intimate View of Urban Politics* (New York 1970).
Michelke, Horst and Jeanmaire, Claude, *100 Jahre Frankfurter Straßenbahnen: 1872–1899–1972* (Brugg/Switzerland 1972).
Mills, F., 'Effects of Beltways on the Location of Residences and Selected Workplaces', *Transport Research Board Records*, 8, 12, 1981, 26–33.

Moraglio, Massimo, 'Light Rail Renaissance in European Cities. Urban Mobility Agenda and City Renewals', in Ralf Roth and Paul van Heesvelde, eds, *The City and the Railway in the World 19th to 21st Centuries* (Surrey 2015, forthcoming).

Möser, Kurt, *Geschichte des Autos* (Frankfurt am Main and New York 2002).

Müller-Raemisch, Hans-Reiner, *Frankfurt am Main. Stadtentwicklung und Planungsgeschichte seit 1945* (Frankfurt am Main and New York 1998).

Mumford, Lewis, *The City in History: Its Origins, Its Transformations, and Its Prospects* (San Diego, NY, and London 1989).

Osterhammel, Jürgen, *Die Verwandlung der Welt. Eine Geschichte des 19. Jahrhunderts* (Munich 2009).

Patton, P., *Open Road* (New York 1986).

Pollins, Harold, *Britains Railways: An Industrial History* (Newton Abbot 1971).

Predöhl, Andreas, *Verkehrspolitik* (Göttingen 1958).

Ramachandraiah, Chigurupati, 'Urban Mega Projects and Civic Conflict – The Case of Hyderabad Metro Rail Project (India), in Ralf Roth and Paul van Heesvelde, eds, *The City and the Railway in the World 19th to 21st Centuries* (Surrey 2015, forthcoming).

Reichsverband der Automobilindustrie, ed., *Eisenbahn und Kraftwagen. Zur Denkschrift des Deutschen Industrie- und Handelstags* (Berlin 1930).

Rossberg, Ralf Roman, *Geschichte der Eisenbahn*, sec. ed. (Frankfurt am Main 1984).

Roth, Ralf, 'Interactions between Railways and Cities in Germany – Some examples', in Ralf Roth and Marie-Noëlle Polino, eds, *The City and the Railway in Europe* (Aldershot 2003), 3–28.

Roth, Ralf, *Das Jahrhundert der Eisenbahn. Die Herrschaft über Raum und Zeit 1800–1914* (Ostfildern 2005).

Roth, Ralf, 'Die Eisenbahn verändert die Stadt – die Stadt verändert die Eisenbahn', in Wolfgang Kos and Günter Dinhobl, eds, *Grosser Bahnhof. Wien und die weite Welt* (Vienna 2006), 36–42.

Roth, Ralf, 'Die Eisenbahnen der Welt – formten sie wirklich ein world wide web?', *Zeitschrift für Weltgeschichte*, 12, 2, 2011, 77–106.

Roth, Ralf and Jacolin, Henry, eds, *Eastern European Railways in Transition, Nineteenth to Twenty-first Centuries* (Surrey 2013).

Ruppmann, Reiner, *Schrittmacher des Autobahnzeitalters. Frankfurt und das Rhein-Main-Gebiet* (Pacemaker of the Motorway Age – Frankfurt and the Rhein-Main-Area) (Darmstadt 2011).

Schieder, Theodor, *Staatensystem als Vormacht der Welt 1848–1918* (Frankfurt am Main 1980).

Schimpff, Gustav, 'Wirtschaftliche Betrachtungen über Stadt- und Vorortbahnen', *Archiv für Eisenbahnwesen*, 35, 1912, 597–643, 849–73, 1167–201 and 1456–82, and *Archiv für Eisenbahnwesen*, 36, 1913, 20–53 and 383–416, here *Archiv für Eisenbahnwesen*, 35, 1912, 597.

Schmidt, Gert, ed., *Automobile und Automobilismus* (Frankfurt am Main and New York 1999).

Schulz, Günter, 'Die Deutsche Bundesbahn 1949–1989', in Lothar Gall and Manfred Pohl, eds, *Die Eisenbahn in Deutschland von den Anfängen bis zur Gegenwart* (Munich 1998), 317–76.

SCI Verkehr GmbH, The Worldwide Market for Rail Freight Transport and its Operators: Markets – Trends – Players of 2008, http://www.sci.de/uploads/tx_edocuments/Product_information_MC_SGV_eng.pdf (last accessed on 28 February 2014).

Scott, Mel., *American City Planning Since 1890* (Berkeley, CA 1969).

Seely, Bruce E., Der Pan American Highway – eine Straße zwischen zwei Kontinenten, *Zeitschrift für Weltgeschichte*, 12, 2, 2012, 141–74.

Shank, W.H., *Vanderbilt's Folly: A History of the Pennsylvania Turnpike*, sec. ed. (York, PA, 1973).

Stadt Frankfurt am Main, ed., *Gesamtverkehrsplan Frankfurt am Main, Ergebnisbericht 2004. Studie im Auftrag des Stadtplanungsamts zur zukünftigen Entwicklung Frankfurter Verkehrsnetze* (Frankfurt am Main 2004).

Studienausschuss 'Eisenbahn und Kraftwagen' beim Deutschen Industrie- und Handelstag, ed., *Eisenbahn und Kraftwagen*. Denkschrift March 1930 (Berlin 1930).

Stürmer, G., *Geschichte der Eisenbahnen. Entwicklung und jetzige Gestaltung sämmtlicher Eisenbahnnetze der Erde* (Bromberg 1872).

Tilly, Stephanie and Triebel, Florian, eds, *Automobilindustrie 1945–2000. Eine Schlüsselindustrie zwischen Boom und Krise* (Munich 2013).

Tubbesing, Markus, 'Der Wettbewerb Groß-Berlin: Die Suche nach der Einheit im Großstadt-Chaos', in Harald Bodenschatz et al., eds, *Stadtvisionen 1910/2010* (Berlin 2010), 64–70.

US Department of Transportation and Federal Railroad Administration, Vision for High-Speed-Rail in America, 1 April 2009, http://www.fra.dot.gov/eLib/details/L02833 (last accessed on 3 March 2014).

Veblen, Thorstein, *The Theory of the Leisure Class: An Economic Study of Institutions* (Mineola, NY, 1994, orig. 1899).

Weiner, E., *Urban Transportation Planning in the United States: An Historical Overview.* US Department of Transportation, Department of Transport (Washington, DC 1986).

Weingroff, Richard F., 'Federal-Aid Highway Act of 1956: Creating the Interstate System', *Public Road*, 60, 1, 1996 (online, no pagination), http://www.fhwa.dot.gov/publications/publicroads/96summer/p96su10.cfm (last accessed 28 February 2014).

Whitehill, Walter M., *Boston in the Age John F. Kennedy* (Norman, OH 1966).

Wiedenbauer, Anton, and Hoyer, Hans-Jürgen, *Fahrt in die Zukunft – Die Geschichte der Frankfurter Straßenbahn* (Frankfurt am Main 1968).

Wittig, Paul, *Die Weltstädte und der elektrische Schnellverkehr. Nach dem Vortrag im Berliner Architektenverein am 13. März 1909* (Berlin 1909).

Wolf, Peter M., *The Future of the City: New Directions in Urban Planning* (New York 1974).

World Bank, *World Development Indicators* (New York 2005).
Yago, Glenn, *The Decline of Transit. Urban Transportation in German and U.S Cities, 1900–1970* (Cambridge 1984).

PART I
Rails and Roads Between Competition and Interdependency

Chapter 1

Rails and Roads Between Competition and Interdependency: a Long and Winding Relationship with Many Innovations That Failed

Ralf Roth

Over the course of the two centuries that led up to 1800, road travel made great progress. Coaches and carriages improved, as did logistical organisation. Post companies enhanced their services to passengers. Then, at the turn of the nineteenth century, a discussion began of some innovative ideas regarding a particular transport system for goods traffic. The ideas concerned iron rails and iron wheels.[1] At the beginning of this discussion stood very fundamental considerations. Problems facing transport included the tendency of vehicles to sink in mud, and the fact that they lost energy on unpaved roads due to friction. Smooth, hard surfaces seemed to be needed. It made sense to experiment with paved roads (*Steinstraßen*), as in the Netherlands, where road builders had become aware of the advantages of hard roads of stone or bricks. But experts spoke more and more of a kind of road made of iron, and in this context there emerged a new form of transport whose speed inspired the imagination of the public at the turn of the nineteenth century.

The railway consisted essentially of three components: rails, flanged wheels and steam engines for propulsion. The wheel-rail system was of fundamental importance. The rolling of the iron wheel on an iron surface brought large savings in energy compared with street transport. The railway was the nineteenth century's answer to the rough streets of the previous centuries. The new system could be

[1] This article is based on a presentation in the panel 'From Rails to Roads (and vice versa?)' at the Seventh International Conference on the History of Transport, Traffic and Mobility: Energy and Innovation, in Lucerne, Switzerland from 5 to 8 November 2009. A similar publication in German entitled 'Zwischen Wettbewerb und Abhängigkeit: Ein langes und kompliziertes Verhältnis von Straße und Schiene mit vielen fehlgeschlagenen Innovationen' is included in Christoph Siepermann and Michael Eley, eds, *Logistik – gestern, heute, morgen, Festschrift für Richard Vahrenkamp* (Berlin 2011), 15–42.

Figure 1.1 Map of Central Europe including postal coach services around 1714

Source: Postroutenkarte from Johann Peter Nell and Johann Baptist Homann 1714. Museumsstiftung Post und Telekommunikation Berlin.

loaded heavily, and had the advantage of 'minimal friction of the rail'.[2] On this point, all the pioneers of railways agreed. Joseph von Baader, for example, pointed out the advantages very clearly:

> Instead of rough, bumpy gravel and macadam, or tough and bottomless mud and sludge piles, over and through which the loaded cars often need to be hauled, sometimes when they are sunk up to the hubs of the wheels, a process which is extremely tedious and involves the most violent shocks, the railways approach the ideal of unchanging perfection, independent of the weather's influence, along permanent paths and mirror-smooth, hard, flat surfaces on which the wheels of the carriages constructed for them roll continuously without shaking.[3]

The beginning of the system can be traced back to mining in early modern times. In his *Cosmographia Universalis*, Sebastian Münster described a wooden railway that had been used in silver mines of the Alsatian Leberthal in the sixteenth century.[4] In the eighteenth century, English coal mining entrepreneurs successfully made use of iron fittings on wooden planks and flanged wheels. Here the term 'railroad' appeared for the first time; the system achieved considerable success. The first iron rails were relatively thin strips of sheet metal which were nailed on along planks laid down in the direction of travel. The German term for these was *Straßbäume*; they formed fairly efficient rails. Later on, cast-iron rails were used, including in the British village of Coalbrookdale. John Curr introduced the L-shaped flanged rails made with cast-iron plates in hard-coal mines in Sheffield

2 Friedrich Harkort, *Die Eisenbahn von Minden nach Cöln*, ed. by Wolfgang Köllmann (Hagen 1961), 38. See also A.L. Crelle, *Einiges allgemein Verständliche über Eisenbahnen insbesondere als Privat-Unternehmungen* (Berlin 1835), 6, and Joseph von Baader, *Ueber die Vortheile einer verbesserten Bauart von Eisenbahnen und Wagen* (Munich 1826), 23.

3 Joseph von Baader, *Die Unmöglichkeit, Dampfwagen auf gewöhnlichen Strassen mit Vortheil als allgemeines Transportmittel einzuführen, und die Ungereimtheit aller Projekte die Eisenbahnen dadurch entbehrlich zu machen* (Nuremberg 1835), iii–iv. See also Ludwig Henz, *Bericht über Project und Vorarbeiten zu der Anlage einer Eisenbahn von Elberfeld über Hagen nach Witten* (Elberfeld 1836), 132. Ludolf Camphausen agreed with them and opined: 'The improvement of transport capacities depends only minimally on the improvement of carriages, but above all on the reduction of friction at the surface of the streets'. Ludolf Camphausen, *Die Eisenbahn von Köln nach Antwerpen* (Cologne 1835), 34.

4 See Georgius Agricola, *De re metallica.* Bergwerksbuch (Basel 1557), and Sebastian Münster, *Cosmographia universalis* (Basel 1541). At this time the term *Gleis der Trömen* for tracks was created. Some are of the opinion that this was the origin for the English term 'tramway' which was taken over into German language as *Trambahn*, an old expression for the German *Straßenbahnen*. See Ralf Roman Rossberg, *Geschichte der Eisenbahn*, new ed. (Frankfurt am Main 1984), 12.

in 1776.[5] In the late 1760s, the Coalbrookdale Company began to fix plates of cast iron to the wooden rails. These (and earlier railways) had flanged wheels as on modern railways, but another system was introduced, in which unflanged wheels ran on L-shaped metal plates – these became known as plateways. John Curr, a Sheffield colliery manager, invented the flanged rail, though the exact date of this is disputed.

Beginning in 1770, cast-iron rails were laid on stone blocks, first at the Derby Canal Railway in Great Britain.[6] According to some sources, in the 1730s, the Briton Ralph Allen invented an iron flanged wheel that allowed a more secure drive on rails. According to other sources, iron flanged wheels were not introduced before 1789. Together with flanged wheels came rails with a mushroom-shaped profile, and a strengthening of the network. But the relatively short cast-iron rails were not suitable for the high pressure of the wheels of a running locomotive. In 1820, John Berkinshaw of Durham succeeded in producing rails by rolling. This enabled the creation of rails out of more durable material and in great length – at that time, 15 English feet, that is, 4.575 metres:

> The cross-sectional shape was initially the same mushroom shape and support the same also with cast iron chairs on stone blocks. Oddly, it was believed, also of the fish belly shape in the longitudinal direction should not vary and rolled with great difficulty, the wave guide. These tracks are first rolled on a small part of the web-Stocton Darlington [sic] (1825) and on the first large railway locomotive, Liverpool-Manchester (1826–30).[7]

The advantages of rails were considerable. One horse could now pull several coal wagons at the same time.[8] This inspired the imagination of transport reformers. Friedrich Glünder argued that horses used on rails could provide multiples of their current performance.[9]

Shortly after the first English railway company successfully commenced operation on the line between Liverpool and Manchester, the first railway line in Germany also went into business, running between Nuremberg and Fürth in 1835. But for it to come this far, a series of problems had to be solved.

---

[5] John Curr, *The Coal Viewer, and the Engine Builder's Practical Companion*, 2nd ed. (London 1970).

[6] Rossberg, *Geschichte*, 10–12.

[7] Bibliographisches Institut, ed., *Meyers Großes Konversations-Lexikon*, 6th ed. (Leipzig and Vienna 1905–09).

[8] See F. Glünder, *Kurze Darstellung einiger der wichtigsten Verhältnisse bei Eisenbahnen mit besonderer Beziehung auf solche Anlagen zwischen Hamburg, Bremen und Hannover* (Hannover 1834), 7. On the importance of the flanged wheel see Anonymous, *A History and Description of the Liverpool and Manchester Railway* (Liverpool 1832), 6, and Rossberg, *Geschichte*, 14.

[9] See Glünder, *Darstellung*, 12, and Baader, *Vortheile*, 39.

The railway committee had to manage a period of intense work at the construction site, coping with extremely difficult logistical problems there; they had to manage the transport of English locomotives that they would use; and they had to find convincing answers in a fundamental debate about whether a railway was even necessary for the modernisation of the transport infrastructure, or if it would be better to let steam carriages run directly on the streets. Indeed, there were technical alternatives to steam locomotives on rails. Up to the 1840s, discussions went on about the possibility of using compressed air as a driving force.[10] Above all, the view persisted that steam engines could drive direct on country roads (*chausseen*), either as they were, or once they were improved with great effort.

Between 1810 and 1830, that is, parallel to the construction of the first experimental railways, the interest of English transport reformers was attracted by numerous attempts to develop a self-propelled street carriage, a dream that had attracted attention since the Middle Ages. In the thirteenth century, Roger Bacon, a monk and educated person, noted:

> One day it will be possible to construct a carriage which moved and will keep moving without being pushed or pulled from any sort of animal.[11]

Starting in 1447, so-called *Muskelkraftwagen* (muscle-powered carriages) appeared on the scene. In 1490, Leonardi da Vinci drew a sketch of an armoured carriage that could be mechanically propelled. A bit more than 100 years later the Dutch mathematician Simon Stevin constructed some land yachts powered by wind that could transport up to 30 people, but these vehicles had some difficulties to keep the direction. From 1650 to 1660, the German mathematician Johann Hautsch sold ornate mechanical carriages (*Prunkwagen*) which were propelled by muscle force.

In 1674, the Dutch physicist Christiaan Huygens constructed a motor that was driven by gunpowder. Therefore he is seen as a pioneer of the internal combustion engine and one of the inventors of the piston engine. Most automobile motors of today work on Huygens' principles. But he himself never took his work beyond the experimental stage. Shortly later, in 1680, Sir Isaac Newton presented the concept of a steam mobile, which was realised 80 years later by the Scottish engineer James Watt. In the 1760s Watt enriched the debate about a steam engine with some fundamental suggestions and in 1768 he constructed a first working model of his

---

10 See contemporary publications of Andraud Motay and Tessié, *Ueber die comprimirte Luft als universelle Triebkraft und unentgeltliches Ersatzmittel der Dampfkraft* (Weimar 1841); Clegg and Samuda, *Mallets Bericht über die atmosphärische Eisenbahn von Dublin nach Dalkey in Irland* (Darmstadt 1844), and Friedrich Becker, *Die atmosphärische Eisenbahn. Nach den Berichten von Smith, Mallet, Samuda, Pim etc. und englischen Quellen bearbeitet* (Frankfurt am Main 1844).

11 Quoted from Nationales Automobilmuseum, ed., *Die großartigsten Autos des Jahrhunderts* (Straßburg 2005), 130. See also Günther Mensching, *Roger Bacon* (Münster 2009).

Figure 1.2 Land yacht made by Simon Stevin for Prince Maurice of Orange, 1649

Source: Wikimedia Commons (http://de.wikipedia.org/w/index.php?title=Datei:Simon_Stevins_zeilwagen_voor_Prins_Maurits_1649.jpg) (last accessed 14 March 2012).

Simon Stevin built two land yachts for Prince Maurice, who used them on the beach to entertain his guests.

ideas. He patented both his invention of a steam engine and its use as a carriage drive. From this moment on it was only a short step to the construction of a self-propelling unit by transferring the kinetic energy back to the transport mechanism of the engine. Indeed, the first attempt followed soon, only two years later but not by Watt.

In 1770 Josef Cugnot experimented with a steam carriage that would serve as a tractor for cannons. It was envisioned that the carriage he invented could also serve on roads. Independent from him and independent from James Watt, Oliver Evans had thought about the concept of a steam mobile and took a ride with his own experimental model through the streets of Philadelphia in 1797.[12]

---

12 The smith and boat builder Oliver Evans published an article about the value of railways, which he foresaw as shuttles for canals. A bit later he started building steam mobiles, with which he travelled through the streets of Philadelphia. His idea of a railway between Pittsburgh and New York did not find public support. See Rossberg, *Geschichte*, 151.

The previous year, William Murdoch, an engineer employed by Watt, had built a small model carriage; this inspired Richard Trevithik, another inventor, to become interested in steam mobiles. In 1801 Trevithick built the first steam coach and drove it through Camborne near Plymouth. Later on he introduced the machine to the public in London. Other inventors followed between 1814 and 1830, including Major Pratt, John Stevens, William Palmer, Thomas Tindall, Joseph Reynolds, David Gordon, Julius Griffiths, Burstall of Edinburgh and J. Hill of London.[13] Their experiments were not without success. Gordon and Burstall undertook serious attempts to develop steam coaches to technical and commercial functionality and Goldsworthy Gurney installed a regular steam omnibus transport between the city of London and some suburbs in 1822. A bit later Walter Hancock followed with the establishment of the London and Paddington Steam Carriage Company.[14] All these attempts were carefully monitored by Michael Alexander Lips, one of the 'busiest apostles of highway steam transport (*Chaussee-Dampffahrt*)' as von Baader ironically wrote.[15]

The outlook was indeed promising because there were some attractive arguments for a rail-less steam transport system. All of these arguments seemed to solve a problem of the rail system. Railways as transport facilities are a directed system with limited possibilities for individual and free use. In the 1820s and 1830s this disadvantage directed the attention of transport reformers to steam carriages without rails. With such carriages it would have been possible to make

13 Albert Edward Richardson and Harold Donaldson Eberlein, *The English Inn Past and Present: A Review of its History and Social Life* (Manchester 1980), 64.

14 See Wolfgang von Hippel, 'Gut Ding will Weile haben. Die Eisenbahnpläne von Ludwig Newhouse und Friedrich List und die Reaktion von Regierung, Landtag und Öffentlichkeit', in Wolfgang von Hippel et al., eds, *Eisenbahnfieber. Badens Aufbruch ins Eisenbahnzeitalter* (Mannheim 1990), 35–59, here 36–8, Artur Fürst, *Die hundertjährige Eisenbahn. Wie Meisterhände sie schufen* (Munich 1925), 28–30, and 34, and Max Maria von Weber, *Aus dem Reich der Technik*, 2 vols (Berlin 1928), vol. 2, 121–6. On the contemporary discussion about the beginning of the railway age see Baader, *Unmöglichkeit*, 6–8. In 1816, Ritter von Reichenbach, the director of a salt production operation, who was the opponent of initiatives for the construction of canals, announced the first steam mobile in Germany. But his announcement was not followed by action. Also in England many public promises and applications for patents for the construction of steam carriages had no consequences. See Joseph von Baader, 'Ueber den gegenwärtigen Zustand und die künftigen Aussichten der Dampfwagen', *Polytechnisches Journal*, 14, 7, 1833, 1–39, here 34.

15 Baader, *Unmöglichkeit*, 50. Baader referred to the pamphlet of Michael Alexander Lips, *Die Unanwendbarkeit der englischen Eisenbahnen auf Deutschland und deren Ersatz durch Dampffuhrwerk auf verbesserten Chausseen* (Marburg 1833). Because the idea of steam mobiles or steam carriages seemed to be plausible, many initiators of railway lines as Ludolf Camphausen and also Johannes Scharrer had to take it seriously. See Camphausen, *Die Eisenbahn*, 16–31, and Johannes Scharrer, *Deutschlands erste Eisenbahn mit Dampfkraft oder Verhandlungen der Ludwigs-Eisenbahn-Gesellschaft in Nürnberg. Von ihrer Entstehung bis zur Vollendung der Bahn* (Nuremberg 1836), 43.

use of existing roads and streets, and therefore to avoid heavy investments in a totally new and costly infrastructure of rails. The renovation could have been limited to a modernisation of the fleet of coaches and carriages. Moreover, and probably of even greater importance, this would have allowed the mechanisation of independent and individual transport. It would have made it easy for existing companies in the post and freight sectors to transform themselves into a modern transport industry. It would have paved the way for individual mobility 100 years before mass motorisation began in the 1950s.[16]

This was the core of the debate over the relative advantages of steam rail cars and steam mobiles at the end of the 1820s and beginning of 1830s. In Germany, the main debaters were Joseph von Baader on the rail side and Michael Alexander Lips on the street side. Both stood in more or less close connection to the railway committee of Nuremberg, which would later construct the first German railway line in 1835.[17] As long as the public debate remained unresolved and uncertainty remained about the new transport system, there would be little investment into it. A decision had to be taken. It is interesting to step a bit deeper into the controversy.

Joseph von Baader was convinced that all accounts of successful journeys with steam coaches and steam mobiles were 'deceptions, boasts, and fairy tales (*Täuschungen, Gasconnaden und Märchen*)'.[18] Transport by steam traction without rails could not work because the great weight of the steam engines and the poor condition of the streets would cause heavy shocks and vibrations that would lead to the destruction of both. Additionally, Baader argued, one must take into consideration the destructive effects of dust and thrown-up street filth (*aufgeworfenem Straßenkoth*).[19] To avoid shocks one could only diminish the speed (*Mäßigkeit der Geschwindigkeit*), in which case the advantage over horse-drawn coaches and carts would vanish.[20] The only way out of this dead end would be to construct much better streets, either using the 'macadam' model invented by the Scotsman John Loudon McAdam, or as 'stoneways' (*Steinbahnen*) or by

---

16 This discussion reappeared later on and the German railway engineer Max Maria von Weber wrote several contributions about it in the 1870s. See Max Maria von Weber, *Die Induvidualisierung und Entwickelbarkeit der Eisenbahnen* (Leipzig 1875).

17 See Ralf Roth, 'It Began 175 Years Ago – the First German Railway Line and Its Importance for the City of Nuremberg and for the National Railway Network', paper presented at the Fourth International Conference on Railway History: Cities, Users and their Railways of the International Railway History Association, Mechelen, 27–29 May 2010.

18 Baader, *Unmöglichkeit*, 10 and VI.

19 See Baader, *Unmöglichkeit*, 15 und 51. See also Baader, *Zustand*, 7 and 24.

20 Baader, *Unmöglichkeit*, 15. The list of his criticisms was underlined by a long list of necessary repairs whose frequency could not diminished by 60 years of experiments. See Baader, *Unmöglichkeit*, 13, and Elfriede Rehbein et al., *Zu Wasser und zu Lande. Die Geschichte des Verkehrswesens von den Anfängen bis zum Ende des 19. Jahrhunderts* (Munich 1984), 194.

paving the surface (*Pflastern der Oberfläche*). However, this would not only cost a lot of effort and time, but also more money than laying iron rails.[21]

Baader's next argument was that if one did not take into consideration the problems with the street's surface, steam engines would be dangerous for passenger and other participants of street traffic. Because

> even if it were really possible or practicable, however, to go with such steam wagons on ordinary streets just as fast as on iron rails, without the machine being in danger of breaking down at any point, or else flipped over and smashed upon running over a stone in the middle of the street, not only would the people sitting in the wagon be in constant danger of breaking their necks or bones, but also everyone else who went on the same street on foot, on horseback, or on ordinary wagons would not be safe at any moment of their lives.[22]

For mental history this argument is of great interest, because streets at this time were seen as an open public space for all, where all traffic participants could freely move between slow driving carts and coaches. Streets had not become the dead zones of today in which pedestrians are banished to a small strip on either side of the street to support a speedy flow of motor vehicles. It was, in Baader's opinion, a significant argument for railways that faster transport would be separated from slower and more leisurely transport, for the benefit of safety.[23]

But more than technical problems and dangers for life and limb, Baader stressed the economic disadvantages of his opponents' ideas. The more power steam mobiles would need for a ride on ordinary streets – 40 times that of a railway – would, according to Baader, vice versa mean that one would have to buy 40 steam mobiles for the same transport achievements as of one train. Furthermore, engines more robust than those currently in use would have to be built in order to withstand the numerous shocks. Those new engines would need more water and

---

21 See Baader, *Unmöglichkeit*, 42–3. A similar verdict was expressed by Ludolf Camphausen, who referred in that context to an account of the introduction of a steam-carriage connection on the route from Holyhead to London. Experiments there had been successful and led to the foundation of a steam carriage company between Birmingham and London, but only on the condition that a 'particular way', that is, a 'road with ashlars (*Fahrbahn von Quadersteinen*)' would be built, costing £300,000. See Camphausen, *Die Eisenbahn*, 25–7 and 30. On English railway history see Terry Coleman, *The Railway Navvies* (London 1965), Michael J. Freeman and Derek H. Aldcroft, eds, *Transport in Victorian Britain* (Manchester 1988), Michael J. Freeman, *The Railway and the Victorian Imagination* (Yale 2000), Ellis C. Hamilton, *British Railway History*, 2 vols (London 1957), H. Pollins, *Britain's Railways: An Industrial History* (Newton Abbot 1971); Jack R. Simmons and Gordon Biddle, *The Oxford Companion to Railway History* (Oxford 1997), and Jack R. Simmons, *The Victorian Railway* (London 1995).

22 Baader, *Unmöglichkeit*, 16–17. On numerous accidents with steam mobiles, see ibid., 13 and 22.

23 See ibid., 24.

more coal and bigger boilers, and therefore could provide less transport capacity. Taking this into consideration Baader calculated the cost for commercial use of steam mobiles on the route between Manchester and Liverpool and compared the result with the statistics from the railway line that had just been put into operation. The results spoke for themselves. To replace the six trains that were in use at this time, no fewer than 2,160 steam mobiles would have to be put into service. The cost for such an investment would have been the enormous sum of £1.8 million. That was three times the cost of the railway line, including all infrastructure and buildings.[24] This was a devastating result and Baader drew the conclusion

> that the annual expenditure of a route of the length of 30 miles (48.3 kilometres) based on steam mobiles would require the interest of around 27 million pounds sterling in capital. With such an amount of money one could build a double track railway of the most valuable construction type of the length of no less than 675 miles (1087 kilometres).[25]

The Bavarian railway pioneer's arguments were convincing. His opponent Lips gave in and confessed: 'that steam mobiles have not yet acquired the power to withstand the friction of a good road'.[26]

The result of the debate was that steam transport and steam mobility could not have been realised on the existing road network; it needed a new one: the railway system. But the victory of the railway system in the public debate was not over. One reservation continued, which would later fall into oblivion because of the success of railways – the fact that they could not be used for individual transport. But at the beginning of the railway age Lips was not alone in expressing the hope for a later renaissance of steam mobiles, when 'the construction of smooth and solid street surfaces would be possible by making use of better construction material – notably by procuring and using the splendid basalt'.[27]

Together with Lips, Ludolf Camphausen, the great railway investor of the Rhineland, opined 'that the solution of this wonderful but difficult task should be awaited in the future'.[28]

Thus steam engines on rails were viewed as an interim solution until individual transport could be placed on a secure technical base. This reservation was carried away by the railway pioneers and was later forgotten when the railways became the most successful transport facility of the nineteenth century, bringing an immense new type of infrastructure, a parallel transport network. The model for this was, of course, the line between Liverpool and Manchester. Lines between Brussels

---

24 See ibid., 30.

25 Baader, *Unmöglichkeit*, 36. See also Baader, *Zustand*, 36.

26 Michael Alexander Lips, *Die Nürnberg-Fürther Eisenbahn in ihren nächsten Wirkungen und Resultaten* (Nuremberg 1836), 5.

27 Lips, *Nürnberg-Fürther Eisenbahn*, 6–7.

28 Camphausen, *Die Eisenbahn*, 31.

and Mechelen in Belgium and Nuremberg and Fürth in Germany followed within several years after the debate between Lips and Baader was decided.

The rail network expanded rapidly in the following decades alongside the street network.[29] In fact, the networks for land transport doubled, and these two networks with all their transport facilities competed fiercely from the beginning. We all know which of them was the winner in the nineteenth century – in the so-called age of railways.

Figure 1.3a Railway network of Europe 1870

Source: Theodor Schieder, *Staatensystem als Vormacht der Welt 1848–1918* (Frankfurt am Main, Berlin and Vienna 1977), 424–5.

29 On the discussion see Ralf Roth, *Das Jahrhundert der Eisenbahn. Die Herrschaft über Raum und Zeit 1800–1914* (Ostfildern 2005), 14–32.

Figure 1.3b Railway network of Europe 1913

Source: Theodor Schieder, *Staatensystem als Vormacht der Welt 1848–1918* (Frankfurt am Main, Berlin and Vienna 1977), 424–5.

In a period of six decades in the German states and later in the German Empire, tens of thousands kilometres of tracks were laid. In Europe the length of tracks amounted to several hundred thousand kilometres.

Together with the spread of the system, more and more locomotive and carriage factories were founded in Europe and North America. The import of locomotives from United Kingdom declined in the 1850s and was replaced by national production. Independent technical solutions and steady increases in speed and capacity soon followed. Enormous capital investments took place. In Germany alone, capital investments in the railway sector amounted to 60 million Marks in 1840 and swelled to two billion Marks by 1913. In the 1880s, railways absorbed up to two-thirds of all German investments. Rail construction not only required vast amounts of money but also strained the financial market to the limit. This was why railways also fostered the modernisation of the stock market and the establishment of large banks. Not all investors were successful. Many shareholders had to gain experience and some lost their shirts. The construction boom itself led to many feedback effects (*Rückkoppelungseffekte*) on the German economy. It massively sped up iron production and coal mining. The railway sector not only had a great demand for iron and coal but also increased the efficiency of distribution. Between the railways and the steel industry, interactions piled up that contributed enormously to an expansion of the economic fundament of German society, that is, it improved the economy. Coal mining skyrocketed from two million tons in 1840 to 190 million in 1913. In the same decades, iron and steel production grew from 0.3 to 19.3 million tons, and freight transport multiplied from 3.2 million to 61 billion ton-kilometres, an increase even higher than that of passenger transport, which increased from 62 million to 41 billion person-kilometres. Railways transported more and more people and freight over ever greater distances.[30]

Railway distribution made goods cheaper in two ways, first through its role in increasing production, that is, through greater efficiency in exchange of material and goods between factories, and second through lowering costs for goods transport from manufactures to retailers and consumers. In general, the speed and reliability of all transportation increased. There was also an increase in travel comfort. The railway was a transport system that could be used in multifunctional ways. Accordingly, impacts could be found in many areas. We can mention only a few of them here. Railways made possible a greater decentralisation and more complex division of labour in industry, because they linked industrial locations and regions in Germany, Europe and the Americas. They contributed to a worldwide network for the shipment of goods. On land, railways were the medium for business travel. They increased the efficiency of administrations and governmental activities (*Staatshandeln*), and even the efficiency of warfare. They connected local and regional political movements, enabled the formation of national organisations and contributed to the creation of national cultures – including by enabling all kinds of artists to travel freely around their countries. They facilitated summer-time tourism to spas and other destinations. For some social classes, they introduced the culture of tourism. With cheaper transport, the mobility of the poor increased tremendously, both for play and for work. This resulted in enormous waves of migration from the countryside to growing cities or to distant regions, and, in combination with modern shipping, to other continents. Railways connected cities like Augsburg, Esslingen and Berlin with regions of heavy industry where the necessary coal, iron and steel were produced, and with their markets. For centres of trade like Frankfurt and harbour cities like Hamburg and Bremen, railways became absolutely necessary both for goods transport and for business travel. Educated people made use of railways to visit cultural monuments or beautiful

30 Roth, *Das Jahrhundert*, 130–33.

landscapes, and those who were looking for leisure travelled via railways to baths and contributed to the upswing in many spas and tourist cities.[31]

This is why railways also affected people's environments. This was especially true in the knots of the network – big cities and metropolises. Railways often changed the functions, the sizes and of course the shapes of those cities. Big cities needed railways, because they made it possible to unite growing urban landscapes. In many cases the centre of power of such cities shifted from the traditional marketplace, the exclusive housing area and the city hall to the railway station, the new gateway to the surroundings.

In most cases, at the edge of the formerly rather small cities, neighbourhoods grew, and the square in front of the train station became a place for exclusive development. Here settled exclusive hotels and major business districts. The station street became a high-class address in the nineteenth century.

The modernised cities stretched out much farther into the region than they had at the beginning of the century. This is why railways can be thought of as developers of the surrounding country.[32] This is clearly illustrated by the example of Berlin. Around 1870 planners discussed the concept of a railway ring around the city to solve the problem of limited housing areas for a speedily growing population:

> In our opinion, only railways (*Locomotiv-Eisenbahnen*) are able to satisfy all the demands of regular mass passenger transport because of their capacity to provide all classes of people with cheap transport (*Communication*) from the entire surroundings of the city to the centre and from the latter to all areas of the periphery.[33]

This statement is from a petition to the Ministry of Trade, Industry and Public Works of 23 October 1871, by the magistrate of Berlin, who requested a circle line around the city with a connection to the city centre. This was justified by the need for urban passenger traffic and for the opening of the region for development. The purpose was to make possible healthy and inexpensive housing for all classes 'with all the amenities of country living and the incomparable joys of Mother Nature'.[34] The intention was 'to colonise on a large scale'.[35] This line of argumentation shaped the bulk of the public discussion in which leading members of the railway and

---

31 Ralf Roth, 'Vom Adler zum ICE', *Damals*, 33, 7, 2001, 14–21.

32 Ralf Roth, 'Die Eisenbahn verändert die Stadt – die Stadt verändert die Eisenbahn', in Wolfgang Kos and Günter Dinhobl, eds, *GROSSER BAHNHOF. Wien und die weite Welt. Ausstellungskatalog* (Vienna 2006), 36–42.

33 Petition of the magistrate of Berlin from 23 October 1871, quoted from Hermann Schwabe, *Berliner Südwestbahn und Centralbahn. Beleuchtet vom Standpunkt der Wohnungsfrage und der industriellen Gesellschaft* (Berlin 1873), 7–9. See also *Berlin und seine Eisenbahnen 1846–1896*, 2 vols (Berlin 1896), vol. 2, 76–7.

34 Petition of the magistrate from 23 October 1871, 7–9.

35 Ibid.

city administration participated. The different projects developed in this context envisaged a ring of settlement, ten kilometres in diameter, for 200,000 households, that is, a million people.[36] Indeed, the *Wilhelminischer Ring* (Wilhelmine Ring of Settlement) for a population of around two million people based on the City and Ring Railway was built between 1877 and 1882. In all larger cities, branches of the main arteries of the long-distance railway network stretched out from the cities into the region and formed complex networks of suburban railway lines. They tied the city with suburbia. City planning was powerfully influenced by the railway.

In time, as the process of industrialisation accelerated more and more and developed on an ever-broader basis, the cities in Germany, Europe and North America grew enormously. The ever-larger urban landscapes were laboratories for the development of ever-more complex railway systems. They had to be adapted to the conditions of the new densely populated urban spaces. These conditions included speedy acceleration to serve short distances between two stations, less noise, less emissions and separation from street traffic. A search began for new technical solutions. Siemens presented a model of an electric train at the 1879 Berlin Industrial Exposition. Two years later the company introduced the first tramway in Lichterfelde, a suburb of Berlin. Soon there followed a second line from Offenbach to Frankfurt.

In the 1890s tramways spread rapidly in the cities of the Western world. But in metropolises like Berlin, Paris and London they were only half of the solution. They conflicted with the increasing street traffic, and the great distances of the new urban landscapes demanded speedy electrical railways (*Schnellbahnen*). Such systems were not developed in Berlin but in America's large urban environs. In the 1890s, the elevated trains of metropolises like Boston, Chicago and New York were redesigned and appeared around 1900 in Europe as subterranean railways in London and Paris and then in Berlin. In this form they contributed enormously to diminishing the noise, and they did not conflict with street transport as tramways did. From these beginnings originated our contemporary U- and S-Bahn systems, and one cannot imagine the existence of modern metropolises without them. They solved not only the problems of distances in modern urban environments but also the problem of a great bulk of emissions of the old railway system. They did not conflict with street traffic and they did not separate city quarters with a dense network of rails. All in all they were a serious and successful attempt to minimise the potential of conflicts between railways and densely populated living environments, although the development of housing areas for settlement only

[36] See E. Engel, 'Die Wohnungsnoth: Ein Vortrag auf der Eisenacher Conferenz am 6. Oktober 1872', *Zeitschrift des kgl. Statistischen Bureaus*, 1872, 392–4. On the social background and on the fear of a 'coherent Berlin mass of stone' see Dieter Radicke, 'Öffentlicher Nahverkehr und Stadterweiterung: Die Anfänge einer Entwicklung beobachtet am Beispiel von Berlin zwischen 1850 und 1875', in Gerhard Fehl and Juan Rodriguez-Lores, eds, *Stadterweiterungen, 1800–1875: Von den Anfängen des modernen Städtebaues in Deutschland* (Hamburg 1983), 345–57, esp. 350.

functioned alongside these iron lines and not in the whole area. In any case, it was assumed that railways would be *the* transport means of the twentieth century for long-distance passenger travel, goods transport and intra-city transport. This assumption proved incorrect, as we know 100 years later. The question is why? To find an answer, we must view the world network of railways a little closer.

Table 1.1 Length of railways in the world, 1850 to 1930 (in kilometres)

Year	USA	Russia	Canada	India	Germany	France	UK
1850	14,500	500	100		2,100	900	3,900
1870	85,000	11,000	4,000	9,000	19,000	16,000	21,000
1890	335,000	31,000	23,000	27,000	43,000	33,000	28,000
1910	566,000	67,000	51,000	53,000	61,000	40,000	32,000
1930	692,000	78,000	91,000	71,000	58,000	42,000	33,000

Source: The table is based on Daniel Headrick, *Tentacles of Progress* (New York 1988), 55, and John R. McNeil and William H. McNeill, *The Human Web: A Bird's-Eye View of World History* (New York and London 2003), 220.

First, strictly considered, there was no world network of railways. Although there clearly was progress in the expansion of the railway network in the world from a length of several hundred kilometres in 1840 to 670,000 kilometres 50 years later, most of that development took place in two regions: Western Europe and the United States. This result does not change even though the improvements outside these two hot spots accelerated later on and showed impressive construction rates. In absolute figures, the networks in Europe and North America grew faster than in the rest of the world. Around 1890 they were the only two areas with networks efficient and dense enough to serve a multitude of purposes – economic, social, cultural, political, administrative and military.[37] This means that in many parts of the world the railway networks did not replace the road and river networks that remained as legacies of the ancient world.[38]

There is another line of development to consider. It is well known that the power relationship between railways and streets reversed during the twentieth century, even in those regions where the railway system was dominant and formed a very dense network. Instead of a steadily increasing railway network, citizens were confronted with a renaissance of the road system in all industrialised and developed economies of the Western world.

Before modern electric railways spread from city transport into the whole transport field, coaches reappeared on the scene, and with them, individual transport. The situation was very similar to the rise of railways at the beginning

[37] See Michael Geistbeck, *Weltverkehr. Die Entwicklung von Schiffahrt, Eisenbahn, Post und Telegraphie bis zum Ende des 19. Jahrhunderts* (Reprint Leipzig 1986), 342–3.

[38] See Ralf Roth, 'Die Eisenbahnen der Welt – formten sie wirklich ein world wide web?', *Zeitschrift für Weltgeschichte*, 12, 2, 2011, 77–106.

of the nineteenth century. At the beginning of the twentieth century, some very small beginnings and technical experiments led the roadways to compete with railways for passenger and goods transport. When the motorcar became a facility for mass transport, many phenomena which accompanied the breakthrough process of railways took place again. This new period started with fundamental technical innovations – not, as one might think, the internal combustion engine, but the development of streets with a hard or paved surface and the innovation of pneumatic tyres. The system did not reach the low level of friction of the iron rail and iron wheel system, but achieved some very clear improvements in comparison with the former systems of street transport. At any rate it was enough for a revision of the decision about the technological path in transport – for railways over roadways – which had been taken in the 1830s.[39]

This was why railways, then the dominant transport facility for land transport, got a serious competitor. In an astonishing way, the reason for the paradigm shift leads back to the dawn of the railway age and on to the struggle in the environment of the Nuremberg committee: because together with technological improvements of the motorcar, we can consider a metamorphosis of the street as transport medium – not from one day to the next, of course, but in the decades that followed the automobile's appearance around the 1890s. Streets became not only more robust but also capable of rapid transportation of motorised coaches and carts – exactly as Lips and Camphausen had envisioned: 'When the construction of smooth and solid street surfaces becomes possible by making use of better construction material … then one can again think about a Locomobile'.[40]

The process of implementation and the transformation of modern individual transport into a serious competitor of railways was a process that took several decades. In Europe this process was interrupted twice by world wars, but in the end the result was clear.

In the 1930s we find serious plans for a continental network of particular routes for high speed traffic of motorcars across Europe, as the example of Kurt Gustav Kaftan shows. Parallel to the rail net, a second transport network for land transport developed. But unlike the rail network, it was an additional component of the very dense network of streets and indeed a part of it. The map (Figure 1.5) included the main lines of Kaftan's plan, which were oriented to the traditional transport routes. He foresaw three lines from Southwest to Northeast (with a variation from Paris to Warsaw), three lines from Northwest to Southeast (with a variation from Calais over Strasbourg and Munich to Belgrade) and three direct lines from North to South.

39 See Maxwell G. Lay, *Die Geschichte der Straße. Vom Trampelpfad zur Autobahn* (Frankfurt am Main and New York 1994), 160–62, and 219–38.

40 Lips, *Nürnberg-Fürther Eisenbahn*, 6–7.

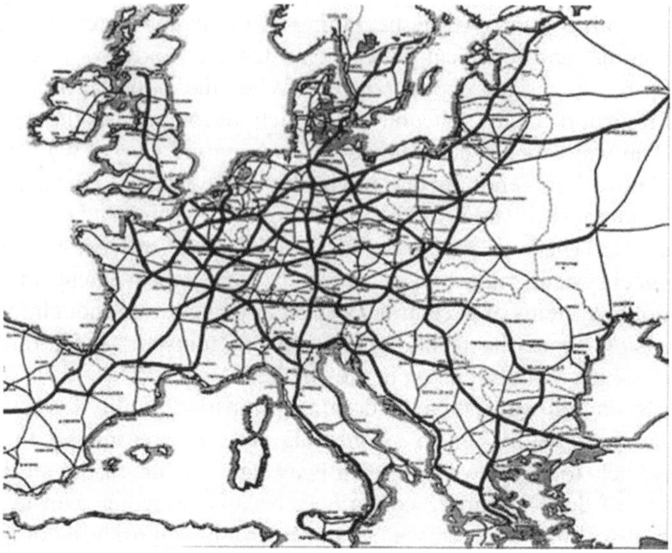

Figure 1.4 Road network of Europe: the vision of Kaftan in 1937 …

Source: Kurt Gustav Kaftan, 'Von der Reichsautobahn zur Europa-Autobahn', *Der Straßenbau*, 28, Nr. 4 of 15 February 1937.

Figure 1.5 … and the outcome: the International E-Road Network in 1990

Source: http://en.wikipedia.org/wiki/File:International_E_Road_Network _green.png (last accessed 29 September 2009).

In the second half of the twentieth century, most of the ever-increasing traffic volumes of land transport shifted into these modern roads. In contrast to this development, in the former hot spots of the transport revolution, the railway network stagnated and in many cases rail transport declined. Numerous lines had to be closed, and the total length of the rail network shrank in more or less all countries of the Western world. But despite this tendency, the decline was, in most cases, relative. In absolute figures the railway companies were able to defend their transport volume. In some cases they even succeeded in increasing it. But the share of the market fell steadily. In Europe, railways carried only 13 per cent of all transports in 2002. Similar developments took place in all the so-called developed countries of the Western world.[41]

What were the reasons for such success on the part of vehicular transport? Why did road construction attract such enormous investments? It was not – as one might assume – the technical safety, security, efficiency or travel comfort which made the motorcar attractive. Similarly, the attempt to explain motorcar transport as the culmination of the nineteenth century's obsession with speed leads us astray. These explanations are not convincing because for a long time railways were faster, more comfortable, secure and safer than automobiles. What then was the reason? Let us listen to an early motorcar enthusiast, Otto Julius Bierbaum, a professor in art history and a great German agitator for motorcars. He was sent from the *Adlerwerke* in Frankfurt, a motorcar manufacturer, to Italy in 1902. His mission was to demonstrate the usefulness and the qualifications of motorcars for touristic long-distance travel. He wrote a travelogue on the experiences of his journey, titled *Eine empfindsame Reise im Automobil* (*A Gentle Journey by Automobile*), and subtitled *Lerne Reisen ohne zu rasen* (*Learn to travel without racing*). Bierbaum compensated for the obvious disadvantages of a motorcar in comparison with the speed of ordinary railways at the time by praising the benefits.[42] Bierbaum's core argument was as follows:

> The railway ticket is paid for not only by money but also by an abandonment of one's self-determination for a certain period of time. But with a motorcar we determine whether we will drive fast or slow, where we will stop and where we will drive through without stopping.[43]

Self-determination: that was the dream of Alexander Lips and many railway opponents at the dawn of the railway age. That was why they agitated for steam mobiles.[44] Some 80 years after Lips' debate with Baader, the desire to take easy

[41] See on Germany http://www.gesis.org/fileadmin/upload/dienstleistung/ daten/soz_indikatoren/Schluesselindikatoren/V002.pdf (last accessed on 1 March 2011).

[42] See Otto Julius Bierbaum, *Eine empfindsame Reise im Automobil. Von Berlin nach Sorrent und zurück an den Rhein* (Reprint Munich 1955), 11.

[43] Otto Julius Bierbaum, *Yankeedoodlefahrt und andere Reisegeschichten* (Munich 1910), 20 and 467.

[44] See Roth, *Das Jahrhundert*, 50–57.

and unbounded trips increased as the new vehicle gained technical maturity and transport capacity. On the horizon, the possibility of individual transport shone brightly.

But it was not only the tempting freedom for self-determined travel and temporal flexibility. There was another reason connected to a second systemic disadvantage, namely, the low density of the network. The railway network was not only inflexible but also – despite all construction efforts – quite coarsely meshed, which meant that those who settled near a railway knot were at an advantage. For that reason, nearly all transport processes, of both passengers and goods, ended with a transfer by train or a reloading of goods. That problem deserves a closer look. Starting in the 1830s, the construction of railways alongside roads meant a doubling of transport networks. The two were in competition from the beginning. But this competition was only one part of the story. The second part was that the two networks needed each other. The railway system could not exist without a network of roads that was always much denser and had already achieved what the planners of railways longed for but never achieved: a density that would allow the connection of every village and city of a country – and even every house of a village or city.

In the railway timetable for Germany from 1854, we see, beside some singular railway lines, busy networks of numerous postal courses. This gives an impression of the density of the postal service at the time. The railways could not replace it for many years because the railway network consisted only of some main arteries for transport and – crucially – always remained wide-meshed, never close-knit. Around the mid-1850s, numerous cities were not connected with the net of railway lines, and they still relied totally on postal services or freight cart entrepreneurs. Würzburg, for example, a medium-sized city and a prince-bishopric, had 12 postal routes at its disposal. Göttingen, a university city, could only be reached by foot or one of its six postal routes. Mainz, a bishopric too, had only a single railway line, but seven postal connections for all directions. Even Frankfurt with its four railway companies was approached by five main routes of postal service.[45] Despite all efforts to expand the railway network in the decades following the 1830s, and despite the success that more or less all cities were plugged in, the situation for smaller locations and villages remained unchanged, as we can see on the maps from 1854. The next station could only be reached on streets via coaches or later by buses. That is the reason why railways have always needed streets.[46]

---

45 See Heidemann, *Die Eisenbahnen*, map IV. In 1856 post companies in Prussia travelled no less than 4.3 million German miles (32.25 million kilometres) and railways only 1.3 million German miles (9.75 million kilometres). Gottfried Nort, 'Das Reisen mit der Post', in *Postkutschen* (Frankfurt am Main 1983), 4–8, here 8. See also Klaus Herrmann, 'Die Personenbeförderung bei Post und Eisenbahn in der ersten Hälfte des 19. Jahrhunderts', *Scripta Mercaturae* 11, 1977 3–25, and Klaus Herrmann, *Thurn und Taxis-Post und die Eisenbahnen* (Kallmünz 1981).

46 And that is also the reason why – contrary to the assumptions some decades before – there were more horses at the end of the nineteenth century than at its beginning.

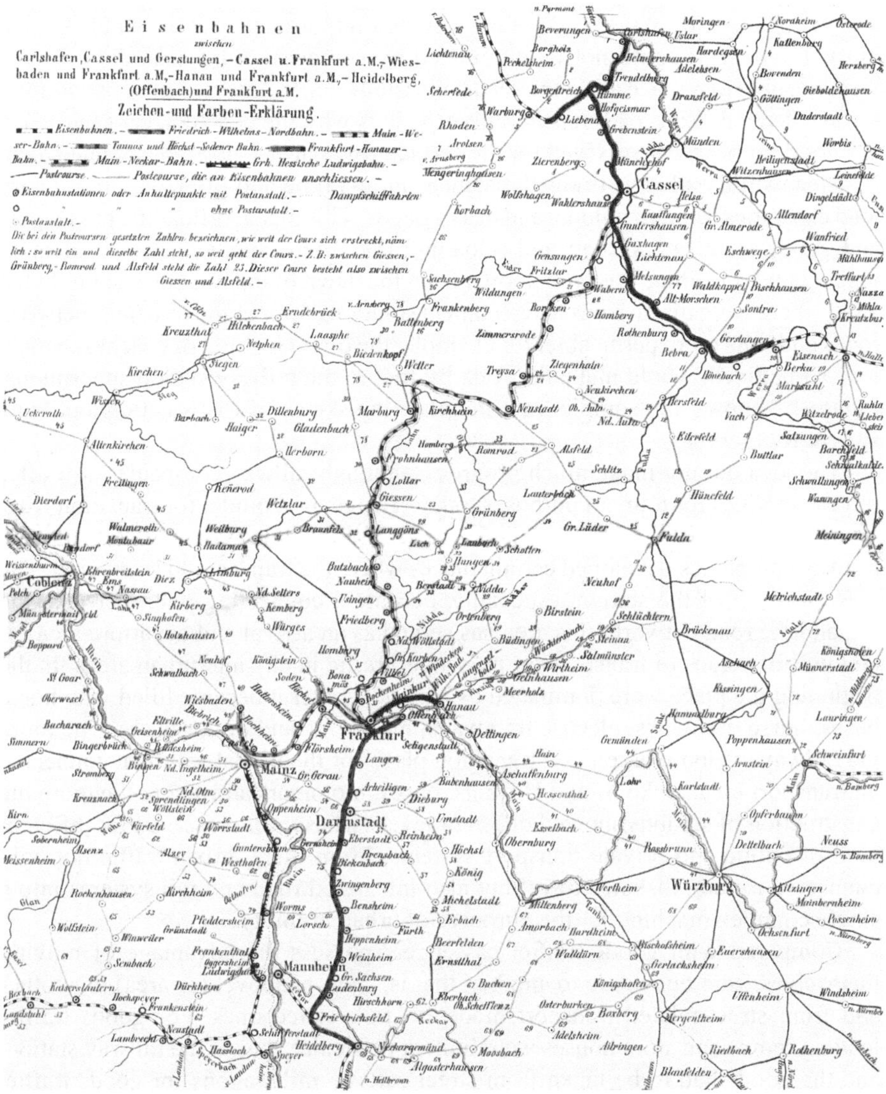

Figure 1.6 Part of the railway network and postal coach services on streets in the environment of Frankfurt around 1850

Source: F.W. Heidemann, *Die Eisenbahnen nebst den dazu gehörenden Post-Coursen und die Dampfschiffahrten in Deutschland* (Merseburg 1854), map IV.

They needed roads and transport facilities to bring passengers and goods to the next railway station. In this respect, competition was reduced to a question: when does it make sense to make use of railways? The success story of railways in the nineteenth century gives an answer to that question. As the rail network expanded, transport on roads was driven back to a regional and sometimes only local level.

The national routes of the road system lost their importance. But the whole system did not vanish; it could not be eliminated by competition because the railways were not able to replace all of the roads' functions. Furthermore, rail transportation always depended on road transportation. This is why the coach driver (*Kutscher*) did not disappear, but survived for the services of coaches, horse buses and so on.

Meanwhile, railways bridged distances in less time and offered extraordinary load capacities for high volume and heavy goods. This meant offloading passengers and goods from one system and reloading them onto another. The problem of loading and reloading was well known from the dawn of the railway age on. In the 1830s there were discussions and technical solutions for making transport between roads and rails more permeable: for example, the direct loading of coaches, which, it was imagined, would make the walk by foot to the railway station superfluous. Figure 1.7 shows an example from the planning sketch of List's national railway system for Germany.

The idea did not make much progress, although railway companies still offer rail car services for tourism purposes today. The general model for transition from road to rail and vice versa has become standardised. On the model of post stations, railway companies developed certain places where the trains could be entered. The place in front of the station, especially, became a connecting point between the rail and the road network; this area has served as an arrival and departure area for all kinds of means of transport for passenger traffic in city and urban areas. In the beginning the place were dominated by coaches. Later it became filled with horse buses, horse tramways, electric tramways, motorcars and motor buses. The more the railway station worked as a transition place for the modal split that connected all transport means like S- and U-trains, buses, motorcars and so on, the more the construction of stations showed different levels. These were reserved for different kind of public and private transport systems. From there, urban traffic not only connected to long distance travel but also integrated road and rail systems into a single complex machine for the purposes of urban mobility.

Compared with goods traffic, passengers possess the advantage of moving themselves from one mode to another, that is, from one level (or area) to another and from street-related transport modes to rail-related ones. For goods traffic, loading ramps and store houses were built at particular sites at the railway station, and the goods had to be taken from street carts to rail wagons for goods traffic. They had to be loaded on and offloaded. This was a hard and time-consuming job, which, in most cases, had to be done twice per shipment. The loading process doubled and that reduced the time and money saving achieved by speedy rail transport compared with the traditional form of road transport.[47]

This was why many attempts were made to put the train at the beginning of the transport chain. Big factories were built directly on railway lines, or else an

[47] Otto Blum, *Personen- und Güterbahnhöfe*, 2nd ed. worked over by Kurt Leibrand (Berlin, Göttingen and Heidelberg 1961), and Berthold Grau, *Bahnhofsgestaltung*, 2 vols (Berlin 1968).

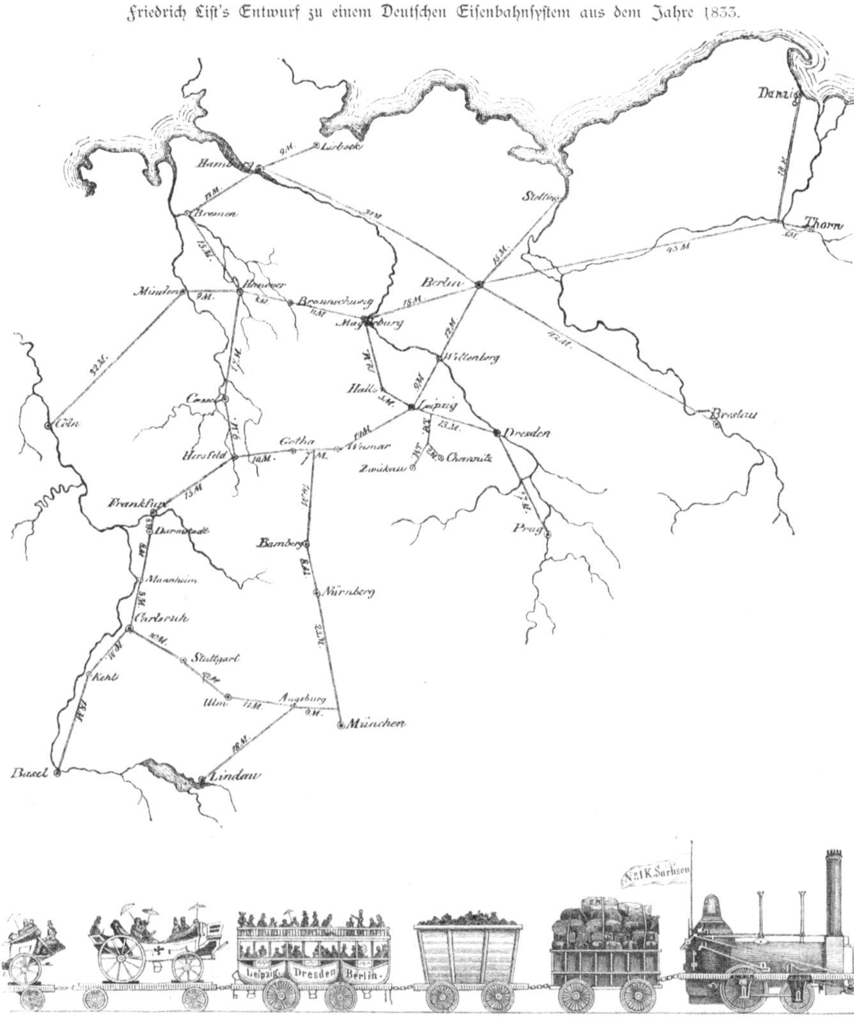

Figure 1.7 Coaches on rail in the planning sketch of List's national railway system for Germany

Source: Robert Krause, Friedrich List und die große Eisenbahn Deutschlands. Ein Beitrag zur Eisenbahngeschichte (Leipzig 1887), 24f.

extension of the network connected the plant with the network. Large companies even developed railway sites inside their factories and connected them with the network. In some cities, particular networks of railways developed which connected many factories and industrial sites with the main railway lines. The Ringbahn of Berlin, for example, was used for such purposes, as were railway rings in even medium-sized cities. In industrial areas at the outskirts of other cities, stations for goods traffic were built, in order to avoid excessive noise in parts of

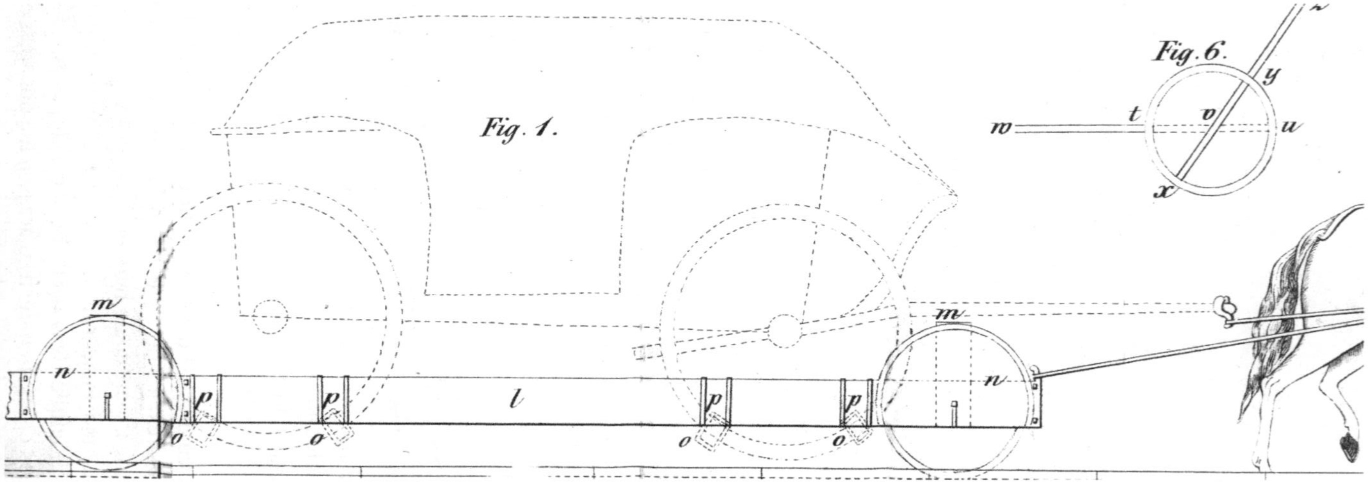

Figure 1.8 Freight car carried on a rail car: sketch from a memorandum for a horse railway from Dürrenberg to Leipzig, 1828

Source: Anonymous, *Darstellung einer anzulegenden Eisenbahn von der K. pr. Saline Dürrenberg und der schiffbaren Saale daselbst bis nach Leipzig auf den Wageplatz vor dem Halleschen Thore* (Schneeberg 1826), attachment.

the city that were more densely populated. These transfer points from road to rail are what we are familiar with today.

For the transport of goods coaches on rail, there were several variations. In 1828 a committee engaged for the introduction of a horse-powered railway connection from the saltworks of Dürrenberg to Leipzig proposed a special railway car on which a normal freight cart for the transport of salt would be carried. Like the passenger coaches mentioned before, this system was not realised and failed as a means of making mass transport more comfortable. The question is why. First, together with the goods, the transport vehicle would have been carried away and would have to be transported back on a costly extra load. Second, the carts were not standardised. Every loading would have had to be handled as a discreet action. All in all, not a very economical transport mode from road to rail. However, the transport and logistics problems repeatedly forced operators to return to these approaches.[48]

An even stranger example of the switch from road to rail and vice versa was the loading of a railway carriage on a cart. This was impossible for a long time, because the horse-driven coaches and carts could not carry a pretty much heavier railway wagon. But in the time of motorisation and the development of special cars for the transport of goods – trucks – with increasing power and capacity, the idea was realised. Indeed, this was the answer of the *Deutsche Reichsbahn Gesellschaft*, the German national railway in the interwar period, to the increasing use of trucks in goods transport. The advantages of trucks were obvious. They could manage the door-to-door transport that railway companies could only dream of. With a transport vehicle that could load a complete railway freight car on air-pressured tyres, the *Deutsche Reichsbahn* was able to solve the problem of missing door-to-door connections.

This was the Culemeyer Street Roller, developed by the *Reichsbahn* engineer Johann Culemeyer. Culemeyer lived from 1883 to 1951. He studied technology at the Hannover Technical University. He was hired by the *Reichsbahn*, and climbed the ladder until reaching the level of a *Streckenbaumeister* (Master of Rail Construction). In 1921 he earned the title of *Regierungsrat* (Councillor), studied machine construction and moved to the central railway construction department of the *Reichsbahn* in Berlin. Here he took over responsibility for the construction of freight wagons and was promoted to *Reichsbahnoberrat* (Senior Councillor) at the *Reichsbahn-Zentralamt für Maschinenbau* (Central Department of Mechanical Engineering) in Berlin. One of his projects in 1931 was the improvement of English carriages and French changeable carriages for use on both rail and road. This project was quickly named *Fahrbares Anschlussgleis* (Moveable Connecting Rail) and had a strategic background. At the international congress on motorcars in Rome in 1928, the *Reichsbahn* announced a competition for the construction of standard boxes for transport purposes. This led to a fundamental

48 Anonymous, *Darstellung einer anzulegenden Eisenbahn von der K. pr. Saline Dürrenberg und der schiffbaren Saale daselbst bis nach Leipzig auf den Wageplatz vor dem Halleschen Thore* (Schneeberg 1826), attachment.

Figure 1.9 *Deutsche Reichsbahn* Street Roller, or *Culemeyer-Straßenroller* R40 of 1935

Source: http://upload.wikimedia.org/wikipedia/commons/c/c5/Culemeyer_1935_Nürnberg.JPG (last accessed 20 March 2014).

strategic discussion about *Haus-zu-Haus-Verkehr* (door-to-door transport) of the *Reichsbahn* and to the foundation of the International Container Bureau.[49] In this context Culemeyer developed the Street Roller, later known simply as the 'Culemeyer'. The Reichsbahn patented the Street Roller in 1933. In the same year a public demonstration took place at Anhalter Station in Berlin. This cart enabled the transport of railway freight cars and other heavy loads on streets. That meant a railway freight car could be brought to a customer of *Deutsche Reichsbahn*, loaded directly at his location with goods, brought to a train, transported, reloaded at the arriving railway station onto a second Culemeyer and brought to the final address of the transport. All in all this resulted in a more tightly organised transport chain that was fully in the hands of the *Reichsbahn*. Reloading the goods was not necessary any more. Culemeyer developed different variations of the Street Roller for different purposes.[50] All in all, the *Deutsche Reichsbahn* built 59 of such carts

[49] See Walter Meyercordt, *Behälter und Paletten. Handbuch zur inner- und außerbetrieblichen Transportrationalisierung* (Darmstadt 1960), 13–17.

[50] He earned his PhD with a dissertation entitled 'Das Straßenfahrzeug für Eisenbahnwagen, eine Verkehrsaufgabe und ihre Lösungen' ('The street vehicle for railcars. A problem in traffic and its solution'). In 1935 he became a *Reichsbahndirektor* at the department *Bau, Einkauf und Betrieb von Straßenfahrzeugen für Eisenbahnwagen* and took

Figure 1.10 Remains of the LR 40.9S, among them the *Deutsche Bahn*'s last operable *Culemeyer Roller* (DB 80–671/ DB 67–071) at the railway museum in Darmstadt-Kranichstein

Source: http://www.culemeyer.de/actuell3.htm (last accessed 16 July 2011).

and set them into business. After the war and after Culemeyer had died in 1951 the *Bundesbahn* ran 250 of them up to 1963.[51] Could we therefore call Culemeyer's machine a success story? Of course we could not.

The Culemeyer rapidly vanished from the street in an era of increasing motorisation in the Western part of Germany. Although it survived for some years longer in the German Democratic Republic, its failures were obvious. The vehicle was too heavy for the road system. Its imbalanced proportions made it slow. This was why planners' thoughts again returned to the beginning of the railway age and the idea of the loading of trucks on rail (when not loading railways on trucks). Indeed we have several modern variations of the salt-train coaches of Dürrenberg. They are nowadays called Rolling Road (*Rollende Landstraße*, or *RoLa*). Above all the Austrian, Swiss and German Railways took up this old idea.

---

over the leading position of the *Kraftwagenabteilung*. In 1945 he moved to Göttingen. After the end of the war, together with the railway car manufacturer *Uerdingen*, he managed the export of Street Rollers to Scandinavian countries. See Johann Culemeyer, *Die Eisenbahn ins Haus (Berlin 1939). On the background see Alfred B. Gottwaldt, Deutsche Reichsbahn 1935* (Stuttgart 1975), and Matthias Hengst, 'Eisenbahn ins Haus', *Eisenbahn Journal*, June 2001.

51 Thomas Zeller, 'Kombinierter Verkehr – die ewige Zukunftshoffnung', in Harry Niemann and Armin Hermann, eds, *100 Jahre LKW. Geschichte und Zukunft des Nutzfahrzeugs* (Stuttgart 1997), 378–94, here 379.

Figure 1.11 Rolling Road (RoLa) at the Southern ramp of the Lötschberg line, pulled by two Re 465 of the BLS *Lötschbergbahn* in Switzerland

Source: http://de.wikipedia.org/wiki/Rollende_Landstraße (last accessed 16 July 2011).

The Rolling Road works with a modal split (*kombinierter Verkehr*). In this system, complete trucks are loaded on rail. They are set on special low-floor train cars (*Niederflurwagen*). The drivers travel in normal passenger cars that are part of the train. The trains depart from and arrive at terminals with special facilities to load and unload the trucks. The advantages of the Rolling Road system are economic and environmental. The truckers save fuel and fees for highway use, and do not lose time caused by traffic jams at regular bottlenecks or because of regulations that limit their working hours at night, at the weekend and holidays. The Rolling Road was developed as a solution for connections passing through environmentally sensitive regions such as the Alps.[52]

But on the other side, it seems to be uneconomical to have a complete motorcar system – that is, a truck – costing several hundred thousand Euro only for the transport from and to the railway station, which is then only dead weight for the

[52] In most cases, RoLa serves transit routes from North to South Europe or to Eastern Europe. For Austria, a traditional transit country, RoLa is of interest for environmental reasons. In 1999 the *Östreichische Bundesbahn* (Austrian state Railway) carried 254,000 trucks with a freight volume of 8.5 million tons. In 2007 nearly 20,000 trains transported 288,776 trucks. In Switzerland RoLa trains took the route via Gotthard and the Lötschberg-Simplon axis. See http://de.wikipedia.org/wiki/Rollende_Landstraße, and http://www.schiene2010.de/web/de/ projekte/rollende-landstrasse.html (last accessed 16 July 2011).

transport and incurs additional costs. Also, the transport agencies depend on a schedule and are confronted with long loading times. These disadvantages forced the transport industry to look for other solutions. One of them has been seen in so-called piggyback transport (*Huckepackverkehr*), when only the trailers of the truck are loaded and the cab stays at the location and can made use of for other purposes. But still, the process is time-consuming, and time is money.

That is why further improvements are being considered. One of them is the Automatic Loading System, developed at the turn of the millennium. In this system, the equipment for loading and unloading is carried by rail car, so that there is no extraordinary infrastructure necessary at the station. These loading robots move under the trailer to be loaded, lift it and carry it to the rail car.[53]

However, even when loading is automated, it takes a certain amount of time. So transport agencies were forced back to think about the loading and reloading again, and making this more comfortable and not so time-consuming. It showed that a different path in the logistic of goods transport had more potential than the transport of lorries or trailers – the standardisation of transport boxes. Since the 1920s we know of experiments with standard boxes, that is containers; and containerisation is even today the solution to the problem of transfer of goods between different transport modes. Containerisation has contributed enormously to increasing the permeability of the systems of water, road and rail transport. The well-known story goes like this. In 1937, Malcolm McLean, the son of a farmer, stayed at the harbour of Hoboken in New Jersey, where he had to deliver a load of cotton. He watched the loading of a ship. The transport workers entered a truck, one after another, loaded up a package on their shoulders and carried them to the ship. What a waste of time, thought McLean. Why not carry the whole car onto the ship without taking any notice of the content? Twenty years later, his vision became reality. McLean ordered an old oil tanker, loaded it with 56 steel containers, and directed it from New York to Houston, and that was the beginning of container shipping.[54]

The real story is a bit longer and more complicated. The container was actually invented in Europe many years before McLean. In the days of the Moveable Connecting Rail mentioned above, ideas rather similar to McLean's were being discussed in the UK, The Netherlands and Germany, and were realised as the

---

[53] Jens Biere, Thorsten Flerlage and Volkhard Nölle, *Kombinierter Verkehr. Straße/Schiene*. Downloaded from: www.mcl.fh-osnabrueck.de/~articles/.../Kombinierter%20 Verkehr.ppt (last accessed 29 September 2009).

[54] See Petra Steinberger, 'Angst vor der Schachtel. Der Container hat die Globalisierung vorangetrieben – jetzt aber bringt er sie in Gefahr', *Süddeutsche Zeitung* of 15 and 16 June 2002, and Marc Levinson, *The Box. How the Shipping Containers Made the World Smaller and the World Economy Bigger* (Oxford 2006). On the literature see Alex Roland, 'Containers and Causality (Review Essay)', *Technology & Culture*, 48, 2, 2007, 386–92.

'standard container' (*Standardbehälter*). There was even an institution for such efforts, the International Container Bureau in Paris.[55]

When we look closer at the problem, we find many attempts to make a practical container solution. In 1937 when Malcom McLean first faced the problem, there was already an international office for containers in the International Chamber of Commerce in Paris.[56] In the Netherlands, the State Railway developed the so-called pa boxes ('pa' stands for *Porteur Aménagé*). Later the *Deutsche Bundesbahn* invested heavily in the standardisation of such transport boxes, and saw them as a means of competition with increasing good transport on road. Indeed, the transport with pa boxes increased.[57] But why then, if the idea was not new, was it McLean who achieved the breakthrough? First, his steel boxes were wider and twice as long as pa boxes, and second, they became normalised earlier by the International Organisation for Standardization (ISO). The international standardisation was the reason for his success.[58] Only when all containers are of equal size or could be combined effectively was it possible for such a system to have a chance to become an important part of the international transport chain.[59]

Three decades passed by before Mc Lean's container system was adopted by Europe and the world. The first container ship arrived in Rotterdam in May 1966, and three days later in Bremen.[60] Both events caused a sort of container-mania. The system had been seen as not profitable before – for example by *Deutsche Lloyd.* The figures of transported containers skyrocketed. Whereas the *Deutsche Bundesbahn* carried only 120 containers in 1966, it carried 3,800 two years later.[61] In 1969, 61,000 Twenty-foot Equivalent Units (TEU) arrived at the harbour of Hamburg, and by 2004 this figure had increased to seven million TEUs.

Containerisation sparked many subsequent innovations such as total reconstructions of harbours to include container terminals, special container cranes and automatic loading systems – and of course, not only in harbours but also in railway station infrastructure.

The classical goods station with storehouses, loading docks and gigantic track areas where the freight trains were assembled was replaced by container terminals

---

55 See Keith Harcourt, 'Rail Containerisation in the United Kingdom and Europe during the 1920s and 1930s' in this volume.

56 Meyercordt, *Behälter*, 13–17.

57 See Zeller, 'Kombinierter Verkehr', and Meyercordt, *Behälter*, 120–21.

58 Gerd Wolff, *Kombinierter Ladungsverkehr*, 2 vols (Freiburg i. Br. 2005), vol. 1, S. 5.

59 McLean succeeded although his container does not fit very well together with the earlier norm of the European standard pallet. See Wolff, *Kombinierter Ladungsverkehr*, vol. 2, 11, and the website of *Gütergemeinschaft Paletten, Portrait der Gütergemeinschaft Paletten e. V.* at http://www.gpal.de/index.php?&id=39 (last accessed 7 October 2008).

60 Hans Jürgen Witthöft, *Container: die Mega-Carrier kommen* (Hamburg 2004), 22.

61 Michael Hascher, 'Die low-tech-Revolution: Container und Pipelines', in Ralf Roth and Karl Schlögel, eds, *Neue Wege in ein neues Europa. Geschichte und Verkehr im 20. Jahrhundert* (Frankfurt am Main 2009), 428–48.

for the transfer from ship to train, or for reloading from train to train and from train to truck. For the last four decades there has been a flow of innovations to rationalise and automate this reloading process.[62]

Figure 1.12 Container Terminal Altenwerder (CTA) in 2004

Source: http://de.wikipedia.org/wiki/Hamburg-Altenwerder (last accessed 29 September 2009).

A typical container terminal (CT) is a place where containers are loaded and reloaded between ships, trucks and railways. They are knots or hubs of international transport networks.

In some container terminals, such as in Altenwerder (in Hamburg) and in Rotterdam, automatic loading is offered. Automatic loading requires higher investments and the terminal is less flexible than with manually handed facilities. There are also systems that promise to load a train while it moves at five miles per hour. This seems progress indeed in the permeability between rail and road.[63]

Conclusion

The container is the modern medium for the exchange of goods between three major transport networks of the world, that is, waterways, railways and roadways.

62 See Levinson, *Box*, 64–5.

63 Biere/Flerlage/Nölle, *Kombinierter Verkehr*.

Ultimately, the container demonstrates that despite their competition, all these networks belong together, and that transport and mobility can be arranged to the advantage of every part of the worldwide communication and transport networks. History has seen a long and winding development of the relationship between road and rail, including the development of facilities that make intermodal transport comfortable and speedy.

The example of railway goods transport and its relationship to other transport systems shows, furthermore, that it is essential to think in terms of networks, and to take their interdependence into consideration. Important parameters for success in a fluid and sometimes volatile transport market are speed, permeability to other systems, capacity and environmentalism. Moreover, it is important to consider how any system fits in into global networks, how it fits into the urban spaces of the world, and how successful the intra- and intercontinental connections are. In this context, the contemporary dominance of road and air transport is not necessarily the end of the story. Factors such as energy, emissions, limited resources of space and gaps in capacity might suddenly shift the whole system of global networks into another direction.

References

Agricola, Georgius, *De re metallica.* Bergwerksbuch (Basel 1557).

Albert Edward Richardson and Harold Donaldson Eberlein, *The English Inn Past and Present: A Review of its History and Social Life* (Manchester 1980).

Anonymous, *A History and Description of the Liverpool and Manchester Railway* (Liverpool 1832).

Anonymous, *Darstellung einer anzulegenden Eisenbahn von der K. pr. Saline Dürrenberg und der schiffbaren Saale daselbst bis nach Leipzig auf den Wageplatz vor dem Halleschen Thore* (Schneeberg 1826).

Baader, Joseph von, *Ueber die Vortheile einer verbesserten Bauart von Eisenbahnen und Wagen* (Munich 1826).

Baader, Joseph von, 'Ueber den gegenwärtigen Zustand und die künftigen Aussichten der Dampfwagen', *Polytechnisches Journal*, 14, 7, 1833, 1–39.

Baader, Joseph von, *Die Unmöglichkeit, Dampfwagen auf gewöhnlichen Strassen mit Vortheil als allgemeines Transportmittel einzuführen, und die Ungereimtheit aller Projekte die Eisenbahnen dadurch entbehrlich zu machen* (Nuremberg 1835).

Becker, Friedrich, *Die atmosphärische Eisenbahn. Nach den Berichten von Smith, Mallet, Samuda, Pim etc. und englischen Quellen bearbeitet* (Frankfurt am Main 1844).

Berlin und seine Eisenbahnen 1846–1896, 2 vols (Berlin 1896).

Bibliographisches Institut, ed., *Meyers Großes Konversations-Lexikon*, 6th ed. (Leipzig and Vienna 1905–09).

Bierbaum, Otto Julius, *Yankeedoodlefahrt und andere Reisegeschichten* (Munich 1910).
Bierbaum, Otto Julius, *Eine empfindsame Reise im Automobil. Von Berlin nach Sorrent und zurück an den Rhein* (Reprint Munich 1955).
Biere, Jens, Flerlage, Thorsten, and Nölle, Volkhard, *Kombinierter Verkehr. Straße/Schiene*. Download from: www.mcl.fh-osnabrueck.de/~articles/.../Kombinierter%20Verkehr.ppt (last accessed 29 September 2009).
Blum, Otto, *Personen- und Güterbahnhöfe*, 2nd ed. worked over by Kurt Leibrand (Berlin, Göttingen and Heidelberg 1961).
Camphausen, Ludolf, *Die Eisenbahn von Köln nach Antwerpen* (Cologne 1835).
Clegg and Samuda, *Mallets Bericht über die atmosphärische Eisenbahn von Dublin nach Dalkey in Irland* (Darmstadt 1844).
Coleman, Terry, *The Railway Navvies* (London 1965).
Crelle, A.L., *Einiges allgemein Verständliche über Eisenbahnen insbesondere als Privat-Unternehmungen* (Berlin 1835).
Culemeyer, Johann, *Die Eisenbahn ins Haus* (Berlin 1939).
Curr, John, *The Coal Viewer, and the Engine Builder's Practical Companion*, 2nd ed. (London 1970).
Engel, E., 'Die Wohnungsnoth: Ein Vortrag auf der Eisenacher Conferenz am 6. Oktober 1872', *Zeitschrift des kgl. Statistischen Bureaus*, 1872, 392–4.
Freeman, Michael J., and Aldcroft, Derek H., eds, *Transport in Victorian Britain* (Manchester 1988).
Freeman, Michael J., *The Railway and the Victorian Imagination* (Yale, CT 2000).
Fürst, Artur, *Die hundertjährige Eisenbahn. Wie Meisterhände sie schufen* (Munich 1925).
Geistbeck, Michael, *Weltverkehr. Die Entwicklung von Schiffahrt, Eisenbahn, Post und Telegraphie bis zum Ende des 19. Jahrhunderts* (Reprint Leipzig 1986).
Glünder, F., *Kurze Darstellung einiger der wichtigsten Verhältnisse bei Eisenbahnen mit besonderer Beziehung auf solche Anlagen zwischen Hamburg, Bremen und Hannover* (Hannover 1834).
Gottwaldt, Alfred B., *Deutsche Reichsbahn 1935* (Stuttgart 1975).
Grau, Berthold, *Bahnhofsgestaltung*, 2 vols (Berlin 1968).
Hamilton, Ellis C., *British Railway History*, 2 vols (London 1957).
Harkort, Friedrich, *Die Eisenbahn von Minden nach Cöln*, ed. by Wolfgang Köllmann (Hagen 1961).
Hascher, Michael, 'Die low-tech-Revolution: Container und Pipelines', in Ralf Roth and Karl Schlögel, eds, *Neue Wege in ein neues Europa. Geschichte und Verkehr im 20. Jahrhundert* (Frankfurt am Main 2009), 428–48.
Heidemann, F.W., *Die Eisenbahnen nebst den dazu gehörenden Post-Coursen und die Dampfschiffahrten in Deutschland* (Merseburg 1854).
Hengst, Matthias, 'Eisenbahn ins Haus', *Eisenbahn Journal*, June 2001.
Henz, Ludwig, *Bericht über Project und Vorarbeiten zu der Anlage einer Eisenbahn von Elberfeld über Hagen nach Witten* (Elberfeld 1836).

Herrmann, Klaus, 'Die Personenbeförderung bei Post und Eisenbahn in der ersten Hälfte des 19. Jahrhunderts', *Scripta Mercaturae*, 11, 1977, 3–25.

Herrmann, Klaus, *Thurn und Taxis-Post und die Eisenbahnen* (Kallmünz 1981).

Hippel, Wolfgang von, 'Gut Ding will Weile haben. Die Eisenbahnpläne von Ludwig Newhouse und Friedrich List und die Reaktion von Regierung, Landtag und Öffentlichkeit', in Wolfgang von Hippel et al., eds, *Eisenbahnfieber. Badens Aufbruch ins Eisenbahnzeitalter* (Mannheim 1990), 35–59.

Kaftan, Kurt Gustav, 'Von der Reichsautobahn zur Europa-Autobahn', *Der Straßenbau*, 28, Nr. 4 of 15 February 1937.

Krause, Robert, *Friedrich List und die große Eisenbahn Deutschlands. Ein Beitrag zur Eisenbahngeschichte* (Leipzig 1887).

Lay, Maxwell G., *Die Geschichte der Straße. Vom Trampelpfad zur Autobahn* (Frankfurt am Main and New York 1994).

Levinson, Marc, *The Box. How the Shipping Containers made the World smaller and the World Economy bigger* (Oxford 2006).

Lips, Michael Alexander, *Die Unanwendbarkeit der englischen Eisenbahnen auf Deutschland und deren Ersatz durch Dampffuhrwerk auf verbesserten Chausseen* (Marburg 1833).

Lips, Michael Alexander, *Die Nürnberg-Fürther Eisenbahn in ihren nächsten Wirkungen und Resultaten* (Nuremberg 1836).

Mensching, Günther, *Roger Bacon* (Münster 2009).

Meyercordt, Walter, *Behälter und Paletten. Handbuch zur inner- und außerbetrieblichen Transportrationalisierung* (Darmstadt 1960).

du Motay, Andraud and Tessié, *Ueber die comprimirte Luft als universelle Triebkraft und unentgeltliches Ersatzmittel der Dampfkraft* (Weimar 1841).

Münster, Sebastian, *Cosmographia universalis* (Basel 1541).

Nationales Automobilmuseum, ed., *Die großartigsten Autos des Jahrhunderts* (Straßburg 2005).

Nort, Gottfried, *Das Reisen mit der Post*, in *Postkutschen* (Frankfurt am Main 1983).

Pollins, H., *Britain's Railways. An Industrial History* (Newton Abbot 1971).

Radicke, Dieter, 'Öffentlicher Nahverkehr und Stadterweiterung: Die Anfänge einer Entwicklung beobachtet am Beispiel von Berlin zwischen 1850 und 1875', in Gerhard Fehl and Juan Rodriguez-Lores, eds, *Stadterweiterungen, 1800–1875: Von den Anfängen des modernen Städtebaues in Deutschland* (Hamburg 1983), 345–57.

Rehbein, Elfriede, et al., *Zu Wasser und zu Lande. Die Geschichte des Verkehrswesens von den Anfängen bis zum Ende des 19. Jahrhunderts* (Munich 1984).

Roland, Alex, 'Containers and Causality (Review Essay)', *Technology & Culture*, 48, 2, 2007, 386–92.

Rossberg, Ralf Roman, *Geschichte der Eisenbahn*, new ed. (Frankfurt am Main 1984).

Roth, Ralf, 'Vom Adler zum ICE', *Damals*, 33, 7, 2001, 14–21.

Roth, Ralf, *Das Jahrhundert der Eisenbahn. Die Herrschaft über Raum und Zeit 1800–1914* (Ostfildern 2005).

Roth, Ralf, 'Die Eisenbahn verändert die Stadt – die Stadt verändert die Eisenbahn', in Wolfgang Kos and Günter Dinhobl, eds, *GROSSER BAHNHOF. Wien und die weite Welt. Ausstellungskatalog* (Vienna 2006), 36–42.

Roth, Ralf, 'It Began 175 Years Ago – the First German Railway Line and Its Importance for the City of Nuremberg and for the National Railway Network', paper presented at the Fourth International Conference on Railway History: Cities, Users and their Railways of the International Railway History Association, Mechelen, 27–29 May 2010.

Roth, Ralf, 'Die Eisenbahnen der Welt – formten sie wirklich ein *world wide web*?', *Zeitschrift für Weltgeschichte*, 12, 2, 2011, 77–106.

Roth, Ralf, 'Zwischen Wettbewerb und Abhängigkeit: Ein langes und kompliziertes Verhältnis von Straße und Schiene mit vielen fehlgeschlagenen Innovationen', in Christoph Siepermann and Michael Eley, eds, *Logistik – gestern, heute, morgen, Festschrift für Richard Vahrenkamp* (Berlin 2011), 15–42.

Scharrer, Johannes, *Deutschlands erste Eisenbahn mit Dampfkraft oder Verhandlungen der Ludwigs-Eisenbahn-Gesellschaft in Nürnberg. Von ihrer Entstehung bis zur Vollendung der Bahn* (Nuremberg 1836).

Schieder, Theodor, *Staatensystem als Vormacht der Welt 1848–1918* (Frankfurt am Main, Berlin and Vienna 1977).

Schwabe, Hermann, *Berliner Südwestbahn und Centralbahn. Beleuchtet vom Standpunkt der Wohnungsfrage und der industriellen Gesellschaft* (Berlin 1873).

Simmons, Jack R., *The Victorian Railway* (London 1995).

Simmons, Jack R. and Biddle, Gordon, *The Oxford Companion to Railway History* (Oxford 1997).

Steinberger, Petra, 'Angst vor der Schachtel. Der Container hat die Globalisierung vorangetrieben – jetzt aber bringt er sie in Gefahr', *Süddeutsche Zeitung* of 15 and 16 June 2002.

Weber, Max Maria von, *Die Induvidualisierung und Entwickelbarkeit der Eisenbahnen* (Leipzig 1875).

Weber, Max Maria von, *Aus dem Reich der Technik*, 2 vols (Berlin 1928).

Witthöft, Hans Jürgen, *Container: die Mega-Carrier kommen* (Hamburg 2004).

Zeller, Thomas, 'Kombinierter Verkehr – die ewige Zukunftshoffnung', in Harry Niemann and Armin Hermann, eds, *100 Jahre LKW. Geschichte und Zukunft des Nutzfahrzeugs* (Stuttgart 1997), 378–94.

Chapter 2

Shaping British Freight Transport in the Interwar Period: Failure of Foresight or Administration, 1919–34?

Roy Edwards

Debating the organisation and administration of transport policy has been a constant feature of the British political landscape since the late eighteenth century and the coming of canals. The development of the railways further embedded transport regulation in the British state as their construction required powers of compulsory purchase, similar to canals. Competing proposals between railways along the same or similar route would in most cases result in insufficient revenue to cover the cost of construction, nevermind make an adequate return on investment once the line was operating. Hence railway organisation tended toward monopolistic conditions and, once open, there were real concerns over both the quality of service and price level. These concerns dominated the first 130 years of government intervention in rail transport.

By 1919, the experience of indirect wartime control had encouraged the pre-war trend toward the advantages of amalgamation, and even nationalisation was briefly considered a possibility. It was argued that an integrated management structure would enable the companies to take advantage of the economies inherent to a natural monopoly and the benefits associated with the closer working of the network. But at the same time, the war had led to the increased use of the internal combustion engine as motive power for road-hauled transport and this technical development would alter, far more than legislation, the future development of the haulage industry. Terry Gourvish in his study of the nationalised railway notes that some of the difficulties faced in the late 1940s had their origin in the first two decades of the twentieth century, and this chapter supports this view.[1]

The twentieth century saw three parliamentary acts which substantially rearranged how the network was organised, in 1921, 1947 and 1993. The 1993 Railways Act has been the subject of an apology by the party who passed it, and the 1947 Transport Act has been regarded by scholars as a commendable attempt at coordinating transport, but deeply flawed in its execution.[2] This chapter

---

1 T.R. Gourvish, *British Railways 1948–1973: A Business History* (Cambridge 1986), 1.

2 M. Bonavia, *The Nationalisation of British Transport: The Early History of the British Transport Commission, 1948–1953* (London 1987), 163–7.

will explore the 1921 Railways Act, and more particularly the circumstances surrounding its passing and the consequences surrounding the failure to recognise the rise of road competition. This chapter will not cover the specific operating and commercial issues surrounding the emergence and growth of road freight haulage, as this has been examined by Peter Scott.[3] His findings also reject the charge that the railways did not develop appropriate responses to road competition or manage their affairs in an unscientific fashion.[4] However, in his discussion of the 1921 settlement he notes that 'the significance of road competition was not taken into account' when drafting the Act.[5] This chapter will demonstrate that this is not strictly true, as the Speaker of the House of Commons had ruled that a clause granting road powers under the 1921 Railway Act was not within the scope of the Bill.[6] The sin was therefore of commission rather than naive omission. This chapter will present evidence that it was the agency of regulation and the evidence presented to a committee of the House of Commons that prevented a more unified approach to haulage being developed. This would have consequences that echoed through much of the twentieth century as government struggled to achieve a coordinated transport policy. The chapter begins with a review of the background to the post-war settlement, before examining the first attempt to get road powers by the combined London North Western Railway (LNWR) and Midland Railway companies. This provides evidence of the difficulty faced by business in reshaping markets in the face of competition from new forms of technology.

Background to Regulation

The British railway network developed piecemeal in the nineteenth century, with very little government planning, but a great deal of regulation.[7] Established by private Act of Parliament, much of the initial cost of promotion was consumed by the process of sending Bills to committees, and ensuring that all constituencies affected in the construction of a line were supportive of the proposal. This, and the attendant legal morass that often resulted, were costly and contributed to the high costs of construction.[8] Regulation of the industry gradually extended from construction to operation to deal with safety, and the creation of a Railway Clearing House in 1842 led to some standardisation of wagon design, signals and

---

3 C. Reid and P. Scott '"The white slavery of the motor world": opportunism in the interwar road haulage industry', *Social History*, 12, 2000, 300–315, P. Scott, 'British railways and the challenge from road haulage: 1919–1939', *Twentieth Century British History*, 13, 2002, 101–20.

4 P. Scott, 'British railways', 102.

5 P. Scott, 'British railways', 104.

6 Hansard of 27 July 1921, column 489.

7 See M. Casson, *The World's First Railway System* (Oxford 2009).

8 R.W. Kostal, *Law and English Railway Capitalism 1825–1875* (Oxford 1994).

brakes.[9] Aside from the parliamentary chamber and investigations by departmental committees and royal commissions, the key agent of regulation was the Board of Trade Railway Department.[10] Rates were set through the individual Act of Parliament for each company, but over time, mergers resulted in different rates being imported into the new company rating structure. The resulting confusion as to the basis for establishing the price of haulage and associated services such as carriage and delivery led to the Railway Clearing House codifying the disparate rates classes into a General Rates Classification. While this eventually became the basis for the statutory setting of price, traders still suspected the railways of abusing their monopoly position. This culminated during the latter 1880s and early 1890s in a stand off between parliament and the railways over the appropriate level of charges with the railways immediately charging the statutory maximum for all traffic.[11] As the railways matured, dissatisfaction from traders, shareholders and government grew with questions being asked over the effectiveness of management. For example, there was a debate on the use of information for management control conducted through the press, and culminating in 1906, with the establishing of a Departmental Committee of the Board of Trade to investigate railway accounts and statistics.[12]

The experience of war was to alter the organisation of railways forever, as they were run as a unified entity, albeit through a Railway Executive Committee rather than by direct government ownership. A Ministry of Transport in 1919 and Railways Act in 1921 were introduced to reconfigure the industry in an attempt to ensure financial stability, and it was the structuring of this settlement, and in particular the ability of government to shape the market, that led to a false start in developing railway-owned road services. Even before the arrival of road haulage there was recognition in government and industry that the railways would have to change. The issue of rail-hauled road powers was not a deliberate part of this reformulation of regulation. It was instead a response to enquiries from the road haulage industry regarding services offered under wartime conditions that were still operating in peacetime which first prompted investigation.

The 1921 Act continued with the existing principles of price and service regulation where high-value goods cross-subsidised low-value services and added

---

9 P. Bagwell, *The Railway Clearing House in the British Economy 1842–1922* (London 1968).

10 H. Parris, *Government and the Railways in the Nineteenth Century* (London 1965).

11 See in general the work of Peter Cain, 'Railway Combination and Government, 1900–1914', *Economic History Review*, 25, 1972, 623–41, ibid., 'Traders versus Railways: The Genesis of the Railway and Canal Traffic Act of 1894', *The Journal of Transport History*, New Series 2, 2, 1972, 65–84, ibid. 'Railways and Price Discrimination: The Case of Agriculture, 1880–1914', *Business History*, 28, 2, 1976, 190–205, and ibid., 'The British Railway Rates Problem 1894–1913', *Business History*, 20, 1978, 87–100.

12 For background to this see R.J. Irving, *The North Eastern Railway 1870–1914* (Leicester 1976).

a Railway Rates Tribunal to adjudicate disputes and monitor performance against a net revenue target. The principle underlying pricing remained 'what the traffic could bear' where price was set according to a rates classification. The ranking of a commodity or product in the classification was determined by the bulk to weight characteristics of the load, the likelihood of damage occurring in transit, the amount likely to be hauled and finally the regularity of the business. This complex system contrasted with road hauliers who had only to price at cost plus a given margin, and were not subject to such intrusive regulation of decision-making processes as rail hauliers. Furthermore, railway rates had to be available for public inspection at the local station, so road hauliers in competition with the railways could 'skim' the best traffic, leaving the railways with an uneconomic rump that could not in pay its way in the long run. Additional constraints of common-carrier status and restrictions relating to 'undue preference' further eroded commercial freedom. The former required that all traffic offered had to be carried, unless a very good reason could be provided in a court of law, while undue preference was designed to give all customers access to equal service. This had the effect of complicating managerial decision-making, as traders, the term universally used to describe railway customers, were often willing to challenge railway operating decisions where it seemed the competition were getting cheaper rates, irrespective of the underlying operating conditions. Economies of scale in loading, for example, were recognised, but their existence was often challenged by those other traders who were unable to take advantage of large consignments.

This had a twofold effect on rail transport and distribution: firstly the regulatory environment prevented the railways from responding in general to changes in commercial and operating conditions because they did not have freedom to set price independently of the General Rates Classification. Secondly, the lack of specific regulation relating to road transport, allowed hauliers to run services that were dangerous to both drivers and other road users, when the railways had to invest heavily in safety. A further complaint of the railways was that road haulage had its 'permanent way' paid for out of property rates – and railway companies as property owners were significant contributors to this local tax. All these issues taken together added considerably to the constraints within which railway managers had to make decisions regarding commercial and operating strategy.

The evidence presented here makes it clear that officials from the new Ministry of Transport were well aware of the possible impact of road on rail haulage and warned of the consequences. However, the 1921 Railways Act explicitly failed to address the issue, and investigation into the matter of roads powers for railway companies foundered. Further attempts to legitimate road-hauled rail services were prevented not by traders or even road hauliers, but by opposition from the Ministry of Transport. Not only did regulation stifle the response of the railways to the overall competitive environment, but the policy 'process' in formulating these constraints was unable to deal with the degree of change implied by the new technology, or recognise the speed with which it would change the market for haulage. This flawed process is the subject of the next section.

Road Powers and Transport Policy in the Ministry of Transport, 1919–22

This section examines the policy discussion surrounding the use of lorry-hauled road transport by railway companies where consignments of freight could be transported throughout the journey solely by road. This emerges as an issue at the end of 1919, when the National Alliance of Commercial Road Transport Associations and Federations reported that railway companies had been using lorries loaned by the government to haul traffic without authority from the Ministry. They were anxious to avoid 'irregular forms of competition', and noted that this was unfair as the railway services were 'more or less' subsidised by government.[13]

The Ministry of Transport sought legal opinion that concluded specific road powers were required. Counsel further noted that railways were entitled to use road vehicles as 'auxiliary' to rail services 'conducive to efficient and economical working' and legally much depended upon how such auxiliary services were defined.[14] The Midland Railway reported back that their service was experimental, although they were hoping to save on handling at local stations, and the Lancashire and Yorkshire stated that they utilised lorries only to relieve congestion when demand was high, therefore supplementing the rail network, rather than as an out and out substitute. At the time it was noted by the Ministry that 'there is no question of perpetuating throughout road services by railway companies'.[15] The Director General of Transport, Phillip Nash, commented that such powers would not be 'in accord with the policy of this ministry', noting that there would be considerable opposition to the introduction of such services.[16] Nevertheless, many road hauliers were alive to the potential threat that this offered, and unsurprisingly sought to prevent it – hence the complaint to the Ministry. This prompted considerable discussion within the Ministry as to what might be done. The records of this debate reveal that the civil servants recognised the coming importance of road haulage both in and of itself, but more importantly as a competitive threat to the railways.

In March 1920 a minute examining this situation noted that 'the advent of mechanical transport is ... certain to bring about great changes' as regarding carriage and delivery traffic, observing how uneconomical it must be to maintain small goods warehouses. The authors suggested that the railways ought to be allowed to 'centralise their collection and delivery by mechanical transport at large transhipment centres' thereby anticipating so-called 'zonal' distribution.[17] In response, Nash observed in a letter to the Rates Advisory Committee that was advising the Minister that it was a matter for 'serious consideration ... whether

---

[13] The National Archive (TNA): PRO MT 33/1 Minute TR 64 letters, 18 December 1919 and 29 December 1919. This was presumably referring to the control then exercised by government over the railways. Needless to say the railways did not take this view.

[14] TNA: PRO MT 33/1 Minute TR 64, 12 March 1920.

[15] TNA: PRO MT 33/1 Minute Kissan, 12 March 1920.

[16] TNA: PRO MT 33/1 Minute to Minister, 20 April 1920.

[17] TNA: PRO MT33/1 Minute, 15 March 1920, signed by Pichard and Kissan.

on the grounds of economy and efficiency in transport' throughout road powers might be 'extended with advantage'.[18] He explicitly linked the emerging of road transport and the future position of the railways, and stated that mechanical road haulage had been encouraged by the war: 'to a state of development which in the normal course it would probably not have reached for many years', noting that road competition 'is a serious factor in the Railway situation'. He stated that the issue would, before too long, be 'acute' and that it would arise in the detailed negotiations for the settlement of the new policy of grouped railways, thereby recognising the reality of road-hauled transport.[19] He went on to suggest one alternative would be to support the railways' quest for powers as 'a logical extension of the arrangements now in contemplation' with rates being separated out into their component parts – conveyance, terminal and Carriage and Delivery. A response was provided by one of Nash's colleagues, Charles de Bartolome, who provided an analysis for the Minister. If Nash's view was correct, railways would have to 'resign' traffic to roads or lower rates by a considerable amount against traffic competitive with road and raise rates by similar amounts where there was little competition. This would apply particularly to coal and mineral traffic, with the outcome being higher rates for a poorer service, and was an inevitable outcome as the higher valued service explicitly subsidised the low:[20] this failure to recognise the importance of road services would erode the long-term viability of the post-1923 grouping, postponing indefinitely dealing with business consequences of moving to a cost-based pricing mechanism.

This mattered because road hauliers were not regulated as to price and charged at cost plus, leaving the railways with the un-remunerative traffic, and it was this perceived unfairness that rankled so much with the railway companies throughout the interwar period. They believed that competition with road haulage was unfair because they could not charge on the same basis as road. In addition it was clear that for many consignments and routes, road haulage was better suited for the task – and a cheaper alternative.[21]

The Ministry, or at least the civil servants, noted that there was the possibility that the railways would be a counterweight to the road hauliers, who may well be tempted to combine to force up prices. In other words railways could make the market for road-hauled transport more competitive. This point is crucial: there was explicit recognition that the granting throughout of road powers would aid competition in transport, not rail or road in particular, but transport *in general* between road and rail companies. What the framers of the 1921 Railways Act

18 TNA: PRO MT 33/1 Memo to Rates Advisory Committee, 20 April 1920.

19 TNA: PRO MT3/1 Confidential Memo, Nash to the Minister, 18 June 1920

20 TNA: PRO MT33/1 Note to the Minister C.M. de Bartolome, 18 June 1920.

21 The railways 'Square Deal' campaign of the 1930s would eventually secure an agreement with government in principle to remove the restrictions on pricing, but these were never introduced as war intervened, resulting in government control leading, eventually, to nationalisation.

would fail to do is view railways as firstly part of a transport network where the monopoly, insofar as it had ever existed, was being eroded, therefore rendering the financial arrangements of the 1921 Act problematic. Charles de Bartolome's report concluded that railways should be given road powers for this and another reason: 'Because they already posses an efficient organisation, which is the result of years of experience in meeting the transport requirements of trade, and we would be most unwise not to take full advantage of it and so avoid duplication'.[22]

Of course, he noted, there would have to be safeguards, but also, private road services could be established if the railways quoted extortionate road and rail rates. That this was not pursued is indicative of the confusion surrounding policy, as the amalgamation of the railways was to encourage economies of working through the rationalisation of facilities. Having the option to use road services would enable the railway company to decide which mode of transport was best in terms of both cost and quality of service for the traffic being offered. There was clearly a fear that a new monopoly of transport would result, similar to that which existed for much of the nineteenth and into the twentieth century. But it only required the span of regulation to include similar safeguards with reference to road transport operated by rail companies as existed for rail-hauled services, and the issue would be dealt with: this was the view of some within the Ministry. One official responded that although it was difficult to see what safeguards could be introduced, especially to protect the 'small undertaking', separate accounts could be kept, with 'similar machinery' as that used to regulate rail transport by railway companies to regulate road transport by rail companies. And he noted further that concern for the small undertaking should not stand in the way of the greater gain for the wider economy.[23]

But there were still lingering doubts about the reality of implementing these powers. Despite his analysis of the consequences of road haulage upon railways by October 1920, Nash's response to road powers was at best lukewarm. In a note to the Rates Advisory Committee, whose members were investigating the issue, he stated that there is 'presumably' to be no departure from the general view that 'the object of railways is the carriage of goods by rail'. He further suggested that the problem might be solved by regulating road-hauled rail services so that they were self-supporting, and perhaps more bizarrely, that railways should charge rail rates but for road haulage.[24] Given Nash's prescient analysis of the market for transport, this last suggestion reveals either a lack of understanding regarding the consequences of road-hauled technology, or perhaps more likely, an attempt to proffer a solution acceptable to traders, road hauliers and railways, and indeed colleagues in his own Ministry. In the event, as we shall see, even this compromise went too far for some.

22 TNA: PRO MT 33/1 Note to the Minister C. M. de Bartolome, 18 June 1920.

23 TNA: PRO MT33/1 Minute Pickard, 5 August 1920.

24 TNA: PRO MT33/1 Note to Railway Advisory Committee, 20 October 1920.

Commenting on the proposed Departmental Committee, other officials noted that there would be 'strenuous opposition' to railroad operations, but went on to say that the issue as to whether powers should be given for railways to carry goods by road as an alternative to rail 'had not received sufficient consideration'. In a letter to the Minister, Nash stated that the reason for this was the manner in which the railways presented their evidence. They stated that they wished to 'recover traffic', implying that the perception of a rapacious railway monopoly had led to less support for the idea. He noted that even if railway rates were charged for road haulage, efficient and economical working would result because the lowest cost mode would be used, thereby enhancing the railways' financial position.[25]

Ultimately, what seems to have concerned the Ministry was the need to obtain for the country a suitable transport service at a reasonable price, but with no appreciation of how the business model worked, whether steam or internal combustion engine. With the potential for road competition, there loomed the prospect of wasteful competition and the difficulty of hundreds of millions of pounds of railway capital not receiving an adequate return, and this prospect filled government with horror. Given that the Speaker of the Commons had ruled against considering road powers in 1921, the government sought to examine the issue in a Departmental Committee of the Board of Trade.

The Committee to investigate was ostensibly part of the Rates Advisory Committee but was chaired John Hutton Balfour Browne. The Committee took the title of its chairman, who was well versed in railway matters having been chairman of the Railway and Canal Commission, and so appreciated both the positions of traders and railways in matters regarding commercial policy. Two representatives each from traders, road hauliers, unions and the railways were brought together and evidence was heard from road hauliers such as Carter Paterson, and their representative bodies, and included the National Alliance of Commercial Road Transport Associations and Federations, and the Commercial and Motor Users' Federation, both important lobbyists on behalf of hauliers. Traders were well represented by the Federation of British Industry, and various specific manufactures associations – and 14 Chambers of Commerce, and the railway companies, also submitted evidence. When the Committee finally reported, there were three, split along what we might call the interest of the members and their constituency. Both road hauliers and traders came out against road powers, while the representative of labour rejected separate road powers per se, and instead suggested nationalisation. The Chairman and railway companies supported the introduction of railway road powers, but with regulatory caveats: in reports it was noted that difficulties surrounded the granting of rail-operated services, and in particular the need to then monitor such activity as part of the *quid pro quo* for allowing road haulage. Perhaps unsurprisingly since the railway members supported the report, the

---

[25] TNA MT33/1 Minute Kissane to Nash, 22 March 1921, and letter from Nash to Minister, 4 April 1921.

Committee could not 'contemplate' the destruction of an estimated £1.3 billion nominal capitalisation of railway assets.[26]

The separate report from the road haulage interests and traders went some way to denying the importance of this new technology, and the institutional structure surrounding the market for haulage. These authors stated that the existing infrastructure was sufficient for all 'legitimate purposes' of a railway company, expressing a concern that even with statutory restriction, a monopoly might ensue.[27] Perhaps inevitably, the Balfour Brown Committee findings were ignored by government. While the evidence presented brought up many of the issues involved in freight haulage, the failure to agree on an approach, if unsurprising, offered no easy solution to government. However, it is what happened next that forms the heart of this chapter's argument: that it was the administrative process that failed rather than railway management.

Attempts at Road Powers for Railways 1921–22

The failure of both the Railways Act and the Balfour Brown Committee to address road haulage by railway companies left the latter in a quandary. Carriage and delivery services had long been part of the service offered, and management was well aware of the advantage to using road delivery. But if road haulage was to be used in any other capacity this would be ultra vires unless existing legislation was amended, or new law was introduced. The North Western & Midland Group, the company that represented the merged interests of the London & North Western Railway and the Midland Railway, decided to proceed with legislation through Parliament, in an attempt to acquire such powers. This was clearly a test case as a successful outcome would lead to others seeking similar powers, and the railways shared information through meetings in the Railway Clearing House and at the Railway Companies Association. This section of the chapter examines the 1922 Bill from the minutes of the London & North Western Railway. It will be argued that the Committee proceedings for this Bill were yet another opportunity missed to reshape the institutional arrangements surrounding the organisation of transport and distribution. Failure to grant road powers in 1922 only postponed their eventual awarding in 1928.

Throughout 1922, the minutes of the Railway Clearing House reveal that the LNWR was considering 'adopting a rail head system of distribution' that might use 'throughout' road services, with the LNWR acting as an agent for the trader. The service would also be open to competition from road hauliers, although probably only if railway assets were unavailable, and be on a 'non-competitive' basis between railway companies. In other words, private hauliers would be used

[26] TNA: PRO MT 33/9 1921 Road Committee Road Conveyance by Rail, paragraphs 7 and 9.

[27] TNA PRO: MT 33/9 Draft Report 'B', paragraph 11.

to haul traffic if railway assets – road or rail – proved insufficient. The scheme was limited to a 20-mile radius of the terminal, and for a period of six months.[28] Such arrangements were not unusual, as the railways often experimented with services, but in this case, without the excuse of wartime congestion, such a proposal in peacetime conditions would require a change in the law. The decision to seek such a change seems to have been made at the end of 1921 when first mention is made in the minutes of the company. Once the intention to obtain powers had been announced, the solicitors of the company noted that 65 petitions against the Bill had been received, but were from either a misunderstanding of what was intended, or a result of vested interest. What they meant exactly by this is not clear from the minutes and they may, especially in the light of subsequent events, have been deluding themselves. The LNWR believed they could explain in greater detail to those objecting what was proposed, but against entrenched interest, such as owners of road haulage businesses, there was little to be done. By May 1921, the solicitors confirmed that 'safeguards' would be required, but noted that the company 'had always intimated their willingness to provide' these.[29] By the end of May the solicitors were of the understanding that the climate of opinion was as favourable as might be expected, but time was pressing, and concerns were expressed over the time-wasting of the opposition. In May 1921 it was noted that George Beharrell of the Ministry of Transport was expected to give evidence concerning the form of accounts required for the regulation of rail-hauled road services, and this was expected to be in broad support of the company proposals.[30]

What grounds there were for this optimism regarding such evidence is not clear from the archival record.[31] The LNWR managers and directors certainly seem to have received a shock when Beharrell's evidence effectively sank the proceedings and the minutes report on the events expressed barely concealed anger at the turn of events. Beharrell had 'brought forward a most serious and vital criticism against the principle of charging rates laid down in the Bill'. The LNWR was intending to charge railway rates for road services, but Beharrell thought this 'improper and impracticable'. Beharrell's objection was that the railways had to maximise their revenue, but that if they were competing by road, this could not be the case. Railways were just that, railways, not roads, and such business would therefore be ultra vires. This was a curious interpretation of the spirit if not the letter of the law, and in any event the legislation was seeking power to change the legal status quo, and by definition allowing road powers. This view ignored both the fact that

[28] TNA: PRO RAIL 1080/218 Minutes of Meetings of Goods Managers, the Railway Clearing House, Minute Number 4505, 25 May 1922.

[29] TNA: PRO RAIL 418/4 LNWR Board Minute, Minute 65, 24 February 1922; Minute 169, 28 April 1922.

[30] TNA: PRO RAIL 418/4 LNWR Board Minute, Minute 210, 26 May 1922.

[31] For what follows see TNA: PRO RAIL 418/4 LNWR Board Minute, Minute 254, 30 June 1922.

railways had been allowed to expand into the owning of docks from the nineteenth century, and that road carriage and delivery services were also allowed.

Unsurprisingly, the LNWR was indignant: the Board noted that the Ministry had had 'abundant opportunity' to express doubts, both publicly and privately, but had not done so. There seems to be some support for this view in that the committee of the House responsible for managing the legislation through Parliament censored the Ministry for the way the matter had been handled. The LNWR Board were presented with three choices. They could accept the amendment of the Ministry, but it was thought that this would not pass the standing orders of the House of Commons, and would break faith with traders who had supported the railway cause. Another option was to fight the Ministry, but this would undoubtedly lose the support of the government and the Bill would not pass. The only other alternative was to withdraw the Bill, and this was the course eventually decided upon. At the end of July the Board sought counsel's advice as to the next step. The company could promote numerous local road hauliers, but this was not recommended. Government could be approached for general legislation, but, perhaps due to recent experience this did not appeal either. The final option was to renew the 'application'.[32] In the event, the LNWR let matters drop until, under the auspices of the LMS, and the other amalgamated companies, road powers were applied for and obtained in 1928. However it is the consequences of these events, and what they reveal of the administrative process that are the concern of this chapter.

Consequences

This episode points to one of the main difficulties faced by the railways during this period, the inability of regulators to appreciate how the freight haulage business worked. In the case of road powers this was compounded by a somewhat cavalier attitude to consultation. Even if the Ministry was legally correct to block the railway's application, the process by which this was accomplished was seen as heavy-handed at the time. In an editorial, the recently formed periodical *Modern Transport* regarded the loss of the Bill as entirely down to Beharrell's evidence that any road haulage by a railway company was a diversion from rail. The editor went further: 'This may be true' but was not traffic 'already being diverted to the roads by the independent haulier. We know very well that it is, and in all probability it will be so to an increasing extent in the future'.[33] So Beharrell was correct, but

> with the anomaly that whereas the traffic diversion but for his opposition to the bill, would still have brought in revenue on the road side of the railway

[32] TNA: PRO RAIL 418/4 LNWR Board Minute 301, 28 July 1922. RAIL 418/4 LNWR Board Minute.

[33] *Modern Transport* of 17 June 1922, 1.

> undertaking, it will in future be lost to the railway, and the companies will be still more badly placed in their efforts to earn a standard revenue.[34]

Despite the concerns expressed by its own civil servants, noted earlier, the Ministry of Transport was clearly not disposed to take matters any further. The Beharrell view was repeated when, ten years later, the then Minister of Transport John Pybus saw fit to refer to the incompetence of the railways on this matter:

> [T]he bill embodying the old LNWR application for road powers in 1922 was killed, not as suggested by the action of government, but by the weight of its own imperfections. The parameters of the Bill proposed to adopt a basis of charge … which would have put the company in an impossible position.[35]

Pybus then noted that the Bill was withdrawn by 'some unrevealed bargain with certain opponents', presumably referring to the negotiations with traders that the LNWR had entered into.

What are we to make of these events? It reveals how difficult it was for the railway companies to manage in an environment where the casual conduct of administrative procedures had very real consequences for business practice. It is sometimes noted that railway management should have behaved differently, that they interpreted their statutory obligations too narrowly. But time and again the experience of regulation was to disappoint management and make railway operating and commercial activity more difficult.[36]

These decisions had more significant consequences than most others made during this time. An opportunity was lost to develop a more integrated road/rail service, where the decision as to what mode was best would be made on business grounds relating cost of haulage to the appropriate technology. As it was, many railway managers saw themselves as doing just that, and Michael Bonavia presents evidence from the passenger business suggesting that this was a tension.[37] A speculative counterfactual would be that had the railways been granted road powers even with legislative safeguards, not only would a more integrated transportation network have developed earlier, but it would also have enabled a smoother switch from a dominant but outdated rail-based system, to a new road technology.

---

34 *Modern Transport* of 17 June 1922, 1.

35 TNA: PRO PREM 1/140 Memo to Prime Minister Ramsey McDonald from Minister Pybus, 23 January 1933.

36 See R.A. Edwards, 'Is management accounting just what Management Accountants do? Implicit Cost Analysis on Britain's Railways c. 1923–1939', *Accounting, Business and Financial History*, 8, 1998, 331–49; ibid., 'Conceptualising Cost: The Analysis of Management Information on Britain's Railways c. 1935–1956', *Contemporary British History*, 13, 1999, 72–81, and ibid., 'Job analysis on the LMS: mechanisation and modernisation c. 1930–c. 1939', *Accounting, Business and Financial History*, 20, 2010, 91–105.

37 M. Bonavia, *Railway Policy Between the Wars* (Manchester 1981).

Conclusion

This chapter has explored just one of the many regulatory decisions affecting the railways in the period 1918 to 1923. The failure to properly consider the impact of road haulage on the dominant existing rail technology reflects badly on the administrative process. However, much more research remains to be done in this area. The parliamentary records contain detailed information of the evidence presented to both the Balfour Browne and parliamentary committees. Further investigation of this evidence would reveal a great deal more on the nature of the relationship between road and rail services, but more importantly on the nature of administrative process and whether a realistic perspective on market conditions was ever presented.

In establishing a post-1918 settlement that neglected road haulage, government failed to address the changing technology of the internal combustion engine running not on rails but the road. Although it is probable that there were both civil servants and railway staff who regarded road transport as a minor player in the nation's transport, others were well aware of its future role including those such as Nash in the Ministry of Transport. In a history of the road haulage industry written by one of the protagonists, the author noted that the government should 'certainly' have known what effect the internal combustion engine would have had on the market for haulage.[38]

The real failure of administration in this period was an inability to understand what would now be known as the 'business model' of the industry. The Ministry of Transport insisted that road and rail haulage should be pursued by separate companies, because they were separate and different technology. This failure to recognise that the internal combustion engine would change the market for freight transport and distribution led to many of the difficulties faced by railway companies in the interwar period, a fact recognised by the appointment of a Royal Commission on Transport only eight years after the passing of the Act, and the eventual granting of rail-hauled road powers in 1928.

References

Aldcroft, D., 'The Efficiency and Enterprise of British Railways', *Explorations in Entrepreneurial History*, 5, 1968, 158–74.

Bagwell, P., *The Railway Clearing House in the British Economy 1842–1922* (London 1968).

Bagwell, P., and Lyth, P., *Transport in Britain: From Canal Lock to Gridlock* (London 2002).

Bonavia, M., *The Four Great Railways* (Newton Abbott 1980.

Bonavia, M., *Railway Policy Between the Wars* (Manchester 1981).

38 C.S. Dunbar, *The Rise of Road Transport 1919–1939* (London 1981), 9.

Bonavia, M., *The Nationalisation of British Transport: The Early History of the British Transport Commission 1948–1953* (London 1987).
Burtt, P., *The Principal Factors in Freight Train Operating* (London 1926).
Cain, P., 'Railway Combination and Government, 1900–1914', *Economic History Review*, 25, 1972, 623–41.
Cain, P., 'Traders versus Railways: The Genesis of the Railway and Canal Traffic Act of 1894', *The Journal of Transport History*, New Series 2, 2, 1973, 65–84.
Cain, P., 'Railways and Price Discrimination: The Case of Agriculture, 1880–1914', *Business History*, 28, 2, 1976, 190–205.
Cain, P., 'The British Railway Rates Problem 1894–1913', *Business History*, 20, 1978, 87–100.
Casson, M., *The World's First Railway System* (Oxford 2009).
Crompton, G., '"Efficient and economical working"? The performance of the railway companies 1923–1933', *Business History*, 27, 1985, 222–37.
Crompton, G., '"Squeezing the pulpless orange": labour and capital on the railways in the inter-war years', *Business History*, 31, 1989, 66–83.
Crompton, G., 'The railway companies and the nationalisation issue', in R. Millward and J. Singleton, eds, *The Political Economy of Nationalisation in Britain 1920–1950* (Cambridge 1995), 116–43.
Dunbar, C.S., *The Rise of Road Transport 1919–1939* (London 1981).
Dyos, H.J. and Aldcroft, D., *British Transport: An Economic Survey from the Seventeenth Century* (Harmansworth 1969).
Edwards, R.A., 'Is management accounting just what Management Accountants do? Implicit cost analysis on Britain's railways c. 1923–1939', *Accounting, Business and Financial History*, 8, 1998, 331–49.
Edwards, R.A., 'Conceptualising Cost: The Analysis of Management Information on Britain's Railways c.1935–1956', *Contemporary British History*, 13, 1999, 72–81.
Edwards, R.A., 'Job analysis on the LMS: mechanisation and modernisation c.1930–c.1939', *Accounting, Business and Financial History*, 20, 2010, 91–105.
Gourvish, T.R., *British Railways 1948–1973: A Business History* (Cambridge 1986).
Hare, T., Bernard, *British Railway Operating* (London 1946).
Irving, R.J., *The North Eastern Railway Company, 1870–1914* (Leicester 1976).
Kostal, R.W., *Law and English Railway Capitalism 1825–1875* (Oxford 1994).
Paish, G., *The British Railway Position* (London 1902).
Parris, H., *Government and the Railways in the Nineteenth Century* (London 1965).
Pollins, H., *Britain's Railways: An Industrial History* (Newton Abbott 1971).
Reid, C. and Scott, P., '"The white slavery of the motor world": opportunism in the interwar road haulage industry', *Social History*, 12, 2000, 300–315.
Robertson, W.A., *Combination Among the Railway Companies* (London, 1912).
Scott, P., 'British railways and the challenge from road haulage: 1919–1939', *Twentieth Century British History*, 13, 2002, 101–20.

Chapter 3

Conceiving Distribution in the United Kingdom: the (London and) North Eastern Railway's Discursive Response to Road Haulage, 1921–39

Colin Divall

Despite the long shadow cast by the Great Depression of the early 1930s which so badly affected the UK's railways, from the point of view of the consumer the interwar years were generally good ones, with a steadily increasing range of retail goods from which to choose. Such consumption was underpinned by an increasingly sophisticated network of distribution operating at a range of geographical scales, dealing not only with finished goods going from producers to wholesalers and then retailers but also the intermediates generated by manufacturers. Before the First World War the railways had dealt with almost all of this traffic moving more than a few miles, but once the immediate post-war economic boom started, road haulage emerged as a competitor, limited at first but rapidly inflicting serious damage on railway finances. This chapter starts to address the question of how the Big Four railway companies, formed in 1923 under the 1921 Railways Act, and their predecessors understood and thought about responding to this threat.

Although the mobility turn in transport history over the past 15 years has largely ignored freight, this neglect tells us more about scholars' fascination with the semiotics of passenger travel than the comparative importance of moving things. Granted, it is not easy to think about freight in other than utilitarian terms – there is little of the glamour or other social symbolism of attributes such as comfort and speed that encourage people to move.[1] On the other hand, three of the Big Four

---

1 G. Mom, C. Divall and P. Lyth, 'Towards a paradigm shift? A decade of transport and mobility history', in G. Mom, G. Pirie and L. Tissot, eds, *Mobility in History: The State of the Art in the History of Transport, Traffic and Mobility* (Neuchâtel 2009), 13–40; C. Divall, 'The modern passenger: constructing the consumer on Britain's railways, 1919–1939', in M. Pinheiro, ed., *Railway Modernization: An Historical Perspective (19th and 20th Centuries)* (Lisbon 2009), 111–25; C. Divall, 'Civilising velocity: masculinity and the marketing of Britain's passenger trains, 1921–1939', *Journal of Transport History*, 3rd series 32, 2011, 164–91; H. Shin, 'Business strategy and corporate image: Britain's railways, 1872–1977', in H. Mäki and J. Korjus, eds, *Railways as an Innovative Regional Factor* (Kouvola 2009), 63–84.

railway companies (the exception was the smallest, the Southern) earned most of their income before the Second World War from freight, much of it high-value general merchandise. Peter Scott has demonstrated the seemingly inexorable rise of road competition in this sector (the railways' 'natural monopoly' of bulk-haul materials such as coal and minerals was another matter), while Thomas Gibson has traced some of the main technical, economic, statutory and regulatory factors underpinning this success.[2] An earlier generation of historians regarded road distribution's ascendancy as either near-inevitable or, at best, in no small measure a consequence of the railways' poor management.[3] But starting in the 1980s with Gerald Crompton's series of nuanced articles on the Big Four's business performance, such views have become increasingly untenable.[4] Most recently, Scott's spirited defence extends Crompton's point that railway managers were hamstrung by the 1921 Act's inappropriate regulatory framework, arguing that they acted rationally in seeking to obtain legislative redress through the regulation of road haulage.[5] Basing his case mostly on the largest company, the London Midland & Scottish Railway (LMS), Scott demonstrates that freight pricing was generally sound and that managers were fairly innovative, particularly from the late 1920s, with regard to technology and service quality. These views bear some parallels with those of the interwar transport economist, Gilbert Walker, whose 1942 book *Road and Rail* remains an invaluable guide to the regulatory and commercial context of distribution from the perspective of one who believed strongly in market pricing.[6]

This chapter develops the line taken by Crompton and Scott by exploring how, once freed from state control in August 1921, the North Eastern Railway (NER) and its successor, the London and North Eastern Railway (LNER), thought about competition from road distribution. The LNER was certainly hard hit. Covering parts of the sparsely populated Scottish Highlands and the industrialised Scottish central belt, the company's territory, all north of London, also included the largely

---

[2] P. Scott, 'The growth of road haulage, 1921–58: an estimate', *Journal of Transport History*, 3rd series 19, 1999, 138–55; T. Gibson, *Road Haulage by Motor in Britain: The First Forty* Years (Aldershot 2001). Gibson's narrative is supplemented by a handful of studies of individual hauliers, for example, G.L. Turnbull, *Traffic and Transport: an Economic History of Pickfords* (London 1979). See also J. Armstrong et al., eds, *Companion to British Road Haulage History* (London 2003).

[3] The classic exponent is Derek Aldcroft. See, for example, D.H. Aldrcroft, *Studies in British Transport History, 1870–1970* (Newton Abbot 1974).

[4] G. Crompton, '"Efficient and economical working?" The performance of the railway companies 1923–33', *Business History*, 27, 1985, 222–37. See also M. Bonavia, *Railway Policy Between the Wars* (Manchester 1981).

[5] P. Scott, 'British railways and the challenge from road haulage: 1919–39', *Twentieth Century British History*, 13, 2002, 101–20. See also Roy Edwards, 'Shaping British Freight Transport in the Interwar Period: Failure of Foresight or Administration, 1919–1934' in this volume.

[6] G. Walker, *Road and Rail: An Enquiry into the Economics of Competition and State Control* (London 1942; 2nd ed. 1947).

agricultural English region of East Anglia as well as the heavily industrialised areas of Yorkshire and the north-east between the rivers Tyne and Tees, this last once served by the prosperous NER and particularly badly hit in the Depression. As a proportion of its total (freight and passenger) revenue in 1923, the LNER's merchandise traffic was second only to the LMS's, at 27.1 per cent, although by 1938 it had fallen into third place behind the LMS and the new frontrunner, the Great Western Railway. Over the same period, the LNER's merchandise receipts fell from just over £15.7 million to just under £12 million, tons-lifted from around 27.4 to 19.8 million and ton-miles from 1.78 to 1.57 billion.[7] It is not my intention, however, to explain this disappointing business performance. Instead I make a start on 'opening up the black box' of the company's thinking by analysing how managers understood the nature of road competition and hence the ways in which the railways might have retained a role in a distribution system that would inevitably involve a strong element of road transport. More particularly, I explore two themes: first, the conceptualisation of railway workers as both a gigantic marketing-cum-sales force and agents of quality control; and, secondly, an understanding of rail-based distribution[8] as a truly national network spreading the economic returns of cheap transport around the country in contrast to the more parochial benefits of road haulage.

The degree to which the managerial black box is opened is limited by the fact that my evidence is taken chiefly from the *LNER Magazine* (published from January 1927) and its variously named predecessors originating with the NER. It remains to be seen from other records what kind of managerial thinking went on behind closed doors. On the other hand, the railway company magazines extend our understanding of management in at least two ways. In the first place, these monthly periodicals were a kind of discourse, a set of discursive practices shaping – or at least attempting to shape – the attitudes and hence the behaviours of their readers, chiefly railway workers but also their families, friends and even parts of the wider public. By the mid-1920s managers were using the magazines to try to circumvent the growing power of the trade unions by rhetorically (re)constructing the interests of labour and capital as one.[9] And the readership was extensive. Although no figures are available for the *LNER Magazine*, its circulation was probably on a par with that of the *LMS Magazine*, also sold to staff cheaply at a subsidised price, which

7 J.W.E. Helm, 'The grouping years (1923–1938): a comparative study of the railways in crisis', part 2, 'Traffic results', *Backtrack*, 11, 1997, 74–80. Caution is needed: some intermediate years were better although only in 1927 did the LNER take more revenue than in 1923.

8 Rail-*based* because of course the railways had to rely on road vehicles to extend their reach beyond the goods yard.

9 D. Howell, *Respectable Radicals: Studies in the Politics of Railway Trade Unionism* (Aldershot 1999); M. Heller, 'Company magazines 1880–1940: an overview', *Management and Organizational History*, 3, 2008, 179–96; M. Heller, 'British company magazines, 1878–1939: the origins and functions of house journals in large-scale organisations', *Media History*, 15, 2009, 143–66; M. Esbester, 'Organizing work: company magazines and the discipline of safety', *Management and Organizational History*, 3, 2008, 217–37.

settled down to sales of roughly 70–79,000 in the later 1930s, with a readership estimated to be about three times this figure.[10] The magazine's content – a mix of editorials, articles and other pieces such as short stories, verses and cartoons, many contributed and ranging from official railway business to entertainment and news about railway staff, families, sport and social events – allowed the company 'to talk to itself', building workers' loyalty and promoting effective day-to-day working.[11] This is particularly important for understanding managers' perceptions of the nature of road competition and the role of workers in fighting it. Thus the *LNER Magazine* sensitised the workforce to the intensifying competition, informed about managerial policy, gave out news about initiatives and, to some degree, acted as a forum in which workers could debate the future of rail-based distribution, both by reporting discussions held elsewhere, such as in railway debate and lecture societies, and by publishing letters and contributed articles.

In the second place, the *LNER Magazine* offers an insight into the company's development of what we should now call public relations, part of the blurring of boundaries between the corporation and its stakeholders.[12] Because it was sold to the public, the *Magazine*'s contents were a resource that could help mobilise wider opinion in favour of the legislative redress sought by the Big Four. Although there is no way of assessing the *Magazine*'s effectiveness, this wider readership was offered not only a taste of what senior management thought but also a glimpse of the range of debate within the company, including opinions on rail-based distribution that did not always fit neatly with the LNER's policies.

The Scale and Nature of the Challenge

Road competition for general merchandise after the First World War was unlike anything previously faced by the railways and so required an exceptional response. Merchandise was traffic of small consignments, averaging under three tons per wagon, and conveyed (in the late 1930s) on average for just over 100 miles (160 kilometres).[13] Such flows suited a retailing and manufacturing system increasingly keen to minimise stockholding costs, and in 1923–24 were worth about £50 million in revenue to the Big Four.[14] Before the war the railways had largely competed for

---

[10] *LMS Magazine* (hereafter *LMSM*), 3 July 1926, 181; 11 December 1934, 513; 12 July 1935, 323; 12 December 1935, 583; 13 January 1936, 1; 13 June 1936, 1; 15 January 1938, 1; 15 May 1938, 211; 15 August 1938, 375; *North Eastern and Scottish Magazine* 14 July 1924, 210.

[11] Heller, 'Company magazines 1880–1940', 187.

[12] Heller, 'Company magazines 1880–1940', 187–8; Esbester, 'Organizing work', 219.

[13] Helm, 'Traffic results', 75. Distances calculated from Walker, *Road and Rail*, 128, table 10. Helm suggests a figure some 25 per cent or more lower.

[14] Walker, *Road and Rail*, 1, and Helm, 'Traffic results', 74.

this traffic amongst themselves; price competition was heavily regulated so service quality was the key. Indeed by comparison with continental Europe, Britain was renowned for short transit times gained at the high cost of running more frequent, if less economically loaded, trains. Nor was motorised road haulage an entirely new competitor – it had been growing rapidly in some areas since the early 1900s. But the situation was transformed from 1919 by the arrival of large numbers of small road hauliers. Prices were slashed as one- or two-lorry operators sought to gain traffic from the railways and each other. Service quality was also often better, with quicker transit, less pilferage and fewer breakages amongst the advantages widely cited.[15] By 1921 the railways' annual loss of freight (mostly merchandise) was already estimated at some six million tons.[16] Given the highly fragmented nature of the road haulage industry and its low entry costs, in the short-to-medium term the railways could hope neither to eradicate their competitors nor collude with them. In the longer term, the companies hoped that cooperation might be possible if road haulage became dominated by large firms, particularly if the industry were to be regulated by the state.[17] But for the time being state policy towards the railways was distinctly unsympathetic; the rejection in 1922 of a test application for powers to run lorries independently of their trains was a significant defeat for the companies.[18] Although they finally succeeded in 1928, the delay further blunted the railways' competitive edge, forcing them to continue operating expensive short-haul rail services which some managers wanted to abandon. Estimates of the continued losses to road vary. Walker thought that by 1935 over half of rail merchandise had gone, although a recent estimate based on official returns is less pessimistic, putting the decline between 1923 and 1938 at 19.5 per cent by revenue, 16.5 per cent for tons-lifted and 8 per cent for ton-miles.[19] What is certain is that market share had plummeted as road hauliers captured new flows generated by the burgeoning consumer economy, particularly as nationally marketed branded goods increasingly replaced non-branded, regionally sourced commodities.

Much of the Big Four's case against road haulage was that it was 'unfair competition', particularly in the form of subsidised roads, unregulated labour and lack of statutory pricing controls. As Scott has detailed they sought, with some success in the later 1920s and 1930s, to have this moderated through legislation, most notably with the 1933 Road and Rail Traffic Act which introduced the licensing of road haulage. As already noted, gaining public support for such measures was vital and helps to explain why from the early 1920s the companies worked

---

15 Gibson, *Road Haulage*, 1–186, especially 150.

16 Gibson, *Road Haulage*, 150–55.

17 The pre-war railways had sometimes colluded with coastal shipping and inland navigation in regard to bulk flows such as coal.

18 R. Edwards, this volume; Gibson, *Road Haulage*, 150–55. The companies could already operate road services to collect and deliver goods to and from their stations and depots.

19 Walker, *Road and Rail*, 124–9, and Helm, 'Traffic results', 74–5.

together in developing publicity emphasising the critical role played by rail-based distribution. In response to political uproar over high food prices, for example, in 1923 the industry-wide Railway Clearing House (RCH) issued a pamphlet detailing the low cost of distributing a wide range of foodstuffs. The exercise was repeated in 1927, in the run-up to the second attempt to gain road powers.[20] In the same year, and still in response to the charge 'that Railway Companies are responsible for the high cost of food', the Big Four mounted a display at the Advertising Exhibition, 'a combined effort to make known facts about the railway business in relation to the trade of the country, and to establish the importance of railways to the national well-being'.[21] Such cooperative public relation was slowly – perhaps too slowly – complemented by joint marketing of rail-based distribution, particularly once revenue-pooling and traffic-sharing became legal in 1928, resulting in a decline in inter-company competition. By the mid-1930s joint marketing was increasingly prominent,[22] and according to Walker by the end of the decade the companies 'co-operate so closely that they are often regarded as one organisation'.[23] In short, although it remains appropriate to analyse the railways' thinking about the future of distribution at the level of an individual company, for a fuller picture we are going to have to follow Roy Edwards' lead and look at the ways in which the Big Four worked together, particularly through the RCH.

Constructing Workers as Agents of Sales and Quality-Control

While the small scale of early road hauliers had its own disadvantages, owner-operators were closer than the large, bureaucratic railways to their customers and therefore had a head start both in securing business and ensuring rapid, reliable and secure delivery. These advantages tended to continue even as haulage firms increased in size, because drivers still found it easier to keep contact with traders or distribution managers and maintained personal control over the goods they delivered.[24]

---

20 Railway Clearing House, *Railway Rates: How They Affect the Cost of Living (London 1923), and Railway Clearing House, Railway Rates: How Little They Affect the Cost of Food* (London 1927).

21 *London and North Eastern Railway Magazine* (hereafter *LNERM*), 17 August 1927, 342. The display featured mock ups of a shop-window and breakfast room showing the household necessaries carried for a penny. Over a 100,000 members of the public visited this exhibition alone. The breakfast-table display was later exhibited during the Gateshead Empire Shopping Week and, in the form of a window-display, at the North-East Coast Exhibition, Newcastle, attended by nearly 4.4 million, in 1929. *LNERM*, 17 October 1927, 469; 19 July 1929, 363–5, and 19 December 1929, 644.

22 *LNERM*, 25 November 1935, 632–3; 26 February 1936, 76–7; 27 November 1937, 630–31.

23 Walker, *Road and Rail*, 140.

24 Walker, *Road and Rail*, 115–20.

The NER and LNER's managers responded by encouraging railway workers to think of themselves as part of the solution, employing the idea of 'team spirit' so central to contemporary ideologies of managerial control. For instance in 1928, the LNER's Chief General Manager, Ralph Wedgwood argued that

> properly viewed, what is the Company's business is the business of each and all of us. The credit of the Company for progress and efficiency inevitably appeals to every member of the staff who has pride in his calling, and in the long run it is on the welfare of the Company that salaries and wages alike depend.[25]

Such exhortations were hardly disinterested: they served partly to inculcate a feeling of loyalty to the company which might then be exploited by pursuing financial viability through pay and job cuts.[26] More positively, managers understood workers partly as lobbyists for the legislative relief sought by the Big Four.[27] They were also seen as a free supplement to the railway's specialist sales force, unpaid agents extending the company's intelligence of the numerous retailers, wholesalers and manufacturers spread across the (L)NER's extensive territory. Within a month of being freed from state control, for instance, NER managers, inspired partly by US practice, were promoting the idea that workers should see themselves as part of the sales initiative.[28] Such pleas probably found a ready audience among those such as the station master conjured up in 1922 by 'C.V.M.', a man facing a very different competitive situation than his pre-war equivalent, 'the sole district agent, blessed with a cheap selling line. His task was easy'.[29] Continuing this line in the *LNER Magazine* of the late 1920s, readers were told about a trial scheme covering 60,000 workers in the North Eastern Area (essentially the old NER), 'inviting every railwayman to be a canvasser of the Company' by returning a postage-paid postcard whenever one heard of potential traffic.[30] Moving into the 1930s, the language of retailing, already apparent from the early 1920s, became common, with pleas for railway workers to think of themselves as 'selling transport to our customers' often coming from well below senior or middle management.[31]

Management's invocation of a 'team spirit' was also intended to meeting the charge that road hauliers often provided a better service – quicker, more reliable,

25 *LNERM*, 18 April 1928, 154. For similar sentiments, see also *LNERM*, 18 April 1928, 162.

26 G. Crompton, '"Squeezing the pulpless orange": labour and capital on the railways in the interwar years', *Business History*, 31, 1989, 66–83.

27 *LNERM*, 22 April 1932, 202; 23 February 1933, 79, and 29 February 1939, 88–9.

28 *North Eastern Railway Magazine* (hereafter *NERM*), 11 September 1921, 158.

29 *NERM*, 12 June 1922, 141.

30 *LNERM*, 17 July 1927, 294. This scheme was also borrowed from the USA. See also *LNERM*, 18 April 1928, 154. The postcards were reported as having generated about £900 worth of business in the first two months. *LNERM*, 17 September 1927, 347.

31 *NERM*, 12 June 1922, 141; 16 April 1926, 127; *LNERM*, 21 May 1931, 241; 22 February 1932, 73; 23 January 1932, 31; 26 November 1936, 646.

less pilferage, fewer breakages. Although rail's disadvantages were apparent by the early 1920s, LNER managers seem to have become more concerned about this from the mid-1920s. In 1926, for instance, a middle-ranking official argued that 'we have a commodity for sale, i.e. transport, which is useless unless it gives satisfactory service to the customer at a cost he can pay, a service which by cheapness, despatch and safety, will attract the trader'.[32]

Similarly, the following year the Assistant General Manager, Robert Bell, told the Great Central Debating Society that '[a]part from cost, it was poor deliveries which drove traffic to the road'.[33] Although cooperation between management and labour was still a key – 'Every man should be treated, not as a hand, but as part of the railway team …'[34] – this was no longer seen as enough. Organisational schisms within the company, particularly between the commercial (including marketing) and the operating divisions, needed to be healed, with the reliability – 'punctuality' – of goods trains a key area where managers saw room for immediate improvement.[35] Thus service delivery was linked to marketing, revenue and financial stability, and hence the maintenance of wages and jobs.

While these messages, often repeated, appear to have been sympathetically received by many workers, the battle for service quality was unceasing.[36] Despite the introduction of quantity licensing of road haulage in 1933, the LNER's marketeers still found it necessary to address the workforce in terms remarkably similar to the previous decade. Thus in 1936, 'L.M.' argued that traders remained deeply dissatisfied: 'That word "service" does more harm to the railways … than you in the marshalling yard, the staff on the bench, or the trainmen realise. Capital has … been made of the damage which is said to occur on our railways, and not on the road'.[37]

Repeating the message that all railway workers were 'virtually … Salesman of transport' upon whose 'efficiency of their labours' depended 'the amount of business the railways of this country secures [sic]', L.M. thundered:

> In whatever sphere you operate consider yourself the shopkeeper selling your wares, 'Transport', and give an efficient service, and so enable those fighting your cause, because it is your cause, in the Traffic [licensing] Courts to secure you more customers. No apathy, Mr. Railwayman; if you have no customers

32 *NERM*, 16 April 1926, 127.

33 *LNERM*, 17 May 1927, 188. For similar remarks, see *LNERM*, 17 April 1927, 140–41 (by 'J.I.T'.); 19 January 1929, 2 (by William Whitelaw, Chairman, Board of Directors).

34 *NERM*, 16 April 1926, 127.

35 For example, *LNERM*, 18 May 1928, 226; 18 August 1928, 391 (by R. Wedgwood, Chief General Manager); 24 January 1934, 2 (by Thomas Hornsby, Divisional General Manager, North Eastern Area).

36 For example, *NERM*, 16 February 1926, 47–8.

37 *LNERM*, 26 November 1936, 646.

> you will have to close shop – so backs to the wall and give the trader what he requires – EFFICIENT SERVICE.[38]

Not helped by a general increase in freight prices in October 1937, this was a fight the railways continued slowly to lose.

Geographies of Distribution

Rail-based distribution might have been widely seen, even within the industry, as providing a more expensive and inferior service to road haulage. But there was still considerable scope for managers, and others, to try to define ways in which rail and road might best complement each other. In particular, rail freight was construed as the only network capable of providing a *national* service and thus spreading transport's wider economic benefits on a more spatially equitable basis than road haulage.

This definition took some time to emerge: as long as road haulage was seen as only viable within a radius of 20 or 30 miles, rail-based distribution was easily understood as the key way in which inland transport would contribute to the UK's economic development. For the NER's General Manager, Ralph Wedgwood, the most important facet of British economic geography in the early 1920s was competition between regions; it was the railways' task to provide efficient service within their respective territories and hence to develop the competitiveness of each. (That Wedgwood should tend to this view is no surprise given that the NER had – uniquely – served precisely this territorial function before First World War.)[39] On this perspective, the railways' national reach mattered less than the territorial integrity that the 1921 Railways Act was thought – wrongly as it turned out – likely to produce. In any case, the lack of a network of trunk roads, the technical shortcomings of lorries and their high operating costs meant that it was not implausible for Wedgwood and his ilk to maintain that road competition was geographically circumscribed, 'a factor of secondary importance'.[40] Indeed in 1921 at least one ordinary railwayman welcomed the fact that road haulage could already relieve the railways of 'not very remunerative' traffic over a 30-mile radius of operation, reducing congestion at freight terminals, and allowing trains to provide a better long-distance service.[41]

---

38 *LNERM*, 26 November 1936, 646. See also the Chairman's New Year Message, *LNERM*, 29 January 1939, 3.

39 R.J. Irving, *North Eastern Railway Company, 1870–1914: An Economic History* (Leicester 1976).

40 *NERM*, 12 October 1922, 258, and Gibson, *Road Haulage*, 142–50.

41 *NERM*, 11 March 1921, 55, and Gibson, *Road Haulage*, 135–6.

Figure 3.1 By the Railway C.O.D. Service. Advertisement of British Railway Companies, 1920s

Source: National Railway Museum, York.

Figure 3.2 Use Road-Rail Containers for Every Form of Freight Traffic. Advertisement of British Railway Companies, 1920s

Source: National Railway Museum, York.

Figure 3.3 Railway Country Lorry Service. Advertisement of British Railway Companies, 1920s

Source: National Railway Museum, York.

Views changed rapidly as road competition bit and, particularly in the 1930s, as the domestic, consumer-driven economy came to take a larger role compared with Britain's staple export industries. By the mid-to-late 1920s, railwaymen of all grades accepted that road hauliers operated economically over an increasingly large radius. The emphasis switched to containing competition by constructing a picture of the railways' uniquely national reach. In the 1930s, railway managers argued for the advantages of the 'speed and reliability' of a nationwide, door-to-door distribution system delivered through technological innovations such as containers, fully braked trains and the increasingly widespread coverage of railway-operated collection-and-delivery by road.[42] As the LNER's road-services manager for the North Eastern Area boasted in 1938 'Whether in town or country, our aim is to provide efficient and reliable road-transport services in connection with rail which will add to the attractiveness of the complete transport service which the company has to offer its customers …'[43]

[42] For example, *LNERM*, 25 October 1935, 565. See also Walker, *Road and Rail*, 173–5.

[43] *LNERM*, 28 September 1938, 505. See also P. Butterfield, 'Unfair competition?', *Journal of the Railway and Canal Historical Society*, 35, 2007, 807–8. We do not have a good idea of just how geographically comprehensive or economically significant rail-based distribution was by comparison with that of road haulage in 1939. In particular, own-account operations (C-licence holders), such as those of the food retailer J. Sainsbury,

Although easy to criticise in retrospect, the still-common – if not universal[44] – assumption by railway managers and workers that rail would remain at the core of a countrywide network was not unreasonable given the very slow progress towards a trunk-road system and road hauliers' failure to offer a truly nationwide service.[45] Thus as consumer markets increasingly took on a national character, the claims of 'British Railways' to operate across the whole country was an important selling point, and arguably helped to maintain wider political support for the industry.[46]

Rail's nationwide reach was intimately tied up with the sharply contrasting ways in which rail and road priced their services, differences vigorously debated by contemporaries and much discussed by historians.[47] What is of interest here is the spirited defence in the 1930s of the railway's methods on the grounds that in a rough-and-ready way they evenly distributed the wider economic benefits of cheap transport around the country.

Road hauliers operated in a free market, generally charging, or attempting to charge, prices which at least covered movement and other variable costs. Prices therefore varied even for ostensibly similar loads (some were more expensive to haul than others), and thus traders' costs might differ considerably, particularly from region to region.[48] By contrast the railways' statutory scheme of 'standard rates' (applicable from January 1928, but in their fundamental principles very similar to the previous charging regime) did not pay close regard to costs, charging instead on the basis of a highly complex classificatory system which gave most weight to the economic value of, and hence the supposed benefits to traders of moving, a particular good. While prices were related to distance, this was on a tapering scale. In theory, this statutory framework prevented discrimination between traders and between places.[49] Thus firms engaged in similar businesses in the same region should have paid the same rate for distributing any given commodity over a given distance. And distribution costs for firms situated in different parts of the country should have varied only in terms of the distance goods travelled, and even then not fully in proportion. The overall effect was to cross-subsidise flows and hence to reduce disparities in distribution costs between firms.

---

made up an increasingly large proportion of the competition. By 1937, at least one LNER manager held that C-licence hauliers were becoming the determining long-term factor in setting charges across road and rail, although Walker did not believe that was yet the case. *LNERM*, 27 March 1937, 158–9. Walker, *Road and Rail*, 121–3.

44 See the opposition to a motion at the North Eastern Area Federation of Debating Societies, 'That the railway system of this country is essential to its Commercial Life'. *LNERM*, 21 February 1931, 68.

45 *LNERM*, 21 February 1931, 68; 23 January 1933, 2, and 25 January 1935, 3.

46 *LNERM*, 23 October 1933, 538; 25 February 1935, 88; 28 September 1938, 502–5; 28 October 1938, 546–8; 28 November 1938, 618–19, and 29 August 1939, 452–3.

47 See Scott, 'British railways' for a summary.

48 Walker, *Road and Rail*, 94–106.

49 Walker, *Road and Rail*, 36–93.

I am not concerned here whether this pricing regime was fully applied in practice (there is plenty of evidence that it was not).[50] The point is that proponents and opponents of standard rates agreed on what the system *should* have delivered but disagreed about its desirability: there was a choice to be made. Although the analogy was not perfect even in terms of the ideal, proponents argued that it was a good thing that railways were 'so regulated by Parliamentary control that everyone takes for granted that, like the Post Office, they will treat all customers alike'.[51] Detractors such as Gilbert Walker argued that this was a disadvantage precisely because it reduced the comparative locational advantage of one firm over another.[52] At root, the battle between the two pricing regimes and their associated modes of transport was one between competing conceptions of economic spatial justice.

The long-term implications of this debate were to be so profound that it is worth unpicking the contemporary arguments. In the 1930s, to argue in favour of statutory pricing and minimising inequalities in distribution costs was to place rail at the core of the national distribution system. The key advocate in the *LNER Magazine* was A.S. Sewell, a rising star in the goods department.[53] Writing first in 1933, Sewell knew his transport economics: that cross-subsidies and hence a national network were unsustainable if road hauliers continued to cherry-pick profitable flows. He knew too that road competition was pushing the railways 'from a "classification" towards a "cost" basis of charging'.[54] But he argued on the basis of interviews with some 2,000 firms that most preferred statutory regulation because 'it adds stability to their business'.[55] This position was essentially that assumed by traders a decade earlier when the proposals that led to the 1928 charging regime had been under debate.[56] The desired stability included not only constant and spatially consistent standard prices (indeed, there was only the one general increase, that in October 1937), but also an extensive, geographically comprehensive distribution network. Thus in 1933 and again in 1938, Sewell argued that cross-subsidy was necessary

[50] Walker argued that in practice the railways were not prevented from charging any rate they deemed advantageous. By 1935 nearly 84 per cent of all freight was charged at 'exceptional' rates below the standard. Thus in reality rail pricing could be spatially discriminatory; for example, a railway might offer a manufacturer favourable prices in order to secure the location of a new works on its system. Walker, *Road and Rail*, 67–8, 73–4.

[51] *LNERM*, 23 April 1934, 187. The Post Office did not vary its prices with regard to distance.

[52] Walker, *Road and Rail*, 251–2. Although written in 1947, Walker's comments here were clearly at one with the analysis of the rest of his book, based largely on the pre-war situation.

[53] Sewell rose from Assistant Goods Manager, Southern Area in 1931 to Goods Manager, Southern Scottish Area by 1937. He drew the analogy with the Post Office.

[54] *LNERM*, 23 January 1933, 15.

[55] *LNERM*, 23 January 1933, 16. Unfortunately nothing is known about the firms surveyed.

[56] Walker, *Road and Rail*, 47–8.

if 'unremunerative and sparsely populated districts' were to continue to be served,[57] thereby providing 'a national transport system at low rates'.[58] Consistent with this perspective, Sewell was a very reluctant supporter of 'agreed charges', a scheme legalised in 1933 which allowed the railways to charge traders on the basis of the alternative cost of road distribution.[59] He argued, correctly, that by shadowing road pricing, agreed charges distorted the railways' spatial logic of providing a national network that minimised locational inequalities in distribution costs.[60]

Thus for Sewell, the choice facing the state and business alike was stark. Since 'the country cannot do without railways', firms should abandon their short-term, individual interests and 'pay more for transport than the very cheapest at which they can get it done' by road in order to ensure the long-term survival of the national network.[61] The corollary was that road haulage prices should be regulated – deregulation of railway prices in the prevailing competitive context would, he argued, inevitably lead to a market-led system of shifting prices, confidential rates, preference granted to particular firms and localities and the closure of '[u]nremunerative branch lines ... without the provision of alternative facilities'.[62]

Within a quarter of a century, Sewell was, of course, to be proved wrong in his assumption that Britain could not do without its railways for distribution, or at least a large proportion of them, but this is not the point here.[63] His propositions might have been politically unrealistic and unpalatable to many firms, but even opponents of his way of thinking did not question the basic logic of the argument: there *was* a choice to be made. Gilbert Walker, for instance, a powerful advocate of market pricing, accepted this in *Road and Rail*:

> To remove the 'unfairness' and place road and rail on an equal competitive footing, road charges and railway rates must be made on the same set of principles. Either the road haulier must be required to apply a classification of goods by value and make his charges on that principle, as the railways do, or the railways must leave the value of the goods out of account when fixing rates and follow the current practice of road hauliers, who make cost the basis of transport charges.[64]

---

57 *LNERM*, 23 April 1933, 186–7, quote at 186.

58 *LNERM*, 28 March 1938, 145.

59 Walker, *Road and Rail*, 82–93. By 1937 over 530 schemes were in operation, producing an annual income of nearly £4 million. *LNERM*, 27 April 1937, 214.

60 *LNERM*, 25 March 1935, 137.

61 *LNERM*, 23 April 1933, 186–7, quotes at 187.

62 *LNERM*, 23 April 1933, 187.

63 He was right about the consequences of price deregulation – although we should bear in mind that the quickening decline of rail distribution from the 1950s happened after many years of these very different charging regimes for rail and road, punctuated by the abnormal – and arguably damaging – commercial and operating conditions of the Second World War.

64 Walker, *Road and Rail*, 115.

For Walker, the latter was not only 'simpler to administer', it also had 'the additional recommendation of being economically more justifiable'.[65] And as the evidence of the *LNER Magazine* shows, even within the railway industry many argued by the mid-to-late 1930s that there was no realistic prospect of maintaining the old pricing system wholesale, although their preference was not for all-out competition and market pricing. At the most senior level, railway managers preferred to see voluntary agreement with road hauliers on regulated pricing, keeping compulsory state regulation at bay. In 1938 the Big Four launched the 'Square Deal' campaign, aimed at securing further concessions from the state along these lines in order to maintain financial viability. While the outbreak of war stopped both lobbying and any chance of reform, both this campaign and the companies' negotiations in 1938–39 with various haulage and business interests merit closer study; reports in the *LNER Magazine* suggest that all parties saw the maintenance of a *national* distribution network involving all transport operators – not only rail and road but also coastal shipping and inland navigation – as desirable.[66]

Conclusion

It was, of course, one thing for LNER managers to understand their workforce as a spatially extended network of sales and quality-control agents, or to advocate a spatially 'non-discriminatory' national system of rail-based distribution based on regulated pricing, quite another to turn such ideas into reality. The aim of this chapter has not been to assess managers' effectiveness in promoting these proposals – if indeed such a goal is sensible. In particular, I doubt whether it would be possible to gain more than a very general sense of how seriously LNER employees took the notion that they had a key role to play in attracting and retaining general merchandise to rail, although here the autobiographies and oral histories of railway workers might prove useful sources.

Nevertheless, I want to stress that the railway-company magazines enrich our understanding of the *possibilities* envisaged by the industry for a rail-based system of distribution tailored to the needs of a consumer economy that was both growing rapidly and taking on a national character. The LNER's managers, for example, at least thought hard about rail's shortcomings with regard to quality of service. Merely exhorting workers to 'pull together' as a 'team' might well be criticised as an inadequate response to the rigidities of departmental divisions – but the case needs to be argued on the basis of further research like that of Scott's study of the LMS, not merely taken as read. Archival sources will have their place in such work, particularly when it comes to debates at a senior managerial level. But the magazines hint at a range of views that remind us of the value of looking at

[65] Walker, *Road and Rail*, 115.

[66] *LNERM*, 28 December 1938, 682–3; 29 February 1939, 88–9; 29 March 1939, 152–3, and 2 May 1939, 328–9.

debates and decisions about distribution in terms of bounded rationality or, more broadly, as processes in which the construction of a debate's parameters could have an important (if not determining) bearing on which policy was eventually chosen. It is too easy to assume that the simple fact that road distribution grew rapidly in the interwar years spelt the eventual demise of a rail-based alternative. A knowledgeable critic of the railways such as Gilbert Walker, writing in the 1940s, thought this neither necessary nor desirable.[67] We should do more to explore the options that were on the table, and the reasons why they came to nothing – a task which will require a more detailed knowledge of the business practices and traffic operations of the Big Four and associated organisations such as the RCH, and a more sophisticated understanding of the legislative, regulatory and commercials context in which the railway's policies were formed and enacted.[68]

References

Aldcroft, D.H., *Studies in British Transport History, 1870–1970* (Newton Abbot 1974).

Armstrong, J., et al., eds, *Companion to British Road Haulage History* (London 2003).

Bonavia, M., *Railway Policy Between the Wars* (Manchester 1981).

Butterfield, P., 'Unfair competition?', *Journal of the Railway and Canal Historical Society*, 35, 2007, 807–8.

Crompton, G., '"Efficient and economical working?" The performance of the railway companies 1923–33', *Business History*, 27, 1985, 222–37.

Crompton, G., '"Squeezing the pulpless orange": labour and capital on the railways in the interwar years', *Business History*, 31, 1989, 66–83.

Divall, C., 'The modern passenger: constructing the consumer on Britain's railways, 1919–1939', in M. Pinheiro, ed., *Railway Modernization: An Historical Perspective (19th and 20th Centuries)* (Lisbon 2009), 111–25.

Divall, C., 'Civilising velocity: masculinity and the marketing of Britain's passenger trains, 1921–39', *Journal of Transport History*, 3rd series 32, 2011, 164–91.

Edwards, R., 'Job analysis on the LMS: mechanisation and modernisation c.1930–c.1939', *Accounting, Financial and Business History*, 20, 2010, 91–105.

Esbester, M., 'Organizing work: company magazines and the discipline of safety', *Management and Organizational History*, 3, 2008, 217–37.

Gibson, T., *Road Haulage by Motor in Britain: The First Forty Years* (Aldershot 2001).

---

67 Walker, *Road and Rail*, especially 250–253.

68 For example, R. Edwards, 'Job analysis on the LMS: mechanisation and modernisation c. 1930–c. 1939', *Accounting, Financial and Business History*, 20, 2010, 91–105.

Heller, M., 'Company magazines 1880–1940: an overview', *Management and Organizational History*, 3, 2008, 179–96.

Heller, M., 'British company magazines, 1878–1939: the origins and functions of house journals in large-scale organisations', *Media History*, 15, 2009, 143–66.

Helm, J.W.E., 'The grouping years (1923–1938): a comparative study of the railways in crisis', part 2, 'Traffic results', *Backtrack*, 11, 1997, 74–80.

Howell, D., *Respectable Radicals: Studies in the Politics of Railway Trade Unionism* (Aldershot 1999).

Irving, R.J., *North Eastern Railway Company, 1870–1914: An Economic History* (Leicester 1976).

Mom, G., Divall, C. and Lyth, P., 'Towards a paradigm shift? A decade of transport and mobility history', in G. Mom, G. Pirie and L. Tissot, eds, *Mobility in History: The State of the Art in the History of Transport, Traffic and Mobility* (Neuchâtel 2009), 13–40.

Railway Clearing House, *Railway Rates: How They Affect the Cost of Living* (London 1923).

Railway Clearing House, *Railway Rates: How Little They Affect the Cost of Food* (London 1927).

Scott, P., 'The growth of road haulage, 1921–58: an estimate', *Journal of Transport History*, 3rd series 19, 1999, 138–55.

Scott, P., 'British railways and the challenge from road haulage: 1919–39', *Twentieth Century British History*, 13, 2002, 101–20.

Shin, H., 'Business strategy and corporate image: Britain's railways, 1872–1977', in H. Mäki and J. Korjus, eds, *Railways as an Innovative Regional Factor* (Kouvola 2009), 63–84.

Turnbull, L., *Traffic and Transport: an Economic History of Pickfords* (London 1979).

Walker, G., *Road and Rail: An Enquiry into the Economics of Competition and State Control* (London 1942; 2nd ed. 1947).

Chapter 4
Railway Containers in the United Kingdom and Europe during the 1920s and 1930s

Keith Harcourt

The adoption of methodologies for freight transport was, like the development of rail transport itself, an evolutionary process with multiple starting points. In the UK the government had allowed railways to develop as private companies with differing local agenda, whereas in Belgium by 1835 the railways were being engineered as state-owned enterprises, hence differences in modus operandi, technology and management across and within countries were almost inevitable.[1] Thus it may come as no surprise that development of a method of secure delivery, packed at the point of origin, moved by more than one mode of transport and unpacked by its consignee also had a long and varied development. As Silvio Crespi noted in 1934:

> Broadly speaking, a container is any contrivance that 'contains' any kind of commodities or loose units. The use of boxes as a means of transport dates back to the most ancient times of human history. As an example, it may be recalled that this means was used for the transport of wild beasts for the Roman circus games. More recently containers were used for goods traffic between England and the Continent.[2]

From the earliest development of railways in the UK, the movement of goods has been shaped with the desire to move goods as safely and as efficiently as possible. In all nations, the placement of goods inside an open-topped or closed vehicle became the norm. This offered railway companies great flexibility in being able to use a given vehicle to carry a wide range of traffic. However, transferring goods into and out of railway vehicles, shunting and other movements increased the possibility of damage and pilferage. The railways were legally liable for these and investigated ways to minimise them. The idea of using a container that could be transported unopened from shipper to consignee was attractive to railway companies.

---

1 P. Bagwell, *The Railway Clearing House in the British Economy 1842–1922* (London 1968).

2 S. Crespi, 'What a container is', *The Container*, 1, 1934, 3–4.

House removals in the UK and abroad had been achieved by the use of 'lift vans' (an early form of container) packed at the shipper's 'old' house, transported by road, rail and sometimes ship, and then unpacked at the new one, since the late nineteenth century. Lift vans were owned in the most part by removal companies. Some commercial companies also had similar containers. Roy Horniman notes Lyons (Tea Merchants) and others as using them.[3]

Some of the earliest intermodal containerisation of commercial traffic took place on British tramways and canals about 1775 with Joseph Butler's creation of wagons with detachable boxes for the Lings Colliery Line in Derbyshire UK. Benjamin Outram's Little Eaton Gangway copied Butler's system using wagons which

> consisted of two sections, an undercarriage or chassis and a body or box. … When the wagons were loaded … a team of horses would take them down the railway to the wharf at Little Eaton. Here, a crane was used to lift the laden bodies off the undercarriages and place them into a boat for onward carriage.[4]

Technology transfer onto the newly evolving railway system in the early nineteenth century did not take long. The Liverpool and Manchester Railway (LMR) began using containers for both coal and goods in the 1830s. 'Simple rectangular timber boxes, four to a wagon, they were used to convey coal from the Lancashire collieries to Liverpool, where they were transferred to horse drawn carts by crane'.[5]

Paul Wohl whilst noting the above developments in the 1830s states that 'no serious development of containers took place during the greater part of the 19th century owing to the lack of adequate crane and elevating equipment'. He goes on to note that 'towards the end of that century, however, we already see very substantial containers (sic!) employed regularly between England and France'.[6] However, the British railway standard loading gauge has always been much smaller than that of its continental counterparts. As the Secretary of the Railway Research Bureau, Charles Sherrington, stated in 1930:

> The pioneer, simply because he is a pioneer, suffers in comparison with those who profit by his pioneering developments. This is the pioneering railway country of the world and as a consequence, it suffers from the small loading gauge by which the size of its rolling stock is limited.[7]

---

[3] R. Horniman, *How to Make the Railways Pay for the War* (London 1916), 99.

[4] D. Ripley, *The Little Eaton Gangway and Derby Canal* (Usk 1993), 24–5.

[5] R.J. Essery, D.P. Rowland and W.O. Steel, *British Goods Wagons from 1887 to the Present Day* (New York 1970), 92.

[6] P. Wohl, 'The Twin Problems of Transportation – the container has come to stay', *The Container Bulletin*, 1 January 1934, 11–12.

[7] C.E.R. Sherrington, 'British and Foreign Rolling Stock Compared', *Journal of the Institute of Transport*, 11, no. 4 February 1930, 180–84.

Interchange of UK containers with the continent was possible but, at least for large continental containers, the reverse was problematic. Wohl also notes that from 1929

> a fast speed container service has been in operation between Basle and London. Containers used on these lines have wheels and are loaded four on a special flat car 16.7 metres long and with a net weight of 27 tons ... These cars are used jointly between the London, Midland and Scottish Railway and the Northern French Railway; they run in the fast train which leaves Basle at 13.30 and arrives at Dunkirk at midnight; thus the containers are in London the next day at 8 am.[8]

The quotation, though interesting and an early ideal use of the international intermodal technique, hides the fact that the containers could not be to the full European railway dimensions and this disparity was to bedevil UK railways' participation in European container standardisation efforts until Malcolm Maclean's invention of the intermodal 'box' in 1956 led to the development of the International Organisation for Standardisation (ISO) regulations between 1968 and 1970. Containers built under the ISO regulations then superseded earlier designs and even the British railways were forced to find ways of accommodating them within their restricting infrastructure.

As Michael Hascher notes, though the ways in which containers and their use were developed in the various countries and continents where they flourished differed, there was a common thread. In his words: 'the key players were not to be found in governmental circles, but in private businesses'.[9] This was certainly the case in the United Kingdom, Italy, France, Switzerland, Austria and the USA.

Prior to the First World War the UK's private railway companies held a virtual monopoly on inland transport. After hostilities ceased, government, the emerging motor industry and the road hauliers were determined not to let the pre-war situation reassert itself. The resulting regulation occupied differing timescales and took several forms, especially in countries where railways were state-owned, but a report in the January issue of the International Chamber of Commerce (ICC) journal *World Trade* gives a flavour of the anti-rail feelings prevalent at the time. It notes that railways should not be allowed to 'freeze out' road hauliers, stating that

> powerful corporations such as Railways would be able to do by running their motor transport at a loss for a certain time and, after having killed off all motor

[8] P. Wohl, 'Containers in Action in America and Europe', *Container Supplement in World Trade*, 4, 2 January 1932, 3–6.

[9] M. Hascher, 'The Lowtech Revolution: Containers and Pipelines', in R. Roth and C. Schlögel, eds, *Neue Wege in ein neues Europa. Geschichte und Verkehr im 20. Jahrhundert* (Frankfurt am Main and New York 2009), 431–51.

> transport competition, withdraw their own motor transport services so as to restore the railway monopoly.[10]

By the time this was written the UK railways had, via legislation, won the right to own and operate road haulage services, but the European debate to resolve the issue was very much alive.

With this political background in mind it is worthy of note that in Europe it was the World Motor Congress held in Rome in 1928 that suggested that the intermodality of containers was an area where the interests of road and rail might best be served by cooperation. This notion was taken up by the ICC who formed an International Container Committee. Hence the European development of containers, unlike that in the UK, appears to have been the result of a move by road hauliers to cooperate with the railways, though it would be surprising if their micro-political intention was not to grow traffic. The development of the container movement in the UK and Europe was a lengthy, complex and political process. The next section reviews developments in the United Kingdom.

Containerisation in the United Kingdom

The close of hostilities in 1918 left some 48,000 motor lorries surplus to UK government requirements together with a ready supply of services trained, but now unemployed, drivers.[11] Private motoring was also a rapidly developing factor; the Morris Motor Company alone increased production of their cars from 337 per annum in 1919 to 48,712 in 1925.[12] In terms of freight transport, according to Alfred Plummer, 'goods vehicles numbered 151,000 in 1922 and 334,000 in 1930'.[13]

The government at the end of the war, faced with the large numbers of unemployed soldiers returning from the Continent, started schemes of public works, including a large road improvement programme. In these circumstances, almost, it might be said, with government sponsorship, commercial road transport in a few short years became a major competitor to the railways in the short haul and specialist freight market. As Peter Scott has argued, the 'failure to prevent

---

[10] P. Wohl, 'The Work of the International Chamber', *World Trade*, 1, no. 1, January 1929, 103–7.

[11] The National Archive (TNA), Goods Department 'Freight Transportation in Container Trucks' – London Midland & Scottish Railway Company internal publication, Rail 421/146.

[12] L.A. Smith, 'The Evolution of the Automobile', in *The Transactions of the Swindon Engineering Society*, 30 November 1926 (Swindon 1926), 5–28.

[13] A. Plummer, *New British Industries in the Twentieth Century* (London 1937), 103.

rapid loss of traffic to the roads was the inevitable consequence of the regulatory framework under which the railways had been returned to private control in 1921'.[14]

The arrival of road transport competition to rail in the UK post-1918 was also complicated by the fact that the railways had been under government control throughout the war. Any return to the commercial position before the war was not to be. The public and the politicians had pre-war memories which characterised the railway companies as greedy capitalists, and often as inefficient. Determined that this should not be the case again, the government, whilst stopping short of nationalisation, with the Railways Act 1921 merged 120 companies into just four large commercial groups. The grouping originating from the Act did not come into force until the 1st January 1923, but much of the management expertise needed to fight the challenge of road competition was, initially at least, engaged with making staff of what had been different and proud companies work together as members of the new groups.

John Droege in his textbook of US freight operations in 1912 has a whole chapter on 'British Freight Service' and notes: 'One such country will suffice for the purposes of comparison, and England has been selected because its railroads are most interesting to us … because they are privately owned and operated like our own'.[15]

The railway companies, even when grouped post-1923, were privately owned, but since 1842 they had been necessarily, though often unwillingly, cooperating. Some initially stood aside, but by 1870 the majority of railways in the British Isles were members of The Railway Clearing House (RCH). This organisation was responsible for the through booking across different railways, of freight, passengers and, in the early days, the carriages and horses of the latter.

The RCH also divided the revenue from freight booked to travel from one area to another across the companies involved and settled inter-company debts. In terms of rolling stock the RCH set standards for goods wagons and later was set to play an important role in the standardisation and development of containers in the UK. Further research is required, but it may be that the London, Midland and Scottish Railway (LMS) encouraged this via their membership of the Goods Managers' Committee of the RCH, in order to get their new idea accepted on a national basis.

Early Developments

The largest of the grouped companies to emerge from the 1921 Act was the LMS. This was a grouping of companies linking the industrial regions of the English

---

[14] P. Scott, 'British Railways and the Challenge from Road Haulage: 1919–1939', *Twentieth Century British History*, 13, 2, 2002, 101–20.

[15] J.A. Droege, *Freight Terminals and Trains – Including a Revision of Yards and Terminals* (New York 1912), 299.

Midlands and North-west with Scotland and London; the LMS was entrepreneurial, innovative and had immense capital. One constituent, the Lancashire and Yorkshire Railway (L&Y), had a huge trade in cotton, both the raw material and the finished fabrics. To deal effectively with the traffic it had, as Coates has shown, developed containerisation as early as 1894, in the form of 'flat bottoms'.[16] The pioneering work of the L&Y was credited by the International Container Committee in 1934,[17] but had been noted still earlier by the industry press, in 1916:

> Reference may be made to the use of flatbottoms, which have been used by the Lancashire & Yorkshire Railway for a very long period in dealing with the Lancashire cotton trade. Their use is of interest in view of the stress which is being laid upon the use of containers as a feature of the Goods Clearing Scheme.[18]

Indeed, containers were high on the agenda in the UK by this date, possibly due largely to the Goods Clearing Scheme proposals of Mr Alfred Gattie, promulgated widely and set out in detail in Roy Horniman's book, *How to Make the Railways Pay for the War*, which were generating much debate and comment.[19] For the purposes of this chapter it will suffice to say that Gattie wanted to create a vast Goods Clearing House, which physically would have dwarfed St Paul's Cathedral, in an effort to make the railway goods operations efficient enough to 'pay for the War'. Gattie's scheme was not frivolous; Hansard shows questions still being asked in the House of Commons about the scheme in June 1919 when Horniman's book reached its third edition.[20] The Gattie Scheme was the subject of a departmental enquiry in 1920 which found against it, but the railway press noted another Parliamentary question asking for the revival of the scheme in 1940.[21]

LMS Container Developments

The LMS was the railway that drove the introduction of containers. During 1925–26 it built and tested two types of container as well as commissioning a report on the results. The major internal and unpublished LMS report entitled

---

16 N. Coates, 'Lurries and Flat Bottoms', *LYR Focus. Journal of the Lancashire and Yorkshire Railway Society*, 61, 2007, 22–35.

17 Anonymous, 'The State of Container Traffic throughout the World 1933', *The Container Bulletin*, 1 January 1934, 13–72.

18 Anonymous, 'Goods Loading and Unloading', *The Railway News*, 4 November 1916, 540.

19 R. Horniman, *How to Make the Railways*, 80–114.

20 Goods Clearing House (Mr Gattie's scheme), Hansard, '*HC Deb 05 June 1919, vol 116 cc 2217–8*'. http://hansard.millbanksystems.com/commons/1919/jun/05/goods-clearing-house-mr-gatties-scheme (last accessed: 16 September 2011).

21 Anonymous 'Traffic Congestion and the Gatty Scheme', *The Railway Gazette*, 72, 11, 1940, 392.

'Freight Transportation in Container Trucks' dated 31 December 1926 puts the road threat very clearly:

> Under the present legal situation the Road Haulier has the initial advantage of a gratuitous permanent way together with a subsidised maintenance of that permanent way, which factors are sufficient to enable him, under certain conditions of wide application, to carry merchandise at rates below railway charges. … It is patent, therefore, that there has arisen a new and powerful system in the sphere of transport which, if allowed to develop under existing disparity of conditions, may seriously disturb the financial structure of the railways in the course of the next few decades.[22]

More of the traditional freight movement methods would not answer the problem and the report recommended that 'Improved facilities and conditions corresponding as nearly as possible to road transport' needed to be provided.[23] It is worth noting that aside from the externally obvious changes, the recommendations were to have an impact on one of the railway's most labour-intensive and therefore costly facilities, the Goods Terminals. Goods Terminals were a subject to which LMS Vice-President Ernest J.H. Lemon, together with the Canadian consultant Louis G. Ord, returned in 1933.[24]

Road haulage was winning customers because it provided door-to-door service without intermediate handling, thus eliminating much packing and loss or breakage. The road hauliers were under no obligation to carry a load that they might find commercially unviable. The railway as a common carrier had to carry whatever the consignee wished to send. The railways thus found themselves left with the low-rate, difficult-to-handle and often small-consignment traffics. One of the aims of containerisation was to win back the door-to-door traffic. The container, the report contended, provided a possible means of competition. Three types were currently in use: 'lift vans', open containers and flat-bottom containers, the last being an obvious reference to the L&Y developments described above. The authors stressed that a change of view of the container was necessary, and possibly for the first time in a UK company document, describes the philosophy of intermodal traffic:

> It is most important that the hybrid character of the container as an integral part of a road or railway VEHICLE (sic) should be fully appreciated and accepted,

22 TNA, Goods Department 'Freight Transportation in Container Trucks' – London Midland & Scottish Railway Company internal publication, Rail 421/146, paragraphs 3 and 4.

23 TNA, Goods Department 'Freight Transportation in Container Trucks' – London Midland & Scottish Railway Company internal publication, Rail 421/146.

24 H.G. Smith, *Notes on Mr Lemon's Achievements*, unpublished MS (London 1933). From The Lemon Papers held in The Archive of the Institution of Mechanical Engineers.

> as this conception of the appliance as opposed to the view that it is a substitute for a packing case has a vital bearing upon the facts and arguments contained in this review.[25]

The report also suggested that containers should be kept to as few types as practicable to facilitate their interchange with other railway companies. This gives an important hint as to the source of the RCH's success in standardising containers. The LMS was able to influence the RCH Goods Managers' Committee which recommended, in what might be seen as a short amount of time in RCH terms, that the specifications be approved. Thus containers became an RCH Standard and indeed remained so, as Don Rowland comments: 'British Railways containers followed pre-nationalisation designs very closely, so much so that in many cases construction was still to RCH drawings a long time after 1948'.[26] Indeed, RCH Diagram Numbers for containers were still being revised as late as 1963.

Unsurprisingly, given the trans-Atlantic influences on the company's senior management, the LMS report considered the use of containers in America as well as in Germany and Switzerland.[27] Though interested in all of these international experiments, the authors felt that because of the 'similarity to English conditions', the small Swiss experiment was worthy of special study and had arranged with the Railway Information Bureau at the London School of Economics to research the full details.[28] The report provisionally concluded that:

> Railway Companies appear to have reached the parting of the ways, where a progressive outlook, with due regard to the sale of transportation in the form demanded by the Public, will conserve their revenue and enhance their prestige, whilst a rigid adherence to the prescriptions of an era which has closed will leave the Companies with only that business which others cannot carry … increasing time and labour values demand a readjustment of the factors of production – especially at Goods terminals.[29]

It continued to note that the existing charging system in general needed readjustment and that it was difficult to see real progress without such change. Combining a rate reappraisal with containerisation, as long as the railway plant could be adapted to meet the new demands, 'should leave little doubt as to the future'.[30] It is significant

---

25 TNA, Goods Department 'Freight Transportation in Container Trucks' – London Midland & Scottish Railway Company internal publication, Rail 421/146, paragraph 122.

26 D. Rowland, *British Railways Wagons – the First Half Million* (London 1996), 136.

27 TNA, Goods Department 'Freight Transportation in Container Trucks' – London Midland & Scottish Railway Company internal publication, Rail 421/146, paragraphs 328 to 334.

28 Ibid., paragraph 334.

29 Ibid., paragraphs 336/7.

30 Ibid., paragraph 340.

that in the opening sentence of the Provisional Conclusions, the authors used the plural: 'Railway Companies'.[31] Here were LMS employees stating what they believe to be the future not just for their company, but for all British Railways.

The report was presented to the LMS board of directors in early 1927 and was enthusiastically received. Almost immediately, containerisation began to be embraced as company policy. Just over 4,000 (4077 to be precise) containers were built between 1926 and 1930; 760 Type A, 1067 Type B, 1827 Type C and 423 Type D. After that date, almost inevitably, the four types of containers envisaged by the progenitors of the plan increased as new traffics were gained. By 1933 the LMS had eight container types and by 1936 18 types and subtypes were in use.[32]

The LMS produced a leaflet in 1933 in three colours and on an art paper stock, not a cheap publication by any measure. Though publicity leaflets inevitably are biased, it is worth quoting this one:

> The L.M.S Container Service has developed amazingly. The traffic carried in 1933 shows a 770% increase over that of 1927 in spite of the unprecedented depression of recent years. Every month more and more businessmen are using the L.M.S Container Service in preference to any other method of transport .... Why? It is reliable. Your goods, loaded into a container in your own works, are not touched until they are unloaded at your customers' premises. That makes breakage and pilferage next to impossible. When covered containers are used, you can padlock the door and post the key to your customer.[33]

And similarly:

> The LMS Container Service is quick. Containers are conveyed on fast trains. It is economical. You save considerably on packing costs, labour and materials. Thus, the LMS Container System enables you to give better service to your customers and at the same time to reduce your overhead costs.[34]

The Aftermath of the 1926 Report

Commercial figures for new developments are often difficult to find. However, in 1934 the LMS's president, Sir Josiah Stamp, made the following statement:

---

31 Ibid., paragraph 336.

32 R.J. Essery and K.R. Morgan, *The LMS Wagon* (Newton Abbott 1977), 119–21.

33 TNA, Goods Department 'Freight Transportation in Container Trucks' – London Midland & Scottish Railway Company internal publication, Rail 421/146.

34 TNA, LMSR Publicity Department 'Why You Should Use LMS Containers', 1933 RAIL 429/30.

> Thus in 1928, the inaugural year of the container service by all the main line railways, the L.M.S carried 25,248 container loads representing a tonnage of 46,553 tons. By 1930 these figures had expanded to 66,754 loads and 129,003 tons, while in 1932, (the last full year for which figures are available) the L.M.S. conveyed 101,692 container loads representing a tonnage of 196,496 tons.[35]

These figures suggest that in four years containers had gone from carrying no general goods traffic to about two per cent of it. Williamson writing contemporaneously stated:

> The system has been an unqualified success from its inception, the demand by the trading interests is increasing year by year and 'container operation' by both passenger and freight trains is, in fact, now an established practice of international railway working.[36]

As its progenitors had foreseen, the container as a means of freight handling could not be ignored: the London North Eastern Railway (LNER) and the Southern Railway had introduced containers by 1927, with the Great Western Railway joining in around 1928. This company had a number of innovative schemes, including so-called Rotanks, that is, milk tanks that could be placed on rail or road chassis.[37] By 1931 the Southern Railway had introduced similar milk containers, and in 1937 a fleet of six wheel Dyson Road-Rail milk tanks 'generally similar to those already in use by United Dairies …' was introduced for use on the LMS.[38]

All the railway companies used and promoted containers and by 1933, 7,150 were in service. The numbers for each company being: LMS (3717), London North Eastern Railway (1606), Great Western Railway (1233) and the Southern Railway (SR) (594). The latter's small fleet was particularly intensively used, perhaps because it carried much of the continental export traffic, which was well-suited to the container. Contemporary figures show that in July 1933 the SR expedited 2,410 container journeys with a fleet utilisation of 70 per cent, at the time thought to be optimal.[39] In 1936, Lloyd Wilson, in an American review of British container working, stated:

---

35 J. Stamp, 'Some results of Container Operations in Great Britain', *The Container*, 1, 1934, 7–8.

36 J.W. Williamson, *A British Railway Behind the Scenes* (London 1933), 154.

37 J.H. Russell, *Great Western Wagons* (Oxford 1974), appendix.

38 Anonymous, 'New Dyson Road-Rail Milk Tank Containers', *The Railway Gazette*, 66, 15, 1937, 712–13.

39 M.S Charlton, 'The Rise of Container Service in Great Britain', in The International Container Bureau, ed., *Le Container No. 2* (Paris 1934), 1–2. This quotation is taken from a proof copy, (manuscript) in French of what presumably went on to be the journal, *The Container*, no. 2. No published copies have yet been found. This proof copy is in the British Library.

> The significance of the container car services of the British railway in developing freight traffic is indicated by the fact that the number of containers in service, the number of container loads transported, and the tons of goods transported in containers have increased steadily and rapidly in each year since 1928, despite the general decrease in traffic between 1929 and 1932.[40]

New traffic sometimes demanded special provisions. For instance, by 1937 the production of pedal cycles for home and export markets reached two million per annum. The railways developed containers capable of holding 76 cycles. The fittings were arranged at two levels so that bicycles could be double-stacked.[41]

Figure 4.1 Southern Railway container No. A337

Source: Photograph reproduced courtesy of the Historical Model Railway Society and comes from their BC&W Collection, Catalogue No. AA426.

The picture is clearly showing the three end door method of construction. The strength of this arrangement was commended in the tests at the International Container Competition in Venice, 1931.

---

40 L.G. Wilson, 'The Use of Freight Containers by British Railways', *Annals of the American Academy of Political and Social Science*, 187, September 1936, 173–9.

41 Anonymous, 'Rail Conveyance of Pedal Cycles', *The Railway Gazette*, 68, 4, 28 January 1938, 160.

By 1938, the LMS found it necessary to develop their Earlestown Works, which constructed all the company's containers, by converting what had previously been the wheel shop into a mass production facility for containers having an 'output capacity of 800 to 1000 wagons per annum'.[42] The *Railway Gazette* commented in July 1939: 'At the end of 1938 they numbered 15,521 as against 1,574 in 1928. From 1930 to 1934 the number of journeys by containers increased by 146 per cent. The 1938 figures showed an increase of 41 per cent compared with 1934'.[43]

The final container usage figures for the period in question that have been discovered by the author so far, come from the same journal as above but at a later date and state:

> Increase in the use of LNER Containers. – Loadings of LNER containers of all types during 1939 totalled 114,968, against 23,473 during 1930, representing an increase of no less than 390 per cent. The largest individual increase was with insulated meat containers, the loadings of which have risen by 5,544 per cent. Loadings of large open containers rose by 322 per cent., large covered by 267 per cent., and small covered by 217 per cent. By the end of 1928 450 containers were in use by the LNER and by 1930 the stock had risen to 710; and today no fewer than 4,569 containers of seven principal types are owned by the company.[44]

The UK container had shown a dramatic rise in construction and use. The next section will look at developments in Europe.

The Container in Europe

The years 1928 to 1932 seem to have been seminal for the container in Europe. All that will be attempted here is to give an overview, awaiting further research in individual countries.

In 1928 the World Motor Transport Congress in Rome adopted a resolution that led the International Chamber of Commerce, based in Paris, to form the International Container Committee (ICC). The Container Committee was formed to find 'which is the most practical solution of the problem of carrying goods in a combination of road and rail transport'.[45] Here then is an apparent paradox: in the UK the LMS were designing, building and promoting containers as a means

---

[42] Anonymous, 'New L.M.S.R. Container-Building Plant at Earlestown', *The Railway Gazette*, 69, 8, 1938, 340.

[43] Anonymous, 'Cartage and Containers', *The Railway Gazette*, 71, 4 1939, 135.

[44] Anonymous, 'Increase in the use of LNER Containers', *The Railway Gazette*, 72, 4, 1940, 135.

[45] S. Crespi, and P. Wohl, 'General Report on the International Container Competition', *Container Supplement in World Trade*, 4, 2, January 1932, 10–21.

of fighting road competition, whilst in Europe, the road lobby saw the very same artefact as a means of gaining traffic.

The Committee set out to fulfil its remit by holding an International Competition based in Venice. A description of the competition, together with its results was published as a supplement to *World Trade*, the ICC's journal, in 1930.[46] Commenting on the methods of moving the containers to be entered for the competition C. Grahame points out that

> the Committee of Experts consider the most desirable system would be of a nature that would enable the 'container' to be transferred from one conveyance to another with the minimum of external force. It would particularly favour a system where the 'container' could be transferred without its (sic) being necessary to utilize a crane.[47]

Fourteen manufacturers, seven from Germany, three from France, two from England and one each from Switzerland and Italy, all submitted drawings of containers of varying types for the competition. Following the deliberations of the competition jury six manufacturers were chosen to submit containers for testing. The manufacturers were: Butterley Iron Works, Derby, UK; Gesellschaft M.B.H für Oberbauforschung, Berlin, Germany; Gloucester Carriage and Wagon Works, Gloucester, UK; Gothaer Wagonfabrik. A.G. Gotha, Germany; Officine Mechaniche Italiane, Milan, Italy; and *Siegener Eisen-Bahnbedarf Aktiengesellschaft*, Siegen, Germany.

The containers were subjected to:

1. Ventilation tests
2. Waterproof Properties tests
3. Special tests for collapsible containers
4. Tests of handling
5. Tests for securing containers to vehicles
6. Resistance tests.

These tests were described exhaustively in the *World Trade Supplement*. Crespi and Wohl in their summation made 14 conclusions and the supplement gives valuable photographic and technical evidence. At the end of the competition:

> the Jury did not consider it possible to make a distinct classification of the containers submitted and to award prizes … however, by virtue of the extensive study and effort devoted to the second stage by the competitors, there was justification for making awards to them, taking into consideration the number of

---

46 Crespi and Wohl, 'General Report', 10.

47 C. Grahame, 'A Novel Competition', *World Trade*, 11, 1929, 329–30.

> containers submitted by each competitor and the valuable ideas which might be retained and used later for development of transport by containers.[48]

It is possible that the high number of containers supplied for the competition needing cranes for transhipment led to the jury's decision not to classify them.

Figure 4.2 A 5-ton hand crane No. 200 at Derby, 1938

Source: Picture reproduced courtesy of Peter Tatlow and comes from an original in The Tatlow Collection.

This picture of 5-ton hand crane No. 200 at Derby, was taken in 1938 to demonstrate the inadequacy of existing cranes for use in handling containers. The jib of the crane is not long enough to lift the LMS BX type container into the wagon.

Despite this seemingly low-key set of results, the Venice trials had an effect and Crespi and Wohl's conclusions were all potentially useful to manufacturers and users of containers. Indeed, many of the ideas passed into construction practice, particularly the use of pressed sheet metal ribs and the three-door (two vertical and one horizontal) arrangement, which the trials found to be resistant to distortion and practical in use.

Articles about containers continued to appear in *World Trade* throughout 1932 and by 22 February 1933 the International Container Bureau had been set up under the auspices of the ICC. In June 1933 it was reported that: 'The Container

48 Crespi and Wohl, 'General Report', 15.

Bureau is actively interested in everything relating to container traffic, including the equipment for handling containers such as cranes, travelling elevators ...'[49]

It may be that the widespread handling of containers by crane had changed attitudes in Paris. The problem of handling containers by crane, particularly at small stations with few facilities, was ever present and in the following review of container activities in various countries it surfaces again and again.

1934 saw the publication of the first two issues of *The Container*, the bulletin of the International Container Bureau (ICB). Italian Senator Silvio Crespi who had chaired the International Container Committee was also the ICB's President. Crespi was well suited for the post, having sat on the Allied Maritime Transport Council from 1917.

Given Crespi's involvement internationally it may be seen as no surprise that Italy appeared at this stage to be very active in container operations. He was Chairman and Managing Director of the *Società Italiana Casse Mobile* (SICON) formed in September 1932, which had sole rights to use containers on Italian State Railways. The reports and photographs of SICON experiments occupied 24½ pages of the first two issues of *The Container* (1934), indeed photographically, diagrammatically and in terms of technical calculations, Italy was the best represented of any country.

All of the different kinds of Italian containers shown were capable of movement either by Fenwick fork lift trucks (French made under licence from the American company Yale), or by hand truck and purpose-made ramps. All the Italian containers represented photographically, however, retained the four lift rings necessary for movement by crane. In 1934 the *Railway Gazette* reported that SICON had been taken over by the Italian State Railways.[50] By 1936 the Italian State Railway are reported as owning some 1,000 containers, 300 of which were insulated and had been in use for the transport of fruit to London, Paris and Hamburg. However, in that year, all the insulated containers had been shipped to East Africa and were in use shipping meat to the Italian troops fighting the Ethiopian war.[51]

Germany had a long tradition of the use of what the *Deutsche Reichsbahn-Gesellschaft* (DRG) called large containers, for house removals.[52] In the early 1930s the individual area railway administrations, particularly Köln and Frankfurt am Main were developing container traffic. The Köln administration developed mainly small containers with a capacity of 1,000 to 1,200 kilograms which were suited for movement by hand or fork lift truck. Most of the small containers of the DRG appear from photographic evidence to be 'semi-open' and the written

---

49 Anonymous, 'The Container Bureau Goes Ahead', *World Trade*, 5, 6, 1933, 4.

50 Anonymous, 'Containers in Italy', *The Railway Gazette*, 69, 10, 11.

51 Anonymous, 'Containers on the Continent', *The Railway Gazette*, 64, 17, 815.

52 See German Furniture Container 1886, illustrated in Richard Vahrenkamp, *The Logistics Revolution – The Rise of Logistics in the Mass Consumption Society* (Frankfurt am Main 2012), 54.

report notes difficulties in getting them unloaded if the weather was inclement, especially where access to raised, covered platforms was not available. Almost all small containers had retractable wheels and corner projections that would engage with a railway wagon or lorry bed to prevent slippage, thus increasing the door-to-door services of the railway and the safety of goods in transit. By 1933 German railways had 3543 small containers in use for such services.

DRG report many experiments with large containers having some form of retractable wheels, stating that: 'the German State Railway completely disapproves of the principle of designing containers for handling by cranes or travelling elevators only'.[53] The reason was that the lack of such equipment precluded certain stations from using them. By 1934 DRG had decided that all their large containers would conform to the international specifications laid down by the ICB and in addition they would be fitted with retractable rollers which would fit between the required basal longitudinal beams. The rollers could be lowered using a winch mechanism, thus enabling the container to be rolled in all lateral directions. The total numbers of such containers in use in 1934 were reported as being 191, of which 80 were used for lime and limestone transport. Large containers were also in use for new furniture, clay, iron, enamelled goods, stone goods, batteries and amalgamated freight, but no statistics were given.

A new type of four-tonne payload containers was built by the *Gothaer Wagonfabrik* company around 1934 which had four pneumatically tyred road wheels which swivelled upwards when not in use. These containers could be drawn by a horse or by a truck as a trailer. The containers were made of stiffened steel sheet reinforced with ribs, and though smaller than twenty-first-century containers, do not look dissimilar.[54]

The development of containerisation continued in Germany and by 1937 the DRG was reported as considering itself to be 'the largest user of containers in the world'.[55] Whilst statements such as this have to be weighed against the political and propaganda situation at the time, it seems reasonable to state that containers and their handling equipment were being developed rapidly in Germany. For instance, Saar Railways owned 42 containers and worked 11 more privately owned ones in 1934. Sixteen of the railway containers were used internally whilst the remainder of the stock were in international use, travelling to France and Germany. Traffics carried are reported as including fragile items such as pottery but groceries, hardware, glassware and personal items were also shipped.

Containers had been used by the seven principal railway companies in France since 1929 and by 1934 they had 249 containers with a further 119 on order. Private commercial companies also had 2,200 containers in use in France. International

---

53 Anonymous, 'The State of Container Traffic across the World', in The International Container Bureau, ed., *The Container No. 1* (Paris 1934), 13–71.

54 Anonymous, 'The State of Container Traffic', 13–71.

55 Anonymous, 'Container Handling in Germany', *The Railway Gazette*, 69, 1, 1938, 19.

traffic was noted with England, the commodities being given as building materials and electrical apparatus though cross-Channel luggage traffic also appeared. Container traffic to North Africa in sanitary ware, bath tubs and heating apparatus was also reported. All French containers were built to the international standards of the ICB; however photographic evidence suggests that most of them were capable of transhipment by crane. Of all railway companies the *Chemin de Fer du Nord* had the most containers in use. The privately owned containers were technologically interesting especially for their use of refrigeration. These were involved in the transport of meat from Algeria, Morocco, the Irish Free State, Poland and Belgium as well as fish from Marseilles and England.

Other tank or citerne containers had been developed for the domestic transport of milk, and significantly this had meant that 'the railways have succeeded in recovering the milk transport for Paris, which had passed over to a considerable extent to motor lorries'.[56] This is the first evidence found so far of the container's successful deployment in the face of road competition in a Continental context. By 1935 the seven main French railway companies were declaring their intention to develop container traffic in 1936 and by April 24th of that year the Railway Gazette announced: 'France has now over 10,000 of the standard large type (containers) partly railway owned and partly privately-owned; a further 1000 new containers are also under construction'.[57]

Post-nationalisation in 1938 the *Société Nationale des Chemins de fer français* (SNCF) continued to use and experiment with various types of container and associated trans-shipment equipment. By 1939 small containers of one, two- and three-cubic-metre capacities were available for hire at 24 hours' notice from the departure station and could 'be hired for a single journey or by the month or year'.[58] Whilst not owned by the SNCF, tank containers were available for hire from specialist companies and carried by the railway.

During 1934 a satisfactory beginning to container use was reported in Spain. Six containers each loaded to 1,550 kilograms were carried on ordinary freight wagons and a regular service was in place between Madrid and Barcelona.[59]

Belgian railways experimented with seven small containers and as these were obviously successful, in 1934 they ordered 500 more, all of which were built to the international standards laid down by the ICB. Development continued and by 1936, 1100 small containers were in use with a further 500 on order.

The Dutch railways did not use large containers, but had 440 open small containers used for the transport of cheese, dairy products, preserves and fruit. The small distances involved and a lack of organisation of international traffic was, in 1934, felt to be holding back developments.

---

56 Anonymous, 'The State of Container Traffic', 13–71.

57 Anonymous, 'Containers on the Continent', 815.

58 Anonymous, 'Containers in France', *The Railway Gazette*, 70, 10, 1939, 413–16.

59 Anonymous, 'Containers in Spain', *The Railway Gazette*, 60, 21, 1934, 922.

Figure 4.3 A 75 horsepower Ford Tractor with the special conveyer trailer

Source: Photograph reproduced with the permission of the Editor of Railway Gazette International.

The trailer was developed jointly by the engineering staff of Netherlands Railways and van Doorne Aanhangwagenfabriek (Trailer Factory).

The provision of door-to-door delivery was for the Dutch, as for every other railway operator, very important. But the Dutch railways found, in common with all other countries using the container, 'one of the difficulties being that many clients do not possess cranes or lifting tackle able to handle the loading and unloading at their premises'.[60] The mechanical engineering staff of the railway with the staff of the Van Doorne trailer works at Eindhoven therefore developed in 1939 specially adapted Ford 75 horse-powered trucks with machinery designed to substitute for a crane. These so-called demount trucks could pull up a container from ground level and at the rail yard, match the height of the container to the wagon and then push the container onto it. If the container was of the end-door tipper type, the trailer mechanism allowed its contents to be tipped onto the ground. A history of Van Doorne, later DAF, notes this ground breaking development, but seems to imply that during the Second World War the firm concentrated on preparing for the post-war mass production of trucks and does not mention the demount trailer again.[61] Interestingly, a very similar mechanism had been suggested by an LMS officer in Northern Ireland five years previously.[62]

According to the 1934 ICB report, the Swiss railways owned no containers, but had 25 in service which were privately owned by chocolate manufacturers. Interestingly, the report does not mention the LMS's Basle to London service

60 Anonymous, 'Handling Containers on the Netherlands Railways', *The Railway Gazette*, 70, 10, 1939, 417.

61 A history of DAF http://www.daf-macedonia.com.mk/index.php?m=about&p=history&l=en (last acessed 31 March 2012).

62 Anonymous, 'Containers', *The Railway Gazette*, 61, 1, 1934, 17.

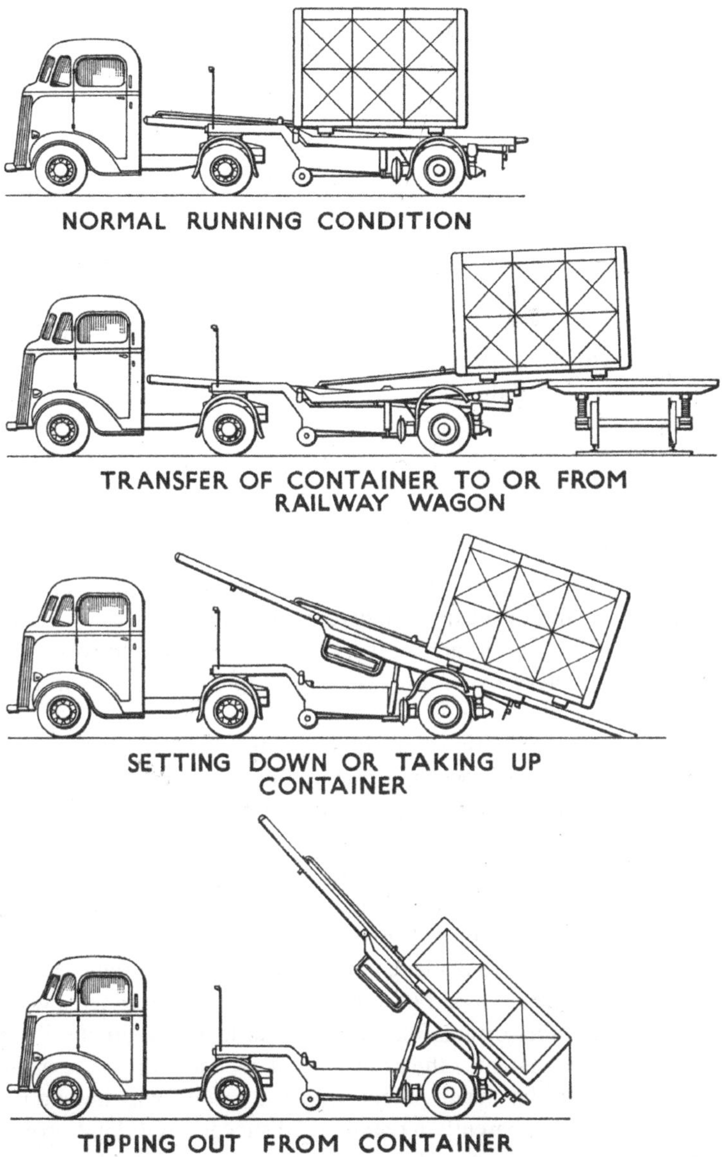

Figure 4.4 Diagrams about the use of a conveyor trailer in loading and unloading containers

Source: Diagrams reproduced with the permission of the Editor of Railway Gazette International.

Four diagrams showing the flexibility of the Netherlands designed conveyor trailer in loading and unloading containers.

discussed earlier and this leaves open the question as to whether it had been discontinued. However, in 1938 the Swiss railways introduced small, one- and two-cubic-metre capacity wheeled containers which could be used for international traffic, 150 being in use by January 1939.[63] Austria had milk traffic in tank containers, and began in 1929 using privately owned containers; by 1934, 23 were in regular use. Cranes were the preferred method of transfer from road-to-rail vehicles. By 1935 Swedish State Railways had 42 containers in parcels service. Contemporary reports held that the traffic 'has met with considerable success'.[64] In 1937 a new insulated container for fish traffic which had integrated but retractable wheels was reported as having been introduced in Sweden.[65] The *Railway Gazette* reported in 1936 that the Hungarian Railways had introduced refrigerated containers with which they were exporting poultry to London. Unfortunately no firm figures for the size of the traffic were reported.[66]

Conclusion

The 1920s and 1930s were times of rapid container development in Britain and elsewhere in Europe. Despite differing national commercial and political factors, the competition for freight business between rail and road was a significant and constant driver of innovation across the Continent. But the history of container development in the interwar period was not a simple progression from a need to its inevitable fulfilment.

Hascher is correct in stating that the original containers were developed by private companies.[67] What should not be forgotten, however, is that governments across Europe had a very significant impact on the shape of railway-freight operations. At various junctures governments prepared for and waged war, attempted to allay public unrest and provide jobs for the unemployed, and regulated what were, publicly and in some political circles, seen as monopolistic, greedy and manipulative railway companies. It may be, as the UK's railways claimed, that governments handed the road haulage industry an unfair advantage early in its life. However, the container was a part of a raft of commercial initiatives which, in the later part of the era under discussion, in the UK at least, included railway-owned country lorry services that gave the railways a chance to redress the balance.

The container's initial development in Great Britain was innovative and, at least in a modest way, apparently a commercial success. It did not provide a total solution to the challenges posed for cross-Channel or other international traffic

63 Anonymous, 'Containers on the Swiss Federal Railways', *The Railway Gazette*, 70, 2, 1939, 70.

64 Anonymous, 'Containers in Sweden', *The Railway Gazette*, 63, 24, 1935, 999.

65 Anonymous, 'Insulated Containers in Sweden', *The Railway Gazette*, 67, 13, 528.

66 Anonymous, 'Containers on the Continent', *The Railway Gazette*, 64, 17, 815.

67 Hascher, 'The Lowtech Revolution', 431–51.

by the UK's tight loading gauge. Nevertheless the use of containers enabled the interwar railways of the UK and the rest of Europe to provide intermodal door-to-door delivery systems which their customers were reported as welcoming.

It is, however, important to differentiate between the use of containers by the UK railways in this era and the full ISO containerisation concept which developed later. The LMS officers who produced the report which led to their development did however stress the germ of later concepts when they stated that the container needed to be seen as more than a 'packing case' and more an 'integrated part of a road or railway vehicle'.[68] The types of containers developed from the LMS's 1926 initiative were used by the railways in this period, as part of a more general rationalisation programme, to unitise loads, minimise losses from theft and damage in transit and also generate much needed revenue by fighting the competition. These containers were not a complete solution to competition with road haulage, however, they were an important part of the railways' response, as the rapidly rising usage of the 1930s demonstrates.

References

a) Anonymous articles, author not known

'Cartage and Containers', *The Railway Gazette*, 71, 4, 1939, 135.
'Container Handling in Germany', *The Railway Gazette*, 69, 1, 1938, 19.
'Containers in France', *The Railway Gazette*, 70, 10, 1939, 413–16.
'Containers in Italy', *The Railway Gazette*, 69, 10, 1938, 11.
'Containers in Spain', *The Railway Gazette*, 60, 21, 1934, 922.
'Containers in Sweden', *The Railway Gazette*, 63, 24, 1935, 999.
'Containers on the Continent', *The Railway Gazette*, 64, 17, 1936, 815.
'Containers on the Swiss Federal Railways', *The Railway Gazette*, 70, 2, 1939, 70.
'Containers', *The Railway Gazette*, 61, 1, 1934, 17.
'Goods Loading and Unloading', *The Railway News* of 4 November 1916, 540.
'Handling Containers on the Netherlands Railways', *The Railway Gazette*, 70, 10, 1939, 417.
'Increase in the use of LNER Containers', *The Railway Gazette*, 72, 4 1940, 135.
'Insulated Containers in Sweden', *The Railway Gazette*, 67, 13, 528.
'New L.M.S.R. Container-Building Plant at Earlestown', *The Railway Gazette*, 69, 8, 1938, 340.
'Rail Conveyance of Pedal Cycles', *The Railway Gazette*, 68, 4, 28 January 1938, 160.
'Road-Rail Milk Containers', *The Railway Gazette*, 66, 15, 1937, 703 and 712–13.
'The Container Bureau Goes Ahead', *World Trade*, 5, 6, 1933, 4.

[68] TNA, Goods Department 'Freight Transportation in Container Trucks' – London Midland & Scottish Railway Company internal publication, Rail 421/146, paragraph 122.

'The State of Container Traffic across the World', in The International Container Bureau, ed., *The Container, No. 1* (Paris 1934), 13–71.
'The Work of the International Chamber', *World Trade*, 9, January, 1929, 104–5.
'Traffic Congestion and the Gatty Scheme', *The Railway Gazette*, 72, 11, 1940, 392.

b) Named articles and monographs

Bagwell, P., *The Railway Clearing House in the British Economy 1842–1922* (London 1968).
Charlton, M.S., 'The Rise of Container Service in Great Britain', in The International Container Bureau, ed., *Le Container No. 2* (Paris 1934), 1–2.
Coates, N., 'Lurries and Flat Bottoms', *LYR Focus. Journal of the Lancashire and Yorkshire Railway Society*, 61, 2007, 22–35.
Crespi, S., 'What a container is', *The Container*, 1, 1934, 3–4.
Crespi, S. and Wohl, P., 'General Report on the International Container Competition', *Container Supplement in World Trade*, 4, 2, January, 1932, 10–21.
Droege, J.A., *Freight Terminals and Trains – Including a Revision of Yards and Terminals* (New York 1912).
Essery, R.J. and Morgan, K.R., *The LMS Wagon* (Newton Abbott 1977).
Essery, R.J., Rowland, D.P. and Steel, W.O., *British Goods Wagons from 1887 to the Present Day* (New York 1970).
Grahame, C., 'A Novel Competition', *World Trade*, 11, 1929, 329–30.
Hascher, M., 'The Lowtech Revolution: Containers and Pipelines', in R. Roth and C. Schlögel, eds, *Neue Wege in ein neues Europa. Geschichte und Verkehr im 20. Jahrhundert* (Frankfurt am Main and New York 2009), 431–51.
Horniman, R., *How to make the Railways Pay for the War* (London 1916).
Plummer, A., *New British Industries in the Twentieth Century* (London 1937).
Ripley, D., *The Little Eaton Gangway and Derby Canal* (Usk 1993).
Rowland, D., *British Railways Wagons – The First Half Million* (London 1996).
Russell, J.H., *Great Western Wagons* (Oxford 1974).
Scott, P., 'British Railways and the Challenge from Road Haulage: 1919–1939', *Twentieth Century British History*, 13, 2, 2002, 101–20.
Sherrington, C.E.R., 'British and Foreign Rolling Stock Compared', *Journal of the Institute of Transport*, 11, 4, February 1930, 180–184.
Smith, H.G., Notes on Mr Lemon's Modernisation of Goods Terminals, unpublished Ms. (London 1933) (part of The Lemon Papers now deposited in The Archive of the Institution of Mechanical Engineers, London. UK).
Smith, L.A., 'The Evolution of the Automobile', in *The Transactions of the Swindon Engineering Society*, 30 November 1926 (Swindon 1926), 5–28.
Stamp, J., 'Some results of Container Operations in Great Britain', *The Container*, 1, 1934, 7–8.
Vahrenkamp, R., *The Logistics Revolution – The Rise of Logistics in the Mass Consumption Society* (Frankfurt am Main 2012).
Williamson, J.W., *A British Railway Behind the Scenes* (London 1933).

Wilson, L.G. 'The Use of Freight Containers by British Railways', *Annals of the American Academy of Political and Social Science*, 187, September 1936, 173–9.

Wohl, P., 'Containers in Action in America and Europe', *Container Supplement in World Trade*, 4, 2, January 1932, 3–6.

Wohl, P., 'The Twin Problems of Transportation – the container has come to stay', *The Container Bulletin*, 1, January 1934, 11–12.

Chapter 5
The Sea Container Revolution and Road-Rail Competition in Britain: a Preliminary Assessment of Freightliner

Terry Gourvish

Introduction

The emergence of the sea container business has been one of the most significant developments in both international and domestic freight transport since the Second World War.[1] Making its appearance in the 1950s, but gaining ground from the 1970s, container transport has reduced unit costs and journey times and secured productivity gains that are particularly high on the sea part of the journey.[2] Growth has sprung from the investment in larger ships and in port handling methods, and from a shift in the origin of European manufacturing imports, where there has been an increasing reliance on Asia. The container itself has grown in size. In the 1950s there was a variety of sizes – 10, 20, 30 and 40 feet long, though usually eight feet high. But the key attributes of the modern ISO container are the standardisation of dimensions and handling, and stackability. Containers are customarily 20 or 40 feet long and 8 foot 6 inches or 9 foot 6 inches high. In 2010 the favoured size was 40 feet long and 9 foot 6 inches high; these containers account for 40 per cent of those arriving by ship in the UK, and are expected to account for half of the total in 2011.[3] The challenge for inland transport has been to handle ever larger consignments and take these from the ports to their final destination, either by road, rail or water transport.

---

1 My thanks to John Dodgson, Roy Edwards and those who commented on an earlier version presented to the Association of Business Historians Conference in York in July 2010.

2 Cf. Frank Broeze, *The Globalisation of the Oceans: Containerisation from the 1950s to the Present* (St Johns 2002); Marc Levinson, *The Box: How the Shipping Container Made the World Smaller and the World Economy Bigger* (Princeton, NJ, 2006), and Brian Cudahy, *Box Boats* (New York 2006).

3 On the emerging standard see Levinson, *The Box*, 129–49; Bernard Warner and Stewart Joy, 'The Economics of Rail Container Operation in Britain', *Rail International*, 4 April 1971, 345–56, here 346, 348 (my thanks to John Dodgson for this reference), and *Modern Railways*, 67, September 2010, 56. The container statistics are based on 'TEU's, that is, 20-foot equivalent units.

Following the growth of national and international motorway systems and the parallel development of the modern heavy goods road vehicle in the period 1950 to 1970, railways have generally been a minority provider of inland freight transport, other than for heavy minerals and coal. In 2000, for example, their share of European (EU 15) freight traffic (in tonne-kilometres) had fallen to only 8 per cent, compared with the 20 per cent share enjoyed in 1970.[4] Moreover, in the United Kingdom the challenge for rail has always been much tougher because of the relatively short distances between major centres. Rail transport's share of total freight movements is lower than the European average, partly due to this factor. It fell from 18 per cent in 1970 to 7 per cent in 2000, and was below 6 per cent in 1994 and 1995.[5] Clearly, road transport has dominated inland freight flows since the 1950s. This competitive asymmetry has been aided by the British government's substantial investment in the development of a motorway network. The first major motorway, the M1, was opened from Watford to Rugby, a distance of 61 miles or 98 kilometres, in November 1959; the road was extended by 112 miles to Leeds in 1965–68.[6] By 1965, 354 miles of new motorway had been constructed, and by 1970 the network amounted to 660 miles or 1,057 kilometres. The most rapid period of expansion was in the 1970s, when the network increased by 150 per cent, such that by 1980 there were 1,600 miles or 2,556 kilometres of improved road. Thereafter, growth was slower. Britain had 1,870 miles of motorway in 1988, 2,138 miles in 1998 and 2,224 miles or 3,559 kilometres in 2008.[7] At the same time there was a progressive increase in the permissible dimensions and weights of lorries operating in Britain. The maximum permitted weight of both rigid 4-axle and articulated vehicles was 24 tons in 1955. By 1973 the limits had risen to 30.49 and 32.52 tonnes respectively. There were further increases from the 1980s, encouraged by Britain's membership of the European Union, and the harmonisation of weight restrictions therein from January 1993.[8] The maximum weight of rigid four-axle vehicles was lifted to 32 tonnes in 1993; the maximum for articulated vehicles (with five/six axles) was raised to 38 tonnes in 1983, 40/41 tonnes in 1999 and 44 tonnes since 2001 (90 per cent higher than in 1955). Over the same period the maximum length of an articulated lorry was increased from 10.7 metres in 1955 to 16.5 metres since 1990 (an increase of 54

[4] Michel Beuthe, 'Intermodal freight transport in Europe', in Thomas R. Leinbach and Cristina Capineri, eds, *Globalized Freight Transport: Intermodality, E-Commerce, Logistics and Sustainability* (Cheltenham 2007), 54–99, 57.

[5] Department for Transport, Transport Statistics Great Britain (TSGB) 2009, Table 4.1.

[6] The first new motorway was the Preston by-pass, opened December 1958, and now part of the M6.

[7] TSGB 2009, Table 7.6; David Starkie, *The Motorway Age: Road Traffic Policies in Post-war Britain* (Oxford 1982).

[8] The UK enjoyed an exemption from some of the regulations until 1 January 1999.

per cent).[9] Engine capacity and performance has matched the increase in size and weight.[10] The provision of a motorway network made larger lorries even more competitive: as much as 60 per cent of the mileage travelled by vehicles over 32 tonnes was on motorways.[11] By contrast, while railway technology also made progress in increasing the power of diesel and electric freight locomotives, and there were corresponding improvements in wagon size and technology, the British railway authorities, nationalised from 1947, made a less substantial investment in freight facilities than they did for passenger traffic. The explanation for this lies partly in the government's preference for road investment; and partly in policy mistakes by railway managers. Thus, faith was placed on improving the efficiency of British railways' wagon-load traffic, once the mainstay of continental rail freight flows. Under the Modernisation Plan of 1955, a number of expensive and ultimately unproductive investments were undertaken in the form of larger marshalling yards, notably at Carlisle (Kingmoor), Healey Mills (Wakefield) and Tinsley (Sheffield).[12] And there was no investment in new or improved freight routes. It is not an exaggeration to assert that rail freight was the Cinderella of railway services in Britain.[13] This comparative neglect was significant in that the increase in the height of maritime containers presented problems for railways in Britain, where the loading gauge was generally more restricted than that in use in Continental Europe.

However, despite the fall in the railways' overall share of the freight market, the concentration of the growing container traffic at a small number of major ports offered a new opportunity to the sector, since railways are best suited to the movement of high volume traffics. In the period since privatisation in the mid-1990s its share has increased slightly thanks mainly to longer average lengths of haul. In 2006 it amounted to 8.8 per cent, and in 2008 was 8.6 per cent.[14] Further progress is not assured, of course. First, the current recession has halted traffic growth. Second, as the recent manifestos of the Rail Freight Group and Network Rail have pointed out, a more supportive environment is required if railway freight

---

9 A gesture towards equalisation of competition between road and rail was made in 1994, when the higher weight of 44 tonnes was permitted for 6-axle articulated lorries carrying intermodal container traffic from/to rail terminals.

10 John Armstrong et al., eds, *Companion to British Road Haulage History* (London 2003), 102–3, 428; Statutory Instruments, SI 1955/482, 1963/1646, 1964/1169, 1978/1017, 1982/1576, and 1986/1078; Louise Butcher, 'Lorry sizes and weights', House of Commons briefing note SN/BT/654, 23 November 2009.

11 TSGB 2009, Table 7.4.

12 Terry R. Gourvish, *British Railways 1948–1973: A Business History* (Cambridge 1986), 270, 288–90.

13 Ibid., 288–93, 579; Terry Gourvish, *British Rail 1974–1997: From Integration to Privatisation* (Oxford 2002), 283–9, and Terry Gourvish, *Britain's Railways 1997–2005: Labour's Strategic Experiment* (Oxford 2008), 163.

14 TSGB 2009, Table 4.1. See also Network Rail, ed., *Value and Importance of Rail Freight* – July 2010 (London 2010), 12.

is to flourish. This would entail help in developing a freight network, support for sustainable distribution, more terminals, a more encouraging planning framework and the maintenance of controls on large, heavier lorries.[15]

The movement of freight offers the challenge of reconciling efficient and cost-effective transport goals with congestion avoidance and sustainable energy requirements. Over the past half-century there has been a continuing debate about the prospects for both 'intermodal' and 'combined' traffic, where sea, rail and road transport are used, and we should note the contributions, for example, of Yehuda Hayuth, Geerke van den Berg and Arjen van Klink and Y.M. Bontekoning et al.[16] Intermodal transport is customarily defined as the movement of goods by stackable sea containers, where at least two transport modes carry the same loading unit or vehicle without handling. 'Combined' or 'swap-body' transport, in contrast, involves the carriage of non-stackable containers by more than one mode with transhipment into another unit or vehicle, usually from rail to road.[17] Here I am concerned primarily with Britain's stackable container traffic carried by rail, though it is sometimes difficult to distinguish it from intermodal and combined operations taken together. Container traffic has clearly matched the growth elements in rail freight since privatisation. Allan Woodburn's data for domestic and port-based intermodal traffic indicates a 29 per cent increase from 3.53 billion tonne-kilometres in 1998/9 to 4.56 billion in 2006/7, though most of the growth was from 2004. We should note that most of this was sea container business growth, since in 2007 the port-based business accounted for about 85 per cent of the total business (based on a count of train services).[18] And most of the sea container business – again around 85 per cent – went through two ports – Felixstowe and Southampton. However, an increase in coal import flows has also been important, with substantial consignments from countries such as Poland and Australia arriving at Immingham and Hunterston, for example, and this traffic is carried over much longer distances than, for example, British Rail's domestic 'Merry-Go-Round' traffic from the Yorkshire pits to the coal-fired power stations.

---

15 Rail Freight Group, ed., Manifesto for rail freight growth – October 2009 (London 2009); Network Rail, *Value and Importance*.

16 Y. Hayuth, *Intermodality: Concepts and Practice. Structural Changes in the Ocean Freight Transport Industry* (London 1987); H. Arjen van Klink and Geerke C. van den Berg, 'Gateways and intermodalism', *Journal of Transport Geography*, 6, 1, 1998, 1–9; Y.M. Bontekoning, C. Macharis and J.J. Trip, 'Is a new applied transportation research field emerging? – A review of intermodal rail-truck freight transport literature', *Transportation Research*, A 38, 2004, 1–34.

17 Cf. European Council of Ministers of Transport, ed., *Benchmarking Intermodal Freight Transport* (Paris, 2002).

18 Allan Woodburn, 'Intermodal Rail Freight in Britain: a Terminal Problem?', *Planning Practice & Research*, 23, 2, August, 2008, 441–60, here 447.

Figure 5.1 Freightliner train, circa 2009

Source: Courtesy of the author.

Consequently intermodal's share of the total freight carried has remained fairly constant at about 20 per cent.[19]

The literature on intermodal transport is comparatively abundant, with studies of both a theoretical and an empirical nature. But the focus has been mainly on logistical problems, and in particular on identifying the optimum methods of handling, though there is also a smaller, policy-related strand of research which examines the relationship between freight transport and public policy, including land-use planning. Comparatively little has been written on the business history of the major companies involved in rail freight. However, some practitioners have published histories or memoirs. Graham Zeitlin, for example, has written a short but perceptive contribution on his time as a railway manager. He joined British Rail's Freightliner subsidiary shortly before its transfer to the National Freight Corporation in 1969 (see below), returned to British Rail with the business in 1978 and, having retired from British Rail, organised an unsuccessful bid for Freightliner when it was privatised in 1996.[20] There are also some more general works which deal with British Rail's freight activities, including Freightliner, notably the several pioneering contributions of Geoffrey Freeman Allen from

[19] Woodburn, 'Intermodal Rail Freight', 447; Gourvish, *British Rail 1974–1997*, 286; Gourvish, *Britain's Railways 1997–2005*, 163.

[20] Graham Zeitlin, *Staying on Track: The Reflections of a Railwayman* (Lancaster 2002).

1959 to 1984, Michael Collins' short book on Freightliner itself in 1991, and David Lowe's survey of intermodal freight in 2005.[21] Books are now appearing on container shipping, notably the recent account of one of the leading players and one of Freightliner's most important customers, Overseas Containers Ltd (OCL), edited by Alan Bott, who was a director of the company from 1976 to 1996.[22]

The Freightliner Story, 1965–68

This chapter is concerned with charting the institutional development of rail-based sea container transport in Britain. Essentially, it is the story of a single enterprise, Freightliner. This subsidiary of the nationalised British railway corporation, the British Railways Board (BRB), was established in 1965. The initiative came only two years after the Board itself had been created, following the break-up of the British Transport Commission (BTC), which had presided over the whole of post-war nationalised transport since 1947. Freightliner was planned and launched during the chairmanship of the reforming rationaliser, Dr Richard Beeching, once of Imperial Chemical Industries, the move being part of his efforts to reform the operation of the railways' freight business. However, the idea was older, the notion of despatching containerised traffic in dedicated train loads having been promoted for some time. One of the more influential enthusiasts was Hugh Barker, a part-time member of the BTC since 1951. A director of the engineering firm Parkinson & Cowan, Barker stayed on as a part-timer in Beeching's time when the BRB was established in 1963, and continued to advise the Board until the end of 1967. Freeman Allen, in a review of British railways published in 1959, referred to plans for a 'fast Freight-Liner service between principal industrial centres, devoted entirely to container traffic'. The first experiment was the high-speed 'Condor' service between Hendon (London) and Glasgow, operated by the London Midland Region from the spring of 1959. The trains used converted engineer's flat wagons, and a 10-hour transit time contributed substantially to its eventual success. Competitive rates, 16 to 18 pounds per container, were also charged.[23] Whatever the origins, the Freightliner concept was clearly consonant with Beeching's *Reshaping* reform of British railways, and enjoyed the full support of internal managers who had been attracted to the Beeching formula of rationalisation and cost control. The leading disciples of Beeching were: Fred Margetts, General Manager of the North Eastern Region, 1961–62, then a key member of the reforming British Railways

---

21 Geoffrey Freeman Allen, *British Railways Today and Tomorrow* (London 1959), 105–26, Geoffrey Freeman Allen, *British Railways After Beeching* (Shepperton 1966), 240ff., and Geoffrey Freeman Allen, *British Railfreight – Today and Tomorrow* (London 1984); Michael J. Collins, *Freightliner* (Sparkford 1991) and David Lowe, *Intermodal Freight Transport* (London 2005).

22 Alan Bott, ed., *British Box Business: A History of OCL* (Godalming 2009).

23 Freeman Allen, *British Railways*, 121, and Freeman Allen, *After Beeching*, 281.

Committee of 1962, and Board Member responsible for operating, 1962–67; and James Ness, General Manager of the Scottish Region, 1955–62, and a Board Member from 1963 to 1966.[24]

Almost before the new subsidiary could show its potential, it was caught up in one of the many shifts in the political economy of the railways. The incoming Labour Government of 1964, which took office after 13 years of Conservative administration, developed a more integrationist approach to the problem of nationalised transport, and from 1965 to 1968 entrusted the Transport Ministry to the feisty and determined politician, Barbara Castle. Castle's anxiety to make her mark at the Ministry produced several clashes with the British Rail chairman, by this time Stanley Raymond, and his colleagues. Here, the main bone of contention was her decision to transfer Freightliner as a limited company, along with the loss-making small consignment or 'sundries' business, to the National Freight Corporation, a body created by new legislation, the Transport Act of 1968.[25] Why was the separation, effective from 1 January 1969, made? It has been suggested that one of the reasons was concern within Whitehall about lurches in the freight policy of British Railways, whose managers had first enthusiastically endorsed the notion of a modernised wagon-load service, and then quickly changed horses to support train-load freight, including Freightliner. Treasury suspicions, based on prior experience of the Modernisation Plan, that the potential profitability of these activities would be exaggerated, and possibility inflated by accounting devices, encouraged the move to NFC on the grounds that it would prevent Freightliner from being cross-subsidised within BRB.[26] But clearly the main thrust was organisational. The creation of the NFC would, it was hoped, encourage the elimination of wasteful competition between publicly owned road and rail services, and help to persuade road hauliers to use rail for the trunk portion of their transits. While well-intentioned, neither aspiration bore fruit.[27]

How well did Freightliner perform before its enforced transfer? The first thing to note is that it quickly built up a network of services. Starting with the London-Glasgow route in November 1965, Freightliner introduced services to terminals in Manchester (Longsight), Liverpool (Garston) and Aberdeen in 1966, then in 1967 to Cardiff, Heysham (for Belfast), Birmingham, Sheffield, Leeds, Newcastle and Stockton. Terminals in Hull, Edinburgh and Southampton followed in 1968, and a West Country service to Plymouth and Par (Cornwall) began in June.

---

24 Gourvish, *British Railways 1948–1973*, 329–31.

25 On BRB opposition to the move see British Railways Chief Executive (Railways) file on Organisation: Freightliners Ltd and National Carriers Ltd, 1968–1978, The National Archives, The National Archives (TNA) ref. AN156/71.

26 Stewart Joy, *The Train That Ran Away: A Business History of British Railways 1948–1968* (Shepperton 1973), 136–7.

27 Zeitlin, *Staying on Track*, 18–19.

There were no fewer than 33 services by this time.[28] The number of containers carried rose from 27,000 in 1966 to 281,000 in 1968; the tonnage carried increased from modest 0.2 million tons in 1966 to 2.4 million in 1968. Most of the early traffic was in the form of inland container flows, rather than the distribution of sea containers. The maritime business, which began at Felixstowe and Harwich (Parkeston Quay), was negligible at first, amounting to only 3,000 containers in 1967. But two years later 87,000 sea containers were carried, 22 per cent of the total.[29] In business terms, this was no overnight success. Stanley Raymond had claimed that Freightliner was: 'the brightest jewel in BR's crown'. But it failed miserably to meet the internal targets set for it. Stewart Joy, a critic of British railway management and chief economist to BRB from 1968 to 1972, notes that there were gung-ho expectations of a potential Freightliner traffic of 26 million tons year, 16 million of which would be new traffic, but, as we have seen, in 1968 the figure was only 2.4 million, and in 1969, 3.9 million.[30] Financial estimates for the business, included in Beeching's famous *Reshaping* Report published in 1963, indicated that Freightliner would cover its direct costs plus 21 per cent by 1968, and direct costs plus 37 per cent by 1973. Unpublished forecasts were more optimistic, suggesting that the contribution might be higher at 56 per cent. But none of these proved remotely accurate, and losses were the order of the day to 1968. Although it seems that no separate profit and loss accounts were prepared for railway subsidiaries such as Freightliner, a rudimentary management accounting calculation for 1968, reported in BRB's Report and Accounts for that year, revealed that on a turnover of £6.4 million Freightliner failed to cover its full operating costs, 'including interest, administration, and an appropriate charge for the use of track and railway rolling stock by about £3m'. However, the actual loss was greater than this, and Margetts suggested in an internal memorandum that it was probably as high as £4.6 million.[31]

Why was this? A number of reasons for the disappointing results have been advanced, some internally, some externally. Many of them were attributable to imperfections in the railways' supply-chain. The first is an old business history favourite: Marvin Frankel's concept of the 'drag of inter-relatedness'.[32] Container services demanded associated investment, not only in containers and the trucks for carrying them, but also in loading and unloading facilities at the docks and at inland terminals, and of course a network of terminals at major distribution points.

---

28 BRB, *Report and Accounts 1965* (London 1966), 26–7, *1966* (London 1967), 18–19, *1967* (London 1968), 8–9, *1968* (London 1969), 14; Gourvish, *British Railways 1948–1973*, 491–2.

29 Data from Richard Pryke and John Dodgson, *The Rail Problem* (London 1975), 86.

30 Joy, *Train That Ran Away*, 141, and Pryke and Dodgson, *Rail Problem*, 86.

31 BRB, ed., *The Reshaping of British Railways*, 2 parts (London 1963), part 1, 147, BRB, *Report and Accounts* 1968, 32; Gourvish, *British Railways 1948–1973*, 394, 492–3.

32 Marvin Frankel, 'Obsolescence and Technological Change in a Mature Economy', *American Economic Review*, 45, 3, 1955, 296–319.

The British Railways Board *did* invest, introducing 5,370 containers and 1,266 container-carrying wagons over the period 1965–68, but the possibilities were clearly limited by investment constraints on one of Britain's largest nationalised industries.[33] It seems that the business was held back, at least until early 1967, by a shortage of containers. There were also technical problems with both the flat wagons carrying the containers and the American Drott 'Travelift' cranes, the mobile cranes which lifted the containers from one mode to the other. All this clearly affected the pace of change. At Glasgow's Gushetfaulds terminal, the quality of service declined sharply when the volume of business over-stretched the capacity of the equipment in use.[34]

Second, there were serious industrial relations problems in developing this innovation in railway intermodal traffic. The rail unions opposed the change, and were particularly hostile to the proposal to open British Rail's container terminals to private hauliers as well as public ones for the onward transmission of containers. The dispute also involved the road haulage industry and the road transport workers' unions. The details are as follows. Beeching had intended that the Freightliner terminals be open to all road haulage interests, but Sidney Greene, General Secretary of the National Union of Railwaymen (NUR) made it clear from the start, in 1964, that he was opposed to the move, which, he argued, would threaten railway staff with redundancies. The Labour Government failed to influence the union's stance, and the Freightliner terminals were initially worked on a 'rail only' basis, with no access for private road hauliers and 'C' licence (own-account) vehicles. Further efforts to resolve the dispute in 1966 came to nought. The issue came to a head in the following year with the activities of Tartan Arrow, a small long-distance haulier operating between London and Glasgow. The firm proposed to build its own terminals on railway land and use rail for the trunk part of the journey. However, before anything was done the Transport Holding Co., a government-owned business which owned the nationalised road haulage businesses, British Road Services and Pickfords, took a controlling stake in, then full control of Tartan Arrow, thereby giving the latter legitimate access to the terminals. This angered the NUR, and eventually its opposition was bought off by a settlement, in June 1967, which involved generous employment guarantees and a change of ownership for Tartan Arrow, with British Rail taking a 50 per cent stake. Even then there was militancy at a new international freight depot at Stratford, in East London, which extracted further guarantees from railway management. There is no doubt that these costly concessions made it harder for Freightliner to cover its costs.[35]

---

33 BRB, *Report and Accounts 1965–68.*

34 Gourvish, *British Railways 1948–1973*, 492, 545, and Zeitlin, *Staying on Track*, 16–17.

35 Gourvish, *British Railways 1948–1973*, 544–7. See also Barbara Castle, *The Castle Diaries 1964–70* (London, 1984).

However, the essential problem was one of fundamental railway economics, a point emphasised by transport economists such as Anthony J. Harrison, Stewart Joy, Bernard Warner, Richard Pryke and John Dodgson. As early as 1964 Harrison exposed conceptual weaknesses in the case for Liner Trains presented in Beeching's *Reshaping* report. No attempt had been made to estimate indirect costs or to calculate an expected rate of return on the planned investment. Criticising some of British Rail's assumptions about the relative costs of road and rail transport over given distances, Harrison argued that there were grounds for believing that the new services would fail to cover their full costs.[36] After a number of years of operating, critics with experience of the business, such as Warner and Joy, were able to ask further questions about the economics of container trains. They argued that Freightliner in its full form was a relatively high-cost service, and could be exposed where volumes were low and distances were short. Furthermore, prices were pitched too low, and certainly low in relation to costs. Under-pricing was a common fault within British Rail at this time, applying to many other commodities. But in the case of Freightliner the initial strategy, according to Joy, had been to set rates lower than road hauliers' back-haul rates to try to make them transfer their efforts to the collection and delivery work to/from rail terminals. As we have seen, this strategy created industrial relations difficulties until at least 1968. But the real problem was that the initial rates had been set far too low.[37] Internal management files support this contention. In November 1968 Margetts conceded that rates had been set low in order to win business for Freightliner, but as Stanley C. Robbins, British Rail's Freight Marketing Manager, explained, it was also the case that costs were rising, and pricing strategies had patently failed to take this into account.[38] Zeitlin's autobiography is also critical about the legacy of British Rail pricing methods and, in particular, the inflexibility in using a scale of charges based on size of consignment, frequency and forwarding, which was adjusted periodically for inflation. This approach did not take account of market conditions, and often led to unprofitable charging.[39]

---

36 A.J. Harrison, 'Investment in Liner Trains', *Bulletin of the Oxford University Institute of Economics and Statistics*, 26, 3, August, 1964, 205–22, cit. in Joy, *Train That Ran Away*, 135–6.

37 Joy, *Train That Ran Away*, 135–6, 140, and Warner and Joy, 'Economics of Rail Container Operation', 345–56.

38 Fred Margetts, Memo to BRB, 30 November 1968, S.C. Robbins, Memo on 'Freightliner Profitability', 13 December 1968, TNA AN167/19.

39 Zeitlin, *Staying on Track*, 27–8. Zeitlin claims that he addressed this problem by introducing a more flexible, decentralised approach to charging and overheads allocation, though no dates are given: ibid., 28–30.

The National Freight Corporation and Freightliner, 1969–78

From 1 January 1969 the Freightliner business, organised as a limited company, Freightliners Ltd, was managed as a subsidiary of the National Freight Corporation (NFC), with BRB as a large minority shareholder (49 per cent). The company was responsible for marketing, owned and operated most of the terminals, provided containers and undertook collection and delivery by road where necessary. Despite railway managers' opposition to the transfer to NFC, the change of ownership did not dampen the expansion of the container business, much of which was maritime traffic. Pryke and Dodgson show that after the NFC takeover, the network was extended to embrace 29 terminals and 175 daily services by 1973. New destinations served included Swansea, Nottingham and Holyhead (for Ireland). The number of containers carried increased by 60 per cent from 397,000 in 1969 to 634,000 in 1973; the sea container share of this rose from 22 per cent in 1969 to 39 per cent in 1972, boosted by the handling of Far Eastern containers from Southampton in that year, following an agreement with OCL, Associated Container Transportation and Ben Line. Total tonnage was 62 per cent higher, rising from 3.9 million in 1969 to 6.3 million in 1973.[40] A more modest growth was reported in the difficult trading conditions which followed the oil crisis of 1973: an 11 per cent increase from 1974 to 1978, by which time there were 36 terminals in operation and seven million tonnes of traffic was being moved.[41] However, financial results continued to disappoint (Table 5.1). Losses were made in 1969 and 1970, and although the NFC reported a break-even position for 1971, on the return of Freightliner to BRB in 1978 the business had accumulated losses of 13.9 million pounds on a capital of £26 million.[42]

A review of British Rail's subsidiaries in 1979 highlighted its weakness. In 1978 its 'operating margin', defined as 'net profit & loss before interest as a percentage of gross income', was a disappointing 1.7 per cent of a turnover of £51 million.[43]

Why was this? It is clear that in the domestic market Freightliner was experiencing difficulty in winning market share, even over the relatively longer distances (above 100 miles) where rail might be expected to hold a competitive

---

40 Pryke and Dodgson, *Rail Problem*, 85–6 (no maritime figure given for 1973); BRB, *Report and Accounts 1970*, 10, and *1971*, 5.

41 Gourvish, *British Rail 1974–1997*, 79, and Freightliner press release, 3 August 1978, TNA AN156/624.

42 Gourvish, *British Rail 1974–1997*, 40; BRB, *Report and Accounts 1969*, 15. The figure for accumulated losses comes from R.B. Reid, Memo 28 July 1978, TNA AN156/624. The audited accounts for 1978 provided a restated figure of £12.7 million, or £15.1 million including a negative capital reserve of £2.4 million: TNA AN192/894.

43 BRB, *Report and Accounts 1979*, 47 (the operating margin for 1978 reported on page 75, and quoted in Gourvish, *British Rail 1974–1997*, 42, appears to be in error).

Table 5.1 Freightliners Ltd results, 1969–78

Year	Turnover in million pounds	Operating Margin in million pounds/ per cent of turnover	Profit or loss after interest plus taxation per cent	Profit or loss after extraordinary items per cent	TEUs handled
1969	10.54	n.a.	–2.24	–2.24	n.a.
1970	14.26	n.a.	–0.84	–0.84	n.a.
1971	15.98	n.a.	–0.09	–0.08	n.a.
1972	20.32	n.a.	–1.86	–0.38	n.a.
1973	25.12	1.11 / 4.4	–0.18	–0.38	n.a.
1974	27.62	0.24 / 0.9	–1.00	–1.30	n.a.
1975	31.22	–1.07 / –3.4	–3.09	3.09	[e]810,000
1976	38.20	1.3 / 3.4	/	/	/
1977	46.11	1.4 / 3.0	–1.05	–1.05	870,000
1978	50.96	0.86 / 1.7	0.29	#	843,000

Note: In the 3rd column Operating Margin means operating surplus or loss before interest.
[e] = estimated
[#] = financial reconstruction
Source: Freightliners Ltd. Reports & Accounts 1969–78 (incomplete), in TNA AN192/894.

advantage over road haulage.[44] Pryke and Dodgson, writing in 1975 and drawing on the 1971 cost analysis of Warner and Joy, suggested that the comparative costs of the two modes were critical. The distances at which Freightliner was competitive with road increased substantially where the goods carried were bulkier in comparison with their weight. Collection and delivery costs were also important, and competitiveness often rested on the comparative distance of the rail and road terminals from the customer's delivery/collection point. The competitiveness of Freightliner, it was argued, would have been improved had the company adopted the newer, 40-foot containers in preference to those measuring 20 feet. Even so, the inland container traffic between major British centres was often insufficient to give railways profitable volumes. In contrast, the expansion of the sea container business, evident by the mid-1970s, was a more promising prospect for the railways. The break-even distance for this traffic was only around 50 miles, since unlike the domestic business it required only one of the costly collection and delivery operations.[45]

There were also organisational obstacles to Freightliner growth. As Zeitlin makes clear in his autobiography, the transfer to NFC may have introduced ex-British Rail managers to some of the managerial freedoms enjoyed by their counterparts in the private sector, but it should not be assumed that they enjoyed a level playing field in the market. Potential Freightliner business was sometimes

44 Pryke and Dodgson state that Freightliner had captured only 11 per cent of the freight market over 100 miles: Pryke and Dodgson, *Rail Problem*, 85.

45 Ibid., 86–9, and Warner and Joy, 'Economics of Rail Container Operation', 355–6.

retained by one of NFC's road haulage subsidiaries, because in that way they would retain a 100 per cent of the profit, instead of having to share it with British Rail. At the same time, British Rail, while happy to provide rail haulage for Freightliner, retained potential Freightliner traffics for themselves, such as domestic refuse and waste. This clear contradiction of the intentions of the 1968 Transport Act served to constrain the growth of container traffic.[46] Finally, the legacy of Freightliner's development within British Rail was to introduce some 'path dependency' elements into the routines of operational management that acted as a further constraint. Thus, Zeitlin refers to the separate treatment of the road and rail transits and the management accounting surrounding them. The train function was handled by the head office, but a considerable degree of autonomy was enjoyed by the managers of the terminals, in line with the experience of the first MD, George Gibb, who had joined Freightliner from British Road Services. As a result, Zeitlin argues, depot managers were allowed to 'take the first bite' when allocating revenues to cost functions, and the road function tended to show a profit while the train transit appeared to be less successful. Initial investment allocations tended to reflect this imbalance.[47]

Back to British Rail, 1978–88

In August 1978 the Freightliner business, now employing 2,400 staff, was returned to British Rail on the grounds that it would do better if more closely aligned with the rest of railway freight, a reversal of the argument accepted by government a decade earlier. The change of ownership was effected by the Transport Act 1978. There had been some strong lobbying of the Department of Transport by British Rail, led by Peter Parker.[48] The main plank of the argument, according to BRB's Railway Executive Committee, was 'the strength of the total freight marketing package'.[49] But Freightliner's sharply deteriorating financial position provided an equally pressing reason for change. Unsecured loan stock amounting to £16 million was due for repayment on 1 December 1978, and since, as we have seen, the accumulated losses were approaching this figure, the business was unable to

46 Zeitlin, *Staying on Track*, 18–19, 22–3.

47 Ibid., 25. Zeitlin also claims that road vehicle and driver utilisation was sub-optimal. See ibid., 25–6.

48 *Transport Act 1978*, c.55, s.15–20; Gourvish, *British Rail 1974–1997*, 40. See also correspondence between Sir Peter Parker (Chairman, BRB) and William Rodgers (Secretary of State for Transport), December 1977–August 1978, and especially Rodgers-Parker, 7 August 1978, TNA AN156/624.

49 BRB, *Railway Executive Committee Minutes*, 13 February 1978, extract in TNA AN156/624.

provide for this.[50] There may also have been a political motive. Zeitlin suggests that the Labour Government bowed to pressure from the largest rail union, the NUR, to the dismay of Freightliner managers, the proviso being that the business should be run as a separate entity within British Rail.[51] Whatever the reasons, the move necessitated a substantial financial reconstruction – with a bail-out to the extent of over £18 million – and during the 1980s Freightliner was subject to a firmer control of its cash flow and investment requirements. This was not, however, accompanied by an increase in the amount of public information about its trading. Indeed, there was a distinct lack of transparency about rail freight in the 1980s (and arguably beyond), and it is difficult to extract details about the sea container portion of Freightliner's activity. Gross revenue (turnover) and the operating margin are revealed in British Rail's published annual reports and accounts, along with references to the number of containers moved (Table 5.2). Taking the business as a whole (sea containers, inland containers, European Traffic [from 1983]), turnover increased by 76 per cent from £60 million in 1979 to £106 million in 1985/6.

Table 5.2 Freightliners Ltd results, 1979–87/88

Year	Turnover in million pounds	Operating margin in million pounds / per cent of turnover	TEUs handled	Reported share of deep sea container market
1979	60.32	2.03 / 3.4	871,000	n.a.
1980	68.95	1.37 / 2.0	866,000	n.a.
1981	72.10	0.09 / 0.1	824,000	n.a.
1982	69.60	–4.36 / –6.3	778,000	n.a.
1983	97.60	1.46 / 1.5	#975,000	n.a.
1984/85	126.20	1.5 / 1.2	/	40 %
1985/86	106.30	0.1 / 0.1	/	n.a.
1986/87	104.70	–6.4 / –6.8	/	–
1987/88	97.7	–6.2 / –6.3	800,000	30 %

Note: In the 3rd column Operating Margin means operating surplus or loss before interest. For 1984/1985 the figures refer to a period of 15 months. In 1987/88 the number of TEUs included 507,000 deep sea containers.

Freightliners Ltd figure [968,000 in BRB].

Source: BRB, *Report and Accounts 1979–87/8*; Freightliners Ltd, Report and Accounts 1981–84/5 (incomplete), TNA AN192/894.

50 See auditors' concerns expressed in 1975, and BRB, *Railway Executive Committee Minutes*, 21 March 1977, TNA AN192/894.

51 Zeitlin, *Staying on Track*, 71.

However, the operating margin remained small, declining from a highpoint of £2.0 million (3.3 per cent of turnover) to average only 0.36 per cent per annum in 1981–85/86. The margin was negative in 1982, when there were disruptions to services as a result of industrial action in Southampton docks and Millbrook terminal, and in 1986/7 and 1987/8 the results were poor, the operating margin averaging *minus* £6.3 million. BRB's accounts for 1986/7 referred to 'a difficult trading year', and a 'need for change'. In 1987 the subsidiary embarked on a major rationalisation exercise. Eight depots were closed, but the move produced no major turnaround in the operating results.[52] Some published data exist on the number of containers moved, in TEUs (Table 5.2). The figures are difficult to interpret as they stand since they are incomplete. However, we can say that by 1979 Freightliner was carrying 871,000 containers, 37 per cent more than in 1973, and that although the traffic fluctuated with the trade cycle, 975,000 containers were moved in 1983, an increase of 12 per cent on 1979. The disappointing financial results of 1986 and 1987 seem to have been associated with lower volumes, with only 800,000 containers in 1987/8. Only a glimmer of light was shed on the importance of the sea container market in Freightliner's overall operations. However, British Rail claimed that it enjoyed a 40 per cent share of that market in 1984/5 and 30 per cent in 1987/8, when the number of sea containers moved – 507,000 – represented 63 per cent of the total (Table 5.2). Zeitlin suggests that attention to quality of service was important in strengthening Freightliner's share of sea container movements. In January 1985 'Masterhaul' was launched, an overall package of services offered to shipping companies, embracing logistical control, container storage, cleaning and repair. A partnership with the Felixstowe road hauliers, Russell Davies, produced speedier decisions about whether to move a consignment by rail or road.[53] Here, comparative margins were important, and it is clear that ports such as Felixstowe affected modal choice via the charges they levied for the movement of containers from the ship to the railhead within the port (loading on and off road vehicles was conducted free of charge).[54] These considerations warn us of the dangers of making the simple assumption that the public sector was always inferior to the private sector in terms of management quality, innovation or speed of response. Of course, further research will be required to strengthen the tentative conclusions advanced here.

Railfreight Distribution and Freightliner, 1988–96

In October 1988 the loss-making freight businesses of British Rail, Freightliners, Railfreight International (international traffic) and Speedlink (wagon-load freight) were grouped together in a new institutional entity, Railfreight Distribution

52 BRB, *Report and Accounts 1986/7*, 27, and *1987/8*, 27.

53 Ibid., 40ff.

54 Ibid., 43–4.

(RfD). The move was suggested by the Department of Transport as a means of encouraging British Rail to be more transparent about the financial results of its profitable and unprofitable activities.[55] Henceforth separate results were published for 'Trainload Freight', that is, the profitable bulk traffics such as coal and aggregates, and RfD. But while the position of the railways' *overall* freight business was henceforth more transparent, the performance of the component parts of RfD was barely revealed in the published data, principally BRB's annual reports and accounts. Consequently, this dataset contains very little additional information for our purposes. The expectations were that by unifying investment and train planning decisions for the three bi-modal freight activities, their financial performance would improve. British Rail's senior managers were also keen to exploit the opportunities presented by European deregulation and the building of the Channel Tunnel. This optimism was to prove largely unfounded, however. Table 5.3 gives RfD's limited published results from 1988/9 to 1995/6, viz. gross revenue (turnover), and the operating margin. The business performed poorly in the long recession of 1989 to 1993, posting very large operating losses.

Table 5.3 Railfreight Distribution results (including Freightliner), 1988/9–95/6

Year	Turnover in million pounds	Operating Margin in million pounds
1988/89	n.a.	–64.6
1989/90	176.7	–73.4
1990/91	172.8	–152.3
1991/92	174.9	–118.7
1992/93	172.3	–90.1
1993/94	159.5	–62.2
1994/95	130.7	–60.9
1995/96	87.9	–58.6
1995/96	70.4	–20.2

Note: For year 1995/96 only Freightliner included.

Source: BRB, Report and Accounts, 1988/9–95/6.

The operating margin was negative to the extent of £65 million in 1988/89, and in the worst year, 1990/91, the loss was more than double this at £152 million. Speedlink, RfD's struggling wagon-load business, was responsible for much of the deficit. Internal documents show that it lost £51 million on a turnover of £39 million in 1990/91; its accumulated losses were put at £211 million since 1982.[56] Certainly, RfD's losses were reduced after Speedlink was axed in July 1991. But Freightliner's more recent results were scarcely impressive either, and

[55] Gourvish, *British Rail 1974–1997*, 140, 283.

[56] BRB, *Minutes*, 7 March–6 December 1990, 6 June 1991, TNA AN167/56–7.

an ambitious plan to revitalise the business in 1987 seems to have failed.[57] The Channel Tunnel proved to be an enormous distraction. Months of management time was taken up in planning for a large continental rail traffic which failed to materialise. Under half of the expected traffic by train – 3.1 million tonnes – had materialised by 1998, and the total fell to only 1.5 million tonnes in 2002.[58] In the last year of public ownership, 1995/6, RfD posted an operating loss of £59 million, and with Freightliner's results separated in the build up to privatisation, one can see that its £20 million loss was only a third of the total (Table 5.3).

How did the sea container portion of RfD/Freightliner's business fare doing this disappointing period? Further research will be required to answer this question, but there are references to the fact that this portion of the business was more buoyant. Indeed, a belated £40 million investment in 700 new wagons was authorised in 1990 and delivered in 1991–93. This was the only major investment in freight vehicles made by British Rail (the Channel Tunnel excepted) in the last decade of nationalisation.[59]

Conclusion and Research Issues

Freightliner was privatised in May 1996, when the business was sold to Management Consortium Bid Ltd in a management buy-out. The purchasers benefited from a payment of £4.9 million from British Rail, which made a loss on the deal of £13 million over asset value. The MBO also enjoyed a substantial government subsidy in the form of £77 million to cover track access charges to be paid to Railtrack for the five years to March 2001.[60] The initial indications were that the move freed the business from the straightjacket of the public sector, enabling losses to be converted into profits. Is there any truth in this? Certainly, improved results were reported, a profit of £2.2 million was announced for 1997/8, and more entrepreneurialism was displayed in the winning of new business outside the company's core activities.[61] On the other hand, Freightliner continued to enjoy state support, including more generous treatment of track access charges, and the railways' renaissance after privatisation owed much to the benefits of a long boom

57 Gourvish, *British Rail 1974–1997*, 283.

58 Terry Gourvish, *The Official History of Britain and the Channel Tunnel* (Abingdon 2006), 369–70; Gourvish, *British Rail 1974–1997*, 285, 618; Zeitlin, *Staying on Track*, and the issues of *Modern Railways*, May 1988, 308–11, and July 1999, 476. Lorry traffic carried on Eurotunnel's freight shuttle services proved to be a more successful venture.

59 Gourvish, *British Rail 1974–1997*, 307–10.

60 Mike Anson, Appendix L1, in Gourvish, *British Rail 1974–1997*, 511–16, here 439, 512 (loss figure calculated after the completion accounts process, taking account of net assets, page 516), and Gourvish, *Britain's Railways 1997–2005*, 164.

61 Paul Shannon, *Railway Freight Operations* (Shepperton 1999), 89, and www.freightliner.co.uk (last accessed 1 January 2010).

rather than to any intrinsic superiority of the change in ownership. Nevertheless, under private control the railways' share of the sea container business grew from about 17 per cent to 25 per cent in the decade after privatisation.[62]

Our preliminary survey of Freightliner and British railways' sea container traffic raises questions about the ability of the public sector both to effectively develop a new technology, and to cost and price its services in competition with road transport. The latter was a potent competitor. Also benefiting from technological change, it was able to increase its average length of haul from 42 miles in 1980 to 59 miles in 2001.[63] Did the public sector, in the shape of British Rail, fail containerised rail freight? Were the financial difficulties experienced by Freightliners Ltd in the 30 years from 1965 avoidable? How sympathetic should we be to railway management? These are challenging issues, but a preliminary assessment of the senior managers allocated to Freightliner indicates that there was no shortage of managerial quality, in theory at least. It could not be said that the Freightliners Board lacked expertise, particularly after 1978, when Bob Reid (later BRB Chairman) became its Chairman and Cyril Bleasdale continued as its Managing Director (he was first appointed in 1975). Bleasdale was succeeded by the equally able Bryan Driver in 1982; Reid, arguably the most effective railway manager of his generation, was succeeded by Geoffrey Myers (in 1980), then by James Urquhart (1983), both successful members of BRB. Other members of the Freightliner Board included Alec Tait, David Kirby, Peter Land, Henry Sanderson and Frank Paterson.[64] On the other hand, these managers were unable to transform Freightliner's bottom-line, and some aspects of the business could have been pursued with more vigour and sophistication.

Has Freightliner performed better in the private sector, and, if so, why is this? Are we dealing with an improved performance in private hands, increased investment, or merely the result of market forces, with the huge growth of container imports from Asia, and China in particular gathering pace after privatisation in 1996? Have the railways become more competitive vis-à-vis road transport, and is this critical in the modal choices made by customers of container transport? These issues require further consideration. Here, our review of Freightliner operations since 1965 suggests that during the period of nationalisation investment shortages were important in constraining traffic growth. For example, when 370 containers were ordered on 1978, they were the first of such acquisitions since 1974.[65] And, as we have seen, investment in new container-carrying wagons was delayed until the early 1990s. The tardy way in which both public and private sector railway infrastructure managers responded to the constraints on moving larger

62 Gourvish, *Britain's Railways 1997–2005*, 163–4.

63 Alan C. McKinnon, 'The economic and environmental benefits of increasing maximum truck weight: the British experience', *Transportation Research*, D10, January 2005, 77–95, here 78.

64 See Freightliner files, TNA AN156/71, AN156/626, and AN192/894.

65 Freightliner News Line No. 5 (1 February 1978), in TNA AN156/624.

sea containers from the critical ports of Felixstowe and Southampton was also significant.[66] Not before 2010 the benefits of improvements to key rail routes from Felixstowe (first via the North London Line, then via Nuneaton) and Southampton (to the West Midlands) had been realised.[67] And yet it was also the case that railway managers were prepared to under-price their product and run up operating losses, particularly in the periods from 1975 to 1978 and from 1986 to 1996. Over-optimistic expectations about the potential long-run profitability of intermodal traffic especially through the Channel Tunnel were also a factor. The tentative conclusion here is that the railways' competitive advantage was limited not only by investment constraints and pricing weaknesses, but also by technical changes, such as the growing popularity of 40-foot containers, and the introduction of larger, heavier lorries in the UK. Larger containers have had a deleterious impact on the railways' route availability given the restricted loading gauge of the UK infrastructure, while making road haulage more competitive.

References

Anson, Mike, Appendix L1, in Gourvish, *British Rail 1974–1997*, 511–16.

Armstrong, John, et al., eds, *Companion to British Road Haulage History* (London 2003).

Beuthe, Michel, 'Intermodal freight transport in Europe', in Thomas R. Leinbach and Cristina Capineri, eds, *Globalized Freight Transport: Intermodality, E-Commerce, Logistics and Sustainability* (Cheltenham 2007), 54–99.

Bontekoning, Yvonne M., Macharis, Cathy and Trip, Jan J., 'Is a new applied transportation research field emerging? – A review of intermodal rail-truck freight transport literature', *Transportation Research*, A 38, 2004, 1–34.

Bott, Alan, ed., *British Box Business: A History of OCL* (Godalming 2009).

BRB, ed., *The Reshaping of British Railways*, 2 parts (London 1963).

BRB, *Report and Accounts 1965* (London 1965–1967).

Broeze, Frank, *The Globalisation of the Oceans: Containerisation from the 1950s to the Present* (St Johns 2002).

Butcher, Louise, 'Lorry sizes and weights', House of Commons briefing note SN/BT/654, 23 November 2009.

Collins, Michael J., *Freightliner* (Sparkford 1991).

Cudahy, Brian, *Box Boats* (New York 2006).

[66] Containers grew from 20-foot containers with a length of 19 foot 10.5 inch, a width of 8 foot and a heights of 8 foot 6 inch to 40-foot containers with a length of 40 foot, 8 foot in width and 8 foot 6 inch or in the high-cube model even 9 foot 6 inch in heigths. The volume grew from 33.1 cubic metres to 75.3 or 86.1 cubic metres.

[67] For example the £70.7 million. Southampton-West Midlands project: *Modern Railways*, September 2010.

European Council of Ministers of Transport, ed., *Benchmarking Intermodal Freight Transport* (Paris, 2002).

Frankel, Marvin, 'Obsolescence and Technological Change in a Mature Economy', *American Economic Review*, 45, 3, 1955, 296–319.

Freeman Allen, Geoffrey, *British Railways Today and Tomorrow* (London 1959).

Freeman Allen, Geoffrey, *British Railways After Beeching* (Shepperton 1966).

Freeman Allen, Geoffrey, *British Railfreight – Today and Tomorrow* (London 1984).

Gourvish, Terry R., *British Railways 1948–1973: A Business History* (Cambridge 1986).

Gourvish, Terry R., *British Rail 1974–1997: From Integration to Privatisation* (Oxford 2002).

Gourvish, Terry R., *The Official History of Britain and the Channel Tunnel* (Abingdon 2006).

Gourvish, Terry R., *Britain's Railways 1997–2005: Labour's Strategic Experiment* (Oxford 2008).

Harrison, Anthony J., 'Investment in Liner Trains', *Bulletin of the Oxford University Institute of Economics and Statistics*, 26, 3, August, 1964, 205–22.

Hayuth, Yehuda, *Intermodality: Concepts and Practice. Structural Changes in the Ocean Freight Transport Industry* (London 1987).

Joy, Stewart, *The Train That Ran Away: A Business History of British Railways 1948–1968* (Shepperton 1973).

Levinson, Marc, *The Box: How the Shipping Container Made the World Smaller and the World Economy Bigger* (Princeton, NJ 2006).

Lowe, David, *Intermodal Freight Transport* (London 2005).

McKinnon, Alan C., 'The economic and environmental benefits of increasing maximum truck weight: the British experience', *Transportation Research*, D10, January 2005, 77–95.

Network Rail, ed., *Value and Importance of Rail Freight* – July 2010 (London 2010).

Pryke, Richard and Dodgson, John, *The Rail Problem* (London 1975).

Rail Freight Group, ed., *Manifesto for Rail Freight Growth* – October 2009 (London 2009).

Shannon, Paul, *Railway Freight Operations* (Shepperton 1999).

Van Klink, H. Arjen and van den Berg, Geerke C., 'Gateways and intermodalism', *Journal of Transport Geography*, 6, 1, 1998, 1–9.

Warner, Bernard, and Joy, Stewart, 'The Economics of Rail Container Operation in Britain', *Rail International*, 4, April, 1971, 345–56.

Woodburn, Allan, 'Intermodal Rail Freight in Britain: a Terminal Problem?', *Planning Practice & Research*, 23, 2, August, 2008, 441–60.

Zeitlin, Graham, *Staying on Track: The Reflections of a Railwayman* (Lancaster 2002).

Chapter 6
Trucking in Germany: Rise and Restricted Growth, 1900–1938

Richard Vahrenkamp

Introduction

Between 1900 and 1938, road haulage rapidly supplemented the traditional freight carriers by water and railway. This chapter investigates how new technology made a difference to the German road transport business between 1920 and 1938. It aims to demonstrate the special conditions under which truck transport and the trucking trade developed in Germany. After the depression following the First World War, the German economy boomed only in the short period between 1925 and 1929, providing good conditions for the rise of trucks. But Chancellor Brüning's emergency decree in October 1931 and Nazi rule severely restricted road haulage for hire and forwarding in favour of the railway. In the 1920s, private transport companies had already had to stave off competition from state-run transport companies. Thus, an important branch of the economy could not develop as fully as it did in the United States or in Britain, where trucks gained a great share in the transport trade of the 1930s.

Business history research in Germany has focussed on large enterprises, for example, German railways or German banks. But the numerous small trucking and forwarding companies have attracted little attention. There are only two studies in this field.[1] Frank Lippert's book is on the rationalisation of truck production in the 1920s. He does not distinguish between, for example, own-account transport and that for hire and forwarding. Heidi Rohde's research discusses the restriction of truck transport under Nazi rule, but does not provide an account of the forwarding trade in the 1930s. This chapter aims to close these gaps in our understanding.

The analysis is based on the evaluation of trade journals, national statistics and various archives, including the archives of the *Industrie- und Handelskammern* (IHK) (Chambers of Industry and Commerce) in Cologne, Leipzig, Munich and Darmstadt, as well as the considerable IHK records held in the *Institut für Stadtgeschichte* (Institute for Urban History) in Frankfurt am Main. But these sources have certain limitations. The archives only provide a fragmentary picture

1 Frank Lippert, *Lastkraftwagenverkehr und Rationalisierung in der Weimarer Republik* (Frankfurt am Main and New York 1999), and Heidi Rohde, *Transportmodernisierung oder Verkehrsbewirtschaftung?* (Frankfurt am Main and New York 1999).

of the trucking trade. The data are sparse, sketchy and heterogeneous. The haulage industry consisted of small companies and weak umbrella organisations, none of which preserved any archives. Trade journals did not publish aggregate data about the industry, for example the number of companies, the number of employees, the turnover and the amount of cargo delivered. These data are lacking until Nazi rule forced the trade to publish statistics on their member companies.

Following a description of the legal constraints on truck traffic and the instruments of regulation, the chapter investigates the traffic policy of the Weimar Republic. This included the provision of road infrastructure for increased car and truck traffic, marking the first conflicts between the German National Railway Company (*Deutsche Reichsbahn*) and the road haulage industry. The chapter demonstrates how the German National Railway Company was able to bring about regulation for its own benefit, and how truck traffic was nearly strangled during the Nazi period. The later rapid growth of road haulage, specifically own-account and commercial carrying, despite the difficult competitive conditions, are then analysed.

The emergence of buses and trucks gave rise to new legal terms in transport policy. For the first time, the term 'local traffic', defined as traffic travelling on roads up to 50 kilometres, was defined by law in 1925. Local traffic (of buses and trucks) was permitted without approval, and was distinguished from long-distance traffic: that going beyond 50 kilometres and offering frequent connections between two places. According to the 1925 law, long-distance traffic had to be approved by the *Reichsbahn*. Chancellor Brüning's emergency decree in October 1931 then distinguished between commercial carriers by road (transport for hire and reward) and transport on own account. Consequently, the term 'transport on own account' was introduced into German transport policy.[2] The term 'commercial carriers by truck' described a business sector that consisted of both carrying and forwarding firms. Unlike in the United States, there was no distinction in Germany between common carriers and contract carriers.[3] Both were included in the term 'commercial carrier'.

The military contributed decisively to the initial proliferation of trucks. By 1908, the Prussian army administration had supported the purchase of trucks by private companies, at 4,000 marks each, subsidising operations with 1,000 marks

[2] 'Dritte Verordnung des Reichspräsidenten zur Sicherung von Wirtschaft und Finanzen und zur Bekämpfung politischer Ausschreitungen vom 6. Oktober 1931, Kapitel V, Überlandverkehr mit Kraftfahrzeugen (Ordinance on 9 October 1931) vom 9. Oktober 1931', *Reichsgesetzblatt*, 1931, vol. I, 572–7.

[3] The difference between common carriers and contract carriers in the US regulation of road carriers is explained by R. William Childs, *Trucking and the Public Interest* (Knoxville 1986), and Mark H. Rose, Bruce E. Seely and Paul Barrett, *The Best Transportation System in the World: Railroads, Trucks, Airlines, and American Public Policy in the Twentieth Century* (Columbus, OH 2006).

annually for four years.[4] However, the mechanisation of army transport was not decisively achieved until 1914. The First World War helped the truck gain acceptance in three ways. Technologically, it gave impulse to the development of greater carrying capacity and engine power. Secondly, it clearly revealed the truck's significance as an alternative to railway transport. Truck transport was implemented both for the supply of material, for example at the Austrian-Italian front in the Alps or by the French for their front near Verdun, and for the alleviation of the logistical crisis experienced by the German railways in 1916. To do this, the German army requisitioned or bought up approximately 18 per cent of the 5,361 trucks of greater than 16 horse power that were registered to private German companies in 1914.[5] Thirdly, the First World War led to a widespread distribution of trucks; after the war, all parties involved in the war had a large number of ex-military trucks available for civilian use.[6] This fleet provided an incentive to search for new fields of operation.

Another demonstration of the capability of road haulage was at the Battle of the Ruhr. In 1923, when French troops occupied the Ruhr area and commandeered the railway, the resulting shortfall in freight capacity was filled by the truck.[7] Similarly, until 1930, allied forces occupied the left bank of the Prussian province Rhineland and reduced the capacity of the railway. Thus, road haulage substituted for railway transport, and moreover showed its advantages. By 1929, 30 per cent of the trucks in Prussia were located in the Rhineland.[8] To make use of this modern transport technology (as well as that of cars and buses) *Autobahn* projects were planned to connect Aachen with Cologne, Düsseldorf with Cologne and Bonn with Cologne; the first *Autobahn*, from Bonn to Cologne, was opened in 1932.[9]

---

[4] Emil Merkert, *Der Lastwagenverkehr seit dem Krieg, insbesondere sein Wettbewerb und seine Zusammenarbeit mit den Schienenbahnen* (Berlin 1926), 3.

[5] Frank Schipper, *Driving Europe – Building Europe on Roads in the Twentieth Century* (Amsterdam 2008), 69; Peter Kirchberg, 'Technik und Verkehrswirksamkeit der Lastkraftwagen in Deutschland bis zum Ende der 1930er Jahre', in Harry Niemann and Armin Hermann, eds, *100 Jahre LKW. Geschichte und Zukunft des Nutzfahrzeuges* (Stuttgart 1997), and Christoph Merki, *Der holprige Siegeszug des Automobils 1895–1930: Zur Motorisierung des Straßenverkehrs in Frankreich, Deutschland und der Schweiz* (Vienna 2002), 72–87.

[6] Lippert, *Lastkraftwagenverkehr und Rationalisierung*, and Deutscher Industrie- und Handelstag, ed., *Eisenbahn und Kraftwagen* (Berlin 1930). Scott reports that some 60,000 army trucks were released in Great Britain. See Peter Scott, 'British Railways and the Challenge from Road Haulage: 1919–39', *Twentieth Century British History*, 13, nr. 2, 2002, 101–20, here 103. See also Schipper, *Driving Europe*, 69.

[7] Otto Cohausz, 'Der französisch-deutsche Eisenbahnkrieg im Ruhrgebiet 1923', *Jahrbuch für Eisenbahngeschichte*, 6, 1973, 5–25.

[8] 'Der Lastkraftwagen und die Rheinlande', *ADAC-Motorwelt*, 27, nr. 27, 1930, 9–10.

[9] Richard Vahrenkamp, *The German Autobahn – Hafraba Visions and Mega Projects* (Cologne 2010).

Trucking firms were mostly engaged in the field of contract carriers. They worked with certain large enterprises in the production or commercial sector to move regular, full truck loads. In contrast, forwarding firms mainly combined small shipments from different companies into full loads; this business sector was known as 'common carriers'. But these firms also sometimes worked as contract carriers. Thus, unlike in the USA, no barriers existed in practice or in law between common carriers and contract carriers. In this respect, German truck regulation was not as rigid as in the USA. Forwarding firms could either use their own trucks or those of subcontractors. While in the USA, the Motor Carrier Act of 1935 had to include a special clause exempting truck transportation of unmanufactured agricultural goods from regulation, in order to give farmers an opportunity to transport their products into cities, no such measure was necessary in Germany.[10]

Since road haulage at the beginning of the 1920s was not yet regulated by law and liability insurance was not yet obligatory, haulage companies were considered gamblers carrying 'wild traffic'. Both the Chamber of Industry and Commerce and the umbrella organisation for forwarding companies asked for the formulation of minimum standards of quality and security, partly to help stabilise the road haulage industry: the financially weak members were unable to weather the cyclical fluctuations of the transport demand, leading to ruinous competition.[11] On the other hand, the railways regarded trucks as a new competitor and called for a legal framework that would provide either protection against the new threat or the chance to enter and compete in the new sector. Around 1930, similar problems with road haulage across Europe led to widespread calls for state regulation.[12] Policy could rely on a broad array of measures designed to regulate short- and long-haul trucking regarding safety, price, timetables, licences and routes. The goal was to protect the national railway against the truck or to restrict the railway to its traditional business field.

The resulting regulations were implemented differently throughout Europe. For instance, in Great Britain a licence became necessary for private carriers, but not in Germany. Sweden did not distinguish between private carriers and professional carriers, but all other countries did. The Netherlands pursued a policy of flexible adaptation. Because of growing demand, the Dutch allowed more

[10] Shane Hamilton, 'The Populist Appeal of Deregulation: Independent Truckers and the Politics of Free Enterprise, 1935–1980', *Enterprise & Society*, 10, nr. 1, 2009, 137–77, here 145.

[11] Deutscher Industrie- und Handelstag, *Eisenbahn und Kraftwagen*, 41. The journal of the chamber of commerce in Cologne reported on 'wild' competition under the truckers. See *Westdeutsche Wirtschaftszeitung* of 5 July 1929, 408, and of 11 January 1929, 34, Rheinisch-Westfälisches Wirtschaftsarchiv Cologne.

[12] Paul Wohl and A. Albitreccia, *Road and Rail in Forty Countries. Report prepared for The International Chamber of Commerce London* (Oxford 1935).

trucks to operate.[13] The opposite policy was implemented in France, where in 1934 the government heavily restricted the foundation of new transport companies and long-distance road haulage in favour of the railways.[14] The reason for this policy was the railways' high financial losses, which were blamed on automobile competition.[15] In France, the automobile industry was more advanced than in other European countries. Moreover, since the road-building programme in the nineteenth century, French roads were very good; they were wide and had a hard macadam surface. Therefore, long-distance road transport developed well in France. Nazi policy also restricted trucking, but not because the national railway company incurred financial losses as the result of their operation. The number of long-haul trucks allowed to operate was capped at 11,400 – far below the demand of the booming economy.

The question whether railway companies should be allowed to enter the trucking industry was also answered differently throughout Europe. In Great Britain the business activities of railway companies were prescribed by acts of Parliament. If a railway company wanted to operate lorries, it had to apply to Parliament. But in Germany no such restrictions prevented the national railway company from entering the trucking business. A broad public debate arose when, in 1932, the *Reichsbahn* bought the forwarding company Schenker in a secret purchase. Small- and medium-sized trucking and forwarding companies and their umbrella organisations wrote numerous protest letters to state authorities, as the files of the Chambers of Industry and Commerce reveal.

The German long-haul trucking companies operated not only under severe regulatory charges and restrictions but also had to meet competition arising from state-run transport companies. When railway bottlenecks endangered the food supply to German cities in 1916, the army deployed trucks to secure the supply. At the end of the war, these trucks were transferred from the army to state-run transport companies.[16] Between 1920 and 1923, when strikes, coal shortages, the financial burden of reparation payments and the occupation of the Ruhr district strained the railway, these state-run transport companies met the shortfalls. But in the years of economic recovery, 1924 until 1929, the states and provinces continued to support the companies, prompting numerous protest letters from private carriers about the distortion of competition. For example, the West German association of forwarders founded the *Rheinische Verkehrsgesellschaft*, claiming self-protection

13 Ruud Filarski, *The Rise and Decline of Transport Systems. Changes in a Historical Context* (Rotterdam 2004).

14 See the contribution of Bruno Carrière, 'Road-Rail Competition in France in the 1930s: From a Railway Perspective' in this volume.

15 Joseph Jones, *The Politics of Transport in Twentieth-Century France* (Kingston and Montreal 1984), 51.

16 Angela Zatsch, *Staatsmacht und Motorisierung am Morgen des Automobilzeitalters* (Konstanz 1993), 120, and Merki, *Siegeszug*, 2.

in their battle with the state-owned company *Kraftverkehrs AG Westfalen*; the latter company was accused of being unfairly supported by the tax-payer.[17]

The Conflict Between Rail and Truck

The federal German states both controlled traffic policy and were owners of their respective railways until 1920. In the transition from the imperial *Reich* to a republic, the new Weimar constitution of 1919 demanded the unification of the several state-owned German railway organisations into an umbrella organisation, the *Reichsbahngesellschaft* (the German Railway Company; hereafter *Reichsbahn*). This was codified by the *Reich* in 1920.[18] In 1924, this organisation was converted into a private company under the control of the victorious powers. This was agreed on in the Dawes plan in 1924, negotiated between Germany, France, England and the USA after it proved impossible for Germany to pay the reparations required by the Treaty of Versailles. After the economic breakdown during the catastrophic inflation of 1923, Germany demanded a reduction in its yearly payments. At the same time, the USA demanded that France and England repay their wartime loans. The latter countries linked both payment streams, demanding that Germany's payments should be at least as high as the money they owed the USA. At a conference chaired by the US finance expert Charles Gates Dawes in London in August 1924, the countries agreed upon a new schedule of payments. Germany got a loan of 800 million Reichsmarks from the USA to stabilise its economy. The victorious powers exercised control over the *Reichsbahn* to secure the annual German reparation payments, which amounted to 660 million Reichsmarks.[19] Thus, the *Reichsbahn* became a cash cow for reparations. According to Mierzejewski, the Dawes plan had the aim of converting the *Reichsbahn* from a commonweal organisation into a profit-orientated company based on the Western model; the railways in France, Great Britain and the USA were run by private companies.

In the nineteenth century, the railway had been a monopolistic carrier in many regions without sea harbours or canal systems.[20] Both inland navigation and the railway focussed on bulk cargo transport. When motorised road transport for passengers and cargo emerged at the beginning of the twentieth century, the

---

17 Institut für Stadtgeschichte Frankfurt am Main, IHK 854.

18 'Gesetz über den Übergang der Eisenbahnen auf das Reich vom 30. April 1920 (Act to unite the German state railways from on 30 April 1920)', *Reichsgesetzblatt*, 1920, vol. I, 773–90.

19 Alfred Mierzejewski, *The Most Valuable Asset of the Reich: a History of the German National Railway*, 2 vols (Chapel Hill 1999 and 2000), vol. 1, chapter 4.

20 Andreas Kunz, 'The economic performance of inland navigation in Germany, 1835–1935: a reassessment of traffic flows', in Andreas Kunz and John Armstrong, eds, *Inland Navigation and Economic Development in Nineteenth Century Europe* (Mainz 1995), 47–78.

railways not only had a new competitor but also the challenge of dealing with a new kind of freight: manufactured goods. These goods were packed in wooden boxes, baskets and cartons and shipped in small amounts. Since these loads did not fill a 20-ton railway wagon, they were particularly suitable for small trucks.[21] There are no data on shipments of packaged goods by road hauliers in Germany in the 1920s. Only data for the German railway network demonstrate the new significance of packaged goods; shipments rose from 14.6 million tons in 1925 to 20.4 million tons in 1929.[22]

Rail and road had completely different operating conditions, cost and ownership structures. Since the state financed the road system, motor transport did not have to bear high, fixed costs but was only responsible for its individual share of road wear; being proportional to driving distances, this was paid for by the petrol tax as a variable cost. Therefore, road hauliers had to bear only the low fixed costs of the truck (or, for that matter, the car). Motor transport could operate according to individual decisions made at any time of the day, regardless of a timetable, and could reach each destination on the road network, even those poorly maintained. The property structure of motor transport was individual. In contrast, the railway was state-owned, had to cover high, fixed costs (the large network of tracks, and safety and signal systems); was organised as one big organisation; operated according to a timetable; had to coordinate its different trains at railway stations and on lines; and was tied to its network of rails. The pricing system for cargo was not based on production costs, but rather on the value of the goods. As with all other countries, Germany had a detailed list of different classes and prices. Cargo of high value paid high prices ('tariffs'), cargo of low value, low prices.[23] This price system provided no incentive for management to be concerned with production costs and was regulated by the authorities, even in countries with privately run railways: management was tied to this system and could not set market prices. The price system for road haulage was much simpler: the customer paid the cost of transport and a margin for the carrier's profit, independent of the kind of goods.[24] Besides this simple price model, road haulage had another, more important advantage with regard to high-value goods, that is, finished goods,

---

21 Richard Vahrenkamp: *The Logistic Revolution – The Rise of Logistics in the Mass Consumption Society* (Cologne 2012).

22 Statistisches Amt, ed., *Statistisches Jahrbuch für das Deutsche Reich 1929*, vol. 48 (Berlin 1929), 152, and Statistisches Amt, ed., *Statistisches Jahrbuch für das Deutsche Reich 1933*, vol. 52 (Berlin 1933), 163.

23 For the rate structure of the US railways in the 1850s see Alfred Chandler, *The Visible Hand – The Managerial Revolution in American Business* (Cambridge 1977), 125.

24 Many authors maintain that truck transport charges marginal cost (for example: Scott, 'British Railways', 101–20). But his assertion is incorrect. Marginal cost is the increase of cost if the truck loads one additional unit or drives one additional mile. But the costs a truck incurs consist of fixed costs (insurance, tax, depreciation by aging) and variable costs depending on load and distance driven (consumed fuel, wear of tires, wage for the driver, maintenance, depreciation by driven kilometres).

a fast growing segment of the transport market in the emerging mass consumption society: it was much cheaper than rail transport.

Road-rail competition became an issue of public debate at the end of the 1920s. Before 1928 this topic was barely discussed in German transport publications, but thereafter there were many articles in this press.[25] The memorandum '*Reichsbahn und Kraftwagenverkehr*' ('*Reichsbahn* and Motor Traffic') was published by the German corporation of the *Reichsbahn* in January 1930. It argued that increasing motor traffic caused a considerable loss of income for the *Reichsbahn*, both in passenger transport due to bus competition, and in the traffic of goods due to competition with the truck. The *Reichsbahn* justified its tariff system for goods in macro-economic terms: by charging higher prices for high-value goods, the transport of bulk goods could be reduced in price. This policy was said to be necessary to maintain the competitiveness of peripheral production sites that depended on cheap transport of raw materials.[26] Since commercial truck traffic focussed on profitable business, it did not offer the cross-subsidisation inherent in the macro-economic tariff system.[27]

In the memorandum, the *Reichsbahn* argued for limiting privately run commercial truck traffic, giving itself a monopoly of long-distance haulage. Just the local hauls of up to 50 kilometres were to be left to private companies. Here, for the first time, the idea of a transport policy controlled by a centralised large-scale corporation was presented: the *Reichsbahn* followed the model of a large-scale or monopolistic corporation that was such an important model of 1920s economic policy, both for the private trusts and the consumer cooperatives of the German labour movement, as well as for the industrialising Soviet regime.[28] Rationalisation profits were expected thanks to increasing flows, without taking into account the disadvantages that might result from the elimination of competition, such as deficiencies of production and services, slow technical progress and excessive prices. Not surprisingly, in reaction to the memorandum many trade associations and Chambers of Commerce published warnings against the *Reichsbahn*'s threatened monopoly.[29]

25 Deutsche Reichsbahngesellschaft, ed., *Reichsbahn- und Kraftwagenverkehr* (Berlin 1930), and Deutscher Industrie- und Handelstag, ed., *Eisenbahn und Kraftwagen* (Berlin 1930).

26 This coordination of rates is similar to the pricing system of US railroads under the regulation of the Interstate Commerce Commission (ICC), see J. Albert Churella, 'Delivery to the Customer's Door: Efficiency, Regulatory Policy, and Integrated Rail-Truck Operations 1900–1938', *Enterprise & Society*, 10, 1, 2009, 98–132, here 127. See also Chandler, p. 125, in note 23.

27 Deutsche Reichsbahngesellschaft, *Eisenbahn und Kraftwagen.*

28 D. Alfred Chandler, *Giant Enterprise* (New York 1964), and Klaus Novy and Michael Prinz, *Illustrierte Geschichte der Gemeinwirtschaft* (Bonn 1985).

29 In 1932 more than 30 Chambers of Commerce passed resolutions against the *Reichsbahn* monopoly. See Deutsche Wirtschaftszeitung 1932, Saxonian Economic Archive, Leipzig,

In the following, the arguments of the *Reichsbahn* are evaluated. Motorised transport was barely competitive with rail by 1929. In that year the *Reichsbahn*'s turnover reached an all-time high for the decade and so none of the predicted losses of income due to road competition are found in the data.[30] Mellerowicz's figures also show that the competitive pressure road haulage put on the *Reichsbahn* cannot have been very strong. He says that in 1931 there were 11,000 trucks available for long-distance haulage. In another publication, he shows that in the same year commercial road hauliers handled only 2.6 per cent of the *Reichsbahn*'s 51 billion tons-kilometres.[31] This weak competition did not imply that in later years road haulage could not become a more formidable competitor, as the experience of other countries such as the USA and UK shows.[32] But in fact the global financial crisis of 1929–33 and the regulation of truck transport by the Nazi regime between 1933 and 1939 stopped the expansion of road transport for hire.

It should be remembered that the *Reichsbahn* was only arguing against long-distance haulage by commercial carriers (scheduled services), and not transport on own account, which also took away cargo from the railways. According to Mellerowicz's data, own-account transport carried twice the local and long-distance traffic of that carried by commercial road hauliers.[33] In its memorandum, the *Reichsbahn* had to acknowledge that a struggle against own-account transport was hopeless because it was central to the vast majority of large, reputable companies, upon which the *Reichsbahn* was unable to exert pressure.[34] However, with long-distance haulage the balance was in favour of the *Reichsbahn*, since the truck entrepreneurs were fragmented, had a meagre capital base, and their umbrella organisation had little political influence.

If one looks at contemporary press accounts of competition between the automobile and railway, it becomes clear that the *Reichsbahn* had a significant influence on the terms of debate. In 1930, the *Reichsbahn* was by far the biggest German company, with 713,000 employees. With its 29 authorities spread across the country, it had a number of higher-ranking executives who presented their point of view in the local and national press.[35] For this reason, the Imperial Federation of the Automobile Industry complained in a letter to the Chamber of Industry and Commerce on 22 April 1929, that the 'permanently repeated portrayals of the

---

30 'Die Reichsbahn im Jahre 1933', *Die Reichsbahn*, 10, 1, 1934, 4.

31 Karl Mellerowicz, 'Der Stand des gewerblichen Güterfernverkehrs', *Die Strasse*, 2, 5, 1935, 143–7, and Karl Mellerowicz, 'Autobahnen und Kraftverkehrswirtschaft', *Die Autobahn*, 2, 9, 1934, 368–73, here 370.

32 Scott, 'British Railways'. And Childs, *Trucking and the Public Interest*. See also Rose, Seely und Barret, *The Best Transportation System in the World*.

33 Mellerowicz, 'Der Stand des gewerblichen Güterfernverkehr', 143–7. The transport for own account was primarily local traffic.

34 Deutsche Reichsbahngesellschaft, *Reichsbahn- und Kraftwagenverkehr*, 85–6.

35 Hans Baumann, *Deutsches Verkehrsbuch* (Berlin 1931), 80 and 301.

Reichsbahn' with various personalities of the *Reichstag* and umbrella organisations led to views which are 'in contrast to real circumstances'.[36]

In 1925, a law on road haulage became the first regulatory measure in favour of the railway.[37] This prompted the protest of various Chambers of Industry and Commerce; they feared the railway would gain a traffic monopoly.[38] Although this law proved ineffective because it was not policed at the municipal level, the legal framework within which road hauliers operated became unclear. The forwarding firms refrained from advertising their services so as not to draw the attention of the courts. Instead, they communicated directly with their customers. Prosecutors nevertheless brought some cases before municipal courts because they perceived a violation of the law; but most courts argued that this law did not apply to the forwarding firms because they only organised transport that was then conducted by road hauliers.[39]

The regulation was tightened by an emergency decree under Chancellor Brüning in October 1931. It stipulated that long-distance traffic by truck or bus should be made subject to approval by the *Reichsbahn*, and that minimum prices in road haulage for the two higher tariff classes for finished goods (A and B) were to be regulated and tied to the higher level of railway tariff.[40] These minimum prices, although intended to favour the *Reichsbahn*, can be also interpreted as a measure to stabilise the road haulage industry.

While in the USA the railways were considered monopolistic and the aim of railway regulation was to protect the public, railways in Europe were more widely perceived as serving the public interest. In this sense, German policy to protect the railway against motorised transport was an obvious measure to take. In addition, the consequences of the Versailles peace treaty made further protection necessary; the state needed to ensure that the *Reichsbahn* generated the 660 million Reichsmarks required under the Dawes plan.[41] In September 1930, the governing board of the *Reichsbahn* asked the *Reich*'s Minister of Transport to provide appropriate protection.[42] The *Reichbahn*'s dramatic drop in turnover during the world economic crisis from 1929 to 1933 put additional pressure

36 Hessisches Wirtschaftsarchiv Darmstadt, Abt. 6/1949.

37 *Reichsgesetzblatt*, 1925, vol. I, 319.

38 Protest resolution of the Saxonian Chambers of Commerce on 3 February 1926, Stadtarchiv Frankfurt, file IHK 854.

39 Deutsche Reichsbahngesellschaft. *Reichsbahn- und Kraftwagenverkehr*, 66. *Das Auto-Ferntransportgewerbe*, 1, 1930, 6.

40 'Dritte Verordnung des Reichspräsidenten zur Sicherung von Wirtschaft und Finanzen und zur Bekämpfung politischer Ausschreitungen vom 6. Oktober 1931', *Reichsgesetzblatt*, 1931, 558–77, here Kapitel V, Überlandverkehr mit Kraftfahrzeugen.

41 Mierzejewski, *The Most Valuable Asset of the Reich*, vol. 1, chapter 4.

42 See 39. Tagung des Verwaltungsrats (39th meeting of the advisory board), *Die Reichsbahn*, 6, 40, 1930, 1053.

on the government to find ways of safeguarding the railways' revenue.[43] Since long-distance road haulage was not in fact much of a competitor, the regulation brought about by the emergency decree was probably both disproportionate and unsuccessful: the world economic crisis was the fundamental problem, regulation something that the state introduced in order to be seen to be acting. In any case, the consequence was a crisis in government policy, with the two previously separate aims of regulating road haulage and stabilising the *Reichsbahn*'s finances now conjoined. On the other hand, the world economic crisis proved favourable for the *Reichsbahn*: it meant that a protectionist policy for the railways could be presented as measure necessary in the national interest.

However, the emergency decree did not achieve the desired reduction in competition between road and rail, since the regional authorities were unable to enforce the forwarding agencies' adherence to the regulated tariffs (*Reichskraftwagentarif*).[44] The conflict between the *Reichsbahn* and independent road haulage companies increased after the *Reichsbahn* took over the forwarding agency Schenker, intending to found a monopoly-like railway forwarding agency. In the summer of 1931 the magazine of the German association of forwarders published special editions arguing against this 'monopoly agreement'.[45] The *Reichsbahn* intensified the conflict by using the rail transport contract (*Bahnspeditionsvertrag*) on 1 March 1932 to tie some 3,000 trucking companies into its operations and to undercut the prices of the independent haulers.[46] Like the railways in the USA, the *Reichsbahn* offered integrated rail-truck operations as a means of competing.[47]

In 1933, the forwarding associations started a 'work committee against traffic monopoly' in Berlin and addressed urgent petitions against the pricing policy of the *Reichsbahn* to the Minister of Transport and to Hitler. They warned that the drift of transport policy risked threatening middle-class interests.[48]

---

43 The turnover of the Reichsbahn amounted to 5.3 billion RM in 1929. It dropped to 3.8 billion RM in 1931 and to 3.5 billion RM in 1933, see: 'Die Reichsbahn im Jahre 1933', 4. In the 1920s the exchange rate was 1 US-Dollar to 4.20 RM.

44 'Besprechung im Reichsverkehrsministerium zum Entwurf des Gesetzes über den Güterfernverkehr mit Kraftfahrzeugen am 16.4.1935 (Meeting in the transport administration concerning the long haulage act on 16 April 1935)', in Hans Günther Hockerts, ed., *Akten der Reichskanzlei, Regierung Hitler 1933–1945*, vol. II: *1934/1935* (Munich 1999), 532.

45 Bayrisches Wirtschaftsarchiv München, K9/1486.

46 Paul Beck, 'Der Bahnspeditionsvertrag und das Abkommen mit den Auftragsspediteuren', *Die Reichsbahn*, 8, 1932, 1142–7.

47 For the US case see Churella, 'Delivery to the Customer's Door'.

48 'Telegramm des Arbeitsausschusses an Hitler vom 18. Februar 1933 (Telegram of the working committee to Hitler on 18 February 1933)', *Der Kraftwagen-Güterverkehr*, 2, 4, 1933, 3. Letter of the top representatives of the transportation trade to the minister of traffic on 8 March 1933 and letter of the association of Germans forwarders to the chancelor on 23 March 1933, Bayrisches Wirtschaftsarchiv, K9/1486. See also the protest letters of

On 16 March 1933, Hitler summoned the General Director of the *Deutsche Reichsbahngesellschaft*, Julius Dorpmüller, to the Chancellery for a lecture on competition between the *Reichsbahn* and road haulage.[49] Dorpmüller supported the arguments in the memorandum of the *Reichsbahn*, stating that it would make sense macro-economically to subsidise the transport of bulk goods by rail with revenue from the dispatch of high-value goods, and to eliminate price competition with the independent forwarding agencies that mainly transported valuable goods.[50] Moreover, due to the rules of the Rail Transport Ordinance (*Eisenbahnverkehrsordnung*), the *Reichsbahn* was obliged to transport all goods and to treat all traders equally, and was therefore disadvantaged by comparison with independent forwarding agencies, which could choose to take only profitable contracts. Hitler opposed Dorpmüller, saying that the *Reichsbahn* would have to accept that trucks would increasingly transport high-value goods since the truck offered the advantages of door-to-door traffic. Promotion of road haulage was also desirable in order to ensure the *Reich* would have enough vehicles for warfare and to enable technical progress in motor construction. As a consequence, the *Reichsbahn* could not be allowed to let truck traffic wither. Initially, Hitler required the *Reichsbahn* to take over the transport of freight with trucks as a monopoly; in this he was following the idea of a large centralised transport company proposed in the *Reichsbahn*'s 1930 memorandum.[51] However, he emphasised that the *Reichsbahn* should use road haulage instead of continuing to operate unprofitable railway lines – a development that was considered 'self-motorisation', and was also found in Great Britain and in the USA.[52]

The transport administration drafted a Bill that aimed to create a monopoly of long-distance haulage controlled by the *Reichsbahn* and which would satisfy the military. The latter saw an advantage in a monopoly since it would only have

documents 64 and 95 in Konrad Repgen, ed., *Akten der Reichskanzlei, Regierung Hitler 1933–1945*, part I: *1933/34*, 2 vols (Boppard am Rhein 1983), vol. 1, 225 and 329.

49 'Vermerk des Oberregierungsrats Willuhn über einen Vortrag des Generaldirektors der Deutschen Reichsbahngesellschaft zur Frage des Wettbewerbs zwischen Reichsbahn und Kraftverkehr am 16.3.1933 (Report of Willuhn on the lecture of Dorpmüller on 16 March 1933)', in Repgen, *Akten der Reichskanzlei*, 225–31.

50 See Deutsche Reichsbahngesellschaft. *Reichsbahn- und Kraftwagenverkehr*, 64.

51 'Vermerk des Oberregierungsrats Willuhn über einen Vortrag des Generaldirektors der Deutschen Reichsbahngesellschaft zur Frage des Wettbewerbs zwischen Reichsbahn und Kraftverkehr am 16. März 1933 (Report of Willuhn on the lecture of Dorpmüller on 16 March 1933)', in Repgen. *Akten der Reichskanzlei*, 229.

52 See the report 'Lastkraftwagen in den USA', *Archiv für Eisenbahnwesen*, 48, 1925, 424, and Karl Busemann, 'Schiene und Landstrasse', *Die Autobahn*, 1, 11, 1932, 3–4, here 4. See also Rudolf Meyer, 'Die Reichsbahn auf Schiene und Strasse!', *Die Reichsbahn*, 10, 25, 1934, 607–9. For the policy of motorisation of the railway see Mierzejewski, *The Most Valuable Asset of the Reich*, vol. 2, chapter 2.

to deal with one organisation in the event of war.[53] In anticipation of this law, as early as July 1933 the transport administration stopped issuing concessions for commercial road hauliers.[54] Yet right up until the ratification of the 1935 law, associations of the automobile industry and of truck-forwarding companies tried to ward off the anticipated restrictions on commercial long-distance haulage and the *Reichsbahn*'s impending monopoly.[55] It is a sign of how little transport policy was brought into line with the Nazi regime prior to 1934 that in January that year the association of the German truck and forwarding companies (the *Reichsverband des gewerblichen Kraftverkehrs und der Fuhrbetriebe Deutschlands e.V.*) was able to organise public demonstrations against the *Reichsbahn*'s monopoly and the Schenker treaty in Dortmund, Duisburg, Cologne and Mannheim.[56] However, the public effect of these demonstrations was limited, since a free press and open debates in Parliament no longer existed. Out of the public eye, Fritz Todt, the Inspector General for German Roadways and responsible for the construction of *Autobahnen*, was resisting the *Reichsbahn*'s plans: he pursued the objective of concentrating road transport on the motorways that were to be built, and refused to allow this potential traffic to fall within the *Reichsbahn*'s monopoly.

The long-distance haulage law of 1935 contained very restrictive measures against truck entrepreneurs, but did not give the *Reichsbahn* its desired monopoly, thanks to the objections of the forwarding associations and Todt.[57] They successfully claimed that a total elimination of competition would be harmful for economic and technical development – an argument with which Hitler agreed.[58] Yet for the first time in Germany, market access to long-distance road haulage became regulated, and the independent haulers were required to apply for registration with the *Reichs-Kraftwagen-Betriebsverband* (RKB) (Council of Truck Operators), which tied tariffs to the railways' high rates. Supervision by the transport administration would prevent tariffs being undercut. However long-distance haulage companies were relieved from the elementary business functions of issuing invoices and handling

[53] Christopher Kopper, 'Modernität oder Scheinmodernität nationalsozialistischer Herrschaft – Das Beispiel der Verkehrspolitik', in Christian Jansen, Lutz Niethammer and Bernd Weisbrod, eds, *Von der Aufgabe der Freiheit. Festschrift für Hans Mommsen* (Berlin 1995), 399–411, here 401.

[54] Rohde, *Transportmodernisierung*, 199.

[55] Ibid., 197–224. Kopper, 'Modernität', 403.

[56] Without author, *Der Kraftwagen-Güterverkehr*, 3, 2, 1934, 3. This journal was the organ of Gedekra Reichsverbandes.

[57] 'Gesetz über den Güterfernverkehr mit Kraftfahrzeugen vom 26. Juni 1935', *Reichsgesetzblatt*, 1935, vol. I, 788–93, and 'Verordnung zur Durchführung des Gesetzes über den Güterfernverkehr mit Kraftfahrzeugen vom 26. Juni 1935', *Reichsgesetzblatt*, 1936, vol. I, 320–26.

[58] 'Besprechung im Reichsverkehrsministerium zum Entwurf des Gesetzes über den Güterfernverkehr mit Kraftfahrzeugen am 16. April 1935 (Meeting in the transport administration concerning the long-haulage act) vom 16 April 1935', in Hockerts, *Akten der Reichskanzlei*, 531–5. See also Kopper. 'Modernität', 404.

payments, which were transferred to the RKB.[59] For this reason, evasion of set freight tariffs was considerably reduced. Moreover, the RKB strictly controlled the registration of operators and the number of licensed trucks was severely limited. By bringing road hauliers within the control of the RKB, truck traffic was effectively integrated into the wider economic and social policies of the Nazi state: these limited the economic freedom of the middle class by requiring the licensing of trades and professions through compulsory membership of new chambers. Such measures were partly connected with the aim of excluding political enemies and, from 1936, with that of focusing business activity on large-scale enterprises that would produce weapons within the framework of the Four-Year Plan.[60]

Although the president of the *Reichsbahn*, Julius Dorpmüller, could have been satisfied with the weakened position of long-distance road haulage, he continued the fight against the truck. When he became Minister of Transport in 1937, he reintegrated the *Reichsbahn* as a state-run company into his administration. The number of trucks licensed for long-distance haulage decreased from an all-time high of 13,400 in 1933 to 11,400 in 1937, falling even below the number of 11,500 in 1932. This drop occurred despite the higher demand for transport services caused by rearmament, demonstrating deep contradictions within the Nazi transport policy.[61] There was no attempt to exploit the truck as a highly productive means of transport for industrial logistics, particularly in light of the developing *Autobahn* network which, since 1936, had provided high-performance roads. The plans by the promoters of *Autobahn* construction to use the *Autobahnen* for freight traffic failed due to the resistance of the transportation administration, which was responsible for licensing truck traffic.[62] As a result of this restrictive transport policy, German economy experienced severe transport bottlenecks in the years 1937 and 1938, when fortifications at the French border were being built, requiring large volumes of material.[63] Martin Bormann, Hitler's secretary, exerted pressure on the transportation administration to supply more licences for trucks.[64]

The expansion of long-haul services was impeded despite its being only weak competition for the railway. In 1938, long-haul road services accounted for 2.8 billion tons-kilometres, compared with 76 billion tons-kilometres for the railway.

59 'Gesetz über den Güterfernverkehr mit Kraftfahrzeugen', *Reichsgesetzblatt*, 1935, vol. I, 788–93.

60 Ludolf Herbst, *Der Totale Krieg und die Ordnung der Wirtschaft* (Stuttgart 1985), and Heinrich August Winkler, 'Der entbehrliche. Stand. Zur Mittelstandspolitik im "Dritten Reich"', *Archiv für Sozialgeschichte*, 17, 1977, 1–40.

61 Wilhelm Scholz, 'Die Entwicklung des Kraftfahrzeugbestandes im gewerblichen Güterfernverkehr', *Die Strasse*, 5, 4, 1938, 106–8, here 106.

62 Oswald Lutz, '3000 Kilometer Reichsautobahn für den gewerblichen Kraftverkehr', *Die Strasse*, 5, 24, 1938, 772–3, here 772. Also Mellerowicz. 'Autobahnen und Kraftverkehrswirtschaft', 368–73.

63 Rohde, *Transportmodernisierung*, 281.

64 Letter of Bormann to Dorpmüller on 19 May 1938, Bundesarchiv R5, 8126. Bormann wrote that Hitler expects 60,000 more trucks.

The suppression of long-haul road services impeded the development of a powerful logistics industry serving the division of labour among the industrial branches. Industrial and trading companies substituted the scarce capacity of long-haul services with own-account transport. But this mode was more costly the longer the distance to the customer since the truck had no back-haul. On the other hand, the forwarders were tied to the high prices of the railway and they could not give the price advantages of their business model to their customers. So state regulation made truck transport far more expensive than under market conditions, leading to a loss in gross national product.

Conclusion

This chapter shows that the early period of road haulage in Germany mainly focused on own-account transport, providing new business models for delivery. In contrast, the evolution of long-distance haulage, with only about 11,000 heavy-weight trucks, was stymied by the intervention of the *Reichsbahn*, underpinned by state regulation of the financially weak transport industry combined with its protection of the *Reichsbahn* required by the Dawes Plan. Between 1925 to 1929, when it was allowed to flourish, long-distance road haulage was not able to reveal its full potential as a logistics provider for manufacturing industry. Partly for these reasons, traffic policy in the 1930s failed to exploit the potential of long-distance haulage: the principal focus of policy on overcoming economic crisis and rearmament was skilfully exploited by the *Reichsbahn* to maintain its dominance. The development of long-distance haulage was also hindered by the wider policies of the Nazi dictatorship.

So far, historians have given scant attention to the fact that between 1925 and 1929 the competition between the *Reichsbahn* and road hauliers was mostly marginal and that the world economic crisis was the fundamental reason for the railways' faltering finances. The *Reichsbahn*'s contemporary claim that its losses were due to competition with the truck should therefore be interpreted as rhetoric intended to secure its monopoly of freight traffic. This was to a large extent achieved as a consequence of the road haulage law (*Güterkraftverkehrsgesetz*) of 1935. As a political entity, road haulage was strikingly weak: despite numerous resolutions against the *Reichsbahn*'s monopoly made by the industry's associations and Chambers of Commerce, the *Reichsbahn* was largely able to achieve its goals.

During the Nazi period, traffic policy was characterised by an unsystematic coexistence of different, often opposed, interests, and a lack of strategic planning. This meant that it was not until 1938 that due recognition was given to the importance of having a large civilian fleet of heavy trucks for the purpose of war. The *Reichsbahn* took advantage of this situation, and was able to continue to marginalise long-distance road haulage up to the transport crisis of 1938. Beginning in 1931, the railway's dominant position hindered the emergence of a powerful forwarding sector, an essential element of the slowly developing 'tertiary sector' of services. This was to have long-term consequences, weakening the service sector in the Federal Republic of Germany since 1949 right up to the beginning of the deregulation of road haulage in the 1980s.

References

a) Anonymous articles, author not known

'Besprechung im Reichsverkehrsministerium zum Entwurf des Gesetzes über den Güterfernverkehr mit Kraftfahrzeugen am 16.4.1935 (Meeting in the transport administration concerning the long-haulage act) vom 16 April 1935', in Hans Günther Hockerts, ed., *Akten der Reichskanzlei, Regierung Hitler 1933–1945*, vol. II: *1934/1935* (Munich 1999), 531–5.

'Gesetz über den Güterfernverkehr mit Kraftfahrzeugen vom 26. Juni 1935', *Reichsgesetzblatt*, 1935, vol. I, 788–93.

'Gesetz über den Übergang der Eisenbahnen auf das Reich vom 30. April 1920 (Act to unite the German state railways from on 30 April 1920)', *Reichsgesetzblatt*, 1920, vol. I, 773–90.

Der Kraftwagen-Güterverkehr, 3, nr. 2, 1934.

'Lastkraftwagen in den USA', *Archiv für Eisenbahnwesen*, 48, 1925, 424.

'Der Lastkraftwagen und die Rheinlande', *ADAC-Motorwelt*, 27, nr. 27, 1930, 9–10.

'Die Reichsbahn im Jahre 1933', *Die Reichsbahn*, 10, nr. 1, 1934, 4.

'39. Sitzung des Verwaltungsrats (39th meeting of the advisory board)', *Die Reichsbahn*, 6, nr. 40, 1930, 1053.

'Telegramm des Arbeitsausschusses an Hitler vom 18.2.1933 (Telegram of the working committee to Hitler on 18 February 1933)', *Der Kraftwagen-Güterverkehr*, 2, nr. 4, 1933, 3.

'Dritte Verordnung des Reichspräsidenten zur Sicherung von Wirtschaft und Finanzen und zur Bekämpfung politischer Ausschreitungen on 6. October 1931', *Reichsgesetzblatt*, 1931, 558–77.

'Verordnung zur Durchführung des Gesetzes über den Güterfernverkehr mit Kraftfahrzeugen vom 26. Juni 1935', *Reichsgesetzblatt*, 1936, vol. I, 320–26.

b) Named articles and monographs

Baumann, Hans, *Deutsches Verkehrsbuch* (Berlin 1931).

Beck, Paul, 'Der Bahnspeditionsvertrag und das Abkommen mit den Auftragsspediteuren', *Die Reichsbahn*, 8, 1932, 1142–7.

Busemann, Karl, 'Schiene und Landstrasse', *Die Autobahn*, vol. 1, nr. 11, 1932, 3–4.

Chandler, D. Alfred, *Giant Enterprise* (New York 1964).

Childs, R. William, *Trucking and the Public Interest* (Knoxville, TN 1986).

Churella, J. Albert, 'Delivery to the Customer's Door: Efficiency, Regulatory Policy, and Integrated Rail-Truck Operations 1900–1938', *Enterprise & Society*, 10, nr. 1, 2009, 98–132.

Cohausz, Otto, 'Der französisch-deutsche Eisenbahnkrieg im Ruhrgebiet 1923', *Jahrbuch für Eisenbahngeschichte*, 6, 1973, 5–25.

Deutsche Reichsbahngesellschaft, ed., *Reichsbahn- und Kraftwagenverkehr* (Berlin 1930).

Deutscher Industrie- und Handelstag, ed., *Eisenbahn und Kraftwagen* (Berlin 1930).

Filarski, Ruud, *The Rise and Decline of Transport Systems. Changes in a Historical Context* (Rotterdam 2004).

Hamilton, Shane, 'The Populist Appeal of Deregulation: Independent Truckers and the Politics of Free Enterprise, 1935–1980', *Enterprise & Society*, 10, nr. 1, 2009, 137–77.

Herbst, Ludolf, *Der Totale Krieg und die Ordnung der Wirtschaft* (Stuttgart 1985).

Hockerts, Hans Günther, ed., *Akten der Reichskanzlei, Regierung Hitler 1933–1945*, vol. II: *1934/1935* (Munich 1999).

Jones, Joseph, *The Politics of Transport in Twentieth-Century France* (Kingston and Montreal 1984).

Kirchberg, Peter, 'Technik und Verkehrswirksamkeit der Lastkraftwagen in Deutschland bis zum Ende der 1930er Jahre', in Harry Niemann and Armin Hermann, eds, *100 Jahre LKW. Geschichte und Zukunft des Nutzfahrzeuges* (Stuttgart 1997), 16–40.

Kopper, Christopher, 'Modernität oder Scheinmodernität nationalsozialistischer Herrschaft – Das Beispiel der Verkehrspolitik', in Christian Jansen, Lutz Niethammer and Bernd Weisbrod, eds, *Von der Aufgabe der Freiheit. Festschrift für Hans Mommsen* (Berlin 1995), 399–411.

Kunz, Andreas, 'The economic performance of inland navigation in Germany, 1835–1935: a reassessment of traffic flows', in Andreas Kunz and John Armstrong, eds, *Inland Navigation and Economic Development in Nineteenth Century Europe* (Mainz 1995), 47–78.

Lippert, Frank, *Lastkraftwagenverkehr und Rationalisierung in der Weimarer Republik* (Frankfurt am Main und New York 1999).

Lutz, Oswald, '3000 Kilometer Reichsautobahn für den gewerblichen Kraftverkehr', *Die Strasse*, 5, nr. 24, 1938, 772–3.

Mellerowicz, Karl, 'Autobahnen und Kraftverkehrswirtschaft', *Die Autobahn*, 2, nr. 9, 1934, 368–73.

Mellerowicz, Karl, 'Der Stand des gewerblichen Güterfernverkehrs', *Die Strasse*, 2, nr. 5, 1935, 143–7.

Merkert, Emil, *Der Lastwagenverkehr seit dem Krieg, insbesondere sein Wettbewerb und seine Zusammenarbeit mit den Schienenbahnen* (Berlin 1926).

Merki, Christoph, *Der holprige Siegeszug des Automobils 1895–1930: Zur Motorisierung des Straßenverkehrs in Frankreich, Deutschland und der Schweiz* (Vienna 2002).

Meyer, Rudolf, 'Die Reichsbahn auf Schiene und Strasse!', *Die Reichsbahn*, 10, nr. 25, 1934, 607–9.

Mierzejewski, Alfred, *The Most Valuable Asset of the Reich: a History of the German National Railway*, 2 vols (Chapel Hill, NC 1999 and 2000).

Novy, Klaus and Prinz, Michael, *Illustrierte Geschichte der Gemeinwirtschaft* (Bonn 1985).

Repgen, Konrad, ed., *Akten der Reichskanzlei, Regierung Hitler 1933–1945*, part I: *1933/34*, 2 vols (Boppard am Rhein 1983).

Rohde, Heidi, *Transportmodernisierung oder Verkehrsbewirtschaftung?* (Frankfurt am Main and New York 1999).

Rose, Mark H., Seely, Bruce E. and Barrett, Paul, *The Best Transportation System in the World: Railroads, Trucks, Airlines, and American Public Policy in the Twentieth Century* (Columbus, OH 2006).

Schipper, Frank, *Driving Europe – Building Europe on Roads in the Twentieth Century* (Amsterdam 2008).

Scholz, Wilhelm, 'Die Entwicklung des Kraftfahrzeugbestandes im gewerblichen Güterfernverkehr', *Die Strasse*, 5, nr. 4, 1938, 106–8.

Scott, Peter, 'British Railways and the Challenge from Road Haulage: 1919–39', *Twentieth Century British History*, 13, nr. 2, 2002, 101–20.

Statistisches Amt, ed., *Statistisches Jahrbuch für das Deutsche Reich 1929*, vol. 48 (Berlin 1929).

Statistisches Amt, ed., *Statistisches Jahrbuch für das Deutsche Reich 1933*, vol. 52 (Berlin 1933).

Vahrenkamp, Richard, *The Logistic Revolution – The Rise of Logistics in the Mass Consumption Society* (Cologne 2012).

Winkler, Heinrich August, 'Der entbehrliche. Stand. Zur Mittelstandspolitik im "Dritten Reich"', *Archiv für Sozialgeschichte*, 17, 1977, 1–40.

Wohl, Paul, and Albitreccia, A., *Road and Rail in Forty Countries. Report Prepared for The International Chamber of Commerce London* (Oxford 1935).

Zatsch, Angela, *Staatsmacht und Motorisierung am Morgen des Automobilzeitalters* (Konstanz 1993).

Chapter 7
Road-Rail Competition in France in the 1930s: from a Railway Perspective

Bruno Carrière

The first reflex when addressing the issue of competition between the two modes in France in the 1930s is to describe it simply as brutal confrontation, the revenge of road over rail, with road transport and the advent of the motor car symbolising all that is modern and desirable and rail a debt-ridden relic from a bygone era unable to adapt to the times. Obviously this description is a vast over-simplification and far too superficial to be true. At the beginning of the twentieth century, relations between the 'new' road transport and rail were far from confrontational and tended on the whole to be cordial, each recognising the other's welcome complementarities. By replacing horse-drawn carriages, motor vehicles were able to take up where railway lines left off, giving rail access to places hitherto beyond its reach and a chance to modernise its operations. In return, trains were helpful to motor vehicles by creating traffic flows and entering into official partnership agreements.

While motor vehicles may have truly come into their own during the First World War, the big private railway companies and state-owned networks, true to their pre-war policy, continued to use the roads to their own ends to develop their tourist services and, in a new departure, bail them out on secondary lines by replacing loss-making services virtually on the hoof.

It was only at the end of the 1920s that the railways finally woke up to the danger represented by the roads. A slight economic downturn was enough to spark the first serious cases of competition from the latest generation of 'heavy goods vehicles', that is, lorries equipped with low-pressure tyres, heavy-duty diesel oil engines. The railways blamed this budding competition on the enviable position of the roads, unburdened by the many restrictions and obligations they themselves had to endure. With no hope of rapid intervention on the part of the public authorities to achieve a fairer balance between the rights and duties of road and rail, the railways decided to take matters into their own hands by setting up their own road subsidiaries, while being constantly careful not to engage in direct conflict with the sector by continuing to treat road operators as privileged partners.

This policy began, however, to come apart at the seams at the time of the Great Depression, the first effects of which were felt in France at the end of 1930. As the economic crisis hit the automobile industry, manufacturers shifted their production from private cars towards the seemingly more promising bus and lorry sector, where sales had been made easier with the widespread extension of credit facilities. This sparked a proliferation in the number of road haulage companies, which, with their creditors breathing down their necks, often resorted to price-cutting to stay in business. This sudden shift from gentlemanly to cut-throat competition was to have a disastrous effect on the bottom-line results of the railways, the first victims of their rivals' commercial practices, in particular that of 'creaming off' the best for themselves, in other words the smaller, higher value goods, and leaving the bigger, less valuable products to rail. In addition, road hauliers, who since 1928 had joined forces in a powerful union lobby, had no compunction in using their new powers to urge the public authorities to stamp on the initiatives of the railways' road subsidiaries. They were backed up by manufacturers, and some of which had set up their own transport companies.

Under fire from their critics and other, frankly speaking unfair, attacks on their disastrous management, the railway companies changed their approach, asking instead for greater freedom of movement to enable them to counter competition more effectively, and a fairer split among traffic flows. The response to the first of these demands was the so-called 'Paganon' amendment to the state-railway agreement of 1921, which sparked a thorough overhaul of their working methods and brought a plethora of administrative, technical and commercial innovations.[1] This is, however, a different subject and it is inappropriate to expand on it here.[2] The second demand, namely coordination of shipments between rail and road on the basis of 'agreements' freely negotiated between carriers, failed to achieve the desired results. A first rail-road committee that met in 1932 was almost immediately abandoned by the road hauliers, who sensed it to be nothing more than a frontispiece for the railways that had prompted its creation. A second attempt, this time at the instigation of the public authorities, made little progress before being 'put on ice' in 1936, following accusations that it had failed to take account of the needs of the local communities and users. Weary of the whole business, the Popular Front (*Front populaire*) governments decided to impose authoritarian and 'regulated' coordination. But, with the outbreak of war, the process had to be put on the back-burner until after the hostilities ceased.

Cars, a Welcome Backstop

The big French railway companies had always kept a close eye on the development of automobiles. They had sent observers to the various 'heavy goods vehicle' contests regularly organised by the French Automobile Club since 1897, a sure sign of their interest in this emerging mode of transport. Not content just to sit back and watch the coach and lorry builders fight it out among themselves,

---

1 The 'Paganon' amendment was named after the Minister of Public Works Joseph Paganon (1880–1937) who led the ministry from 1933 to 1935.

2 See for instance Joseph Jones, *The Politics of Transport in Twentieth-Century France* (Montreal 1984), 45.

the railways soon launched some experiments of their own. For example, the *Compagnie du chemin de fer du Nord* (Nord) which, in 1906, launched a service using Purrey-type steam lorries to supply coal to the Paris premises of the Public Hospital Administration, *Assistance Publique* from its depot at La Chapelle. All in all they transported 51,000 tonnes per year. Ironically, the lorry drivers were selected from the team at La Chapelle station by taking those who 'knew how to handle a hammer and file or had seen agricultural machines at work'.[3]

For its part, the *Compagnie des chemins de fer de Paris-Lyon-Méditerranée* (PLM) gave its tacit blessing to private operators prepared to offer bus services from its stations. Some of the first were Joseph Magnat and Louis Debon who, in 1906, were authorised by PLM to offer onward bus services from Brides to Pralognan, albeit unsubsidised.[4] Doubtless lured by the popularity of this new type of transport and its many advantages, PLM did not hesitate in going one step further and subsidising its first bus services in 1909 from Grasse to Thorenc and 1910 from Saint-Flour to Pierrefort. That same year, it also set the foundations for its famous *Route des Alpes*, the precursor of its grand coach tours, and urged its correspondents to follow suit: 'By increasing existing or introducing new subsidies, we have helped to convert horse buses into motor bus services, considering that there is much to be done along these lines'.[5] Shortly before the Second World War, nearly 33 per cent of all services connecting with PLM trains, that is, 46 out of a total of 140, were operated using motor buses.

As for the state-owned *Réseau Ouest-État* (state network), in 1911 it acquired three four-seater limousine coupés and three six-seater omnibuses to provide door-to-door passenger services in Paris and its suburbs alongside its horse buses.[6] It also began to develop an interest in using motor vehicles, in districts just outside Paris, for 'ordinary' or 'express' goods deliveries. After a number of successful tests, the following year it purchased 15 Panhard-Levassor and Delahaye delivery vans and five Berliet 'lorries' to add to its fleet of 580 horse-drawn vehicles. Just before the First World War, *Ouest-Etat* may admittedly still only have had a modest collection of these road vehicles – seven coupés, five omnibuses, 21 vans and 13 lorries – but its interest in these new-fangled machines was clear.

---

3 Chambelin, 'Note sur l'emploi des camions automobiles à la livraison de la houille, à domicile, dans Paris (Memorandum on the use of motor lorries for domestic coal deliveries in Paris)', *Revue générale des chemins de fer*, 31 March 1908, 211–15.

4 Joseph Magnat and Louis Debon were associated since 1893 in the manufacture of cycles and motor vehicles in Grenoble. *Archives nationales du monde du travail* (National Labour Archives, ANMT), Compagnie du Paris-Lyon-Méditerranée (PLM), 77 AQ 200, Minutes of the Board meeting on 13 July 1906. Brides-les-Bains was at the time the terminus of a tram originating at the PLM station of Moutiers-Salins.

5 PLM, Board of Directors' report made to the General Assembly of Shareholders (GAS) on 14 April 1912, printed report published by Paul Dupont, 137 pages.

6 The French State had bought up the bankrupt Western Company in 1908 and added it to its previous state-owned small network.

Figure 7.1 PLM company's subcontractors waiting for engagement, 1934

Source: Coll. AHICF (Le Bulletin PLM, no. 34, July 1934, p. 98).

In the Interwar period, the PLM company's subcontractors in charge of home delivery went for modernisation, trading their horse drawn carts for lorries.

In the early days of the automobile, rather than treating it with disdain, the big railway companies were quick to build it into their strategies. As proof of this contention, the Deputy Head of Operations at PLM, Auguste Pourcel, addressed the assembled gathering of manufacturers and operators at the First National Congress on Public Transport by Motor Vehicle on the 'general organisation of well-managed permanent and seasonal services' on the basis of PLM's experience with the *Route des Alpes*.[7] There were even those who thought that road and rail could work more closely together, for example D. Duaner, a columnist in the engineering journal *Génie civil*, who, in 1912, expressed his regret at the 'general ignorance of the possible uses of these forms of transport, which should not be seen as rivals to the railways but as ancillary service providers capable of taking over where rail services are insufficient or impossible'. To underscore his point, he highlighted the trend towards lorries capable of carrying 3.5 tonne payloads 'since, in three trips, they can clear the load of an ordinary railway wagon, while remaining sufficiently economical on the many occasions when they operate with less than maximum loads'.[8]

That was impossible with a five-tonne vehicle. For motor vehicles the war was a blessing in disguise, since it gave them the chance to develop beyond all imaginings by demonstrating their speed and capacity. Examples for this were the Marne taxis in 1914 and the trucks on the 'Sacred Way', that is, *Voie Sacrée*, during the Battle of Verdun in 1916. In addition, from 1920, in the wake of demobilisation, thousands of lorries poured on to the roads, in particular the 30,000 vehicles sold off at cut-rate prices by the American Expeditionary Forces, and an equivalent number of qualified drivers, to the great distress of the manufacturers who, having boosted their production capacities, were now faced with an abruptly shrinking market. Berliet, to name but one of them, found itself on the brink of bankruptcy. Yet this interlude was to prove the opportunity for the heavy goods vehicle industry to give itself a new lease of life. According to G. Delanghe, another columnist in the *Génie civil*, in an article published at the time of the 1924 Automobile Show, 'the crisis was nearing its end; manufacturers with time on their hands had used it wisely to conduct thorough research and prepare more sophisticated vehicles, far better than their wartime models'.[9]

In practice, the result was a proliferation of road passenger and goods services, in some cases subsidised by the state and/or the local authorities, always ready to pander to the wishes of their electorate. In 1930 there were an estimated

---

7 Lucien Périssé, 'Ier Congrès national des transports en commun par automobiles sur route, Paris, 18 au 20 décembre 1912 (1st national congress of public transport by motor vehicle – Paris, 18 to 20 December 1912)', *Le Génie civil* of 28 December 1912.

8 D. Duaner, 'Les véhicules industriels au Salon de l'Automobile à Paris, en 1912 (Industrial vehicles at the Paris Motor Show in 1912)', *Le Génie civil* of 21 December 1912.

9 G. Delanghe, 'XIXe Salon de l'automobile. Section des véhicules industriels, 22–31 octobre 1924 (19th Motor Show. Industrial vehicles section, 22–31 October 1924)', *Le Génie civil*, of 22 November 1924.

20,000 road transport companies on the market, mostly small businesses whose development was facilitated by lack of regulations, the minimal investment needed and the growing availability of loans. There was, however, one exception, namely the *Société générale des transports départementaux* (SGTD) founded in 1919 for the organisation and operation of public road transport services, which, by 1924 was serving some 7,000 kilometres of regular lines in 44 French *départements*.[10] But even these road services were still, for the most part, complementary to rail. And while it is true that, in 1921, the *Compagnie du Nord* did talk of the need for a 'fair and rational distribution of traffic' between the two modes of transport, there was as yet no mention of open warfare.[11]

On the contrary, the big railway companies, whose passenger and goods services had never been so flourishing, had no qualms in harnessing the roads to their own ends. As early as in 1918, in an effort to modernise its collection and delivery operations, *Compagnie des chemins de fer de Paris à Orléans* (PO) began to give 'serious thought to ways of adopting automobile traction for such services'.[12] The first practical result of these efforts was the acquisition of 20 tractors and 50 trailers for ordinary (*petite vitesse*, PV) and express (*grande vitesse*, GV) delivery services from Paris-Ivry station, each unit replacing two horse-drawn pairs. In 1923, the *Compagnie de l'Est* (Est) replaced the horse-drawn carriages reserved for passengers at its Paris station by motorcars. All the railways were at pains to urge companies offering connecting services to withdraw their horse-drawn vehicles at once and opt for road tourers instead, if they had not already done so.[13] Here again, PLM set the standard: 78 services over a total of 8,700 kilometres in 1923 (990,000 kilometres-vehicle, 150,200 passengers); 224 services over a total of 10,900 kilometres in 1929 (3,200,000 kilometres-vehicle, 324,000 passengers). In 1928, referring for the first time to the effects of road competition on the company's results, its managers made no bones about the benefits of these services:

> There is no denying the progress made in recent years in the development of motor vehicles and we have even taken advantage of this progress ourselves to improve our many coach operations, taking services on beyond our lines in

---

10 Subsidiary of the *Société anonyme des transports automobiles industriels et commerciaux* (SATAIC) founded in 1908. The SAT and the SGTD merged in 1971 to form the Générale de Transport and d'Industrie (named VIA GTI) which subsequently joined forces with Cariane to form Keolis in 2001.

11 After André Waru, member of the Board of the *Compagnie du Nord*, report made in 1921, quoted by François Caron, *Histoire des chemins de fer en France*, vol. 2: *1883–1937* (Paris 2005), 752.

12 De Lalande, 'Note sur le camionnage automobile pour chemin de fer (Memorandum on road haulage for the railways)', *Revue générale des chemins de fer*, 39, December 1920, 294–8.

13 PO from 1910 (Auvergne), *Compagnie des chemins de fer du Midi* (Midi) in 1913 (Pyrenees), *Compagnie des chemins de fer de l'Est* (Est) in 1922 (Vosges), and so on.

> a way beneficial to our traffic, and now cover a road network greater in length than our rail network.[14]

More significantly, the railway companies had no compunction in using buses to replace trains on heavily loss-making routes. PO was the first to move in this direction 'to avoid running little-used trains on certain lines', but also 'to improve links between places with no direct rail connections'.[15] In 1926, the following featured among the lines concerned: Busseau-sur-Creuse to Felletin, Quimper to Douarnenez-Tréboul, Saint-Nazaire to Le Croisic, Villefranche-sur-Cher to Romorantin, followed, in 1927, by the Evaux-les-Bains to Parsac-Gouzon line. PO's example was soon followed by other railways. In 1928, PLM introduced replacement bus services on its Carpentras-Avignon (from 15 May) and Cavaillon-Avignon (from 1 August) lines for each of two trains carrying only 'insignificant' parcels traffic, the cost of which was totally out of proportion to their earnings. The new services were subcontracted to one of PLM's official correspondents, Prosper Aubert, a garage owner in Avignon.[16] Buses were also sometimes a way of avoiding the need to put on extra trains. For example, with the closure of many minor tribunals and sub-prefectures creating new travel needs, in 1927 PLM launched a 'small number of bus services on local routes to offer the communities concerned new facilities, this being more economical than running new trains for such limited passenger flows'.[17]

From Replacement Services to Competition Between Modes: Railway Companies Enter the Road Business

The first replacement services, for which special permission had to be obtained, occurred during a period of economic depression linked to Raymond Poincaré's efforts to stabilise the franc. They also coincided with the first allusions to the effects of competition. An example of such allusions is to be found in the conclusions of the commission in charge of auditing the PLM accounts for 1926, in its report

---

14 PLM, GAS of 20 April 1928, Paris: Paul Dupont, 104 pages.

15 PO, GAS of 31 March 1927, Paris: Chaix, 101 pages, and PO, GAS of 22 March 1929, Paris: Chaix, 111 pages.

16 In an advertising insert in 1926, Prosper Aubert claimed to be a 'correspondent' of PLM and the Vaucluse Syndicat d'Initiative. His garage proposed the rental of very comfortable tyred cars and Alpine coaches (private collection, published in digital auction catalogue, 2012, see: http://www.delcampe.net/item.php?id=60514365&var=PLAN-D-AVIGNON-PUBLICITE-DU-GARAGE-PROSPER-AUBERT&language=F&sessionToken=sslLogin_e51682b07f6c9d2759723e75ef09e498, last accessed 25 April 2012).

17 PLM, GAS, 20 April 1928. The reference here is to the closure of 106 sub-prefectures on economic grounds on 10 September 1926, a part of the so-called 'Poincaré reform'). Raymond Poincaré (1860–1934), Prime Minister (President of Council) and Minister of Finance from 23 July 1926 to 11 November 1928, left his name to a financial reform which culminated in a 75 per cent devaluation of the Franc.

of 15 November 1927. After emphasising the excellent results obtained that year (revenues were in excess of expenditure for the first time since the signature of the 1921 agreement between the state and the railway companies in an attempt to reduce their debts), the commission expressed concern about the drop in traffic in 1927. In its opinion, the current national economic difficulties were not the only cause for this downturn:

> The strongly adverse effects of the (economic crisis; B.C.) on our traffic should not prevent us from discerning other reasons for the current trend, albeit modest at this stage, in particular the development of inland waterway shipping, air transport and motor vehicles. These latter are increasingly well adapted to business requirements, for French and foreign manufacturers, in vying to outdo each other, are doing everything they can to increase the comfort, durability and range of their cars, to reduce sales prices, oil and fuel consumption. These methodical efforts, all heading in the same direction, have not been in vain and their success is at our expense; progress and savings made to date are such that many long distance travellers and parcels shipments now journey by road.[18]

Having made its point, the Commission then goes on to say that the problem is not specific to PLM: 'Since the growing competition between rail and motor cars cannot be stopped, finding ways of living with it is one of the biggest challenges for the railways, and one now under serious consideration'.[19]

A view shared by the shareholders of *Compagnie du Midi*:

> We are well aware that one of the reasons for the drop in our traffic lies in competition from public road services. A number of pricing measures are under consideration to compensate for certain specific points. However, the only possible way we can see of resolving the problem overall would be close cooperation between rail and road, in which each would handle those traffics for which it is most suited, and which would, through harmonisation, enable the needs of the public to be best met, without useless sacrifice on the operators' part.[20]

'Harmonisation', the notion, was finally out in the open. In 1926, the Management Committee of the leading railway companies talked of the latent dangers and raised the problem of equal fiscal and legal treatment for road and rail.[21] Unlike the railway, road transport at the time was subject to minimal taxes and enjoyed

---

[18] Ibid.

[19] Ibid.

[20] Midi, GAS of 27 April 1928, Paris: Villain et Bar, 104 pages.

[21] This body, which was set up by the 1921 agreement, 'to ensure coordination among the different operations' (28 June 1921 agreement enforced by the law on 29 October 1921), was a gathering of directors of the big railway companies, where they could discuss matters of common interest.

complete commercial freedom, without the slightest public service obligation. These inequalities would only be partially eliminated in 1933 with the amendment to the 1921 agreement (see below).

In the meantime, the big railways imagined that the best way round the obstacle would be to set up ancillary road transport companies that they would both patronise and subsidise to protect themselves from the ambitions of the road companies. The idea was set out in a report drafted for the Management Committee in 1928 by Pourcel, then PLM's Deputy Chief Engineer, from which it is perfectly clear that the railways' intention was to 'annexe the motor vehicle to use it as a feeder, as a complement to their main business'.[22] The Ministry of Public Works, André Tardieu, subscribed to the proposal and urged the larger railways to adopt a practice perfectly justified in law, since under the concession agreement with the state and the legal practice, railway companies were entitled to create any services that were 'naturally complementary or ancillary to their main operations'.[23]

In the months and years that followed, a whole spate of railway-owned road companies came into existence: in 1928, SATOS (*Société auxiliaire de transports de l'Ouest and du Sud-Ouest*), SATE (*Société auxiliaire de transports automobiles de l'Est*), STAM (*Société des transports auxiliaires des chemins de fer du Midi*), STARN (*Société de transports auxiliaires de la région du Nord*), SATAL (*Société auxiliaire de transports d'Alsace et de Lorraine*); in 1929, TPLM (*Société auxiliaire de transports du réseau* PLM, which chose an abbreviated logo) and, in 1931, STAPO (*Société de transports auxiliaires du réseau Paris-Orléans*). Local railway and tram companies were invited to take a stake in these new enterprises. In the case of SATOS, for example, of a total capital of 12 million francs, one-third was put up by five local operators, and in the case of TPML (20 million francs) nine operators accounted for 25 per cent.[24] Faithful to its policy, PLM invited its

---

[22] ANMT, Nord Archives, 48 AQ 5975. Quoted by François Caron, *Histoire des chemins de fer en France*, vol. 2: *1883–1937* (Paris 2005), 753.

[23] Ibid., 754.

[24] For SATOS capital was put up by *Société générale des chemins de fer économiques*, *Société centrale de chemins de fer and de tramways*, *Société des chemins de fer du Calvados*, *Compagnie des chemins de fer des Côtes-du-Nord* (together totalling 2.5 million francs) and *Société générale des chemins de fer départementaux* (1.5 million francs). For TPML capital was put up by *Compagnie générale française des tramways* (1.2 million francs), *Compagnie des omnibus et tramways de Lyon* (1.09 million francs), *Compagnie des chemins de fer de la Provence* (1 million francs), *Compagnie des chemins de fer départementaux* (1 million francs), *Société générale des chemins de fer économiques* (200,000 francs), *Société grenobloise de tramways électriques* (100,000 francs), *Compagnie des chemins de fer de la Camargue* (50,000 francs), *Compagnie des chemins de fer de l'Est de Lyon* (50,000 francs), *Société des tramways de Grenoble à Chapareillon* (10,000 francs), making a total of 4.7 million francs. See Archives Nationales (AN), Dautry Archives, 307 AP 68, Board of the *Chemins de fer de l'État*, meeting on 18 July1930: SATOS operating results for 1929 and ANMT), *Compagnie du Paris-Lyon-Méditerranée* (PLM), 77 AQ 218, Minutes of the Board meeting on 31 May 1929, f 240.

subsidiary to work with its existing local correspondents. In 1932, it explained that, although TPLM 'organised and controlled' the motor vehicle services under its responsibility, it did not operate them directly but 'had them performed by local firms offering all the necessary guarantees, a solution deemed preferable in all respects'.[25] This approach, also adopted by the other railway companies, was the most cost-effective in that it enabled overheads to be kept to a minimum, and the most productive in that it turned companies that could have been working against the interests of the railways into companies working for them. The only exception was the state-owned railway, for although the state encouraged its road subsidiary to sign 'attractive contracts' with its local correspondents, it also allowed it to operate a number of services for itself. Indeed, in 1929, SATOS already had its own fleet of some 50 coaches.[26] The railways' ambitions were no longer simply to use road services to replace occasional loss-making trains. For example, the state expected SATOS to 'organise tourist excursions by road and operate regular bus lines between (its) stations and places without means of communication by creating fast links between centres poorly served by rail'.[27]

On 15 October 1928, just six months after its foundation, SATOS inaugurated a 'fast service' between Rennes and Caen – 330 kilometres covered in a little less than four hours by road, in other words half the time for the same journey by rail! – including halts in the main towns on the route and connections in Rennes, in both directions, with express trains between Bordeaux, Nantes and Cherbourg and vice versa. Other such services were to follow in 1929: Evreux to Rouen, Elbeuf to Louviers, Dinard to Rennes. The same year, trains were taken out of service and replaced by buses on secondary lines from Coutances to Régneville, Nogent to Courtalain and so on, whilst a *de luxe* coach service was placed in operation twice a week between Cherbourg and Paris (and back) for transatlantic customers anxious to reach the capital as fast as possible 'in the most comfortable and agreeable style'.[28]

STAPO, the role of which was 'to manage all motor vehicle services, tourist or otherwise, coordinate the operation of lines with those of the regional railways and offer forwarders door-to-door delivery solutions' on behalf of PO, was in a very similar situation to SATOS.[29] There is no evidence to show that it took over responsibility from SGTD for the 'fast service' inaugurated in 1928 between Poitiers and Limoges, a three-hour journey compared to the just over seven hours

---

25 PLM, GAS of 22 April 1932, Paris: Paul Dupont, 109 pages.

26 AN, Dautry Archives, 307 AP 68, Board of the *Chemins de fer de l'État*, meeting on 18 July1930: SATOS operating results for 1929.

27 *Chemins de fer de l'État*, Administrative account for 1928 (*Compte d'administration. Exercice 1928. Rapport sur l'exécution des opérations (...) pendant l'année 1928* (Paris 1929), 13.

28 Anonymous, 'Un nouveau service automobile: Paris-Cherbourg (A new bus route : Paris-Cherbourg)', *Revue illustrée des Chemins de fer de l'État*, 31 September 1929.

29 PO, GAS of 22 March 1932, Paris: Chaix, 127 pages.

by train, at its parent company's behest. By contrast, it is a known fact that the *départements* of Corrèze (from 1 January 1932) and Lot (from 1 April 1934) had no hesitation in placing it in charge of their bus and tram services. We also know that, to prevent the asparagus produced in the Loir-and-Cher from being shipped to Paris by road, in 1932, with the logistical backing of the *Société anonyme des transports industriels et commerciaux*, it launched a system of road collection based on three circuits centred on the stations of Blois and Mer, the actual number of rounds completed depending on demand.[30]

As for TPLM, its replacement bus services, parallel to the railway or offering feeder services, continued to expand through until 1937: 111 services covering 4,228 kilometres, just over 4.8 million passengers and 5,017 tonnes of freight. This was in line with the wishes of PLM, which made no secret of its desire to develop this type of service as fast as possible 'whenever it would enable (the company; B. C.) to achieve attractive savings or improve its loss-making services at little cost'.[31] In 1931, PLM even went as far as to request the authority to have TPLM carry out an experiment taking goods by road between Paris and Clermont-Ferrand to counter competition from two rival road hauliers. For its director, the time had come 'to operate freight vehicles on the roads under the PLM subsidiary label to show road hauliers that we are able to compete with them using similar weapons and thus have an effect on our rivals' morale'.[32]

But this request was rejected by the Minister of Public Works, who had to be consulted on any proposals for changes in the services provided by the railway companies. The results of the major railways' road subsidiaries were all the more remarkable in that the sector had been experiencing major difficulties since 1930 and the first effects of the Great Depression. Between 1928 and 1938, rail's share of goods traffic fell from 75.5 per cent to 53.2 per cent of all tonne-kilometres, while its share of passenger traffic went from 88.5 per cent to 72.2 per cent of all passenger-kilometres.[33] While it may have pierced the defences of the major railways, the Depression cannot be made to take all the blame. Conversely, there is no denying that the early 1930s marked a major breakthrough on the part of road traffic. In 1931, *Génie civil* reported that 'today (in France; B.C.) there are some 15 times more saloon cars and 85 times more industrial road vehicles than before the war'.[34]

---

30 On 21 May, 12 rounds were made for a total of 67 tonnes of asparagus.

31 PLM, GAS of 24 April 1931, Paris: Paul Dupont, 115 pages.

32 ANMT, PLM, 77 AQ 220, meeting on 7 August 1931.

33 Jean-Claude Toutain, *Les transports en France de 1830 à 1965* (Transport in France from 1830 to 1965), *Économies and sociétés, Série AF, Histoire quantitative de l'économie française*, vol. 9 (Paris 1967), 250. At the same time, road's share rose from 11.1 per cent to 24.7 per cent of all goods transported and from 11.5 per cent to 27.8 per cent of all passengers travels.

34 G. Delanghe, 'Le XXVe Salon de l'automobile. Voitures de tourisme, Paris, 1–11 August 1931 (The 25th Motor Show Sedan vehicles, Paris, 1–11 August 1931)', *Le Génie civil*, of 17 October 1931.

Lorries were not only more numerous but their performance had also improved. Launched on the market by Michelin in 1926, the low-pressure tyre was a boon in raising vehicle speeds from 25 to 50 kilometres per hour, with the result that lorries could now be used over longer distances. The advent of the heavy duty diesel engine in 1929 with vehicles attaining weights and speeds comparable to those of ordinary motorcars resulted in a drop in the consumption and cost of fuel, diesel oil being five times cheaper than petrol. That had positive effects on running costs. Another key factor was, of course, the improvements made to the national road system, maintained at the expense of the state. Once it had completed work on the 40,000 kilometres of the old network of national roads started in the early 1920s – straightening alignments, closure of level crossings, metal foundations, asphalting, etc. – ten years later the state set about improving the 40,000 kilometres of secondary and local roads placed under its authority by the 16 April 1930 Act.

'Heavy goods vehicles' were also able, at the time, to take advantage of the problems facing the French automobile industry, which, prosperous until then, was suffering the backlash of the 1930 crisis. The resulting sudden slump in private car sales had hit production hard. Car plants started to close one after the other, their number shrinking from about 100 to less than two dozen in the space of just a few years. By 1936, after 'long having brilliantly occupied second place', France had fallen to fourth position among the world's leading manufacturers, trailing behind the United States, Great Britain and Germany.[35] Faced with enormous difficulties in selling their production, even the most robust firms decided to enter the coach and lorry market, which seemed to offer brighter, short-term prospects. Berliet, for its part, virtually ceased its car production, Renault developed a range of industrial vehicles and Citroën (whose production had dropped by 50 per cent) embarked on the manufacture of a coach soon to proliferate on the highways and byways of France. The future seemed so bright that Laffly, until then a road equipment manufacturer, decided to start producing 'fast lorries', copying in the process a number of railway manufacturers dismayed at their dwindling order books, as the manufacturer Coder did in Marseilles, Carde in Bordeaux or Fouga in Béziers. Their target was not so much the big road hauliers as the smaller one-man firms, 'duped' by the tempting credit facilities generously extended by establishments often tied to the manufacturers themselves. In the unhappy position of having to work below cost price to service their loans, their cut-price policies were to have the effect of artificially bringing prices down, creating a spiral of which they were the biggest victims. The bigger players, always ready to swallow their less fortunate rivals, were merciless in their power games. The most noticeable of these was Citroën, which in exchange for its neutrality, as Citroën was also a fully-fledged

---

[35] G. Delanghe, 'Le XXXe Salon de l'automobile, Paris, 7–17 octobre 1937 (The 30th Motor Show, Paris, 7–17 October 1937)', *Le Génie civil* of 23 October 1937.

Figure 7.2 Two views of the rail-road wagon ‘Willème-Coder’, 1933

Source: Author’s collection.

The rail-road wagon ‘Willème-Coder’ may be used both on road and railway track. When on the road, two wheels are equipped with tyres and the wagon is hauled by a tractor. On tracks, it is just an ordinary wagon.

carrier through its subsidiary, Transports Citroën, managed to convince local independent hauliers only to use vehicles from its works.[36]

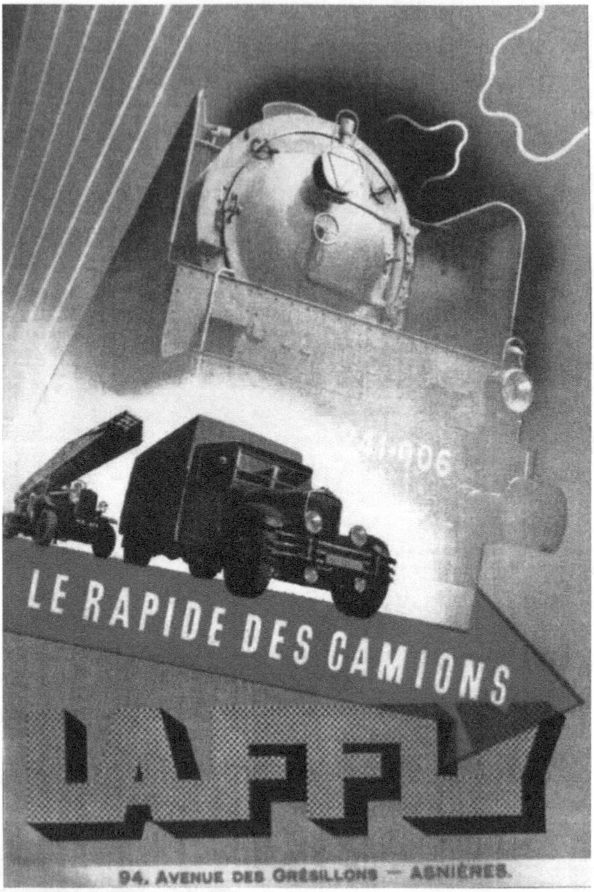

Figure 7.3 Advertisement of the car manufacturer Laffly, 1929

Source: Collection of AHICF.

This advertisement published by the car maker Laffly implies that his lorry is equal to railway transport speed and performance, whatever be the power of the engine.

Against this backdrop, the road subsidiaries of the big railways could doubtless have played a much greater role, if they had not been under constant attack from a front probably manned behind the scenes by the big automobile manufacturers and the brand new National Federation of Road Hauliers, founded in 1928 and chaired

[36] See Maurice Wolkowitsch, *L'Économie régionale des transports dans le Centre and le Centre-Ouest de la France* (Regional transport economics in the Centre and Centre-West of France) (Paris 1960), 125.

by René Musnier, manager of the *Société des messageries nationales*, a company specialising in express goods. Parliamentarian Lionel de Tinguy du Pouet, was one of the most virulent opponents of rail company intervention in road transport. Expressing his indignation that the 'railway companies should have become road transport operators', he vociferously denounced the fact that PLM had managed somehow to assume the status of 'public service allocating authority, or the next best thing'. But the worst was probably the Railways Director at the Ministry of Public Works, by extension government representative of the Management Committee of the major railways, a certain Cyrille Grimpret, who on 3 March 1931 announced his opposition to the 'generalisation of this method of locomotion (automobiles), to the extent of it now being an integral and essential part of railway operations'.[37]. For him, the railways' road subsidiaries should only handle 'feeder services' and not services 'in replacement of trains'. This negative attitude was later to be condemned by François Caron:

> He (Grimpret; B.C.) single-handedly prevented the development of the road subsidiaries by multiplying the prohibitions and controls. At a time when the initiative taken by the big railways was the only way to ensure their salvation, their efforts were stymied by the very administration that had encouraged and approved them at the start.[38]

Economic Crisis and Regulated Competition: the State Intervenes

Unable to bring any great influence to bear on the road transport system, the big railways next sought to go further than the fiscal and legal harmonisation so necessary in the sector and tried to promote the idea of contract-based 'coordination' to ensure a fair distribution of traffic between rail and road. In 1933, after running through the various initiatives already taken by railways to offset competition from the roads, Marcel Peschaud, Secretary General of the Management Committee, went on to say that

> all these measures, however necessary they may be, cannot be enough. They are little more than defensive measures by rail vis-à-vis the roads. But the railway neither can nor should kill off motor vehicles any more than the roads can or should kill off the railway. What is important for the nation is that transport be coordinated, something rightly demanded on all sides.[39]

---

[37] ANMT, Archives of the Chemin de fer du Nord, 48 AQ 5975. Quoted by Caron, *Histoire des chemins de fer*, vol. 2, 755.

[38] Caron, *Histoire des chemins de fer*, vol. 2, 755.

[39] Marcel Peschaud, 'La question du rail & de la route en France et dans les principaux pays étrangers (The issue of rail and road in France and in the main foreign countries)', *Revue générale des chemins de fer*, 52, September 1933, 171–231.

In reality, it was almost exclusively the big railway companies that were demanding coordination, in the face of the reluctance of the public authorities to address the central issue, even though the first texts curbing the excessive freedoms of road transport had been published, for example the 28 February 1933 Act imposing taxes on lorries in proportion to their weights and dimensions.

Nationally, the idea had been defended since 1931 by Raoul Dautry, Administrative Director of the state-owned railways, and by his former mentor Paul-Emile Javary, Operations Director at the *Compagnie du chemin de fer du Nord* (Nord). In 1932, the railways had attempted to introduce a system of coordination on an amicable basis: on 30 May, André Lebon, Chairman of PLM, had even pulled off the exploit of managing to gather together representatives of the various interested parties. But the withdrawal, one month later, of René Musnier on the grounds that, for him, the programme of work set by the big railway companies would preclude any real exchange, had brought a premature end to discussions in this first 'rail-road coordination committee'. However, before parting company, the members of this committee had approved several recommendations, including that freight traffic should be shared between rail, to whom belonged bulk shipments over long distances, and road, which should take over part-loads over shorter distances, in three-party 'regional conferences' (where deputies of carriers, users, and state were to meet), the decisions of which could be taken to appeal before a 'Higher Transport Committee' (*Conseil supérieur des transports*). Put to the Management Committee on 7 July 1932, these recommendations had caused a furious Grimpret to protest loudly in the name of the minister that the railways should have taken such an initiative outside the Management Committee's control and the *Conseil supérieur* remained on paper.

In fact, while several other European countries, Great Britain and Germany in particular, had bitten the bullet and taken steps to split the rights and obligations between rail and road, the French political authorities were still determinedly seeking a purely railway solution to the crisis affecting the big railways, including, if the worst came to the worst, 'revocation', as demanded in 1931 by the Socialist Jules Moch.[40] Fortunately, the position of the International Chamber of Commerce (ICC), officially expressed in June 1933, in favour of 'coordinated competition' obtained through agreements among the industries concerned (ICC Vienna Congress of 1933) was to make the government show greater common sense. In the wake of the work subsequently carried out by the National Economic Council (*Conseil national économique*), the idea of coordination among the different transport modes began to make headway.[41] The decisive impetus was given by Gaston Doumergue who, asked to lead a government of 'national reconciliation'

[40] On the German case see the contribution of Richard Vahrenkamp, 'Trucking in Germany: Rise and Restricted Growth, 1900–1938' in this volume.

[41] Consultative body set up in 1925. The CNE had 47 members selected by the most representative economic organisations and the forerunner of the present Economic and Social Committee.

following the political upheaval of 6 February 1934, took advantage of the exceptional powers granted him for restoring budgetary equilibrium as quickly as possible to ask Pierre-Etienne Flandin, his Minister of Public Works, to draft decrees based on the NEC's conclusions and submit them to him without delay.[42] Doumergue, who had supported the work of the first 'rail-road coordination committee' set by Lebon in 1932, was in fact convinced that the only way to drive down the railways' deficit was through transport coordination. The actual task of drafting the decrees was left to Dautry who, apart from being Director of the state-owned railways (state network), had also just been asked, in his capacity as technical advisor to the Chairman of the Board, to produce a programme of budget cuts.

In the meantime, the big railways had been busy taking part in the discussions on the amendments to the 1921 agreement, which, in their view, stacked the cards against rail in its competition with the roads. They argued that, unlike the road hauliers, they had to bear the cost of building and maintaining their infrastructure, that they were not free to set their own rates, which not only had to be approved by the Ministry but were also fixed in relation to the value of the goods carried and not in relation to the real cost of providing the transport service. Lastly, they were bound by the obligation to carry and could not, like their rivals, turn away goods tendered for carriage, even in peak periods, which forced them to maintain extra capacity all too often otherwise unused. It was these inequalities of treatment that had been the main issue in the open letter that they had sent to the Minister of Public Works on 13 March 1931 in response to the polemic and the criticisms surrounding their financial situation. The amendment to the 1921 agreement dated 6 July 1933, instigated as said before by the Minister of Public Works, Joseph Paganon, and endorsed by the Act of 8 July 1933 in an 'attempt to adapt the general conditions applicable to the major general interest railways to the technical and economic necessities of the time', went some of the way towards meeting their request.[43] The new legislation included changes of a contractual nature (Art. 1) geared towards increasing state controls and more economical management as well as amendments to the organic laws and specifications (Art. 2) conductive to more modern and more commercial operations.[44] This part was the most interesting in that it empowered government to issue decrees authorising exceptions to:

---

42 Nicolas Neiertz, 'La coordination des transports en France de 1918 à nos jours (Coordination of transports in France from 1918 to today)', thesis submitted for a doctorate in history under the guidance of François Caron, University of Paris IV-Sorbonne, École doctorale Mondes contemporains, September 1995, 80–84.

43 After the title of the Act itself, see: 'Revue documentaire. Chronique des chemins de fer. Loi du 8 juillet 1933', *Revue générale des chemins de fer*, 52, October 1933, 366–71.

44 State controls and more economical management were to be obtained through the inclusion of government officers on the Boards of Directors of the companies, merger of PO and Midi operations and so on.

- the specifications on the following points: obligation to keep lines in working order; number of coaches and classes of travel; special compartments
- notice required for posting and applying rates; transport times, station opening and closing times; agreements over connecting services with road and waterway carriers and so on
- the 1883 agreements on the minimum number of trains to be worked over the lines
- the Act of 15 July 1845 regarding the erection of barriers and fences and of buildings along the side of the track
- the Act of 9 April 1898 regarding consulting the Chambers of Commerce on the charges raised for services under concession.

The Act also made provision for tax allowances (Art. 3), in the form of a cut in the rate applicable to transport which, on 1 November 1933, was reduced from 32.5 per cent to 12 per cent.

Two decrees adopted in application of Article 2 were designed to relax state control over fares and rates and over operating conditions. The first, promulgated on 30 December 1933, relaxed the procedure for producing and amending rates, in particular by allowing the railways to enforce a rate on a provisional basis and maintain it, if the Administration did not demand its withdrawal within one month, and increase the particular rate three months after its introduction as opposed to the requirement settled in 1921, which was 12 months. It also accepted rates that included a maximum and a minimum between which the railways could select their price at will. The second decree, issued on 19 January 1934, removed the obligation to work three trains per day and per line imposed by the 1883 agreements and authorised a reduction in the number of classes available in coaches. It also gave the railways the right to set certain transport rates on other bases than the distance by kilometre or weight fraction categories in force.

This relaxation of the regulations seemed to satisfy the railway companies: 'We hope they (the decrees; B.C.) will give the railway a little of the freedom so liberally dispensed to rival modes'.[45] They were however fearful that application of the new regulations could prove difficult or be limited given its dependency on the goodwill of the Minister of Public Works.

It was on the basis of the decree of 19 January 1934, which gave the railways permission not to apply the rule of three trains per day, that, on behalf of the state-owned railways, Dautry embarked on negotiations with road hauliers in the *Seine-Inférieure département*. These negotiations, which started even before he had been asked by the government to draft the decrees on coordination, were to form a basis for the new legislation. The proposal put by Dautry to road hauliers in Normandy was simple, namely that they cease their long-distance operations and, in return, the state railway would give them exclusive rights to the short-haul services to be created in replacement of trains to be withdrawn, and would

45 PLM, GAS of 27 April 1934, Paris: Paul Dupont, 111 pages.

also grant them financial guarantees in respect of these services. The ‘agreements’ thus reached between industry professionals (in particular, in the absence of local authority representatives) would simply require the approval of the Minister of Public Works. This last stipulation meant that road services would have to be frozen during the time elapsing between the signature of the agreements and the Minister’s approval. The purpose behind this was to prevent any changes made to existing services from rendering the agreement null and void even before it could come into application.

Signed on 27 March 1934 by 80 per cent of those concerned, the Rouen agreements made provision for the closure to traffic of 16 secondary lines out of 23, to be replaced by road services, and the closure of 60 stations which were two-thirds of their number, leaving only the central stations between which solely express trains would run. In the months that followed, the Rouen agreements served as a model for other local agreements involving all the railway companies. However, in the face of general outcry from the local authorities, which were violently opposed to the disappearance of stopping trains and demanded to be party to negotiations at the Chambers of Commerce and Chambers of Agriculture supposedly representing users, these various agreements could not be enforced, the Minister of Public Works refusing to endorse them on the grounds that they had no basis in law.

This did not stop the principles underlying the ‘Rouen agreements’ from serving as an inspiration for the texts drawn up in application of the decree of 19 April 1934, in which rail-road coordination was to be based on a system of direct agreements between carriers. The task of conducting negotiations was given to a coordination committee made up of representatives of the five different categories of road and rail carrier. These included the major railways, local interest lines, subsidised road hauliers, independent road passenger carriers and independent road goods carriers. The committee was completed by an arbitrator named by the Minister of Public Works. The agreements dealt with such things as routes, timetables, fares and rates and public service obligations such as operating continuity, equal treatment for all users, postal transport. They were endorsed by ministerial order. Throughout the duration of negotiations, services could not be altered (‘frozen’) and any new service subsequently created had to be approved by the committee and authorised by the Minister. All infringements were to be punishable through fines and, in the event of repeated infringement, an offending vehicle could be temporarily impounded.

While this solution may have suited those directly involved – for PLM, it was ‘the most liberal of all those envisaged in this connection in the different countries’ – it was not as popular in other circles.[46] By eliminating control on the part of the local authorities and user influence, the system was based solely on the goodwill of the carriers of the two modes. And such goodwill was by no means

46 ‘La coordination des transports en France (Coordination of transport in France)’, *PLM Journal* of July 1934 (no pages).

readily available, given their diverging interests. Maurice Wolkowitsch regretted that 'right from the start, coordination appeared not so much a way of ensuring the harmonious use of two techniques but more a palliative in an attempt to reconcile irreconcilable interests'.[47]

Chaired by Dautry, the coordination committee met for the first time on 20 August 1934. On the strength of its experience with the Rouen agreements, it began by examining passenger transport and agreed the general principles for its coordination on 20 October. All that remained was to put these principles into practice. For this, technical transport committees at *département* level were brought into action to prepare the necessary agreements, the details of their membership and working arrangements having been set in a decree dated 25 February 1935, and submit their findings to the coordination committee. Contrary to the original regulations, the General Councils and Chambers of Commerce were now entitled to table their recommendations on the plans of the individual *départements* before referring them on to the higher echelons.

The first individual plans were submitted to the coordination committee in September 1935. Not all of them had the support of the General Councils: on 22 November 1935, of the 56 recommendations tabled, only eight were unreservedly in support of the agreements drawn up locally and 22 rejected them out of hand. This prompted Dautry to ask the Minister to intervene with the 'prefects' to speed up the procedure and remind the 'recalcitrant' General Councils of the 'absolute need' for coordination. Dautry went on to add that in the event of it being impossible to create a 'favourable climate', the government would be well advised to 'carry on regardless in the face of last-ditch opposition'.[48] His request was to prove futile and, on 31 December, the coordination committee was only able to put five plans to the Minister for signature.

Such widespread opposition was also an impediment to the application of the measures connected with the Paganon amendment, as PLM reported to its shareholders in April 1935:

> In addition, the many of the exceptions to the legal requirements, specifications and agreements for which provision was made, subject to ministerial agreement, in the Act of 8 July 1933 and the decree of 19 January 1934, most of which concern operations on smaller lines, have only had limited effect, since most of

[47] Wolkowitsch, *L'Économie régionale*, 114.

[48] AN, Dautry Archives, 307 AP 79, letter from Raoul Dautry to the Minister of Public Works, 22 November 1935. Quoted by Nicolas Neiertz, 'La coordination des transports en France', 1995, 111. See also 'La coordination des transports dans les années trente (Coordination of transport in the 1930s)', *Revue d'histoire des chemins de fer*, 9, Autumn 1993, 130–43; 'La révision du régime de 1921 (Revision of the 1921 system)', included in 'Le statut des chemins de fer français and leurs rapports avec l'État 1908–1982 (The status of the French railways and their relations with the State 1908–1982)', *Revue d'histoire des chemins de fer hors série*, 4, February 1996, 69–87.

> the measures regarding the reorganisation of these lines are on hold, awaiting the decisions on rail-road coordination.[49]

It did, however, also mention that it had been possible in 1934 to cut down the number of trains from three to two on 16 of its smaller lines and that TPLM was now offering services on 65 routes, 36 parallel to the railway.

Criticism of coordination was becoming more virulent. It included that of goods transport when the deadline for drawing up a list of existing road transport services had to be extended. The conditions had been set out in a decree dated 13 July 1935. The final blow came from the Upper House where, on 27 February 1936, Senator Robert Thoumyre took the government to task, roundly condemning coordination that 'culminated in agreement among private interests all set to enjoy a de facto monopoly'.[50] Following his recent appointment to the Ministry of Public Works, Camille Chautemps, who had given Dautry to understand that he had no intention of immediately approving the *département* plans in his possession, took advantage of the opportunity to announce that rail-road coordination was suspended *sine die*. When this became known, each of the two parties accused the other of not having played the game and of being to blame for this setback. In response to criticism from the *Fédération nationale des transports français* (FNTF), the syndicate of road transport business, chartered in 1933), the railways stated that, since coordination on the basis of agreements had failed, the only other option was for authoritarian solutions to be imposed.

'Regulated' coordination would in fact be introduced by the Popular Front. In a decree dated 14 November 1936, Albert Bedouce, Minister of Public Works in the first government under Léon Blum, broadened the membership of the coordination committee and local technical committees (now under the chairmanship of the 'prefects') to include user representatives. The new coordination committee only became effective on 1 March 1937, under the chairmanship of Senator Yves Le Trocquer, a former Minister of Public Works between 1920 and 1924. But the committee was no longer empowered to act and had little more than consultative status, making recommendations with which the Minister had no obligation to comply. The new bases for coordination were set out in a legislative decree dated 31 August 1937. This was also the date on which the *Société nationale des chemins de fer français* (SNCF) was founded, bringing together the previously separate companies. Passenger services were targeted as a priority. The General Councils (*départements*) were invited to draw up transport plans that would include axing railway lines judged loss-making and scrapping duplicate bus services. Failure to do so would result in the government intervening to decide on the measures to be taken. On 1 December 1938, the contributions of 33 *départements* were accepted,

---

49 PLM, GAS of 30 April 1935, Paris: Paul Dupont, 125 pages.

50 AN, F14 12510, *JO Sénat* (printed proceedings of the Senate house debates), 27 February 1936, 145–50, quoted by Neiertz, 'La coordination', 1995, 114.

with, as a result, the outright closure to passenger traffic of 4,600 kilometres of general interest lines, a further 1,700 kilometres being partially axed.

Contrary to popular belief, the disastrous results of the large railway companies in the 1930s cannot be blamed solely on competition from the roads. Far from condemning motor vehicle transport, they made repeated attempts to adopt it for themselves and advocated close cooperation with road transporters. Despite their apparent mutual enmity, the two modes of transport actually shared substantial common interests – as evidenced by the development by the automobile industry on behalf of the big railways of the so-called 'coach on rails', a motor coach train intended as a replacement for buses – which earned them the dubious privilege of being accused of trying to establish a shared monopoly over transport.

However, by forcing the big railways to face up to real competition and develop the resources necessary to be on an equal footing with the roads, the latter contributed to the 'rehabilitation' of the railway which, dispossessed of its almost absolute monopoly on the transport market, showed unprecedented levels of innovation, especially commercially, in this pre-war period.

This then begs the question of the real scale of road competition at the time. At the end of 1930, the chief operations engineer at PLM, Eugène Mugniot, reported to company board members on the latest developments of road competition. He announced that, although such competition was growing, 'it was only becoming serious in a few regions and for some types of traffic', whereas in other cases 'it was dwindling or disappearing altogether'.[51] He even reported that industrial firms were 'beginning to realise the limits to the benefits of using road lorries, which were already travelling more slowly than before and were therefore becoming more expensive with every passing year', and that, 'when their sites so allowed, they were increasingly applying for private siding concessions'.[52]

Then, taking the example of high-speed goods services between Paris and Lyon and vice-versa, he recalled that since autumn 1928 when it had launched its first road service, PLM had never stopped fighting to win back traffic lost to the roads through rates adjustments and other benefits. And successfully, since in September 1930, the four road companies in this market had announced mixed results: 'In all, the traffic they handle is little more than the equivalent over the year of some 2,500 to 3,000 tonnes, whereas rail can boast as much as 13,500 tonnes'. From this, Mugniot came to the following conclusion: 'Furthermore, we will soon come to the point where our road rival will reach its cost price limit and will no longer be able to cut its rates'.[53]

This type of statement about how customers were flocking back to rail was to proliferate throughout the 1930s. In a lecture given in 1932, Dautry was unable to resist quoting an article published in the *Bulletin des Halles* on 14 October 1931 alluding to the use of lorries to carry perishables over long distances:

---

51 ANMT, PLM, 77 AQ 219, meeting of 4 December 1930.

52 Ibid.

53 Ibid.

> At the beginning, all was perfect, but then the service started to worsen to the extent that it is now frankly poor. All too often the goods arrive late or even too late to be sold on the same day. Whence the need to store them overnight, with the risk of poorer sales the following day, and other similar misadventures. It is quite clear that producers who let themselves be tempted by this mode of transport have had to rethink their decisions and go back to 'the good old puffer train'.[54]

This is hardly defeatist language. One final quotation from Raymond Godfernaux, Editor of *La Revue générale des chemins de fer*, who, in his analysis of the situation of the big railways in 1932, wrote the following words:

> No other mode of transport can rival the railway for regularity, throughput, comfort and safety. (Recalling that; B.C.) a goods train can convey 500 tonnes with a four-man crew. To move the same amount, you would need fifty 10-tonne lorries and as many drivers and deliverymen.[55]

His views on this point were shared by Dautry who, in the abovementioned lecture, after noting 'without bitterness' that the big railways no longer had and would never again have a monopoly over the production and sale of transport and that 'nobody is interested in our short-distance services (except in the suburbs)', declared that 'for our long distance or bulk services, we are better equipped than the roads and our cost prices are lower'.[56]

It is impossible at this point not to make comparisons with the current situation of SNCF Fret, whose local traffic is on the wane. The big difference, however, is that the company has had the intelligence (and the ability) to secure itself a powerful road freight division (Geodis Group), a possibility not available to the big railways in their day.

References

Anonymous, 'La coordination des transports en France (Coordination of transport in France)', *PLM Journal* of July 1934 (no pages).

Caron, François, *Histoire des chemins de fer en France*, vol. 2: *1883–1937* (Paris 2005).

[54] Raoul Dautry, 'Regards sur les transports (A Look at Transport). Lecture at Zurich University on 16 March 1932', published as a supplement to the December 1932 issue of the magazine *L'État, notre réseau*, 19.

[55] R. Godfernaux, *Les Grands Réseaux de chemins de fer français. Année 1932* (*The Big French Railways – Year 1932*) (Paris 1933), 12–13.

[56] Dautry, 'Regards ...'

Chambelin, 'Note sur l'emploi des camions automobiles à la livraison de la houille, à domicile, dans Paris' (Memorandum on the use of motor lorries for domestic coal deliveries in Paris), *Revue générale des chemins de fer* (RGCF), 31, March 1908, 211–15.

Dautry, Raoul, 'Regards sur les transports (A Look at Transport). Lecture at Zurich University on 16 March 1932', *L'État ... notre réseau*, December 1932, 19.

De Lalande, 'Note sur le camionnage automobile pour chemin de fer (Memorandum on road haulage for the railways)', *Revue générale des chemins de fer*, 39, December 1920, 295–8.

Delanghe, G., 'XIXe Salon de l'automobile. Section des véhicules industriels, 22–31 octobre 1924 (19th Motor Show. Industrial vehicles section, 22–31 October 1924)', *Le Génie civil*, of 22 November 1924.

Delanghe, G., 'Le XXVe Salon de l'automobile. Voitures de tourisme, Paris, 1–11 August 1931 (The 25th Motor Show Sedan vehicles, Paris, 1–11 August 1931)', *Le Génie civil*, of 17 October 1931.

Delanghe, G., 'Le XXXe Salon de l'automobile, Paris, 7–17 octobre 1937 (The 30th Motor Show, Paris, 7–17 October 1937)', *Le Génie civil* of 23 October 1937.

Duaner, D., 'Les véhicules industriels au Salon de l'Automobile à Paris, en 1912 (Industrial vehicles at the Paris Motor Show in 1912)', *Le Génie civil*, of 21 December 1912.

Godfernaux, Raymond, *Les Grands Réseaux de chemins de fer français. Année 1932* (The big French Railways. Year 1932) (Paris 1933).

Neiertz, Nicolas, 'La coordination des transports dans les années trente (Coordination of transport in the 1930s)', *Revue d'histoire des chemins de fer*, 9, Autumn 1993, 130–143.

Neiertz, Nicolas, 'La coordination des transports en France de 1918 à nos jours (Coordination of transports in France from 1918 to today)', thesis submitted for a doctorat in history under the guidance of François Caron, University of Paris IV-Sorbonne, École doctorale Mondes contemporains, September 1995.

Neiertz, Nicolas, 'La révision du régime de 1921 (Revision of the 1921 system)', included in 'Le statut des chemins de fer français and leurs rapports avec l'État 1908–1982 (The status of the French railways and their relations with the State 1908–1982)', *Revue d'histoire des chemins de fer hors série*, 4, February 1996, 69–87.

Périssé, Lucien, 'Ier Congrès national des transports en commun par automobiles sur route, Paris, 18 au 20 décembre 1912 (1st national congress of public transport by motor vehicle – Paris, 18 to 20 December 1912)', *Le Génie civil* of 28 December 1912.

Toutain, Jean-Claude, *Les transports en France de 1830 à 1965* (Transport in France from 1830 to 1965), Économies and sociétés, Série AF, Histoire quantitative de l'économie française, vol. 9 (Paris 1967).

Wolkowitsch, Maurice, *L'Économie régionale des transports dans le Centre and le Centre-Ouest de la France* (Regional transport economics in the Centre and Centre-West of France) (Paris 1960).

Chapter 8
Containerisation in the United States During the Interwar Period

Albert J. Churella

In October 1931, 25 years before intermodal pioneer Malcom McLean launched the container ship SS *Ideal-X*, a truck carrying a cargo container departed from a loading dock in Baltimore, Maryland.[1] At the harbour, a crane lifted the box onto a ship, which then sailed across Chesapeake Bay to a rail terminal on the opposite shore. Another crane transferred the container to a railroad car for the journey to Salisbury, Maryland, where a truck delivered the cargo to its destination. The entire operation, under the management of the Pennsylvania Railroad (PRR), was a technological triumph of coordinated intermodal service, under the management of the nation's largest rail carrier. PRR President William Wallace Atterbury, arguably the most influential railroad executive in the United States, if not the world, predicted that there would be even more intermodality in the years to come. 'My idea of the railroad', Atterbury announced, 'is that it should be definitely co-ordinated with every sound economic agency of transportation', including trucks, buses, ships, and aircraft.[2] Six years later, Federal Coordinator of Transportation Joseph B. Eastman, one of the most influential regulators in the United States, predicted a similarly rosy future for intermodal operations. He foresaw 'rail-water, highway-water, or rail-highway-water movements of traffic in carload lots'.[3]

Although historians have largely accepted McLean's iconic status as the father of containerisation, McLean did not develop any of the constituent technological

1 The author acknowledges the assistance of Christopher Baer and Marjorie McNinch, at the Hagley Museum and Library, which has also provided generous research support. Thanks, too, to Keith Harcourt, who has given me excellent advice on the parallel British experience with containers, during the interwar period. Portions of this work appeared previously in Albert J. Churella, 'Delivery to the Customer's Door: Efficiency, Regulatory Policy, and Integrated Rail-Truck Operations, 1900–1938', *Enterprise and Society*, 10, March 2009, 98–136, and Albert J. Churella, 'Saving the Railroad Industry to Death: The Interstate Commerce Commission, the Pennsylvania Railroad, and the Unfulfilled Promise of Rail-Truck Cooperation', *Business and Economic History On-Line*, 4, 2006 (last accessed on 30 March 2012).

2 Atterbury remarks, 24 April 1930, reprinted in H.C. Oliver, 'Co-Ordinated Transport: How it Represents The Trend of the Times', *The Mutual Magazine*, March 1934, 12.

3 *New York Times* of 15 June 1936.

or organisational elements that made that service possible.[4] Containerisation – and its attendant potential for global economic and social change – antedated McLean's career. In their focus on the post-war history of the container, many historians give short shrift to the largely unrealised potential of containerisation during the interwar period. They typically attribute the container's lacklustre performance during the 1920s and 1930s to adverse regulatory factors, particularly the reluctance of Interstate Commerce Commission (ICC) commissioners to sanction the development of a new transportation technology. In that context, it was hardly surprising that the PRR's pioneering intermodal experiment took place entirely within the state of Maryland, and was thus exempt from ICC oversight.[5]

The reality is somewhat more complex. ICC officials manifested an extraordinarily high degree of competency during the interwar period, particularly after President Woodrow Wilson appointed Eastman as a commissioner, in 1919.[6] Ironically, it was the ICC's competence, and not its intransigence, that helped delay containerisation. Many of the commissioners, and Eastman foremost among them, astutely recognised that railroad executives had little interest in employing containerisation to increase operating efficiency, as they had claimed. Instead, managers of large carriers, particularly the PRR and the New York Central (NYC), envisioned containers as a mechanism for fracturing the long-established railroad rate structure and threatening the long-term financial health of the railroad industry.

Early Containerisation

The First World War induced the first use of intermodal container services, in order to alleviate terminal congestion in the Ohio River gateway city of Cincinnati. In 1917, railroads serving the congested Cincinnati terminal area pioneered the use of large freight containers, also referred to as 'demountable truck bodies'. Benjamin Fitch, a salesman at the White Motor Company, devised a system whereby workers at railroad freight houses loaded less-than-carload-lot (LCL) freight into

---

[4] Brian J. Cudahy, *Box Boats: How Container Ships Changed the World* (New York 2006), and Marc Levinson, *The Box: How the Shipping Container Made the World Smaller and the Economy Bigger* (Princeton 2006).

[5] For various perspectives on this issue, see Stephen B. Goddard, *Getting There: The Epic Struggle between Road and Rail in the American Century* (New York 1994), 64; Albro Martin, *Enterprise Denied: Origins of the Decline of American Railroads, 1897–1917* (New York 1971); Michael W. Blaszak, 'Intermodal – Railroading's Indispensible Adaptation', *Pacific RailNews*, 394, September 1996, 26–37; and Brian Solomon, *Intermodal Railroading* (St Paul, MN 2007), 26.

[6] This view comports with the 'new institutionalism' school, particularly as depicted by Keith D. Revell, 'Cooperation, Capture, and Autonomy: The Interstate Commerce Commission and the Port Authority in the 1920s', *Journal of Policy History*, 12, 2000, 177–214; and Keith D. Revell, *Building Gotham: Civic Culture and Public Policy in New York City, 1898–1938* (Baltimore, MD 2003).

containers destined for specific railroads and then hoisted them onto trucks for cartage to various freight houses. By 1921, the Cincinnati, Lawrenceburg & Aurora interurban railway had initiated a small-scale intermodal service, transferring the demountable truck bodies to rail cars.[7]

During the period immediately following the First World War, as railroad executives became increasingly concerned at truck competition, containerisation constituted a mechanism for resisting motor carrier incursions into the railroads' LCL business. Managers claimed that containers offered several distinct advantages. Cargo containers, generally sized so that between four and ten individual units could be placed on a standard 50-foot-long flatcar or gondola, represented a substantial decrease in the size of the minimum shipping unit, compared to a boxcar.[8] Companies that might take a week to generate enough merchandise to fill a boxcar could load a container within a day, thus reducing demurrage charges. Because shippers loaded the containers at the point of origin, the railroads could reduce congestion at freight stations. Most importantly, with containers loaded and locked by the consignor and unlocked and loaded by the consignee, the railroads minimised claims for lost and damaged merchandise. Containers, as the *New York Times* observed, were 'individual travelling safe-deposit vaults' and 'sectional steel safes'.[9]

The New York Central, the only trunk-line carrier with direct freight rail service to Manhattan, was particularly well positioned to offer a container service. On 19 March 1921, the Less Than Carload Lot Corporation, a subsidiary of the NYC, began operations. A freight car equipped with four containers travelled between Chicago and Cleveland, while a similar car transported shoes to destinations around Boston. Another type of car, 61 feet, 3 inches long, and fitted with nine containers, carried express shipments on such high-priority passenger trains as the Twentieth Century Limited. Shipments travelled at standard LCL rates, subdivided into the same six classes that applied to boxcar LCL traffic.[10]

Shipper response was poor, however, and NYC managers experimented with a variety of pricing strategies. The most significant breakthrough occurred thanks to the influence of the United States Post Office, under the direction of Postmaster General Will H. Hays. Hays, best known for implementing the restrictive 1930

[7] John H. White, Jr, *On The Right Track: Some Historic Cincinnati Railroads* (Cincinnati 2003), 36–51; *Railway Age* of 25 February 1928, 499–502, and 16 February 1929, 419–22. See also *Coordination of Motor Transportation*, 182 ICC 263 (1932), at 342–3.

[8] Interestingly, however, containers did little to reduce the important ratio of payload weight to tare (empty weight). A fully equipped container car weighed about as much as a standard boxcar, but accommodated a maximum of 10.5 tons (two large containers holding 7,000 lbs. and two small containers holding 3,500 lbs.) on a 50-foot flatcar – even though many 40-foot boxcars could carry almost four times that load, even if they rarely did so in LCL service.

[9] *New York Times* of 3 April 1921 and 21 January 1922.

[10] *New York Times* of 3 April 1921 and 8 January 1922.

Hays Code that sharply curtailed sex and violence in early Hollywood films, was particularly concerned at thefts of the mails. He valued the 'burglar-proof' characteristics of the container, 'primarily because of the great safeguards it afforded against banditry'.[11] Such concerns were not to be taken lightly, inasmuch as losses to the United States Mail had reached 100 million US dollars in 1920 (equivalent to more than one billion US dollars in 2010). The inaugural trip between New York and Chicago, on 6 May 1921, proved so successful that NYC officials predicted that thousands of container cars would soon be in service, replacing more than twice as many mail storage cars and LCL boxcars.[12]

The service provided at the request of the Post Office encouraged NYC officials to adopt a new pricing strategy for LCL freight moving in containers. Beginning on 24 August 1922, NYC managers authorised a rate structure based on the mileage travelled multiplied by the weight of the container, irrespective of the cargo that it contained. In traditional LCL service, small shipments travelled in boxcars at one of six class rates, calculated in cents per hundredweight. Only when a shipment reached a certain size (5 tons, for example) was it eligible to travel at much lower carload rates. Under the NYC's new tariffs, shipments in containers travelled at uniform Freight-All-Kinds (FAK, also known as all-commodity rates), regardless of the contents of the container. High-value commodities, ordinarily subject to the top tiers of the class-rate structure, now moved at a lower uniform container rate. Shippers could thus dispatch small shipments at a lower cost than traditional LCL service.[13]

The FAK rates thus enabled the NYC to pull business away from competing railroads and even from motor carriers.[14] By October, the NYC had introduced tank containers for milk and other bulk liquids, and had offered a service, in conjunction with the Chicago & North Western Railway, as far west at Minneapolis. Under the new rate structure, the NYC's traffic increased rapidly, from 278 containers in 1922 to 10,217 in 1927 and 47,886 in 1930.[15]

Pennsylvania Railroad officials soon emulated the NYC service. In October 1928, after attempting, unsuccessfully, to acquire partial ownership of the L.C.L. Corporation, PRR managers established the Keystone Container Car Company. On 20 June 1929, with an initial complement of 500 containers and 75 specially equipped container cars, Keystone initiated a service linking New York,

---

11 *New York Times* of 21 January 1922.

12 Despite the success of the tests, regular container mail service did not begin until January 1922, probably owing to the absence of sufficient equipment. *New York Times* of 8 May 1921 and 21 January 1922.

13 Levinson, *The Box*, 30.

14 David J. DeBoer, *Piggyback and Containers: A History of Rail Intermodal on America's Steel Highway* (San Marino, CA 1992), 15.

15 See *New York Times* of 1 October 1922; ICC, *Coordination of Motor Transportation*, at 342; *In the Matter of Container Service*, 173 ICC 377, at 382–5; and *Railway Age* of 25 February 1928, 499–502 and 16 February 1929, 419–22.

Baltimore, Pittsburgh, Cleveland, and Buffalo, followed by Philadelphia on 20 October and South Kearney, New Jersey on 15 November. The PRR employed essentially the same rate structure as the NYC, and it experienced a similar increase in container shipments, with 63,084 handled between 20 June 1928 and 3 January 1931.[16]

The rapid expansion in container service caught the attention of the Interstate Commerce Commission, whose regulators were increasingly concerned at the container rate structure employed by the railroads. In December 1928, the Missouri Pacific Railroad and the affiliated Texas & Pacific Railway requested authority from the Railroad Commission of Texas to establish a container service within Texas. Although this was a matter of intrastate commerce, the NYC and the Lehigh Valley Railroad shortly thereafter filed proposed tariffs with the ICC, for expanded interstate container operations, causing the Texas Commission to defer to the ICC's judgement in all of the cases.[17]

ICC Examiner Harry C. Ames evaluated the proposed rates, and his subsequent report, issued in August 1929, set the tone for the hearings that followed. Ames concluded that the Missouri Pacific experienced little competition from trucks, and therefore had no need to haul containerised freight at reduced rates. In the East, however, Ames conceded that trucks had severely eroded the railroads' freight business. In that instance, he approved of a container service in principle, but found unacceptable the rate structure that the railroads had proposed. Newspapers reported that 'the present schedule of charges is too low', but that was not strictly the case.[18] Ames concluded that container rates were skewed in favour of short-haul shippers, largely to combat motor carrier competition. As such, they conferred an unfair advantage on short-haul shippers in certain communities.[19] Ames suggested that a container service be permitted, but that the associated rate structure was unlawful. With container rates held in abeyance, railroad officials appealed the matter to the ICC commissioners. The future of container service depended on their ruling.[20]

16 The Lehigh Valley also offered container service, effective 9 January 1928, in cooperation with the NYC and the L.C.L. Corporation. In 1935 Keystone transferred all of its equipment to the PRR, and ceased to exist as a corporate entity. See ICC, *Coordination of Motor Transportation*, at 342; *Container Service*, at 385–6; Pennsylvania Railroad Collection at the Hagley Museum and Library, Wilmington, Del. (hereafter, HML), Box 374, folder 9, PRR response to ICC questionnaire, 'In the Matter of Container Service', 11 January 1929, and *New York Times* of 20 June 1929.

17 D. Philip Locklin, 'Reorganization of the Railroad Rate Structure', *The American Economic Review*, 36, May 1946, 466–78.

18 *New York Times* of 27 August 1929.

19 *New York Times* of 25 August 1929.

20 *New York Times* of 6 October 1929.

The Regulatory Context

Between late 1929 and 1931, just as the Great Depression was descending on the nation, the ICC heard testimony on the proposed container rates. That investigation, 'In the Matter of Container Service', soon revealed the carriers' intent to use containers to undermine two key pieces of legislation, the Transportation Act of 1920 and the Hoch-Smith Resolution. In that context, ICC commissioners were acting responsibly to fulfil a set of Congressional mandates regarding the health of all of the constituent carriers in the railroad industry, as well as the interrelationship of the transportation, agrarian and industrial sectors of the economy. Those mandates enjoyed an extraordinarily brief existence in the long span of public-policy history in the United States, coming into being just after the First World War and fading from the scene as the Great Depression settled over the nation. Unfortunately for the advocates of containerisation, that period coincided almost precisely with the rapid rise of motor-carrier competition, and its tendency to deprive the railroads of one of their most profitable markets, LCL traffic.[21]

The Transportation Act of 1920 required the ICC to develop a plan for the development of regional railroad systems, a process similar to the 'grouping' that was occurring in Britain, at roughly the same time. ICC officials and eminent transportation economists such as Harvard's William Z. Ripley were particularly concerned about what was commonly referred to as the 'strong road – weak road problem'. Simply put, some carriers, such as the PRR and the NYC, served major industrial centres and other generators of traffic, and thus enjoyed high traffic densities and revenues that were sufficient to permit the maintenance and expansion of the physical plant. Other carriers suffered from short average hauls, high terminal costs, steep gradients and alignments that bypassed large cities. The resulting combination of high costs and low revenues discouraged investors from committing additional capital to such weak carriers, compounding their inability to undertake the types of betterments that would permit more efficient operation.[22]

Since the Supreme Court's 1898 ruling in *Smyth v. Ames*, railroad executives had been careful to base their proposed rates on differences in the cost of service. As such, NYC and PRR officials argued that the inherent efficiency of containerisation justified low tariffs. Their strongest arguments came from the container's ability to reduce labour-intensive handling at terminals and, more importantly, to lower

---

21 ICC, *Container Service*, at 380, 386; *New York Times* of 7 April 1929 and 20 June 1929.

22 For treatments of the effects of the Transportation Act of 1920 see Richard Saunders, Jr, *Merging Lines: American Railroads, 1900–1970* (DeKalb, Ill. 2001), 47–72, and the multiple volumes of the *Investigation of Railroads, Holding Companies, and Affiliated Companies: Report of the Committee on Interstate Commerce: Railroad Combination in the Eastern Region* (Washington, DC 1940).

claims for loss and damage in transit. As such, low rates were not only justified by the reduced cost of service, they also benefited shippers, a situation that was clearly in the public interest. Furthermore, executives asserted, containers enabled the railroads to fend off truck competition, increasing their financial health in conformity with the intent of the 1920 Transportation Act.[23]

The proposed container rates were based solely on weight and distance, and not on the value of the commodity. They were also gradated in 500-pound increments: that is, a shipper paid a lower rate, in cents per hundredweight, on a minimum shipment of 6,000 pounds than on a shipment of 4,000 pounds, and a lower rate still on an 8,000-pound or a 10,000-pound minimum shipment. Incredibly, none of the railroad representatives attending the hearings were able to provide any evidence that more heavily laden containers incurred a lower per-pound handling cost. There was thus no basis for the railroads' favouritism toward large shippers, and their concomitant discrimination against smaller consignors.[24] It was instead up to Commissioner Eastman to assert, in a dissenting opinion, that 'differences in cost of transportation inevitably attend differences in loading'.[25] Without any cost data to substantiate this conclusion, however, Eastman's recommendations did little to persuade his fellow commissioners.

What railroad officials seldom admitted to the ICC or the press was that containers did little to lower the actual cost of transportation and may well have increased line-haul costs. In a few select cases, most notably the transportation of building bricks, containers offered a service that was far superior to traditional boxcar freight.[26] For most commodities, however, the benefits were far less clear. Unlike later cargo containers, such as those that Malcom McLean loaded aboard the S.S. Ideal-X, those constructed during the 1920s and 1930s were fabricated from heavy-gauge steel, and so greatly increased the tare weight of

---

23 *New York Times* of 27 August 1929.

24 ICC, *Container Service*, at 434–5. See also Robert A. Emery, 'The Cult of Smallness: The Early ICC and Volume Shipments', *Journal of Transportation Law, Logistics and Policy*, 73, 2006, 313–19.

25 ICC, *Container Service*, at 449.

26 Despite their seemingly robust nature, bricks are actually quite fragile, and will break or spall if handled too roughly. Containers minimised the need to restack bricks during shipment, and enabled brick makers in various parts of the country to supply major markets, such as New York, at a time when local manufacturers often suspended operations during winter months. Keith Harcourt has noted that, in Britain, containers were particularly useful for transporting bricks, tiles and firebacks (the rear of a fire grate, cast as a single piece), which were also subject to breakage caused by rough handling during shipment. Keith W. Harcourt and T.C. Cornille, 'A Comparative International Study of Technology and Policy in the Development of Railway Freight Containerisation in the US & UK', http://bit.ly/Harcourt_Cornillie_LisbonPaper (last accessed on 28 March 2012); G. Lloyd Wilson, 'The Use of Freight Containers by British Railways', *Annals of the American Academy of Political and Social Science*, 187, 1936, 173–9. *New York Times* of 3 March 1930.

each shipment.[27] Furthermore, the containers employed by the PRR and the NYC were manufactured to differing designs, and could not be interchanged.[28] On most routes, containers were therefore inherently less efficient than a conventional line-haul rail service.[29] Moreover, in overland service, containers offered little benefit vis-à-vis trucks. The true potential associated with containers lay in combined land-water operations. Yet, the lack of international container standards retarded the development of trans-Atlantic intermodal shipping, while the definition of per-package liability limits, first developed under the 1924 Hague Rules, was not implemented in the United States until 1936, with the passage of the Carriage of Goods at Sea Act.[30] The 1912 Panama Canal Act, which prohibited railroads in the United States from offering coastwise or Great Lakes shipping competitive with rail service, further discouraged integrated rail-water container operations. Under the circumstances, the railroaders' claims of extraordinary efficiency gains associated with containers fell somewhat flat.[31]

ICC regulators were accordingly unconvinced by railroaders' arguments that containers would generate the increased efficiency necessary to offset their lower rate structure. Instead, they suspected that the stronger carriers, particularly the NYC and the PRR, would employ containerisation to poach traffic from the weaker railroads in the Northeast. Those weak carriers, unable to afford investments in container service, would potentially lose the bulk of their profitable LCL traffic, and would thus be at risk of bankruptcy. Such developments would conflict with

---

27 Beginning in 1931, the PRR employed lightweight composite steel and aluminium Fitch containers, but railroad officials concluded that the reduced weight did not offset the higher initial cost, and elected to retain all-steel containers.

28 The containers used by the PRR's Keystone subsidiary were based on the same technology as the NYC's L.C.L. Corporation containers – so much so that the in 1932 the L.C.L. Corporation filed a patent infringement suit against Keystone. It appears that Keystone designers had made just enough changes in L.C.L. technology to skirt the patent issue, but those changes were sufficient to make the container designs incompatible. *New York Times* of 10 January 1932.

29 Levinson, *The Box*, 29–32.

30 For information on the development of European container standards at this time, see Keith Harcourt, 'Rail Containerisation in the United Kingdom and Europe during the 1920s and 1930s' in this volume.

31 Ship owners argued that the 500 US dollars 'per customary freight unit' liability limit specified by the Carriage of Goods by Sea Act (COGSA) applied to the entire container, regardless of the number or value of items in that container. US courts did not address that issue until 1971, however. *International Convention for the Unification of Certain Rules of Law relating to Bills of Lading* ('Hague Rules') *and Protocol of Signature* (Brussels, 25 August 1924), Admiralty and Maritime Law Guide, http://www.admiraltylawguide.com/conven/haguerules1924.html (last accessed on 12 January 2011); *Carriage of Goods by Sea Act*, 46 U.S.C. 1300 (1936); John Furness Wilson, *Carriage of Goods by Sea*, 2nd ed. (London 1993), 195; Craig Still, 'Thinking Outside the Box: The Application of COGSA's 500 US dollars per-package Limitation to Shipping Containers', *Houston Journal of International Law*, 24, September 2001, 81–137.

the Transportation Act of 1920 and its mandate that the ICC set minimum rates, in order to guarantee a reasonable rate of return to the railroads and protect the weaker carriers from competition by their stronger brethren. In that context, low container rates might well imperil the health of the railroad industry.

On 30 January 1925, moreover, Congress had adopted the Hoch-Smith Resolution, giving the ICC the authority to redistribute rates in order to ensure the overall health of the railroad industry. Hoch-Smith codified into federal law the value-of-service pricing that the railroad industry had adopted over the preceding decades, with high-value commodities (and this included most LCL traffic) travelling at high rates, and bulk commodities, most notably agricultural products, commanding substantially lower charges. In 1927, and in keeping with the terms of the Hoch-Smith Resolution, the ICC launched a sweeping investigation into railroad rate structures.[32] On 1 July 1930, the ICC issued a new rate schedule, to go into effect on 1 October. Carrier representatives protested, arguing that after the hearings ended in September 1928, the onset of the Great Depression had substantially altered competitive conditions. On 4 January 1932, the Supreme Court (in *Atchison, Topeka & Santa Fe Railway Company v. United States*) ruled in favour of the carriers, nullifying the key provisions of the Hoch-Smith Resolution. The Court's ruling came too late to save railway container operations, which fell victim to exceptionally unfortunate timing. Hoch-Smith required the ICC to safeguard the value-of-service tariffs established by the railroads, at precisely the same time when containerisation enabled the railroads to abandon that type of pricing.[33]

The debate over the terms of the Transportation Act of 1920 and the Hoch-Smith Resolution came to the fore, during the 'In the Matter of Container Service' hearings. The managers of weak railroads, particularly the New Haven and the Erie, opposed a container service and, ICC officials noted, 'expressed doubt of its economy'.[34] Representatives from the smaller railroads contended, correctly, that containerisation would not permit the elimination of urban freight terminals, and would thus increase the per-unit cost of handling merchandise at those locations. In addition, they argued, cash-strapped railroads would face the necessity of constructing container terminals and purchasing containers and carrier cars, at a time when they faced a surplus of boxcars. As a result, those carriers that had inaugurated a container service 'caused a selection of desirable

32 Mark H. Rose, Bruce E. Seely and Paul F. Barrett, *The Best Transportation System in the World: Railroads, Trucks, Airlines, and American Public Policy in the Twentieth Century* (Columbus 2006), 14.

33 ICC, *Container Service*, at 433; *Atchison, Topeka & Santa Fe Railway Company v. United States*, 284 US 248 (1932); Robert A. Emery, 'Social Engineering through Ratemaking: Value of Service and Hoch-Smith', *Journal of Transportation Law, Logistics and Policy*, 71, 2004, 167–74, and Patrick S. McCarthy, *Transportation Economics, Theory and Practice: A Case Study Approach* (Malden, MA 2001), 220.

34 ICC, *Container Service*, at 412.

tonnage for container traffic, leaving the bulkier and less desirable traffic to the box cars' operated by the weaker carriers.[35] The commissioners thus believed 'that the present and proposed container rates, taken as a whole, would be so low as to throw an unnecessary burden upon other traffic'.[36]

Under those circumstances, the executives of the Erie and the New Haven alleged that the impressive gains in LCL traffic reported by the NYC and the PRR had not come at the expense of trucks – it had come at the expense of the weaker railroads, through the reduction in boxcar rates. 'Clearly where this occurs', the ICC commissioners observed, there would be 'dire consequences to the revenues of the (weak; A. Ch.) carriers'.[37] Regulators were particularly concerned that the L.C.L. Corporation and Keystone Container permitted the NYC and the PRR to disguise the actual expenses associated with container operation. Had L.C.L. and Keystone charged fair market rental rates to their parent companies, the commissioners noted, the NYC would have barely broken even, while the PRR's container operations would have lost money.[38]

The commissioners agreed that the container, in principle, was 'a commendable piece of equipment', in that it afforded railroads the opportunity to lower costs and increase the efficiency of their operations, while more effectively meeting motor-carrier competition.[39] The ICC thus accepted the railroads' arguments that containerisation increased the quality of transportation, by reducing loss and damage in transit. As a result, regulators insisted that containers merited an increase, rather than a decrease, in freight rates. 'In other words', they asserted, 'being a distinctly superior service, the container should, other things being equal, command a higher price than boxcar service'.[40] That seemingly perverse logic did not reflect any intent on the part of the ICC to deprive railroads of the opportunity

---

35 Ibid., at 408.

36 Ibid., at 442.

37 Ibid., at 482.

38 The experience of British railways, particularly the Great Western and the Southern, substantiated the Commissioners' assertion that container service was in reality far more expensive than PRR and NYC officials claimed. During the early 1930s, British carriers set container rates by applying a surcharge ranging from 5 per cent (for tools and construction equipment) to 33½ per cent (for aviation gasoline) over and above standard freight rates – an indication that cost accountants had concluded that containers actually cost more to operate than conventional rail service. Containers nonetheless reduced packaging costs, increased the ease of lading, and minimised loss and damage in transit, indicating why shippers were willing to pay a premium for such services. G. Lloyd Wilson, 'The Use of Freight Containers by British Railways', *Annals of the American Academy of Political and Social Science*, 187, September 1936, 173–9, here 178; *Railway Age* of 22 December 1928, 1230; 16 February 1929, 421–2, and 13 April 1929, 833–7; HML, Box 374, folder 9, James Regis Downes to John F. Deasy, et al., 11 February 1929, and ICC, *Container Service*, at 401.

39 ICC, *Container Service*, at 442.

40 Ibid., at 438.

to handle freight efficiently in a container service. Rather, the commissioners were endeavouring to ensure that the increased efficiency associated with containerisation rebounded to the interests of the carriers, in the form of remunerative rates, rather than to shippers.

On 14 April 1931, the ICC disallowed the proposed container rates. Because FAK rates afforded 'no consideration to the value of the commodity, long an important factor in the making of rates', the commissioners required the railroads to charge class rates, which varied according to the type of cargo being transported.[41] The Commission further stipulated that container rates must be set at or above the carload tariff for the relevant commodity, while establishing a threshold rate for a container service, set no lower than the third-class LCL tariff. The new rate schedules, which took effect on 30 July 1931, imposed a 4,000-pound minimum weight per container shipment. That stipulation ensured that most of the smaller containers were uneconomical for all but the heaviest bulk commodities, such as sand and bricks.[42]

The ICC's ruling in 'In the Matter of Container Service' did not affect all railroads equally. Officials on the PRR, a railroad accustomed to bulk shipments of heavy, low-value goods, adapted most easily to the new rate structure. In July 1931, three months after the ICC's decision, the railroad's managers ordered 3,000 new containers, each with a capacity of 10,000 pounds, and planned to double the number of locations where a container service was available.[43] Rival NYC executives responded less successfully, probably because their railroad's traffic base was more heavily skewed to smaller, diverse shipments of high-value manufactured goods. The NYC's container traffic dropped precipitously, causing the commissioners to reconsider their stance on container rates.

Yet, it was the PRR that induced regulators to re-examine container rates. In October 1931, the railroad filed a request for new rates covering the transportation of demountable truck bodies between New York, Philadelphia, Baltimore and Richmond, Virginia, to take effect on 5 November 1931. These were all-commodity (that is, FAK) rates, in which a single consignor dispatched multiple types of cargo in a single container to a single consignee. Such rates were based solely on the cost of service, and not the value-of-service pricing that the 1925 Hoch-Smith Resolution had written into federal law.[44]

---

41 Ibid., at 445.

42 DeBoer, *Piggyback*, 15; John H. Mahoney, *Intermodal Freight Transportation* (Westport, Conn. 1985), 8.

43 *New York Times* of 19 July 1931 and 20 July 1931.

44 *Railway Age* of 17 October 1931, 608; 7 November 1931, 720, and 2 July 1932, 7; HML, Box 374, folder 10, 'Corrected Report of the Interstate Commerce Commission, No. 21723, In the Matter of Container Service, decided July 11, 1932'; *Wall Street Journal* of 27 May 1932; National Transportation Committee, *The American Transportation Problem* (Washington, DC 1933), 677; Edward S. Lynch, 'Railroad Pick-Up and Delivery', *The Journal of Land & Public Utility Economics*, 14, May 1938, 120–32, here 126.

The PRR's timing was excellent, as the Great Depression had eroded the ICC's commitment to Hoch-Smith, as well as to its narrowly constructed definition of value-of-service pricing. In January 1932, when the Supreme Court overturned the Hoch-Smith Resolution, it ended the ICC's responsibility to maintain value-of-service pricing and to redistribute rates in order to protect the health of the railroad industry. In February 1932, the Chicago, North Shore & Milwaukee Railroad submitted a proposed rate schedule, for a container service similar to that operated by the NYC, the PRR and the Lehigh Valley. By the time of the hearings, the commissioners noted that 'The clear demonstration upon this record of the increasingly severe motor-truck competition which respondent has had to meet leaves little to the imagination'. More importantly, the North Shore's managers were able to supply detailed cost information, showing that the per-unit expense associated with container operations varied according to the weight of the container. On 14 March 1932, the commissioners ruled that the North Shore's rates were lawful, that they did not unduly burden other traffic and that they were necessary to meet the threat of truck competition.[45]

Beginning in 1932, the ICC's willingness to liberalise container rates in order to more effectively meet motor carrier competition enabled railroads such as the PRR and the NYC to continue and even expand their container operations – thus undermining assertions that 'In the Matter of Container Service' crippled the railroads' efforts to embrace intermodal operations. By August, five months after the North Shore rate hearings, reporters announced that 'Container-car service and a new rate schedule started by the New York Central Railroad to recover freight traffic from the highways have already given indication of succeeding in their object'.[46] On the PRR, shippers in 70 origination cities dispatched thousands of containers to a variety of destinations. Classified and standardised in typical Pennsylvania Railroad fashion, containers ranged from the small, 64-cubic-foot Class DD64A, which a single worker could roll through a freight terminal, to the more common 7' × 9' × 8' Class SD, intended for sectionalised boxcar service. The largest container was the 20-foot long Class TD demountable truck body, similar to a modern cargo container, which could be transferred, by crane, directly from a railcar to a fifth-wheel truck trailer. The PRR also purchased drop-bottom containers for stone, cement and other bulk cargoes, and managers even contemplated building refrigerated containers for perishables. The containers rode on modified flat and gondola cars (nearly 900 by 1936), with deck heights that allowed container doors to be set at the same level as both loading docks and conventional boxcars.[47]

The PRR's massive Enola yards near Harrisburg served as a centralised sorting and dispatching facility. Large cranes plucked containers from their carrier cars, then transferred them to other cars (and, rarely, to truck chasses), depending upon

45 ICC, *Container Service*, at 659.

46 *New York Times* of 13 August 1932.

47 Pennsylvania Railroad, *Container Car Service* (Philadelphia, PA 1929).

their destination city. Opened in November 1932, the new container terminal handled 800 containers on an average day, with a maximum capacity nearly double that figure. Containers could make train connections as short as 40 minutes – far less than the 24 hours required at a typical boxcar LCL transfer station. By 1934 the PRR was handling nearly 200,000 containers a year in this fashion, at a cost of little more than eight cents per container. Total transfer costs amounted to 15,000 US dollars per year, compared to the 135,000 US dollars it would have cost the railroad to sort and transfer LCL shipments sent in conventional boxcars.[48] By 1939, the PRR transported nearly 160,000 container loads each year.[49]

However, the type of container service that emerged after 1932 was very different than the one developed during the 1920s. The all-commodity rates approved in 1932 gave a powerful advantage to freight forwarders (also referred to as consolidators), companies that occupied a nebulous zone between the users and the providers of transportation. Forwarders solicited small shipments and bundled them into container- or boxcar-sized lots, earning a profit based on the differential between container shipping rates and the higher LCL package rates; they could in turn pass part of this savings on to LCL shippers (in the form of a 4 to 19 per cent rate reduction) as an inducement to gain their business. The consolidators also added their marketing and clerical expertise to the equipment and facilities provided by railroads, greatly reducing the paperwork associated with a typical LCL shipment. They also accepted all liability for shipments, ensuring that a railroad would be responsible for loss or damage only in the rare event that a catastrophic occurrence – such as a train wreck – caused significant damage to the container itself. Consolidators benefitted from the all-commodity rates because they were exempt from ICC authority, and thus could do something that the railroads could not do – accept multiple unique shipments of different freight classifications and bundle them together into a single shipment travelling at a uniform rate.[50]

The ICC's acceptance of the 1932 all-commodity rate structure on container shipments was not the only regulatory factor that facilitated the shift of container traffic from the railroads to the freight forwarders. Since the late nineteenth century, several railroad companies serving Baltimore and Philadelphia (principally the PRR, the Baltimore & Ohio (B&O), and the Reading) circumvented the

---

48 *Railway Age* of 19 December 1931, 954, and 18 January 1936, 143–5.

49 HML, Box 374, folder 9, Downes to Deasy 26 March 1929; 'In the Matter of Container Service': 'Merchandise or Less-than-Carload Freight', testimony of Deasy, 17.

50 In 1917, the Supreme Court ruled, in *Lehigh Valley R.R. v. United States* (243 U.S. 444), that railroads must treat forwarders as shippers, and that railroads could not offer preferential rates to forwarders. See Rose, Seely and Barrett, *Best Transportation System,* 70, 115; and Anonymous, 'Intermodal Transportation and the Freight Forwarder', *The Yale Law Journal*, 76, June 1967, 1360–1396, here 1362–3, 1381, 1389–90. See also Giles Morrow and G. Lloyd Wilson, 'Some Problems of Freight Forwarders', *Annals of the American Academy of Political and Social Science*, 230, November 1943, 110–15, here 110–11, and Lynch, 'Railroad Pick-Up', 126.

anti-rebating provisions of the 1887 Interstate Commerce Act by contracting with nominally independent warehouses, designating them as 'freight stations' and using those facilities to consolidate shipments.[51] The PRR, for example, maintained a symbiotic relationship with the Merchants Warehouse Company in Philadelphia, maintaining tracks adjacent to the various Merchants warehouses and paying Merchants an allowance for grading, sorting and storing merchandise. In return, Merchants agreed to use the PRR as a preferential shipper. In effect, the Pennsylvania Railroad billed shippers at LCL rates, while using Merchants as a consolidator, with that company assembling small shipments into boxcar lots for delivery to the PRR. The PRR could then move that traffic at much lower full-boxcar rates, passing the savings on to shippers and thus luring business away from competing railroads. For decades, the ICC acquiesced to this legal subterfuge, largely because no one complained of its inherently discriminatory nature. As Supreme Court Justice Benjamin Cardozo later observed,

> the history of the relation between (the) Pennsylvania (Railroad) and Merchants indicates strongly that the illegal discrimination, far from being a symptom of a larger combination, was the product of a mistake of law, which was shared for many years by the regulatory commission … (and represented; inclusions by the author) the concession of a privilege which has turned out to be forbidden.[52]

Regulator acquiescence ended in 1928, when an independent warehouse operator in Philadelphia filed a protest with the ICC. In McCormick Warehouse v. Pennsylvania Railroad, the commissioners concluded that the 'preferential allowances … in our opinion, are nothing more than a device to attempt to lend legality to the payment of rebates'.[53] Warehouses that were not contractually tied to the PRR, the B&O or the Reading were bound to suffer, inasmuch as shippers using those unallied facilities would be required to pay LCL rates, rather than the lower full-car rates. Such practices violated Rule 14 of the 1919 Consolidated Freight Classification, which limited carload rates to instances where a single shipper filled an entire car, and Rule 23 of the Classification, which prohibited railroads from assembling LCL shipments into carload lots at carload rates.[54]

---

51 *Keystone Warehouse Company v. Pennsylvania Railroad Company and Director General*, 53 ICC 335 (1919); *Keystone Elevator & Warehouse Company v. Director General, as Agent, and Pennsylvania Railroad Company*, 73 ICC 273 (1922); *McCormick Warehouse Company v. Pennsylvania Railroad Company et al.*, 95 ICC 301 (1925).

52 *Terminal Warehouse Company v. Pennsylvania Railroad Company*, 297 U.S. 500 (1936).

53 *McCormick Warehouse Company v. Pennsylvania Railroad Company*, 148 ICC. 299 (1928), at 306.

54 Frank L. Barton, 'Uniform Freight Classification and the Interstate Commerce Commission', *The Journal of Land & Public Utility Economics* of 18 August 1942, 312–22, and Charles A. Taff, *Management of Physical Distribution and Transportation*, 7th ed. (Homewood, IL 1984), 353–5.

In that light, railroads could not employ their contractually favoured warehouses for the purpose of consolidating small shipments. In 1931, the Supreme Court affirmed the ICC's decision in *McCormick*, ruling that

> The service rendered by appellants' warehouses in distributing and assembling package carload freight is thus one which a carrier is not authorized or permitted to render, even at its own public freight stations, and, if performed by it, would nullify its published rates for carload transportation service.[55]

The ICC and Supreme Court rulings associated with the *McCormick* case thus prevented the railroads from consolidating their own shipments, through the medium of contractual ties with independent warehouses. Railroad executives accordingly reasoned that their next best option was to permit freight forwarders to take on that function, accepting small packages from multiple shippers and bundling them into container loads that the railroads could carry at a uniform rate. The nearly contemporaneous 'In the Matter of Container Service' and McCormick rulings thus reinforced one another, giving railroad managers twin incentives to shift container use from their own account to that of independent consolidators. Consolidator container rates thus bore the entire burden of the discriminatory pricing practices that railroad executives thought necessary, in order to meet competition from other railroads, and from trucks. To put the situation in a different way, the carriers encouraged massive discrimination by consolidators, because they could not engage in rate discrimination on their own account.

The shift in discriminatory pricing practices quickly attracted the ICC's scrutiny, however, inasmuch as the railroads controlled the freight forwarders. Universal Carloading & Distributing, the largest of the consolidators, was a subsidiary of the United States Freight Company, which was in turn a subsidiary of the New York Central, the company that also controlled the L.C.L. Corporation. The Van Sweringen Lines (consisting of the Nickel Plate Road and other railroads) owned the Standard Carloading Corporation. The Pennroad Corporation, an investment subsidiary of the Pennsylvania Railroad, controlled the National Freight Company (subsequently renamed the National Carloading Corporation, following a merger with Standard Carloading), which in turn utilised the equipment supplied by the Keystone Container Car Company, another PRR subsidiary.[56]

---

55 *Merchants' Warehouse Company v. United States*, 283 US 501 (1931). See also: *Terminal Warehouse Company v. Pennsylvania Railroad Company* and 'Regulation by the Interstate Commerce Commission of Railroad Terminal Trucking Facilities', *Columbia Law Review*, 32, December 1932, 1373–83, here 1374.

56 *New York Times* of 3 May 1929, 27 August 1929, 4 September 1929, 29 January 1930 and 10 January 1932. See also Meyer H. Fishbein, 'The Trucking Industry and the National Recovery Administration', *Social Forces*, 34, December 1955, 171–9, at 177; and Lynch, 'Railroad Pick-Up', 126–43.

As ICC officials had suspected, the freight forwarders appropriated most of the net revenues created by the added efficiency of containerisation.[57] The chief difficulty, at least for the PRR, seems to have been that the NYC's freight-forwarder subsidiary, Universal Carloading & Distributing, soon came to dominate the national consolidator market. That company filled between 90 and 95 per cent of the containers used on both the PRR and the Lehigh Valley, and three-quarters of those on the NYC. Even though the PRR originated 363 containers at Baltimore during January 1929, only two shippers used the service, with one of them, Universal, responsible for all but a dozen of the containers. Universal used the PRR's container cars as compartmentalised boxcars, assembling loads at the railroad's freight houses. By the late 1930s, containers rarely left their carrier cars, providing fairly convincing evidence that the technology was merely a regulatory subterfuge to permit partial carloads that would otherwise have moved at LCL rates to instead travel at lower all-commodity tariffs.[58]

Containerisation did not stop the shift of high-value LCL traffic to the highways, however, nor did it prove remunerative to the railroads. Because forwarders such as Universal possessed no innate loyalty to the Pennsylvania Railroad, or even to the railroad industry in general, they readily transferred their business to other carriers or to trucks. By the summer of 1933, Universal Carloading shifted its operations from the PRR to the New York Central. By the late 1930s, forwarders had diverted virtually all LCL traffic between New York and Chicago, the two largest cities on the PRR, to other railroads or to motor carriers. As a result, PRR managers withdrew most of the Keystone containers from service, permitting them to be converted to tool sheds or to simply rust in storage yards. What little service remained ceased when the ICC required that shippers (including forwarders), and not the railroads, own all containers used in rail service.[59]

The ability of the freight forwarders, rather than the railroads, to oversee container operations reflected the fragmentation that has long shaped transportation regulation in the United States. Since 1887, and particularly after passage of the

---

[57] According to the ICC, 'The New York Central found that in New York City there are some 18,000 potential shippers of less-than-carload freight', yet only 140 to 150 shippers (mainly consolidators) actually used the NYC's container service. 'It is also significant', the ICC noted, 'that in 1928, after the Universal began operating, the number of containers handled by other shippers was only 5,088, as compared with 10,217 for the preceding year'. ICC, *Container Service*, at 389–90.

[58] *Railway Age* of 20 April 1929, 901–5, 31 August 1929, 554, 14 November 1931, 762, and 12 December 1936, 878–80.

[59] HML, Box 374, folder 11, 'Performance of Container Car Service June 20th, 1928 to January 3rd, incl., 1931'; HML, Box 380, folder 5 'Memorandum of Conference with Mr. Bradley of the Acme Fast Freight, Inc., in their New York Office, June 6, 1933', and John B. Large to H.W.B., 3 July 1933; HML, Box 334, folder 7, Testimony of Walter S. Franklin, 'Merchandise or Less-than Carload Freight'; Howell T. Cover to James M. Symes, 13 November 1950; Richard Burg, 'Container Service on the Pennsylvania R.R'., *The Keystone*, 18, Spring 1985, 7–50.

Transportation Act of 1920, ICC regulators were committed to the oversight of a mature railroad industry, one in which the weak carriers had to be protected from their stronger rivals. With the passage of the Motor Carrier Act of 1935, the ICC gained authority over interstate trucking, an immature industry characterised by cutthroat competition, and the rapid turnover of firms. The ICC could not regulate water carriers, a situation that did not change until Congress passed the Transportation Act of 1940. The Freight Forwarder Act of 1942 ultimately brought consolidators under regulatory control. Even then, the ICC regulated separately the various modes of transportation, making effective regulatory coordination a difficult, if not impossible task.[60]

The compartmentalisation of the regulatory apparatus – a situation created by Congress, and not the ICC – left regulators unable to devise a mechanism that might provide a container service across all three modes of transportation. In 1933, when President Franklin Delano Roosevelt selected Joseph Eastman as the Federal Coordinator of Transportation, the long-time ICC official took on the responsibility for developing industry-wide plans to reduce costs and increase efficiency, in order to offset the deleterious effects of the Great Depression. By the summer of 1936, Eastman had concluded that containers offered the potential to carry 100 million tons of freight each year. The problem, he noted, was precisely the feature that made containers such an attractive method of transportation. Through their control of freight forwarders, the railroads owned the container companies, yet containers were also employed by other modes of transportation. Sole railroad ownership, Eastman claimed,

> would be manifestly inappropriate, in view of the fact that the containers are also to be used by water carriers and motor carriers. A joint, tripartite ownership by the three classes of carriers would be logical, but as a practical matter it would be exceedingly difficult to work out any such arrangement, owing to the great number of the motor carriers and the lack of organization of the water carriers.[61]

And he concluded,

> For the present … (I) am inclined to think that the best course to pursue is to await developments. It will afford an opportunity to private enterprise to show what it can do in the absence of governmental interference.[62]

By 1936, however, the Great Depression had severely restricted the ability of private enterprise, and particularly the railroads, to show what they could do in the absence of governmental interference. The war that followed taxed the railroads'

60 The best coverage of this regulatory fragmentation is in Rose, Seely and Barrett, *Best Transportation System*, esp. 30–75.

61 *New York Times* of 15 June 1936.

62 Ibid.

carrying capacity, but discouraged such innovative practices as containerisation. The war also generated fundamental changes in maritime commerce and the global economy, and created substantial incentives for the more efficient transportation of oceangoing freight. As such, it was no surprise that Malcom McLean launched containerisation on the high seas. Only later did containers come back to land, to the railroads that had first developed them.

It would be difficult to surmise what might have been, had the ICC permitted companies such as the New York Central and the Pennsylvania Railroad unfettered authority to set rates on container traffic during the interwar period. The railroads might well have proved more successful at holding back the onslaught of truck competition, although that seems doubtful. They might even have emerged as the guiding force in global shipping, bringing to fruition PRR President Atterbury's vision of coordination 'with every sound economic agency of transportation'. But that was Eastman's intent, as well. Government and business, the regulators and the regulated, shared an appreciation for the potential of containerisation. Yet, their intents were substantially at odds with one another. Railroaders were prepared to set container rates in such a way as to seize traffic from weaker railroads, imperilling Congressional mandates to protect the railroad industry from self-destruction. When the ICC prevented them from doing so, railroad executives shifted responsibility for container services to nominally independent freight forwarders, who were until 1942 exempt from regulatory oversight. Eastman and ICC officials soon spied those attempts to thwart the will of Congress, and in enforcing the law they limited the scope of container operations, even as they acknowledged the immense potential of a container service.

References

Anonymous, 'Intermodal Transportation and the Freight Forwarder', *The Yale Law Journal*, 76, June 1967, 1360–96.

Anonymous., 'Regulation by the Interstate Commerce Commission of Railroad Terminal Trucking Facilities', *Columbia Law Review*, 32, December 1932, 1373–83.

Barton, Frank L., 'Uniform Freight Classification and the Interstate Commerce Commission', *The Journal of Land & Public Utility Economics* of 18 August, 1942, 312–22.

Blaszak, Michael W., 'Intermodal – Railroading's Indispensible Adaptation', *Pacific RailNews*, 394, September 1996, 26–37.

Burg, Richard, 'Container Service on the Pennsylvania R.R', *The Keystone*, 18, Spring 1985, 7–50.

Churella, Albert J., 'Delivery to the Customer's Door: Efficiency, Regulatory Policy, and Integrated Rail–Truck Operations, 1900–1938', *Enterprise and Society*, 10, March 2009, 98–136.

Churella, Albert J., 'Saving the Railroad Industry to Death: The Interstate Commerce Commission, the Pennsylvania Railroad, and the Unfulfilled Promise of Rail-Truck Cooperation', *Business and Economic History On-Line*, 4, 2006 (last accessed on 30 March 2012).

Committee on Interstate Commerce, ed., *Investigation of Railroads, Holding Companies, and Affiliated Companies: Report of the Committee on Interstate Commerce: Railroad Combination in the Eastern Region* (Washington, DC 1940).

Cudahy, Brian J., *Box Boats: How Container Ships Changed the World* (New York 2006).

DeBoer, David J., *Piggyback and Containers: A History of Rail Intermodal on America's Steel Highway* (San Marino, CA 1992).

Emery, Robert A., 'Social Engineering through Ratemaking: Value of Service and Hoch-Smith', *Journal of Transportation Law, Logistics and Policy*, 71, 2004, 167–74.

Emery, Robert A., 'The Cult of Smallness: The Early ICC and Volume Shipments', *Journal of Transportation Law, Logistics and Policy*, 73, 2006, 313–19.

Fishbein, Meyer H., 'The Trucking Industry and the National Recovery Administration', *Social Forces*, 34, December 1955, 171–9.

Goddard, Stephen B., *Getting There: The Epic Struggle between Road and Rail in the American Century* (New York 1994).

Harcourt, Keith W. and Cornille, T.C., 'A Comparative International Study of Technology and Policy in the Development of Railway Freight Containerisation in the US & UK', http://bit.ly/Harcourt_Cornillie_LisbonPaper (last accessed on 28 March 2012).

Levinson, Marc, *The Box: How the Shipping Container Made the World Smaller and the Economy Bigger* (Princeton, NJ 2006).

Locklin, D. Philip, 'Reorganization of the Railroad Rate Structure', *The American Economic Review*, 36, May 1946, 466–78.

Lynch, Edward S., 'Railroad Pick-Up and Delivery', *The Journal of Land & Public Utility Economics*, 14, May 1938, 120–132.

Mahoney, John H., *Intermodal Freight Transportation* (Westport, CT 1985).

Martin, Albro, *Enterprise Denied: Origins of the Decline of American Railroads, 1897–1917* (New York 1971).

McCarthy, Patrick S., *Transportation Economics, Theory and Practice: A Case Study Approach* (Malden, MA 2001).

Morrow, Giles and Wilson, G. Lloyd, 'Some Problems of Freight Forwarders', *Annals of the American Academy of Political and Social Science*, 230, November 1943, 110–5.

National Transportation Committee, *The American Transportation Problem* (Washington, DC 1933).

Oliver, H.C., 'Co-Ordinated Transport: How it Represents The Trend of the Times', *The Mutual Magazine*, March 1934, 12.

Pennsylvania Railroad, ed., *Container Car Service* (Philadelphia, PA 1929).

Revell, Keith D., 'Cooperation, Capture, and Autonomy: The Interstate Commerce Commission and the Port Authority in the 1920s', *Journal of Policy History*, 12, 2000, 177–214.

Revell, Keith D., *Building Gotham: Civic Culture and Public Policy in New York City, 1898–1938* (Baltimore, MD 2003).

Rose, Mark H., Seely, Bruce E. and Barrett, Paul F., *The Best Transportation System in the World: Railroads, Trucks, Airlines, and American Public Policy in the Twentieth Century* (Columbus, OH 2006).

Saunders, Richard Jr, *Merging Lines: American Railroads, 1900–1970* (DeKalb, Ill. 2001).

Solomon, Brian, *Intermodal Railroading* (St Paul, MN 2007).

Taff, Charles A., *Management of Physical Distribution and Transportation*, 7th ed. (Homewood, IL 1984).

White, John H. Jr, *On The Right Track: Some Historic Cincinnati Railroads* (Cincinnati, OH 2003).

Wilson, G. Lloyd, 'The Use of Freight Containers by British Railways', *Annals of the American Academy of Political and Social Science*, 187, September 1936, 173–9.

PART II
Mobility on Roads: an Innovative Success Story of the Twentieth Century – But Rail Survived

Chapter 9
Creative Destruction? A Schumpeterian View of Innovation in Car Transportation

Reiner Flik

The Kondratiev Cycle

In his *Business Cycles*, published in 1939, Joseph Alois Schumpeter developed an analysis of history which describes the evolution of the capitalistic economies as a sequence of cycles of innovation. Fundamental new products and completely new production techniques each cause periods of prosperity, which last approximately a quarter of a century.[1] Periods of poor innovation are accompanied with a decrease in investment, income stagnation, an increase of unemployment and social unrest.

These super-cycles are termed Kondratiev waves, after the Russian economist who studied the development of capitalistic societies in the 1920s in order to develop the Socialist command economy. Kondratiev based his findings on price statistics including wages and interest rates. The following figure shows an attempt to detect a Kondratiev-like pattern in the time series of the US national income (see Figure 9.1). The USA is an ideal object for studying this problem: first, because its national product statistics go back to 1790, and second, because its economy was able to function comparatively unaffected by war, revolution and state intervention.

If we do not make exorbitant demands to accuracy, we can view the trend line (moving average) as some kind of wavy line showing fluctuations in the long-run average growth rate of the per capita income. In any case, the result is vague, and the existence as well as the length of such a cycle is disputed. The limited space of this chapter does not permit a detailed discussion of the problem of the correct measurement of long-term business cycles.[2]

---

1 Joseph A. Schumpeter, *Business Cycles: A Theoretical, Historical, and Statistical Analysis of the Capitalist Process* (New York 1939).

2 See Rainer Metz, *Auf der Suche nach den Langen Wellen der Konjunktur* (Stuttgart 2008).

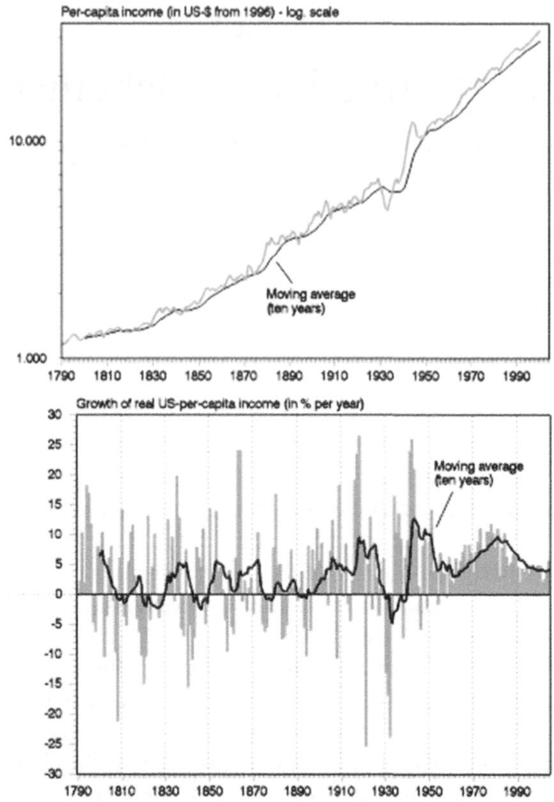

Figure 9.1 Real US-per-capita income – log. scale, 1790–2000

Source: Created by the author. Data taken from Richard Sutch, ed., *Historical Statistics of the United States*. Part C: *Economic Structure and Performance* (Cambridge 2006), vol. 3, 23–6.

Basic Innovations and Leading Industries, 1750–2000

Industrialisation started at the end of the eighteenth century in Great Britain when the textile crafts were mechanised. On the one hand, this created new centres of economic activity based on machine-made textiles and on the construction of textile machines; Manchester became a symbol for this. On the other hand, it brought distress and unemployment to regions and businesses that could not switch quickly enough from medieval methods of production to industrial production. Manual spinning died off quite calmly, because it was essentially a sideline occupation for women within the rural economy. But when handicraft weaving was being squeezed out of the market by the power loom in the 1810s, Great Britain experienced a radical movement of skilled textile artisans who destroyed

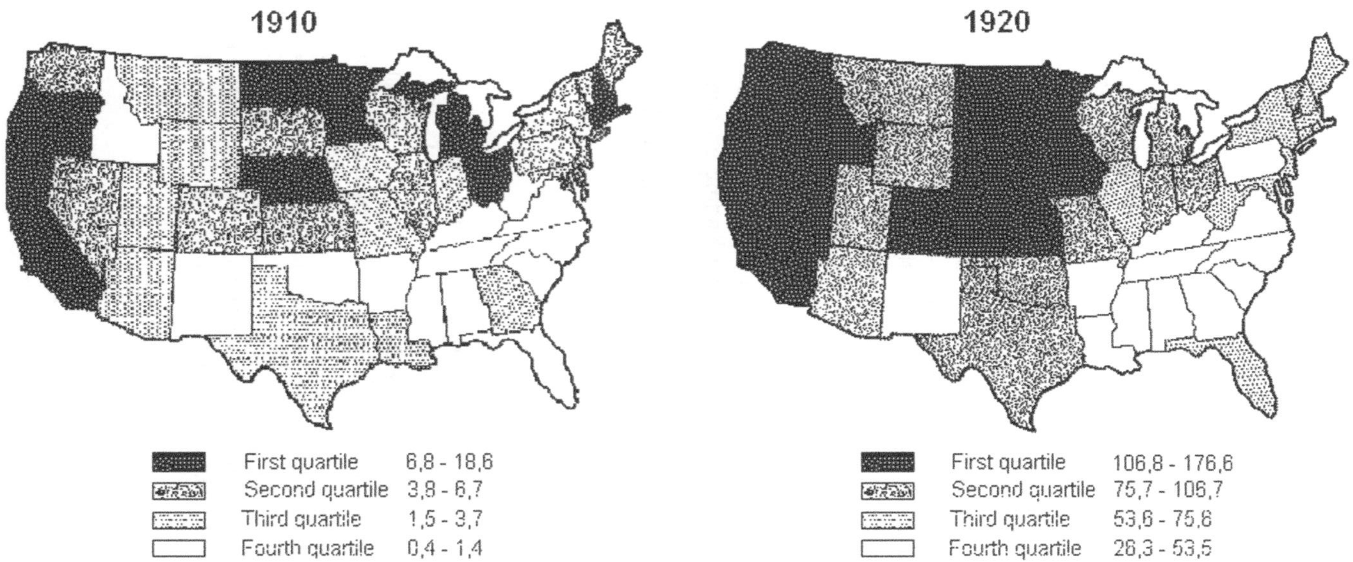

Figure 9.2 Car density in the USA, by states (1910 and 1920)

Source: Created by the author. Data taken from George Kirkham Jarvis, *The diffusion of the automobile in the United States: 1895–1969, University of Michigan*, Ph.D. thesis (Ann Arbor, MI 1972), 184 and 189.

the textile mills that were putting them out of business.[3] In Silesia, a province of Prussia, linen weavers, demoralised by long-term wage pressure, revolted against their employers in 1844. In German social history, the period from 1815 to the revolution of 1848 is called the Age of Pauperism (*Zeitalter des Pauperismus*).

The second third of the nineteenth century was the heyday of the iron and steel industry – the age of steam engines, steamships and railroad trains. The recovery period of the 1850s and 1860s is referred to as the Railway Kondratiev (*Eisenbahn-Kondratjew*). The boom collapsed in a stock market crash in 1873, allegedly due to excessive speculation in railway company shares. Afterwards came nearly two decades of stagnation – in German social history called the Great Depression or the Long Depression of the Bismarck era.

Around the turn of the century, another group of innovations again revitalised the global economy: electrification, the internal combustion engine, advances in pharmaceuticals and synthetic chemistry, the radio, the motorcar and the airplane. New infrastructure networks sprang up involving electricity, telephones, motorways and airports. New mass media like radio broadcasting and moving pictures emerged. New knowledge-based industries linked academic research and business more closely than ever before. Electrical engineering and chemical industry were the fundaments of the prosperity of the German economy in the Wilhelminian Era, and they made the USA the leading economic power in the world in the years leading up to 1914.

Car production became a substantial job-creator in the USA, especially in the 1920s, when America entered the age of the mass motorisation and mass consumption. Walt Whitman Rostow describes the impact of the car on the American society as follows:

> With the automobile the United States began a vast inner migration into newly constructed, single-family houses in the suburbs; and these new houses were filled increasingly with radios, refrigerators, and the other household gadgetry of a society whose social mobility and productivity had all but wiped out personal service. Within these houses Americans shifted their food consumption to higher-grade foods, increasingly purchased in cans – or, later, frozen. Automobiles, single-family houses, roads, household durables, mass markets in higher-grade foods – these tell a good deal of the story of the transformation of American society in the 1920s, a transformation which supported the boom of the 1920s and which altered the whole style of a continent's life, down to its courting habits.[4]

---

[3] These craftsmen-vandals were known as Luddites. Eric Hobsbawm has called the Luddites' actions 'collective bargaining by riot'. Eric Hobsbawm, 'The Machine Breakers', *Past and Present*, 1, 1952, 57–70.

[4] Walt Whitman Rostow, *The Stages of Economic Growth. A Non-communist Manifesto*, 3rd ed. (Cambridge, MA 1990), 77.

At the end of the 1920s, the newly created consumer good markets approached market saturation in the USA and the power of the aforementioned industries to stimulate economic growth slackened. Schumpeter regards this as the main cause for the Great Depression of the 1930s. He wrote his *Business Cycles* in a climate of widespread pessimism regarding the question of whether the capitalistic economy could constantly revitalise herself by continuous innovation. At that time, theories of stagnation had come into fashion. According to these theories, the state is the repair shop of a late-stage capitalistic system suffering from a lack of new ideas. This is where John Maynard Keynes' theory of the business cycle summarise Schumpeter's ideas. If creative destruction, initiated by private enterprise, fails to constantly produce the amount of net investment which secures full employment, then it is the state's responsibility to close the gap between aggregate demand and aggregate supply through its own investment.

The inventiveness of the scientists in the universities and in the laboratories of big business postponed the settlement of this issue for at least two Kondratiev waves. After the Second World War, transistor technology, used in TV, audio equipment and mainframe computers, along with both petrochemistry and the pent-up demand of Europe and Asia for motorcars, initiated a fourth Kondratiev wave. Microelectronics initiated a fifth by enabling personal computers, the Internet and mobile telephony. Contestants for initiating a sixth long wave include environmentally sensitive energy technologies like renewable energy and fuel cells, as well as bioengineering and medical engineering.

Basic Innovations in Transportation

Basic innovations are alterations that affect wide swaths of the economy, modifying, among other things, production techniques, consumer habits and styles of living. So far, their most important impacts on the economy have come from innovation in infrastructure networks, that is, the energy sector, communications and transportation. This book deals with transportation, so I will focus my discussion of Schumpeter's theory of innovation on this topic. To this end I will cut down my scheme of innovation cycles to three essentials, each standing for a century, or, rather, a Kondratiev cycle:

- channel transportation (first Kondratiev cycle)
- railway transportation (second Kondratiev cycle)
- automobile transportation (third and fourth Kondratiev cycle).

Schumpeter describes the construction of artificial waterways as 'one of the great features' of the period from 1787 to 1842, which defines the first long Kondratiev wave of prosperity in his time scheme.[5] Channels prepared Britain for

[5] Schumpeter, *Business Cycles*, 275.

the Industrial Revolution. The first true artificial waterways in eighteenth-century England were built at the end of the 1750s in the Manchester area. 'The distinction is usually given to the Bridgewater Canal running from the Duke of Bridgewater's estates at Worsley outside Manchester into the city itself, a distance of 10½ miles (17 kilometres)'.[6]

The Bridgewater Canal was built from 1759 to 1761 for getting coal from the Duke's mines in Worsley into the city. 'With the coming of the canal to Manchester, the cost of coal in the city dropped by almost half'.[7] Cheap transportation by channel allowed the British economy to shift swiftly from wood and charcoal to coal, and was a precondition of the profitable use of steam power outside the coal-mining fields. And the steam engine ended the attachment of factories to rivers. At that point, the iron producing and processing industries as well as the iron ore and steel trades migrated from the wooded, mountainous districts to the coal-mining areas and the seaports, forming urban agglomerations of industry.

In the twentieth century, electrification and the internal combustion engine again made the choice of location more free. Motor transportation partly undid the concentration of manufacturing plants and settlements which had happened in the nineteenth century.

Schumpeter calls the entrepreneur a pioneer because he must promote his project against the resistance of mighty interest groups. A new product or method of production, even if it is obviously suitable, is confronted by the repudiation of those groups who are affected adversely by it in their social position, their income and their wealth. Schumpeter therefore defines innovation as the pushing through of a new combination of means of production against resistance. Transportation history provides many examples of this. The railways allowed the US and German economies to catch up; both were far more dependent on land transportation than Britain's economy was. But 'it was', as Schumpeter ironically commented, 'in general not the postmasters who founded the railways'.[8] Railways were also a menace to the channel companies. It is said that during the railway mania in Britain, channel operators bought pieces of real estate only to impede railway lines that were threatening their business. For a time, the two transportation systems operated side by side. Channel operators even benefited from the new competitor, for instance by carrying building material and taking away the soil. In some cases railway companies took over channel operators and ran a combined transportation system. But in the long run, the railway trounced channel transport in matters of capacity, velocity and costs of maintenance.

---

6 Michael E. Ware, *Canals and Waterways* (Ashbourne 1989), 5. Ware considers the St Helens Canal, an artificial branch of the Sankey Brook, which made this water course navigable down to the Mersey River, to be the first artificial waterway in Great Britain.

7 Ibid., 6.

8 Joseph A. Schumpeter, *Theorie der wirtschaftlichen Entwicklung. Eine Untersuchung über Unternehmergewinn, Kapital, Kredit, Zins und den Konjunkturzyklus*, 2nd ed. (Berlin 1926), 101.

The crowding out of the channels by the railways is a good example of Schumpeter's concept of creative destruction. Channels were the precondition for the diffusion of the steam engine. But, when put on wheels, the steam engine outmoded the channels.

The same thing happened when motor transport appeared. There were many forms of resistance to it, which seem embarrassing in retrospect, and which are only comprehensible when we remember that the way progress is introduced to the society is that the good is crowded out by the better. Resistance to motor transport mainly came from social groups that were excluded from its use due to its high costs but who had to bear its social costs.[9] Again, as with the relationship between channel and rail, there was as well rivalry as cooperation between two business sectors serving the same purpose. In the 1920s, the invention of durable pneumatics for heavy vehicles allowed fast and flexible intercity transportation of goods and passengers, and trains had to compete and cooperate with trucks and buses. In Germany this issue was called the Road-Track Conflict (*Straße-Schiene-Konflikt*). In 1931, the state-owned *Reichsbahn Gesellschaft*, the German railway company, secretly took over Germany's most important trucking company, Schenker, in order to create a mixed building-to-building transportation system that would secure the long-distance transport monopoly of the railway.[10] The Road-Track Conflict was the main reason Adolf Hitler placed the control of the highway system in Germany (*Reichsautobahnprojekt*) into the hands of the *Reichsbahn*.[11]

The resistance to the motorcar at the outset of its life cycle has been thoroughly investigated by historians from Germany and Switzerland in recent years.[12] There is also a lively debate on motorised freight transportation and highway construction in the German literature on economic history.[13] Therefore I will not go deeply into

---

[9] The term 'social costs' includes the destruction of gravelled roads, traffic accidents and the disturbance of pedestrians and horse-drawn vehicles by dust, noise and exhaust. See Ralf Roth, *Das Jahrhundert der Eisenbahn. Die Herrschaft über Raum und Zeit 1800–1914* (Ostfildern 2005), chapter Die Gegner der Eisenbahn und der Beginn der Arbeiten am Netz, 50–70.

[10] See Richard Vahrenkamp's article in this volume.

[11] See Alfred Gottwald, *Julius Dorpmüller, die Reichsbahn und die Autobahn* (Berlin 1995), 29–41.

[12] Barbara Haubner, *Nervenkitzel und Freizeitvergnügen. Automobilismus in Deutschland 1886–1914* (Göttingen 1998); Christoph Maria Merki, *Der holprige Siegeszug des Automobils 1895–1930. Zur Motorisierung des Straßenverkehrs in Frankreich, Deutschland und der Schweiz* (Vienna 2002) and Uwe Fraunholz, *Motorphobia. Anti-automobiler Protest in Kaiserreich und Weimarer Republik* (Göttingen 2002).

[13] See Richard Vahrenkamp, *Autobahnbau in Hessen bis 1943* (Darmstadt 2007); Richard Vahrenkamp, 'Planning and Constructing the Autobahn Network in Germany During the Nazi Period – Styles and Strategies', in Gijs Mom and Laurent Tissot, eds, *Road History, Planning, Building and Use* (Neuchâtel 2007), 87–98, and Richard Vahrenkamp, *The German Autobahn 1920–1945. Hafraba Visions and Mega Projects*

these issues. Instead I will turn to the very interesting phenomenon of the spread of the automobile overseas, and the pioneering role played by the farming regions.

Motorisation of Road Transport in Europe and in the USA

When I started my research about motorisation I did some exploratory statistical work. Figures 9.2 and 9.3 show the outcome. It was a surprise to me because these results are not in harmony with two assumptions commonly accepted in the literature about transport history:

1. Innovations are first accepted in urban areas and diffuse from there to the hinterlands.
2. New products require a certain level of infrastructure to become innovations. Therefore, a highly developed road system is a precondition for, or at least fosters the spread of, the automobile.

The second argument, usually based on the French case, is especially incompatible with my findings. The automobile density, that is, the number of cars and lorries registered for use on public roads in relation to the total population, grew fastest in countries that did not possess a European-like dense road network at all. Figure 9.3 shows the increase in automobile density in Europe and overseas. It grew fastest in the USA and some overseas agricultural economies. But around 1914, roughly 90 per cent of the US road network still consisted of dirt roads.

In 1919 a German commercial attaché in Argentina was asked by German automobile producers how to increase the sales of German cars in South America to the pre-war level. His major piece of advice, published in the journal of the manufacturers' association, was to reduce the track width of German cars. In Argentina, he wrote, country roads were made by the cars themselves. The standard had been set by Ford's Model T, which dominated the world market then. So the wider German cars had to drive with two wheels in the track and two wheels out.[14]

These findings led me to study the role of the car in rural America.[15] I explain the pioneering role of the North American farmlands using a comparison of the benefits, the private costs and the social costs of car ownership. Benefits include the savings of time and the increases of income which farmers and rural businesspeople derived from their cars. This was why the number of railway tracks per square kilometre in the USA was about one-third of the railway density in Germany, and what the Midwest States particularly lacked were regional and

---

(Lohmar 2010). See also Reiner Ruppmann, *Frankfurt und das Rhein-Main-Taunus-Gebiet – Schrittmacher für das Autobahn-Zeitalter* (Darmstadt 2011).

[14] Anonymous, 'Argentinien als Markt für Kraftwagen', *Motorwagen*, 22, 1919, 127.

[15] See Reiner Flik, *'Von Ford lernen?' Automobilbau und Motorisierung in Deutschland bis 1933* (Cologne 2001), 30–61.

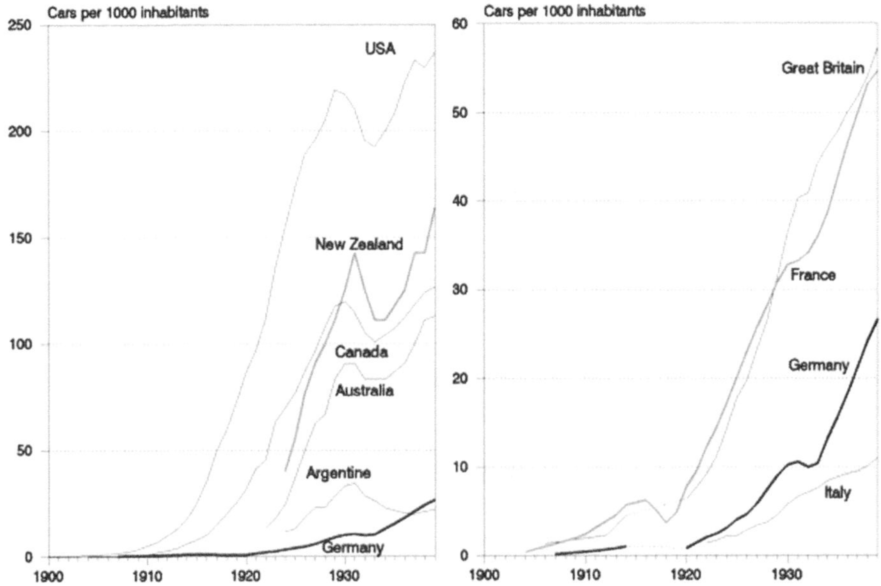

Figure 9.3 Car density in Europe and overseas, 1900–1939

Source: Created by the author.

linking railways that connected country towns to the main lines. It is obvious that the motorcar brought about an enormous improvement in productivity and the standard of living in these thinly-populated areas, although the roads that existed were in a bad shape. But less investments in road construction enabled a low level of social costs of this transport system. The limited size of this chapter does not allow me to go into details of this explanatory model. Therefore I will restrict myself to its main topics: roads and income.

Road Construction and Car Density

Let me explain in a few words my thesis about the influence of road construction on car density: the relationship should not be regarded as a unidirectional causal connection – in the sense that a highly developed road system fostered the spread of motor vehicles. It was rather an interaction of the two factors. Bad roads were not a big argument against buying cars. They simply challenged design engineers to develop low-weight, all-terrain cars. The men at Ford did this best. And in early motorised regions there rapidly emerged interest groups that campaigned for the improvement of the road system.

In the USA, motor vehicles actually drove the construction of roads, which had been neglected since the appearance of the railway.[16] The Good Roads Movement had started before the First World War. At first it advocated for better country roads to improve transportation between farms and markets. During the war, Congress decided to create a network of federal highways. The US railways were overburdened by the increased needs for transportation due to the war. Seaports and railway intersections had to cope with huge waiting queues. The transportation crises made everyone aware that a network of intercontinental roads, suitable for heavy lorries, was needed not only for business but also for the military. At the end of the 1920s, the USA had the world's densest and most modern highway network.[17]

In the case of Germany, the relation between car density and the development of road infrastructure is not as clear. Germany had a network of gravelled roads that was hundreds of years old, and with respect to the HaFraBa (*Verein zur Vorbereitung der Autostraße Hansestädte–Frankfurt–Basel* / Association for the Preparation of the Motorway Hanseatic cities–Frankfurt–Basel), founded in 1926, and the *Reichsautobahnprojekt*, initiated in 1933, we can even say that Germany had both highways and interest groups who worked to improve them before it had a noteworthy stock of cars. But this by itself is not enough evidence for us to conclude that things went in the opposite direction in Germany, that is, that road construction was an important driver of car density. And the fact that the initially better condition of roads in Germany did not translate into more car registrations is another argument that roads do not matter much in explaining the diffusion of the automobile. With respect to the Federal Republic of Germany, it is indisputable that road construction was mainly driven by car density.[18]

Income and Car Density

Apparently income is the most prominent factor in explaining car density. But once again it must be presumed that the nexus seems to be more an interaction (a mutual self-augmenting process) than a causation: high income increases the demand for cars, and cars increase the productivity of the economy, and, therefore, the income. In rural countries, where railway density was low, cars and lorries were the precondition to create integrated markets. Once they became established, motor vehicles provided tremendous power to supplier industries – iron and steel,

---

[16] Hans Lopinski, 'Die Entwicklung des Straßenbauwesens in den Vereinigten Staaten von Amerika', *Mitteilungen des Reichsverbands der Automobilindustrie*, 3, 1927, 315–16.

[17] See Werner Feilchenfeld, *Kraftverkehrswirtschaft, Kraftfahrzeugsteuern und Landstraßenfragen in U.S.A. Denkschrift der Studienkommission des Deutschen Industrie- und Handelstages und der Industrie- und Handelskammer zu Berlin zur Prüfung von Kraftfahrzeugsteuerfragen* (Berlin 1929).

[18] See Dietmar Klenke, 'Freier Stau für freie Bürger', *Die Geschichte der bundesdeutschen Verkehrspolitik, 1949–1994* (Darmstadt 1995).

machine building, petroleum and so forth – and to other interrelated branches of economic activity such as road construction, suburb settlement and tourism.

The excerpt from Rostow's 'Stages of Economic Growth', cited above, sums up the car's overall contribution to the Roaring Twenties in the USA – a period, according to Schumpeter, that was a late stage of the third Kondratiev cycle. Some statements from a survey of US farmers about the impact of the automobile on their business may illustrate why just rural America was the vanguard in the process of mass motorisation.[19] Most of the farmers consulted for this study judged the use of motorcars as profitable: 25 per cent emphasised that the size of their market had been tripled; 50 per cent were able to eliminate one job, and bigger farms even two jobs by the use of motor cars;[20] and motorisation compensated in a certain sense for the slow progress of the electricity grid, which had not yet penetrated deeply in the countryside. Farmers used cars (with supplementary tools and the help of a transmission belt) as power plant for grinding, milling, pumping, sawing and threshing, and for pulling harvesters and haycarts. In a pre-war US automobile journal I found an advertisement for a tool which allegedly enabled cars to plough fields. In about 1915, Ford and International Harvester came out with a low-priced tractor, an offshoot of car construction. The tractor 'invites the combination of operations that were previously quite distinct, ploughing and the preparation of the seedbed, for instance, and thus steadily leads to ever-increasing mechanization'.[21]

From 1920 to 1929 the number of tractors in the USA increased from 246,000 to 920,000. This expansion was principally on the Great Plains, where mechanised farming with tractors and combine threshers could be brought to its full advantage.

Therefore we can summarise: for the average farmer overseas, the motorcar was not a mere gadget for escaping the boredom of rural life, that is, a consumer good. It was principally an investment good, which enhanced productivity and increased income. In Henry Ford's words: 'The citizens of the United States do not own automobiles because they are wealthy. They are wealthy because they own automobiles and use them as a device to extend their abilities'.[22]

From 1910 to 1929 the per capita income in the USA more than doubled. Farmers' average net gains increased from 652 US-dollars in 1910 to 1,395 US-dollars in 1919, partly due to the abnormal rise in agricultural prices during the war. During the crisis of 1920 and 1921, agricultural prices and farmer incomes

---

[19] In 1929 'about 60 per cent of all farms were equipped with motor vehicles, and about one-quarter of all trucks were in farm use', Schumpeter, *Business Cycles*, 774. According to the figures given in Anonymous, 'Agrarkrise und Agrarpolitik in den Vereinigten Staaten von Amerika', *Vierteljahreshefte zur Statistik des Deutschen Reichs*, 45, 4, 1936, 124, and Feilchenfeld, *Kraftverkehrswirtschaft*, 265, in 1920 about one-third of all US farmers owned a motorcar. By 1929 this figure had reached almost 90 per cent. (The average combines personal cars and lorries.)

[20] Flik, 'Von Ford lernen?', 48.

[21] Schumpeter, *Business Cycles*, 735.

[22] Henry Ford, *Und trotzdem vorwärts!* (Leipzig 1930), 261.

fell sharply and did not fully recover. In 1929 a farmer's income averaged 945 US-dollars. In the decade of the 1920s, the index of agricultural prices peaked in 1925, then gradually declined, while fluctuating, up to the eve of the world crises.[23]

Agricultural Credit and Business Cycle

The characteristics of the motorcar as an investment good, which was worth running into debt to acquire, leads us to an aspect of Schumpeter's theory that has been neglected here so far – the role of banking and credit creation in the process of evolution. Innovators are rarely rich enough to initiate their project by their own means; an exceptional case may be the investment of the British gentry in channels. An entrepreneur usually needs financing to be able to buy the means of production he needs – labour, raw materials, machinery and the like. Therefore he needs the banker as a partner to jointly push the development of the capitalist economy. The railway Kondratiev would be hardly imaginable without the concurrent emergence of modern investment banking.

A Kondratiev prosperity is therefore almost necessarily a period of credit creation and growing debt. Schumpeter considers this healthy as long as borrowing is confined to entrepreneurs and serves only to improve the productive apparatus and to lower the cost per unit of a product. But innovators generally attract competitors (that is, imitators), if access to the market cannot be restricted effectively, such as by using patents. And:

> Once a prosperity has got under sail, households will borrow for purposes of consumption, in the expectation that actual incomes will permanently be what they are or that they will still increase; business will borrow merely to expand on old lines, on the expectation that this demand will persist or still increase; farms will be bought at prices at which they could pay only if the prices of agricultural products kept their level or increased. In these cases there is no increase in productivity at all, and it is this fact … alone which is responsible for a fall in prices sometimes spelling disaster.[24]

These effects almost of necessity lead to overproduction when the newly created capacity comes fully into operation. Because increases in consumption and hence in income normally lag by some years that in production, firms are forced to cut prices in order to stimulate demand and an initially sound debt position becomes unsustainable.

This seems an appropriate description of the development of the US economy in general and of US agriculture in particular during the 1920s. The growth of US industry relied already heavily on sales financing in these days; more than

---

23 See Schumpeter, *Business Cycles*, 734, and Flik, *'Von Ford lernen?'*, 49.

24 Schumpeter, *Business Cycles*, 147.

50 per cent of the new cars were sold on instalment plans, and other markets for consumer durables showed a similar picture. Private households and corporations piled up a formidable stock of debt, amounting to nearly 160 per cent of the gross domestic product (GDP) in 1929. Total farm mortgages almost tripled from 1910 to 1928 (1910: 3.3 billion US-dollars; 1928: 9.5 billion US-dollars). This proved to be untenable for many when competition diminished income:

> Agriculture had been ... an innovative industry, or rather an industry that had innovations forced upon it which originated elsewhere, such as the internal combustion engine, specifically agricultural machinery, electric power and appliances, new fertilizers. As ... these innovations fully conquered and came to fruition ... they ... sectionally reduced costs to a level on which large sectors were unable to compete. ... After 1926 ... the agrarian situation became increasingly unsatisfactory, but the only *general* cause of this was the pressure of unproductive debt.[25]

Conclusion and Outlook

According to the model developed in Schumpeter's *Business Cycles*, the downturn of the US economy at the end of the 1920s was not the result of some 'meaningless and functionless disturbances of economic life and of the march of progress', but a normal reaction of the economic system during a long-lasting growth cycle. One could also speak of a debt cycle, this one largely based on the spread of the motorcar.[26]

Those inherent recessions can lead to depression, but they don't have to. To provide a full understanding of the Great Depression of the 1930s, the analysis provided here would have to be supplemented by other information on how competition between countries was accelerated by the First World War, on the role of trade barriers, international capital flows and so on. But that task lies beyond the ambition of this chapter.

There is evidence that income was also the main driving power of the motorisation of the Western European economies after the Second World War during the fourth Kondratiev. In Figure 9.4 I have extended some of the time series from Figure 9.3. None of the national car markets depicted there showed a strong tendency of market saturation until the end of the twentieth century. Additionally, I have plotted Angus Maddison's estimations of the development of the real income per capita in these nations (measured in the so-called Geary-Khamis dollar – a hypothetical unit of currency which provides a valid measure to compare the standard of living between countries and over time). A comparison of the time series shows a nearly perfect positive correlation with coefficients of one

25 Schumpeter, *Business Cycles*, 733–4.

26 Schumpeter, *Business Cycles*, 146.

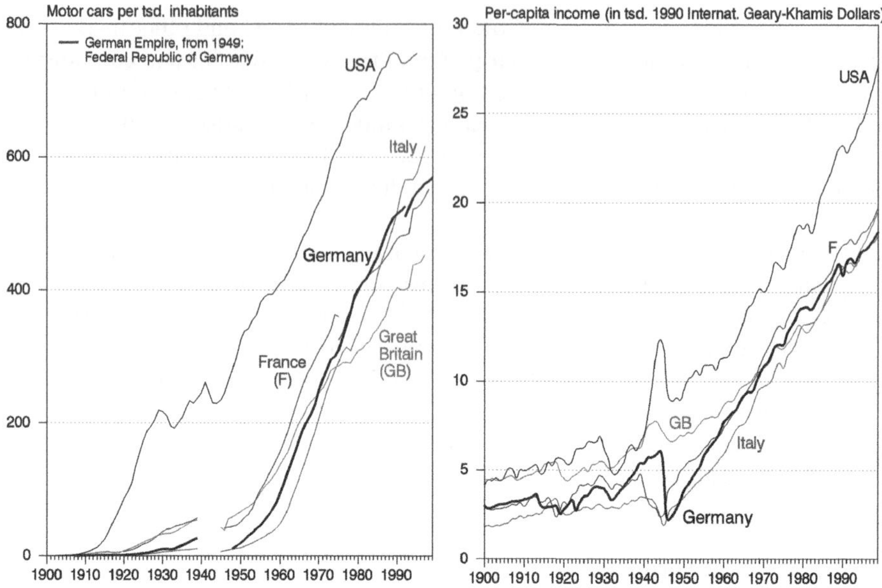

Figure 9.4 Real per capita income and car density in Western Europe and in the USA, 1900–1999

Source: Created by the author. Data taken from B.R. Mitchell, *International Historical Statistics. The Americas 1750–2000*, 5th ed. (Basingtonstoke and New York 2003); Statistisches Bundesamt, ed., *Statistisches Jahrbuch für die Bundesrepublik Deutschland*, vol. 1950–1999 (Wiesbaden 1951–2000). Angus Maddison, *Historical Statistics of the World Economy: 1–2008 AD*, ggdc.net/Maddison/Historical_Statistics/horizontal-file_02–2010.xls (last accessed 12 September 2012).

or close to one. However, correlation gives us no hint about the direction of the relationship. But it seems a reliable assumption that the interaction between the increase of car density and the *Wirtschaftswunder* (economic miracle) in Western Europe was similar to that shown above in the case of the USA.

References

Anonymous, 'Agrarkrise und Agrarpolitik in den Vereinigten Staaten von Amerika', in *Vierteljahreshefte zur Statistik des Deutschen Reichs*, 1936, 4, 123–37.

Anonymous, 'Argentinien als Markt für Kraftwagen', *Motorwagen*, 22, 1919, 127.

Buhr, Hermann de and Regenbrecht, Michael, eds, *Industrielle Revolution und Industriegesellschaft* (Frankfurt am Main 1983).

Feilchenfeld, Werner, *Kraftverkehrswirtschaft, Kraftfahrzeugsteuern und Landstraßenfragen in U.S.A. Denkschrift der Studienkommission des Deutschen*

Industrie- und Handelstages und der Industrie- und Handelskammer zu Berlin zur Prüfung von Kraftfahrzeugsteuerfragen (Berlin 1929).

Flik, Reiner, *'Von Ford lernen?' Automobilbau und Motorisierung in Deutschland bis 1933* (Cologne 2001).

Ford, Henry, *Und trotzdem vorwärts!* (Leipzig 1930).

Fraunholz, Uwe, *Motorphobia. Anti-automobiler Protest in Kaiserreich und Wiemarer Republik* (Göttingen 2002).

Gottwald, Alfred E., *Julius Dorpmüller, die Reichsbahn und die Autobahn* (Berlin 1995).

Haubner, Barbara, *Nervenkitzel und Freizeitvergnügen. Automobilismus in Deutschland 1886–1914* (Göttingen 1998).

Hobsbawm, Eric, 'The Machine Breakers', *Past and Present*, 1, 1952, 57–70.

Jarvis, George Kirkham, *The Diffusion of the Automobile in the United States: 1895–1969, University of Michigan*, Ph.D. (Ann Arbor, MI 1972).

Klenke, Dietmar, *'Freier Stau für freie Bürger.' Die Geschichte der bundesdeutschen Verkehrspolitik, 1949–1994* (Darmstadt 1995).

Lopinski, Hans, 'Die Entwicklung des Straßenbauwesens in den Vereinigten Staaten von Amerika', *Mitteilungen des Reichsverbands der Automobilindustrie*, 3, 1927, 315–16.

Maddison, Angus, *Historical Statistics of the World Economy: 1–2008 AD*, http://www.ggdc.net/Maddison/Historical_Statistics/horizontal-file_02–2010.xls. (last accessed on 12 September 2012).

Merki, Christoph Maria, *Der holprige Siegeszug des Automobils 1895–1930. Zur Motorisierung des Straßenverkehrs in Frankreich, Deutschland und der Schweiz* (Vienna 2002).

Metz, Rainer, *Auf der Suche nach den Langen Wellen der Konjunktur* (Stuttgart 2008).

Mitchell, B.R., *International Historical Statistics. The Americas 1750–2000*, 5th ed. (Basingstoke and New York 2003).

Rostow, Walt Whitman, *The Stages of Economic Growth. A Non-communist Manifesto*, 3rd ed. (Cambridge, MA 1990).

Ruppmann, Reiner, *Frankfurt und das Rhein-Main-Taunus-Gebiet – Schrittmacher für das Autobahn-Zeitalter* (Darmstadt 2011).

Schumpeter, Joseph A., *Theorie der wirtschaftlichen Entwicklung. Eine Untersuchung über Unternehmergewinn, Kapital, Kredit, Zins und den Konjunkturzyklus*, 2nd ed. (Berlin 1926).

Schumpeter, Joseph A., *Business Cycles. A Theoretical, Historical, and Statistical Analysis of the Capitalist Process* (New York 1939).

Sutch, Richard, ed., *Historical statistics of the United States*. Part C: *Economic Structure and Performance* (Cambridge 2006).

Statistisches Bundesamt, ed., *Statistisches Jahrbuch für die Bundesrepublik Deutschland*, vol.: *1950–1991* (Wiesbaden 1950–90).

Vahrenkamp, Richard, 'Planning and Constructing the Autobahn Network in Germany During the Nazi-Period – Styles and Strategies', in Gijs Mom and

Laurent Tissot, eds, *Road History, Planning, Building and Use* (Neuchâtel 2007), 87–98.
Vahrenkamp, Richard, *Autobahnbau in Hessen bis 1943* (Darmstadt 2007).
Vahrenkamp, Richard, *The German Autobahn 1920–1945. Hafraba Visions and Mega Projects* (Lohmar 2010).
Ware, Michael E., *Canals and Waterways* (Ashbourne 1989).

Chapter 10
Inventing the American Road: Innovations Shaping the American Freeway[1]

Bruce E. Seely

The usual starting point for exploring American transportation mobility is the automobile, since vehicles allow citizens the opportunity to go where they want, when they wish. Railroads may have started Americans thinking this way, but the current vision of mobility clearly relies upon motor vehicles. Yet it is also a truism that the drivers of those motor vehicles rely upon the road to realise their unfettered assumptions about mobility. The road and car system is rather tightly coupled, but such a simple formulation of automotive transport misses much of the enormous complexity that is related to the automotive right of way, the highway. Indeed, the highway deserves attention in its own right as a pivotal element in the American concept of mobility.

The American highway system developed during the twentieth century is the largest public works project ever undertaken. The network includes rural dirt roads, city streets, the tracks providing access to National Forests and National Parks, the secondary and primary roads linking cities. But at the pinnacle are the high-speed, limited-access roads of the National System of Interstate and Defense Highways. For American motorists, the 46,000 miles of Interstate roads are fundamental to their concept of individual mobility delivered via the internal combustion-powered automobile, the epitome of 'the Freedom of the American Road'.[2] As with all complex technical systems, the shape and designs of these roads did not emerge fully formed with the decision to fund the massive construction programme approved by the Congress in 1956. Rather, they are the product of efforts to develop what many engineers once labelled freeways, and involved many small, incremental steps over a span of 40 to 50 years. The freeway is a complex

---

1 This chapter grew out of a lecture originally presented in the series 'The Freeway in America' sponsored by the Rice Design Alliance and the Hines College of Architecture at the University of Houston, 13 October 2000. I appreciate the assistance of Richard Weingroff at the Federal Highway Administration in conducting the research about the many developments discussed in this chapter.

2 The linkage was made apparent in a publication by the Ford Motor Company, ed., *Freedom of the American Road* (Dearborn, MI 1956), which was produced as part of the public relations campaign conducted during the mid-1950s to secure passage of legislation funding construction of the Interstate highway system.

socio-technical system composed, like other large-scale technologies, of many components. Importantly, not all of them are technical; indeed it is impossible to ignore the political, financial, social, cultural and organisational elements that are tightly interwoven into the technical features.[3] These technical, political, structural and financial challenges all called for original solutions. Some of the resulting 'inventions' were physical components of the modern freeway and adjacent roadside, what we might call the 'material culture' of the American freeway. But more than hardware had to be invented in order to bring the freeway into existence. A combination of technical and non-technical elements were required to make the freeway a functioning system and the basis of American mobility.

Organisational and Financial Innovations

While freeways were a product of the middle decades of the twentieth century, this type of highway also rested upon a number of organisational and financial features that supported the more general development of the American road system during the twentieth century. Certain of these organisational elements took shape more than a century ago.

At the end of the nineteenth century, American roads were the responsibility of local governments, and had been since railroads came to dominate American transportation after 1850. This combination of railroads and local control also explained why most American roads of the 1880s and 1890s were unimproved, muddy quagmires in spring and fall and dusty and rutted the rest of the time. Getting Americans out of the mud – the battle cry of road improvement supporters – required organisational innovations that improved and expanded the capacity of state and local governments to construct better roads, of which freeways were a later culmination.[4]

---

3 Among the scholars who have discussed the concept of socio-technological system, see Thomas P. Hughes, *Networks of Power: Electrification in Western Society, 1880–1930* (Baltimore, MD 1983); Wiebe Bijker, et al., *Shaping Technology/Building Society: Studies in Sociotechnical Change* (Cambridge, MA 1992); idem, *Of Bicycles, Bakelites, and Bulbs: Toward a Theory of Sociotechnical Change* (Cambridge, MA 1995); and Ronald R. Kline, *Consumers in the Country: Technology and Social Change in Rural* America (Baltimore, MD 2000).

4 Much of the information that follows is drawn from my study of the Bureau of Public Roads, the federal government's highway agency after 1893. See Bruce E. Seely, *Building the American Highway System: Engineers as Policy Makers* (Philadelphia, PA 1987). That study rested heavily upon the Records of the BPR, RG-30, National Archives Records Center II, College Park, MD. A general account of nineteenth century roads and their administration can be found in George Rogers Taylor, *The Transportation Revolution, 1815–1860* (New York 1951); see also US, Department of Transportation, Federal Highway Administration, *America's Highways, 1776–1976: A History of the Federal-Aid Program* (Washington, DC 1976). Hereafter cited as US FHWA, *America's Highways*.

One myth can be exploded right away – the American road system was not simply a response to the automobile. The car was a very important factor, no doubt. But the pressure for road improvements started with bicyclists in the 1880s. And bicycle advocates were supported by railroad executives who believed a network of farm-to-market roads would expand their reach into the countryside. Lobbying efforts bore fruit in 1893, with the formation of the Office of Road Inquiry (ORI) in the Agriculture Department to gather and disseminate information leading to better roads. In short order, the ORI established itself as 'THE' source of information about road improvement. Its pamphlets and bulletins promoted the value of better roads. Its laboratory, opened in 1900, tested materials for free. The engineers in the laboratory prepared material standards and construction specifications as guides to best practice. They also drafted model state legislation establishing state highway departments. The ORI consistently argued that engineers as apolitical experts should control the road system to prevent graft, insure efficiency and remove politics from the process. This image of road engineers being above politics survived as the foundation of the American highway construction programme until the early-mid 1960s.

This principle of engineering control was enshrined into federal law when Congress provided funds for a national road construction programme in 1916 and 1921, under the direction of a renamed Bureau of Public Roads (BPR). Federal funding grew from 25 million US dollars per year in 1920 to 75 million US dollars and then to 100 million US dollars and more annually during the 1920s. While only a fraction of the total expended for roads in the US, federal dollars were highly significant because of the organisational structure that accompanied the funding. State and federal highway engineers proved very influential in shaping Congressional thinking about highway administration, successfully convincing Congress to specify a federalist structure. Specifically, the law required the states and the BPR to share equally in funding this road system. Road construction was similarly divided, with the states expected to design, build and maintain roads, while the BPR approved all plans, helped set construction and materials standards, ensured that competent state highway departments existed under engineering control and inspected completed roads.[5]

This federal-aid highway programme was an apparent model of federalism, a partnership between state highway engineers and the BPR. But the reality was a great deal more complicated, for federal engineers were more knowledgeable than most state engineers and less subject to political interference. Moreover, BPR researchers had the time and the facilities to study the problems facing road builders, a luxury denied most state road engineers. As a result, the BPR became the arbiter of this relationship, but the skilful administration of Thomas H. MacDonald, chief of the BPR from 1918 to 1953, insured that state officials

[5] Organisationally, this structure still governs the American highway programme, with the states building roads whose plans have been approved by federal officials, even though funding is no longer equally provided.

had few reasons to complain about BPR domination. Above all, BPR reliance upon various cooperative organisations, including the American Association of State Highway Officials (AASHO), enabled federal engineers to lead without dictating policy to the states. Moreover, BPR engineers genuinely sought to strengthen and enhance the capacities of state highway departments. By the 1930s, BPR engineers had developed working partnerships with their state counterparts that allowed both to work toward a national road network.[6]

Among the many political consequences of this organisational structure was the substantial agreement concerning the direction of American highway policy from Congress at the top through the state highway departments. All agreed that the primary imperative was completion of a national road system linking the cities. Indeed, the House and Senate road committees worked closely with the BPR and AASHO engineers during the drafting of every biennial highway Bill into the 1950s. The sense of common purpose in the highway community was backed by a strong but amorphous public support, resting upon the American love affair with the automobile.

This organisational structure could not, however, guarantee the complete removal of political controversy and interference over road questions, so long as the key question of paying for road construction was unresolved. Before the onset of either the federal-aid programme or mass automobility, local and state road builders employed several funding approaches. In most locales, property owners were responsible for the roads that abutted their property, either through property taxes or through a direct road tax paid by working on the roads for a few days every a year. The first method initially caused many farmers to oppose road improvements for fear of increased property taxes. The second approach created many wonderful social occasions, as farmers gathered to work off their road tax obligations, but provided only minimal improvements in the roads. Even less effective was convict labour, a preferred alternative in Southern states, because the workers lacked both the knowledge and the desire to produce serious improvements in local roads.[7]

---

[6] The BPR's sense of partnership was evident in its oversight of federal-aid projects, as well as its role in the establishment of construction and material standards and specifications, and the expansion of research capabilities at the state level. See Seely, *Building the American Highway System*, chapters 4–6; also National Academy of Sciences, National Research Council, *A History of the Highway Research Board, 1920–1970* (Washington, DC 1970); and American Association of State Highway Officials, *AASHO: The First Fifty Years, 1914–1964* (Washington, DC 1965).

[7] Contemporary information on highway financing can be found in Thomas H. MacDonald, 'The Financing of Highways', *Annals of the American Academy of Political and Social Science*, 116, November 1924, 160–68; Thomas R. Agg and John E. Brindley, *Highway Finance and Administration* (New York 1927), 108–221; John H. Bateman, *Highway Engineering: A Textbook for Students of Civil Engineering* (New York 1928), 35–54. The annual reports of the ORI and its successor organisations within the US Department of Agriculture routinely discussed highway finance issues. The years of the various reports are: ORI (1893–98); Office of Public Road Inquiry (1898–1904); Office of

State funds, which eventually became the most important source of road support before 1950, appeared in tandem with highway departments to oversee those funds. The first state-wide road agencies were established in Massachusetts and New Jersey in the early 1890s, and the idea slowly spread west and south before the federal-aid legislation made them a condition for receiving federal funds in 1916. Usually state funds were limited to designated systems of the most important roads, although some states assisted counties that adopted engineering control and the higher construction standards advocated by state engineers. But it was not easy for the counties to find the funds needed to match state-aid packages. When federal-aid began in 1916, the states encountered similar problems matching federal-aid dollars. The states initially relied upon general tax revenues for road construction funds, a situation that exposed road programmes to competition with other activities and occasional political manipulation.[8]

State and local road organisations discovered three possible solutions to the problem of funding road construction. The first and initially the most important source was license and registration fees, which jumped from 100 million US dollars in the states in 1921 to 259 million US dollars in 1928. By the latter year, another 50 million US dollars from registration went into the coffers of local road agencies. Despite the rate of increase, these sums could not support construction programmes, so highway builders also relied upon a second major strategy – bond financing. In 1921, about 27 per cent of the state funds available for road work, and 43 per cent of local funds came from bond sales, but these proportions had dropped to 14 per cent and 18 per cent by 1928, although actual revenues increased steadily.[9] Borrowing money was always a touchy political subject, however, and over-reliance on these funds could leave a highway department in trouble. In Pennsylvania in 1913, for example, the defeat of a 50-million-US dollars-bond issue left the highway department's engineering staff 'threatened with disintegration'.[10]

A third revenue source quickly proved much more appealing – taxes on gasoline. Oregon enacted the first fuel tax in 1919 and the idea quickly spread. In 1921, gas taxes generated only 3.2 million US dollars, or 0.8 per cent of the states funds used for road construction, but by 1928, the total had risen to 254 million US dollars, or 27.6 per cent of the total. Every state had enacted a gas tax by

---

Public Roads (1905–17); Bureau of Public Roads (1918–38). For summaries, see Leonard S. Goldberg, 'Local Government Highway Finance Trends, 1984–1993', *Public Roads*, 60, Summer 1996, 24–8; Charles L. Dearing, *American Highway Policy* (Washington, DC 1942), 100–110; and US, FHWA, *America's Highways*, 243–6.

8 The expansion of state highway departments is traced in Seely, *Building the American Highway System*, 12–34.

9 Information from Thomas H. MacDonald, 'How Highway Financing Has Evolved', *Engineering News-Record*, 104, 2 January 1930, 4–7; see also US, FHWA, *American Highways, 1776–1976*, 238–43.

10 'Highway Repair Work', *Engineering News*, 72, 2 July 1914, 52.

1936. The American Petroleum Institute was never completely happy about this mechanism, but one historian called this the only popular tax in American history. Of central importance was increasing public acceptance of the proposition that gas tax revenues should be earmarked strictly for road improvements. Motorists felt they received immediate benefits, while the rate of a couple of pennies per gallon of gas seemed almost painless. Indeed, gas taxes were so painless that they were the only state revenue source that did not diminish during the Depression, and they attracted attention from legislators looking to 'divert' these funds to pay for other services. By the mid-1930s, the road and automobile communities were united in support of constitutional amendments requiring the use of these revenues for road work.[11] The BPR persuaded Congress to punish states guilty of diversion by withholding a portion of federal-aid funds, but state constitutional amendments were more effective.[12]

Restricting gas taxes solely to road construction was a pivotal innovation that largely freed road engineers at the state level from worrying about the source of funds to match federal-aid. Right after the Second World War, however, some states encountered new problems matching the suddenly-increased federal appropriations for road construction that emerged from Congress beginning in 1944. Available federal-aid funds passed 500 million US dollars per year in 1946 and accelerated upward. State legislatures could not raise gas tax rates high enough or fast enough to keep up, and a few states could not obligate their complete share of federal-aid funds.

Several states turned to tolls as a means of financing the much more costly, large-scale intercity roads. Federal and state engineers had always opposed toll financing as double taxation on motorists who already paid gas taxes. In the mid-1920s, they had persuaded Congress to require the removal of tolls on any bridge on the federal-aid system after construction bonds had been paid off.[13] But the demand for road improvements was so great after 1945 that highway officials failed to block toll financing at this time. A key reason was the success of the Pennsylvania Turnpike, which opened in 1940 and immediately refuted BPR arguments that motorists were unwilling to pay extra for improved roads. Truckers

[11] See John Chynoweth Burnham, 'The Gasoline Tax and the Automobile Revolution', *Mississippi Valley Historical Review*, 48, 3 December 1961, 435–59. Literally hundreds of articles appeared in the late 1920s and 1930s urging the end of gas tax revenue 'diversions'. See as examples of Thomas H. MacDonald, 'Crisis Demands Engineering Statesmanship', *Engineering News-Record*, 108, 24 March 1932, 429; 'Fight Gas Tax Diversion, Ruinous Regulation, Unfair Taxation', *Roads and Streets*, 75, October 1932, 423–4; and Charles H. Upham, 'Diversion – The Highway Handicap', *Civil Engineering*, 9, January 1939, 1–2.

[12] See, for example, the comments in BPR, *Annual Report*, 1939, 8–9. The BPR had pressed this point through the 1930s in its annual reports, in various studies of highway financing, and in its research journal, *Public Roads*, by printing tables showing state gas tax receipts and diversions. See Seely, *Building the American Highway System*, 103.

[13] This episode is related in Seely, *Building the American Highway System*, 79; see also BPR, *Annual Reports*, 1921–30.

especially loved the road over the Allegheny Mountains. So after 1945, New York, New Jersey, Maine, Oklahoma, West Virginia, Ohio, Indiana, Illinois and a few other states used toll financing for specific large-scale systems. By the mid-1950s, more than 3,500 miles of toll roads were open or under construction.[14]

The end of the toll financing era began in 1956, however, with the emergence of an alternative strategy for raising funds for freeway construction. This financial innovation was embedded in the legislation that funded the Interstate highway system.[15] With an initial price tag of 25 billion US dollars, the Interstate construction programme had been hung up in Congress for about six years by disagreements about how to pay for it; several Congressmen feared the programme would bankrupt the government. The funding package of 1956 had two important elements. First, the Interstate Highway Act created a highway trust fund by allocating all federal gas tax revenues, excise taxes on tyres and other minor 'road-user fees' to road construction. The trust fund mirrored state constitutional requirements and provided an assured stream of revenue for this expensive road programme. And as in the states, one side-effect that appeared at the federal level was the ending of the rancorous fights about annual appropriations that had dominated the highway debates from 1945 through 1956.

The second financial innovation of the 1950s was the provision that the federal government provide 90 per cent of the cost of the Interstate system. This element marked a substantial change, ending federal-aid as an equal partnership. The logic was that these expensive roads were designed to serve the entire nation, and construction progress could not be held up by the difficulties that a few states had experienced matching federal-aid appropriations in the late 1940s. In the short term, the change in the funding formula allowed every state to participate fully in the massive new road programme, at the cost of greater control over the system by federal engineers. But the most real 'beneficiaries' of this new financial structure were cities, where the most expensive sections of the systems were located. Most state highway departments had always focused on intercity primary highways and had shown little enthusiasm for urban freeways before 1956 because of their cost. This situation had forced a few pioneering cities to consider tolls as a means of paying for these projects. The 1956 legislation largely eliminated these difficulties by altering the financial equation concerning urban freeways with substantially greater sums of money.

These funding mechanisms did more than allow the Interstate system of limited-access, high-speed roads to be built, both inside and outside cities. To be sure, the

---

[14] Post-war toll financing is discussed in Seely, *Building the American Highway System*, 204–8; for general overviews, see Charles L. Dearing and Wilfred B. Owen, *Toll Roads and the Problem of Roll Road Modernization* (Washington, DC 1951); and FHWA, *America's Highways*, 166–70 and 190–92.

[15] The financial elements of the 1956 legislation are dealt with in Mark H. Rose, *Interstate: Express Highway Politics, 1914–1956*, 2nd ed. rev. (Knoxville 1989); see also Seely, *Building the American Highway System*, 208–23.

trust fund covered expenditures of 93.5 billion US dollars on Interstate roads alone between 1954 and 1986. As importantly, these financial innovations also removed much of the political wrangling about these roads that had earlier focussed on financing. Highway funding did not resurface as a significant political issue until the late 1970s, after the energy crisis had lowered both gasoline consumption and gas tax receipts in many states. Some public complaints followed the resulting increases in gasoline tax rates, as federal levies jumped from 4 cents per gallon in 1975 to 9 cents per gallon in 1985, with diesel taxes increasing to 15 cents per gallon, even as the average state tax rate rose from 7.65 cents per gallon to 11.11 cents. Even with these adjustments, funding for roads lagged through the 1980s, as state highway departments tried to persuade voters to provide the revenue they needed. An apparent solution appeared in 1991, when Congress passed the Intermodal Surface Transportation Efficiency Act, which sharply increased highway expenditures as part of a 151 billion US dollars legislative package.[16] But funding has not been increased during the twenty-first century, given a political climate that will not countenance even discussion of tax increases. The only palatable idea broached during the past 15 years is the public-private partnership, a phrase describing financial arrangements that revive toll financing in a new guise.[17]

Pavements and Earthmovers: Road Construction Technology

These organisational and financial innovations were every bit as important as technical inventions in terms of the development of the freeway in America. The federal-aid programme encouraged the growth of state organisations with the increasing levels of technical competence, and the gas tax and trust fund allowed implementation of construction plans. But constructing a rural network of two-lane paved roads was not the same as building freeways. The expertise and knowledge required to build these much more complex highways did not appear overnight. Over the course of the twentieth century, better and more durable pavements were developed for multi-lane roads carrying cars and trucks at high speed, even as the entire construction process was mechanised. Both innovations were typical of the

---

16 Statistics from US, Department of Transportation, Federal Highway Administration, ed., *Highway Statistics: Summary to 1985* (Washington, DC ca. 1987), 125, and 132–4. See also T. Ichinowski, 'States are Raising Gas Taxes', *Engineering News-Record*, 222, 18 May 1989, 13; 'President Bush Signs $151 Billion Transportation Bill', *New York Times* of 19 December 1991, B:19, 1; and Charles L. Miller, 'Intermodal Surface Transportation Efficiency Act of 1991', *Public Roads*, 55, March 1992, 102–6.

17 Cesar Queiroz, 'Public-private partnerships in highways in transition economies: recent experience and future prospects', *Transportation Research Record*, 1996, 2007, 34–40; and Hiroyuki Iseki, Brian D. Taylor and Kansai Uchida, *Are Public Private Partnerships a Good Choice for U.S. Highways? A Review of the Literature* (Berkeley, CA 2009).

incremental advance of many American technologies driven more by the efforts of teams of researchers and engineers than by the work of heroic individuals. In this environment, it is often impossible to credit a person with a specific invention.

Engineering knowledge about highway pavements was rudimentary before the automobile appeared as the primary road vehicle. The French *École Nationale des Ponts et Chaussées* (School of Bridges and Roads) led the world in the construction of good roads in the eighteenth and nineteenth century, although British engineer John Macadam developed a durable hard-surfaced rural road by preparing many layers of carefully measured small stones, compacting the layers with heavy rollers, and binding them together with water and earth. But with large numbers of automobiles on highways, American highway engineers faced unique challenges. The Bureau of Public Roads borrowed both European machinery and testing techniques in an effort to discover how automobiles destroyed macadam surfaces. They discovered that the powered rear wheels were loosening the earth binding, which then blew away in clouds of dust. This and other situations forced US road engineers to reinvent the construction of durable, hard-surfaced roads.[18]

Most large cities had paved streets by the 1880s, built using a variety of expensive surfaces including brick and stone. The cost of these materials ruled out their extension into the countryside. Federal and state engineers therefore experimented with materials suited to local conditions, ranging from oyster shells in the coastal south to sand-clay roads elsewhere. Sometimes clay was made usable by 'burning' – building fires to harden the road surface. A more promising rural road improvement process was borrowed from urban experiments with bituminous materials such as tar and asphalt. Often a simple coating of heavy oil on a dirt road kept down the dust and provided a temporarily smooth surface. It was a short step to combining bituminous materials and the macadam process, so that the tar bound together the rock to create a hard surface. Bituminous macadam quickly became a favoured pavement for many rural roads.[19]

Another alternative was concrete, with experiments beginning during the 1890s in several places. Residents of Bellefontaine, Ohio, claimed to have built

---

18 On European road building capabilities, see Melvin Kranzberg and Carroll Pursell, *Technology and Western Civilization*, 2 vols (New York 1967), vol. 1, 212–13; on macadam, see Thomas Codrington, *The Maintenance and Use of Macadmized Roads* (London 1902); and Frederick P. Spalding, *A Textbook on Roads and Pavements*, 3rd ed. (New York 1908), 180–288. The BPR was charged with gaining an improved understanding of roads from its earliest days, and the organisation's efforts can be followed in its annual reports (1895–1940); in its pamphlets and circulars; and in articles in its research journal, *Public Roads* (1918–40). See also articles published in engineering and popular journals such as Logan Page, 'The Motor Car and the Road: Destructive Effect of High Speed', *Scientific American*, 102, 15 January 1910, 46–7.

19 See for example, Quincy Adams Gilmore, *A Practical Treatise on Roads, Streets, and Pavements* (New York), 137–209; Thomas R. Agg, *American Rural Highways* (New York 1920); and John Henry Bateman, *Highway Engineering, A Textbook for Students of Civil Engineering* (New York 1928).

the first concrete pavement in 1894, and other experiments followed. In 1909 Wayne County outside Detroit, Michigan, constructed the first concrete road with steel reinforcing bars to add strength. Concrete became the pavement of choice on heavily used intercity routes constructed during the 1920s, although asphalt remained an option and the two materials began a competition that continues to the present day.[20]

The federal-aid partnership was pivotal in improving road-building techniques, as the BPR slowly built a highway research community that learned how to build more durable roads. Research projects were directed by federal engineers but conducted cooperatively with state highway departments, university engineers and trade association laboratories. A few studies had been launched in the mid-1890s, but the start of systematic highway research came in 1918, after trucks carrying war materiel from Mid-West factories to Atlantic ports destroyed some of the best roads in the country. BPR and state engineers moved quickly to determine why. The research programme they launched has since continued without any real pause.[21]

Those early investigations highlighted the basic factors that cause road failures. Most seriously, BPR and state engineers found water in the foundation was the primary culprit in winter highway damage. This danger has long been recognised, but studies of the failed roads and tests on sample pavements demonstrated that water damage was much more likely in clay soils. These findings launched federal engineers on long-term studies of soils and road foundations, and one of the eventual outcomes was soil mechanics, the engineering manipulation of soil conditions. Also implicated in the 1918 pavements' failures were heavy trucks. Researchers found that the problem was not simply their weight, but the force created by truck springs accelerating into a pavement slab after wheels lifted over pavement irregularities. This dynamic element caused much more damaging impact forces than expected.

The reactions of the engineers to these findings were instructive. Even in 1920, road engineers knew they were engaged in a race with ever heavier trucks. They faced a classic engineering challenge – find the balance between economy of construction and durability. Early on, they decided not to seek strict regulations governing truck size and weight, recognising how much political controversy

---

20 On concrete pavements, see Thomas J. Pasko, Jr, 'Concrete Pavements – Past, Present, Future', *Public Roads*, 62, July/August 1998, http://www.tfhrc.gov/pubrds/julaug98/concrete.htm (last accessed 20 March 2012); Board of County Road Commissioners, Wayne County, ed., *Third Annual Report* (1909); and Bateman, *Highway Engineering*.

21 The BPR's research programme was chronicled in its annual reports (1918–40), and in articles in its magazine, *Public Roads*. See Seely, *Building the American Highway System*, chapter 5; idem, 'The Scientific Mystique in Engineering: Highway Research in the Bureau of Public Roads, 1918–1940', *Technology and Culture*, 25, October 1984, 798–831; and Highway Research Board, *Ideas and Actions*. The following section is largely drawn from these sources.

might result from such an approach. Instead, they professed to welcome the challenge of building roads to withstand rapidly increasing traffic demands. This decision was endorsed by most transportation experts, who argued that engineers had a duty to design roads to traffic requirements rather than to limit vehicle size.[22]

With this goal in mind, researchers soon offered design recommendations for more durable pavements. By 1920, Illinois Highway Department engineers proposed thickening the edge of concrete slabs to better withstand impact forces. Every study showed the value of steel reinforcing bars in concrete pavement slabs, for they allowed thinner yet stronger and thus more economical pavements. Ironically, steady increases in vehicle size and numbers always threatened construction specifications, as larger vehicles required thicker pavement slabs, a trend that continued throughout the century. More useful recommendations included using dowels to connect slabs, a step that helped prevent failures at slab edges. Studies of airport runways during the Second World War also advanced knowledge of pavement thickness. During the post-war period, as attention focussed on Interstate roads, highway engineers built a series of test roads that subjected sample pavements to real vehicles under various soil conditions. Those findings confirmed the need for even more massive pavements and better soil treatments. Concrete slabs had been seven inches thick in the 1930s, but by the mid-1970s standards for Interstate roads called for eight or more inches of reinforced concrete on top of an asphalt foundation 12 inches thick, laid on several inches of specially prepared soil.[23]

Highway design remains an uncertain business, however, for the interface of soils, foundations, pavements and vehicles creates an extraordinarily complex system with too many variables to model perfectly. But the research programme, now headed by the Federal Highway Administration (FHWA) in partnership with the states, continues to produce incremental improvements in materials, standards and construction procedures. For example, asphaltic materials now include recycled rubber from old tyres that produce pavements that are flexible and more durable. In the 1990s, the FHWA encouraged states to adopt a design process called 'Superpave' that promised to increase asphalt pavement life substantially, while pursuing the development of high-performance concrete that is not only

[22] BPR engineers embraced this logic, as can be seen in the BPR, *Annual Reports* (1918–40); and in the files related to the research project, which included interaction with the National Automobile Chamber of Commerce, a vehicle manufacturer's trade group: File 890 Tests: Motor Truck. Classified Central File, 1912–1950, Records of the Bureau of Public Roads, RG 30, National Archives and Record Center II, College Park, MD. See also comments in engineering and trade journals, such as 'Fitting the Highways to Modern Transportation Needs', *Automotive Industries*, 43, 26 August 1920, 407.

[23] Information on the geometric design of pavements can be traced in BPR, *Annual Reports* (1950–68); see also Bruce E. Seely, 'Urban Freeway Development and the Bureau of Public Roads, 1930–1950', *SCA* (Society for Commercial Archaeology) *Journal*, 15, Spring 1997, 12–20; Pasko, 'Concrete Pavements', and US, FHWA, *American Highways, 1776–1976*, 324–35, and 381–400.

strong, but durable.[24] But even now, the basic factors identified in the first studies in 1918 continue to guide efforts to build better roads – isolate the pavement from most soil environments.

The process of actually building those pavements has witnessed a series of inventions that have completely reshaped the construction industry. In 1900, engineers chose rights of way that required moving as little earth as possible. As a result, highways bore little resemblance to railroads, which used cuts and fills to produce flat grades with gentle slopes and curves. Horse-drawn scrapers were the primary tool of road builders, while steam rollers and stone crushers were necessary to construct macadam-type roads. Steam shovels assisted on some excavations. After 1920, however, road construction followed the American pattern of industrial mechanisation via the application of the internal combustion engine. One historian labelled that process 'the earth moving revolution'.[25]

The first steps came in the farm fields of California's Imperial Valley after 1900, where two different machine builders introduced tractors running on endless tracks to keep from bogging down in wet, heavy soils. 'Caterpillar' tractors soon found other users, including the Army during the First World War and highway departments that acquired war surplus machines after 1919. In 1925, the two original producers of tracked agricultural tractors combined forces to create the Caterpillar Tractor Company, the long-time industry leader. Among the early innovations by Caterpillar were self-propelled motor graders and the use of diesel engines, both in 1931, as the company began to develop a complete line of road building machinery. Caterpillar also introduced 'HiWay Yellow', the standard colour even today of most earthmoving equipment.[26]

The use of trucks rather than small industrial trains to carry excavated earth was another important development during the 1920s, but an invention by Robert

---

24 See Michael Halladay, 'The Strategic Highway Research Program: An Investment that Has Paid Off', *Public Roads*, 61, March/April 1998, 4–8, and David C. Smith, 'The Promise of High-Performance Concrete', *Public Roads*, 60, 2, Autumn 1996, 31–41.

25 Eugene S. Ferguson coined the term; see E.S. Ferguson, 'Technology and its Impact on Society', in *Tekniska Museet Symposia on the History of Technology* (Stockholm 1979), 273–80, here 276. The introduction of road-building machinery was eagerly reported in engineering journals; for example, O.L. Kipp, 'Evolution of Road Construction and Maintenance Equipment', *Roads and Streets*, 63, February 1925, 229–40; S.T. Henry, 'Trend in the Design of Construction Equipment', *American Highways*, 8, April 1929, 8–9, and 12; H.J. Spelman, 'Machinery Revolutionizes Highway Grading', *Engineering News-Record*, 108, 7 January 1932, 10–13; W. Vance Boise, 'Development of Highway Equipment', *American Highways*, 17, October 1939, 45–51, and 53. For an overview, see Charles W. Wixom, *American Roadbuilders Association Pictorial History of Roadbuilding* (Washington, DC 1975).

26 See Reynold M. Wik, *Benjamin Holt and Caterpillar: Tracks and Combines* (St Joseph, MI 1984); William R. Haycraft, *Yellow Steel: The Story of the Earthmoving Equipment Industry* (Urbana, IL 2000), 49–67; and Caterpillar, Inc., *The Caterpillar Story* (Peoria 1900).

G. LeTourneau rendered dump trucks superfluous on many projects. His business supplied optional equipment for Caterpillar tractors – huge ploughs to pull stumps, cable-controlled bulldozer blades and so forth. In 1926, he began experimenting with a scraper pulled by a Caterpillar. After the scraper bowl was filled, the front edge, or apron, lifted and the tractor pulled the wheeled scraper to where the earth could be dumped. Over the next decade, LeTourneau tinkered with his scraper, adding electric motors, a blade to push dirt out of the scraper and huge pneumatic tyres. Then in 1938, he built a wheel-mounted, diesel-powered tractor that, when hooked to his Carryall scraper, became the prototype earthmover. LeTourneau's machine moved much faster than crawler tractors and was thus more efficient; it soon became an indispensable tool for road builders.[27]

The full capabilities of Caterpillar and LeTourneau machines were proven during the Second World War, especially by Navy Seabees in the South Pacific. As a result, during the late 1940s road builders adopted other large, diesel-powered machines, including front end loaders, back-hoes and hydraulic excavators from Europe. But excavation was not the only road-building process to be mechanised, as paving operations followed a similar trajectory. Both asphalt and concrete paving started out as a batch process, with equipment from firms such as Barber-Greene, the pioneer in asphalt spreading machines. Portable batch plants, rollers and trucks for carrying asphalt completed one mechanisation process during the 1920s, while on-site concrete mixers grew into a collection of spreaders, levellers and finishing machines tended by more than 100 men. These paving trains rode upon the metal forms that held concrete in place, using the forms as rails. After 1945, slip-form pavers that used moving forms and fast-setting concrete eliminated the slow, labour-intensive process of erecting forms. Trains laying a mile of pavement a day with a crew of only 25 workers were available just in time to build the Interstates![28]

Incremental technical innovation continued in the post-war period, with the most obvious feature being the ever-increasing size of the machines. The pressure to construct the 44,000-mile Interstate system, originally scheduled for completion in 15 years, stimulated many of these developments, but also encouraged organisational changes designed to increase the efficiency of state highway departments. For example, the Ohio Highway Department adopted photogrammetry, the use of stereo aerial photographs to assist in the preparation of drawings and plans. The possibilities had been explored in the late 1940s, but

---

[27] Robert Haralson Selby, 'Earthmovers in World War II: R.G. LeTourneau and his Machines', Ph.D. diss., Case Institute of Technology, 1970; Robert G. LeTourneau, *Mover of Men and Mountains: Autobiography of R.G. LeTourneau* (Englewood Cliffs, NJ 1960); Philip G. Gowenlock, *The LeTourneau Legend* (Brisbane 1996); Haycraft, *Yellow Steel*, 67–76.

[28] See Barber-Greene Company, *Silver Anniversary, 25th, 1916–1941* (n.p. 1941); idem, *Our First Five Decades* (n.p. 1966); and Pasko, 'Concrete Pavements'.

Ohio found that the technique allowed them to programme many of their projects far more rapidly than ever before.[29]

In recent decades, other changes have come as well. Lasers have been adopted to achieve higher levels of accuracy in the placement of pavements, while specialised machines carefully prepare the subgrade and foundation to prevent moisture from destroying the pavement from below. Computers monitor materials to insure quality. In the 1990s, global positioning systems offer further opportunities for improvements in the planning of the construction work. These tools guided the work of newer machines invented to rehabilitate Interstate roads, which were nearing the end of the original design life. The machinery stripped off and recycled layers of pavement, broke up old slabs and prepared the subgrade for new pavements. Hardly a hand labourer is required.

With all of this equipment at their disposal, road engineers have largely ignored topography and terrain since 1945, for it is economically feasible to move millions of cubic yards of earth. This capability, so in keeping with 1950s America, was essential for realising the goal of the freeway – driving across the country without encountering a stoplight. The tools were perfect symbols of American technological machismo, providing an ability to reshape nature to fit the needs of traffic.

Highway Design and Planning: Inventing Express Highways

The most obvious difference between regular roads and freeways is their design, that is, their location and layout on the landscape. The primary point is that substantial innovation occurred in highway design and planning as road builders moved from the typical, narrow, two-lane American road of the 1920s to freeways. The keys design features would be grade separations and limited access.

The form of freeways emerged from several antecedents. One vital influence was the parkway concept developed by nineteenth-century city-beautiful planners such as Frederick Law Olmsted – winding, tree-lined roads built in city parks, like Central Park in New York and along the Brandywine River in Wilmington, Delaware. In 1907, the Bronx River Parkway in New York City became the first parkway built with the automobile in mind. From this pioneering effort sprang the Long Island and West Chester parkways built by Robert Moses in the 1920s.[30]

---

[29] Duane L. Cronk, 'Ohio Pioneers in Better Use of Aerial Engineering', *Roads and Streets*, 98, December 1955, 79–85.

[30] Elizabeth Stevenson, *Park Maker: A Life of Frederick Law Olmsted* (New Brunswick, NJ 2000); Charles E. Beveridge, David Larkin and Paul Rochleau, eds, *Frederick Law Olmsted: Designing the American Landscape*, rev. ed, (New York 1998); Christopher Tunnard and Boris Pushkarev, *Man-Made America: Chaos or Control?* (New Haven, CT 1963), 160–65; and J. Downer, 'Parks and Parkways of Westchester County, New York', *Municipal and County Engineering*, 72, February 1927, 57–8.

Apart from their scenic beauty and prohibitions of commercial traffic, the most unique feature of parkways was a design element that would largely define the freeway – separation of the road from all crossing traffic.[31]

Parkways sought separation for scenic beauty, but another reason for separating traffic streams was to avoid collisions between cars and trains. Railroad grade crossings were the most dangerous intersection of the 1920s, and became more even more dangerous as motor vehicle speeds increased. But grade separations were costly, and few were constructed even though many states obliged railroad corporations to pay for bridges or underpasses. Railroad executives disliked this situation, especially after trucks and buses began siphoning away traffic and revenue in the 1920s. As a result, substantial progress was not made until the 1930s, when federal relief funds became available from the Public Works Administration.[32]

Congestion in many cities soon encouraged road builders to examine traffic separation in order to increase vehicle flow at major intersections. Traffic lights controlled movement safely, but interrupted traffic flow. Several eastern states built traffic circles, or roundabouts, but they were not without safety problems. New Jersey examined the options systematically in the early 1930s, constructing 'flared' intersections that had extra lanes for turning traffic in addition to traffic circles. Then in 1931, the New Jersey highway department constructed one of the earliest 'four-leaf clover' intersections near Paramus to eliminate all turns across traffic. The now-ubiquitous cloverleaf is a costly way to eliminate intersections, especially in terms of land, so a variety of configurations have evolved. Whatever its shape, the cloverleaf remains a crucial element of freeway design.[33]

The other design feature that defined freeways was control of access from adjoining property. Designers cited several reasons for favouring this development, including the safety gained by reducing the points of entry for merging cars. A side-effect was maintenance of higher driving speeds. But many designers also noted that limited-access designs allowed control over roadside development. Even in the 1930s, many critics abhorred the 'ribbon' commercial developments that sprang up

---

[31] See R.H. Gilman, 'Divided Highways are Safer Highways', *Civil Engineering*, 8 April 1938, 258–60; also Timmothy Davis, 'The American Motor Parkway', *Studies in the History of Gardens & Designed Landscapes*, 25, 4, 2005, 219–50.

[32] See 'New Approach to the Grade Separation Problem', *Railway Age*, 93, 8 October 1932, 494–7; M.W. Harrison, 'Urges Use of P.W.A., Funds for Crossing Eliminations', *Railway Age*, 97, 13 October 1934, 451–2; and 'Grade Crossing Programs Approved by President', *Railway Age*, 99, 16 November 1935, 643–4; see also BPR, *Annual Report* (1928–40).

[33] 'Intersection Design is Primary Highway Problem in New Jersey', *Engineering News-Record*, 107, 26 April 1931, 843–8; H.S. Swan, 'Separating Grades at Highway Intersections', *Civil Engineering*, 3, February 1933, 79–83; E.W. James, 'Highway Safety', *Engineering News-Record*, 114, 17 January 1935, 102–5; H.W. Griffin, 'Current Highway Problems: Freeways at Intersections', *Engineering News-Record*, 117, 8 October 1936, 514–17; and 'Canada's First Cloverleaf', *Canadian Engineering*, 74, 15 February 1938, 6–10.

alongside most main roads. Road builders, who might not have shared the aesthetic concerns of planners, agreed because commercial strips slowed traffic flow.[34]

Unfortunately, a legal barrier prevented designers from simply adopting limited access. Under common law, landowners who abutted a road had rights of access, so only on traditional parkways could access be restricted easily. In the late 1920s and 1930s, the BPR launched several well-publicised projects that reinforced the value of this technique, starting with the Mount Vernon Memorial Highway from the District of Columbia to Mount Vernon, the Blue Ridge Parkway, the Natchez Trace Parkway and various roads in National Parks.[35] More importantly, by the end of the decade the BPR's legal staff had developed model state legislation that removed legal obstacles to limited-access roads. Under this legal innovation, safety, speed and convenience for motorists were given more weight than the tradition of public access. Colorado and Rhode Island were among the first states to adopt such legislation, which removed a barrier to expansion of the freeway design.[36]

Even as these design elements were being worked out, many cities began building express highways. In a few instances, they added features that eventually become standard elements of freeway design. Robert Moses in New York was especially influential because he was building the only extensive urban freeway system in the country before 1940. Moses was much in demand as a consultant, especially after the Second World War, and knowledge of New York City's experience spread widely.[37] But in the 1930s, few cities shared Moses'

[34] See Charles M. Noble, 'Modern Express Highway', *Proceedings of the American Society of Civil Engineers*, 62, September 1936, 1013–23, and November 1936, 1473–85; also correspondence in File 740.1.2 (1934–38), Classified Central File, 1912–50, RG 30, Records of the BPR; and L.E. Boykin, 'Interregional Highways: Legal and Right-of-Way Problems', *Roads and Streets*, 83, January 1940, 57–60. A summary of these developments can be found in Ross D. Netherton, *Control of Highway Access* (Madison, WI 1963).

[35] These activities are treated in the BPR, *Annual Report* (1928–40), in numerous official publications, and in articles in the engineering and professional journals. See also Timmothy Davis, Todd A Croteau and Christopher H Marston, *America's National Park Roads and Parkways: Drawings from the Historic American Engineering Record* (Baltimore, MD 2004).

[36] See Seely, 'Urban Freeway Development', 16–17. The BPR's role is best seen in correspondence in File 740.1.2, 1934–38, Classified Central File, 1912–50, RG-30, Records of the BPR; in US, Federal Works Administration, Public Roads Administration, ed., *Public Control of Highway Access and Roadside Development*, David R. Levin (Washington, DC 1943); and Timmothy Mark Davis, 'Mount Vernon Memorial Highway and the Evolution of the American Parkway', (Ph. D. diss., University of Texas, Austin, TX 1997).

[37] Moses' work is critically chronicled in Robert Caro, *The Power Broker: Robert Moses and the Fall of New York* (New York 1974). There is little truth to Caro's story that Moses deliberately designed parkway bridges to keep buses carrying blacks and other minorities from reaching Jones Beach. This outcome reflected the original expectation that no parkway would carry commercial traffic.

access to money, including large grants from New Deal relief agencies, the Works Progress Administration (WPA) and the Public Works Administration (PWA). Moreover, until 1938 urban sections of the US-numbered system of primary highways were not eligible for federal-aid funds. Finally, state highway departments rarely showed willingness to devote scarce resources to very expensive urban expressways. So urban-road experiments tended to be local and small. Detroit, for example, began planning better roads in the 1920s, laying out wide boulevards with integrated street car lines. These boulevards were generally built by the early 1930s, but without transit features. Late in the decade, the Wayne County road department in Detroit began improvements on Davison Avenue that included four lanes of limited-access highway, sunk below grade and crossed by seven bridges. Exits carried traffic onto parallel access roads that separated the avenue from surrounding streets, thereby allowing limited access. As an indication of the difficulties these projects faced, Detroit's early freeway caused 69 buildings to be destroyed and another was moved. The price tag was 1.45 million US dollars for 7,000 feet of superhighway.[38]

Other cities also had launched road experiments during the late 1930s. The most notable efforts occurred in Los Angeles, which had adopted a road and transit plan similar to Detroit's in the 1920s and built the Arroyo Seco Freeway with parkway features and limited access in the 1930s. Chicago also made large-scale plans for express highways in the 1930s, and actually constructed the Outer Drive along Lake Michigan.[39] But the real excitement was found at the 1939–40 New York World's Fair, specifically at the hugely popular Futurama exhibit in the General Motors pavilion. Industrial designer Norman Bel Geddes offered throngs of visitors a vision of American roads in 1960: highways 12 lanes wide with vehicles moving at 120 miles per hour under automatic control. The public was

---

[38] On Detroit's efforts in the 1930s, see in Seely, *Building the American Highway System*, 149–56; Leroy C. Smith, 'Trunk Line Highways in Metropolitan Areas', *Civil Engineering*, 7, October 1937, 685–6; Wayne County, Michigan, Leroy C. Smith, 'Roads Become Superhighways in Wayne County, Michigan', *Engineering News-Record*, 119, 25 November 1937, 857–60; Wayne County, Michigan, Board of Road Commissioners, ed., *Thirty-third Annual Report* (1939); and Harry A. Shuptrine and Julian C. Mead, 'Davison Limited Highway, Wayne County, Michigan', *Civil Engineering*, 12, December 1942, 673–6.

[39] See Seely, ibid.; 'Transportation – Progress on Large Projects', *Engineering News-Record*, 114, 6 February 1936, 214. The Historic American Engineering Record, part of the National Park Service, prepared a report on the Arroyo Seco Parkway in 1999, including a monograph and measured architectural drawings. See Historic American Engineering Record, *Historic American Engineering Record: Arroyo Seco Parkway*. Historic American Engineering Record, 1999. On Chicago, see 'Superhighways (and Subways) for the City of Chicago', *Engineering News-Record*, 123, 23 November 1939, 696–7.

fascinated, even if many highway engineers considered the vision deeply flawed and outrageously expensive. But Bel Geddes got people thinking about roads.[40]

Two other developments during the late 1930s perhaps prepared motorists to accept the highway visions presented in Futurama. First, in 1935 Germany opened the first sections of the *Autobahn* and by early 1938, drivers could utilise 2,000 kilometres of this national system of express highways. American engineers were jealous, even as they stressed that American highway needs were quite different.[41] Reinforcing the excitement about the freeway style was the opening of the Merritt Parkway in Connecticut in 1939, followed by the initial 160 miles of the Pennsylvania Turnpike in 1940. Such highly publicised roads provided an American version of limited-access motor roads. Both roads attracted the attention of a public committed to the automobile, especially as motorists and truckers gladly paid tolls to use the road over the Allegheny Mountains. In this way, they defied BPR predictions that traffic would not generate sufficient toll revenue to pay off government construction loans.[42] Clearly, public interest in freeways was growing. Yet the most important interwar development related to freeways involved neither the Futurama nor actual construction. The key development was the highway planning process that the Bureau of Public Roads had set in motion during in the 1920s and which culminated in a comprehensive national planning effort during the 1930s. The BPR first studied traffic patterns in Cleveland and in Cook County, Illinois, by counting vehicles, determining the purposes of travel and estimating the value of improved roads in terms of time lost and freight damaged. These regional projects grew into a state-wide project in Michigan in the early 1930s,

---

[40] Thomas MacDonald, chief of the BPR, really disliked Bel Geddes' ideas, but President Franklin Roosevelt was intrigued and invited the designer to the White House. See letters in Official File 129 (Roads and Highways), Papers of Franklin Delano Roosevelt, Roosevelt Library, Hyde Park, New York; Rose, *Interstate*, 1–2. On Bel Geddes and Futurama, see Jeffrey L. Meikle, *Twentieth Century Limited: Industrial Design in America, 1925–1939* (Philadelphia, PA 1979); Norman Bel Geddes, *General Motors Highways & Horizons: New York World's Fair* (New York 1939), and Norman Bel Geddes, *Magic Motorways* (New York 1940).

[41] Information on the *Autobahnen* drawn from Kurt Kaftan, *Der Kampf um die Autobahnen* (Berlin 1955); and from numerous articles in engineering and professional journals, including 'German Motor Roads', *Engineer*, 164, 20 August 1937, 199–202, 206, and 225–8; John Poulter, 'The New German Highway System', *Roads and Streets*, 80, May 1927, 31–5; and H. Seidel, '2000 km fertige Kraftfahrbahnen', *Zeitschrift des Vereines Deutscher Ingenieure*, 82, 15 January 1932, 73–5.

[42] See C.G. Nichols, 'The Merritt Parkway', *Engineering News-Record*, March 1940, 66; 'Designing the Roadway: Pennsylvania's Turnpike', *Roads and Streets*, 82, October 1939, 40–48, and 67–71; H.H. Allen, 'Pennsylvania Turnpike; Longest Toll Superhighway in the United states', *Civil Engineering*, 10, February 1940, 79–82; S.W. Marshall, 'Planning the Pennsylvania Turnpike', *Civil Engineering*, 10, June 1940, 337–9; C.M. Noble, 'Design Features; Pennsylvania Turnpike', *Civil Engineering*, 10, July 1940, 437–40; and 'Turnpike Birthday', *Business Week* of 1 March 1941, 31.

with the aim of determining where future road needs were greatest. Working with the Michigan Highway Department, BPR engineers developed uniform methods, reporting forms and procedures, and with IBM's assistance developed counting devices. In 1936 Congress required every state to inaugurate state-wide planning projects on the Michigan model.[43]

The resulting information mattered enormously to freeway construction in the US, but most significantly the mountains of data informed a BPR report, *Toll Roads and Free Roads*, that shaped national highway policy for several decades. The key finding was that the nation's most pressing highway needs existed in and near cities. Political leaders recoiled from this conclusion, for the same reason that state highway departments had resisted extending their responsibilities to urban areas. President Roosevelt, in particular, refused to endorse an expensive programme of urban road building and ordered the report's executive summary to downplay this finding. Yet the message of the report could not be disguised that easily. At the same time, the planning and survey data also undermined alternative express highway plans that had surfaced in Congress after 1935. Inspired by the German *Autobahn* and the need to put men to work, several bills proposed to create a national highway commission to construct a grid of toll roads (three east/west, five or six north/south). Backed by the planning survey data, BPR engineers claimed such a national toll-road system could not be self-liquidating and proposed instead a 33,000-mile system of 'free' roads serving existing and future traffic running into and between cities.[44]

Finally, the planning process and *Toll Roads and Free Roads* institutionalised the BPR's emphasis upon vehicle counts and economic criteria in subsequent highway planning efforts. Indeed, the next steps in that process followed closely upon the release of the 1939 report. A year later, President Roosevelt appointed a National Interregional Highway Planning Committee to pursue the issues raised in *Toll Roads and Free Roads*. The BPR's Thomas MacDonald chaired this committee, which met during the war years and drafted a blueprint for post-war road building that Congress endorsed as the 1944 Highway Bill. Included were

[43] The development of regional and then state planning surveys can be traced in BPR, *Annual Reports* (1922–40); records in File 481 Correspondence-FAS Michigan and File 710.6 Michigan (1931–38), Classified Central File, 1912–50, Records of the BPR; H.S. Fairbank, 'Statewide Highway Planning Surveys', *Civil Engineering*, 7, March 1937, 178–81; and US, Department of Agriculture, Bureau of Public Roads, *Rules, Regulations, and Recommendations for Carrying Out Federal Aid Highway Programs* (Washington, DC 1939). See also Frederick W. Cron, 'Highway Design for Motor Vehicles – A Historical Review, Part 2: The Beginning so Traffic Research', *Public Roads*, 38, March 1975, 163–8.

[44] See Bureau of Public Roads, *Toll Toads and Free Roads: Message from the President of the United States (...)* 76th Cong., 1st sess., 1939, H. Doc. 272; and Memo: FDR to MacDonald, 16 February 1928, Official File 1E (Bureau of Public Roads, 1938), FDR Papers; 'Toll Superhighway System Rejected', *Engineering News-Record*, 122, 11 May 1939, 655–8; and H.S. Fairbank, 'Interregional Highways: Indicated by State-Wide Highway Planning Surveys', *Roads and Streets*, 83, January 1940, 37–44.

significant increases in Federal-aid funds and authorisation of a system of 40,000 miles of Interstate freeways. Congress did not fund that new system, considering them another element of the federal-aid programme. Indeed, even the highway community did not envision a network of uniformly high-standard roads, and assumed that lightly travelled rural sections would remain two-lane pavements. But urban sections clearly were to be freeways, as the BPR and the states showed in 1947 when they issued the first map of the system.[45]

Importantly, despite Franklin Roosevelt's apprehension about the cost of building urban roads, the BPR quickly became intimately involved in planning and developing urban highways and freeways. During the war, planning for multi-lane limited-access highways started in more than 100 cities, and BPR urban design specialist Joseph Barnett was a frequent adviser who urged planners to emulate the BPR's style of economic and traffic-orientated analysis. When traffic exploded after the war as returning soldiers purchased new cars, few citizens voiced doubts about the highway engineers' call to construct freeways.[46]

During these years, Barnett also influenced design standards for these freeways while chairing the state highway officials' committee that proposed the standards for urban arterial highways and Interstate highways. Before the war, many competing design ideas circulated, including aesthetic elements drawn from the parkway tradition. But the post-war focus almost exclusively emphasised the movement of vehicles, so standards emphasised high speeds, long sight distances, shallow grades and sweeping curves, with exits spaced at least one mile apart. Limited access and separation of traffic were taken for granted.[47]

Even more important for urban freeways than design standards was funding, but significant amounts did not materialise until the mid-1950s. As a result, progress on most sections of the Interstate network was slow after 1947. Most cities combined municipal, state and federal funds to begin acquiring some

45 See Seely, *Building the American Highway System*, 166–91.

46 The main alternatives – urban transit in cities, railroads between them – realistically were out of the picture in most cities, thanks to a decades-long combination of public apathy and even antipathy, poor management, rigid regulation and public fascination with the automobile. The best book on what happened to transit – Paul Barrett, *The Automobile and Urban Transit: The Formation of Public Policy in Chicago, 1900–1930* (Philadelphia, PA 1987) – showed the public policy choices favoured roads from the 1920s on, leaving few alternatives to roads by the 1940s. The conspiracy theories touted by Bradford Snell and others, who argued that auto and tyre companies conspired to replace streetcars with buses and run the companies into the ground, is simply not necessary to explain what happened in most cities. See also Robert C. Post, 'The Myth Behind the Streetcar Revival', *American Heritage*, 49, May 1998, 95–101.

47 Barnett's pivotal role is evident in the correspondence between city officials and the BPR during and after the war – he ran the BPR's urban programmes from the 1940s until his retirement in 1963, and chaired the standards committees that entire time. Seely, 'Urban Freeway Development', 16–17; and American Association of State Highway Officials, *Standards for Urban Arterial Highways* (Washington, DC 1957).

property and to launch planning efforts, but only a few, including Los Angeles and Detroit, launched major construction programmes. State highway departments generally preferred to build the easier and less expensive rural routes, especially in eastern states that resorted to toll financing for core routes such as the New York Thruway and the New Jersey Turnpike. Serious funding finally came for the National System of Interstate and Defense Highways in the 1956 legislation passed by Congress. The miles of urban freeways that finally appeared in every major city reflected a common design mindset that signalled the federal influence on urban freeways.[48] That national system of freeways owed much more to the planning programme conducted by the BPR during the 1920s and 1930s than to GM's Futurama exhibit.

Safety Considerations

The organisational and financial innovations, the technical knowledge and construction tools, the planning surveys all came together in the 1950s in the form of the Interstate construction programme in every major city and across the landscape. As the roads themselves began to be built, another group of inventions helped shape the material culture of American freeways. Many were directly related to highway safety.

Safety – or the lack thereof – has been a significant issue on American highways throughout the automobile era. Safety concerns were often evident in many early discussions of freeway design elements, such as grade separations and limited access. The annual death toll on American roads exceeded 25,000 in the 1920s, leading Secretary of Commerce Herbert Hoover to convene the first national meeting on highway safety in 1924. Yet fatalities climbed unchecked to 37,000 in the late 1930s. By the 1990s the annual death toll stood at about 41,000, although fatalities per vehicle mile had plunged.[49] Two schools of thought existed on how to reduce carnage: modify driver behaviour (cut speeding, drinking and so on) or improve the car and road environment. Early on, the prevailing view resembled the logic of the American workplace – injured parties were to blame for accidents

[48] See the Public Roads Administration, *Annual Report* (1946–49); BPR, *Annual Report* (1950–68). An endless string or articles appeared on urban road programmes after 1946 in *Roads and Streets* and *Engineering News-Record*. Also see David Brodsly, *L.A. Freeway: An Appreciative Essay* (Berkeley, CA 1981). On the state highway departments, see Mark Rose and Bruce E. Seely, 'Getting The Interstate System Built: Road Engineers and The Implementation of Public Policy, 1955–1985', *Journal of Policy History*, 2, Winter 1990, 23–56.

[49] 'National Conference on Street and Highway Safety', *Engineering News-Record*, 93, 25 December 1924, 1038–42, and 94, 1 January 1925, 15–20. Statistics from Christine M. Johnson, 'The National ITS Program: Where We've Been and Where We're Going', *Public Roads*, 61, no. 2, September/October 1997, 6–14.

and injuries. Thomas MacDonald summarised the views of many in an article in 1937 entitled 'Highways Will be Safer; Driver Remains a Problem'.[50] But over time, engineers began to recognise the need to provide safe environments, leading to the design of recessed knobs and padded dashboards and seat belts in cars, and efforts to design safer highways. Many of resulting safety innovations significantly shaped the appearance of modern roadsides.

The evolution of highway signs is one example of the changes in the appearance of highways. A century ago, motorists worked hard to find their way, and confusion led to accidents. Location and directional signs were necessary, but most were placed by highway supporters like the Lincoln Highway Association or the American Automobile Association. Such signs could be hard to read, especially amidst the welter of signs located at most crossroads.[51] In 1918, Wisconsin's highway department's pioneering effort labelled all 500 miles of state roads using a uniform numbering system. Other states followed suit, with Minnesota introducing the first state shield in 1921. Problems still remained at state boundaries, until the BPR and state engineers implemented a national numbering system for the federal-aid highway network, and by 1925 the familiar shield and numbers were found on all US-numbered roads.[52] This system still prevails, with east-west roads on the US system given even numbers, starting with US 2 in the north. North-south roads have odd numbers beginning with US 1 on the East Coast. Interstate routes start numbering plans in the south and west sides of the country.

State-federal cooperation also produced a uniform manual for traffic signs in 1927. Basic principles included using yellow for warning signs and white for directional signs. Red was rejected for the stop sign because neither paint nor baked enamel produced a durable red colour. Similarly, round signs were used at railroad crossings, stop signs were octagonal, warning signs were diamonds and information was on rectangles. The goal was to be sure that drivers interpreted signs and the hazards they represented quickly by both shape and colour.[53]

The 1928 supplement to the sign manual first mentioned luminous materials and reflecting elements, a new and significant invention. Until the late 1920s, 'cat's eyes', which used a glass lens to focus light onto a mirror, were the only reflectors. The largest were an inch across, so many of these buttons were installed

---

50 Thomas H. MacDonald, 'Highways Will be Safer; Driver Remains a Problem', *Scientific American*, 156, March 1937, 213.

51 Institution of Traffic Engineers (ITE), *Traffic Devices: Historical Aspects Thereof* (Washington, DC 1971), 79–81; and 'Historical Note: Signs of Fifty Years Ago', *Traffic Engineering*, 38, October 1967, 10–11.

52 Ibid.; and A.E. Johnson, 'A Story of Signing', in *AASHO: The First Fifty Years*, 129–46.

53 ITE, 'Traffic Devices', 90–92; also James, 'Highway Safety', 104–5; A.E. Johnson, 'Highway Signs for the Interstate System', *Civil Engineering*, 27, April 1957, 251–5; and J.O. Martineau, 'Buoys and Lifelines of Highways', *Roads and Bridges*, 84, April 1946, 87–9, 114, 116, and 118.

on each sign. Occasionally cat's eyes distracted drivers or obscured the letters. Improvements came from an inventor named Stimson, who introduced a plastic device he called the 'cube-corner' reflector. Stimsonite-brand reflectors used lucite plastic, not silvered mirrors, and so were much cheaper and larger. At about the same time, inventor Ernest Gill developed reflecting signs by placing tiny glass spheres into paint or sign material. With his 1933 patent, he formed the Prismo Holding Corp. But Minnesota Mining and Manufacturing (3M) shortly thereafter introduced 'Scotchlite' – plastic reflective sheeting containing glass spheres that had better optical efficiency than Gill's. Now the whole sign could be reflective, especially after 3M introduced an improved material called 'Flat Top' in the 1940s, with glass beads premixed in the binder and coated with plastic to remain reflective even in rain.[54]

These new signs in turn forced substantial research into how drivers perceived signs, how far away they could be seen and how large letters needed to be. The problems became acute on high-speed freeways, for it was imperative to know how to make a sign that drivers could comprehend at 60 miles per hour. Overhead signs came into increasing use, as they seemed less distracting and also marked appropriate lanes. The BPR also investigated sign colours in the mid-1950s, testing green, blue and black signs. All were visibly acceptable, but drivers subjectively favoured green, so that became the standard Interstate sign colour. The BPR also required reflectorised backgrounds on all overhead signs, and strongly recommended this treatment on all others as well. Since the 1960s, nearly all signs have been self-luminescent, while human factors engineering carefully examines sign designs and placement.[55]

Road signs could not, however, keep drivers in their appropriate lane, a major problem on multi-lane highways. One answer – pavement markings – is a good example of the often-unnoticed small developments that proved crucial to the development of the freeway. Road markings may have been used in Mexico City as early as 1600, where different colour paving materials marked the centre of the street. That strategy is occasionally used today, but marking pavements took longer to emerge. In the late-nineteenth century, several cities painted lines to mark safe clearance zones for street cars, while officials at the Brooklyn Bridge marked a centre-line by locating street cars between lanes of oncoming vehicles. The first painted traffic lines might have been used in Portsmouth, Virginia, in 1907, as stop lines at a few intersections. New York City might have had painted cross walks in 1911, followed by Providence in 1913 and Minneapolis in 1914.

54 ITE, 'Traffic Devices', 126–8.

55 ITE, 'Traffic Devices', 140–42; R.E. Holaday, 'The Overhead Sign: Its Development, and Future for Traffic Control', *Public Works*, 87, November 1956, 99–101; Johnson, 'Highway Signs for the Interstate'; 'Self Luminous Signs Suggested for Highways', *Civil Engineering*, 30, September 1960, 93; P.L. Connolly, 'Adapting Vehicle and Highway to Suit Man's Visual Limitations Can Bring Big Safety Dividends', *SAE Journal*, 74, August 1966, 44–8; and numerous articles cited in *Industrial Arts Index* (1970–90).

Wayne County, Michigan, near Detroit, claims to have used the first centre-line markings in 1911, and by 1922 its entire county road system was painted. But California claimed credit for striping the first state highways in 1924.[56] Still, none of the painted lines could be seen at night, inspiring several solutions. In the late 1920s, Stimonite introduced the first raised pavement markers, buttons 1⅝ inches in diameter. These reflective plastic dots could be placed on the shoulder to mark the edge of the road. Michigan first tried them, but because snow ploughs ripped them, raised markers found limited use in northern states. Even in warmer climates, poor adhesives were a problem, as was the tendency of the reflector to be obscured by mud and dirt. But by the 1960s, reflective buttons found wider use thanks to various adjustments. Some were shaped with a metal 'keel' that raised snow plough blades; others tried recessing the marker into the pavement. Neoprene snow-blow blade edges also promised help, and by the 1970s the BPR encouraged the use of raised markers everywhere.[57]

Another type of highway marker had its first trial in Michigan, which opened the first 'reflectorized highway' in 1938. Highway officials installed 6,900 plastic reflectors at 100-foot intervals on 3-foot poles over 70 miles of highway between Detroit and Lansing. These marked the road ahead further than headlights could show. This idea has been widely copied almost everywhere now, not just on freeways.[58] Also widely adopted has been yet another approach to marking roads – reflective paint. The same year that Michigan installed reflectors, tiny glass beads (0.015 inches in diameter) were mixed with paint, and early trials in New Jersey, Massachusetts and on Long Island proved successful. Over the years, the process spread everywhere and by 1965, state highway department used 12 million gallons of traffic paint; cities and counties applied another 9.5 million gallons. Together they added 107 million pounds of reflector beads to that paint. Today, acrylic stripes are placed on the road for the same purpose.[59]

Lighting proved to be an even more important safety development on roads. During the 1920s, city streets were lit by gas, arc lights and even the first incandescent bulbs with tungsten filaments. Improvements in electric lights opened new possibilities over the next decade, first with gas-filled incandescent bulbs in 1930, and then mercury vapour lamps and sodium vapour lights in 1934.

---

56 ITE, 'Traffic Devices', 101–5; see also 'Saga of Highway Striping in Black and White', *Public Works*, 102, August 1971, 72–3; and Bernard Chaiken, 'Traffic Marking Materials – Summary of Research and Development', *Public Roads*, 35, December 1969, 251–6.

57 'Raised Pavement Markers as a Traffic Control Measure at Lane Drops', *Public Roads*, 39, June 1975, 1–6.

58 'First Reflectorized Highway', *Engineering News-Record*, 120, 14 April 1938, 541–2; 'Making Night Driving Safe', *Mechanical Engineering*, 60, July 1938, 568–9.

59 'Making Night Driving Safe', *Mechanical Engineering*, 60, July 1938, 568–9; and Chaiken, 'Traffic Marking Materials', 251–2; and 'Saga of Highway Striping in Black and White', *Public Works*, 102, August 1971, 72–3.

All offered much more light per watt, but the sodium bulbs bright produced 50 lumens per watt, compared to 35 for mercury vapour and gas-filled fluorescent bulbs and 20 lumens for conventional bulbs. Improved holders with aluminium reflectors called luminaires further brightened roads and allowed lights to be mounted twice as high (25–30 feet), cutting the number needed. These developments made it possible to consider lighting regular roads.[60]

The potential benefit of this development was suggested by the mortality statistics for 1937, when 39,700 people were killed on the nation's highways. Almost 60 per cent of those lives were lost at night (23,800) when only 20 per cent of traffic moved. Vehicle headlights, which had not improved since 1917, offered about 150 feet of visibility. At 55 miles per hour (81 feet per second) drivers had less than two seconds of sight. The new streetlights, however, extended visibility to 700–1,200 feet. The new lights, in other words, allowed higher speed night driving without feeling blind on the road.[61]

After the Second World War, further changes brought improved night visibility. Newer and larger bulbs packed more power, while mercury vapour bulbs with red coatings on the inside of the glass globe eliminated their characteristic blue-green tint. The newest idea was the use of fluorescent lights in some urban installations, beginning in Oakwood, Ohio in 1952. These lights proved especially useful for tunnels and underpasses.[62] The larger and more powerful bulbs also allowed the breakthrough innovation in lighting during the post-war period – 'high mast' lights. Very high poles – at first 100–150 feet and later 200-feet high – were able to light large areas, reducing the number of poles even while they eliminated much of the glare. The basic idea was not new, for a number of cities had tried tower lighting in the nineteenth century. Austin, Texas, for example, had 'moonlight' lights by the 1890s, while Germany tried tower lighting on highways in the late 1950s. The idea spread to Holland, France, Italy and the UK, but Americans only adopted this approach after test installations by the Texas Transportation Institute at College Station in the mid-1960s. Trials on Interstate interchanges in San Antonio and Texarkana proved the concept, as did parallel investigations in Seattle. The Washington test used metal halide bulbs in a special luminaire mounted on 150-foot high towers to produce a brilliant circle of light that helped even in fog. Additional tests in Nebraska and North Dakota followed and showed

60 'Street Lighting Then and Now', *Illuminating Engineering*, 51, January 1956, 86–96; 'Demonstration of High Intensity Mercury Vapor Street Lighting', *Roads and Streets*, 78, June 1935, 195; 'Sodium Vapor – The Modern Highway Light', *Electrical Journal*, 32, July 1935, 289; and Edward M. Rice, 'Lighting and the Modern Highway', *Roads and Streets*, 81, March 1938, 45–6.

61 Rice, 'Lighting and the Modern Highway'.

62 'Street Lighting Then and Now', also 'Test of Fluorescent vs. Filament', *Journal of the Franklin Institute*, 41, February 1946, 105–30; and 'New Developments in Light Sources', *Electrical Engineering*, 77, October 1958, 903–7.

that installation and operating costs were much lower. The Washington interchange required 23 poles, for example, instead of 240 regular light poles.[63]

All of these safety innovations make Interstates and freeways safer than regular highways, especially when measured in terms of accidents per mile travelled. Night is little different than day on roads lit in this way. Yet those same light poles were potentially lethal hazards. Before the 1950s, obstacles like this were accepted as a fact of life. But the elimination of roadside hazards could pay dividends. On one stretch of new superhighway in Cook County, Illinois, for example, 89 drivers died from striking light poles over five years – more than one per month. After county highway engineers installed short, hollow poles 6½ feet high, no one was killed.[64]

This development fitted into a change of outlook on the part of highway engineers during the 1960s, as they embraced the idea of developing a 'forgiving roadside'.[65] Among the most dangerous elements of the roadside were light posts and sign supports. Engineers set out to design poles that support lights and signs in strong winds but give way when hit. Rhode Island introduced a collapsible post in the mid-1960s, but the most commonly used form emerged from research at the Texas Transportation Institute (TTI) starting in 1963.[66] Seeking to prevent injury-causing sudden deceleration, TTI engineers designed a 'slip-joint' base that broke clean when hit by a vehicle. For sign supports, a second hinge just below the sign allowed the post to pivot upward and out of the way of the car.[67] In one test period, 77 accidents involving breakaway poles caused only five serious injuries, while 72 incidents at rigid posts caused 26 major injuries. Another study reported only one fatality in 117 collisions with breakaway supports. So promising were the results that 13 other highway departments joined the test programme, even before theoretical and mathematical analyses were started. By 1968, the BPR mandated

[63] Louis J. Horn, 'Making Highway Safety Practical', *Public Works*, 99, December 1968, 64; 'Cloverleafs Get High Lights', *Electrical World*, 173, 5 January 1970, 74–6; 'High Level Lighting System Tested at Cloverleaf Interchange', *Public Works*, 100, January 1969, 80–82; 'High Poles, Metal Halide Lamps Cut Roadway Lighting Contrast', *Electrical World*, 171, 26 May 1969, 85–6; and 'Light Poles are Growing Taller', *Illuminating Engineering*, 65, March 1970, 127–9.

[64] 'New Collapsible Lighting Standards Designed to Cut Highway Fatalities', *Engineering News-Record*, 136, 27 June 1946, 995. Even in the 1930s, *Fortune* magazine had commented on the danger posed by bridge abutments, trees and poles. See 'Unfit for Modern Traffic; US Highway System', *Fortune* of 14, August 1936, 85–92.

[65] Richard Weingroff at the FHWA noted that a TV repairman from the Bronx helped identify dangerous design features being built into Interstate roadsides. But the idea was not new. See J.L. Bauer, 'Building Safety into the Rural Road', *Civil Engineering*, 2, December 1932, 767–70; Weingroff e-mail correspondence with the author, 27 September 2000.

[66] H.R. Cooke, 'Safety Hardware on Freeways', *Civil Engineering*, 38, September 1968, 56–60.

[67] N.J. Rowan and R.M. Olson, 'The Development of Safer Highway Sign Supports', *Traffic Engineering*, 38, 11 November 1967, 46–51.

breakaway posts for all new Interstate road signs, and urged retrofitting older installations. A last chapter came in the late 1970s, when an updated new design was introduced to allow for smaller compact cars.[68]

Another safety invention is truly mundane – barriers. Yet few elements of the roadside are more important for freeways. Highway safety barriers started as simple posts along the roadside. The next versions included wooden cross bars and then steel cables between the posts. Metal guard rails, which were strongly promoted by the steel industry in the early years of the Depression, proved more durable. They could keep cars from running off the road, but also could prove highly dangerous to drivers because of their rigidity and strength.[69]

Head-on collisions were even more frightening than running off the road, especially on high-speed highways. Median strips or other dividers were an early design feature of freeways, but they were not completely effective. By the 1960s, 616,500 head-on accidents of all types occurred annually, 8,760 of them resulting in fatalities. Seeking to prevent such crashes on their turnpike, in 1955 New Jersey engineers began experimenting with a concrete barrier to keep streams of traffic separated. Engineers at the General Motors proving ground pursued a separate study, and both groups devised barriers about 32 inches high that sloped up from the base before becoming a vertical wall. That taper is the crucial element, for wheels hit that sloping base before the body touched the barrier and are turned, moving the car away from the barrier before full impact. Cars cannot jump these barriers. And they proved to require almost no maintenance. The 'Jersey barrier' slowly spread across the country; only 200 miles had been installed by 1967, although 33 states and provinces had tried it. Today, however, they are a ubiquitous element of the roadscape, as bridge railings, median and temporary lane guides at construction projects.[70]

Other barriers were improved as well. The traditional W-shaped steel guard rail remains in wide use. In many locations, these are fabricated from Cor-Ten

---

68 Horn, 'Making Highway Safety Practical', see also 'Safety Effects of Breakaway Signs', *Traffic Engineering*, 38, August 1968, 12; 'Breakaway Luminaires Pay Dividends', *Public Works*, 100, September 1969, 128–9; 'Breakaway Poles Changed to Fit Smaller Cars', *Highway and Heavy Construction*, 123, April 1980, 28–30.

69 H.F. Mattimore and F.P. Woodruff, 'Trend of Highway Guard Fence Design', *Public Works*, 60, March 1929, 119–20; H.L. Whittemore, 'Setting Wire Rope Guard Rails', *Public Works*, 60, August 1929, 301; 'Large Uses of Steel in Small Ways; Wire Rope Highway Guards', *Steel*, 93, 7 August 1933, 38; 'Steel Guard Rail Provides Safe, Strong Economical Protection for Motorist', *Steel*, 88, 28 May 1931, 38; S.B. Slack, 'Design Of Highway Guard-Rail Dictated by Tests', *Engineering News-Record*, 108, 9 June 1932, 824–6; and R.C. McKnight, 'Visibility, Road Signs, and Guard Rails', *Canadian Engineer*, 73, 16 November 1937, 7–8.

70 'Making a Safe Highway Safer?', *Engineering News-Record*, 163, 12 November 1959), 28; Cooke, 'Safety Hardware on Freeways', 56–60; 'Concrete Safety Barriers Win Wider Acceptance', *Roads and Streets*, 112, July 1969, 70 and 95; also http://www.roadstothefuture.com/Jersey_Barrier.html (last accessed 29 May 2012).

steel introduced by US Steel in the early 1960s because this material develops an oxidised coating of rust that never needs painting. More importantly, current support posts are made of lightweight steel that allows the rail to give way but not break under vehicle impact, thereby deflecting the car back onto the highway. In addition, the ends of the rails are turned away from traffic and buried to prevent cars from being impaled on the rails.

Another element in the forgiving roadside concept is crash barriers, or 'impact attenuators', in the parlance of road engineers. Installed where sudden deceleration accidents are possible, these devices come in a variety of forms. Some barriers consist of 30–40 steel drums, or water-filled vinyl cells held in place by panels (the Hi-Dro Cushion). The Tor-Shok system used cylindrical tubes that deform to absorb energy, while someone even proposed the Dragnet, a system that resembling the nets used to catch aircraft in emergency landings on aircraft carriers. Sand- or water-filled plastic drums can stop cars travelling 65 miles per hour in 18–30 feet, as moviegoers learned in the action film Speed when a Mercedes convertible created a marvellous fountain of water by ramming a set of barrels. Finally, a vermiculite-filled concrete barrier stops cars moving 60 miles per hour in about 9 feet. Another idea is not new, but novel variations have appeared for runaway truck ramps on steep hills. Some simply use the slope to slow the vehicle, but more recently, beds of gravel are used to slow heavy trucks.[71]

Safety concerns clearly have inspired a number of innovations that make freeways today the safest roads in the country. Not all inventions have been adopted, however. In the 1930s, for example, Edwin Land began promoting the use of polarising materials, his first major invention, to eliminate headlight glare. He showed that by placing such material in headlight covers and in windshields or in visors placed in front of the driver's eyes, the glare disappeared. One possible benefit was the ability to install much stronger headlights and increase the range of visions for drivers. Demonstrations convinced many and attracted much attention in the late 1930s, but Land was stymied by his inability to make durable materials that would not discolour in sunlight. When that problem was solved, Land failed to persuade the auto industry, much to his disappointment.[72]

Two other innovations that did not catch on had futuristic tendencies. Many dreamed about a flying car in the late 1930s and 1940s, as historian Joe Corn has demonstrated in his study of American fascination with aviation. A few

---

[71] F.J. Taminini and John G. Viner, 'Energy Absorbing Roadside Crash Barriers', *Civil Engineering*, 40, January 1970, 63–7; John G. Viner, 'Experience to Date with Impact Attenuators', *Public Roads*, 36, October 1971, 209–18; James R. Kircher, 'Impact Attenuators: A National Survey', *Public Works*, 117, January 1986, 73–6; 'Roadside Bunkers to Trap Runaway Trucks', *Public Works*, 103, July 1972, 55; and 'Runaway Truck Ramps are Saving Lives and Reducing Damage', *Institution of Traffic Engineers Journal*, 49, November 1979, 20–23.

[72] See Victor K. McElheny, *Insisting on the Impossible: The Life of Edwin Land* (Cambridge, MA 1998), 86–107, and figures 1 and 2.

manufacturers demonstrated 'simple' ways to cars that could fly, but from traffic control issues to landing strips, there was nothing simple about flying cars.[73] Similarly, a few enthusiasts proposed the use of low-level nuclear waste to de-ice highways. In 1969, the Federal Highway Administration issued a contract to study the use of fission waste to heat fluids circulating through pipes in bridge ramps and pavements, thereby melting ice and snow. An account of this plan concluded,

> unfortunately, a wide application of the nuclear waste system was not possible because of the limited availability of fission waste and safety problems associated with its use. Subsequent disposal, when the nuclear waste no longer produce enough heat to be effective, would be difficult for a highway agency to handle.[74]

Not surprisingly, salt continues to eat away at our cars!

Environmental Issues

If the impetus to many highway inventions of the 1950s and 1960s was safety, a more recent concern for the environment has encouraged other changes in the material culture of freeways. To be sure, environmental considerations were not simply a product of the 1960s. Occasional articles in highway magazines from the 1920s onward had called for the landscaping of roads.[75] Parkways, whether built in the 1880s or the 1930s, were by definition landscaped for scenic beauty. Freeway designers at first paid attention to aesthetic considerations, as witnessed by the designs of the Arroyo Seco, the Merritt Parkway and other early freeways. But after the Second World War, freeways were generally defined by the goal of moving traffic. Landscaping was not completely ignored, but it remained on the back burner until Lady Bird Johnson launched her highway beautification campaign against billboards in the mid-1960s. After passage of the National Environmental Policy Act of 1970, the entire process of road building changed, as public hearings were required to inform people of engineering plans. In addition, highway departments were required to prepare environmental impact statements as part of more thorough-going reviews of proposed roads and their routes.

---

73 Joseph Corn, *The Winged Gospel: America's Romance with Aviation, 1900–1950* (New York 1987).

74 'Space Age Technology for Deicing Hazardous Highway Locations', *Public Roads*, 38, December 1975, 89–95.

75 For example, see 'Serving the Traveler by More Attractive Roads', *Engineering News-Record*, 102, 3 January 1929, 32–4; E. McCaffey, 'Uglification of America's Highways', *Professional Engineer*, 14, March 1929, 5–6; 'Highway Beautification', *Proceedings of the American Society of Civil Engineers*, 55, December 1929, 2580–87; W.E. Burton, 'Beautiful Roadsides', *Scientific American*, 59, 23 September 1930, 18–19; 'Landscaping Made Integral Part of Planning', *Roads and Streets*, 89, January 1946, 97.

A new outlook almost immediately became apparent in the work of road builders and highway engineers. As late as 1967, an author writing in the journal Public Works worried that highway beautification was 'No Bed of Roses for the Maintenance Division', and he feared the landscaping craze would complicate mowing and other maintenance chores: yet only a year later, another author in that journal claimed, 'Roadside Beauty is the Maintenance Engineer's Friend'. And by the mid-1970s, Virginia celebrated a cooperative effort with the state's garden clubs to expand plantings on interstate roads while Minnesota and North Dakota studied roads as wildlife habitats. The change was largely generational in most highway departments; senior engineers complained loudly about the imposition of new rules and wasteful practices while younger engineers accepted environmental and social factors as valid design constraints and often concluded that the new considerations actually led to better designs. By the 1990s, the Federal Highway Administration even celebrated Earth Day![76]

As highway engineers added environmental challenges to the list of factors they considered in designing freeways, adjustments appeared in the city as much as in the countryside. Highways sprouted bike paths, footpaths, small parks and immaculate landscaping programmes. In rural areas, designers sought to minimise the impact of roads on areas of natural beauty. Perhaps the premier example of the new approach is I-70 through Glenwood Canyon in Colorado. Major law suits forced Colorado highway engineers to completely redesign the road to mitigate damage to the scenic beauty of the canyon. The resulting highway is a spectacular engineering project, for which a range of innovative construction techniques were tried, all with an eye to environmental sensitivity. In 1993, the completed project was named the American Society of Civil Engineer's Outstanding Civil Engineering Achievement.[77]

A more obvious sign of environmental sensitivity was the appearance of another now-common feature of urban freeways – noise barriers. These fences appeared rather suddenly beginning in the early 1970s, as many Interstate sections entered urban and suburban neighbourhoods. As late as 1972, there was no category for road noise in a leading engineering index, but the National Environmental

[76] 'Highway Beautification – No Bed of Roses for the Maintenance Division', *Public Works*, 98, October 1967, 140–42; 'Roadside Beauty is the Road Maintenance Engineer's Friend', *Public Works*, 99, November 1968, 102; see also 'Beautification as Well as Building is Highway Department Goal', *Public Works*, 101, November 1970, 77–8; Phil W. Baker and James R. Barrett, 'Roadside Wildflower Program Pays Big Dividends', *Public Works*, 117, March 1986, 71; Robert B. Oetting, 'Wildlife Habitat Development on Highway Rights-of-Way', *Public Works*, 117, March 1986, 72–4; 'Turnpike Goal; Harmony with the Environment', *Public Works*, 107, October 1976, 88. On changes in highway departments, see Rose and Seely, 'Getting the Interstate System Built'. On the FHWA, see a special issue of *Public Roads*, 58, Spring 1995, devoted to highways and the environment.

[77] See Walter D. Munn, 'Glenwood Canyon: A Showcase for Innovation', *Highways and Heavy Construction*, 129, May 1986, 30–39; and 'Pioneer Highway', *Civil Engineering*, 63, July 1993, 36.

Policy Act of 1970, mandated impact statements and reviews, opened the door to a range of new devices. California experimented with barriers in 1973, and New Jersey even issued noise regulations in 1974. Noise barriers took numerous forms, ranging from earth berms to wooden, masonry and metal fences. Ironically, drivers in pursuit of mobility on the open road can find themselves literally fenced in on many urban sections of Interstate highway.[78]

Conclusion

Clearly, the design, construction and material culture of American freeways have changed substantially since they began to appear 70 years ago. That process of change continues even into the new century. A recent excitement within the road-building community concerned the development of the 'automatic highway'. Norman Bel Geddes had envisioned this idea in his 1939 Futurama, but realisation remained the stuff of science fiction until the 1990s. At that time, the Federal Highway Administration, successor to the Bureau of Public Roads, supported a coalition of corporate and academic partners exploring 'intelligent transportation systems'. Between 1992 and 1997, 645 million US dollars was spent on this challenge, prompted by forecasts of a 300 per cent increase in congestion between 1997 and 2005.[79] The centrepiece of this well-publicised project was a prototype 'No Hands, No Feet' automated highway at a test track in San Diego, California. The engineers faced the formidable task of developing road-mounted sensors, various control devices and computer software. But in 1997, a caravan of cars was operated under automatic control at 6.5-metre intervals.[80]

At this very moment of apparent triumph, however, Congress and the FHWA shifted the focus of the project from 'No Hands, No Feet' to less dramatic, but perhaps more important, activities within the automatic highway umbrella. While preparing for the 1997 test, engineers and their funding agencies had realised that intelligent transportation systems offered more immediate utility and direct payoffs in other ways. Software programs designed to improve the efficiency of commercial vehicle operations, especially in terms of safety and regulation, were one example. Others included automatic truck-weighing stations, which have now appeared on many Interstate routes, and urban bus services that can respond to

---

78 'California Tackles Highway Noise', *Civil Engineering*, 43, July 1973, 82–3; 'Highway Noise Control', *Traffic Engineering*, 43, September 1973, 47–53; and 'Noise Reduction by Barriers', *Acoustical Society of America Journal*, 55, March 1974, 504–18.

79 Christine M. Johnson, 'The National ITS Program: Where We've Been and Where We're Going', *Public Roads*, 61, September/October 1997, 6–14.

80 Nina Congress, 'Smart Road, Smart Car: The Automated Highway System', *Public Roads*, 60, Autumn 1996, 46–51; 'DEMO '97: Proving AHS Works', *Public Roads*, 61, July/August 1997, 30–34; and Bob Bryant, 'Actual Hands Off Steering – And Other Wonders of the Modern World', *Public Roads*, 61, November/December 1997, 32–7.

customers and traffic problems. Urban traffic management programmes are now in use in a number of cities, augmenting existing computer-controlled traffic light systems with in-highway sensors, television monitoring, entrance-ramp meters and electronic toll gates on many freeways and urban expressways. These technologies can increase utilisation of existing highways by 8 to 22 per cent. And just now appearing in top-line vehicles are collision avoidance and vehicle safety systems.[81]

The development of the 'automatic highway' is only the most recent chapter in the effort to invent the American freeway and ensure the continued availability of almost unfettered mobility. Like the innovations that have gone before this latest high-tech initiative, a couple of basic patterns are evident. First, like so many other large technical systems, the innovations that resulted in the American freeway have grown from slow, steady incremental activities of mundane elements much more than from the flashy, highly-publicised work labelled revolutionary. Even the 'earthmoving revolution' reflects this pattern of steady improvement that is so reflective of the work of engineers. The technical side of the invention of the freeway demonstrates that success hinges on extremely mundane elements that all but escape public notice. Sweating the details matters enormously. Second, the story of highway inventions also tells us much about the nature of large technical systems. Even amidst the enthusiasm for the science-fiction vision of automatic highways, one reviewer of the Intelligent Transportation System programme correctly noted that 'the primary barriers to using this technology … are not technical but institutional'.[82] In other words, this set of inventions, like all of the others we have examined, are embedded within much more complicated systems with many non-technical dimensions. Technological capabilities count for very little if the other elements – be they organisational, financial, legal and political or social – are not in place. The development of these non-hardware innovations were often more difficult than the so-called technical challenges. In both of these ways, freeways are like the other complicated technical systems on which we depend in modern America. They are visual reminders of the American fascination with the automobile, tied tightly into that even more complex system. Upon such a process rests the basis of the American belief in the mobility of the open road.

---

81 See Johnson, 'National ITS Program'; 'The Intelligent Vehicle Initiative: Advancing "Human-Centered" Smart Vehicles', *Public Roads*, 61, 2, 1997, 18–25; Maria Koklanaris, 'ITS is Already Paying Dividends', *Public Roads*, 61, September/October 1997, 26–9; and William Zaccagnino, 'Technology for Work and Travel', *Public Roads*, 59, Spring 1996, 23–9.

82 Johnson, 'National ITS Program', 1.

References

a) Anonymous articles, author not known

'Beautification as Well as Building is Highway Department Goal', *Public Works*, 101, November 1970, 77–8.

'Breakaway Luminaires Pay Dividends', *Public Works*, 100, September 1969, 128–9.

'Breakaway Poles Changed to Fit Smaller Cars', *Highway and Heavy Construction*, 123, April 1980, 28–30.

'California Tackles Highway Noise', *Civil Engineering*, 43, July 1973, 82–3.

'Canada's First Cloverleaf', *Canadian Engineering*, 74, 15 February 1938, 6–10.

'Cloverleafs Get High Lights', *Electrical World* 173, 5 January 1970, 74–6.

'Concrete Safety Barriers Win Wider Acceptance', *Roads and Streets*, 112, July 1969, 70 and 95.

'DEMO '97: Proving AHS Works', *Public Roads*, 61, July/August 1997, 30–34.

'Demonstration of High Intensity Mercury Vapor Street Lighting', *Roads and Streets*, 78, June 1935, 195.

'Designing the Roadway: Pennsylvania's Turnpike', *Roads and Streets*, 82, October 1939, 40–48, and 67–71.

'Fight Gas Tax Diversion, Ruinous Regulation, Unfair Taxation', *Roads and Streets*, 75, October 1932, 423–4.

'First Reflectorized Highway', *Engineering News-Record*, 120, 14 April 1938, 541–2.

'Fitting the Highways to Modern Transportation Needs', *Automotive Industries*, 43, 26 August 1920, 407.

'German Motor Roads', *Engineer*, 164, 20 August 1937, 199–202, 206, and 225–8.

'Grade Crossing Programs Approved by President', *Railway Age* 99, 16 November 1935, 643–4.

'High Level Lighting System Tested at Cloverleaf Interchange', *Public Works*, 100, January 1969, 80–82.

'High Poles, Metal Halide Lamps Cut Roadway Lighting Contrast', *Electrical World*, 171, 26 May 1969, 85–6.

'Highway Beautification – No Bed of Roses for the Maintenance Division', *Public Works*, 98, October 1967, 140–42.

'Highway Beautification', *Proceedings of the American Society of Civil Engineers*, 55, December 1929, 2580–87.

'Highway Noise Control', *Traffic Engineering*, 43, September 1973, 47–53.

'Highway Repair Work', *Engineering News*, 72, 2 July 1914, 52.

'Historical Note: Signs of Fifty Years Ago', *Traffic Engineering*, 38, October 1967, 10–11.

'Intersection Design is Primary Highway Problem in New Jersey', *Engineering News-Record*, 107, 26 April 1931, 834–8.

'Landscaping Made Integral Part of Planning', *Roads and Streets*, 89, January 1946, 97.

'Large Uses of Steel in Small Ways; Wire Rope Highway Guards', *Steel*, 93, 7 August 1933, 38.

'Light Poles are Growing Taller', *Illuminating Engineering*, 65, March 1970, 127–9.

'Making a Safe Highway Safer?', *Engineering News-Record*, 163, 12 November 1959, 28.

'Making Night Driving Safe', *Mechanical Engineering*, 60, July 1938, 568–9.

'National Conference on Street and Highway Safety', *Engineering News-Record*, 93, 25 December 1924, 1038–42, and 94, 1 January 1925, 15–20.

'New Approach to the Grade Separation Problem', *Railway Age*, 93, 8 October 1932, 494–7.

'New Collapsible Lighting Standards Designed to Cut Highway Fatalities', *Engineering News-Record*, 136, 27 June 1946, 995.

'New Developments in Light Sources', *Electrical Engineering*, 77, October 1958, 903–7.

'Noise Reduction by Barriers', *Acoustical Society of America Journal,* 55, March 1974, 504–18.

'Pioneer Highway', *Civil Engineering*, 63, July 1993, 36.

'President Bush Signs $151 Billion Transportation Bill', *New York Times* of 19 December 1991, B:19, 1.

'Raised Pavement Markers as a Traffic Control Measure at Lane Drops', *Public Roads*, 39, June 1975, 1–6.

'Roadside Beauty is the Road Maintenance Engineer's Friend', *Public Works*, 99, November 1968, 102.

'Roadside Bunkers to Trap Runaway Trucks', *Public Works*, 103, July 1972, 55.

'Runaway Truck Ramps are Saving Lives and Reducing Damage', *Institution of Traffic Engineers Journal,* 49, November 1979, 20–23.

'Safety Effects of Breakaway Signs', *Traffic Engineering*, 38, August 1968, 12.

'Saga of Highway Striping in Black and White', *Public Works*, 102, August 1971, 72–3.

'Self Luminous Signs Suggested for Highways', *Civil Engineering*, 30, September 1960, 93.

'Serving the Traveler by More Attractive Roads', *Engineering News-Record*, 102, 3 January 1929, 32–4.

'Sodium Vapor – The Modern Highway Light', *Electrical Journal*, 32, July 1935, 289.

'Space Age Technology for Deicing Hazardous Highway Locations', *Public Roads*, 39, December 1975, 89–95.

'Steel Guard Rail Provides Safe, Strong Economical Protection for Motorist', *Steel*, 88, 28 May 1931, 38.

'Street Lighting Then and Now', *Illuminating Engineering*, 51, January 1956, 86–96.

'Superhighways (and Subways) for the City of Chicago', *Engineering News-Record*, 123, 23 November 1939, 696–7.

'Test of Fluorescent vs. Filament', *Journal of the Franklin Institute*, 41, February 1946, 105–30.

'The Intelligent Vehicle Initiative: Advancing "Human-Centered" Smart Vehicles', *Public Roads*, 61, 2, 1997, 18–25.

'Toll Superhighway System Rejected', *Engineering News-Record*, 122, 11 May 1939, 655–8.

'Transportation – Progress on Large Projects', *Engineering News-Record*, 114, 6 February 1936, 214.

'Turnpike Birthday', *Business Week* of 1 March 1941, 31.

'Turnpike Goal; Harmony with the Environment', *Public Works*, 107, October 1976, 88.

'Unfit for Modern Traffic; US Highway System', *Fortune* of 14, August 1936, 85–92.

b) Named articles and monographs

Agg, Thomas R., *American Rural Highways* (New York 1920).

Agg, Thomas R. and Brindley, John E., *Highway Finance and Administration* (New York 1927).

Allen, H.H., 'Pennsylvania Turnpike; Longest Toll Superhighway in the United states', *Civil Engineering*, 10, February 1940, 79–82.

American Association of State Highway Officials, *Standards for Urban Arterial Highways* (Washington, DC 1957).

American Association of State Highway Officials, ed., *AASHO: The First Fifty Years, 1914–1964* (Washington, DC 1965).

Baker, Phil W. and Barrett, James R., 'Roadside Wildflower Program Pays Big Dividends', *Public Works*, 117, March 1986, 71.

Barber-Greene Company, *Silver Anniversary, 25th, 1916–1941* (n.p. 1941).

Barber-Greene Company, *Our First Five Decades* (n.p. 1966).

Barrett, Paul, *The Automobile and Urban Transit: The Formation of Public Policy in Chicago, 1900–1930* (Philadelphia, PA 1987).

Bateman, John H., *Highway Engineering: A Textbook for Students of Civil Engineering* (New York 1928).

Bauer, J.L., 'Building Safety into the Rural Road', *Civil Engineering*, 2, December 1932, 767–70.

Beveridge, Charles E., Larkin, David and Rochleau, Paul, eds, *Frederick Law Designing the American Landscape*, rev. ed. (New York 1998).

Bijker, Wiebe, et al., eds, *Shaping Technology/Building Society: Studies in Socio-technical Change* (Cambridge, MA 1992).

Bijker, Wiebe, *Of Bicycles, Bakelites, and Bulbs: Toward a Theory of Socio-technical Change* (Cambridge, MA 1995).

Board of County Road Commissioners, Wayne County, ed., *Third Annual Report* (Detroit, MI 1909).

Boise, W. Vance, 'Development of Highway Equipment', *American Highways*, 18, October 1939, 45–51, and 53.

Boykin, L.E. 'Interregional Highways: Legal and Right-of-Way Problems', *Roads and Streets*, 83, January 1940, 57–60.

Brodsly, David, *L.A. Freeway: An Appreciative Essay* (Berkeley, CA 1981).

Bryant, Bob, 'Actual Hands Off Steering – And Other Wonders of the Modern World', *Public Roads*, 61, November/December 1997, 32–7.

Burnham, John Chynoweth, 'The Gasoline Tax and the Automobile Revolution', *Mississippi Valley Historical Review,* 48, December 1961, 435–59.

Burton, W.E., 'Beautiful Roadsides', *Scientific American*, 59, 23 September 1930, 18–19.

Caro, Robert, *The Power Broker: Robert Moses and the Fall of New York* (New York 1974).

Caterpillar, Inc., *The Caterpillar Story* (Peoria 1900).

Chaiken, Bernard, 'Traffic Marking Materials – Summary of Research and Development', *Public Roads*, 35, December 1969, 251–6.

Codrington, Thomas, *The Maintenance and Use of Macadmized Roads* (London 1902).

Congress, Nina, 'Smart Road, Smart Car: The Automated Highway System', *Public Roads*, 60, Autumn 1996, 46–51.

Connolly, P.L., 'Adapting Vehicle and Highway to Suit Man's Visual Limitations Can Bring Big Safety Dividends', *SAE Journal*, 74, August 1966, 44–8.

Cooke, H.R., 'Safety Hardware on Freeways', *Civil Engineering*, 38, September 1968, 56–60.

Corn, Joseph, *The Winged Gospel: America's Romance with Aviation, 1900–1950* (New York 1987).

Cron, Frederick W., 'Highway Design for Motor Vehicles – A Historical Review, Part 2: The Beginning so Traffic Research', *Public Roads*, 38, March 1975, 163–8.

Cronk, Duane L., 'Ohio Pioneers in Better Use of Aerial Engineering', *Roads and Streets*, 98, December 1955, 79–85.

Davis, Timmothy Mark, 'Mount Vernon Memorial Highway and the Evolution of the American Parkway', (Ph. D. diss., University of Texas, Austin, 1997).

Davis, Timmothy, Croteau, Todd A. and Marston, Christopher H., *America's National Park Roads and Parkways: Drawings from the Historic American Engineering Record* (Baltimore, MD 2004).

Davis, Timothy, 'The American Motor Parkway', *Studies in the History of Gardens & Designed Landscapes*, 25, 4, 2005, 219–50.

Dearing, Charles L., *American Highway Policy* (Washington, DC 1942), 100–110.

Dearing, Charles L. and Owen, Wilfred B., *Toll Roads and the Problem of Roll Road Modernization* (Washington, DC 1951).

Downer, J., 'Parks and Parkways of Westchester County, New York', *Municipal and County Engineering*, 72, February 1927, 57–8.

Fairbank, H.S., 'Statewide Highway Planning Surveys', *Civil Engineering*, 7, March 1937, 178–81.

Fairbank, H.S., 'Interregional Highways: Indicated by State-Wide Highway Planning Surveys', *Roads and Streets*, 83, January 1940, 37–44.

Ferguson, Eugene S., 'Technology and its Impact on Society', paper presented at *Tekniska Museet Symposia on the History of Technology* (Stockholm 1979).

Ford Motor Company, ed., *Freedom of the American Road* (Dearborn, MI 1956).

Geddes, Norman Bel, *General Motors Highways & Horizons: New York World's Fair* (New York 1939).

Geddes, Norman Bel, *Magic Motorways* (New York 1940).

Gilman, R.H., 'Divided Highways are Safer Highways', *Civil Engineering*, 8 April 1938, 258–60.

Gilmore, Quincy Adams, *A Practical Treatise on Roads, Streets, and Pavements* (New York).

Goldberg, Leonard S., 'Local Government Highway Finance Trends, 1984–1993', *Public Roads*, 60, Summer 1996, 24–8.

Gowenlock, Philip G., *The LeTourneau Legend* (Brisbane 1996).

Griffin, H.W., 'Current Highway Problems: Freeways at Intersections', *Engineering News-Record,* 117, 8 October 1936, 514–7.

Halladay, Michael, 'The Strategic Highway Research Program: An Investment that Has Paid Off', *Public Roads*, 61, March/April 1998, 4–8.

Harrison, M.W., 'Urges Use of P.W.A. Funds for Crossing Eliminations', *Railway Age*, 97, 13 October 1934, 451–2.

Haycraft, William R., *Yellow Steel: The Story of the Earthmoving Equipment Industry* (Urbana, IL 2000).

Henry, S.T., 'Trend in the Design of Construction Equipment', *American Highways*, 8, April 1929, 8–9 and 12.

Holaday, R.E., 'The Overhead Sign: Its Development, and Future for Traffic Control', *Public Works*, 87, November 1956, 99–101.

Horn, Louis J., 'Making Highway Safety Practical', *Public Works*, 99, December 1968, 64.

Hughes, Thomas P., *Networks of Power: Electrification in Western Society, 1880–1930* (Baltimore, MD 1983).

Ichinowski, T., 'States are Raising Gas Taxes', *Engineering News-Record*, 222, 18 May 1989, 13.

Institution of Traffic Engineers (ITE), *Traffic Devices: Historical Aspects Thereof* (Washington, DC 1971).

Iseki, Hiroyuki, Taylor, Brian D. and Uchida, Kansai, *Are Public Private Partnerships a Good Choice for U.S. Highways? A Review of the Literature* (Berkeley, CA 2009).

James, E.W., 'Highway Safety', *Engineering News-Record*, 114, 17 January 1935, 102–5.

Johnson, A.E., 'Highway Signs for the Interstate System', *Civil Engineering*, 27, April 1957, 251–5.

Johnson, A.E., 'A Story of Signing', in American Association of State Highway Officials, ed., *AASHO: The First Fifty Years, 1914–1964* (Washington, DC 1965), 129–46.

Johnson, Christine M., 'The National ITS Program: Where We've Been and Where We're Going', *Public Roads*, 61, September/October 1997, 6–14.

Kaftan, Kurt, *Der Kampf um die Autobahnen* (Berlin 1955).

Kipp, O.L., 'Evolution of Road Construction and Maintenance Equipment', *Roads and Streets*, 63, February 1925, 229–40.

Kircher, James R., 'Impact Attenuators: A National Survey', *Public Works*, 117, January 1986, 73–6.

Kline, Ronald R., *Consumers in the Country: Technology and Social Change in Rural America* (Baltimore, MD 2000).

Koklanaris, Maria, 'ITS is Already Paying Dividends', *Public Roads,* 61, September/October 1997, 26–9.

Kranzberg, Melvin and Pursell, Carroll, *Technology and Western Civilization*, 2 vols (New York 1967).

LeTourneau, Robert G., *Mover of Men and Mountains: Autobiography of R.G. LeTourneau* (Englewood Cliffs, NJ 1960).

MacDonald, Thomas H., 'The Financing of Highways', *Annals of the American Academy of Political and Social Science*, 116, November 1924, 160–68.

MacDonald, Thomas H., 'How Highway Financing Has Evolved', *Engineering News-Record*, 104, 2 January 1930, 4–7.

MacDonald, Thomas H., 'Crisis Demands Engineering Statesmanship', *Engineering News-Record*, 108, 24 March 1932, 429.

MacDonald, Thomas H., 'Highways Will be Safer; Driver Remains a Problem', *Scientific American*, 156, March 1937, 213.

Marshall, S.W., 'Planning the Pennsylvania Turnpike', *Civil Engineering*, 10, June 1940, 337–9.

Martineau, J.O., 'Buoys and Lifelines of Highways', *Roads and Bridges*, 84, April 1946, 87–9, 114, 116 and 118.

Mattimore, H.F. and Woodruff, F.P., 'Trend of Highway Guard Fence Design', *Public Works*, 60, March 1929, 119–20.

McCaffey, E., 'Uglification of America's Highways', *Professional Engineer*, 14, March 1929, 5–6.

McElheny, Victor K., *Insisting on the Impossible: The Life of Edwin Land* (Cambridge, MA 1998), 86–107.

McKnight, R.C., 'Visibility, Road Signs, and Guard Rails', *Canadian Engineer*, 73, 16 November 1937, 7–8.

Meikle, Jeffrey L., *Twentieth Century Limited: Industrial Design in Amerca, 1925–1939* (Philadelphia, PA 1979).

Miller, Charles L., 'Intermodal Surface Transportation Efficiency Act of 1991', *Public Roads*, 55, March 1992, 102–6.

Munn, Walter D., 'Glenwood Canyon: A Showcase for Innovation', *Highways and Heavy Construction*, 129, May 1986, 30–39.

National Academy of Sciences, National Research Council, ed., *A History of the Highway Research Board, 1920–1970* (Washington, DC 1970).

Netherton, Ross D., *Control of Highway Access* (Madison, WI 1963).

Nichols, C.G., 'The Merritt Parkway', *Engineering News-Record*, March 1940, 66.

Noble, Charles M., 'Modern Express Highway', *Proceedings of the American Society of Civil Engineers*, 62, September 1936, 1013–23, and November 1936, 1473–85.

Noble, C.M., 'Design Features; Pennsylvania Turnpike', *Civil Engineering*, 10, July 1940, 437–40.

Oetting, Robert B., 'Wildlife Habitat Development on Highway Rights-of-Way', *Public Works*, 117, March 1986, 72–4.

Page, Logan, 'The Motor Car and the Road: Destructive Effect of High Speed', *Scientific American*, 102, 15 January 1910, 46–7.

Pasko, Thomas J. Jr, 'Concrete Pavements – Past, Present, Future', *Public Roads*, 62, July/August 1998, http://www.tfhrc.gov/pubrds/julaug98/concrete.htm (last accessed May 2012).

Post, Robert C., 'The Myth Behind the Streetcar Revival', *American Heritage*, 49, May/June 1998, 95–101.

Poulter, John, 'The New German Highway System', *Roads and Streets*, 80, May 1927, 31–5.

Queiroz, Cesar 'Public-private partnerships in highways in transition economies: recent experience and future prospects', *Transportation Research Record*, 1996, 2007, 34–40.

Rice, Edward M., 'Lighting and the Modern Highway', *Roads and Streets*, 81, March 1938, 45–6.

Rose, Mark H., *Interstate: Express Highway Politics, 1914–1956.*, 2nd ed. rev. (Knoxville 1989).

Rose, Mark and Seely, Bruce E., 'Getting The Interstate System Built: Road Engineers and The Implementation of Public Policy, 1955–1985', *Journal of Policy History*, 2, Winter 1990, 23–56.

Rowan, N.J. and Olson, R.M., 'The Development of Safer Highway Sign Supports', *Traffic Engineering*, 38, 11 November 1967, 46–51.

Seely, Bruce E., 'The Scientific Mystique in Engineering: Highway Research in the Bureau of Public Roads, 1918–1940', *Technology and Culture*, 25, October 1984, 798–831.

Seely, Bruce E., *Building the American Highway System: Engineers as Policy Makers* (Philadelphia, PA 1987).

Seely, Bruce E., 'Urban Freeway Development and the Bureau of Public Roads, 1930–1950', *SCA* (Society for Commercial Archaeology) *Journal*, 15, Spring 1997, 12–20.

Seidel, H., '2000 km fertige Kraftfahrbahnen', *Zeitschrift des Vereines Deutscher Ingenieure*, 82, 15 January 1932, 73–5.

Selby, Robert Haralson, 'Earthmovers in World War II: R.G. LeTourneau and his Machines', Ph.D. diss., Case Institute of Technology, 1970.

Shuptrine, Harry A. and Mead, Julian C., 'Davison Limited Highway, Wayne County, Michigan', *Civil Engineering*, 12, December 1942, 673–6.

Slack, S.B., 'Design Of Highway Guard-Rail Dictated by Tests', *Engineering News-Record*, 108, 9 June 1932, 824–6.

Smith, David C., 'The Promise of High-Performance Concrete', *Public Roads*, 60, Autumn 1996, 31–41.

Smith, Leroy C., 'Trunk Line Highways in Metropolitan Areas', *Civil Engineering*, 7, October 1937, 685–6.

Spalding, Frederick P., *A Textbook on Roads and Pavements*, 3rd ed. (New York 1908).

Spelman, H.J., 'Machinery Revolutionizes Highway Grading', *Engineering News-Record*, 108, 7 January 1932, 10–13.

Stevenson, Elizabeth *Park Maker: A Life of Frederick Law Olmsted* (New Brunswick, NJ 2000).

Swan, H.S., 'Separating Grades at Highway Intersections', *Civil Engineering*, 3, February 1933, 79–83.

Taminini, F.J. and Viner, John G., 'Energy Absorbing Roadside Crash Barriers', *Civil Engineering*, 40, January 1970, 63–7.

Taylor, George Rogers, *The Transportation Revolution, 1815–1860* (New York 1951).

Tunnard, Christopher, and Pushkarev, Boris, *Man-Made America: Chaos or Control?* (New Haven, CT 1963).

Upham, Charles H., 'Diversion – The Highway Handicap', *Civil Engineering*, 9, January 1939, 1–2.

US, Department of Agriculture, Bureau of Public Roads, *Rules, Regulations, and Recommendations for Carrying Out Federal Aid Highway Programs* (Washington, DC 1939).

US, Department of Transportation, Federal Highway Administration, ed., *America's Highways, 1776–1976: A History of the Federal-Aid Program* (Washington, DC 1976).

US, Department of Transportation, Federal Highway Administration, ed., *Highway Statistics: Summary to 1985* (Washington, DC ca 1987).

US, Federal Works Administration, Public Roads Administration, ed., *Public Control of Highway Access and Roadside Development,* David R. Levin (Washington, DC 1943).

Viner, John G., 'Experience to Date with Impact Attenuators', *Public Roads*, 36, October 1971, 209–18.

Wayne County, Michigan, Board of Road Commissioners, ed., *Thirty-third Annual Report* (Detroit, MI 1939).

Wayne County, Michigan, Smith, Leroy C., 'Roads Become Superhighways in Wayne County, Michigan', *Engineering News-Record*, 119, 25 November 1937, 857–60.

Whittemore, H.L., 'Setting Wire Rope Guard Rails', *Public Works*, 60, August 1929, 301.

Wik, Reynold M., *Benjamin Holt and Caterpillar: Tracks and Combines* (St Joseph, MI 1984).

Wixom, Charles W., *American Roadbuilders Association Pictorial History of Roadbuilding* (Washington, DC 1975).

Zaccagnino, William, 'Technology for Work and Travel', *Public Roads*, 59, Spring 1996), 23–9.

Chapter 11

The Development of the European Highway Network: a Literature Survey of Studies on Highway History in European Countries

Reiner Ruppmann

Introduction

In 2007 the topic of road history was presented in an anthology that made public the results of a workshop held 2003 in Neuchâtel, Switzerland.[1] Compared with railway history, this research subject was overdue for scholarly studies. In 2006, German mobility historians organised a conference in Cologne, emphasising the long-term development of the 'modern road'; results were made available in another anthology including some essays on national highways.[2] A third publication, an inventory of current research on the history of transport, traffic and mobility, shed light on the importance of mobility in global historiography, a topic which to a large extent had been ignored by academic historians until then.[3] In addition, several monographs and anthologies regarding the materialisation of transnational European infrastructures and their impact on the unification of Europe have been published. They portray different aspects of bilateral or multilateral processes to build traffic infrastructures across borders.[4] Amazingly, factual historic narratives

1 Gijs Mom and Laurent Tissot, eds, *Road History: Planning, Construction, Use* (Neuchâtel 2007). Swiss scholars interested in the history of traffic and transport published articles concerning the subject as early as in 1999; see 'Strasse und Strassenverkehr – Routes et Circulation Routiere', *Traverse – Zeitschrift für Geschichte – Revue D'Histoire*, 2, 1999.

2 Hans-Liudger Dienel and Hans-Ulrich Schiedt, eds, *Die Moderne Straße. Planung, Bau und Verkehr vom 18. bis zum 20. Jahrhundert* (Frankfurt am Main and New York 2010).

3 Gijs Mom, Gordon Pirie and Laurent Tissot, eds, *Mobility in History. The State of the Art in the History of Transport, Traffic and Mobility* (Neuchâtel 2009).

4 See the article by Johan Schot, 'Building Europe on Transnational Infrastructures', *The Journal of Transport History*, 28, 2, 2007, 167–71. Further Eric van der Vleuten and Arne Kaijser, eds, *Networking Europe: Transnational Infrastructures and the Shaping of Europe, 1850–2000* (Sagamore Beach, MA 2006); Alexander Badenoch and Andreas Fickers, eds, *Materializing Europe: Transnational Infrastructures and the Project of Europe* (Houndmills, Basingstoke, Hampshire 2010). See also Ralf Roth and Karl Schlögel, eds, *Neue Wege in ein neues Europa. Geschichte und Verkehr im 20. Jahrhundert* (Frankfurt am Main and New York 2009).

on the construction of trans-border networks (roads as well as railways) are still rare. For the time being, among the best sources are small booklets with a more technical approach, published by road-building authorities.[5]

But none of these publications has specifically provided an overview of highway history in Europe, although transnational roads were predicted to be an accelerator of European integration since the Commission for European Economy of the United Nations presented the provisional draft of a European road system (E-roads) and set conditions for design and construction of highways in July 1949.[6]

Some historians unfairly describe anthologies as graveyards where academic essays are buried with high-class funerals. In the case of the aforementioned books, this categorisation is not applicable. On the contrary, these compilations give concise descriptions of various aspects of traffic, transport and mobility and show the flourishing culture of discussions in the community. Accordingly, it is evident that the anthologies encouraged further research, which brought to light new insights into the long-term progress of the subject, and contextualised it within the history of political, social and environmental developments, or rather links to economic and urban history.[7]

As is the case with railway history, most scholarly studies of highway history are still national or regional in scope. They usually focus on the history of highway planning and building, whereas the long-term emergence of road networks with its impact on the appearance of the highway idea in European countries and the highway use frequently play a subordinate role or were totally ignored.[8] Gijs Mom

---

5 For example Bundesministerium für Verkehr (BMV), ed., *Bundesautobahn Holland-Linie* (Cologne 1965); BMV, ed., *Erste Autobahn Deutschland – Frankreich. Europastrasse 12 Paris – Saarbrücken – Mannheim* (Saarbrücken 1969); BMV, ed., *Bundesautobahn Duisburg – Venlo. Europastrasse E 3* (Cologne 1975).

6 The term 'highway' in this chapter describes a limited-access road for high-speed and heavy automobile traffic only, with minimum of two unidirectional carriageways and at least two lanes each, separated by a green strip of grass and hedging plants or crash barriers (guardrails), principally with uneven levelled interchanges at crossings of any type, accessible only by particular points of entry, including attached special car parks plus service areas. Some other languages render the term as follows: *Snelwegen/autoroutes* (B), *Nationalstrasse* (CH), *Dálnice* (CZ), *Autobahn* (D), *Hovedvej* (DK), *Autopista*, *Autovia* (E), *autoroute* (F), motorway (GB), *Orzágút* (H), *Autocesta* (HR), *Autostrada* (I), *Hovedvei* (N), *Snelwegen* (NL), *Auto-estrada* (P), *Autostrada* (PL), *Motorväg* (S), *Dial'nica* (SK), *Highway* (SLO), *Freeway/Expressway/Interstate* (USA).

7 See my contribution in this anthology 'The City and the Autobahn, 1926–1956. Frankfurt on Main promoted Road Traffic opposing the Dull Railway Sytem'. For more details see Reiner Ruppmann, *Schrittmacher des Autobahnzeitalters – Frankfurt und das Rhein-Main-Gebiet* (Darmstadt 2011). The monograph of Frank Schipper, *Driving Europe: Building Europe on roads in the twentieth century* (Amsterdam 2008), deals chiefly with the political process of decisions towards a European road network (Europe Roads).

8 Most recently a brief review on this topic was published, regarding developments in six European countries and in the USA. See Bernd Kreuzer, *Vorauseilende Angebotsplanung*

of Eindhoven University wrote a pioneering essay on the subject.[9] Mom showed the four major phases of road history leading to the type of today's highways: road paving; road straightening and improvement of surface; functional road separation by the invention of limited-access roads for automobiles (highways); efforts to develop 'smart' roads/highways in order to guide and control intense traffic and try to avoid traffic congestion. To advance the analysis of road history, Mom additionally drew attention to essential aspects to be integrated into research: 'its multilayered, hierarchical, and multifunctional character', and the recognition of 'expectations and fantasy' in the period of the design process and discussions about the future use of roads/highways.[10]

Regardless, an overview of publications about European highway history has not yet appeared. For researchers, the only choice is to search and check scholarly studies country by country. For reasons of space and work economy, this chapter concentrates on major European countries with high automobile density. The following outline subsumes these countries into two categories: pioneers (Italy, Germany, Netherlands) and followers (Austria, Belgium, Britannia, France, Luxembourg, Portugal, Spain, Switzerland).

This chapter does not make a claim for a complete compilation of literature on highway history, as related essays often are hidden in various books, in remote journals and in anthologies concerning regional or local history.[11] Naturally, it was

---

und Raumerschließung: Die Vor- und Frühgeschichte der österreichischen Autobahnen im internationalen Kontext, in Dienel and Schiedt, *Die moderne Strasse*, 171–201.

9 Gijs Mom is surely the most important driving force in the field of mobility history. He has found equally interested research fellows in his country including Alexander Badenoch, Hans Buiter, Andreas Fickers, Ruud Filarski, Frank Schipper, Johan Schot and Eric van der Vleuten, as well as in other European countries, like Günter Dinhobl and Bernd Kreuzer in Austria, Hans-Liudger Dienel, Christopher Kopper, Ralf Roth and Helmut Trischler in Germany, Mathieu Flonneau in France, Lando Bortolotti, Massimo Moraglio and Claudio Pavese in Italy, Javier Vidal Olivares in Spain, Christoph Maria Merki, Hans-Ulrich Schiedt and Laurent Tissot in Switzerland, Colin Divall, Peter Lyth and Peter Merriman in United Kingdom, and overseas researchers as Clay McShane, Peter Norton and Bruce Seely in the USA and Gordon Pirie in South Africa.

10 Gijs Mom, 'Roads without Rails: European Highway-Network Building and the Desire for Long-Range Motorized Mobility', *Technology and Culture*, 46, October, 2005, 745–72, quotations at 746 and 770.

11 See for instance Christoph Maria Merki, *Der holprige Siegeszug des Automobils, 1895–1930. Zur Motorisierung des Strassenverkehrs in Frankreich, Deutschland und der Schweiz* (Vienna 2002) and Kurt Möser, *Geschichte des Autos* (Frankfurt am Main and New York 2002); Georg Kratz, '50 Jahre Autobahn in Deutschland unter besonderer Berücksichtigung des Alsfelder Raumes', *Mitteilungen des Geschichts- und Museumsvereins*, 13, 1988, 229–38; Herbert Jäkel, 'Der Bau der "Reichsautobahn" bei Alsfeld nach zeitgenössischen Berichtern und Bildern', *Mitteilungen des Geschichts- und Museumsvereins*, 13, 1988, 239–48; Arbeitskreis Dorfchronik Geisenhausen, ed., *Die Holledaubrücke. Geschichte und Geschichten* (Pfaffenhofen 2010).

impossible to discover and quote them all. The aim is to present a useful first bibliography of monographs and important essays regarding the topic.

The Pioneers

In the early 1920s, with the help of the fascist government of Italy, an Italian entrepreneur, Piero Puricelli, built the first expressways from Milan to the lakes north of Milan (*autostrade Milano-Laghi*). In the 1920s, German civil and governmental road engineers developed the blueprints for the design of current motorways. Under the Nazi government, a preliminary nationwide network of about 4,000 kilometres of *Autobahn* was created. Civil engineers in the Netherlands started to think about special roads for the emerging automobiles as early as 1906 and ventured into highway construction in the 1920s. The followers, in contrast, only started to build highways well into the 1950s of last century. The German *Autobahn* was more or less the model for these later highway constructions.

Italian Autostrade

The history of the first automobile-only express road in Italy gets noted in almost every scholarly study on the introduction of highways in Europe. This new traffic route was built between spring 1923 and autumn 1925 with Mussolini's consent. Though it was not built according to standards of highway construction in 1930s or today, it became a Mecca for civil engineers as well as municipal or governmental officials interested in a modern road adapted to automobile traffic. Members of the board of the German *Verein zur Vorbereitung der Autostraße Hansestädte–Frankfurt–Basel* (HaFraBa; Association for the Preparation of the Motorway Hanseatic cities–Frankfurt–Basle) maintained a close relationship with Puricelli, the *spiritus rector* and constructor of the aforementioned first expressway on the continent. To prepare for its foundation in 1926, Frankfurt am Main City Councilman Hermann Uhlfelder and Robert Otzen, later chairman of the HaFraBa executive committee, drove the *autostrada* from Como to Milan and were thrilled by the smooth, swift ride. Puricelli was appointed a member of the association's board and, given his expertise, also acted as consultant to the HaFraBa; his construction company held coporate membership.[12]

While most Italian studies on highway history were published in the journal *Storia Urbana*, some additional information appeared in anthologies not directly

[12] Massimo Moraglio, 'The Highway Network in Italy and Germany Between the Wars: A preliminary comparative study', in Mom and Tissot, *Road History*, 117–32; Massimo Moraglio, 'Real ambition or just coincidence? The Italian fascist motorway project in inter-war Europe', *Journal of Transport History*, 30, 2, 2009, 168–82.

dealing with road history.[13] Compared to their colleagues in other countries, Italian historians were relatively late in coming to highway historiography. It started with an anthology titled *Highways of the First Generation*, in which a portrait of Piero Puricelli can be found.[14] Analogous to German *Autobahn* historiographers in the 1990s, Giuseppe de Luca and Lando Bortolotti followed with a critical analysis of the amalgamation of Italian Fascism and highway construction.[15] Other publications occupied themselves with descriptions of the construction history of Italian highway sections.[16] Between 1923 and 1933, the Italian highway network was built step-by-step by various private companies, becoming a 505-kilometre patchwork of shorter lines connecting large industrialised cities or a city with a seaside resort or other tourist place: Milan-Bergamo (opened 1927), Naples-Pompeii (1929), Bergamo-Brescia (1931), Florence-Viareggio and Torino-Milan (1932), Padua-Venice (1933).[17] The showpiece Rome – Ostia road to the seaside (*via del mare*) – was promoted by the district of Rome and equipped like a triumphal avenue. It was opened by Benito Mussolini on 28 October 1928.[18] The only highway constructed between 1924 and 1935 by the fascist government itself was a carriageway with two unidirectional lanes designed for lorry transports from the port of Genoa to Milan (*autocamionale*). But for the time being the road was

13 Sergio Mattia, 'La costruzione dell'autostrada Milan – Laghi', in Ornella Selvafolta and Aldo Castellano, eds, *Costruire I Lombardia 1880–1980. Rete e infrastrutture territoriali* (Milano 1984), 175–206; Annabella Galleni, 'Strade, autostrade e fascismo. Un memoriale di Piero Puricelli (1940)', *Imprese e storia*, 19, 1999, 47–82.

14 Gianpietro Livini, ed., *1924–1935. Le Autostrade della prima generazione* (Milano 1984). The Puricelli portrait was written by Francesco Aimone Jelmoni, 'Piero Puricelli', in ibid., 20–23. See also Lando Bortolotti, 'Origine e primordi della rete autostradale in Italia, 1923–1933', *Storia Urbana*, 59, 1992, 35–69, portrait of Puricelli 43–7.

15 Giuseppe de Luca and Lando Bortolotti, *Fascismo e autostrade. Un caso di sintesi: la Firenze-mare* (Milano 1994). The close relationship of fascist Italy and Nazi Germany regarding *Autobahn* planning is documented by Lando Bortolotti, 'Fra politica, propaganda e affari: L'Autostrada Roma – Berlino 1927–1942', *Storia Urbana*, 81, 1997, 47–79. For general aspects of the historic and current developments of transport and traffic in Italy see Andrea Giuntini and Claudio Pavese, eds, *Reti, mobilità, trasporti. Il sistema italiano tra prospettiva storica e innovazione* (Milano 2004); Claudio Pavese, 'The Making of the Italian Motorways Network (1924–1974)', *Transportes, Servicios y Telecommunicaciones*, 10, 2006, 97–120.

16 Giuseppe de Luca, 'La construzione della rete autostradale italiana. L'autostrada Firenze–Mare, 1927–1940', *Storia Urbana*, 59, 1992, 71–126, and Massimo Moraglio, 'L'autostrada Torino–Milano (1923–1933). I progetto e la construzione', *Storia Urbana*, 86, 1999, 103–21.

17 Massimo Moraglio, *Storia delle prime autostrade italiane (1922–1943). Modernizzazione, affair e propaganda* (Torino 2007). See also the internet source http://cronologia.leonardo.it/storia/a1950c.htm (last access 12 February 2012).

18 See Piero Puricelli, 'Le Strade dell'Impero Italiano', in Kurt G. Kaftan, ed., *Welt-Strassenwesen 1938* (Berlin 1938), 132–7; pictures see under http://camera.archivioluce.com (last access 12 February 2012).

not finished. It ended at the valley of the river Po. Work on it was resumed well after the Second World War.[19]

Highway building in Italy was not carried out further after 1933 since the private lines did not generate the expected revenues due to low traffic. Thus Puricelli's ventures failed, as did the routes of the other related private companies, except the highway from Turin to Milan. Nevertheless, the 510-kilometre Italian highway system served as an example for modern road construction. Initiators in other European countries used it to support their own arguments.

With mass motorisation and the invasion of tourists after the Second World War, Italy had to restart its road-building activities to provide a basis for economic growth and mobility. The government again pursued the model of constructing highways with private resources.[20] Today, 24 different companies hold concessions to run the toll highways throughout the country, despite about 900 kilometres of toll-free highways in the area of Rome and in the southern part of the country including Sicily. These are operated by the state-owned highway association, A.N.A.S, the *Assozazione Nationale Auto Strade*.[21]

German Autobahnen

Highways interrelate mutually with railways. In nineteenth century the latter inspired people to leave their cramped villages and limiting neighbourhoods to discover distant places and sometimes even to emigrate.[22] Railways expanded the sphere of influence of large cities and the emergence of industrial cities, thus slowly levelling the differences between cities and countryside. Railways fostered the rise of modern industry, contributed to urbanisation and stimulated tourism. Farming villages in the mountains and rustic settlements on the sea coast developed into promising

---

[19] Giovanni da Rios and Savino Rinelli, 'Autocamionale Genova–Valle del Po', in Livini, *1924–1935. Le Autostrade della prima generazione*, 120–37.

[20] E. Santucci, 'Die Entwicklung des Straßenverkehrs und der Ausbau des Straßennetzes bis zum Jahre 1985 in Italien', *Strasse und Autobahn*, 23, 1, 1973, 208–13.

[21] See ibid., 208–13; E. Santucci, *Autostrade per l'Italia S.p.A., La Societa' Autostrade dagli anni della ricostruzione post-bellica all'orrizonte del 2000* (Roma 1996); E. Santucci, *La rete autostradale Italiana 1924–2002* (Roma 2003); S. Vitagliani, *Destination Europe. Autostrada e mobilità in Valle d'Aosta 1962–1992* (Quart 1993); L. Coccia and M.T. Granato, *Ascoli – mare. Una autostrada senza pedaggio* (Napoli 2000); Massimo Morgalio, *Strade e politica. Storia della viabilità in provincia di Torino* (Alessandria 2003); Massimo Morgalio and Michele Bonino, *Inventare gli spostamenti. Storia e immagini dell'autostrada Torino–Savona* (Toino et. al. 2006); Leandra D'Antone, *Senza pedaggio. Storia dell'autostrada Salerno – Reggio Calabria* (Milano 2008); Marco Adorni and Alberto Malfitano, *Un'autostrada per l'Appennino. La superstrada E7–E45 e il dibattito sulla sua costruzione* (Bologna 2006). Questions about the contemporary motorway system in Italy are raised by Giorgio Ragazzi, *I signori delle autostrade* (Bologna 2008).

[22] Ralf Roth, *Das Jahrhundert der Eisenbahn. Die Herrschaft über Raum und Zeit* (Ostfildern 2005).

tourist resorts. But soon people wished to explore places not reachable by railway tracks. The automobile was a new means of transportation that was welcomed and quickly adopted. It offered freedom from timetables and access to remote places. Unfortunately, roads did not keep up with the rise of automobility, the increase of motorised traffic and the desired speed of travel. These and other circumstances led to proposals for roads designed like railway tracks. As the existing roads did not fit into this suggestion, there arose the idea of a new road system. However, it took time and enormous financial effort from national governments to implement these special roads. At first they were far ahead of traffic and transportation demand, but later they had to struggle against an exponentially increasing number of automobiles. In Germany a specific relationship between railway and highway is observable. In this country, the idea, supported by public-private partnerships, to build a new road system adapted for high-speed and heavy automobile traffic in the 1920s gained momentum as a narrow-minded government used the position of power to prevent the German Railway Company from road transport competition.

Narrations on German *Autobahn* history can be divided into three groups: scholarly studies, memorial books and local research. Naturally, the scholarly studies are the focus of the present chapter. Most of them are directly related to the history of Nazi Germany, as, after the Second World War, the *Autobahn* was a remnant of the Nazi period. Post-war historians wanted to fight the opinion of older generations who perceived Hitler's *Autobahn* as a far-sighted 'good deed' and in this respect a helpful forerunner of mass motorisation in West Germany.[23] The following documentation is drawn up without extensive historical remarks.

Karl Lärmer, a historian in the German Democratic Republic where most of the old *Reichsautobahn* files were stored, issued the first relevant study. Naturally, the book had to follow the official Marxist-Leninist opinion of historical developments in the Third Reich. Thus Lärmer used selected documents to prove that *Autobahn* construction was exploited by fascist aggression to prepare for war. The author also presented a large number of interesting details, especially about the labour force at *Autobahn* construction sites.[24] Seven years later, a West German, Rainer Stommer, published a critical anthology on the occasion of the fiftieth anniversary of the *Reichsautobahn*, analysing the mythical term *Autobahn*.[25] In 1989, Claudia Windisch-Hojnacki's Ph.D. thesis addressed the aesthetic side of

---

23 Reiner Ruppmann, 'Das System der Autobahnen und ihre kulturellen Mythen', in Ralf Roth and Karl Schlögel, eds, *Neue Wege in ein neues Europa. Geschichte und Verkehr im 20. Jahrhundert* (Frankfurt am Main and New York 2009), 338–60. Hans-Joachim Winkler, *Legenden um Hitler*. Zur Politik und Zeitgeschichte, H. 7, ed. by Landeszentrale für politische Bildungsarbeit Berlin in Verbindung mit dem Otto-Suhr-Institut an der FU Berlin (Berlin 1963).

24 Karl Lärmer, *Autobahnbau in Deutschland 1933–1945. Zu den Hintergründen* (Berlin 1975).

25 Rainer Stommer, ed., *Reichsautobahn – Pyramiden des Dritten Reiches. Analysen zur Ästhetik eines unbewältigten Mythos* (Marburg 1982).

the *Reichsautobahn*, pointing out in detail how paintings, photographs, sculptures and poetry illustrated the work.[26] *Mythos Reichsautobahn*, by Erhard Schütz and Eckhard Gruber, is considered to be the best book on *Reichsautobahn* history and accordingly gets quoted whenever this highway is mentioned. These authors were among the first who made use of the well-stocked Nazi archives and collections after 1990 then available in reunified Germany.[27] The journal *WerkstattGeschichte* united four papers on the subject of the *Autobahn* before and after the Second World War.[28] Friedrich Hartmannsgruber drew attention to the financing of *Autobahn* construction in the Third Reich. He demonstrated that about 3.5 billion *Reichsmark* was raised from the German unemployment insurance as long-term loans at low rates of interest, and the rest largely was covered through acceptance credits backed by the *Reichsbank*.[29]

There are also other researchers with a more political-historical perspective, for instance Dietmar Klenke, who addressed transport policy decision-making in post-war West Germany in the context of increasing mass motorisation.[30]

Following the so-called 'cultural turn', historical scientists started to approach the *Autobahn* history with comparative studies based on historical-cultural points of view. Thomas Zeller compared the *Autobahn* construction from 1933 to 1945 with post-war road building 1949 to 1970 and the implementation of high-speed railways in West Germany in the period between 1973 and 1991. His objective was to explain the perception of landscape as a mutual and interactive mental process driven by economic, technical and social forces that fundamentally changed the transport of goods and the mobility of persons. With this attempt, he sought to link traffic history with the history of environment.[31] Sylvia Pradel studied

26 Claudia Windisch-Hojnacki, *Die Reichsautobahn – Konzeption und Bau der RAB, ihre ästhetischen Aspekte, sowie ihre Illustration in Malerei, Literatur, Photographie und Plastik*, Ph.D. (Bonn 1989).

27 Erhard Schütz and Eckhard Gruber, *Mythos Reichsautobahn – Bau und Inszenierung der 'Straßen des Führers', 1933–1941* (Berlin 1996).

28 See the special issue of *WerkstattGeschichte*, 21, 1998, on the topic 'Netzwerk Autobahn' edited by Burghard Ciesla.

29 Friedrich Hartmannsgruber, '"... ungeachtet der noch nicht geklärten Finanzierung" – Finanzplanung und Kapitalbeschaffung für den Bau der Reichsautobahnen 1933–1945', *Historische Zeitschrift*, 278, 2004, 625–81.

30 Dietmar Klenke, *Bundesdeutsche Verkehrspolitik und Motorisierung. Konfliktträchtige Weichenstellung in den Jahren des Wiederaufstiegs*. Zeitschrift für Unternehmensgeschichte, Beiheft 79 (Stuttgart 1993); Dietmar Klenke, 'Die deutsche Katastrophe und das Automobil. Zur "Heils"geschichte eines nationalen Kultobjekts in den Jahren des Wiederaufstiegs', in Michael Salewski and Ilona Stölken-Fitschen, eds, *Moderne Zeiten. Technik und Zeitgeist im 19. und 20. Jahrhundert* (Stuttgart 1994), 157–73.

31 Thomas Zeller, *Straße, Bahn, Panorama. Verkehrswege und Landschaftsveränderung in Deutschland 1930 bis 1990* (Frankfurt am Main and New York 2002). See also Thomas Zeller, *Driving Germany. The Landscape of the German Autobahn, 1930–1970* (New York and Oxford 2006).

important legal aspects of highway history; in a lengthy section, she explained the progression of laws concerning trunk roads in Germany.[32] Axel Dossmann in his long-term analyses combined the 'neverending past' of Nazi *Autobahn* works with the post-war history of road infrastructure in the German Democratic Republic, marked by the Cold War and the investments into the *Autobahn* system after the reunification of Germany.[33] The way Benjamin Steininger chose to gain new insight into the *Autobahn* phenomenon was to look at some technical aspects of the traffic.[34] Frank Becker examined the origins and the development of the highway idea in the United States, Italy and Germany during the inter-bellum period. He discovered two major driving ideas: firstly Henry Ford's future-oriented philosophy of industrial efficiency and mass income, and, secondly, John Maynard Keynes' theory of deficit spending.[35] Similarly, Wolfgang Schivelbusch introduced a comparison between, on the one hand, Roosevelt's New Deal, and, on the other hand, the measures of Mussolini in Italy and Hitler in Germany. In his opinion, all three rulers used similar instruments to stimulate the economy against mass unemployment, though only two of them pushed road construction.[36]

Memorial books mirror the professional career of the writer. Kurt Kaftan started this type of *Autobahn* history in 1955 when he recalled the story of the HaFraBa, which had proposed a central *Autobahn* through Germany from the northern cities of Hamburg, Bremen and Lübeck via Frankfurt am Main to Basle.[37] Kaftan was the former chief editor of *HaFraBa*-Mitteilungen, then the leading European motorway journal. All *Autobahn* historians quote his book as a useful and important source, but none has discussed the author's true intentions. First, Kaftan wrote to honour the memory of his friend Willy Hof, former secretary of the HaFraBa and manager of the *Reichsautobahn* company until 1935. Second, he wrote to fight the 'Adolf Hitler's Roads' (*Straßen Adolf Hitlers*) myth, which Nazi officials noisily propagated, claiming that the *Autobahn* was the Führer's idea and glossing over the merits of the HaFraBa. Martin Kornrumpf wrote another

32 Sylvia Pradel, *Entstehung und Entwicklung des Bundesfernstraßenrechts* (Hamburg 2003).

33 Axel Doßmann, *Begrenzte Mobilität. Eine Kulturgeschichte der Autobahnen in der DDR* (Essen 2003).

34 Benjamin Steininger, *Raum-Maschine Reichsautobahn. Zur Dynamik eines bekannt/unbekannten Bauwerks* (Berlin 2005).

35 Frank Becker, 'Autobahnen, Auto-Mobilität. Die USA, Italien und Deutschland im Vergleich', in Wolfgang Hardtwig, ed., *Politische Kulturgeschichte der Zwischenkriegszeit 1918–1939* (Göttingen 2005), 23–59.

36 Wolfgang Schivelbusch, *Entfernte Verwandtschaft. Faschismus, Nationalsozialismus, New Deal 1933–1939* (Munich 2005).

37 Kurt Kaftan, *Der Kampf um die Autobahnen. Geschichte und Entwicklung des Autobahngedankens in Deutschland von 1907–1935 unter Berücksichtigung ähnlicher Pläne und Bestrebungen im übrigen Europa* (Berlin 1955).

memorial book, but with his somewhat untidy collection of facts, he approached the HaFraBa story rather uncritically.[38]

In a sense, the retrospective on 30 years of *Autobahn* building, published 1962 by the German Ministry of Traffic and Transport when the *Autobahn* from Hamburg to Basle was opened, can also be called a memorial book. The articles refer to the history of this important line, which was the origin of German's *Autobahnen*, as well as to the history of its construction.[39]

The books produced by local researchers are largely written for the layperson to satisfy the demand for information of either a mass or a local audience. Accordingly they do not always follow strict scientific standards. Yet, these publications should receive more attention from the scientific community because they supplement scholarly studies with well-conducted investigations, and texts often are illustrated with otherwise-unknown contemporary pictures showing details of construction and road works in progress.[40]

Books written by road and landscape engineers as well as economists are an in-between category. They approach road history with their expertise of their profession and with their extensive know-how; thus, they may tend to put the focus merely on collecting proceedings and actions. Lacking the special research and analysis techniques of transport historians, for them the political, economical and social developments often are of less importance and get short shrift. For that reason the quality of these books is mixed, though they do extend the knowledge

---

38 Martin Kornrumpf, *HAFRABA e. V. – deutsche Autobahn-Planung 1926–1934*. Archiv für die Geschichte des Straßenwesens, vol. 7 (Köln 1990).

39 Bundesminister für Verkehr, Abteilung Straßenbau, ed., HAFRABA – *Bundesautobahn Hansestädte-Frankfurt-Basel. Rückblick auf 30 Jahre Autobahnbau* (Wiesbaden and Berlin 1962).

40 Peter Norden, *Unternehmen Autobahn* (Bayreuth 1983); Hans-Jürgen Mielke, *Die Autobahn Berlin – Helmstedt. Über 160 Kilometer Langeweile?* (Berlin 1984); Hermann Engl and Frank Lämmel, *Highway Deutschland* (Holzkirchen 1996); Franz Semlinger, *Die Autobahn vom Hienberg bis Nürnberg. Bau und Bedeutung bis heute* (Neunkirchen am Sand 1998); Berthold Flessa and Helmut Goller, *Die Geschichte der Autobahn 1934 bis 2000. Abschnitt Bayreuth/Kulmbach bis Landesgrenze Thüringen/Sachsen* (Münchberg 2000); Karl-Heinz Rothenberger, 'Autobahnbau in der Pfalz nach dem Zweiten Weltkrieg', *Mitteilungen des historischen Vereins der Pfalz*, 100, 2002, 533–59; Dieter Stockmann, *Strecke 46 – Die vergessene Autobahn*, 3rd ed. (Veitshöchheim 2007); Gernot Pehnelt, *Das Unternehmen Reichs*autobahn (Dessau 2003); Hans-Jürgen Mielke, *Die Autobahn Berlin – Hirschberg/Hof in Geschichte und Gegenwart. Landeskunde entlang einer deutschen Hauptverbindungsachse* (Halle 2007); Hans-Joachim Weise, *Vom Bau der Autobahn im Schleizer Oberland 1933 bis 1936* (n.l. 2006); Gero Fehlhauer, *Die Geschichte der Reichsautobahn Chemnitz – Hof* (Reichenbach i. Vogtland 2006); Volkhard Stern, *Der Autobahn-Schnellverkehr der Deutschen Reichsbahn* (Freiburg 2007); Britta Eichner-Ramm, *70 Jahre Autobahn Göttingen – Kassel* (Göttingen 2007); Alfred Lambeck, *Die bergisch-märkische Autobahn Leverkusen – Kamen, 1948–1958* (Erfurt 2008); Hans-Jürgen Mielke, *Die Autobahn Berlin – Hamburg. Politik und Geschichte erfahren* (Halle 2010).

of road and *Autobahn* history, shedding light on technical, professional and administrative questions.[41]

Netherlands Autosnelwegen

Highway history in the Netherlands has received almost as much attention from mobility historians as in Italy and Germany. To understand Dutch road history, it seems useful to give a brief summary of its last 200 years. Gijs Mom has published a pioneering overview on this topic with an extensive bibliography.[42] In the old Netherlands, transportation was primarily conducted over waterways; land traffic was poorly developed. There was no centralised governmental agency to look after roads. In 1795, the northern part of the Netherlands founded the Batavian Republic. Marked by French ideas of centralisation, these 'Unitarists' established, amongst other things, the *Bureau voor de Waterstaat*, a governmental office responsible for the waterways. From 1798 until 1813, France occupied the Batavian Republic, which finally was integrated into Napoleon's empire. As a result, the *Waterstaat* had to report to the French *Service des Ponts et Chaussées*, an engineering department responsible for the whole transportation infrastructure in France and in the occupied territories. In 1811 the *Waterstaat* started to plan and build a network of first- and second-class through-roads for trade and defence. At this stage, the connecting roads from Paris to Amsterdam and the key road from Zonder via Breda and Utrecht to Amsterdam were created.[43] After Napoleon's 1815 downfall at Waterloo, the Netherlands came into history (geographically, the new country covered the area of today's Benelux states). The infrastructure organisation, now named *Rijkswaterstaat* (RWS), continued its road-building work following the plans established under French administration.

Once Belgium declared independence in 1830, and finally left the Netherlands in 1839, the *Rijkswaterstaat* concentrated its efforts on the road network (*Rijkswegen*) in the north. It stayed almost unchanged until the end of nineteenth century. With the first steps into the railway network in 1839, roads little by little lost their importance for transport and mobility. Commencing in 1860, the *Rijkswaterstaat*, besides waterways and roads, was also in charge of governmental railway construction,

---

41 See Wolfgang Wirth, ed., *Die Autobahn. Von der Idee zur Wirklichkeit*. Archiv für die Geschichte des Straßen- und Verkehrswesens, vol. 19 (Köln 2005); Roland Gabriel, *Dem Auto eine Bahn. Deutsche 'Nurautostraßen' vor 1933*. Archiv für die Geschichte des Straßen- und Verkehrswesens, vol. 23 (Köln 2010).

42 Gijs Mom, 'Constructing Multifunctional Networks. Road Building in the Netherlands, 1810–1980', in Mom and Tissot, *Road History*, 33–62. Very helpful in this respect is also the internet site http://www.autosnelwegen.nl (last accessed 20 January 2011). Unfortunately, the webmaster has not updated it since 19 April 2007.

43 A. Bosch and W. van der Ham, *Twee eeuwen Rijkswaterstaat. Europese bibilotheek* (Zaltbommel 1998). See also M.J. Ververs, *Kruising, de geschiedenis van pont en brug. Europese biblioteek* (Zaltbommel 1999).

including large bridges and railway stations. The *Rijkswegen* still were kept in a good shape, though the width of some of them was reduced to save money for maintenance. At the turn of the century the overall network of roads was about 8,000 kilometres, some 6,000 kilometres of which were paved with bricks.

As in all other European countries, the beginning of the automobile age considerably altered people's view of public and private transport in the Netherlands. Narrow roads, which often ran on the top of dykes, were not prepared to take that new kind of speedy traffic. In 1906 the Dutch Minister and civil engineer Cornelis Lely predicted mass motorisation and accordingly foresaw the need to split the different road users into adapted kinds of traffic routes. Yet Lely then did not talk about *autosnelwegen*.[44] The *Rijkswegenplan* of 1927, managed by G.J. van den Broek, connected all major cities in the country with by-pass thoroughfares to avoid congested areas.[45] Road construction was financed by a special fund (*Wegenfonds*) remunerated by a road tax (*Wegenbelastingwet*) imposed on car owners starting in 1926.[46] The *Nederlandse Vereeniging voor Autosnelwegen* (NEVA), founded in the fall of 1927, strongly supported this scheme, following the example set by the German HaFraBa association; two leading HaFraBa members had been present at the founding of the NEVA. In 1923, to execute road improvement plans, the *Rijkswaterstaat* organisation formed a department for road construction (*Wegentechniek*), responsible for technology as well as construction management.

In 1929, highway construction started with the Rijswijk-Delft section of the Den Haag – Rotterdam Rijksweg. This was not of the German highway type, but a Dutch version with two non-separated unidirectional carriageways of 5.5 metres width, even levelled crossings and access points, with parallel roads and bicycle paths for local traffic. In the construction phase, from 1936 until the German invasion in May 1940, a total of 60 kilometres of expressways was under construction or ready for use.[47] Astonishingly, 64 kilometres of the route from Utrecht to Emmerich at the German border (today the A12) were built during the Second World War, although the *Reichsautobahnen*, then acting as supervisor of *Rijkswaterstaat*, stopped all construction work in the German Reich in 1942. The last section was opened to the public in February 1944.[48]

---

44 Willem van der Ham, *Verover mij dat land, Lely en de Zuiderzeewerken* (Amsterdam 2007).

45 First comprehensive articles on this subject were published by Marie-Louise ten Horn-van-Nispen, 'Een ideal uit de jaren twintig: autosnelwegen', *De Ingenieur*, 106, 13, 1994, 19–21; Hans Buiter, '"Hoogviadukten in het polderland?" De introductie van de autosnelweg in Nederland', *NEHA-jaarboek*, 60, 1997, 285–306.

46 Marie-Louise ten Horn-van-Nispen, 'Het Rijkswegenplan 1927. De aanpak van het verkeersvraagstuk in de jaren twintig', *Jaarboek voor de geschiedenis van bedrijf en techniek*, 9, 1992, 185–208.

47 See the 1938 *Rijkswegenplan* and interesting photos in the article by L.R. Wentholt, 'Het Nederlandsche Rijkswegennet', in Kaftan, *Welt-Strassenwesen*, 116–23.

48 Adolf Walewijn, *Achter de Bres: De Rijkswaterstaat in oorlogstijd* (Den Haag 1990).

The continuation of *autosnelwegen* construction in the Netherlands after the Second World War anticipated the pattern of highway construction development in European countries. First the damaged bridges had to be repaired and the signs of war devastation had to be cleared away. In 1948 the Dutch transport minister presented a revised *Rijkswegenplan* which contained few changes to its 1938 predecessor. Between 1946 and 1949, the road department of RWS completed 44 kilometres of expressways. In the period of 1952 to 1955, highway construction was accelerated, once government and road construction officials had understood that increasing automobile traffic and the interests of road safety left no alternative. The very first 33 kilometres of modern-type highway between Den Haag and Utrecht were opened on 1 April 1954.[49] In total, 209 kilometres of the combined expressway-highway system was devoted to automobile traffic in the years between 1946 and 1955. The following 18 years (1956–70) was the time of maximum performance, which pushed the highway network to 1,209 kilometres. The next period (1971–2000) added another 1,056 kilometres to the network.[50] Eurostat, the Statistical Office of the European Commission, reported in 2008 a total of 2,631 kilometres of highways in the Netherlands. The second lowest car density, but the second highest traffic share of motorcars of all countries evaluated in this article signifies that highways in the Netherlands are particularly vital for the Dutch economy as well as for individual mobility (see Table 11.1).

The Followers

Some of the follower countries occupied themselves with the problem of road transformation to the automobile traffic in the inter-bellum period. Austria was one of these. Planners knew that something had to be done to attract car tourists; in 1926, civil engineers designed a special road tailor-made for car traffic from Vienna to the tourist region of Semmering in the mountains south of the capital.[51] France had started to construct an expressway from Paris to the Normandy (*autoroute de Normandie*) in about 1938 but had to stop work in 1940. Earlier the French entrepreneur Lucien

---

49 See Hans Buiter and K. Volkers, *Oudenrijn, De geschiedenis van een verkeersknooppunt* (Utrecht 1996).

50 J.W. Tops, 'Die Entwicklung des Straßenverkehrs und der Ausbau des Straßennetzes bis zum Jahre 1985 in den Niederlanden', *Strasse und Autobahn*, 23, 1, 1973, 196–207.

51 See Bernd Kreuzer, 'Die Anfänge der österreichischen Autobahnen', in Verband Österreichischer Historiker und Geschichtsvereine und Niederösterreichisches Landesarchiv, ed., *Tagungsbericht des 25. Österreichischen Historikertag in St. Pölten 2008* (St. Pölten 2010), 202–14. Additionally see Heinrich Schmelz, 'Die Entwicklung des Straßenverkehrs und der Ausbau des Straßennetzes bis zum Jahre 1985 in Österreich', *Strasse und Autobahn*, 23, 1, 1973, 213–23.

Lainé had encouraged the idea of an expressway from Paris to Calais.[52] And the Spanish government planned an *autopista* from Madrid to Irun in the 1920s.

Austrian Autobahnen

The community of road historians in the Western World is rather small. Approximately a dozen specialised contributors supported most of the anthologies mentioned above. One of these competent researchers is the Austrian Bernd Kreuzer, who has examined the history of transport, traffic and mobility in Austria since 1996, integrating himself step-by-step into the international community of traffic historians. In view of this it cannot surprise that he has become the foremost Austrian highway historian. Despite steady research and publication efforts, Kreuzer is not satisfied with the effects of his work on traffic history in his country.[53] 'Still focussing on the railway: Transport and Mobility History in Austria', the author complained in his contribution to the 2009 T2M yearbook.[54] Considering the long list of publications on Austrian railway history and other subjects, he is absolutely right. Kreuzer started his research with an article in Mom and Tissot's anthology *Road History*.[55] His own first book on the history of Austrian highways (*Autobahnen*) was published in 2005 on the occasion of the fiftieth anniversary of *Autobahn* construction after the Second World War and the closure of the last gap in the Austrian highway network which took place in 2004. This pioneering book covers a period of about 70 years from the 1920s until 2004, combining the history of through-roads with intensifying *Autobahn* ideas, *Autobahn* construction in Nazi Germany and the post-Second World War expansion of the first modest lines into a highway network that was to a certain extent based on the old plans of the *Reichsautobahn* organisation. The *Autobahn* is contextualised within the surrounding politics, economy, society and culture.[56] In 2007 Kreuzer finished his Ph.D. thesis, entitled *The country needs fast roads*.[57] More recently, Kreuzer has

[52] Kurt Kaftan, *Europa braucht Autobahnen. Vorschläge und Entwürfe zur Erbauung nationaler Autobahnnetze als Ausgangspunkte zur Errichtung eines europäischen Autobahnnetzes* (Berlin 1936), 14.

[53] See Bernd Kreuzer, 'Transport History in Austria: A literature survey', in Michèle Merger and Marie-Noëlle Polino, eds, *COST 340. Towards a European Intermodal Transport Network. Lessons from History. A Critical Bibliography* (Paris 2004), 1–13.

[54] Bernd Kreuzer, 'Still Focussing on the Railway: Transport and Mobility History in Austria', in Mom et al., *Mobility in History*, 193–200.

[55] Bernd Kreuzer, 'National Road Networks in the 1930s – the Case of Austria's Roads', in Mom and Tissot, *Road History*, 99–116.

[56] Bernd Kreuzer, *Tempo 130. Kultur- und Planungsgeschichte der Autobahnen in Oberösterreich* (Linz 2005).

[57] Bernd Kreuzer, '*Schnelle Straßen braucht das Land*', *University of Vienna Ph.D. thesis, 2007. The thesis is available as an electronic publication. To download, see* http://othes.univie.ac.at/7493 or http://www.gta.arch.ethz.ch/personen/bernd-kreuzer (last accessed 28 December 2010).

addressed functional dimensions of roads that had not been discussed much by transport historians: the development of regions' through-road construction, and the different ways in which various cities have transformed themselves in order to satisfy the demand for swift, smooth flows of automobile traffic.[58]

Belgian Autosnelwegen/Autoroutes

At present, Belgian highway history is a closed book because no valid scholarly studies of the subject can be found. For that reason it seems suitable to give a condensed overview here. The following information is taken from a website entitled 'A site on the construction of roads and motorways in Belgium'.[59]

The start into the planning of the Belgian highway network generally can be located in 1935, but actually the first phase of realisation took place between 1950 and 1965. In 1934, the Belgian Bridge and Road Administration (*l'Administration des Ponts et Chaussées*) planned a general scheme of about 260 kilometres of new roads for the automobile traffic.[60] Undoubtedly, the public opinion in Belgium was influenced positively by Italian and German highway construction, but also by an internationally discussed plan to build a road for long-distance traffic from London to Istanbul. Plans made by the Dutch Highway Association (NEVAS – *Nederlandsche Vereeniging voor Autosnelwegen*) to finance highway construction with a mix of public and private money and expand motorisation gave additional impetus. To defeat the impression that Belgian people were backward in modern road building, in 1935 the Minister of Public Works decided to build a new road from Brussels to Oostende in the form of a highway. At that time some other ideas

---

58 Bernd Kreuzer, 'Stadtumbau für den Verkehr. Stadt- und Verkehrsplanung in Linz im 20. Jahrhundert', in Walter Schuster, ed., *Die Stadt Linz im 20. Jahrhundert* (Linz 2011), 519–618. Currently Kreuzer is working on his habilitation thesis entitled *Auf dem Weg zur 'autogerechten Stadt'. Stadtplanung und Verkehr in europäischen Städten, 1920–1940* (*Towards the 'car-adapted city'. Urban development and traffic in European cities, 1920–1940*).

59 See http://www.wegen-routes.be/ (last accessed 19 January 2011). This website presents the core of R. van de Wall's unpublished historiography thesis, *'Bouwen voor een onbekende toekomst'. De totstandkoming van het Belgische autosnelwegennet (1935–1989)*, Ouitgegeven licentiaatsverhandeling, Katholieke Universiteit Leuven, departement Geschiedenis, 2007 (*'Constructing for a unknown future'. The realisation of the Belgian highway network, 1935–1989*, University of Leuven). See also J. Oosterwall, *Besluitvormingstypes en effectiviteit in het autosnelwegenbeleid in België* (Leuven 1990); Eric van Heesvelde, 'Infrastructuurinvesteringen in de sector vervoer en verkeer', in Vereniging voor Economie, ed., *Verkeer in België in 2000. Mobiliteit of chaos? Twintigste Vlaams Wetenschappelijk Economisch Congres. Gent, 17 en 18 oktober 1991* (Gent 1991), 89–114.

60 The start was described by Paul Deheem, 'Réseau rotier de l'Etat Belge. Routes nouvelles', in Kaftan, *Welt-Strassenwesen*, 123–6.

for smaller projects were taken into consideration but no network was in sight yet. Then the war stopped all projects.

In 1949, responding to a predicted increase in automobile traffic, the Belgian government gave the green light to a highway programme of 930 kilometres covering the whole country, but did not give the project a high priority. In 1955, new statistics about growing automobile traffic inspired the responsible minister to publish a new plan for 1,528 kilometres of highways. He also set up an autonomous road construction fund to finance the projects within the next 15 years. In 1956 the highway from Brussels to Oostende was finally opened. The Belgian road commission soon started another scheme for a highway from Antwerp across the whole country to Luik (Lüttich/Liège) in the southeast. This was the King Baudouin Highway (today E 313). This express road then was not really necessary because traffic was rather light. However, the highway venture was conducted with an eye to the future, offering the port of Antwerp not only fast access to the hinterland with important industrial and commercial places, thus attracting new industry, but also a direct connection to the main industrial area of North Rhine-Westphalia in Germany (*Ruhrgebiet*). It took only four years to finish the highway, which ended at the German border near Aachen. To reduce travel time between the port of Antwerp and Germany, a shortcut was built and opened in 1971.

Like other European countries, Belgium saw a boom in highway growth in the period from 1965 to 1973 due to increasingly dense automobile traffic. It was the time of planning euphoria, feasibility delusions and an anything-goes attitude. During this period, the Belgian government added another 650 kilometres to the existing highway network of 306 kilometres. This addition was financed by rising prosperity and compelled by expanding car sales. The original scheme of a radial highway system with Brussels in the centre was changed into a spiderweb-like network. To maintain economic growth in the wealthy and busy region of Flanders, investments were concentrated there until about 1975. The southbound highway, *De Ardense Autosnelwegen*, runs from Brussels to Luxembourg through the low-populated and hilly region of Wallonia. It was built between 1980 and 1988.

A temporary speciality of Belgian highways was the continuous illumination, which has accompanied road construction after 1969. It raised costs about 20 to 25 per cent. The lights were designed to improve safety, but the results have not lived up to the expectations. At that time almost every large city in Belgium got a city expressway (*autoroutes urbaines*) or through-expressway system (*autoroutes de penetration*), following the opinion to save time entering or leaving centres in the same way as overland traffic can do between conurbations by using motorways.

The first oil crisis in 1973 made Belgians think about pollution and environmental responsibility, as well as about the viability of their existing plans. As a result, the original highway plan was reduced from 2,400 to 1,846 kilometres. The proposed linking highways, which had been intended to fill up the gaps between the main routes, were first downgraded to express roads and then cancelled, as renovation and improvement of existing roads absorbed road funds. Demonstrations of Belgian people against costly highway construction increased, starting in 1973 and intensified in the 1980s. The government had to carry out several cost-cutting measures after the first (1973) and second (1979) oil crises to reduce the burden of interest rates and to redevelop annual budgets. In 1989 the central government handed over responsibility for highway construction to the primary administrative divisions of the three Belgian regions. Highway history in Belgium can be summarised by a look at the augmentation of kilometres provided for the expanding car traffic: in the 23 years from 1950 to 1972, 867 kilometres were built, an average of about 38 kilometres per year; in the following 16 years, from 1973 to 1988, 718 kilometres were realised, an average of about 45 kilometres per year. From then until 2005, a total of only 134 kilometres was added to the existing highway network, of which Flanders today is responsible for 867 kilometres, Wallonia for 869 kilometres and the district of Brussels for 11 kilometres (as of 2005).

Great Britain's Motorways

When the idea of roads devoted exclusively to motor traffic spread across European countries in the 1930s, British road authorities were reluctant to engage with it. On the one hand, the officials saw the urgent need for motorways, but on the other hand, they saw the difficulty of building new roads through a country congested more than others by existing roads, buildings and cultivated open land. Thus the Ministry of Transport started to improve about 7,242 kilometres (4,500 miles) of trunk roads by widening them or modifying them into dual carriageways, and to provide separate tracks for bicycles and pedestrians. The first proposals to construct a motorway network appeared between 1936 and 1938, driven by the impossibility of enlarging trunk roads that ran through largely built-up areas. The answer was the 1936 Trunk Road Act, which included the construction of several bypasses around congested towns where automobile traffic had difficulties to move through; these thoroughfares now were entirely funded by central government.[61] The Lancashire County Council to the Ministry of Transport put forward a primary practical suggestion for a motorway of some 60 miles in length. In this context, the construction of bypasses received high attention. Although public opinion and the British government were ready to embark on the building of motorways, nothing was actually done until after the war.[62]

On 5 December 1958, British Prime Minister Harold Macmillan opened Britain's first dual two-lane motorway, the Preston Bypass. Now part of Motorway

61 Details can be found in the article of Peter Merriman, 'Motorways and the Modernisation of Britain's Road Network', in this anthology. Further see Jonathan Winkler, 'The Role of User Benefits in Deciding to Build Motorways in Britain', paper presented at the Fifth Conference on the History of Transport, Traffic and Mobility, in Helmond, The Netherlands, 25 to 28 October 2007.

62 Gresham Cook, 'The Need for Motorways in Great Britain', in Kaftan, *Welt-Strassenwesen*, 111–15.

M6, it is about eight miles (13 kilometres) long. In 1959 the initial section of the motorway M1 was opened from London to Yorkshire; it was 67 miles, 107 kilometres, long. It had been built as a dual three-lane highway to speed up travel time between Birmingham and London. This was the start of Great Britain's motorway backbone, bridging the gap between the south and the industrial north.[63] The period from 1963 to 1977 was a time of energetic motorway construction; the peak was in the years between 1968 and 1972 with the opening of about 540 miles (865 kilometres) of road. From 1958 to 1977, the total length of new motorways ready for traffic amounted to about 1,620 miles (2,600 kilometres). Due to the oil crises in 1973 and 1978, motorway construction budgets were cut back and the reorganisation of the Public Road Office, which now reported to the Ministry of Environment, made highway construction much more difficult. As a consequence, the average time between the preparation and the approval of construction plans rose from about six years in the 1960s to about 15 years in the 1980s. Accordingly, the construction of motorways slowed to about 670 miles (1,070 kilometres) in the period from 1978 to 2008.[64] While archive material is stored in County Records Offices of the region where motorway sections were built, detailed information about highway history has to be searched for in at least ten different counties of Great Britain. Policy-related and administrative material is stored in the Institution of Civil Engineers, London, and in the Transport Research Laboratory, Crowthorne, Berkshire.[65] Only a very small percentage of the stored material appears in printed volumes.[66] Nevertheless, within the last decade the history of

---

[63] Peter Merriman, *Driving Spaces. A Cultural-historical Geography of England's M 1 Motorway* (Oxford 2007) in a very intelligent manner examines 'different moments and movements in the production and consumption of the landscape of a modern British motorway'. Ibid., 3.

[64] The state of the scholarly literature on British motorways is rather embryonic, apart from semi-official books or reports by engineers and civil servants. The following compilation includes different kinds of studies: W.R. Jeffreys, *The King's Highway: An Historical and Autobiographical Record of the Developments of the Past Sixty Years* (London 1949); Ronald Syme, *The Story of British Roads*, ed. by British Road Federation (London 1950). See also Matthew Dalbey, *Regional Visionaries and Metropolitan Boosters: Decentralization, Regional Planning, and Parkways During the Interwar Years* (Norwell, MA, and Dordrecht 2002); George Charlesworth, *A History of British Motorways* (London 1984); David Nicolas Martin Starkie, *Motorway Age: Traffic Policies in Post-War Britain* (Oxford 1982); William B. Ball, *M63 – Motorway Through a Town: The Story of the Building of the M63 Through Stockport and of Its Impact on the Town* (Congleton 1983). An economic study was provided by Andre de Palma, Robin Lindsey, and Stef Proost, *Investment and the Use of Tax and Toll Revenues in the Transport Sector* (Stamford, CT 2007).

[65] For more information, visit the homepage of United Kingdom Motorway Archive, http://www.ciht.org.uk/motorway/about.htm (last accessed 25 March 2012).

[66] Peter Baldwin and Robert Baldwin, eds, *The Motorway Achievement*, vol. 1: *The British Motorway System – Visualisation, Policy and Administration* (London 2007); Ron Bridle and John Porter, eds, *The Motorway Achievement*, vol. 2: *Frontiers of Knowledge*

Great Britain's motorways received increasing attention from both authors and audiences, especially through the activities of the Motorway Achievement Trust, supported by the Institution of Highways and Transportation, the Institution of Civil Engineers and Thomas Telford Publishing, London.[67]

Luxembourg Autroutes/Voies Express

Highway building in Luxembourg started in 1969 with two short sections of only six kilometres total. One was part of the A1, from Kirchberg to Sennigerberg, and the other was part of the A4, from Pontpierre to Esch/Lallange. In 1970, to finance these roads, the parliament passed a law of guarantee (*loi de garantie*) to back the loans for road construction and to guarantee their repayment with interest by the state. In 1990, another 73 kilometres were built with the help of special highway funds. The goal of these roadworks was the same as it had been elsewhere since the 1950s: adaptation to differences in the various regions of Luxembourg through an unconstrained circulation of road traffic; improvement of the economic situation through easy accessibility of local and foreign markets; integration of Luxembourg into a broader huge highway system of the neighbouring and more distant European countries.[68] Today the total length of highways, free of charge and entirely overseen by a video surveillance system, is 147 kilometres. Some lines still have yet to be completed. Owing to the country's location, two lines to Germany, two lines to Belgium and one line to France dominate the network. The highways form a semicircle in the south of the city of Luxembourg. Typical of

and Practice (London 2004); William J. McCoubrey, *The Motorway Achievement*, vol. 3: *Building the Network* (London 2008); Bill Johnson, *The Motorway Achievement*, vol. 4: *UK Motorway Management – The First Fifty Years* (London 2008). Descriptions of the books can be found on the website http://www.ukmotorwayarchive.org (last accessed 25 March 2012). Details of the enormous efforts since 1996 to establish a motorway archive of the motorway network in the United Kingdom are collected at http://www.icevirtuallibrary.com/docserver/fulltext (last accessed 25 March 2012).

67 Publications in chronological order: Harry L. Yeadon, *Building the Network – The North West of England*, sec. ed. (London, Chichester/West Sussex 2006); Peter Baldwin, Robert Baldwin, and I. Evans, eds, *Building the Network – South East and East Regions* (Chichester/West Sussex 2007); John M. Carrington, *Building the Network – The Midlands* (Chichester/West Sussex 2009); Joe F.A. Sims, *Building the Network in the North East of England* (Chichester/West Sussex 2009); Brian Hawker, Ron Bridle, and Howard Stevens, *Building the Network in Wales* (Chichester/West Sussex 2010). The volume, written by Jackson McCormick, R.R. Ross, J.I. Bill and W. McCoubrey, *Building the Network – Northern Ireland* (The Northern Ireland Roads Service 2002) cannot be purchased. However, a privately run website provides good information: http://www.wesleyjohnston.com/roads/motorwayhistory.html (last accessed 25 March 2012).

68 See Administration des Ponts et Chausses, Luxembourg: http://www.etat.lu/pch (last accessed 21 January 2011).

Luxembourg highways are the very large service areas that are frequently visited by German, Belgian and French car owners to buy cheap gasoline.

French Autoroutes

For one century, France enjoyed a reputation as the nation with the best national road network. This image can be dated back to 17 February 1747 when the French king Louis XV decided to put into operation an office for road planning and the education of road engineers. With that decision, the legendary *École Nationale des Ponts et Chaussées* was founded. Jean Rodolphe Perronet (1708–94) was appointed the first director of this specialised military high school, which still exists today; amongst other things, he constructed the famous Avenue Champs Elysées in Paris. Beginning in 1764, Pierre Trésaguet (1716–96) made decisive progress in road construction techniques; he devised a system of building roads on a firm base of 15 to 20 centimetres of systematically layered rocks or large stones, carefully filled up with hard gravel.[69] Nevertheless, it was the Scotsman John Loudon McAdam (1756–1836) who earned the highest reputation in road engineering throughout the world. As general surveyor of the Bristol Corporation and later of the Bristol Turnpike Trust, he put to practice two important innovations: first, to raise roads above the surrounding ground, and second, to make the profile slightly convex, thus draining rainwater off the road rapidly rather than letting it penetrate and damage the whole construction.[70] 'Macadamisation', or 'macadam' for short, spread quickly across other European countries as state-of-the-art road construction.

With the expertise of well-trained road engineers, Emperor Napoleon I decided to build several trunk roads (*routes imperials*) on December 1811, radiating out of Paris in a clockwise manner. These first-class routes formed the backbones of the French road network until the second half of the twentieth century. Jaques Boulloche, General Inspector of *Ponts et Chaussées* and Director of roads within the French Ministry of Public Works, stressed in 1938 that the density and quality of national roads did not require a new nationwide highway system, apart from one around important urban spaces such as Greater Paris and the densely populated

[69] The Scottish bricklayer Thomas Telford (1757–1834) improved this type of construction when he had to rebuild the road from Shrewsbury to Holyhead in Northern Wales, which was ready for traffic in 1830. He constructed a firm base of about 18 centimetres of very densely layered rocks and about 15 centimetres of hard gravel, but then added another 6 centimetres of intermingled pebbles and sand to harden the surface. This construction is called 'Telford base'. To compress the surface, road engineers used a horse-drawn roller, which was later replaced by steamrollers in the middle of the nineteenth century.

[70] McAdam published two papers about his methods: *A Practical Essay on the Scientific Repair and Preservation of Public Roads* (London 1819), and *Remarks on the Present System of Road-Making* (London 1820).

region of Lyon. He pointed out that France has to invest in the international through-roads (*grands itineraries internationaux*), but in his opinion this could be realised by improving existing roads that would still be accessible to all kinds of road traffic.[71] A special law of 14 May 1932, limited to the region of Paris, stipulated that five radial highways, following a clockwise system, should be built and their ends connected by a beltway named the *Grande Rocade* (today the *Peripherique* has this function).[72] Beginning in 1927, the *Ponts et Chaussée* administration designed the first part of this scheme, the westbound highway to Normandy.[73] Instead of the planned year, 1935, a small section of this highway was opened to the traffic in 1941; the distance of some 50 kilometres from St Cloud to Orgeval went into action only on 9 June 1946.

Because the French government could not provide funds to build highways after the Second World War, it passed a law in 1955 that permitted semi-public or private companies to levy tolls on highways by a governmental concession, but urban highways had to be free of charge, as per a demand from the political left. Based on this law, the first state-run highway company (*Société de l'autoroute* ESCOTA) was established in 1956.[74] Some ten years later, France had finished only 1,000 kilometres of highways. Construction gained momentum in the 1970s after the government legalised public-private partnerships to finance and construct highways.[75]

Surprisingly, important academic studies on French highway history were published mainly by the press of the *L'école nationale des Ponts et Chaussées*.[76] It seems that the authority of this *Grand École* deterred other authors from working on this subject. Thus only a few other publications can be quoted.[77]

---

71 J. Boulloche, 'Les Grades Réalisations du Réseau Routier Français National', in Kaftan, *Welt-Strassenwesen*, 127.

72 In the 1930s, the region of Paris covered about 1/100 of the surface of France; about 1/6 of the French population lived there, owning more than 400,000 automobiles.

73 Presses de l'école nationale des Ponts et Chaussées, ed., *Une Autoroute se Souvient. Histoire de la Société des Autoroutes Paris Normandie* (Paris 1993).

74 Presses de l'école nationale des Ponts et Chausséees, ed., *ESCOTA – Une autoroute dans sa region. Histoire de la Société des autoroutes Estérel-Côte d'Azur-Alpe* (Paris 1995).

75 André Thiébault, 'Die Entwicklung des Straßenverkehrs und der Ausbau des Straßennetzes bis zum Jahre 1985 in Frankreich', *Strasse und Autobahn*, 23, 1, 1973, 186–95.

76 Presses de l'école nationale des Ponts et Chausséees, ed., *Le Plan Routier Breton* (Paris 1996); Valérie Elbaz-Benchetrit, *Autoroutes – Impacts sur l'économie et l'environnement* (Paris 1997); Georges Reverdy, *Les Routes de France du XXe Siecle,* vol. 1: *1900 à 1951* (Paris 2007); Georges Reverdy, *Les Routes de France du XXe Siecle*, vol. 2: *1952 à 2000* (Paris 2007), and Jean-Luc France-Barbou, *La difficile genèse de l'autoroute du sud* (1934–64) (Paris 2010).

77 Michel Millet and Alain Veuve, *Les autoroutes: Conception et réalisation* (Paris 1975); Conseil National des Économies Régionales et de la Productivité, ed., *La France et ses autoroutes: Livre blanc* (Paris 1990); Cherche Midi, ed., *Paris Rhin Rhone. L'histoire et le développement du réseau des autoroutes Paris-Rhin-Rhône* (Paris 2001).

Portuguese Auto-estradas

Portugal is the youngest country with a highway network in Europe. Since scholarly studies about Portuguese highway history are not available, at least some information about the development should be given to complete this report.

During the 1960s, Portugal had no efficient means of transporting goods and people. Most towns were linked by old-fashioned macadam or dirt roads. In 1972 Portugal's right wing government established the listed infrastructure company BRISA (Brisa – *Autoestradas de Portugal*, S.A.) to overcome the country's very poor transportation systems, which were inadequate to serve the growing economy. At present, BRISA is the predominant company in designing, building, managing and maintaining the national network of *autoestradas*, with an exclusive concession until 2035. Since 2000, about 45 per cent of BRISA's stock has been owned by Spanish construction and infrastructure companies.

The first highways of the Portuguese motorway/freeway network were the A1 from Lisbon to Porto and the A2 from Lisbon to southern seaside resorts. Some more lines were added, especially the A3 from Porto to the Spanish border in the north of the country, and the A6 west of Lisbon to the coast, but the total length never exceeded about 300 kilometres through the 1980s as the state tightly controlled BRISA's activities. Compelled by the quickly rising use of automobiles and the increasing logistic traffic, in 1990 the government decided on an intensive program of annual investments into road construction. The largest share of funds went into the extension of the highway system; only some funds were assigned to railroad and subway companies.

Today's freeway system in Portugal is divided into two networks: principal or main highways marked IP1 to IP8 (*itinerários principais*), and 37 complementary or secondary routes marked IC1 to IC37 (*itineraries complementares*). The rest of the Portuguese road network, comprising national roads (*estradas nacionais*) marked with the prefix 'EN', is based on the unchanged 1945 National Roadway Plan.[78] With the help of road construction funds from the European Union, Portugal now has one of the best highway systems of all European countries, including an up-to-date electronic toll payment system (*Via Verde*) which collects charges automatically by an electronic device that communicates directly with BRISA. Still, in some parts of the country, these highways seem somewhat ahead of expected demand.

Spanish Autopistas/Autovias

Spanish road history originates in the poorly developed railway network. In the mid-1960s, the majority of national roads still had macadamised surfaces, though

[78] This information is based on http://en.wikipedia.org/wiki/Brisa_-_Auto-estradas_de_Portugal and http://en.wikipedia.org/wiki/Estradas_de_Portugal (last accessed 28 January 2011).

they were large enough to carry truck traffic without problems. Spain started rather late in the construction of highways, although schemes were discussed as early as in the inter-bellum period.[79] The first three *autopistas* (tool highways) were inaugurated in July 1969 in Catalonia. To raise the country's economic productivity and standard of living to the much higher level of the more central European states, the government developed a very efficient transport system within a short period, supported by funds from the European Union. In 2008 the country had the largest network of high-capacity motorways in Europe, with a length of 13,515 kilometres including *autopistas* (toll highways, reserved for fast automotive traffic and mostly managed by concession companies) and *autovias*. These latter are usually old national trunk roads that have been upgraded by twinning them into dual carriageways; in other cases, they have been newly constructed; they have limited access and semi-loops around cities, have more exits than do *autopistas*, and never charge a toll. These national roads of Spain (*Carreteras Nacionales de España*), supervised by the General Road Directorate (*Dirección General de Carreteras*) of the Ministry of Public Work, are the property of the Spanish state.[80]

In accordance with the fourth General Road Plan of 1939–41, the original trunk roads linking Madrid with the coast and the borders were divided into six clockwise radial sectors with the *Puerta del Sol* in Madrid as centre of the system (N-I – N-VI). Until the turn of the century, traffic suffered from this highly condensed radiality, which frequently blocked Madrid beltways and roads into the city. Today's efforts concentrate on the construction of new radial *autopistas* surrounding Madrid at a greater distance and cross-country highways that link regions without passing through Madrid. Interurban routes form the backbone of the highway network; for identification they carry the sign 'A-' or 'R-', to which a 'P' is added if toll will be charged. In general, the alphanumeric system for naming highways is rather complex. Regional motorways, built by regional authorities, together with the system of beltways, urban highways and city access express roads, make up the national highway/freeway network. Yet scholarly studies on the history of Spanish highway are missing.[81]

---

79 F.J. Rodríguez Lázaro, *Las primeras autopistas españolas* (1925–36) (Ciudas Real 2004). See also the review of Domingo Cuéllar Villar about Francisco Javier Rodriguez Lázaro, 'Las primeras autopistas españoles (1925–1936) (Madrid 2004)', *Transportes, Servicios y Telecomunicaciones*, 9, 2005, 139–43.

80 See http://es.wikipedia.org/wiki/Anexo: Autopistas_y_autovias_de_España (last accessed 28 January 2011).

81 Some books written by economists or jurists are no substitute for the research gap. See Julio-Gaspar Sequeiros Tizon, *A Autopista del Atlántico* (Madrid 1977); E. Perez Touriño, *Infraestructuras y desarrollo regional. Efectos economicos autopista atlantica* (La Coruña 1997); Alfonso Puncel Chornet, *La Autopista del Mideterráneo* (Valencia 1996); Universidade de Santiago de Compostela et Empresa Nacional de Autopistas, ed., *La Autopista del Atlántico. Movilidad, Demanda de Transporte y Localización Empresarial* (Santiago de Compostela 2000); Maria Burzaco Samper and José Maria Abad Liceras, *Leyes de carreteras y autopistas* (Madrid 2002); Pablo Arrias Sierra, *Periferias y Nueva*

Swiss Autobahnen/Autoroutes/Autostrade

Officials in the city and the canton of Basle were enthusiastic about the HaFraBa association's scheme to build an expressway from the North Sea to the Mediterranean. The canton quickly joined the German public-private partnership as a member. In February 1927, together with members of the HaFraBa executive committee, Gustav Wenk, a canton government member, organised an *Autobahn* conference in Basle combined with an exhibition that showed the first schemes of the German *Autobahn* design. At the conference, a Swiss association for the promotion of an *autoroute* from Basle to the Italian border was founded.[82] When the Nazi regime took over the HaFraBa plans in 1933, the promotion of *Autobahn* ideas in Switzerland petered out. In the early 1950s Wenk put the subject on the agenda again, presenting a memorandum on how to finance a Swiss trunk road network.[83]

The Swiss government, following the long tradition of traffic through the country, basically saw the need for a thorough-fare, but refused to build it due to the low automobile density. The officials also recalled the difficult experience their country had had with the Gotthard Railway Line, inaugurated in May 1882. The construction of this line had been incredibly complicated and had required massive investments, originally from the private sphere and later from the public treasury; clearly, building a freeway through the Alps would not be much easier. Michael Ackermann has drawn together the two phases of the emergence of Swiss motorways: first, the period of orientation (1929–50) along with the improvement program for national roads in Swiss valleys, and second, the decade of the beginning of the highway program (1951–61). Ackermann focuses particularly on the political decision-making process to implement a large-scale infrastructure project.[84] The first Swiss *Autobahn*, inaugurated in 1955, was a short section in the Lucerne area. The next steps were a freeway from Lausanne to Geneva on the occasion of the 1964 Expo and the *Autobahn* from Bern to Lenzburg in 1967. Currently, the highway network is dominated by the east-west axis from St Gallen

---

Ciudad. El problema del paisaje en los procesos de Dispersión Urbana (Sevilla 2003), Carlos Padrós Reig and Endrius Eliseo Cocciolo, *Intervencion publica en el sector de las empresas concesionarias de autopista. El caso albertis/autostrade* (Madrid 2009).

82 Documents Schweizer Wirtschaftsarchiv Basel, Sig. Bv L II 6.

83 Gustav Wenk, *Der Ausbau des schweizerischen Hauptstrassennetzes und seine Finanzierung* (Basel 1953), Staatsarchiv des Kantons Basel Stadt, PA 753 Dr h.c. Gustav Wenk, Vorsteher des Innern, Ständerat (1941–1953), Sign. PA 753 3.6. Wenk resigned 1953. See also *Schweizerischer Autostrassenverein*, ibid., Sign. DI-REG 1c 5–8–3.

84 Michael Ackermann, *Konzepte und Entscheidungen in der Planung der schweizer Nationalstrassen von 1927 bis 1961* (Bern et al. 1992). See also Automobil-Club der Schweiz, ed., *Die Planung der Autobahnen in der Schweiz. 4. Vortragstagung 3. März 1959* (Bern 1959); J. Jakob, 'Die Entwicklung des Straßenverkehrs und der Ausbau des Straßennetzes bis zum Jahr 1985 in der Schweiz', *Strasse und Autobahn*, 23, 5, 1973, 223–31.

to Geneva (A1), and the north-south axis from the German border near Basle to the Italian border in Chiasso (A2). The Swiss *Autobahn* system includes 22 routes, some of them partly finished, although Switzerland has one of the highest motorway densities in the world.[85]

Swiss high capacity roads (*Hochleistungs-Strassennetz*) compete with an excellent railway network covering the whole country. In consequence, critical discussions on the relevance of future motorway construction and the substantial alterations of the landscape when freeways and expressways mesh with it are common.[86] Nevertheless, the traffic share of motorcars (individual transport) is still rising, not only due to the immense tourist and through-traffic, but also to the fact that Swiss *Autobahnen* today represent a huge axis of shopping malls located alongside motorways.[87]

Conclusion

The development of the European highway network was not a purposeful course of action based on a central system-building power coordinating a long-term roadmap and a balanced timetable. In the 1920s, far-sighted municipal authorities and civil engineers tried hard, but only suggested investments into highways to solve road traffic problems caused by the increasing number of automobiles. At the same time, early ideas of long-distance through-roads for tourist purposes were suggested.[88] The first motorways erected and run by private Italian engineering companies resembled a patchwork, and, in the end, failed because of economic problems. The German public-private partnership HaFraBa did not get off the ground owing to governmental blockage. Neither venture had the political and financial power to create a nationwide network. In a parallel to railway history, only national road authorities implemented by governments were able to build wide-ranging highway and secondary road networks within a manageable time, because they acted as forceful system builders, backed by parliaments and financed by national budgets. Thus every European country followed its own plan and pace towards an adequate road infrastructure. National decisions to develop and construct trunk road systems more or less followed existing domestic railway connections as well as internalised patterns of ancient cross-country roads.

---

85 Sabine Fischer and Andreas Volk, 'Chronologie der Schweizer Autobahn', in Martin Heller and Andreas Volk, eds, *Die Schweizer Autobahn* (Zurich 1999), 113–46.

86 A variety of viewpoints on this topic were published by Martin Heller and Andreas Volk, eds, *Die Schweizer Autobahn* (Zurich 1999).

87 Christian Felix, 'Shopping Center Rallye', in Heller and Volk, *Die Schweizer Autobahn*, 182–215.

88 Alexander Badenoch, 'Touring between war and peace. Imagining the "trans-continental motorway", 1930–1950', *The Journal of Transport History*, 28, 2, 2007, 192–210.

Except for Germany, which in the 1930s commenced to construct highways with supply-side perspective ahead of demand, most European countries started to invest massively into highway networks only after the Second World War.[89] All countries used similar arguments to highlight the urgent need for motorways: specifications for a forward-looking national through-road system adapted to the future demand of quickly increasing automobile traffic; separation of multi-purpose roads into single purpose routes to achieve the rationalisation advantages of automobile transportation for the national economy; extension of national transport facilities with a more flexible transport system to improve the supplying of industries and the caring for the population; increase in road safety, reduction of injuries and traffic jams; need to disentangle overcrowded areas and to enhance equilibrium of workplaces; development of cultural and recreation areas.

Generally speaking, the development of highway building in Europe can be divided into five major periods: the period of conceptualisation of a West European system of roads for long-distance transportation to fight unemployment through job creation schemes, including the first realisation of a nationwide motorway network in the German Reich (1926–39);[90] the period of reconstruction of damaged roads and first steps towards national motorway networks, in response to incipient mass-motorisation (1949–60), based on the 1950 Declaration on the Construction of Main International Traffic Arteries (European E-road network), which was initiated in 1947 by the United Nations Economic Commission for Europe;[91] the period of comprehensive expansion of national motorways (1961–75), at first financed by the remarkable post-war economic growth throughout Europe, but more and more funded by escalating loans; the period of bilateral interconnection agreements and compression of national through-road networks (1976–85), following the 1975 European Agreement on Main International Traffic Arteries, which replaced the 1950 Declaration and improved road construction standards.

The two decades between 1986 and 2005 saw the long-expected liberalisation of the European transportation market, which national egotism and political motives had prevented for more than 20 years, and on 22 May 1985 was forced by a decision of the European Law Court in the case of the European Parliament against the Conference of European Ministers of Transport (CEMT, founded 1953) requiring the development of a joint transport policy. In this period, hindering

89 Mom, *Roads without Rails*, 745–72.

90 Lando Bortolotti, 'I congressi autostradali internazionali del 1931 e 1932 e le prime proposte di una sistema autostradale europeo', *Storia Urbana*, 75, 1996, 5–27; Ingrid Heckmann-Strohkark, 'Der Traum von einer europäischen Gemeinschaft. Die internationalen Autobahnkongresse 1931 und 1932', in Heller und Volk, *Die Schweizer Autobahn*, 32–45.

91 Seebohm, Hans-Christoph, *Straßenplanung und Forschung*, in BMV, ed., *Die Straßen der Bundesrepublik.* Schriftenreihe des Bundesministers für Verkehr, 5 (Bielefeld 1954), 7–50, here 16–17.

limits of cross-border traffic for goods, persons and services were cleared away.[92] In the Amsterdam Treaty of 1999, European countries approved the Trans-European Road Network (TERN), which forms a key part of the Trans-European Transport Network (TEN-T) accepted in 1990 by the European Commission, and adopted by European Parliament and Council in July, 1996.

Looking at the five periods of motorway construction in European countries, it is evident that West Germany after the Second World War took the lead in the motorway age. No other European country provided better conditions for the European road network; about 2,100 kilometres of passable *Autobahn* routes, the immense technical know-how of the road construction engineers and a fast-recovering industry were outstanding admission tickets for a European road system. Italy was another forerunner, as in the middle of the 1950s the Italian government decided to build a backbone motorway from Milan through the whole country to the south because the railway network was weak and better traffic connections were urgently needed. The result was the *Autostrada del sole*, especially frequently used by German holiday travellers. Surprisingly, transport historians long overlooked the vital impact of the Marshal Plan and the activities of the American Bureau of Public Roads (BPR) on the early road construction after the Second World War, as well as the importance of the International Road Federation (IRF) in the introduction of American planning techniques and road construction machines into European highway projects.[93]

In 1960, only six West European countries had motorways of considerable length: Germany, 2,671 kilometres; Italy, 1,065 kilometres; the Netherlands, 385 kilometres; Great Britain, 202 kilometres; Belgium, 183 kilometres; and France, 174 kilometres. But countries which had been occupied by Germany, like Austria and the Netherlands, where the Germans had begun motorway construction between 1938 and 1942, started investing into their national road networks as soon as possible. All the other countries in West Europe more or less adapted the layout, the dimensions of dual carriageway and the building techniques of the German example.[94] In the 1970s and 1980s, particularly Belgium, France, Italy, the Netherlands, Spain and the Great Britain expanded their motorway system immensely, amounting to an average of 184 per cent between 1970 and 1990.

92 Richard Vahrenkamp, *Die logistische Revolution. Der Aufstieg der Logistik in der Massenkonsumgesellschaft* (Frankfurt and New York 2011), 303–42.

93 See Frank Schipper, 'Changing the face of Europe. European road mobility during the Marshall plan years', *Journal of Transport History*, 28, 2, 2007, 211–28; Pär Blomkvist, 'Roads for Flow – Roads for Peace. Lobbying for a European Highway System', in Eik van der Vleuten and Arne Kaijser, eds, *Networking Europe. Transnational Infrastructures and the Shaping of Europe 1850–2000* (Sagamore Beach 2006), 161–86.

94 An essay by Hermann Kunde entitled 'Autobahnen in Europa', *Strasse und Autobahn*, 9, 1, 1958, 1–8, here 3, discusses the profile of highways in the Netherlands, Belgium, France, Italy, Austria, Sweden and Germany. The width of dual carriageways ranges from 22 metres (Sweden) to 30 metres (Belgium and Germany). The average width comes to 27 metres.

Table 11.1 Highways in Europe in 2009 and comparing figures

Countries	Length of highways kilometres	Length of railways kilometres	Motorcar density per 1,000 citizens	Traffic share motorcars per cent of pkm[5]	Traffic share lorries per cent of tkm[6]
	[1]2009	[1]2009	[2]2009	[3]2008	[4]2009
Austria	1,696	6,256	515	78.6	59.5
Belgium	1,763	3,578	483	78.4	72.9
France	11,163	29,466	489	84.2	81.0
Germany	12,813	37,934	509	85.1	67.0
Great Britain	3,674	15,754	459	86.8	86.7
Italy	6,661	16,686	606	82.4	91.0
Luxembourg	152	657	678	84.4	94.6
Netherlands	2,631	2,888	462	86.5	63.4
Portugal	2,705	2,842	560	85.2	94.3
Spain	14,021	13,354	480	80.1	96.6
Switzerland	1,406	5,159	–	73.4	–
Europe 15	–	–	506	83.8	79.0
Europe 25	–	–	482	83.5	78.1

Notes

[1] Length in kilometres (railway figures of other years: Austria 2007; Netherlands 2008; Switzerland 2002).

[2] Motorcars (private cars) per 1,000 citizens (figures of other years: France 2007; Luxembourg 2008; Portugal 2002).

[3] Percentage of individuals travelling by private cars in relation of total transportation of persons in a country, expressed in person-kilometre – pkm (Eurostat estimation for Italy, Netherlands, Portugal, Europe 15 + 25).

[4] Percentage of road transports in relation of total goods haulage in a country, expressed in ton-kilometre – tkm (Eurostat estimation for Italy, Great Britain, Europe 15 + 25).

[5] pkm means passenger kilometres.

[6] tkm means tons kilometres.

Source: Numbers investigated in tables edited by the Statistical Office of the European Commission (Eurostat) and presented in alphabetical order of the countries described in this article (http://eurostat.ec.eu, last accessed 5 March 2012).

In absolute figures of motorway length, smaller countries like Austria or Switzerland stayed behind, but they put the same exertion into highway construction as the large ones, because they had to surmount greater geographic obstacles. These two countries reached a growth percentage of about 171 per cent within the period of 1970 to 1990. Fast transit routes through the Alps were one of the key issues for establishing an efficient European road system for goods and individual passenger transportation.

The average expansion of 144 per cent of the national motorways of the countries summarised in Table 11.1 between 1970 and 1990 was extraordinary. Looking at the details, Austria, Belgium, France and the Great Britain made the best progress, while Germany, Italy and the Netherlands continued to complete their national systems with growth rates of less than 100 per cent. Beginning in the 1980s, Luxembourg, Portugal and Spain accelerated motorway construction remarkably.

Within the last 30 years, the length of the European highway network has nearly doubled, from 30,747 kilometres in 1980 to 60,578 kilometres in 2009. In this period, Spain showed the most impressive progression, plus 199 per cent, starting from a base of 4,693 kilometres, because the Spanish government invested simultaneously in an extensive system of new highways (*autopistas*) and in the upgrading of former national routes into dual carriage freeways (*autovias*).[95] Table 11.1 shows the state of motorway length of the cited countries and some related figures in 2009.

Even though highways in European countries only have a minor share of the total length of the road system (the overall average is about two per cent), they stand for the most important traffic route of all current transport networks, since motorisation strongly went up in the past 50 years and still has not reached its peak. Both individual travel by motorcar and goods transports by lorry are definitely the principal way of mobility, despite the fact that the use of private cars is decreasing slightly in some of the countries with highly developed networks of express railways. Looking at the traffic shares of motorcars and lorries, we have to take into consideration that in several countries, state-owned railways lost significant shares of the goods transport market because their transport facilities did not provide flexible high-quality services for some decades. As a result, railway goods transportation has declined in competition with escalating long-distance, just-in-time delivery by lorries since the 1980s. The traffic share of lorries in Table 11.1 shows that countries with traditionally weak railway networks – Italy, Luxembourg, Portugal and Spain – transport more than 90 per cent of their goods on roads. But even countries like Belgium, France and Great Britain transport a significant share of goods on roads.

The common attitude in the last two to three decades of lean production and intensifying globalisation was to put stock in the road or on ships, thus saving time and money. With mass motorisation, people have not only got used to driving between home and work, but also to use their cars for shopping, leisure time activities, weekend trips and holiday travels. This attitude will probably be changed in the foreseeable future by rising oil prices, mounting car taxes, road tolls or other governmental charges. But in the meantime, economies round the globe rely on the quick reaction time of component-supplying industries and on-the-spot-production of merchandise at any time. It seems almost impossible to change the current system. For the time being, highways will remain the backbone of European traffic, transport and mobility.

This situation points to some lacuna in road history. Scholars should take up systematically comparative studies addressing topics such as the evolution and organisation of governmental road authorities within the last two centuries; the relationship and dependence of highway profiles and road-building instructions

---

[95] A Spanish law obliges the government to double every new highway by transforming an existing national road into a freeway or building a new one.

in European countries; the development of university-based road research and the related progresses of road construction techniques; the emergence and implementation of heavy road construction machines; the history of important road construction companies; and the influence of university experts and road engineers on political infrastructure decisions.[96]

References

Ackermann, Michael, *Konzepte und Entscheidungen in der Planung der schweizer Nationalstrassen von 1927 bis 1961* (Bern et al. 1992).

Adorni, Marco and Malfitano, Alberto, *Un'autostrada per l'Appennino. La superstrada E7–E45 e il dibattito sulla sua costruzione* (Bologna 2006).

Arbeitskreis Dorfchronik Geisenhausen, ed., *Die Holledaubrücke. Geschichte und Geschichten* (Pfaffenhofen 2010).

Automobil-Club der Schweiz, ed., *Die Planung der Autobahnen in der Schweiz. 4. Vortragstagung 3. März 1959* (Bern 1959).

Badenoch, Alexander, 'Touring between war and peace. Imagining the 'transcontinental motorway', 1930–1950', *The Journal of Transport History*, 28, 2, 2007, 192–210.

Badenoch, Alexander, and Fickers, Andreas, eds, *Materializing Europe: Transnational Infrastructures and the Project of Europe* (Houndmills, Basingstoke, Hampshire 2010).

Baldwin, Peter and Baldwin, Robert, eds, *The Motorway Achievement*, vol. 1: *Visualisation of the British Motorway System. Policy and Administration* (Tonbridge/Kent 2004).

Baldwin, Peter, Baldwin, Robert and Evans, I., eds, *Building the Network in Southern and Eastern England* (Chichester/West Sussex 2007).

Ball, William B., *M63 – Motorway Through a Town. The Story of the Building of the M63 Through Stockport and of Its Impact on the Town* (Congleton 1983).

Becker, Frank, 'Autobahnen, Auto-Mobilität. Die USA, Italien und Deutschland im Vergleich', in Wolfgang Hardtwig, ed., *Politische Kulturgeschichte der Zwischenkriegszeit 1918–1939* (Göttingen 2005), 23–59.

Blomkvist, Pär, 'Roads for Flow – Roads for Peace. Lobbying for a European Highway System', in Eik van der Vleuten and Arne Kaijser, eds, *Networking Europe. Transnational Infrastructures and the Shaping of Europe 1850–2000* (Sagamore Beach 2006), 161–86.

BMV, ed., *Bundesautobahn Holland-Linie* (Cologne 1965).

BMV, ed., *Erste Autobahn Deutschland – Frankreich. Europastrasse 12 Paris – Saarbrücken – Mannheim* (Saarbrücken 1969).

---

[96] The monograph of Manfred Pohl, *Die STRABAG 1923 bis 1998* (Munich and Zurich 1998) is a good example for the history of a road constructing company, today an international group.

BMV, ed., *Bundesautobahn Duisburg – Venlo. Europastrasse E 3* (Cologne 1975).

Bortolotti, Lando, 'Origine e primordi della rete autostradale in Italia, 1923–1933', *Storia Urbana*, 59, 1992, 35–69.

Bortolotti, Lando, 'Perio Puricelli', *Storia Urbana*, 59, 1992, 43–71.

Bortolotti, Lando, 'I congressi autostradali internazionali del 1931 e 1932 e le prime proposte di una sistema autostradale europeo', *Storia Urbana*, 75, 1996, 5–27.

Bortolotti, Lando, 'Fra politica, propaganda e affari: L'Autostrada Roma – Berlino 1927–1942', *Storia Urbana*, 81, 1997, 47–79.

Bosch, A. and van der Ham, W., *Twee eeuwen Rijkswaterstaat. Europese bibilotheek* (Zaltbommel 1998).

Boulloche, J., 'Les Grades Réalisations du Réseau Routier Français National', in Kurt G. Kaftan, ed., *Welt-Strassenwesen 1938* (Berlin 1938), 127.

Bridle, Ron and Porter, John, eds, *The Motorway Achievement*, vol. 2: *Frontiers of Knowledge and Practice* (Tonbridge/Kent 2002).

Buiter, Hans and Volkers, K., *Oudenrijn, De geschiedenis van een verkeers-knooppunt* (Utrecht 1996).

Buiter, Hans, '"Hoogviadukten in het polderland?"' De introductie van de auto-snelweg in Nederland', *NEHA-jaarboek*, 60, 1997, 285–306.

Bundesminister für Verkehr, Abteilung Straßenbau, ed., *HAFRABA – Bundes-autobahn Hansestädte-Frankfurt-Basel. Rückblick auf 30 Jahre Autobahnbau* (Wiesbaden and Berlin 1962).

Carrington, John M., *Buildung the Network – The Midlands* (Chichester/West Sussex 2009).

Charlesworth, George, *A History of British Motorways* (London 1984).

Cherche Midi, ed., *Paris Rhin Rhone. L'histoire et le développement du réseau des autoroutes Paris-Rhin-Rhône* (Paris 2001).

Chornet, Alfonso Puncel, *La Autopista del Mideterráneo* (Valencia 1996).

Ciesla, Burghard, ed., 'Netzwerk Autobahn', *WerkstattGeschichte*, 21, 1998.

Coccia, L. and Granato, M.T., *Ascoli – mare. Una autostrada senza pedaggio* (Napoli 2000).

Conseil National des Économies Régionales et de la Productivité, ed., *La France et ses autoroutes: Livre blanc* (Paris 1990).

Cook, Gresham, 'The Need for Motorways in Great Britain', in Kurt G. Kaftan, ed., *Welt-Strassenwesen 1938* (Berlin 1938), 111–15.

D'Antone, Leandra, *Senza pedaggio. Storia dell'autostrada Salerno – Reggio Calabria* (Milano 2008).

Dalbey, Matthew, *Regional Visionaries and Metropolitan Boosters: Decentral-ization, Regional Planning, and Parkways During the Interwar Years* (Norwell, MA and Dordrecht 2002).

Deheem, Paul, 'Réseau rotier de l'Etat Belge. Routes nouvelles', in Kurt G. Kaftan, ed., *Welt-Strassenwesen 1938* (Berlin 1938), 123–6.

Dienel, Hans-Liudger and Schiedt, Hans-Ulrich, *Die Moderne Straße. Planung, Bau und Verkehr vom 18. bis zum 20. Jahrhundert* (Frankfurt and New York 2010).
Doßmann, Axel, *Begrenzte Mobilität. Eine Kulturgeschichte der Autobahnen in der DDR* (Essen 2003).
Eichner-Ramm, *Britta, 70 Jahre Autobahn Göttingen – Kassel* (Göttingen 2007).
Engl, Hermann and Lämmel, Frank, *Highway Deutschland* (Holzkirchen 1996).
Fehlhauer, Gero, *Die Geschichte der Reichsautobahn Chemnitz – Hof* (Reichenbach i. Vogtland 2006).
Felix, Christian, 'Shopping Center Rallye', in Martin Heller and Andreas Volk, eds, *Die Schweizer Autobahn* (Zurich 1999), 182–215.
Fischer, Sabine and Volk, Andreas, 'Chronologie der Schweizer Autobahn', in Martin Heller and Andreas Volk, eds, *Die Schweizer Autobahn* (Zurich 1999), 113–46.
Flessa, Berthold and Goller, Helmut, *Die Geschichte der Autobahn 1934 bis 2000. Abschnitt Bayreuth/Kulmbach bis Landesgrenze Thüringen/Sachsen* (Münchberg 2000).
France-Barbou, Jean-Luc, *La difficile genèse de l'autoroute du sud (1934–1964)* (Paris 2010).
Gabriel, Roland, *Dem Auto eine Bahn. Deutsche "Nurautostraßen" vor 1933. Archiv für die Geschichte des Straßen- und Verkehrswesens*, vol. 23 (Köln 2010).
Galleni, Annabella, 'Strade, autostrade e fascismo. Un memoriale di Piero Puricelli (1940)', *Imprese e storia*, 19, 1999, 47–82.
Giuntini, Andrea and Pavese, Clausio, eds, *Reti, mobilità, trasporti. Il sistema italiano tra prospettiva storica e innovazione* (Milano 2004).
Ham, Willem van der, *Verover mij dat land, Lely en de Zuiderzeewerken* (Amsterdam 2007).
Hartmannsgruber, Friedrich, '"... ungeachtet der noch nicht geklärten Finanzierung" – Finanzplanung und Kapitalbeschaffung für den Bau der Reichsautobahnen 1933–1945', *Historische Zeitschrift*, 278, 2004, 625–81.
Hawker, Brian, Bridle, Ron and Stevens, Howard, *Building the Network in Wales* (Chichester/West Sussex 2010).
Heckmann-Strohkark, Ingrid, 'Der Traum von einer europäischen Gemeinschaft. Die internationalen Autobahnkongresse 1931 und 1932', in Martin Heller and Andreas Volk, eds, *Die Schweizer Autobahn* (Zurich 1999), 32–45.
Heesvelde, Eric van, 'Infrastructuurinvesteringen in de sector vervoer en verkeer', in Vereniging voor Economie, ed., *Verkeer in België in 2000. Mobiliteit of chaos? Twintigste Vlaams Wetenschappelijk Economisch Congres. Gent, 17 en 18 oktober 1991* (Gent 1991), 89–114.
Heller, Martin, and Volk, Andreas, eds, *Die Schweizer Autobahn* (Zurich 1999).
Horn-van-Nispen, Marie-Louise ten, 'Het Rijkswegenplan 1927. De aanpak van het verkeersvraagstuk in de jaren twintig', *Jaarboek voor de geschiedenis van bedrijf en techniek*, 9, 1992, 185–208.

Horn-van-Nispen, Marie-Louise ten, 'Een ideal uit de jaren twintig: autosnelwegen', *De Ingenieur*, 106, 13, 1994, 19–21.

Jäkel, Herbert, 'Der Bau der "Reichsautobahn" bei Alsfeld nach zeitgenössischen Berichtern und Bildern', *Mitteilungen des Geschichts- und Museumsvereins*, 13, 1988, 239–48.

Jakob, J. 'Die Entwicklung des Straßenverkehrs und der Ausbau des Straßennetzes bis zum Jahr 1985 in der Schweiz', *Strasse und Autobahn*, 23, 5, 1973, 223–31.

Jeffreys, W.R., *The King's Highway: An Historical and Autobiographical Record of the Developments of the Past Sixty Years* (London 1949).

Jelmoni, Francesco Aimone, 'Perio Puricelli', in Gianpietro Livini, ed., *1924–1935. Le Autostrade della prima generazione* (Milano 1984), 20–23.

Johannes, Ralph and Wölki, Gerhard, *Die Autobahn und ihre Rastanlagen. Geschichte und Architektur* (Petersberg 2005).

Johnson, Bill, *The Motorway Achievement*, vol. 4: *UK Motorway Management – The First Fifty Years* (London 2008).

Kaftan, Kurt, *Europa braucht Autobahnen. Vorschläge und Entwürfe zur Erbauung nationaler Autobahnnetze als Ausgangspunkte zur Errichtung eines europäischen Autobahnnetzes* (Berlin 1936).

Kaftan, Kurt, *Der Kampf um die Autobahnen. Geschichte und Entwicklung des Autobahngedankens in Deutschland von 1907–1935 unter Berücksichtigung ähnlicher Pläne und Bestrebungen im übrigen Europa* (Berlin 1955).

Klenke, Dietmar, *Bundesdeutsche Verkehrspolitik und Motorisierung. Konflikt-trächtige Weichenstellung in den Jahren des Wiederaufstiegs. Zeitschrift für Unternehmensgeschichte, Beiheft 79* (Stuttgart 1993).

Klenke, Dietmar, 'Die deutsche Katastrophe und das Automobil. Zur "Heils"-geschichte eines nationalen Kultobjekts in den Jahren des Wiederaufstiegs', in Michael Salewski and Ilona Stölken-Fitschen, eds, *Moderne Zeiten. Technik und Zeitgeist im 19. Und 20. Jahrhundert* (Stuttgart 1994), 157–73.

Kornrumpf, Martin, *HAFRABA e. V. – deutsche Autobahn-Planung 1926–1934. Archiv für die Geschichte des Straßenwesens*, vol. 7 (Köln 1990).

Kratz, Georg, '50 Jahre Autobahn in Deutschland unter besonderer Berücksichtigung des Alsfelder Raumes', *Mitteilungen des Geschichts- und Museumsvereins*, 13, 1988, 229–38.

Kreuzer, Bernd, 'Transport History in Austria: A literature survey', in Michèle and Polino Marie-Noëlle, eds, COST 340. *Towards a European Intermodal Transport Network. Lessons from History. A Critical Bibliography* (Paris 2004), 1–13.

Kreuzer, Bernd, Tempo 130. *Kultur- und Planungsgeschichte der Autobahnen in Oberösterreich* (Linz 2005).

Kreuzer, Bernd, 'National Road Networks in the 1930s – the Case of Austria's Roads', in Gijs Mom and Laurent Tissot, eds, *Road History. Planning, Construction, Use* (Neuchâtel 2007), 99–116.

Kreuzer, Bernd, 'Schnelle Straßen braucht das Land', University of Vienna Ph.D. thesis, 2007.

Kreuzer, Bernd, 'Still Focussing on the Railway: Transport and Mobility History in Austria', in Gijs Mom, Gordon Pirie and Laurent Tissot, eds, *Mobility in History. The State of the Art in the History of Transport, Traffic and Mobility* (Neuchâtel 2009), 193–200.

Kreuzer, Bernd, 'Die Anfänge der österreichischen Autobahnen', in Verband Österreichischer Historiker und Geschichtsvereine und Niederösterreichisches Landesarchiv, eds, *Tagungsbericht über den 25. Österreichischen Historikertag in St. Pölten 2008* (St. Pölten 2010), 202–14.

Kreuzer, Bernd, *Vorauseilende Angebotsplanung und Raumerschließung: Die Vor- und Frühgeschichte der österreichischen Autobahnen im internationalen Kontext, in Hans-Liudger Dienel, Hans-Ulrich Schiedt, Die Moderne Straße. Planung, Bau und Verkehr vom 18. bis zum 20. Jahrhundert* (Frankfurt and New York 2010), 171–201.

Kreuzer, Bernd, 'Stadtumbau für den Verkehr. Stadt- und Verkehrsplanung in Linz im 20. Jahrhundert', in Walter Schuster, ed., *Die Stadt Linz im 20. Jahrhundert* (Linz 2011), 519–618.

Kunde, Hermann, 'Autobahnen in Europa', *Strasse und Autobahn*, 9, 1, 1958, 1–8.

Lambeck, Alfred, *Die bergisch-märkische Autobahn Leverkusen – Kamen, 1948–1958* (Erfurt 2008).

Lärmer, Karl, *Autobahnbau in Deutschland 1933–1945. Zu den Hintergründen* (Berlin 1975).

Livini, Gianpietro, ed., *1924–1935. Le Autostrade della prima generazione* (Milano 1984).

Luca, Giuseppe de, 'La construzione della rete autostradale italiana. L'autostrada Firenze–Mare, 1927–1940', *Storia Urbana*, 59, 1992, 71–126.

Luca, Giuseppe de and Bortolotti, Lando, *Fascismo e autostrade. Un caso di sintesi: la Firenze-mare* (Milano 1994).

Mattia, Sergio, 'La costruzione dell'autostrada Milan – Laghi', in Ornella Selvafolta and Aldo Castellano, eds, *Costruire I Lombardia 1880–1980. Rete e infrastrutture territoriali* (Milano 1984), 175–206.

McAdam, John Loudon, *A Practical Essay on the Scientific Repair and Preservation of Public Roads* (London 1819).

McAdam, John Loudon, *Remarks on the Present System of Road-Making* (London 1820).

McCormick, T.J., Ross, R.R., Bill, J.I. and McCoubrey, W., *Building the network – Northern Ireland* (n. l. 2002).

McCoubrey, William J., *The Motorway Achievement*, vol. 3: *Building the Network* (London 2008).

Merki, Christoph Maria, and Schiedt, Hans-Ulrich, eds, Strasse und Strassenverkehr – Routes et Circulation Routiere', *traverse – Zeitschrift für Geschichte – Revue D'Histoire*, 6, 2, 1999.

Merki, Christoph Maria, *Der holprige Siegeszug des Automobils, 1895–1930. Zur Motorisierung des Strassenverkehrs in Frankreich, Deutschland und der Schweiz* (Vienna 2002).

Merriman, Peter, *Driving Spaces. A Cultural-historical Geography of England's M1 Motorway* (Oxford 2007).

Mielke, Hans-Jürgen, *Die Autobahn Berlin – Helmstedt. Über 160 Kilometer Langeweile?* (Berlin 1984).

Mielke, Hans-Jürgen, *Die Autobahn Berlin – Hirschberg/Hof in Geschichte und Gegenwart. Landeskunde entlang einer deutschen Hauptverbindungsachse* (Halle 2007).

Mielke, Hans-Jürgen, *Die Autobahn Berlin – Hamburg. Politik und Geschichte erfahren* (Halle 2010).

Millet, Michel and Veuve, Alain, *Les autoroutes: Conception et réalisation* (Paris 1975).

Mom, Gijs, 'Roads without Rails. European Highway-Network Building and the Desire for Long-Range Motorized Mobility', *Technology and Culture*, 46, October, 2005, 745–72.

Mom, Gijs, 'Constructing Multifunctional Networks. Road Building in the Netherlands, 1810–1980', in Gijs Mom and Laurent Tissot, eds, *Road History. Planning, Construction, Use* (Neuchâtel 2007), 33–62.

Mom, Gijs and Tissot, Laurent, eds, *Road History. Planning, Construction, Use* (Neuchâtel 2007).

Mom, Gijs, Pirie, Gordon and Tissot, Laurent, eds, *Mobility in History. The State of the Art in the History of Transport, Traffic and Mobility* (Neuchâtel 2009).

Moraglio, Massimo, 'L'autostrada Torino–Milano (1923–1933). I progetto e la construzione', *Storia Urbana*, 86, 1999, 103–21.

Moraglio, Massimo, *Strade e politica. Storia della viabilità in provincia di Torino* (Alessandria 2003).

Moraglio, Massimo, *Storia delle prime autostrade italiane (1922–1943). Modernizzazione, affair e propaganda* (Torino 2007).

Moraglio, Massimo, 'The highway Network in Italy and Germany Between the Wars: A preliminary comparative study', in Gijs Mom and Laurent Tissot, eds, *Road History. Planning, Construction, Use* (Neuchâtel 2007), 117–32.

Moraglio, Massimo, 'Real ambition or just coincidence? The Italian fascist motorway project in inter-war Europe', *Journal of Transport History*, 30, 2, 2009, 168–82.

Moraglio, Massimo and Bonino, Michele, *Inventare gli spostamenti. Storia e immagini dell'autostrada Torino–Savona* (Torino et. al. 2006).

Möser, Kurt, *Geschichte des Autos* (Frankfurt am Main and New York 2002).

Nietfeld, Annette, *Landschaftspflege im Nationalsozialismus am Beispiel der Reichsautobahnen* (Berlin 1985).

Norden, Peter, *Unternehmen Autobahn* (Bayreuth 1983).

Oosterwall, Jörgen, *Besluitvormingstypes en effectiviteit in het autosnelwegenbeleid in België* (Leuven 1990).

Palma, Andre de, Lindsey, Robin and Proost, Stef, *Investment and the use of Tax and Toll Revenues in the Transport Sector* (Stamford, CT 2007).

Pavese, Claudio, 'The Making of the Italian Motorways Network (1924–1974)', *Transportes, Servicios y Telecommunicaciones*, 10, 2006, 97–120.

Pehnelt, Gernot, *Das Unternehmen Reichsautobahn* (Dessau 2003).

Pohl, Manfred, *Die STRABAG 1923 bis 1998* (Munich and Zurich 1998).

Pradel, Sylvia, *Entstehung und Entwicklung des Bundesfernstraßenrechts* (Hamburg 2003).

Presses de l'école nationale des Ponts et Chaussées, ed., *Une Autoroute se Souvient. Histoire de la Société des Autoroutes Paris Normandie* (Paris 1993).

Presses de l'école nationale des Ponts et Chausséees. ed., *ESCOTA – Une autoroute dans sa region. Histoire de la Société des autoroutes Estérel-Côte d'Azur-Alpe* (Paris 1995).

Presses de l'école nationale des Ponts et Chausséees, ed., *Le Plan Routier Breton* (Paris 1996); *Valérie Elbaz-Benchetrit, Autoroutes – Impacts sur l'économie et l'environnement* (Paris 1997).

Puricelli, Piero, 'Le Strade dell'Impero Italiano', in Kurt G. Kaftan, ed., *Welt-Strassenwesen 1938* (Berlin 1938), 132–7.

Ragazzi, Giorgio, *I signori delle autostrade* (Bologna 2008.

Reig, Carlos Padrós and Cocciolo, Endrius Eliseo, *Intervencion publica en el sector de las empresas concesionarias de autopista. El caso albertis/autostrade* (Madrid 2009).

Reitsam, Charlotte, *Reichsautobahn-Landschaften. Das Konzept der 'bodenständigen Gartenkunst' Alwin Seiferts. Fachliche Hintergründe und Rezeption bis in die Nachkriegszeit* (Frankfurt am Main 2001).

Reitsam, Charlotte, *Reichsautobahn-Landschaften im Spannungsfeld von Natur und Technik. Transatlantische und interdisziplinäre Verflechtungen* (Saarbrücken 2009).

Reverdy, Georges, *Les Routes de France du XXe Siecle*, vol. 1: *1900 à 1951* (Paris 2007).

Reverdy, Georges, *Les Routes de France du XXe Siecle*, vol. 2: *1952 à 2000* (Paris 2007).

Rios, Giovanni da and Rinelli, Savino, 'Autocamionale Genova-Valle del Po', in Gianpietro Livini, ed., *1924–1935. Le Autostrade della prima generazione* (Milano 1984), 120–137.

Rodríguez Lázaro, F.J., *Las primeras autopistas españolas (1925–1936)* (Ciudas Real 2004).

Roth, Ralf, *Das Jahrhundert der Eisenbahn. Die Herrschaft über Raum und Zeit* (Ostfildern 2005).

Roth, Ralf and Schlögel, Karl, eds, *Neue Wege in ein neues Europa. Geschichte und Verkehr im 20. Jahrhundert* (Frankfurt am Main and New York 2009).

Rothenberger, Karl-Heinz, 'Autobahnbau in der Pfalz nach dem Zweiten Weltkrieg', *Mitteilungen des historischen Vereins der Pfalz*, 100, 2002, 533–59.

Ruppmann, Reiner, 'Das System der Autobahnen und ihre kulturellen Mythen', in Ralf Roth and Karl Schlögel, eds, *Neue Wege in ein neues Europa.*

Geschichte und Verkehr im 20. Jahrhundert (Frankfurt am Main and New York 2009), 338–60.

Ruppmann, Reiner, *Schrittmacher des Autobahnzeitalters – Frankfurt und das Rhein-Main-Gebiet* (Darmstadt 2011).

Samper, Maria Burzaco and Liceras, José Maria Abad, *Leyes de carreteras y autopistas* (Madrid 2002).

Santucci, E., 'Die Entwicklung des Straßenverkehrs und der Ausbau des Straßennetzes bis zum Jahre 1985 in Italien', *Strasse und Autobahn*, 23, issue 1, 1973, 208–13.

Santucci, E., *Autostrade per l'Italia S.p.A., La Societa' Autostrade dagli anni della ricostruzione post-bellica all'orrizonte del 2000* (Roma 1996).

Santucci, E., *La rete autostradale Italiana 1924–2002* (Roma 2003).

Schipper, Fank, 'Changing the face of Europe. European road mobility during the Marshall plan years', *Journal of Transport History*, 28, 2, 2007, 211–28.

Schipper, Frank, *Driving Europe. Building Europe on Roads in the Twentieth Century* (Amsterdam 2008).

Schivelbusch, Wolfgang, *Entfernte Verwandtschaft. Faschismus, Nationalsozialismus, New Deal 1933–1939* (Munich 2005).

Schmelz, Heinrich, 'Die Entwicklung des Straßenverkehrs und der Ausbau des Straßennetzes bis zum Jahre 1985 in Österreich', *Strasse und Autobahn*, 23, 1, 1973, 213–23.

Schot, Johan, 'Building Europe on Transnational Infrastructures', *The Journal of Transport History*, 28, 2, 2007, 167–71.

Schütz, Erhard and Gruber, Eckhard, *Mythos Reichsautobahn – Bau und Inszenierung der 'Straßen des Führers', 1933–1941* (Berlin 1996).

Seebohm, Hans-Christoph, Straßenplanung und Forschung, in BMV, ed., *Die Straßen der Bundesrepublik. Schriftenreihe des Bundesministers für Verkehr*, 5 (Bielefeld 1954), 7–50.

Semlinger, Franz, *Die Autobahn vom Hienberg bis Nürnberg. Bau und Bedeutung bis heute* (Neunkirchen am Sand 1998).

Sierra, Pablo Arrias, *Periferias y Nueva Ciudad. El problema del paisaje en los procesos de Dispersión Urbana* (Sevilla 2003).

Sims, Joe F.A., *Building the network in the North East of England* (Chichester/ West Sussex 2009)

Starkie, David Nicolas Martin, *Motorway Age. Road Traffic Policies in Post War Britain* (Oxford 1982).

Steininger, Benjamin, *Raum-Maschine Reichsautobahn. Zur Dynamik eines bekannt / unbekannten Bauwerks* (Berlin 2005).

Stern, Volkhard, *Der Autobahn-Schnellverkehr der Deutschen Reichsbahn* (Freiburg 2007).

Stockmann, Dieter, *Strecke 46 – Die vergessene Autobahn*, 3rd ed. (Veitshöchheim 2007).

Stommer, Rainer, ed., *Reichsautobahn – Pyramiden des Dritten Reiches. Analysen zur Ästhetik eines unbewältigten Mythos* (Marburg 1982).

Strohkark, Ingrid, 'Die Wahrnehmung von "Landschaft" und der Bau von Autobahnen in Deutschland, Frankreich und Italien vor 1933', Technical university Berlin Ph.D. thesis, 2001.

Syme, Ronald, *The Story of British Roads*. Ed. by British Road Federation (London 1950).

Thiébault, André, 'Die Entwicklung des Straßenverkehrs und der Ausbau des Straßennetzes bis zum Jahre 1985 in Frankreich', *Strasse und Autobahn*, 23, 1, 1973, 186–95.

Tizon, Julio-Gaspar Sequeiros, *A Autopista del Atlántico* (Madrid 1977).

Tops, J.W., 'Die Entwicklung des Straßenverkehrs und der Ausbau des Straßennetzes bis zum Jahre 1985 in den Niederlanden', *Strasse und Autobahn*, 23, 1, 1973, 196–207.

Touriño, E. Perez, *Infraestructuras y desarrollo regional. Efectos economicos autopista atlantica* (La Coruña 1997).

Universidade de Santiago de Compostela et Empresa Nacional de Autopistas, ed., *La Autopista del Atlántico. Movilidad, Demanda de Transporte y Localización Empresarial* (Santiago de Compostela 2000).

Vahrenkamp, Richard, *Autobahnbau in Hessen bis 1943* (Darmstadt 2007).

Vahrenkamp, Richard, 'Planning and Constructing the Autobahn Network in Germany durig the Nazi-Period – Styles and Strategies', in Gijs Mom and Laurent Tissot, eds, *Road History. Planning, Construction, Use* (Neuchâtel 2007), 87–98.

Vahrenkamp, Richard, *The German Autobahn 1920–1945. Hafraba Visions and Mega Projects* (Köln 2010).

Vahrenkamp, Richard, *Die logistische Revolution. Der Aufstieg der Logistik in der Massenkonsumgesellschaft* (Frankfurt and New York 2011).

Ververs, M.J., *Kruising, de geschiedenis van pont en brug. Europese biblioteek* (Zaltbommel 1999).

Villar, Domingo Cuéllar, 'Review of Francisco Javier Rodriguez Lázaro, Las primeras autopistas españoles (1925–1936) (Madrid 2004)', *Transportes, Servicios y Telecomunicaciones*, 9, 2005, 139–43.

Vitagliani, S., *Destination Europe. Autostrada e mobilità in Valle d'Aosta 1962–1992* (Quart 1993).

Vleuten, Eric van der and Kaijser, Arne, eds, *Networking Europe: Transnational Infrastructures and the Shaping of Europe, 1850–2000* (Sagamore Beach, MA 2006).

Walewijn, Adolf, *Achter de Bres: De Rijkswaterstaat in oorlogstijd* (Den Haag 1990).

Wall, R. van de, 'Bouwen voor een onbekende toekomst. De totstandkoming van het Belgische autosnelwegennet (1935–1989)', Onuitgegeven licentiaatsverhandeling, Katholieke Universiteit Leuven, departement Geschiedenis, 2007.

Weise, Hans-Joachim, *Vom Bau der Autobahn im Schleizer Oberland 1933 bis 1936* (n.l. 2006).

Wenk, Gustav, *Der Ausbau des schweizerischen Hauptstrassennetzes und seine Finanzierung* (Basel 1953).

Wentholt, L.R., 'Het Nederlandsche Rijkswegennet', in Kurt G. Kaftan, ed., *Welt-Strassenwesen 1938* (Berlin 1938), 116–23.

Windisch-Hojnacki, Claudia, *Die Reichsautobahn – Konzeption und Bau der RAB, ihre ästhetischen Aspekte, sowie ihre Illustration in Malerei, Literatur, Photographie und Plastik*, Ph.D. (Bonn 1989).

Winkler, Hans-Joachim, *Legenden um Hitler. Zur Politik und Zeitgeschichte*, H. 7, ed. by Landeszentrale für politische Bildungsarbeit Berlin in Verbindung mit dem Otto-Suhr-Institut an der FU Berlin (Berlin 1963).

Winkler, Jonathan, 'The Role of User Benefits in Deciding to Build Motorways in Britain', unpublished paper presented at the Fifth Conference on the History of Transport, Traffic and Mobility, in Helmond, The Netherlands, 25 to 28 October 2007.

Wirth, Wolfgang, ed., *Die Autobahn. Von der Idee zur Wirklichkeit. Archiv für die Geschichte des Straßen- und Verkehrswesens*, vol. 19 (Köln 2005).

Yeadon, Harry L., *Building the Network – The North West of England*, sec. ed. (Chichester/West Sussex 2005).

Zeller, Thomas, *Straße, Bahn, Panorama. Verkehrswege und Landschaftsveränderung in Deutschland 1930 bis 1990* (Frankfurt am Main and New York 2002).

Zeller, Thomas, *Driving Germany. The Landscape of the German Autobahn, 1930–1970* (New York and Oxford 2006).

Chapter 12
Motorways and the Modernisation of Britain's Road Network, 1937–70

Peter Merriman

Why not a motor-car way through England?

B.H. Thwaite[1]

Writing in *The Nineteenth Century* magazine in 1902, British engineer B.H. Thwaite proposed the construction of an arrow-straight motorway from London to Birmingham. Thwaite's proposal was the first of its kind in Britain, and it appeared 56 years before the first section of motorway was officially opened in December 1958. In this chapter I examine the early history of Britain's motorway network, starting with campaigns for motorways before the Second World War. I examine the history of key motoring lobby groups such as the British Road Federation (BRF) and the German Roads Delegation, before discussing the government's motorway plans which were published in 1946. I trace the tension between road and railway interest groups in the early twentieth century, examining the work of Thomas Lloyd and the Railway Conversion League in the 1950s, when they campaigned for 20,000 miles of British railways to be converted into high-speed motorways. Finally, I discuss the opinions of politicians, government scientists and motorists when Britain finally joined the 'motorway club' in 1958, and I focus on the reactions which followed the opening of the M1 motorway in November 1959 as the motorway quickly entered the public's imagination, and was consumed as an archetypal modern space of travel and consumption.

Campaigning for British Motorways, 1902–45

Britain's first motorways were products of post-war reconstruction, proposed by the new post-war Labour government, put on hold due to successive economic crises and cutbacks in capital investment, and eventually constructed and opened in the late 1950s and 1960s as the country emerged from a decade or more of

---

1 B.H. Thwaite, 'Why not a motor-car way through England?', *The Nineteenth Century*, 52, 1902, 305–8, here 305.

austerity.[2] Britain's motorways were in many ways post-war constructions, but the first motorways followed almost 60 years of plans, parliamentary bills and lobbying by private individuals and organisations pushing for improvements to the nation's road network, and many of these early campaigners faced considerable resistance from railway interests. When Thwaite first proposed a London to Birmingham motor road in 1902, the motorist, publisher and Conservative MP John Montagu of Beaulieu expressed doubt whether railway supporters and shareholders would allow such a scheme to get through parliament.[3] Twenty years later, John, now Lord, Montagu of Beaulieu had seemingly changed his mind, becoming Chairman of a new private company, the Northern and Western Motorway, which proposed a 226-mile (364-kilometre) private toll motorway between London, Birmingham, Liverpool and Salford.[4] At a time when the government were funding new suburban and interurban bypasses to relieve traffic congestion and provide vital employment, Montagu explained how the Northern and Western Motorway would provide vital unemployment relief (directly employing 14,000 and indirectly employing a further 26,000 workers), stimulate agriculture, industry and trade and speed up travel. He was also keen to emphasise that the motorway would complement rather than compete with the railways,[5] which provided a precedent for how private finance and speculation could stimulate the economy and improve trade.[6] The company's private Motorways Bill fell victim to the successive dissolutions of Parliament in December 1923 and October 1924, but the syndicate's parliamentary agent George Blizard continued to campaign for a

2 P. Merriman, *Driving Spaces: a cultural-historical geography of England's M1 motorway* (Oxford 2007); P. Merriman, '"A power for good or evil": geographies of the M1 in late-fifties Britain', in D. Gilbert, D. Matless and B. Short, eds, *Geographies of British Modernity: Space and Society in the Twentieth Century* (Oxford 2003), 115–31.

3 J. Montagu of Beaulieu. 'Editorial jottings: London to Birmingham by motor road', *The Car (Illustrated)*, 2, 20, 8 October 1902, 211; J. Montagu of Beaulieu [The Editor] 1903: 'Motor roads will be opposed', *The Motor Car Magazine*, 1, 2, 1903, 133; B.H. Thwaite, 'Why not a motor-car way through England?', *The Nineteenth Century*, 52 (306), 1902, 305–8; B.H. Thwaite, 'Motor-car ways', *The Car (Illustrated)*, 2, 20, 8 October 1902, 218.

4 Northern and Western Motorway, *Northern and Western Motorway: Direct Lines of Communication Between the Largest Cities and Business Centres of the Country* (London 1923).

5 Lord Montagu of Beaulieu, 'Foreword', in Northern and Western Motorway, *Northern and Western Motorway: Direct Lines of Communication Between the Largest Cities and Business Centres of the Country* (London 1923), 3–6; Lord Montagu of Beaulieu, 'The railways and the motorway: a reply [letter, Daily Mail, 30 October 1923]', in Northern and Western Motorway, *Northern and Western Motorway: Providing Direct Lines of Fast and Cheap Communication by Road Between the Largest Cities and Business Centres of the Country* [revised and extended edition] (London 1923), 49–51.

6 Lord Montagu of Beaulieu, 'To the editor of The Manchester Guardian (letter, 6 November 1923)', in Northern and Western Motorway, *Northern and Western Motorway*, 42–3.

private motorway through the Midlands until the late 1920s, even suggesting that 'the railways might well cut out the cost of stations and signalling on many branch lines by converting them into motor roads'.[7]

As the government's arterial-bypass construction programme was cut back following the financial crisis of 1931, so roads and motorways moved down the political agenda, with very little construction or planning being undertaken in the early 1930s.[8] While the BRF was formed as a lobby group in 1932, their initial aim was not to promote road or motorway construction. The BRF were formed by leading organisations who opposed the increasing taxation and restrictions proposed for motor transport by the Conference on Rail and Road Transport (the so-called 'Salter Conference') in December 1932. Railway and road transport groups began to actively lobby against one another, and the BRF quickly formulated a reply to the Salter Committee, whom they accused of railway bias – due to their decision to increase motor vehicle taxation and their failure to address the inefficiencies of railway companies.[9] According to the Federation, the Salter Conference was charged with the duty of

> establishing a fair basic competition between Rail and Road, and considering the nature and extent of the regulations which should be applied to goods transport by Road and Rail' but what it actually did was to propose most drastic increases in taxation and restrictions in goods transport by road, while entirely ignoring the defects of the Railways. … The constitution of the Conference was itself unsatisfactory; the scales were decidedly weighted on the side of the Railways, and, so far as Road Transport is concerned, important interests were excluded from representation.[10]

The BRF presented themselves as 'the one representative body which is making efforts to combat the sinister and distorted propaganda of the railways in their efforts to enslave British industry',[11] but by the mid- to late 1930s the Federation

[7] British Library of Political and Economic Science (BLPES) at the London School of Economics, Rees Jeffreys Archive (RJ), 16/4, 'Roads specially reserved for motor cars', *Transport Management*, October 1927.

[8] W.R. Jeffreys, *The King's Highway: An Historical and Autobiographical Record of the Developments of the Past Sixty Years* (London 1949); Merriman, *Driving Spaces*; M.J. Law, 'Turning night into day: transgression and Americanization at the English inter-war roadhouse', *Journal of Historical Geography*, 35, 2009, 473–94; M.J. Law, '"Stopping to dream": the beautification and vandalism of London's interwar arterial roads', *The London Journal*, 35, 2010, 58–84.

[9] British Road Federation, *A Statement by the British Road Federation Supplemental to the Case of Trade and Industry Against What is Known as 'The Salter Report'* (London 1933).

[10] British Road Federation, *Roads, Railways and Restrictions* (London 1933), 14.

[11] British Road Federation, *The Motor Industry and the Salter Report* (London 1933), no pagination.

supplemented their strategic defence of the motor industry with calls for the construction of a national network of modern roads and motorways.[12] The impetus for this broadening appears to have been the involvement of senior members of the Federation in a 1937 delegation to study the German *Autobahnen*.

The German Roads Delegation (1937) was organised by the Automobile Association (AA), BRF, Royal Automobile Club (RAC) and Parliamentary Road Group in mid-1937, following an invitation by the German government for a group of expert engineers and politicians to study Germany's main roads and motorways.[13] The delegation of 224 engineers, planners, landscape architects, politicians, motor manufacturers and journalists visited Germany between 24 September and 3 October 1937, touring along 545 miles (877 kilometres) of *Autobahnen*, 280 miles (451 kilometres) of ordinary road, and being entertained by German politicians and officials.[14] On their return the delegation recommended to the British government 'that a national scheme should be formed without delay for a series of motorways', and in a number of subsequent reports, the Delegation, BRF, County Surveyors' Society and the newly formed (but short-lived) Modern Roads Movement, suggested that Britain must implement motorway construction without delay.[15]

In May 1938 the County Surveyors' Society proposed that the government construct 1,000 miles of motorway, while earlier, in late 1937, the BRF proposed a national network of 2,108 miles (3,392 kilometres) of motorway linking major industrial cities and ports.[16] The Federation explained how the motorway network

---

12 British Road Federation, *The Spectre of Monopoly* (London 1938); British Road Federation, *National Motor Roads* (London 1937); British Road Federation, ed., *New Roads or Old?* (London 1937); British Road Federation, *Get a Move On* (London 1937); British Road Federation, *The Crisis and the Roads* (London 1938), and British Road Federation, *From Here to There* (London 1939).

13 Merriman, *Driving Spaces*; P. Merriman, 'Britain and "the motorway club": the effect of European and North American motorway construction on attitudes in Britain, 1930–1960', *Transfers: Interdisciplinary Journal of Mobility Studies*, 2 1, 2012, 106–33.

14 Anonymous, 'German motor roads – British delegation in Berlin', *The Times* of 27 September 1937, 14; The National Archives of the UK (TNA), Ministry of Transport files (MT) 39/96, Report of German Roads Delegation (1937) by Malcolm Heddle, 5 November 1937, 6.

15 German Roads Delegation, *Report Upon the Visit of Inspection and its Conclusions* (London 1938), 12. See also R.G.H. Clements, *The System of Motor Roads in Germany: A Record of Facts and of Technical Details* (London 1937); British Road Federation, *National Motor Roads* (London 1937); British Road Federation, *Get a Move On; British Road Federation, The Crisis and the Roads*; BLPES RJ 16/3, 'Motorways: statement prepared by the County Surveyors' Society in connection with their scheme for motorways', by Arthur Floyd (Secretary of the CSS), with letter dated 30 July 1938; Anonymous, 'Demand for modern motor roads – a new organisation', *The Times* of 18 November 1938, 18.

16 British Road Federation, *New Roads or Old?*; Lord Wolmer, 'Motor roads in Germany – Impressions of a tour – a profitable example', *The Times* of 7 October 1937, 15–16.

would reduce congestion, help industry and commerce, reduce road deaths and aid 'national defence' at a time of rising international tensions and fears about the military potential of Germany.[17] The government considered their options, and Minister of Transport Dr Leslie Burgin suggested that they might authorise the construction of a single, experimental section of motorway where it be proved cheaper than rebuilding an existing section of road.[18] In July 1937, proposals had been received from Lancashire County Council for a 62-mile (100 kilometres) section of North-South motorway between Warrington and Carnforth, and initial surveys were undertaken for a projected London to Birmingham motorway, but the Chancellor of the Exchequer blocked the schemes on financial grounds.[19] Further lobbying occurred throughout 1938 and 1939, and in May 1938 and February 1939 a number of lobby groups who had been represented on the German Roads Delegation's tour advocated motorway construction while submitting evidence to the Select Committee of the House of Lords on the Prevention of Road Accidents.[20] The BRF continued their pressure, and in July 1939 they published *From Here to There*, wherein they highlighted the increasing number of official reports which advanced the construction of experimental stretches or entire networks of modern motorway, and they concluded that immediate action must be taken: 'THERE MUST BE A NATIONAL PLAN AND TIME SCHEDULE'.[21]

With the outbreak of the Second World War, the government's attention focused on more pressing matters, but as early as 1942 reports and plans started to emerge advocating the construction of a national network of motorways as part of plans to reconstruct Britain after the war.[22] In April 1942 the Chief Engineer in the Ministry

---

17 British Road Federation, *National Motor Roads*.

18 TNA MT 39/556, 'Post war planning and motorways', by F.C. Cook, 14 August 1942.

19 See TNA MT 39/145, Minute, E. Bull to Chief Engineer, 'London-Birmingham Motorway', 25 October 1937; TNA MT 39/96, Memorandum, F.C. Cook to The Minister, 3 November 1937; TNA MT 39/145, Minute, Edward Bull to Chief Engineer, 'Investigation into the alignment of a motorway from London to Preston', 4 February 1938, and TNA MT 39/556, 'Post war planning and motorways', by F.C. Cook, 14 August 1942.

20 Select Committee of the House of Lords on the Prevention of Road Accidents, *Report (H.L. 192)* (London 1938); Select Committee of the House of Lords on the Prevention of Road Accidents, *Report (H.L. 2, 52)* (London 1939).

21 British Road Federation, *From Here to There*, 18.

22 The Institution of Civil Engineers, *Post-War National Development Report No. III: Public Works* (London 1942); Institution of Highway Engineers, *The Post-War Development of Highways* (London 1943); The Institution of Municipal and County Engineers, *Post-War Planning and Reconstruction* (London 1942); London Regional Reconstruction Committee of the Royal Institute of British Architects, *Greater London: Towards a Master Plan. Second Interim Report – May 1943* (London 1943); Standing Joint Committee of the RAC, AA and RSAC, *Post-War Roads and Traffic: A Memorandum* (London 1944); British Road Federation, *Roads and Road Transport: Reconstruction of Roads and Development of Road Transport* (London 1944).

of War Transport drafted a 15-page memorandum discussing the potential role of motorways in serving the 'social, industrial and economic needs of the post-war world',[23] while official planning reports such as Forshaw and Abercrombie's *County of London Plan* and Patrick Abercrombie's *Greater London Plan 1944* advocated high-speed arterial roads and motorways radiating from London to help tie the city into its region.[24]

Post-war Plans and Economic Cut-backs

The 1946 'Tea Room Plan'

The first official plan for the construction of a national network of motorways was proposed by the Labour government's Minister of Transport, Alfred Barnes, on 6 May 1946.[25] The proposals formed part of a ten-year plan to reconstruct the nation's main roads, and it was unofficially referred to as the 'Tea Room Plan', as the map outlining the projected motorways was exhibited for Members of Parliament in the House of Commons' Tea Room (Figure 12.1). The plan proposed motorways that would occupy very similar routes to what are now motorways M1, M4, M5, M6 and M62, but despite the release of these plans just a year after the war, and the introduction of the necessary legislation in the Special Roads Bill of 1948 (enacted in 1949), Parliament were quickly informed that construction would be delayed. During parliamentary discussions in late 1948, Alfred Barnes admitted that the government would not start work on the motorways programme in the near future due to the downturn in the economy and subsequent cutbacks in capital investment.[26]

The roads lobby were not pleased by the delays. During the passage of the Special Roads Bill through both Houses of Parliament, the BRF had lobbied hard to ensure that the legislation was passed, forwarding a number of publications to politicians, who in turn referred to the Federation's propaganda.[27] In late 1948 and 1949, many politicians received two editions of the Federation's pamphlet *The Case for Motorways*, along with *The Road Way to Recovery* – written by Christopher Brunner, an economist, General Manager of Shell-Mex, and Chairman of the

23 TNA MT 39/556, 'Post war planning and motorways', by F.C. Cook, 14 August 1942.

24 J.H. Forshaw and P. Abercrombie, *County of London Plan* (London 1943); P. Abercrombie, *Greater London Plan 1944* (London 1945).

25 *Parliamentary Debates, House of Commons*, 'Highway Development (Government programme)', 422, 6 May 1946, cols 590–95, here 591.

26 *Parliamentary Debates, House of Commons*, 'Special Roads Bill – Second reading', 457, 11 November 1948, cols 1737–848.

27 *Parliamentary Debates, House of Commons*, 'Special Roads Bill – Second reading', 457, 11 November 1948, cols 1741, 1761, 1763, 1778.

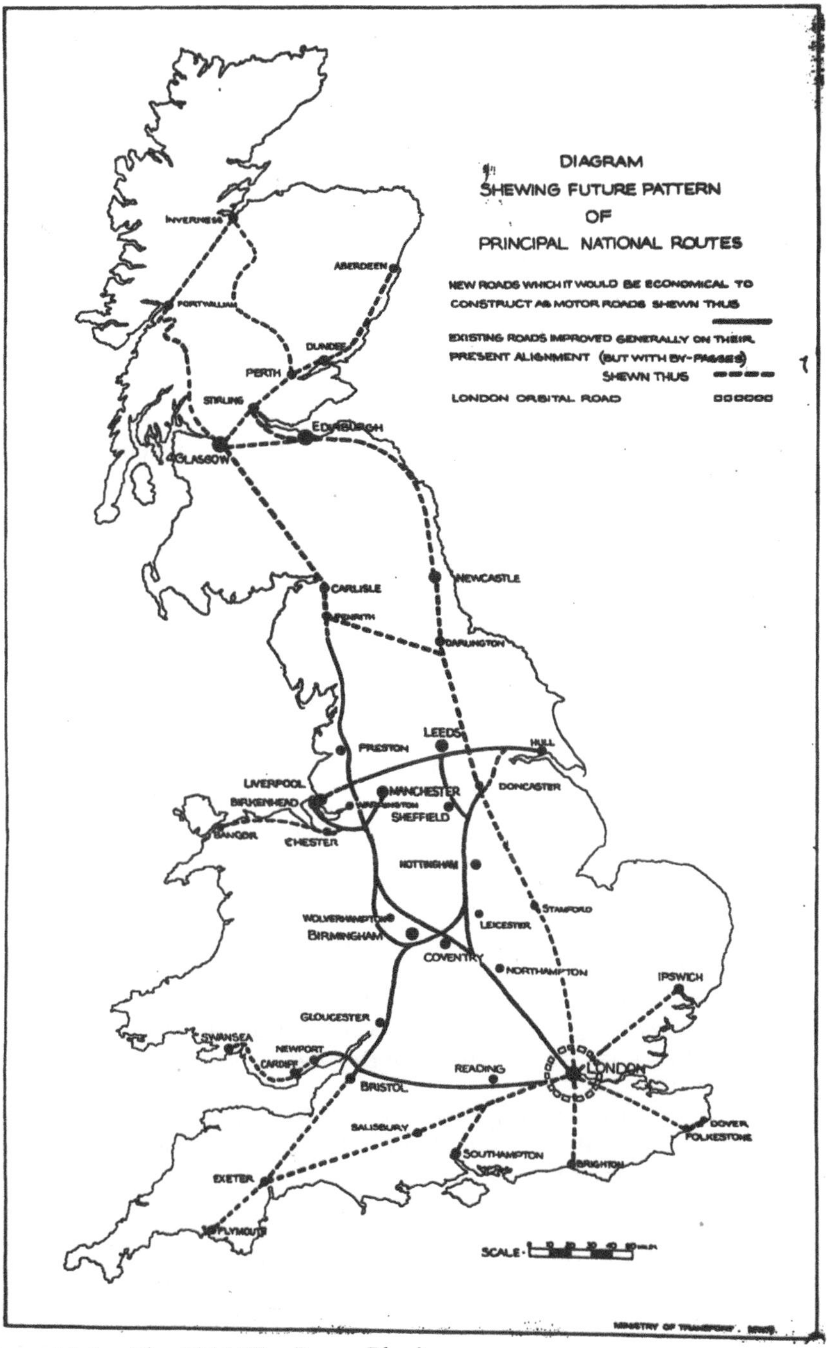

Figure 12.1 The 1946 'Tea Room Plan'

Source: Author's collection.

Federation's Publicity Committee – and a report on the *Economics of Motorways* prepared by a joint committee of the Federation, the Institution of Highway Engineers and the Society of Motor Manufacturers and Traders.[28] Once it had become clear that construction would be delayed, the Federation stepped up their campaigning, emphasising the urgency of motorway construction in Lancashire, and between South Wales and England, as well as the importance of motorways to national defence and the government's rearmament programme.[29] Almost nine years after the 'Tea Room Plan' was first unveiled, the Conservative government's Minister of Transport and Civil Aviation John Boyd-Carpenter announced the start of the 'Expanded Road Programme', which included the Dartford Tunnel under the River Thames east of London, by-passes at Doncaster, Lancaster, Preston and St Albans and the first sections of the M1 London-Yorkshire motorway.[30] The Tea Room Plan was vastly down-sized, and a number of individuals and organisations pushed for more construction. In March 1955 the Royal Automobile Club, BRF and Society of Motor Manufacturers and Traders joined nine other organisations to establish the Roads Campaign Council, whose aim was 'to organise a short, sharp publicity campaign demanding increased expenditure on roads'.[31]

Brigadier Lloyd and the Railway Conversion League

February 1955 also saw the start of a campaign led by Brigadier Thomas Ifan Lloyd, a Deputy Engineer-in-Chief at the War Office. Speaking at a meeting of the Institution of Civil Engineers, Lloyd proposed that the nation's unprofitable and inefficient railways be converted into a network of 20,000 miles (32,180 kilometres) of motorway, and in 1957 he outlined his case in detail in *Twilight of the Railways – What Roads They'll Make!* [32] Lloyd's proposals were radical and controversial. He identified the two key problems with Britain's transport system

---

28 British Road Federation, *The Case for Motorways* (London 1948); British Road Federation, *The Case for Motorways*, 2nd ed. (London 1949); C.T. Brunner, *The Road Way to Recovery* (London 1948); Joint Committee of the British Road Federation, The Institution of Highway Engineers and The Society of Motor Manufacturers & Traders, *Economics of Motorways. Report presented to the Minister of Transport on 18 October 1948* (London 1948).

29 See British Road Federation, *New Roads for Lancashire* (London 1952); British Road Federation, *South Wales Roads* (London 1951), and British Road Federation, *Memorandum on Roads and National Defence* (London 1951).

30 *Parliamentary Debates, House of Commons*, 'Expanded road programme (Government's proposals)', 536, 2 February 1955, cols 1096–109.

31 W. Plowden, 'MPs and the "roads lobby"', in A. Barker and M. Rush, *The Member of Parliament and His Information* (London 1970), 69–96, here 70.

32 See T.I. Lloyd, 'Potentialities of the British Railways' system as a reserved roadway system', *Proceedings of The Institution of Civil Engineers*, 4, 1, 1955, 732–88, and T.I. Lloyd, *Twilight of the Railways – What Roads They'll Make! Railway Conversion as the Cure for Britain's Transport Troubles* (London 1957).

as being 'the ineffectiveness and unprofitability of the railway system [and] the lack of any road system to match the capabilities of modern motor vehicles', and the solution was simply 'for British Railways to cease railway operating and, as they do so, line by line, turn their tracks into roads, thus in time converting the entire unprofitable railway system into the required modern road network'.[33]

Station buildings would be dismantled, providing convenient access points between the new motorways and ordinary roads, and fleets of specially constructed high-speed, high-capacity freight vehicles and buses would run on the system. The new system was forecast to cost considerably less money than the loss-making railways, and conversion would also make strategic sense, as: 'railway routes hardly qualify as strategic in this age of motor transport and nuclear warfare. Indeed, compared with the superb roads they might become, they are positively unstrategic, hampering national mobility'.[34]

Lloyd's proposals gained increasing publicity with the formation of the Railway Conversion League in July 1958, whose express aim was to 'further the proposals of Brigadier Lloyd', and their formation was followed by a very wordy and protracted debate in *The Engineer* about the pros and cons of railway conversion versus railway modernisation/electrification. Almost 80 letters were printed in weekly exchanges in *The Engineer* from February to October 1958, with many of those for conversion being written by Thomas I. Lloyd or Eric C. Gordon-England – a well-known engineer, motor manufacturer and aviator and a founding member of the Railway Conversion League.[35] The League continued campaigning for railway conversion throughout the 1960s and 1970s, building upon Dr Richard Beeching's contentious plans for extensive line and station closures by proposing that abandoned lines be converted into roads rather than sold off to private interests:[36]

> The stage has now been reached when serious consideration must be given to the question of whether the further indiscriminate sale of railway routes and their associated land is in the best interests of the country, faced, as it is, with the formidable problem of creating new routes on a scale adequate to match the rapid expansion of motor traffic.[37]

---

33 Lloyd, *Twilight of the Railways*, 7.

34 Lloyd, *Twilight of the Railways*, 54.

35 See *The Engineer*, 208–9, 1958.

36 British Railways Board, *The Reshaping of British Railways. Part 1: Report* (London 1963).

37 Railway Conversion League, *A Survey of Railway Conversion in Great Britain and Northern Ireland* (London 1969), 3. See also Railway Conversion League, *No Alternative! The Case for Transforming Britain's Railways into Motor Roads. Submitted to the Ministry of Transport, July 1965* (London 1965).

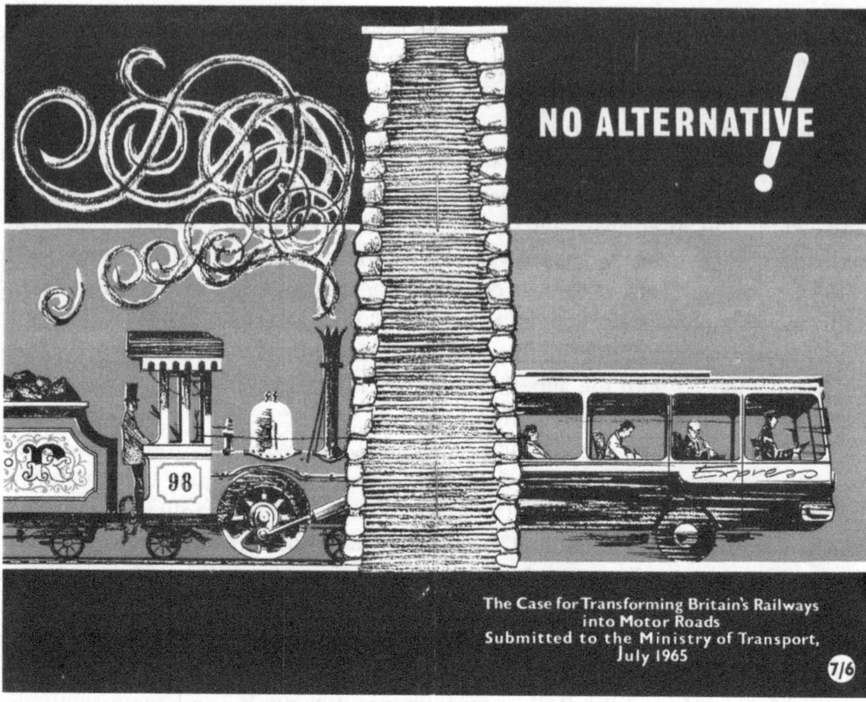

Figure 12.2 Cover of a brochure of the *Railway Conversion League*, 'No alternative!', 1965

Source: Author's collection.

Throughout their campaigning the Railway Conversion League contrasted modern motor transport – with its modern motor roads and motor vehicles – with the antiquated nineteenth-century technology of the railway, and the modernising impulses of the League were vividly captured on the cover of a booklet they submitted to the Ministry of Transport in support of their campaign in 1965 (Figure 12.2). Here, an early steam-train, driven by a top-hatted man, disappears into a tunnel, emerging from the other side as a modern motor coach, travelling at considerable speed. There is only one conclusion for the reader: there is 'No alternative!', no comparison. Motor roads must prevail over railways.[38]

[38] The Railway Conversion League were renamed the Railway Conversion Campaign in the 1970s or 1980s, and they existed as a lobby group until 1994. See P. Withrington, 'Reigniting the railway conversion debate', *Economic Affairs*, 24, 2, 2004, 56–9.

Britain Joins 'the Motorway Club'[39]

At the same time as Brigadier Lloyd was outlining his case for railway conversion, the design and planning of Britain's first motorways was well underway, with the 8¼-mile (13.3-kilometre) Preston By-pass (now part of the M6 motorway) being opened to the public on 5 December 1958, followed almost a year later by the first 72 miles (116 kilometres) of the M1 London to Yorkshire motorway. These early motorways quickly caught the press and the public's imagination. When the M1 was opened on 2 November 1959, thousands of motorists made trips to try out their cars on the new road, and the motorway emerged as a rather unusual tourist attraction.[40] Especially on Sunday afternoons, traffic levels soared and the road became populated with 'heavily laden family cars' and a sprinkling of bus trips organised by London Transport.[41] Britain's first motorways were a distinctly modern and exotic spectacle, and one journalist remarked on how the M1 'has come to this insular nation as an innovation as foreign as a ski-jump course or bull-fight ring'.[42] Here was a dual carriageway road with three lanes in each direction, limited-access flyover junctions, no speed limit, large blue signs and new rules and regulations relating to motorway conduct. The modernity of the motorway was exciting for some, but the government, police and civil servants approached the motorway as a somewhat experimental enterprise, and the performance of its structures and the very first motorists were seen as key to its success or failure.

Engineering Experiments

Britain's first motorways were rather late arrivals on an international scale, appearing several decades after the pioneering projects of the Italians, Germans and Americans, and later than motorway construction projects in Belgium, Denmark, Sweden, the Netherlands, Canada, Mexico and Venezuela, amongst others.[43] Taken in this broader context, Britain's motorways might appear to be far

---

[39] Anonymous, 'Western Europe's 2500 miles of motorways', *The Times* of 2 November 1959, 19.

[40] 'Breakdown rush on M1', *Birmingham Mail* of 2 November 1959; Anonymous, 'Motorway in use', *The Motor*, 116, 11 November 1959, 518; Anonymous, 'Minister "appalled" by new motorway driving', *The Times* of 3 November 1959, 8; '5,000 cars an hour on motorway', *The Times* of 9 November 1959, 10.

[41] Anonymous, '5,000 cars an hour on motorway', *The Times* of 9 November 1959, 10; Anonymous, 'Trips to see motorway', *The Times* of 6 November 1959, 6; and also M.V. Rose, 'After 11 months of M1: good motorway driving rules are still flouted', *Birmingham Post* of 19 October 1960.

[42] W.A. McKenzie, 'Motoring: shedding light all along the motorways', *Daily Telegraph and Morning Post* of 25 November 1959, 13.

[43] Anonymous, 'Western Europe's 2500 miles of motorways', *The Times* of 2 November 1959, 19.

from innovative or novel, and one might even question why engineers and civil servants saw these motorways as experimental rather than predictable. However, despite trips by civil servants, engineers and designers to study motorways abroad, Britain's engineers, politicians and motorists lacked direct experience of these new driving environments. British engineers gained valuable knowledge about the construction of the German *Autobahnen* during the German Roads Delegation's visit in 1937 and through intelligence operations in the British-controlled sectors of Germany in 1946.[44] The BRF sent delegations overseas to study the motorways of Germany, the Netherlands, Belgium and Sweden in the early post-war years, while senior engineers from Sir Owen Williams and Partners – who designed the first section of the M1 – studied the motorways and service areas of Germany and the USA in the mid- to late 1950s.[45] Specialist government committees such as the Advisory Committee on Traffic Signs for Motorways also sent members and civil servants on overseas fact-finding missions to countries such as Belgium, Germany and the Netherlands, and civil servants looked to foreign practices when assessing the pros and cons of many different aspects of motorway design.[46] Experiments were undertaken on roadway composition and construction, sign design, lane markings and other factors by the government's Road Research Laboratory, but the difficulty of carefully testing many design elements meant that the first motorways were themselves designed to serve as experimental structures and spaces, which could in turn be carefully studied by the Road Research Laboratory, police and civil servants once the motorways were opened.

The M6 Preston By-pass motorway and M1 London to Yorkshire motorway both received criticisms from engineers, politicians and journalists when they were opened to the public. The Preston By-pass was opened by Prime Minister Harold Macmillan on 5 December 1958, but just 47 days later it was closed for 34 days after the carriageways cracked up due to severe frost damage. The consulting engineers – Lancashire County Council – blamed the Ministry of Transport for ignoring their recommendations that 'a full drainage system be installed throughout the length of the motorway'.[47] The M1 suffered similar

44 Road Research Laboratory [Department of Scientific and Industrial Research], *The German Motor Roads 1946*, Road Research Technical Paper No. 8, British Intelligence Objectives Sub-Committee Overall Report No. 5 (London 1948).

45 See Anonymous, 'Roads in Sweden', *Roads and Road Construction* of 24 December 1946, 405–8; British Road Federation, *Motorways Tour 1955: Holland, Belgium, Germany* (London 1955); Anonymous, 'Motorways Tour 1955', *Bulletin of the British Road Federation*, 1955, 1. Furthermore, see TNA MT 121/34, Note by Sir Owen Williams and Partners on services at service areas, 10 February 1956; TNA MT 121/33, Minute 1, P.A. Robinson to Mr Gillender, 14 April 1957.

46 TNA MT 121/72, 'Advisory Committee on Traffic Signs for Motorways. Minutes of the 7th meeting held on 25 June 1958'.

47 Anonymous, 'Difference on motorway – county wanted full drainage', *The Times* of 6 February 1959, 8. See also Anonymous, 'New motorway closed after 47 days – surface cracked by frost – better drains to be built', *The Times* of 22 January 1959, 10.

problems with its 'hard shoulders' (emergency stopping lanes), which were fairly narrow and not fully paved. Fifty miles of hard shoulder were comprised of stone covered in tar, and a further 57 miles were made of stone covered in sand and grass seed, but as the first vehicles started to pull over so these marginal areas became rutted and waterlogged, and one section of embankment collapsed just 36 hours after opening.[48] The Ministry of Transport's newly formed Motorways Working Panel and Traffic Engineering Committee investigated many of the M1's early problems, and this modern engineering achievement was approached very much as an experimental, linear laboratory or field-site, as the Road Research Laboratory and numerous committees tested new systems of lighting, signage, lane marking, cat's eye reflector, crash barrier, emergency telephone and junction layout, as well as assessing breakdown and accident rates.[49] While the M1's hard shoulders received critical comments, it was Sir Owen Williams and Partners' motorway bridges which received the most critical attention, whether from architects, landscape architects, engineers, designers or aesthetic commentators, including such luminaries as Nikolaus Pevsner, Reyner Banham, John Betjeman, Brenda Colvin, Sylvia Crowe and Ian Nairn.[50] Sir Owen's distinctive bridges were criticised for their heavy and solid appearance, particularly their central pillars and solid concrete parapets which were seen to block the visual flow of the landscape and the drivers' views along the motorway.[51] After a number of serious collisions with bridge supports on the central reservation in the first few months of operation, the government's Motorways Working Panel and Traffic Engineering Committee recommended that central supports should not be built between the carriageways of future sections of motorway,[52] while in July 1960 the press and politicians focused

---

48 Anonymous, 'Motorway "hard shoulder" slips', *The Times* of 4 November 1959, 9; Sir Owen Williams and Partners, *London Yorkshire Motorway: South of Luton-Watford Gap-Dunchurch Special Road. Report on Widening and Reconstruction of Grass Hard Shoulders, 12th September 1960–21st May 1961* (Birmingham 1961).

49 See the minutes and papers in TNA MT 95/501 and TNA MT 95/642.

50 N. Pevsner, *Buckinghamshire* (Harmondsworth 1960); R. Banham, 'The road to ubiquopolis', *New Statesman*, 59, 1960, 784 and 786; R. Banham, 'New way north', *New Society*, 20, 4 May 1972, 241–3; J. Betjeman, 'Men and buildings: style on road and rail', *Daily Telegraph and Morning Post* of 27 June 1960, 15; B. Colvin, 'The London-Birmingham motorway: a new look at the English landscape', *The Geographical Magazine*, 32, 1959, 239–46; I. Nairn, 'Look out', *The Architectural Review*, 133, 1963, 425–6; Anonymous, 'Discussion on the London-Birmingham motorway', *Proceedings of the Institution of Civil Engineers*, 19, May–August 1961, 61–119. For a broader discussion of these debates see Merriman, *Driving Spaces*; P. Merriman, '"A new look at the English landscape": landscape architecture, movement and the aesthetics of motorways in early post-war Britain', *Cultural Geographies*, 13, 2006, 78–105.

51 Colvin, 'The London-Birmingham motorway'; S. Crowe, *The Landscape of Roads* (London 1960).

52 TNA MT 95/501, 'London-Birmingham Motorway. Second report by the Traffic Engineering Committee', by W.F. Adams, 25 February 1960; reprinted in MT 95/501,

their attention on the role of the bridge supports in the death of 28-year-old Valerie Hopkins who had purportedly seen a shadowy 'phantom menace' under an M1 bridge that caused her to swerve and crash.[53] Broader attention focused on the motorway's accident rate and the location of accident black-spots, while detailed statistics were gathered by the Road Research Laboratory on the movements of vehicles involved in collisions and the role that a central reservation crash barrier might have had in reducing the severity of such crashes.[54]

'Know Your Motorway'[55]

Government scientists, politicians and civil servants were not only concerned with engineering this new space of driving; they also wanted to educate Britain's motorway users, engineering the conduct of motorway man and motorway woman. As early as 1957, commentators started to express concern about how Britain's drivers would behave on these futuristic motorways with no speed limit, multiple lanes, new styles of junction and new rules of conduct. Would Britain's vehicles be able to cope with the speeds and conditions associated with motorway driving? Would Britain's drivers be capable of inhabiting these spaces in a safe and responsible manner?[56] In response to the fears expressed by politicians and journalists, civil servants drafted a series of motorway regulations and a new Motorway Code prior to the opening of the Preston By-pass motorway in December 1958,[57] and this was incorporated into a new version of the Highway Code prior to the opening of the M1 motorway in October 1959.[58] The key concern of civil servants was not only how to get motorists to purchase and read the Code,

---

'London-Birmingham Motorway. Second report by the Working Party', by J.G. Smith, 25 April 1960.

53 Anonymous, 'The phantom of the M1', *Daily Express* of 21 June 1960, 13; Anonymous, 'Is this the phantom van on the M1?', *News Chronicle* of 21 June 1960, 13; TNA DSIR 12/200, 'Phantoms on the M1 motorway', DSIR/RRL Research note no. RN/3860/VJJ, October 1960, BRL263, by V.J. Jehu.

54 W.F. Adams, 'Safety aspects of motorway design', *Traffic Engineering and Control*, 3, 1961, 178–81; R.F. Newby and H.D. Johnson, 'London-Birmingham motorway accidents', *Traffic Engineering and Control*, 4, 1963, 550–55.

55 Royal Automobile Club, *Know your Motorway* (London 1959).

56 Anonymous, 'Motorway code', *Chronicle and Echo*, 26 November 1958; Anonymous, 'Motorways and vehicle design', *The Engineer*, 208, 13 November 1959, 583–4; J.L., 'Topical technics: an engineering notebook', *The Motor*, 116, 9 September 1959, 135; H.F. Ellis, 'M1 for murder', *Punch* of 28 October 1959, 362–3.

57 *Parliamentary Debates, House of Commons*, 'Motorways (traffic regulations)', 592, 23 July 1958, oral answers, cols 402–5; Ministry of Transport and Civil Aviation and the Central Office of Information, *The Motorway Code* (London 1958).

58 Ministry of Transport and Civil Aviation and the Central Office of Information, *The Highway Code Including Motorway Rules* (London 1959).

but how they could ensure that they effectively translated its rules into new modes of conduct and styles of movement. The publication of the paper Highway Code booklet was accompanied by an extensive publicity campaign led by the Ministry of Transport, Central Office of Information and Royal Society for the Prevention of Accidents (RoSPA) which included posters, television and film animations, press releases, bookmarks, pencils, stickers and even adverts on sugar packets.[59] Extracts from the Motorway Code were also reproduced in a large number of guides to the M1 that were distributed by motoring organisations, motor magazines and fuel and tyre companies – including the AA, RAC, Shell, BP, Good-year, and *The Motor* magazine.[60] The RAC's guide was entitled 'Know your Motorway', and like other publications it explained the different forms of knowledge and skill that the motorway driver was required to possess. Drivers were not allowed to stop without due cause, cross the central reservation, or reverse, and they were expected to be fully licensed, to possess an appropriate class of vehicle and to use their mirrors and practise lane discipline.[61] At the opening of the M1, Minister of Transport Ernest Marples insisted that drivers must 'use discipline, common sense and obey the rules',[62] while motoring journalists explained the importance of 'mirror discipline'[63] for drivers, and the necessity of 'a full knowledge at all times of what is going on astern'.[64] Motorway driving was seen to require a very different sense of spatial awareness to ordinary driving, and this spatiality was facilitated by technologies such as wing mirrors and rear-view mirrors which aided the driver in constantly checking the progress and relative position of other vehicles.

Motorway conduct was closely monitored by a range of authorities, from the police and breakdown organisations, to civil servants and scientists working at the Road Research Laboratory. Specially equipped and trained police officers patrolled the M1 from 2 November 1959 onwards, and they were instructed by the Home Office and Ministry of Transport to compile detailed records and statistics on traffic flows, breakdown levels, driving standards and crashes that occurred

---

[59] Automobile Association Archives (AA), Basingstoke, Motorways File, Royal Society for the Prevention of Accidents, 1960, 'Stop Accidents – Honour Your Code', publicity leaflet; P. Merriman, 'Materiality, subjectification and government: the geographies of Britain's Motorway Code', *Environment and Planning D: Society and Space*, 23, 2, 2005, 235–50.

[60] Anonymous, 'Motorway: *The Motor* guide to Britain's first long distance express highway', *The Motor*, 116, 4 November 1959, insert between 508–9.

[61] Ministry of Transport, *The Motorway Code*.

[62] AA Archives, Motorways file, 'Speech of the Rt. Hon. Ernest Marples, Minister of Transport at the opening ceremony of the London-Birmingham Motorway on Monday, November 2nd, at 9.30am', issued with a Ministry of Transport press release, 2 November 1959.

[63] W.A. McKenzie, 'More lane discipline by M1 drivers', *Daily Telegraph* of 4 November 1959.

[64] Anonymous, 'Is your driving advancing? Part 5: on the motorway', *The Autocar*, 111, 6 November 1959, 560–61.

so that politicians and government scientists could assess the performance of the motorway and its users.[65] Motoring organisations such as the AA and RAC operated motorway breakdown patrols which helped stranded motorists, but they also gathered statistics on the performance of Britain's vehicles on this new style of road.

Motorway Popular Cultures

The first motorway users were attracted by the spectacle and excitement of this modern high-speed road with no speed limit, and many of them tested their family saloons and sports cars to their limits. As the national media focused their attention on these exciting new spaces, and increasing numbers of motorists experienced them first hand, so the motorway began to be referenced in all manner of cultural contexts. In 1960 the Ted Taylor Four, a London-based instrumental group, released a seven-inch single entitled 'M1',[66] while the toy companies Marx and Tri-ang both released toy race-car sets with artistic impressions of the new M1 motorway on their covers. Children's authors saw an opportunity to set their latest adventure stories in this exciting new space, with Bruce Carter's *The Motorway Chase* and Robert Martin's *The Mystery of the Motorway* both staging 'racy' adventure stories on and around the motorway. In Bruce Carter's story there is a theft of a Ferrari, a chase, the villain is caught and a hero is born, while in Robert Martin's story a mysterious motorway murder is solved by two teenage boys.[67] In both stories the motorway emerges as a space of masculinity and adventure and as an aspirational space for young boys, and many early advocates and press accounts which feature the M1 construct it as a space for masculine performance.

Motorway driving and masculinity became closely entwined, and the association was not only promoted in children's books and toys but also through advertisements for car accessories and reports about the skill of men driving on the road. When the *Observer* newspaper wanted a report on the performance of the new road, they turned to the quintessentially heroic and masculine figure of the British grand-prix racing driver, employing Ferrari's 27-year-old Tony Brooks to write an article on 'The hazards of M1'.[68] Brooks was a world-class racing-driver who had come second in the 1959 world driver championship, and he had

---

65 Motorway situation reports are held in TNA MT 121/225. See also Merriman, 'Materiality, subjectification and government'; P. Merriman, '"Mirror, signal, manoeuvre": assembling and governing the motorway driver in late fifties Britain', *The Sociological Review*, 54, Supplement 1, 2006, 75–92; Merriman, *Driving Spaces*.

66 D. Burke, 'The Ted Taylor Four story: an interview with Ted Taylor and Bob Rogers', *Pipeline: Instrumental Review*, 12, January 1992, 1–10.

67 B. Carter, *The Motorway Chase* (London 1961); R. Martin, *The Mystery of the Motorway* (London 1961).

68 T. Brooks, 'The hazards of M1', *Observer* of 8 November 1959, 5.

incomparable experience of high-speed driving. The actions of AA patrolmen and motorway policemen, as well as racing drivers and the heroes of children's books, were also frequently discussed in a rather glorified manner, while the first coach journey on the new motorway gave rise to another unexpected hero in the form of a coach driver named Mr Fennel. The first running of Midland Red's new London to Birmingham Motorway Express was widely reported by journalists covering the motorway's opening ceremony, and the unfortunate occurrence of a burst tyre while travelling at high speed on the motorway required the company's experienced driver to save the day: 'Veteran driver Fennel fighting the wheel, forced the 10-ton vehicle on to the safety "hard shoulder" bordering the road'.[69] Mr Fennel was an experienced coach driver who 'coped effectively with a minor crisis', a masculine figure who effectively controlled this high-speed motorway express.[70] Motorway driving and masculinity become entwined in a range of different discourses, and in 1965 the figure of 'motorway man' emerges from another unusual source.

In 1965, British toy manufacturer Pedigree launched a new doll named Paul to be the boyfriend of their successful doll Sindy, who had been launched in September 1963.[71] Paul was a doll who 'likes a good time'; he was described as being 'keen on music and dancing and he and Sindy go to jazz clubs and dances'.[72] When he was launched Paul could be dressed in a number of fashionable and timely outfits reflecting prevailing fashion styles and suggesting activities he might engage in. Paul could be dressed in the fashionable, sharp-suited 'London look', casual jeans and sweater, beach clothes, pyjamas, or an outfit called 'motorway man'. 'Motorway man' carried a flask and was dressed in brown checked trousers, sweater and fur-lined brown driving coat, which cost 25 shillings and 11 pence. 'Motorway man' was a modern man-in-action, a fashionably dressed individual engaged in an exciting, modern past-time: motorway driving.

In many senses, 'motorway man' and Britain's motorway spaces were modern British constructions, but a number of commentators remarked upon the cosmopolitan and European air of these new modernist spaces. In his review of the M1 for the *Observer* newspaper Tony Brooks compared the motorway with other international and cosmopolitan presences in twentieth century England, stating that: 'more than anything – more than Espresso bars, jeans, rock "n" roll, the smell of French cigarettes on the underground, white lipstick – it is of the twentieth century'.[73]

---

69 Anonymous, 'When a tyre bursts on a coach at 70mph', *Daily Express* of 3 November 1959.

70 Anonymous, 'London-Birmingham coach time cut by over two hours', *The Times* of 3 November 1959, 8.

71 C. Mansell, *The History of Sindy: Britain's Top Teenage Doll 1962–1994* (London 1995).

72 The Sindy Set 1965 brochure, cited in: Mansell, *The History of Sindy*, 34.

73 Brooks, 'The hazards of M1', 5.

The M1 had a modernity comparable with fashionable continental European influences or Americanised products, and it was not surprising that the first motorway service areas quickly gained a reputation for being fashionable, modern places to 'hang out'.[74]

The M1's Newport Pagnell service area in Buckinghamshire was operated by Soho café, milk bar and restaurant owner Charles Forte, and motorists from all sectors of society began to frequent its restaurants and cafés.[75] Motorway service areas were exciting and modern for Britain's drivers in the early 1960s, but by the late 1960s the dream had started to fade. Writing in 1968 in *The New Europeans*, author and journalist Anthony Sampson wondered whether Europe's motorway service areas might be the setting for 'a special international motorway life, romantic, seedy, or passionate, like the world of Lolita or The Wild Ones'.[76] The answer was 'no', and during his journeys throughout Europe, he simply found a rather mundane and ubiquitous 'suburban primness':

> All over Western Europe a shiny and uniform superstructure has grown up, of supermarkets, skyscrapers, television towers, motorways. It was the kind of fantasy that post-war children had dreamt of, or glimpsed in Hollywood films. Yet the dream, having come true, had lost its magic; the things turned out to be no more than things, bringing their own problems – motorways brought traffic jams, travel brought tourism, suburbs brought boredom.[77]

Sampson saw Britain and Europe's motorways as one aspect of a rather placeless and ubiquitous modern landscape which was crossing international frontiers, and his remarks predate academic commentaries on the increasing 'placelessness' of modern life and modern landscapes by a decade or more.[78]

Conclusions

The late 1950s and 1960s saw the modernisation of Britain's road and railway networks, but while road modernisation was equated with expansion and

---

74 S. Greaves, 'Motorway nights with the stars', *The Times* of 14 August 1985, 8; D. Lawrence, *Always a Welcome: The Glove Compartment History of the Motorway Service Area* (Twickenham 1999).

75 Greaves, 'Motorway nights with the stars'; C. Forte, *Forte: The Autobiography of Charles Forte* (London 1986).

76 A. Sampson, *The New Europeans* (London 1968/1969), 253.

77 Sampson, *The New Europeans*, viii.

78 E. Relph, *Place and Placelessness* (London 1976); M. Augé, *Non-places* (London 1995); P. Merriman, 'Driving places: Marc Augé, non-places and the geographies of England's M1 motorway', *Theory, Culture, and Society*, 21, 4–5, 2004, 145–67; P. Merriman, 'Marc Augé on space, place and non-place', *Irish Journal of French Studies*, 9, 2009, 9–29.

construction, railway modernisation comprised of rationalisation alongside reconstruction and electrification.[79] In July 1959 the Ministry of Transport released data showing a shift in freight transport from rail to road – with 56 per cent of the nation's freight being transported by road and only 44 per cent by rail[80] – and with increasing numbers of both goods vehicles and private motor vehicles on the nation's roads, road transport came to be seen as the modern mode of short- and middle-distance transport in the post-war decades. By the start of 1960 there were 83 miles (134 kilometres) of motorway in Britain, but this had increased to 672 miles (1,081 kilometres) in 1970 and 1,429 miles (2,299 kilometres) in 1980.[81] Motorways became an accepted part of the British landscape and social and economic life, and in 1968 the M1 even featured in volume five of Samuel E. Ellacott's book, *A History of Everyday Things in England*.[82] Motorways had become ordinary, everyday spaces, but over time they also increasingly came to be depicted as somewhat marginal or dystopian, and at times illicit and edgy, landscapes. In the 1970s, motorways served as the settings for a number of fictional sexualised encounters and dystopian futures,[83] while from the mid-1960s community groups and environmental organisations started to criticise the planning and construction of motorways, particularly in urban areas.[84] Changing attitudes to Britain's motorways appear to mirror broader shifts in the post-war world, from the widespread embrace of reconstruction discourses and modern planning, architecture and design, to concerns about the undemocratic role of the planning process, the effects of motorways on local residents and concerns about the environmental consequences of car travel.[85] While these contexts are clearly important, this chapter suggests that we must not forget that the idea of the motorway has a much longer history in Britain, for just a few years after the first motorcars appeared, proposals emerged for private toll motorways that would separate long-distance, high-speed motor traffic from non-motorised traffic on ordinary roads.

---

79 British Transport Commission, *Modernisation and Re-Equipment of British Railways* (London 1955); British Railways Board, *The Reshaping of British Railways*, part 1: *Report* (London 1963).

80 M. MacEwen, 'Motropolis: a study of the traffic problem. Can we get out of the jam?' *The Architects' Journal*, 130, 1959, 254–75, here 258.

81 G. Charlesworth, *A History of British Motorways* (London 1984), 95.

82 S.E. Ellacott, *A History of Everyday Things in England*, vol. V: *1914–1968* (London 1968), 179.

83 J.G. Ballard, *The Atrocity Exhibition* (London 1970); J.G. Ballard, *Crash* (London 1973); J.G. Ballard, *Concrete Island* (London 1974); P. Nichols, *The Freeway: A Play in Two Acts* (London 1975); P. Enefer, *Girl on the M6* (London 1973); T. Hoyle, *The Man who Travelled on Motorways* (London 1979).

84 J. Tyme, *Motorways Versus Democracy* (London 1978); D. Starkie, *The Motorway Age* (Oxford 1982).

85 Merriman, *Driving Spaces*.

References

a) Anonymous articles, author not known

'5,000 cars an hour on motorway', *The Times* of 9 November 1959, 10.
'Breakdown rush on M1', *Birmingham Mail* of 2 November 1959.
British Road Federation, ed., *Motorways Tour 1955: Holland, Belgium, Germany* (London 1955).
'Demand for modern motor roads – a new organisation', *The Times* of 18 November 1938, 18.
'Difference on motorway – county wanted full drainage', *The Times* of 6 February 1959, 8.
'Discussion on the London-Birmingham motorway', *Proceedings of the Institution of Civil Engineers*, 19, May–August 1961, 61–119.
'German motor roads – British delegation in Berlin', *The Times* of 27 September 1937, 14.
'Is this the phantom van on the M1?', *News Chronicle* of 21 June 1960, 13.
'Is your driving advancing? Part 5: on the motorway', *The Autocar*, 111, 6 November 1959, 560–61.
'London-Birmingham coach time cut by over two hours', *The Times* of 3 November 1959, 8.
'Minister "appalled" by new motorway driving', *The Times* of 3 November 1959, 8.
'Motorway "hard shoulder" slips', *The Times* of 4 November 1959, 9.
'Motorway code', *Chronicle and Echo* of 26 November 1958.
'Motorway: *The Motor* guide to Britain's first long distance express highway', *The Motor*, 116, 4 November 1959, insert between 508–9.
'Motorway in use', *The Motor*, 116, 11 November 1959, 518.
'Motorways and vehicle design', *The Engineer*, 208, 13 November 1959, 583–4.
'Motorways Tour 1955', *Bulletin of the British Road Federation*, 1955, 1.
'New motorway closed after 47 days – surface cracked by frost – better drains to be built', *The Times* of 22 January 1959, 10.
'Roads in Sweden', *Roads and Road Construction* of 24 December 1946, 405–8.
'The phantom of the M1', *Daily Express* of 21 June 1960, 13.
'Trips to see motorway', *The Times* of 6 November 1959, 6.
'Western Europe's 2500 miles of motorways', *The Times* of 2 November 1959, 19.
'When a tyre bursts on a coach at 70mph', *Daily Express* of 3 November 1959.

b) Named articles and monographs

Abercrombie, P., *Greater London Plan 1944* (London 1945).
Adams, W.F., 'Safety aspects of motorway design', *Traffic Engineering and Control*, 3, 1961, 178–81.
Augé, M., *Non-places* (London 1995).

Ballard, J.G., *The Atrocity Exhibition* (London 1970).
Ballard, J.G., *Crash* (London 1973).
Ballard, J.G., *Concrete Island* (London 1974).
Banham, R., 'The road to ubiquopolis', *New Statesman*, 59, 1960, 784 and 786.
Banham, R., 'New way north', *New Society*, 20, 4 May 1972, 241–3.
Betjeman, J., 'Men and buildings: style on road and rail', *Daily Telegraph and Morning Post* of 27 June 1960, 15.
British Railways Board, *The Reshaping of British Railways*, part 1: *Report* (London 1963).
British Road Federation, *A Statement by the British Road Federation Supplemental to the Case of Trade and Industry Against What is Known as "The Salter Report"* (London 1933).
British Road Federation, *The Motor Industry and the Salter Report* (London 1933).
British Road Federation, *Roads, Railways and Restrictions* (London 1933), 14.
British Road Federation, *Get a Move On* (London 1937).
British Road Federation, *National Motor Roads* (London 1937).
British Road Federation, *New Roads or Old?* (London 1937).
British Road Federation, *The Crisis and the Roads* (London 1938).
British Road Federation, *The Spectre of Monopoly* (London 1938).
British Road Federation, *From Here to There* (London 1939).
British Road Federation, *Roads and Road Transport: Reconstruction of Roads and Development of Road Transport* (London 1944).
British Road Federation, *The Case for Motorways* (London 1948).
British Road Federation, *The Case for Motorways*, 2nd ed. (London 1949).
British Road Federation, *Memorandum on Roads and National Defence* (London 1951).
British Road Federation, *South Wales Roads* (London 1951).
British Road Federation, *New Roads for Lancashire* (London 1952).
British Transport Commission, *Modernisation and Re-Equipment of British Railways* (London 1955).
Brooks, T., 'The hazards of M1', *Observer* of 8 November 1959, 5.
Brunner, C.T., *The Road Way to Recovery* (London 1948).
Burke, D., 'The Ted Taylor Four story: an interview with Ted Taylor and Bob Rogers', *Pipeline: Instrumental Review* of 12, January 1992, 1–10.
Carter, B., *The Motorway Chase* (London 1961).
Charlesworth, G., *A History of British Motorways* (London 1984).
Clements, R.G.H., *The System of Motor Roads in Germany: A Record of Facts and of Technical Details* (London 1937).
Colvin, B., 'The London-Birmingham motorway: a new look at the English landscape', *The Geographical Magazine*, 32, 1959, 239–46.
Crowe, S., *The Landscape of Roads* (London 1960).
Ellacott, S.E., *A History of Everyday Things in England*, vol. V: *1914–1968* (London 1968).
Ellis, H.F., 'M1 for murder', *Punch* of 28 October 1959, 362–3.

Enefer, P., *Girl on the M6* (London 1973).

Forshaw, J.H., and Abercrombie, P., *County of London Plan* (London 1943).

Forte, C., *Forte: The Autobiography of Charles Forte* (London 1986).

German Roads Delegation, ed., *Report Upon the Visit of Inspection and its Conclusions* (London 1938).

Greaves, S., 'Motorway nights with the stars', *The Times* of 14 August 1985, 8.

Hoyle, T., *The Man who Travelled on Motorways* (London 1979).

Institution of Civil Engineers, *Post-War National Development Report No. III: Public Works* (London 1942).

Institution of Highway Engineers, *The Post-War Development of Highways* (London 1943).

Institution of Municipal and County Engineers, *Post-War Planning and Reconstruction* (London 1942).

Jeffreys, W.R., *The King's Highway: An Historical and Autobiographical Record of the Developments of the Past Sixty Years* (London 1949).

Joint Committee of the British Road Federation, The Institution of Highway Engineers and The Society of Motor Manufacturers & Traders, *Economics of Motorways. Report presented to the Minister of Transport on 18 October 1948* (London 1948).

L., J., 'Topical technics: an engineering notebook', *The Motor*, 116, 9 September 1959, 135.

Law, M.J., 'Turning night into day: transgression and Americanization at the English inter-war roadhouse', *Journal of Historical Geography*, 35, 2009, 473–94.

Law, M.J., '"Stopping to dream": the beautification and vandalism of London's interwar arterial roads', *The London Journal*, 35, 2010, 58–84.

Lawrence, D., *Always a Welcome: The Glove Compartment History of the Motorway Service Area* (Twickenham 1999).

Lloyd, T.I., 'Potentialities of the British Railways' system as a reserved roadway system', *Proceedings of The Institution of Civil Engineers*, 4, 1, 1955, 732–88.

Lloyd, T.I., *Twilight of the Railways – What Roads They'll Make! Railway Conversion as the Cure for Britain's Transport Troubles* (London 1957).

London Regional Reconstruction Committee of the Royal Institute of British Architects, *Greater London: Towards a Master Plan. Second Interim Report – May 1943* (London 1943).

MacEwen, M., 'Motropolis: a study of the traffic problem. Can we get out of the jam?' *The Architects' Journal*, 130, 1959, 254–75.

Mansell, C., *The History of Sindy: Britain's Top Teenage Doll 1962–1994* (London 1995).

Martin, R., *The Mystery of the Motorway* (London 1961).

McKenzie, W.A., 'More lane discipline by M1 drivers', *Daily Telegraph* of 4 November 1959.

McKenzie, W.A., 'Motoring: shedding light all along the motorways', *Daily Telegraph and Morning Post* of 25 November 1959, 13.

Merriman, P., '"A power for good or evil": geographies of the M1 in late-fifties Britain', in D. Gilbert, D. Matless and B. Short, eds, *Geographies of British Modernity: Space and Society in the Twentieth Century* (Oxford 2003), 115–31.

Merriman, P., 'Driving places: Marc Augé, non-places and the geographies of England's M1 motorway', *Theory, Culture, and Society*, 21, 4–5, 2004, 145–67.

Merriman, P., 'Materiality, subjectification and government: the geographies of Britain's Motorway Code', *Environment and Planning D: Society and Space*, 23, 2, 2005, 235–50.

Merriman, P., '"A new look at the English landscape": landscape architecture, movement and the aesthetics of motorways in early post-war Britain', *Cultural Geographies*, 13, 2006, 78–105.

Merriman, P., '"Mirror, signal, manoeuvre": assembling and governing the motorway driver in late fifties Britain', *The Sociological Review*, 54, Supplement 1, 2006, 75–92.

Merriman, P., *Driving Spaces: A Cultural-historical Geography of England's M1 Motorway* (Oxford 2007).

Merriman, P., 'Marc Augé on space, place and non-place', *Irish Journal of French Studies*, 9, 2009, 9–29.

Merriman, P., 'Britain and "the motorway club": the effect of European and North American motorway construction on attitudes in Britain, 1930–1960', *Transfers: Interdisciplinary Journal of Mobility Studies*, 2, 1, 2012, 106–33.

Ministry of Transport and Civil Aviation and the Central Office of Information, *The Motorway Code* (London 1958).

Ministry of Transport and Civil Aviation and the Central Office of Information, *The Highway Code Including Motorway Rules* (London 1959).

Montagu of Beaulieu, J., 'Editorial jottings: London to Birmingham by motor road', *The Car (Illustrated)*, 2, 20, 8 October 1902, 211.

Montagu of Beaulieu, J., 'Motor roads will be opposed', *The Motor Car Magazine*, 1, 2, 1903, 133.

Montagu of Beaulieu, Lord, 'Foreword', in Northern and Western Motorway, *Northern and Western Motorway: Direct Lines of Communication Between the Largest Cities and Business Centres of the Country* (London 1923), 3–6.

Montagu of Beaulieu, Lord, 'The railways and the motorway: a reply (letter, Daily Mail, 30 October 1923)', in Northern and Western Motorway, *Northern and Western Motorway: Providing Direct Lines of Fast and Cheap Communication by Road Between the Largest Cities and Business Centres of the Country* [revised and extended edition] (London 1923), 49–51.

Montagu of Beaulieu, Lord, 'To the editor of The Manchester Guardian (letter, 6 November 1923)', in Northern and Western Motorway, *Northern and Western Motorway*, 42–3.

Nairn, I., 'Look out', *The Architectural Review*, 133, 1963, 425–6.

Newby, R.F., and Johnson, H.D., 'London-Birmingham motorway accidents', *Traffic Engineering and Control*, 4, 1963, 550–55.

Nichols, P., *The Freeway: A Play in Two Acts* (London 1975).

Northern and Western Motorway, *Northern and Western Motorway: Direct Lines of Communication Between the Largest Cities and Business Centres of the Country* (London 1923).

Pevsner, N., *Buckinghamshire* (Harmondsworth 1960).

Plowden, W., 'MPs and the "roads lobby"', in A. Barker and M. Rush, eds, *The Member of Parliament and His Information* (London 1970), 69–96.

Railway Conversion League, *No Alternative! The Case for Transforming Britain's Railways into Motor Roads. Submitted to the Ministry of Transport, July 1965* (London 1965).

Railway Conversion League, *A Survey of Railway Conversion in Great Britain and Northern Ireland* (London 1969).

Relph, E., *Place and Placelessness* (London 1976).

Rose, M.V., 'After 11 months of M1: good motorway driving rules are still flouted', *Birmingham Post* of 19 October 1960.

Royal Automobile Club, *Know Your Motorway* (London 1959).

Sampson, A., *The New Europeans* (London 1968/1969).

Select Committee of the House of Lords on the Prevention of Road Accidents, *Report (H.L. 192)* (London 1938).

Select Committee of the House of Lords on the Prevention of Road Accidents, *Report (H.L. 2, 52)* (London 1939).

Sir Owen Williams and Partners, *London Yorkshire Motorway: South of Luton-Watford Gap-Dunchurch Special Road. Report on Widening and Reconstruction of Grass Hard Shoulders, 12th September 1960–21st May 1961* (Birmingham 1961).

Standing Joint Committee of the RAC, AA and RSAC, *Post-War Roads and Traffic: A Memorandum* (London 1944).

Starkie, D., *The Motorway Age* (Oxford 1982).

Thwaite, B.H., 'Motor-car ways', *The Car (Illustrated)*, 2, 20, 8 October 1902, 218.

Thwaite, B.H., 'Why not a motor-car way through England?', *The Nineteenth Century*, 52, (306), 1902, 305–8.

Tyme, J., *Motorways Versus Democracy* (London 1978).

Withrington, P., 'Reigniting the railway conversion debate', *Economic Affairs*, 24, 2, 2004, 56–9.

Wolmer, Lord, 'Motor roads in Germany – Impressions of a tour – a profitable example', *The Times* of 7 October 1937, 15–16.

Chapter 13
The Metamorphosis of Public Transport Services in the Paris Region: the Modal and Moral Victory of 'Automobilism' in the 1920s and 1930s

Mathieu Flonneau

This chapter aims to highlight the socioeconomic process of the automobilisation of the public transport system in France. Based on new public and corporate sources, it focuses on the substitution of the automobile for (other) collective modes of transport in the Paris region.[1] The temporary end of tramway services before the Second World War is explained through an analysis of the success of the automobile. We adopt a multi-scale point of view and a multimodal perspective in order to understand how the modern French capital was developed around the automobile system before the post-war boom of the *Trente Glorieuses*, the prosperous years in France between 1945 and 1975.

This contribution aims to shed light on the changes to Paris' ground transport system during the interwar period. Archives held at the media library of the Autonomous Operator of Parisian Transports (*Régie Autonome des Transports Parisiens*, RATP) provided the corpus for an analysis of changes in public transport during this pivotal time. The management was Kafkaesque, but this period offers evidence of the first efforts to unify and direct public transport networks.[2] In this context, we propose a second interpretation to replace the oversimplified conventional explanation of the end of streetcars in Paris and the suburbs. Sources held at the Paris police headquarters and the Paris City Council disprove the accusation that the automobile and its supposed 'lobby' were solely responsible for the disappearance of streetcars as a means of transport.[3]

---

[1] In this article, following French convention, the term 'automobile' is used to include all self-propelled vehicles that use the street, that is, cars and buses.

[2] Dominique Larroque, Michel Margairaz and Pierre Zembri, *Paris et ses transports, XIXe-XXe siècles. Deux siècles de décisions pour la ville et sa région* (Paris 2002).

[3] I have drawn on parts of my doctoral thesis defended at the Sorbonne on 5 January 2002, *The Automobile in the Conquest of Paris, 1910–1977. Urban Forms, the Political Arena and Representations*, 3 vols, University Paris I – Panthéon-Sorbonne, doctoral thesis 2002. For more on the context, see Mathieu Flonneau, *Paris et l'automobile. Un siècle de*

History and Retrospective Theory of the Plot Against the Streetcar

Who killed the streetcar in Paris and the Paris region? In the spirit of technology theorist Bruno Latour's analysis of the drama surrounding the never-completed Aramis project (a personal rapid transit or podcar system that the RATP tested experimentally in the 1970s and 1980s), we would like to argue that there has been both a false irony and a false teleology attached to this story.[4] Unfortunately, the return of the tramway to the Paris region and Paris itself since 1990 'allows some people, using approximate reasoning tinged with historicism, to stigmatise the automobile solution adopted during the 1930s'.[5] The predominant tone adopted is one of denunciation of the biased and short-sighted stupidity of a technocratic structure that was promoted by a lobby.

The interpretation that we propose shifts away from that. It is based on a dynamic perspective and on multiple sources, including the archives of the Society of Public Transportation in the Paris Region (*Société des Transports en Commun de la Région Parisienne*, STCRP). It disproves the accusation articulated by the legendary demographer and economist Alfred Sauvy in his 1968 essay on the automobile, 'The Four Wheels of Fortune'.[6] According to Sauvy, the automobile's victory owed everything to the 'the road, tyre and oil lobby', and occurred through an 'immense hoodwinking of public opinion'.[7]

As the reader will see, this chapter proposes a very different analysis, and endeavours to reconstruct and date the rationale of the process. On this basis, three coherent periods can be distinguished: 1) the automobile's 'raid' on its modal competitor; 2) the reaction of public transport; and finally 3) the logical disappearance of streetcars from the Parisian and suburban network. Between representations of technical determinism and the social construction of their

passions (Paris 2005). This text provides revised arguments already published in French: Mathieu Flonneau, 'La concurrence tramway-automobile au cours de l'entre-deux-guerres à Paris. Pour une relecture des représentations liées à la disparition des chemins de fer urbain', *Revue d'histoire des chemins de fer*, 18, no. 36–7, Spring–Autumn 2007, 279–303. My contribution to Christophe Ramage's film 'Un tramway dans la tête: l'Arpajonnais, 1893–1936', video documentary (Paris 2010) helped round out this analysis. On the bus networks see the recent study of Arnaud Passalacqua, 'Bus and Paris: Flexibility, Public Place and Mobility from the 1900s to 1970s', doctoral thesis defended at University Paris VII – Denis-Diderot, 2009. Parts of this thesis are published in Economica, ed., *Le bus et Paris. Une histoire de mobilité* (Paris 2011). On this chapter's precise focus, see Jean-Marc Offner, 'La disparition des tramways en France', *Revue de l'Association française des amis des chemins de fer*, 388, 1988, 6–10.

4 Bruno Latour, *Aramis ou l'amour des techniques* (Paris 1992).

5 After returning to the suburbs at the beginning of the 1990s, in December 2006 the tramway line along Paris's southern boulevards des Maréchaux was inaugurated.

6 Alfred Sauvy, *Les 4 roues de la fortune* (Paris 1968).

7 Alfred Sauvy, *Mythologies de notre temps* (Paris 1965), chapter XIV: L'automobile, 170–81.

'cycle' or their 'defeat', the interactions among the total Paris traffic, the streetcars and the suburbanites ultimately appear more complex than has been conventionally believed.

The Automobile's 'Raid' on Modal Competition after the First World War

Between the wars, the evolution of Parisian automobile traffic took place against a background of increased mobility using all means of transport within the region. According to the few available surveys, the transformation in commuting (also termed 'daily migrations') in the Paris region was spectacular during this period.

The daily commutes, that is, journeys between places of residence and places of work, were almost exclusively between Paris and its suburbs in the Seine Department. Their numbers rose from about 100,000 in 1901 to 308,000 in 1921 and 448,000 in 1926. They peaked at 572,000 in 1931. In 1936, as all traffic counts show, the total number of commutes had plunged to 372,000.[8]

The subway, which did not to go beyond the city limits of Paris *intra muros* (that is, the area of the 20 Parisian *arrondissements*), could only provide one leg of these commutes, and was supplemented with surface transport by public or private means.[9] The automobile as a stand-alone mode also contributed to this trend – modestly at first, then more significantly (although the available data make it very difficult to quantify automobile traffic in the early stages). The automobile began to disrupt the traditional paradigm of the industrial city that Paris was in part. The city planners' idea to segregate and partition the Paris area was breaking down. Until about 1930, residents appeared to have perceived the western side of the city as more 'residential' and the eastern side as more 'industrial'. Over the long term, proximity between housing and the workplace, while not universal, was

[8] See Louis Bonnier, 'Cartes isochrones de l'agglomération parisienne', *La vie urbaine*, no. 3, 1919, 245–50, and Henri Bunle, 'Migrations alternantes dans la région parisienne', *Annuaire statistique général de la France, juillet-septembre 1932*, in Jacqueline Beaujeu-Garnier and Jean Bastié, *Atlas de Paris et de la région parisienne* (Paris 1967), 245–50.

[9] See Alain Cottereau, 'L'apparition de l'urbanisme comme action collective: l'agglomération parisienne au début du siècle', *Sociologie du travail*, no. 2, 1969, 342–65; Alain Cottereau, 'Les débuts de planification urbaine en France: le métro et les mouvements municipaux', *Sociologie du travail*, 12, 1–2, 1970, 362–92; Alain Cottereau, 'Les origines de la planification urbaine en France: le métro et les mouvements municipaux', in *Politiques urbaines et planification des villes*, colloque de Dieppe, 8–10 April 1974 (Paris 1974), 767–93, and Alain Cottereau, 'Les batailles du métropolitain: La compagnie du chemin de fer du Nord et les choix d'urbanisation', in Sheila Hallsted-Baumert, ed., *Métro-Cité: le Chemin de fer métropolitain à la conquête de Paris, 1871–1945*, under the direction of Francois Gasnault and Henri Zuber (Paris 1997), 75–84.

nevertheless a decisive factor underpinning a degree of integration between the worker and his district, and between the worker and the city.[10]

Despite the remarkable facts that this study has revealed regarding the broader and more democratic use of the automobile, we must make one remark: although it was rapidly gaining ground, the automobile was still confined to niches. To see a typical picture of the daily commute in the early 1930s, we must rely on Jules Romains' description:

> (The metro platforms of) Javel and Billancourt fetch workers out of their beds in Belleville, Plaine-Saint-Denis, Kremlin-Bicêtre. … The worker of October 1933, on his way to work, is likely to be a man standing, packed tightly among many others, on the platform of a suburban streetcar.[11]

Thus, the victory of the automobile must not be projected too far into the past, although obviously, the game was more open and the cards reshuffled after the First World War. However, one fact seems certain during this period: wherever collective transport was inadequate, the automobile in the form of the private motorcar (even if used as a collective means of transport) established itself strongly in the everyday life of the region.

The Delicate Merging of Public Transport with General Traffic: Joint Victories for the Bus and the *Système Automobile*

Faced with unprecedented demographic changes creating new mobility needs for a population – especially in the suburbs – which doubled from one million in 1900 to two million in 1935, and in the midst of unexpected competition from the automobile, decision-makers began to redefine the operating conditions of the Paris public transport system.[12] In so doing, they gave legal backing to the notion

---

10 See Alain Faure, 'Les déplacements de travail entre Paris et sa banlieue (1880–1914): première approche', *Villes en parallèle*, 10, June 1986, 233–48, and Alain Faure, '"Nous travaillons dix heures par jour plus le chemin", les déplacements de travail chez les ouvriers parisiens, 1880–1914', in Susanna Magri and Christian Topalov, eds, *Villes ouvrières* (Paris 1989), 93–107.

11 Jules Romains, *Paris des hommes de bonne volonté* (Paris 1949), and Jules Romains 'Par un joli matin, Paris descend au travail', in Jules Romains, Lise Romains and Pierre Belvès, eds, *Paris des hommes de bonne volonté* (Paris 1949), 110. See also Alain Faure, 'A l'aube des transports de masse. L'exemple des "trains ouvriers" de la banlieue de Paris, 1883–1914', *Revue d'Histoire Moderne et Contemporaine*, 40, no. 2, April–June 1993, 228–55.

12 See Charles Cheape, *Moving the Masses: Urban Public Transportation in New York, Boston and Philadelphia, 1880–1912* (Cambridge, MA, 1980); Sheila Hallsted-Baumert, 'Le Métropolitain: technologie, espace et création d'identités urbaine dans le Paris de fin du siècle', L'École des Hautes Études en Sciences Sociales (EHESS) and New York

of public transport as a public service, formulating their own responsibilities more clearly than ever before. As a result of the simultaneous implementation of several transport policies, public transport in the early 1920s was 'chaotic and old-fashioned'.[13] Numerous inconsistencies in the service provided were caused by partial overlaps between the networks of the dozen private companies dominating the passenger transport market. Hence the decision in September 1920 to lease operating rights for the Paris public transport system to a single operator, the STCRP.

Initially, the concession stemmed from a desire to require a uniform level of service for the entire capital, including maintaining routes that were unprofitable. Naturally, the STCRP, concerned about its profits, was not happy about this. The difficult topic was brought up in the meetings of the City Council, mainly during sessions of the Second Commission on Public Transport (*2e Commission en charge des transports publics*). The first and most complete attempt at transforming a public utility into a governmental department had a painful birth.[14]

The minutes of a meeting held on 24 January 1930 offer a good illustration of the frequent skirmishes between the STCRP's directors and local councillors from the suburbs. The company's directors asked for certain 'parasitic' lines to be shut down, given their poor earnings, and appealed for the 'electoral self-sacrifice of councillors'. They timidly proposed 'reduced lines', with service reduced to the minimum and designed to feed into the more profitable routes. On the other side of the table, one of the elected representatives, Louis Gélis, a city councillor from the 13th Arrondissement of Paris, declared that 'every time [he had] asked for something from the STCRP, he had not received satisfaction'. He argued that 'just because a line is a net financial loss does not mean it's useless' and added, 'if I were a city councillor for the 3rd or 4th Arrondissement, I could find not three or four million francs' worth of savings, but 35 or 40 million'.[15]

In the suburbs, the 'number of lines is completely below what would be needed', Gélis went on, noting that 'only one line exists in the Quartier de la Gare for 60,000 residents'.[16] He concluded that the STCRP had a job to accomplish without necessarily making a profit. This stance was indirectly supported during

University, doctoral thesis, 1999; and Winstan Bond and Colin Divall, eds, *Suburbanizing the Masses. Public Transport and Urban Development in Historical Perspective* (Aldershot 2003).

13 Maurice Daumas, ed., *Analyse historique de l'évolution des transports en commun dans la région parisienne de 1855 à 1939* (Paris 1977), 9.

14 Georges Delavenne, 'La réorganisation des transports en commun du Département de la Seine dans ses rapports avec le plan d'aménagement de Paris', in Société Française des Urbanistes, ed., *Où en est l'urbanisme, en France et à l'étranger, actes du congrès de Strasbourg 1923* (Paris 1923), 381–94, here 383.

15 Archives of the RATP (ARATP), 1R334, 'résultats d'exploitation' (operating results).

16 Located within the 13th Arrondissement, the Quartier de la Gare is the 50th administrative quarter of Paris.

the same session by Léon Riotor, an elected representative from the Saint-Gervais district in the 4th arrondissement, who asked for a clear distinction to be made between 'parasitic' and 'money-losing' lines, with the former purely and simply harmful to the fluidity of general traffic in the city centre, while the former could nevertheless have their usefulness.

The debates held that year were of great importance because the STCRP was gambling on nothing less than the renewal of its contract; every six years the Department had the right to terminate the concession upon giving two years' advance notice. At the request of Louis Sellier, a Socialist elected representative from Suresnes who was in favour of withdrawing the concession, the operating conditions were closely reviewed and reforms were proposed in line with the recommendations of a report drafted in 1927 by Émile Jayot, the Deputy Chief Executive Officer of the STCRP.[17] The first chapter of the new specifications for streetcars and local trains stipulated: 'The Department expressly prohibits, without the Society's being able to refuse, any modification of the services, in particular the routes'.[18]

In the company's defence, and in order to obtain a renewal of the concession, André Mariage, who sat on the STCRP's board, cited all the improvements made compared with the pre-war years. According to him, the automobile (that is, including buses) played a significant role, in several respects.

Table 13.1 Number of STCRP buses in service on the surface network

Year	Number of buses
1921	941
1922	1,041
1923	1,238
1924	1,283
1925	1,296
1926	1,315
1927	1,358
1928	1,376
1929	1,468
1930	1,642
1931	1,942

Source: Annuaire statistique de la Ville de Paris, Imprimerie municipale, 1932.

17 Comité Consultatif des Transports en Commun à la Surface de la Région Parisienne, ed., *Rapport sur la réorganisation des services de transports*, presented by Émile Jayot (Paris 1927).

18 Ibid., Article 3.

First and foremost, Mariage claimed that this promotion of the (collective) automobile was a sure indicator of the company's modernisation. Developing this point, he pointed to the increasing number of STCRP buses in service and equipped with pneumatic tyres, following the famous 'pig advertisement campaign' (*campagne des cochons*) by the tyre maker Michelin in 1924.[19] Mariage also touted the increased standardisation of road and rail fleets. He went on to say that whereas in 1920, streetcars had used 50 types of motors and 40 types of couplings, by 1928, these figures had been reduced to 30 and 20, respectively. Nevertheless, this lack of standardisation, while less marked for buses, was still substantial – a consequence of the multitude of workshops and warehouses, where maintenance could not be optimised. Further rationalisation led to the number of workshops and warehouses being nearly halved during the interwar period, from 40 to 21.[20]

However, what André Mariage omitted to tell his audience – and what everyone knew – was that the improvements to the streetcar fleet had not coincided with an increase in the volume of passengers, which had stagnated at around one billion per year. Indeed, beginning in 1929 the number of passengers travelling by streetcar began to decline steadily following a peak during the Roaring Twenties, until it disappeared with the closure of all tram routes in 1937–38. Conversely, in the interwar period, bus traffic increased continuously. However the nearly threefold increase in bus carryings is proof only of the delayed transfer of passengers from trams, and not of the development of a new market. On the contrary, total volumes carried by road-based public transport constantly decreased from 1931, and particularly after 1937 (although this was an exceptional year, in which the Paris Exposition was held); the network reached its maximum extent in the same year. This decline cannot be attributed to the métro's rise, as métro passenger traffic also stagnated after 1931, only to take off again during the exceptional circumstances of the German Occupation. It was rather the result of the economic crisis, as well as of traffic congestion. Indeed, in the reports on the STCRP's operations, the private automobile was always lurking in the background as a rival to public transport – namely, the motorcar and taxis. On this point, in a report from 1938, André Mariage explained changes in the STCRP's network by citing the

---

19 See René Bellu, *Les autobus parisiens, des origines à nos jours* (Paris 1973). Jean-Paul Machuré and Philippe Vielliard note a proposal from Maurice Levillain: 'Sur l'équipement en pneumatiques des 90 châssis d'autobus nouvellement achetés par le Département et sur les progrès du pneumatique sur poids lourds'. See Jean-Paul Machuré and Philippe Vielliard, *Autobus de Paris* (Paris 1999). See also Mairie de Paris, ed., *Bulletin municipal officiel rapports et documents* (Paris 1928). The pig advertising campaign featured posters showing Parisians climbing on a bus with solid tyres and pigs being driven onto a bus with pneumatic tyres. Bibendum, the Michelin Man, an anthropomorphic figure made of pneumatic tyres, says, 'Parisians! A scandal: pigs traveling on pneumatic tyres, and you on solid ones! Insist on the same treatment!'

20 Noëlle Gerome, *Histoire d'un dépôt d'autobus en banlieue, le dépôt Floréal aux Lilas RATP, Réseau 2000, mai 1987* (Paris 1987).

'requirements of general traffic in Paris', which we can translate as the growing impact of the private automobile.[21]

The coexistence of cars and public transport became hugely problematic. Beginning in 1927, Émile Jayot had noted this worry in presenting his report: 'Paris suffers from another evil: the difficulties of traffic due to the development of the motor car'.[22] The increasing pressure of cars caused considerable disruption to the STCRP's operations and almost marginalised the improvements planned by the company because its vehicles were using roads that were 'swamped' or 'drowned', depending on the metaphor that one chose. Therefore in 1938, faced with serious difficulties in maintaining timetables in some parts of the capital, and following a survey of drivers, the company returned to the Seine Prefecture to request changes to road layouts.[23] All in all, 58 'problematic points' were listed, locations where congestion was particularly acute. For each of these, solutions were suggested, ranging from setting up new road markings to demolishing buildings; for instance at the crossroads of Rue de Turenne and Rue Saint-Antoine.[24]

Another difficulty apparently lay in the new equipment used by the STCRP. In a letter dated 10 March 1938 and addressed to the director of the *Plan de Paris* organisation, the company noted that it was regrettably unable to use its new streetcars on certain routes, the O-line in particular. Expropriation of land was even suggested to facilitate any necessary alterations. The difficulties to establish turning points at their routes were blamed on the 'current state of manufacturing' and were taken very seriously by the officials of the Plan of the Seine Prefecture, up to the highest echelons of the administration of the Works of Paris, which showed a certain degree of impatience: 'This business is very unusual. It would have been preferable to adapt streetcars to the crossroads rather than vice versa. Be that as it may, it is obviously necessary to give satisfaction as soon as possible. But do not neglect the safety of pedestrians by excessively reducing the width of pavements'.[25]

The physical adaptation of the city, desired by some, would not take place at any cost, and the debate proceeded very pragmatically. The private automobile's conquest of the city, if it were to take place, would be achieved step by step. *The Echo of the STCRP*, the company's staff newsletter published from 1929 until 1932, reported on this general deterioration in traffic conditions. In technical articles, including one in December 1932 on 'the traffic capacity of the roadway',

---

21 ARATP, 1R348, note dated 8 April 1938, 'les transports en commun de la région parisienne'.

22 Comité Consultatif des Transports en Commun à la Surface de la Région Parisienne, *Rapport sur la réorganisation.*

23 ARATP, 1R183, file 'Proposition d'amélioration des carrefours présentant des difficultés au passage des omnibus automobiles'.

24 Unsurprisingly, most of them were located in the inner loop of the city.

25 Archives de la Voirie de Paris (Paris Roadway Archives). This is a note from Giraud, head of works in Paris, 29 April 1939.

or further in a series of articles published in several issues in 1931 and 1932 on 'the problem of traffic', this high-quality publication recorded the real working conditions and the fight for space on Paris' streets.

The arguments put forward in *The Echo of the STCRP* were not limited to Paris alone. In an article entitled 'Glances Westward', on transport in the United States during the economic crisis, the newsletter reported on a trip by the company's chapter of *Croix de Guerre* recipients (that is, decorated war veterans), who visited New York, Philadelphia, Louisville (Kentucky), Washington DC and Lafayette (Indiana). These experiences were described by one M. Looten, an operating control engineer at the STCRP. With the approval of the general management, they provided material for rethinking the company's set-up. At the same time, another view of the private automobile had been brought back from America: more a part of daily life, certainly, and more accessible, the American automobile model was the subject of fascination and desire – even, revealingly, for these public transport professionals.

'Air!': the Space Carved Out for the Automobile in the Name of 'Public Interest' and the Natural Decline of the Streetcar[26]

Nevertheless, the questions of congestion remained unresolved. There were some projects to adapt streets, and some revolutionary plans – such as Le Corbusier's far too ambitious and provocative Voisin Plan – but the solution had to be found elsewhere. On a minor note, city councillor Émile Massard, omnipresent on traffic issues in Paris, came out in favour of urban reform in 1928 when he issued this appeal: 'Everything has been done with regard to the major principal measures for safety and ease of movement. But these improvements are lost every day in the rising flood of new cars. At this very moment, Paris is suffocating. … at all costs, we need air and space'.[27]

Elected officials from across the political spectrum initially thought that this space could be found easily, for the benefit of all, by sacrificing another means of transport that had practically no defenders – the streetcar. This point is worth highlighting, because with the modern tramway currently enjoying a spectacular resurrection in French cities, the nature of the debate appears to have changed profoundly. The modern tramway, along with the trolleybus, benefits from a new technological cycle in which its one-time disadvantages are now seen as benefits. Ultimately, the least suitable selling point today is nostalgia for the streetcar of

---

26 Abdelfattah el Kassab, 'Les déterminants techniques, économiques et politiques du démantèlement des tramways dans la région parisienne (Contribution à l'analyse des conditions du démantèlement des tramways dans la région parisienne)', University Paris – XII, doctoral thesis for engineering, 1986.

27 Émile Massard, 'Conclusion', in Mairie de Paris, ed., *Bulletin municipal officiel*, report no. 93 (Paris 1928), 97.

the past, a rose-tinted view, with history accommodatingly rewritten to adorn the streetcar with all the virtues it is given in current public discourse. In reality, by the end of the 1920s, the overwhelming majority of contemporaries no longer supported the streetcar.

The descendants of 'the American' (as the streetcar was known in France) experimented during the interwar period with systems powered by steam, by compressed air and by electricity, but these were anachronistic and poorly received. Hence, the streetcar's domination was disputed, even among the most relentless defenders of public transport, including, notably, the Republican councillor Georges Contenot, who represented the district of Porte Saint-Martin from 1924. Contenot called for 'priority for public transport' in 1929, even if it meant banning private transport, which he felt was responsible for traffic jams in the city centre. He felt it necessary

> That we remove, as demanded by all Parisians, the bothersome streetcar routes; that we establish a 'routing' of heavy trucks; that we start again to extend and specify the measures dealing with the traffic of cars … planned in Article 215 of the ordinance of 15 March 1925; there's nothing better; but in so doing, we must not forget that before being a city of leisure and luxury, Paris is first and foremost a city of business and work, and it is advisable to consider chiefly workers' needs and convenience. … The problem of traffic in the centre of Paris can be resolved only by the use, at certain rush hours, of public means of transport, rather than passenger cars. It is no longer acceptable, at the present day, that a car transporting only one or two people takes the place of sixteen or eighteen people travelling in a collective car. It is not acceptable that employees and businesspeople whose activities bring them to the city centre waste half the time allowed for their meal or rest, waiting vainly [in traffic]. Workers in Paris, who by their labour contribute to making Paris a major centre of production, should also have the right to circulate quickly and in conditions more comfortable than in the metro. A single measure thus seems effective: attributing priority right-of-way to public transportation cars and banning passenger car traffic during certain rush hours and within certain perimeters.[28]

From this new perspective of a selective approach to Paris traffic, the reforms demanded would work against the streetcar, which did not enjoy the support of even the strongest proponents of public transport.

Streetcars, which had first appeared in the capital during the second half of the nineteenth century, peaked during the First World War, then gradually lost out to automotive public transport in the battle for profitability, just as horse-drawn omnibuses had given way to electric trams. The streetcars' eventual demise in 1938 was accelerated after the launch in 1931 of a 50-passenger bus model with

[28] '… in order to govern automotive traffic in Paris'. Bulletin Municipal Officiel (BMO), *Georges Contenot, proposal no. 88, 14 October 1929* (Paris 1929).

pneumatic tyres that could reach speeds of up to 45 kilometres per hour. This model made the bus more profitable, which it had not been in the early 1920s due to its low capacity (38 places) and low speed (using solid tyres, it could only reach a maximum speed of 25 kilometres per hour).

Furthermore, the bus was considered to be a more flexible means of transport. The flexibility of its routes 'allows (it) to follow all forms of economic and social life: exhibitions, fairs, parties, races, sports events'. Besides, an almost sentimental argument was advanced – oddly enough – by the directors of the operating company. Its ability to cut travel time in half on some routes offered users the supreme reward: 'thanks to these time savings, suburbanites were able to return home for lunch'.[29]

The use value of this new mode of public transport, although hard to calculate, was thus very clearly higher, resulting in an 'improvement in service, obvious to whoever uses the new vehicles'. Therefore, the operating company was satisfied, in the mid-1930s, with a partial or complete substitution of the 110 tram lines. The widespread use of flexible and fast omnibuses really came at the right time, because it had become necessary to adapt to traffic growing ever more intense by day with a means of transportation able to move with a maximum of ease. With its high flexibility, the bus enabled traffic to be eased and substantial and sudden variations in traffic to be faced. Operating methods were improved. Revenue collection was largely simplified with the use of stamping machine devices and the launch of ticket books.

Regardless of the criterion used, a comparison of the various means of public transport showed the superiority of buses.[30] They proved better able to meet fluctuations in traffic, not only throughout the day, but also according to seasons and weather conditions. Furthermore, because they became mechanically more reliable, reductions in operating expenses were significantly in their favour: in 1930, the cost per vehicle-kilometre for a motorbus had fallen to 4.07 francs, compared with 4.47 francs for a streetcar.

Lastly, the aim of doing away with the streetcar was based on the obsolescence of its routes and the space it took up in the street, two factors that had been denounced for a long time. 'King of our streets, cumbersome, authoritarian and disabled', the streetcar was considered to be an obstacle to the very delicate traffic of other fashionable modes.[31] This was particularly true for the automobile, which was faster but nevertheless forced to stop behind the streetcar, due to laws

---

29 ARATP, 1R338.

30 In his report for 1927, Champetier de Ribes, chief engineer for the mobility department, noted the positive financial balance of the automotive omnibus network, whereas the streetcar network was mounting increasingly higher losses. ARATP, 1R165/1.

31 ARATP, 1R338, notes quoted. From the first decade of the century, faithful to his aim of emptying and fluidifying the street, Félicien Michotte denounced these 'mobile obstacles' (*chicanes mobiles*). Félicien Michotte, *The traffic in Paris. Its defects. Its remedies* (Paris 1909).

prohibiting passing on the nearside (the right) when passengers were getting on or off the streetcar – sometimes on central platforms, but usually in the middle of the street.

Looking Beyond the Conspiracy Theory: City Space as a Reversible Battlefield for Modal Choices

> Borders – borders-truths, lines of demarcation between white and black, were moved thanks to propaganda. ... Streetcars in good condition serving airy suburbs were put in the rubbish; the car's role in public perception was more important than it should have been.[32]

Alfred Sauvy's conclusion, made well after the events, was concise, with undoubtedly an ounce of truth when speaking about the suburbs, but the point about the 'good condition' of the streetcar fleet was exaggerated. In reality, streetcars did not die in the Paris region just because of the automobile's widespread use and real efficiency, but also (and especially) due to a dearth of investments and the illogical and inefficient way the tramway network was operated.

Recent historical studies, although aware of the possible collusions of interests on the STCRP's board of directors (where tyre makers, car manufacturers and oil men held positions of influence in the late 1920s), generally demonstrate the 'failures of a system that had been unable to take up the challenge of the cycles of innovation'. The economic rationale at work behind this trend disproves the simplistic conventional wisdom of the trams' 'sacrifice to the New Idol' (that is, the automobile) allegedly forced upon Parisians and their elected representatives.[33] As Dominique Larroque wrote, 'the traditional reference to pressures from car manufacturers is not indispensable in the search for the causes of the success of the automobile'.[34]

There was great relief when the last tram operated, and regrets were only very discreetly expressed: at the City Council, no reports asked for the preservation, or called for improvement, of the streetcar network. The STCRP went so far as to

---

32 Sauvy, *Le pouvoir et l'opinion*, 66.

33 This simplistic theory is presented by Jean Robert, *Les tramways parisiens* (n. l. 1959), or Clive Lamming, *Paris Tram. L'histoire mouvementée du tramway parisien et des petits-trains en Île-de-France* (Paris 2003).

34 See Dominique Larroque, 'Les transports en commun dans la région parisienne, enjeux politiques et financiers', École des Hautes Études en Sciences Sociales, Ph.D. thesis, 1980; Dominique Larroque, 'Apogée, déclin et relance du tramway en France', *Culture technique*, special issue: Transports, 19, March 1989, 54–63, and Dominique Larroque, 'Transports urbains et transformation de l'espace parisien', in Danièle Voldman, ed., *Région Parisienne, approche d'une notion, 1860–1980, Cahier de l'IHTP*, no. 12 October 1989 (Paris 1989), 41–56.

organise a 'funeral' on 15 March 1937 for its last routes: numbers 123 and 124. Routes to the suburbs ended 1938. At that occasion, a programme was held, with the 'departure from the head stations of Saint-Cloud and Vincennes of two special, decorated, dressed trains, and if possible with Jazz [sic]'. The press, the League of Travellers, the radio stations, the Friendly Association of Students and the city councillors involved were all informed in advance and asked to supply passengers. Lastly, it was seen as fashionable to exile a streetcar engine – literally! – to the museum. At the same time a judgement formed that history, which does not begin again but moves ahead on the basis of new creations, has proven to be uncertain, at the very least:

> It does not seem very credible that Parisians will ever again see streetcars circulating in the capital; it is even likely that this means of transportation will disappear completely in the immediate future. It seems appropriate to contact the Museum of the Automobile of Compiègne right away and to offer it the last streetcar in service in Paris, or that which is claimed to be.[35]

Now that this judgement has been recontextualised by recent events, it seems unfortunately myopic.

References

Bellu, René, *Les autobus parisiens, des origines à nos jours* (Paris 1973).

Bond, Winstan and Divall, Colin, eds, *Suburbanizing the Masses. Public Transport and Urban Development in Historical Perspective* (Aldershot 2003).

Bonnier, Louis, 'Cartes isochrones de l'agglomération parisienne', *La vie urbaine*, 3, 1919, 245–50.

Bulletin Municipal Officiel (BMO), *Georges Contenot proposal no. 88, 14 October 1929* (Paris 1929).

Bunle, Henri, 'Migrations alternantes dans la région parisienne', *Annuaire statistique général de la France, juillet-septembre 1932*, in Jacqueline Beaujeu-Garnier and Jean Bastié, *Atlas de Paris et de la région parisienne* (Paris 1967), 245–50.

Cheape, Charles, *Moving the Masses: Urban Public Transportation in New York, Boston and Philadelphia, 1880–1912* (Cambridge, MA 1980).

Comité Consultatif des Transports en Commun à la Surface de la Région Parisienne, ed., *Rapport sur la réorganisation des services de transports, presented by Émile Jayot* (Paris 1927).

Cottereau, Alain, 'L'apparition de l'urbanisme comme action collective: l'agglomération parisienne au début du siècle', *Sociologie du travail*, no. 2, 1969, 342–65.

---

35 ARATP, 1R338, 'Historique du réseau'.

Cottereau, Alain, 'Les débuts de planification urbaine en France: le métro et les mouvements municipaux', *Sociologie du travail*, 12, 1–2, 1970, 362–92.

Cottereau, Alain, 'Les origines de la planification urbaine en France: le métro et les mouvements municipaux', in *Politiques urbaines et planification des villes*, colloque de Dieppe, 8–10 April 1974 (Paris 1974), 767–93.

Cottereau, Alain, 'Les batailles du métropolitain: La compagnie du chemin de fer du Nord et les choix d'urbanisation', in Sheila Hallsted-Baumert, ed., *Métro-Cité: le Chemin de fer métropolitain à la conquête de Paris, 1871–1945, under the direction of Francois Gasnault and Henri Zuber* (Paris 1997), 75–84.

Daumas, Maurice, ed., *Analyse historique de l'évolution des transports en commun dans la région parisienne de 1855 à 1939* (Paris 1977).

Delavenne, Georges, 'La réorganisation des transports en commun du Département de la Seine dans ses rapports avec le plan d'aménagement de Paris', in Société Française des Urbanistes, ed., *Où en est l'urbanisme, en France et à l'étranger, actes du congrès de Strasbourg 1923* (Paris 1923), 381–94.

Economica, ed., *Le bus et Paris. Une histoire de mobilité* (Paris 2011).

Faure, Alain, 'Les déplacements de travail entre Paris et sa banlieue (1880–1914): première approche', *Villes en parallèle*, 10, June 1986, 233–48.

Faure, Alain, '"Nous travaillons dix heures par jour plus le chemin", les déplacements de travail chez les ouvriers parisiens, 1880–1914', in Susanna Magri and Christian Topalov, eds, *Villes ouvrières* (Paris 1989), 93–107.

Faure, Alain, 'A l'aube des transports de masse. L'exemple des 'trains ouvriers" de la banlieue de Paris, 1883–1914', *Revue d'Histoire Moderne et Contemporaine*, 40, no. 2, April–June 1993, 228–55.

Flonneau, Mathieu, *The Automobile in the Conquest of Paris, 1910–1977. Urban Forms, the Political Arena and Representations*, 3 vols., University Paris I – Panthéon-Sorbonne, doctoral thesis 2002.

Flonneau, Mathieu, *Paris et l'automobile. Un siècle de passions* (Paris 2005).

Flonneau, Mathieu, 'La concurrence tramway-automobile au cours de l'entre-deux-guerres à Paris. Pour une relecture des représentations liées à la disparition des chemins de fer urbain', *Revue d'histoire des chemins de fer*, 18, no. 36–7, Spring-Autumn 2007, 279–303.

Flonneau, Mathieu, *Interviews in Christophe Ramage, Un tramway dans la tête: l'Arpajonnais, 1893–1936*, video documentary (Paris 2010).

Flonneau, Mathieu, *Un tramway dans la tête: l'Arpajonnais, 1893–1936*, video documentary (Paris 2010).

Gérome, Noëlle, *Histoire d'un dépôt d'autobus en banlieue, le dépôt Floréal aux Lilas RATP, Réseau 2000, mai 1987* (Paris 1987).

Hallsted-Baumert, Sheila, 'Le Métropolitain: technologie, espace et création d'identités urbaine dans le Paris de fin du siècle', L'École des Hautes Études en Sciences Sociales (EHESS) and New York University, doctoral thesis, 1999.

Kassab, Abdelfattah el, 'Les déterminants techniques, économiques et politiques du démantèlement des tramways dans la région parisienne (Contribution à l'analyse des conditions du démantèlement des tramways dans la région parisienne)', University Paris – XII, doctoral thesis for engineering, 1986.

Lamming, Clive, *Paris Tram. L'histoire mouvementée du tramway parisien et des petits-trains en Île-de-France* (Paris 2003).

Larroque, Dominique, *Les transports en commun dans la région parisienne, enjeux politiques et financiers*, École des Hautes Études en Sciences Sociales, Ph.D. thesis, 1980.

Larroque, Dominique, 'Apogée, déclin et relance du tramway en France', *Culture technique, special issue: Transports*, 19, March 1989, 54–63.

Larroque, Dominique, 'Transports urbains et transformation de l'espace parisien', in Danièle Voldman, ed., *Région Parisienne, approche d'une notion, 1860–1980, Cahier de l'IHTP*, no. 12 October 1989 (Paris 1989), 41–56.

Larroque, Dominique, Margairaz, Michel and Zembri, Pierre, *Paris et ses transports, XIXe-XXe siècles. Deux siècles de décisions pour la ville et sa région* (Paris 2002).

Latour, Bruno, *Aramis ou l'amour des techniques* (Paris 1992).

Machuré, Jean-Paul and Vielliard, Philippe, *Autobus de Paris* (Paris 1999).

Mairie de Paris, ed., *Bulletin municipal officiel rapports et documents* (Paris 1928).

Massard, Émile, 'Conclusion', in Mairie de Paris, ed., *Bulletin municipal officiel*, report no. 93 (Paris 1928), 97.

Michotte, Félicien, *The traffic in Paris. Its defects. Its remedies* (Paris 1909).

Offner, Jean-Marc, 'La disparition des tramways en France', *Revue de l'Association française des amis des chemins de fer*, 388, 1988, 6–10.

Passalacqua, Arnaud, 'Bus and Paris: Flexibility, Public Place and Mobility from the 1900s to 1970s', doctoral thesis defended at University Paris VII – Denis-Diderot, 2009.

Passalacqua, Arnaud, *Le bus et Paris. Une histoire de mobilité* (Paris 2011).

Robert, Jean, *Les tramways parisiens* (n. l. 1959).

Romains, Jules, Romains, Lise, and Belvès, Pierre, eds, *Paris des hommes de bonne volonté* (Paris 1949).

Romains, Jules, 'Par un joli matin, Paris descend au travail', in Jules Romains, Lise Romains and Pierre Belvès, eds, *Paris des hommes de bonne volonté* (Paris 1949).

Sauvy, Alfred, *Mythologies de notre temps* (Paris 1965).

Sauvy, Alfred, *Les 4 roues de la fortune* (Paris 1968).

Chapter 14

Rails in the Car Kingdom: Competition, Changes and Continuity in Urban Mobility – the Case of Turin, 1914–73

Massimo Moraglio

The success of car culture and infrastructure has somehow eclipsed all other mobility histories of the twentieth century.[1] The car's success was so rapid and enthusiastically supported that it has often been presented as unavoidable.[2] In Italy, as elsewhere, the automobile was a status symbol and an extraordinary tool for freedom, able to carry people free from train timetables and railway tracks. Meanwhile, summer saw the perfect match between mass motorisation and paid holidays, as – as Italo Calvino wrote in his novel *La speculazione edilizia* (*A Plunge into Real Estate*) – Italians drove *en masse* to domestic beaches. In Italy, as in several other Western countries, car ownership and paid holidays became the pillars of social compromise after the Second World War.[3]

At first it had been believed, even by the automobile's most enthusiastic supporters, that mass motorisation and its accompanying social changes would be limited to the middle class and, eventually, elite workers, but would never spread to the whole population. However, in the 1960s car ownership overtook even the most optimistic predictions, including those of the car industries, and the automobile became an everyday, banal, ubiquitous mobility tool. The Italian transport infrastructure programme reflected this history: in 1952, the first national motorway plan called for massive investment in roads, but also proposed cycle paths and insisted on bicycle parking areas in the main factories, assuming the bicycle would be the main mobility tool for blue-collar workers in the next

1 The research leading to these results has received funding from the People Programme (Marie Curie Actions) of the European Union's Seventh Framework Programme (FP7/2007–13) under REA grant agreement no. 252489.

2 See J.J. Flink, *The Automobile Age* (Cambridge, MA 1988). For a critical approach see P. Wollen and J. Kerr, eds, *Autopia. Cars and Culture* (London 2002).

3 See A. Picon, 'Towards a history of infrastructure', in M. Bonino and M. Moraglio, eds, *Inventare gli spostamenti. Storia e immagini dell'autostrada Torino-Savona / Inventing Movement. History and Images of the A6 Motorway* (Torino 2006), 13–17, here 16. See also the novel from Italo Calvino, *A Plunge into Real Estate* (London 1983; original publication in Italian titled *La speculazione edilizia* in 1963).

decades.[4] Analogous considerations were expressed outside of Italy: the E-road programme, drawn up in 1950, envisioned cycle paths along several E-roads.[5]

The low expectations for car development were also reflected in the confrontation between roads and rails. These two modes should not be seen as mere alternatives. Instead, they have a more complex relationship. In the 1960s and 1970s, at the peak of the automobile trend, many industrialised countries, such as Japan and France, developed massive projects for high-speed train routes. So while it is true that there was competition, there was also overlapping and integration, even coexistence, and railways did not necessarily decline.

Why Analyse the Case of Turin?

This chapter explores the case of Turin during the golden age of roads and car culture, from the First World War to the oil crisis. Although focused on a local case, the chapter seeks to present the example of Turin as a paradigmatic combination of struggle, compromise, integration, continuity and innovation between roads and rails, showing the contradictions, negotiations, limits and strengths of those transport systems and how they met the requirements of mobility. Turin is a truly interesting choice due to the combination of the local car culture – intensified by the presence of Fiat's headquarters and factories – and a public transport system based throughout the century on tramways.

After a short description of land-based transport policy in the Turin area during the eighteenth and nineteenth centuries, the chapter presents the context of mobility in the 1920s and the various schemes to modernise the city's public transport system. In the 1930s, despite the generally reduced reputation of railways and streetcars at a time when many European cities were quickly removing their rails, Turin went through a golden age of trams.[6] Additionally, between the world wars, the Turin network experienced a remarkable increase in routes and passengers, taking advantage of a change of feeling at the level of the national government, which was markedly less enthusiastic about the spread of cars in the wake of the 1929 crisis.[7] In the 1950s trams were still the backbone of the Turin mass transport system, especially for commuting workers. But Turin nevertheless experienced a parallel development. From the 1950s onwards, the city consciously organised

---

4 See F. Paolini, *Storia sociale dell'automobile in Italia* (Rome 2007).

5 See F. Schipper, *Driving Europe. Building Europe on Roads in the Twentieth Century* (Amsterdam 2008).

6 See G. Yago, *The Decline of Transit. Urban Transportation in German and U.S. Cities, 1900–1970* (Cambridge 1984) and C. Divall and W. Bond, eds, *Suburbanizing the Masses. Public Transport and Urban Development in Historical Perspective* (Farnham 2003).

7 See C. Mochi, 'I trasporti', *Annali dell'economia italiana 1930–1938*, 8, 2, 1982, 213–71.

its public spaces for car mobility and managed urban development to facilitate and increase the private use of automobiles.[8] In the 1960s, bus transport became another major factor, but the municipality, tram company management and several mobility experts spoke with foresight about the problems of car mobility in the city and about the cost savings in terms of cheap electricity if trams were maintained in the city.[9]

In 1966, when the industrial and social car development of the city was at its peak, Turin's local government decided to prohibit car access in some central streets, two years after Siena and Split had decided to ban cars in their historical centres. And the paradoxes did not end there: in the 1960s, proposals for three underground lines in Turin were made by a Fiat-affiliated company. And in 1974, when public transport was being relaunched in the wake of the oil crisis and the plan and the money were ready for the underground, the general consensus was that it was better not to go through with it, in order to avoid making problems for the automobile industry.[10]

The Birth of the Tram Tracks

Nowadays Turin proper numbers about 900,000 inhabitants, and there are 1.1 million more in the rest of the metropolitan area. The city, founded in the ancient Roman era, lies in a narrow strip of plains between hills to the East and the Alps to the West. Throughout the centuries the city has preserved its orthogonal structure and, more unusually, continued to follow and reproduce it during the expansions under the House of Savoy during the seventeenth and eighteenth centuries. Napoleon's conquest resulted in the demolition of the city walls and the creation of a new and more spacious urban perimeter which, at the end of the first half of the nineteenth century, was overrun by the city in its ongoing expansion. Already the capital of the Duchy of Savoy, Turin became the capital of Italy during the national unification of 1861. A first crisis for Turin was the transfer of the capital to Florence in 1864, and a second was the economic crisis of the 1870s and 1880s. After these, the successive decades saw the city's first industrial development. This drove urban growth that reproduced the orthogonal structure of the Roman city throughout the entire territory.[11]

---

8 On the public transport in Turin see S. Musso, ed., *Il trasporto pubblico a Torino nel secolo dell'industria: Atm, Satti, Gtt* (Torino 2007).

9 See Archivio Storico della Città di Torino (ASCT), *Atti amministrativi*, minutes of Turin municipal council meetings in the 1950s, especially those of January 1956.

10 See the essay of Alessandro De Magistris, 'L'urbanistica della grande trasformazione (1945–1980)', in N. Tranfaglia, ed., *Storia di Torino*, vol. 9 (Torino 1999), 189–238.

11 See G. Boffa, 'Lo sviluppo urbanistico di Torino', *Atti e rassegna tecnica delle società di Ingegneri e degli Architetti in Torino*, 3–6, 1975, 37–70.

After the first experience with the omnibus in the mid-nineteenth century, the city's public transport expanded, with two private tramway companies operating in 1874. The *Società tramways di Torino* (Tramways Society of Turin), better known in the city as the 'Belga' (Belgian) because it was mostly funded by foreign capital, together with the *Società torinese tranway e ferrovie economiche* (Turin Society of Economical Tramways and Railways), operated six routes. At the end of the nineteenth century there were 18 routes, with a total of 60 kilometres of track, serving a population of around 300,000 inhabitants.

In 1898, according to the general trend in the tramways industry, the municipal council made a very wise decision to proceed with the electrification of the tramway network, and to give a third company, *Società anonima elettricità Alta Italia* (Electric Society of Northern Italy, Ltd.), the right to operate public transport in the city. This new company soon established a network of six routes totalling 31 kilometres, with around 12 million users annually, while the two other competitors together operated around 80 kilometres of route.[12] As noted by John P. McKay in 1976, electrification made it possible to increase the speed of the trams, and reduced, by more than half, the cost of tram car traction: this meant a marked reduction in prices, and faster service.[13] Also in Turin, the bigger extensions of the network corresponded with a decisive lowering of ticket prices, which at the start of the 1900s cost ten Italian lira cents (about two US cents in the 1900s), and with a considerable increase in customers over the preceding decades.[14]

The Foundation of the Municipal Company (1907) and Its Control of All the Urban Lines (1922)

The growth of the city accelerated in the first years of the 1900s, leading the municipal council to approve a new urban plan. The conservative municipal council, with Count Secondo Frola as mayor, launched a massive infrastructure programme based on municipal participation. Transport facilities and electricity production were the key objectives of the Frola's plan. Further,

> the programme of the council was ... a large expansion of the existing lines. It corresponded to the needs of the population, and facilitated the urban development,

[12] See L. Giupponi, *Sviluppo, sistemazione ed organizzazione delle tranvie urbane di Torino* (Torino 1928), 9, and see ASCT, *Atti amministrativi*, minutes of the municipal council, 26 November 1896, 5 December 1896 and 9 June 1897.

[13] See J.P. McKay, *Tramways and Trolleys. The Rise of Urban Mass Transport in Europe* (Princeton, NJ 1976).

[14] Anonymous, 'L'azienda tranviaria municipale ed i suoi risultati finanziari', *Città di Torino – Bollettino mensile dell'ufficio del Lavoro e della statistica*, 1, 1921, 13–16. All the translations from Italian made in this essay are by Erin O'Loughlin.

> consisting of improvement in technical operations, economic improvement for workers, reduction of fares to assist the less wealthy classes, etc.[15]

As an outcome, in 1907 the Turin municipality bought Alta Italia's lines and expanded the tram network. To manage the service, the city created the *Azienda Tranvie Municipali* (Municipal Tramways Company, ATM). Additionally, the two old private companies still operating in Turin merged in order to achieve economies of scale, but, following a global trend in the public transport industry, they intended rapidly to abandon the sector, which was no longer financially attractive.[16]

Given this framework, it is not surprising that in 1922 the Turin municipal council, with a conservative majority, voted almost unanimously for the municipalisation of the entire tramway network, incorporating the routes still in the hands of the private companies into the ATM.[17] This unification brought with it business and managerial problems: the reorganisation of managerial groups and technical offices, the application of a collective contract for the employees and the decision on a single livery for the vehicles and the type of electrical fittings for the overhead wires.[18]

To these problems was added the fundamental reassessment of the routes. It was useless, even counterproductive, to keep all the routes open in their current state. The ATM's lines and the Belga's overlapped throughout the entire city, but in the historical centre, every road, no matter how small, saw trams pass each other through a mish-mash of parallel lines. In 1923 an advisory commission was instituted to satisfy all these needs, and also to ensure that trams met recent legislation requiring them to be driven on the right-hand side of the road.[19] In July 1923 a project for the unification of the tram networks was presented, approved by the ATM management and the municipal council.[20] The project planned to keep 95 kilometres out of the 118 kilometres of routes.[21]

In the preliminary discussions, the possibility of introducing a chequer-board system with orthogonal routes was examined, without a doubt a rational

15 Ibid., 13.

16 See Divall, *Suburbanizing the masses*; for the Argentinean case, similar in many aspects to the Italian one, see R. Garcia Heras, *Automotores norteamericanos, caminos y modernizacion urbana en la Argentina, 1918–1939* (Buenos Aires 1985).

17 See ASCT, *Atti amministrativi*, minutes of the municipal council of 1 July 1922, 23 December 1922 as well as 17 January 1923.

18 The ATM wagons had red livery, while the Belga ones were green.

19 See ASCT, Fondo *Affari servizi pubblici industriali*, Cartella 97 fascicolo 13 and Cartella 106 fascicolo 5.

20 See ASCT, fondo *Atti amministrativi*, deliberations of the prefectural commission of 25 July 1923 and 8 August 1923 and the deliberations of the ATM administration commission of 3 August 1923.

21 On the process of municipalisation see also Giupponi, *Sviluppo*. Partially published in three parts with the same title in *Rivista dell'Azienda Tranvie Municipali di Torino*, 6, 1927, 203–9, 2, 1928, 5–17, and 3, 1928, 74–81.

system when new tracks needed to be laid. However, given the existing lines, the difficulties that would be caused by superimposing one system over another, the travelling habits of the citizens and the economic risk, the best solution was thought to be a merger of the existing lines, with appropriate adjustments.[22] Thus with some regret the idea of a new grid network was abandoned, and the project turned to reorganising the existing lines, maintaining the fundamental layout radiating out from the city centre.[23]

The decision taken in 1923 to keep the radial system was important, and its effects reverberated over a long period. For nearly 60 years the tram and then the bus network preserved that structure. There were many reasons for this choice. Politicians lacked the courage and interest in radically reforming the network, but there were also objective problems. Finally, the creation of a chequer-board network would have been more than a mere technical choice, representing a significant infrastructural investment in the suburbs, partly at the expense of other areas. Keeping the radial structure, however, guaranteed the city centre a primary role, as much in terms of the localisation of administrative and commercial functions as in its symbolic character.

Limit and Success of the Tram System

After the First World War, right in the middle of the reorganisation of Turin's tram network, automobile transport came to be seen as much more than a luxury toy, emerging as a contestant in urban mass mobility. In Turin, the first three urban bus routes were opened in December 1927. A fourth followed in spring 1929. Despite these early attempts, bus routes developed only modestly between the world wars. Certainly, during that period the director of the ATM, Luigi Giupponi, had to respond to a persistent question: if rail transport was becoming a museum relic, why not eliminate the trams in Turin, 'as the modern tendency was toward other means of transport?' In response it was argued that once the tramway existed, the cost of running a bus route was twice that of a tram, not an unimportant element in the choice of transport. Giupponi also asserted that buses were 'the natural complement' to the tramways, while the old trams themselves guaranteed capacious transport and efficient service, which, together with an underground, offered 'the best means of mass transport'.[24]

---

22 ASCT, Fondo *Affari servizi pubblici industriali*, anno 1923, cartella 97 fascicolo 13, 'Progetto attuazione programma unificazione linee', document dated 26 July 1923.

23 See also ASCT, Fondo *Affari servizi pubblici industriali*, deliberations of the ATM administration commission of 3 August 1923, 'Unificazione della rete urbana. Proposte per l'esecuzione del piano di unificazione. Relazione del Direttore sul programma dei lavori'.

24 L. Giupponi, 'L'Azienda Tranvie e le sue vetture', *Rivista dell'Azienda Tranvie Municipali di Torino*, 6, 1930, 77–90.

The ATM's top managers added that Turin's passenger flows rendered the trams unbeatable. The presence of large concentrations of factory workers with fixed shifts and mass movements fully utilised the greater capacity of tram cars compared with buses, justifying the costs of the tracks. Resisting the mounting fortunes of buses, the employees of the ATM argued for the viability of the ATM, according to the company journal. In sum, 'the automobile services must consider how to integrate themselves with the tramway services, which must constitute the principal framework of an urban transport system for a city in which an *urban railway network does not exist*'.[25]

Proposing 'Greater Turin' and Its Failure

The urban railway network was a relevant issue not only for Turin's transport policy, but more widely with regard to Italy's political struggle in the interwar period. As the ATM managers regretted, in Turin the railway system, which was state-owned after 1905, was explicitly not for local purposes. This policy was maintained by the national fascist government in order to control and to limit the autonomy of local authorities and to prevent – or at least reduce – urban growth. This preference fitted perfectly with the fascist ruralist policy, according to which cities were seen as foundries of depravity, known for their Socialist ideas and their lower birth rates.[26] Beyond the propaganda, the central power felt more comfortable restraining local governments, shutting down any proposals to create bigger urban entities.[27] In this way the regime also prevented local Italian municipalities copying the model of the 'Greater Berlin' experience: in 1920 the size of the German capital was greatly expanded through incorporation of many municipalities and giving the City Council greater political autonomy.

In this framework, transport was seen as the most important tool to govern urban development and, consequently, the fascist government strongly limited any further development of railways for local purposes. It is no coincidence that the renovation of the urban railway network in Turin was halted in 1928, nor that the *Ministero delle Comunicazioni* (Ministry of Communication) forbade the municipal transport company to operate outside of the municipal borders.[28] The Turin local elite and ATM managers had to balance these limitations with the demand for urban transport. Without trains for local transport, the tram system seemed to be best for commuting workers. Further supporting this notion was the lower cost of energy in running tramways, due to municipal ownership of the local

---

25 Ibid., 78 (italics added by author).

26 See A. Giuntini, 'Nascita, sviluppo e tracollo della rete infrastrutturale', in L. Segreto, ed., *Storia d'Italia. Annali 15. L'industria* (Torino 1999), 551–617.

27 See P. Aimo, *Stato e poteri locali in Italia 1848–1995* (Roma 1997), and E. Rotelli, *Il martello e l'incudine. Comuni e province fra cittadini e apparati* (Bologna 1991).

28 See S. Maggi, *Storia dei trasporti in Italia* (Bologna 2005), here 38–47.

electricity company, and the fact that it was impossible by diesel bus (as suggested at those time), which used fossil fuel. Discarding the idea of buses, in the 1930s the ATM extended its service toward the distant urban boundaries, addressing 'the need for new institutions of tram lines and extensions of the existing network'.[29]

Consistent development meant that on the eve of the Second World War, the ATM (which was at this point the only company in the market) had 130 kilometres of tram routes in the city, while the lines covered more than 192 kilometres, an increase of 50 per cent over 1924. The 1930s were, for many reasons, the golden era of the trams: between 1923 and 1940 the population of Turin went from 500,000 to 700,000 inhabitants, and in the same period the use of the ATM trams rose from 142 million to nearly 300 million journeys annually. It really was a mass use of public transport, facilitated by the company's fares policy. The maximum development of the service was reached in 1941, in part due to the war, and was a record year for the ATM, reaching a mobility index of 1.68, equal to 339 million passengers annually.[30] In sum, the tram network largely met the mobility needs of the time. Above all, it satisfied the requirements of the great factories that ran on Henry Ford's principles.

The ATM was explicitly forbidden by the national government to operate outside of the Turin boundaries, but at the same time the central authorities did not prevent the private companies leaving the market. Likewise, the Ministry of Communication did not intend to take over private companies with their deficits. The final outcome was an unspoken agreement: the Turin City Council was allowed to take over the old interurban tram firms, but as per previous regulations, the ministry banned the ATM from operating those new lines. The Turin City Council had to create a new limited company called *Società Anonima Tranvie Torinesi Intercomunali* (Turin Inter-urban Tramway Society Ltd, or SATTI) and run it under civil law as a private firm. This double management hindered the design of an integrated system, but despite this, the City Council's control of all the urban and interurban lines allowed economies of scale and encouraged innovation. The reorganisation under SATTI was a business success, moving toward better service, both in terms of car comfort and capacity. This led to a remarkable increase of passengers and income. The passengers of interurban lines run by SATTI rose from 4.5 million in 1938 to 6.4 million in 1939. Those numbers rose further to 8.1 million in 1940 and 9.5 million in 1941 when the war began to show its effects on transport as thousands of inhabitants fled the city daily.

Considering the achievements of 1941, ATM and SATTI, the two municipal transport companies, showed the extent to which they were able to cope with the mobility needs of an expanding urban area, despite (or maybe because of) the 1929

29 'Relazione della commissione di studio dei problemi relativi all'Azienda Tranvie Municipali – Torino, ottobre 1960', vol. 1, typescript kept in Archivio GTT, page 165.

30 For information on passengers and mobility see V. Zignoli, 'Tram e auto: ricerca d'una convivenza', *Torino*, 2, 1966, 47–55. For indexes of mobility, the daily average number of ATM travellers divided by the population resident in the city is intended.

economic crisis. While it is true that the social and infrastructural construction of car-orientated mobility was a monumental programme, with huge changes in landscapes and everyday lives, Italian history shows us that this process was not simple. Increasing the complexity of the road issue, national public policies were not simply directed toward road improvements throughout the twentieth century. Rather, the clash between road and rail intensified after the 1929 crisis, which reduced export possibilities for the car industry. But the national public railway company also lost market share and saw its deficit increase with the crisis. Such uncontrollable losses became, because of their size and unpredictability, a political problem. Facing the loss of competitiveness of the railway system, the government adopted a set of tools to protect it, which also meant somehow revitalising the rail system.[31]

Public Transport and Mass Motorisation

For millions of Italians, the economic boom of the 1950s and 1960s meant a dramatic increase in income and access to a new era of consumption. In this respect, from the users' and customers' side, the car was like the object of a cult, an element of identity, a fetish symbolising the escape from poverty.

Beyond the collective imagination, the possession of a car broke traditional isolation, allowed the populace to discover mobility and radically shortened the travel times of an Italy divided into thousands of villages. Half electrical appliance and half icon, the car was cherished for the values that it incarnated and for its usefulness: for the workers and employees at the end of the 1950s, the car reduced the time needed to get to work to less than half. Women discovered the car as a safer and faster means of mobility, away from the overcrowded trams, buses and trains.[32] For its part, the Italian government were not at all displeased at having to construct a huge motorway network; that was a good objective to present during election times. Neither was the government unhappy to see the electorate speeding by in their Fiat 600s. Last but not least, car and fuel taxation was – and still is – a mainstay of state revenue. Taken by the enthusiasm of the economic 'miracle', lacking the know-how to merge different means of transport and focused on the car industry's needs, the local and national authorities supported mass motorisation and – as just a minor goal – tried to save the public transport system.[33]

Moving back to the Turin case, in the 1950s and 1960s, as in the interwar period, the municipality's choices were the result of a compromise between different pressure groups. The central government, a parliamentary republic after the war, still maintained a strong bureaucratic control over the local authorities and

---

31 See Mochi, 'I trasporti', 217–20. See also Giuntini, *Nascita, sviluppo*, and S. Maggi, *Storia dei trasporti*,

32 See Paolini, *Storia*, here 73–9.

33 See S. Maggi, *Le ferrovie* (Bologna 2003).

the railway system continued to be considered inappropriate for local services; in precisely this period the car culture exploded in all its strength, giving collective mobility a bad reputation, making trams and trains seem archaic.[34] Leaving behind the hesitations of the interwar period, in the 1950s and 1960s, against the objections of the Communist and Socialist opposition parties, the Christian Democrats heavily invested state funds in the renewal and improvement of the road network – including the motorways – at the expense of the other transport means. Interest in the railway system dropped, as did interest in any coordination between road and rail.[35]

The gigantic programme of road construction affected Turin. If at the beginning of the twentieth century there seemed to be too many cars for the roads, in the 1950s the view was that there were not enough roads for the cars and those that existed were inadequate. In the 1950s, as the first wave of motorisation filled urban roads, drivers were suddenly introduced to traffic congestion. An elevated urban motorway seemed an obvious solution, redesigning the city and increasing the infrastructure devoted to the car. In the euphoria of the economic boom, several urban intersections with elevated crossings were proposed, as were three long tunnels under the city centre to lessen traffic jams.[36]

It is also true that the massive investment in the tram sector of the 1930s influenced the choices after the war, making it difficult and onerous to abandon the rails and move over to bus transport. The conscious decision not to develop a bus network before the Second World War meant that after the war the ATM's fleet was almost entirely made up of trams. This inheritance heavily conditioned the choices of the successive decades, making a drastic abandonment of the tramways unadvisable, both because of the need to offset the costs of the rails and tram cars, and because of the high cost of acquiring a fleet of buses. Moreover, as some councillors maliciously highlighted, the management of the ATM was little inclined, due to culture and training, to abandon transport on tracks; others pointed out that electricity, produced by a municipal company, was almost free for the ATM, whereas petrol for the buses was not. Finally, a radical shift of transport services to buses would have put many people out of work, given the less labour-intensive nature of bus operation.[37]

---

[34] See L. Cicognani and C. Mochi, 'I trasporti', *Annali dell'economia italiana 1959–1964*, 12, 2, 1982, 237–301.

[35] See Maggi, *Storia*, here 51–61.

[36] M. Moraglio, 'Le politiche infrastrutturali fra emergenze e squilibri', in F. Levi and S. Musso, eds, *Torino da capitale politica a capitale dell'industria. Il miracolo economico (1950–1970)* (Torino 2006), 169–77.

[37] See ASCT, *Atti amministrativi*, minutes of Turin municipal council meeting, 30 January 1956.

The End of the Suburban Rail Network, but the Tram Is (Again) a Compromise Winner

At the end of the Second World War, the construction of a new tramway system seemed to be increasingly favoured. A few months after the end of the war, the prefect of Turin established a committee to evaluate the public transport system in and around Turin, and to study how to update and integrate it.[38] The committee submitted its work the next year, suggesting a wide range of activities. The main proposal involved enhancing the interurban tram network, even including routes separated from other vehicles, and electrifying all of it.[39] This would relaunch rail-based mass public transport in the Turin area, leading to a network of fast trams connecting at the city centre. With the same goal, in 1946, SATTI's management proposed a massive investment to boost its network. Both these proposals, however, were turned down. Curiously, the main and official justification for this abandonment was not the inadequacy of the proposals themselves, but the expectation that the city would not grow much. The officials imagined Turin as a medium-sized city with no further development, perhaps even with a decrease of population, a situation which did not require massive investment. Of course, behind their decisions, there also lay the dominant transport culture of the times, where automobiles was seen as faster, up-to-date and more flexible – in a word 'modern' and 'efficient', with no extra or hidden infrastructural costs beyond paved public roads.

According to the minutes of the ATM board and of Turin's City Council, the buses' speed was widely appreciated by the passengers who, correctly, saw the ageing tramways – which had not been cared for during the war – as dangerous and slow. The director of SATTI, in an article published in the Turin council magazine in 1946, fatalistically depicted the unavoidable end of the tramway and the 'Darwinian' success of the bus. Even if the tram was cheaper than automobile service in the medium run, he argued:

> Bus service is not much more expensive than tram service, and ultimately such a (small) difference in cost is justified by a better quality of transport for the passengers. Let's put it this way: competition among the means of transport is inevitable and the most advanced and fit one replaces is the one that's out of date.[40]

So despite the higher cost and lower capacity of each unit, the bus offered a faster and more modern service. As for the outskirts, trams in the city appeared to many users and to the social imagination in general as old-fashioned, noisy, slow,

---

38 A. Aloisi, *I servizi ferrotranviari ed automobilistici extraurbani facenti capo a Torino* (Torino 1949), 18.

39 Ibid., 34.

40 F. Giupponi, 'Origine della Satti', *Torino*, 8, 1949, 25–33, here 29.

cumbersome and, particularly in the historical centre, an obstacle for private car circulation.[41] In October 1950, the municipal council, which would be ruled by the Communist and Socialist parties until 1951, commissioned an inquiry on the problems of urban traffic, and it blatantly favoured the buses: 'We cannot help but recognise the advantages of buses: higher speed, less noise, less inconvenience for the road surface leading to more powerful possibilities'. These possibilities included the trolley bus: 'Travel on rubber is today [1956] delayed due only to economic reasons, specifically the great need for capital for the transformation'.[42]

On the outskirts the tracks were accordingly dismantled, but inside the Turin urban area the municipal council, headed by the moderate Christian Democrats party, was orientated toward 'a correct balance' between buses and rails, both to renew the existing tram fleet, and to achieve, with buses, a new zone of urban development.[43] The conservative opposition (among other things faithful to the interests of Fiat) maintained that, given the necessity to get return on investment from the renovation of the trams, they should be kept running within Turin. In effect, in approving this 'correct balance' the municipal council saved the city's rails. Public mobility policies ended up being the same as they had been before the war. At the height of the economic boom, one assessor noted that 'in Turin and Milan it's difficult to shift rapidly from rails to rubber, essentially due to the specific character of urban transport in the two cities, created by the intense industrialisation, which necessitates adequate service at peak time, service that is better suited to rails than to rubber'.[44]

So this choice was the outcome of several factors, including ATM's top management's positive attitude toward tramways, the lower cost of energy in moving trams than buses and the political need to match the workers' demand for mass transit. This unfashionable decision was made against the wishes of city planners and many, but not all, transport technicians who, as elsewhere in Europe, praised 'car-friendly' cities, thought-out and planned for automobiles.[45] However, it was exactly in the car's moment of splendour that the first doubts of the benefits of mobility on rubber came. As stated in 1958, 'some years ago it was hoped that a notable improvement in circulation would be achieved, abolishing transport on rails and almost exclusively using transport on rubber'.[46]

---

[41] See Moraglio, *Le politiche infrastrutturali*.

[42] Reported in ASCT, *Atti amministrativi*, minutes of Turin municipal council meeting of 27 February 1956, by advisor Casalena; italics added.

[43] Said by assessor Curti; see ASCT, *Atti amministrativi*, minutes of Turin municipal council meeting, 30 January 1956.

[44] A. Fogliano, 'Gomma o rotaia?', *Torino municipalizzate*, 2, 1963, 18–25 here 19.

[45] See the classical essay by H.B. Reichow, *Die autogerechte Stadt. Ein Weg aus dem Verkehrs-Chaos* (Ravensburg 1959). See also B. Schmucki, 'Fashion and technological change Tramways in Germany after 1945', *The Journal of Transport History*, 31, 1, 2010, 1–24.

[46] 'Relazione della commissione di studio dei problemi relativi all'Azienda Tranvie Municipali', 213.

In cities that followed the rubber path, the results had been positive when private circulation was not too intense to coexist with public transport. However in the late 1950s, the aforementioned rapid increase of private automobiles had saturated the streets to such an extent that large public vehicles – trolley buses and buses – although independent of tracks, found themselves unable to escape the congestion and had to lower their speed below anything that was acceptable.

The study commissioned by the ATM in 1958 looked at additional problems of the public transport company, such as its uncertain future and its small profit margin. The absolute increase in passengers did not compensate for the expenses incurred by the larger area covered by the service or the salary raises awarded to ATM workers. In the end the 1958 report proposed an ambitious solution, which was reprised in 1974, and then again in 1982 when Socialist and Communist parties again ruled the city:

> The Commission believes that for Turin the moment has not yet arrived for the construction of a proper underground, which may be necessary in thirty years. However it seems very opportune, even necessary, to immediately lighten the circulation in the central zone, implementing in this zone circulation on two levels ... The Commission confirms the convenience of subterranean trams in the entire central zone (keeping cars running on the surface).[47]

In parallel with the fortunes of the automobile, the city was experiencing an extraordinary urban growth; in 1972 there were 1,200,000 inhabitants just within Turin's city limits. The development covered the entire municipal territory, which was spreading out as never before into the hinterland, creating an extended conurbation. Reaching the new areas with public transport were increasingly difficult, in part because of the inefficiency of the radial network inherited from the 1800s.[48]

The Mirage and the Oasis: the Underground and the Oil Crisis

The explosion of private traffic in the late 1950s and early 1960s gave rise to the need to rethink transport policies. If during the 1950s it was the trams that needed to be discarded, in the successive decades it was cars that were cumbersome, especially after the oil crisis put public transport back in fashion.[49] This consciousness was not transformed into consistent action though. The municipality was trapped between the ATM's ever-increasing deficit and the understanding that private

---

47 Ibid.

48 On the public transport policies of the Turin metropolitan area see M. Moraglio, 'Il trasporto extraurbano: la Satti dal 1934 al 2003', in Musso, *Il trasporto pubblico*, 87–131.

49 F. Paolini, *Un paese a quattro ruote. Automobili e societá in Italia* (Venezia 2005), here 189–222.

motorisation was an irreplaceable factor of economic development. Therefore municipal action, conditioned by a national framework favouring the automobile, occurred in a contradictory and limited way, pushed by the ATM's deficit but unable to move against the industrial interests of the city. The best example of the contradiction between the will to intervene and the structural limits of the city government occurred in the events surrounding the underground during the 1960s and 1970s. A 'surface underground' had been talked about in 1956, on the eve of the municipal elections, but was then rejected by the report commission of 1958.

In 1961 the theme of the underground was reprised by Mayor Amedeo Peyron. He proposed to start planning a large project the following year, and then, in 1964, tenders for construction were accepted.[50] In the summer of 1964, the municipality accordingly began to test the Turin subsoil, while in the spring of 1967 the photo on the cover of the local review *Torino municipalizzate* portrayed a prototype of the cars destined for the future underground line:

> In the Lancia factory in Chivasso, they are experimenting with a new model of train with rubber wheels for the underground [in Turin]. The cars (lighter than those of the Milan underground, which have a 230-person capacity) can carry up to 164 passengers at a speed of 100 kilometres an hour. The advantages of this system are silence, adhesion, the absence of vibrations, and the possibility to eliminate the metal tracks. In Paris, two lines of the Metropolitan are already operating with pneumatic wheels.[51]

The formal steps for the construction of the network were all taken between 1969 and 1971:[52]

> But as soon as the working project, drawn by the MT society [Metropolitana Torino Ltd] and by Intermetro [Ltd], was delivered in 1974, the consensus for the operation vanished ... The crisis in the automobile sector contributed in part, at an industrial level, to the cooling of enthusiasm for a work that would have involved great investment and a development of technical know-how, but which could have also eroded a part of the 'local' auto market, ever more essential for the principal Turin companies.[53]

---

50 R. Giardina, 'Stabilito il tracciato e bandito il concorso per la metropolitana', *Torino municipalizzate*, 7, 1964, 24–31.

51 *Torino municipalizzate*, 27, 1967, front cover.

52 See Anonymous, 'La Impresit-Electroconsult prima tra le sette ditte che hanno concorso per il progetto', *Torino municipalizzate*, 37, 1969, 12–25. See also Anonymous, 'Contributo statale di 78 miliardi per la metropolitana torinese', *Torino municipalizzate*, 45, 1970, 45–6 and Anonymous, 'MT. Costituita la società per la metropolitana a Torino', *Torino municipalizzate*, 4, 1971, 85–6.

53 De Magistris, *L'urbanistica*, 231.

The oil crisis of 1973 therefore had the odd effect of sounding the death knell of the underground project, which had come out of a renewal of interest in public transport, a consequence of the increased energy costs.

The rise in fuel costs was not only a low point for the fortune of automobiles, but was above all the end of the model of private mobility based on mass motorisation. Transport on tracks, in this case the tram, no longer had a bad reputation. Overall, the whole sector of mass transport, due to its lower energy costs, saw a decisive revival in terms of users and in the collective imagination. In fact, after the 1970s, tram services got a second wind. In 1982, remarkably, the Turin tram and bus network was completely redrawn, moving toward a grid system. Even more, the 1980s and 1990s witnessed an increasing importance for local authorities and municipalities, and in Turin it meant new fresh proposals for local use of the railway network (a first line was implemented in the late 1990s), a coordination of the ticketing system and a (soft) market-orientated approach to managing the ATM, until all the local public companies operating in the public transport sector were merged into *Gruppo Trasporti Torinesi* (GTT).

But the city was also experiencing a new era, with the massive decline of its industrial production and new markets orientated to services and tourism. The peak came in 2006 when the Winter Olympics were held in Turin. That was also the year of the inauguration of an underground line, a complete new project for the city after several failed proposals.

Which Conclusion?

The history of the success of rail transportation in Turin can be approached from several analytical directions. It is not my intention to suggest an ultimate explanation, but instead to have a closer look at the social and political reasons behind the story and propose further paths of investigation.

From the sources and the literature, we could agree that the main goal of Turin's technical, political and economic elite was to achieve robust industrial development, in order to increase the prosperity of the city in the mobility field. This meant offering an efficient mass transport system able to meet the needs of the thousands of workers typical of a town with factories based on the principles developed by Henry Ford. A well-organised mass transport network had to face overcrowded peak hours four times a day, which, in the technician's view, could be managed best (or least poorly) with a system based on tracks.

The local elite realised quickly that it was impossible to use the ordinary railway network for local purposes. A widespread tram network seemed a good replacement, and constructing it would be easier than struggling against the national railway company and the central government. The tram network was thus an *ersatz*-train system, but it was able to offer good performance throughout the twentieth century, and despite its overcrowded vehicles, it served the industrial workers' needs. This idea of mobility was prioritised throughout the century, though it was thrown into crisis by mass motorisation and the consequent privatisation of mobility. Even when, in the 1960s, car ownership became a mass phenomenon, rail-based mass transport system continued, as the tram was considered an indispensable part of the city's infrastructure.

So the tram, which was seen by the Turin elite as a less efficient substitute for a local train network and a cheaper substitute for an underground, survived the entire twentieth century because it was the best available solution for workers' mass mobility in the industrial city. Its low profile in terms of investment fitted Turin's needs better than an underground. This same low profile also did not face any manifest competition from the car's fortunes, unlike the underground.

To summarise, it seems that in Turin the tram survived because there were no better solutions available for public mass transportation and for a long time it was able to satisfy the demands of industrial development. As a final remark, it is interesting to point out the current state of the Turin tramways. Despite the wider renaissance of public transport, including rails, as of 2010 the Turin network is at its nadir, with only six routes running for a total of about 30 kilometres – far less than in the golden age of car culture.

References

a) Anonymous articles, author not known

'L'azienda tranviaria municipale ed i suoi risultati finanziari', *Città di Torino – Bollettino mensile dell'ufficio del Lavoro e della statistica*, 1, 1921, 13–16.

'La Impresit-Electroconsult prima tra le sette ditte che hanno concorso per il progetto', *Torino municipalizzate*, 37, 1969, 12–25.

'Contributo statale di 78 miliardi per la metropolitana torinese', *Torino municipalizzate*, 45, 1970, 45–6.

'MT. Costituita la società per la metropolitana a Torino', *Torino municipalizzate*, 4, 1971, 85–6.

b) Named articles and monographs

Aimo, P., *Stato e poteri locali in Italia 1848–1995* (Roma 1997).

Aloisi, A., *I servizi ferrotranviari ed automobilistici extraurbani facenti capo a Torino* (Torino 1949).

Boffa, G., 'Lo sviluppo urbanistico di Torino', *Atti e rassegna tecnica delle società di Ingegneri e degli Architetti in Torino*, 3–6, 1975, 37–70.

Calvino, I., *A Plunge into Real Estate* (London 1983; original publication in Italian titled *La speculazione edilizia* in 1963).

Cicognani, L. and Mochi, C., 'I trasporti', in *Annali dell'economia italiana 1959–1964*, 12, 2, 1982, 237–301.

De Magistris, A., 'L'urbanistica della grande trasformazione (1945–1980)', in N. Tranfaglia, ed., *Storia di Torino*, vol. 9 (Torino 1999), 189–238.

Divall, C. and Bond, W., eds, *Suburbanizing the Masses. Public Transport and Urban Development in Historical Perspective* (Aldershot 2003).

Flink, J.J., *The Automobile Age* (Cambridge, MA 1988).

Fogliano, A., 'Gomma o rotaia?', *Torino municipalizzate*, 2, 1963, 18–25.

Giardina, R., 'Stabilito il tracciato e bandito il concorso per la metropolitana', *Torino municipalizzate*, 7, 1964, 24–31.

Giuntini, A., 'Nascita, sviluppo e tracollo della rete infrastrutturale', in L. Segreto, ed., *Storia d'Italia. Annali 15. L'industria* (Torino 1999), 551–617.

Giupponi, F., 'Origine della Satti', *Torino*, 8, 1949, 25–33.

Giupponi, L., 'Sviluppo, sistemazione ed organizzazione delle Tranvie Urbane di Torino', *Rivista dell'Azienda Tranvie Municipali di Torino*, 6, 1927, 203–9, 2, 1928, 5–17, and 3, 1928, 74–81.

Giupponi, L., *Sviluppo, sistemazione ed organizzazione delle tranvie urbane di Torino* (Torino 1928).

Giupponi, L., 'L'Azienda Tranvie e le sue vetture', *Rivista dell'Azienda Tranvie Municipali di Torino*, 6, 1930, 77–90.

Heras Garcia, R., *Automotores norteamericanos, caminos y modernizacion urbana en la Argentina, 1918–1939* (Buenos Aires 1985).

Maggi, S., *Le ferrovie* (Bologna 2003).

Maggi, S., *Storia dei trasporti in Italia* (Bologna 2005).

McKay, J.P., *Tramways and Trolleys. The Rise of Urban Mass Transport in Europe* (Princeton, NJ 1976).

Mochi, C., 'I trasporti', *Annali dell'economia italiana 1930–1938*, 8, 2, 1982, 213–71.

Moraglio, M., 'Le politiche infrastrutturali fra emergenze e squilibri', in F. Levi and S. Musso, eds, *Torino da capitale politica a capitale dell'industria. Il miracolo economico (1950–1970)* (Torino 2006), 169–77.

Moraglio, M., 'Il trasporto extraurbano: la Satti dal 1934 al 2003', in S. Musso, ed., *Il trasporto pubblico a Torino nel secolo dell'industria: Atm, Satti, Gtt* (Torino 2007), 87–131.

Musso, S., ed., *Il trasporto pubblico a Torino nel secolo dell'industria: Atm, Satti, Gtt* (Torino 2007).

Paolini, F., *Un paese a quattro ruote. Automobili e societá in Italia* (Venezia 2005).

Paolini, F., *Storia sociale dell'automobile in Italia* (Rome 2007).

Picon, A., 'Towards a history of infrastructure', in M. Bonino and M. Moraglio, eds, *Inventare gli spostamenti. Storia e immagini dell'autostrada Torino-Savona / Inventing Movement. History and Images of the A6 Motorway* (Torino 2006), 13–17.

Reichow, H.B., *Die autogerechte Stadt. Ein Weg aus dem Verkehrs-Chaos* (Ravensburg 1959).

Rotelli, E., *Il martello e l'incudine. Comuni e province fra cittadini e apparati* (Bologna 1991).

Schipper, F., *Driving Europe. Building Europe on Roads in the Twentieth Century* (Amsterdam 2008).

Schmucki, B., 'Fashion and technological change Tramways in Germany after 1945', *The Journal of Transport History*, 31, 1, 2010, 1–24

Wollen, P. and Kerr J., eds, *Autopia. Cars and Culture* (London 2002).

Yago, G., *The Decline of Transit. Urban Transportation in German and U.S. Cities, 1900–1970* (Cambridge 1984).

Zignoli, V., 'Tram e auto: ricerca d'una convivenza', *Torino*, 2, 1966, 47–55.

Chapter 15

The City and the *Autobahn* 1926–56: How Frankfurt am Main Promoted Road Traffic and Realised an Old Dream

Reiner Ruppmann

Introduction

A remarkable number of scholarly studies have described the changes in urban structures and social life when railways entered cities in the nineteenth century. At this time, many municipal authorities were eager to get a direct rail connection, or at least hoped to be near a railway track. They wished to improve the economic situation of their community, exploiting more distant markets by the use of the faster traffic connection. Railways guaranteed speedy transport of the products demanded by the fast-growing industrial sites and the expanding population in the cities. They boosted the economic revolution in the second half of the century. Both investors and ordinary citizens achieved increasing prosperity through the railway business and the extension of transport range.[1] Therefore municipal authorities accepted the tremendous impact of the new transport system on city planning and urban development, which transformed former medieval towns into hotspots for industry, trade and sightseeing.[2]

Surprisingly, neither road nor traffic historians have yet paid much attention to the interaction between the *Autobahn* and the cities in the twentieth century, although this additional road system dedicated to automobiles faced many of the same issues as the railway did. It seems reasonable to ask certain questions: How did municipalities respond to the potentials and implications of the new road system? When and how did cities connect their municipal streets to the bypassing *Autobahn*? What side-effects did the access roads (*Zubringerstraßen*) have inside

---

1 Rainer Fremdling, *Eisenbahnen und deutsches Wirtschaftswachstum 1840–1879. Ein Beitrag zur Entwicklungstheorie und zur Theorie der Infrastruktur* (Dortmund 1975); Rainer Fremdling, 'Industrialisierung und Eisenbahn. Der Anstoß zur Entwicklung der deutschen Schwerindustrie', in Harm-Hinrich Brandt et al., eds, *Zug der Zeit – Zeit der Züge. Deutsche Eisenbahn 1835–1985*, 2 vols (Berlin 1985), vol. 1, 121–33.

2 Ralf Roth and Marie-Noëlle Polino, eds, *The City and the Railway in Europe* (Aldershot 2003); Ralf Roth, *Das Jahrhundert der Eisenbahn. Die Herrschaft über Raum und Zeit 1800–1914* (Ostfildern 2005).

or in the outskirts of cities? How did the *Autobahn* impact traffic infrastructure in general and town streets in particular? In what ways did it promote or inhibit the development of cities and the evolution of suburban areas? What were the long-term political, economic, social and cultural consequences of the *Autobahn* system?[3]

This article does not attempt to give comprehensive answers to these crucial questions.[4] Its aim is to use the case of Frankfurt am Main to exemplify some aspects of the relationship between the city and the *Autobahn*. The process started after the First World War when car traffic suddenly rushed upon old-fashioned roads, most of them still unchanged since the days of stage coaches. Three key questions are to be explored: When and why did Frankfurt municipal authorities pick up on the idea of a special road only for motorised cars? How did they influence the layout of the *Autobahn*? What consequences did the *Autobahn* network have in the area around Frankfurt?

Frankfurt's Traffic Heritage and Old Dreams

Ideas for improving Frankfurt's traffic situation were influenced by the economic history of the city and the evolution of transport systems in the area. The roots of these systems can be traced back to medieval times.

Before the days of the railways, Frankfurt became rich through trade fairs and the exchange of merchandise, because seven major European trading routes had to pass through the bottleneck of the only bridge over the river Main in Frankfurt. Until the middle of the nineteenth century, the Thurn and Taxis stagecoach company ran its central hub in downtown Frankfurt, serving regional and European relations.

---

3 For questions, see Roth and Polino, *City and the Railway*, xvii.

4 Although Lewis Mumford published his famous collection of essays *The Highway and the City* in 1963, it took a long time before similar projects in Germany started. Competent historical scholarly studies include Barbara Schmucki's 'Schneisen durch die Stadt – Sinnbild der "modernen" Stadt. Stadtautobahnen und amerikanisches Vorbild in Ost- und Westdeutschland 1925–1975', *WerkstattGeschichte*, 21, 1998, 43–63 (the issue has the topic Netzwerk *Auto*-Bahn, and was edited by Burghard Ciesla); and Barbara Schmucki's *Der Traum vom Verkehrsfluß. Städtische Verkehrsplanung seit 1945 im deutsch-deutschen Vergleich* (Frankfurt am Main et al. 2001). Georg Kammann published a Switzerland-based scholarly study, *Mit Autobahnen die Städte retten? Städtebauliche Ideen der Expressstrassenplanung in der Schweiz 1954–1964* (Zurich 1990). Most of the German discussion about cities and road construction after the Second World War took place in specialised magazines for architects, urban planners, traffic and road engineers. Sociologists in general studied the effects of motorcars on personal mobility and the rise of urban sprawl. Naturally they did not look at problems in the same way historians do, and mostly neglected the interdependence of the existing *Autobahn* system and city streets. Since in the 1990s historians took on the long-term development of traffic, transport and mobility as a field of studies, this topic has slowly gathered momentum, but is still greatly undervalued.

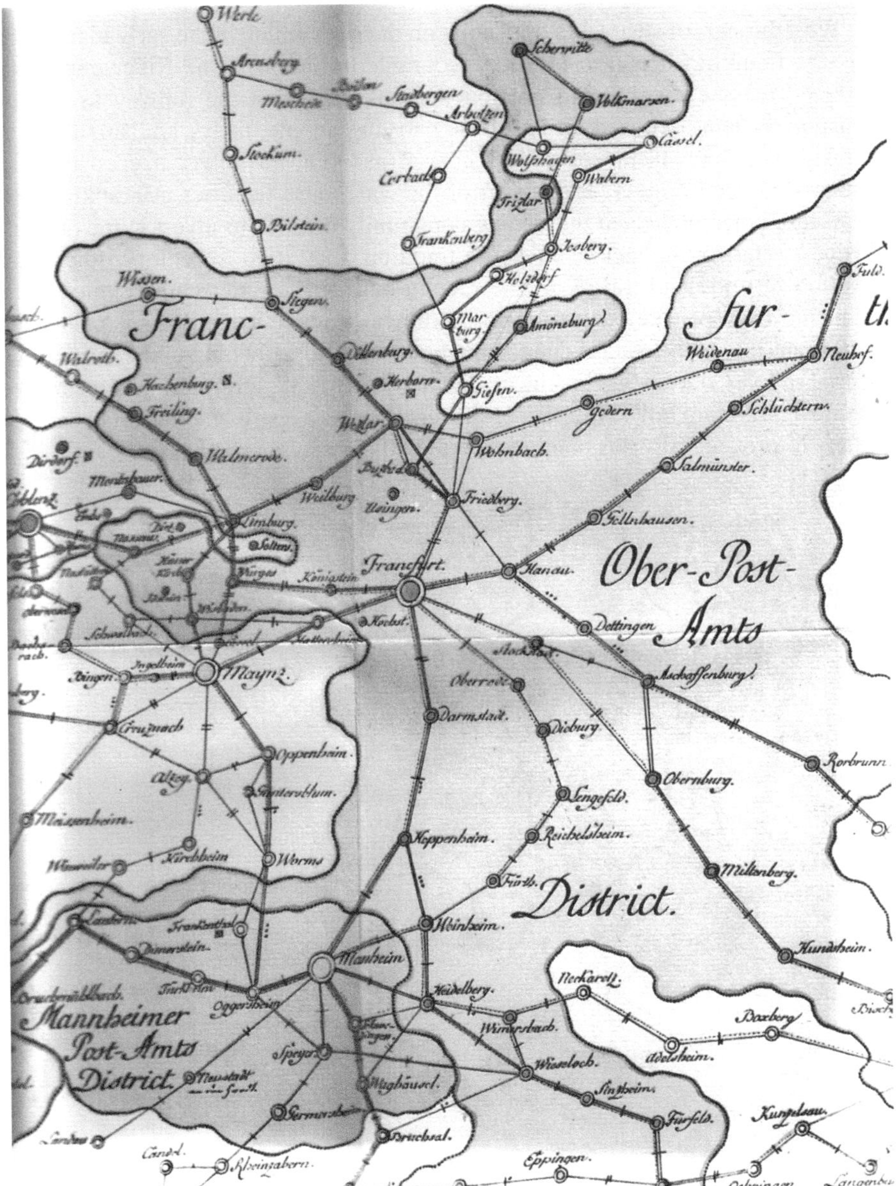

Figure 15.1 Thurn und Taxis stagecoach lines junction at Frankfurt am Main, 1793

Source: Section of the Post-Carte (um Frankfurt) 1793, Reprinted from *Archiv für deutsche Postgeschichte*, 2, 1969, attachment (Museum für Kommunikation, Berlin).

With the start of steamship transports on the river Rhine in the early nineteenth century, Frankfurt began to lose its favourable traffic position.[5] River transports attracted mass cargo but did not touch Frankfurt. Then the railway as a new transport system appeared on the scene carrying people, heavy and small goods quickly over long distances at low cost. Transports no longer needed the old trade roads, the bridge over the river or the warehouse facilities in Frankfurt. So Frankfurt's merchants and the trading community decided to invest in the railway business. Harkening back to their old tradition, they tried to return to their key position in trade and traffic. In the second half of the nineteenth century, with financing from private banks, territorial railway companies built four main lines with Frankfurt as the central connecting point. After the opening of the impressive central railway station outside the medieval wall in 1888, Frankfurt became one of the most important railway junctions in Germany. As a result, the state of economic affairs improved; railways then transported 80 per cent of goods.

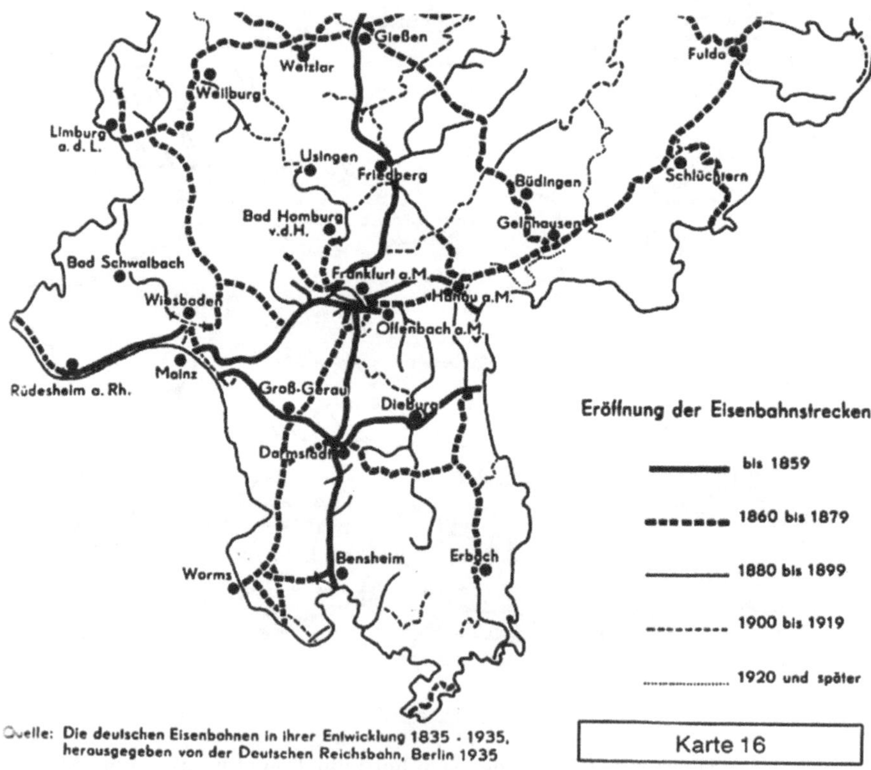

Figure 15.2 Frankfurt am Main railway junction, 1859–1920

Source: Section of a sketch in Walter Heinemeyer, *Das Werden Hessens* (Marburg 1986), 416a.

[5] Ralf Roth, *Die Herausbildung einer modernen bürgerlichen Gesellschaft. Geschichte der Stadt Frankfurt am Main 1789–1866* (Ostfildern 2013), 293–303.

After the occupation of Frankfurt by the Prussian Army in 1866 and its integration into the Kingdom of Prussia in 1867, political and economic conditions changed remarkably. Unfortunately, Frankfurt was not made the capital of the Prussian province of Hessen-Kassel, and lost its importance as a leading banking and exchange place to Berlin. Step by step the former free city (*Freie Stadt*) was downgraded to a regional town at the southern border of the Prussian state. On the other hand, incorporation into Prussia offered new economic opportunities to Frankfurt tradespeople, who were sensible enough to take them. At the turn of the twentieth century, the city expanded quickly through the incorporation of half a dozen surrounding villages, which then hosted modern industries such as chemicals, engine building and electrical appliances, as well as various small manufacturers. Within 20 years, Frankfurt had transformed itself into one of the leading centres for industry in the German Empire. Industrialists of the second industrial revolution started very successful new ventures, especially in the telephone, bicycle and car industries. For a time before the First World War, Frankfurt possessed the largest territory of any German city. Its population grew rapidly. In 1875 the city had over 100,000 residents; by 1914 this number had more than quadrupled.

Railways could not transport urgently needed mass goods any more (for example building materials, coal and corn). So Frankfurt invested in a new river harbour and storage facilities in the west of the city between 1883 and 1886. About 20 years later Frankfurt started another huge port project at the eastern periphery of the city. Transportation had increased considerably and the old west docks were not sufficient any more. At the same time, Frankfurt looked forward optimistically to the connection of the rivers Rhine, Main and Danube by a canal. In 1912 the new eastern harbour went into operation, but there were only two years left to run the business calmly.[6]

In August 1914 Germany went to war and transports declined severely. As a result of the four-year war, Frankfurt lost its former economic strength, due to a large demilitarised district administrated by French Armed Forces which cut off important traffic relations. Once more, Frankfurt had to deal with very problematic circumstances. Ludwig Landmann, mayor of Frankfurt starting in 1923, developed a number of ideas for solving the problems. Far-sightedly, he propagated the prospective advantages of the coming age of overland motorised cross-country and air traffic, which he saw as an important supplement to railway transport. He combined this vision with the idea of a large economic region in the south-west of Germany led by Frankfurt. Preliminary decisions in this vein were taken by forming associations for traffic coordination and urban planning.

[6] For more details concerning this era see Ralf Roth, 'Von der Zollvereinsgründung bis zur Annexion der Stadt, 1834–1870' and Dieter Hein, 'Vom Finanzplatz zur Industriestadt: Frankfurt 1871–1914', in Werner Plumpe and Dieter Rebentisch, eds, *'Dem Flor der hiesigen Handlung'. 200 Jahre Industrie- und Handelskammer Frankfurt am Main* (Frankfurt am Main 2008), 80–102, and 128–55. See also other contributions in the section 'Frankfurt auf dem Weg in die Moderne'.

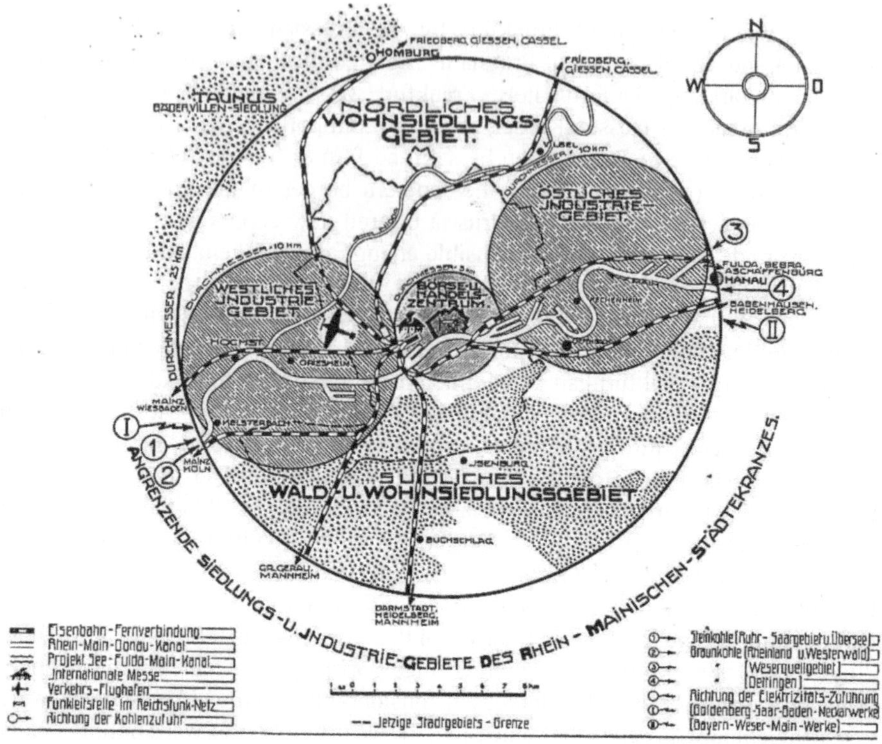

Figure 15.3 Plan of Greater Frankfurt, 1923

Source: Institut für Stadtgeschichte Frankfurt am Main, A. Weitzel, Siedlung und Verkehr Gross Frankfurt a. M., in *Der rhein-mainische Städtekranz mit seiner Zentrale Frankfurt am Main im südwestdeutschen Wirtschaftsgebiet* (Frankfurt am Main 1924), 103. See also Dieter Rebentisch, 'Die kleine Stadt und der große Markt. Regionale und überregionale Zentralitäten der Stadt Frankfurt am Main 1866–1989', in Heinz Jürgen Priamus and Ralf Himmelmann, eds, *Stadt und Region – Region und Stadt. Stadtgeschichte, Urbanisierungsgeschichte, Regionalgeschichte* (Essen 1993) 51–70.

The plan of Greater Frankfurt with strictly separated industrial, housing and recreation areas. Diameter of the circle: 25 kilometres; population about 700,000.

At the beginning of the Weimarer Republic, the effects of motorisation were on the political and economic agenda in all major German cities. The sudden increase in truck traffic in and around large population centres and industrial areas soon became a nightmare for regional and local road construction authorities. They could not provide appropriate roads for the automobile traffic because their cities had lost financial resources in the hyperinflation of 1922 and 1923. The transport ministry of the Deutsche Reich had no authority to supply federal states with road construction funds since the responsibility for all roads was entirely decentralised. Cities had to take care of their streets on their own even if they were thoroughfares. To substitute for the missing commitment of the government, road engineers of the German federal states founded an association called the *Deutscher Straßenbau-Verband* (German Road Construction Association). This association sought to promote a nationwide network of main roads, to define standards of road construction and to organise the exchange of know-how.

At that time, only few of the main roads were prepared for automotive traffic with a paved surface or compressed asphalt. Most of them were still only macadamised. Car traffic bothered people with clouds of dust in the summer and sprays of mud in the winter. With their iron wheels or solid rubber tyres, trucks severely damaged macadam roads and streets. In towns and villages they caused tremendous noise as they jolted over paving stones. To build up new skills as fast as possible, German road experts visited their counterparts abroad, especially in the United Kingdom and the United States of America during the war. With the economic upturn after 1924, road engineers of the German federal states set out into a road-strengthening program mainly financed by international loans. In general, paving was realised by spraying surfaces with a light layer of asphalt; only few important roads with intense lorry *and* car traffic got a bed of tar macadam or concrete.

Meanwhile, urban road engineers experimented with feasible solutions for channelling mixed traffic on main streets leading out of towns by dividing motorcars, slow horse-drawn vehicles, interurban railways, bicycles and pedestrians into single-purpose tracks. Thus ideas to construct main town streets and cross-country roads as well similar to railway tracks gained momentum. However, governmental authorities of the *Deutsches Reich* accepted the need for unique roads for motor vehicles only reluctantly, not only because they did not know how to finance such a huge investment in infrastructure but also because they believed it would be enough to broaden existing roads step by step as the traffic demanded. In the *Zeitgeist* of those times, it seemed foolish to sink limited funds for road building and maintenance into a specialised road for cars only. As a matter of fact, at that time long-range and mass transportation were still dominated by the German Railway Company (*Deutsche Reichsbahn-Gesellschaft*) and water-based shipping companies. Cross-country automotive traffic was not a real problem in the interwar period, because it usually faded away in a distance of 20 to 30 kilometres outside cities.[7] In 1926 Germany had only 291,430 motorised vehicles (cars and trucks, excluding buses and special trucks); by 1932 the number had more than doubled but still did not require expressways.

Frankfurt municipal authorities chose a distinct position to cope with the increasing car traffic in the Rhein-Main region, although the number of motorised vehicles was not really impressive: 27,226 cars and trucks in 1926, 61,120 in 1932 (9.3 and 9.5 per cent respectively of the total numbers in the *Deutsche Reich*). As town councillors had internalised a long-term mental picture of the general influence of traffic and exchange on the economic prosperity of their hometown,

[7] Philipp Rappaport and Karl Heller, *Allgemeine Strassenplanung*, ed. by Hubert Hentrich (Halle a. d. Saale 1928).

Mayor Ludwig Landmann consciously developed a scheme to safeguard the economic future of the city. The Frankfurt counsellors welcomed the automotive age as a chance for future wealth and power, and gladly ventured into the project of a motorway (*Autobahn*).

Like Frankfurt's government officials, progressive entrepreneurs were convinced that trucks and cars should have straight, wide and well-paved roads without crossings on the same level and by-passing all villages. This would maximise their benefits, especially in comparison with slow, expensive railway transportation. In these thinkers' opinion, the small volumes of industrial and consumer goods typical of Frankfurt-based industry could probably be transported (and thus retailed) much faster through the use of motor vehicles. Direct delivery from door to door without the need for the railway timetable, expensive packing materials or reloading charges would save time and money. But decision-makers were confronted with two key problems which hampered truck transport: first, the narrow, curved and poorly paved roads that led through the middle of cities and villages, and second, the scanty motor power of trucks and their comparative inability to carry heavy freight. Nevertheless, to the regret of the powerful *Deutsche Reichsbahn-Gesellschaft*, truck services began to take over a considerable quantity of the profitable segment of railway cargo.[8]

Regarding German *Autobahn* history, the starting point to look more deeply into the idea of a specific road for cars can be located in Frankfurt in 1925, when the city began again to be the 'City of Roads'.

This term reflected the opinion of municipal authorities but was given by a journalist, referring to the city's earlier trading days. It called to mind the economic success of the past that had grown on the intersection of important old trade routes.[9]

Figure 15.4 gives an impression of how Frankfurt spread out in a circle around the old city centre and along the main streets in the west where most of the industrial sites were located. Apart from these sites, the leather industry in the neighbour city of Offenbach and the chemical industry in nearby Höchst also contributed traffic, as did government of the Prussian administrative district in Wiesbaden.

---

8 In Germany, the stock market crash was followed by a vehement dispute between the *Deutsche Reichsbahn* and the truckers' lobby which lasted from 1929 to 1932 without settlement. See for example Deutsche Reichsbahn-Gesellschaft, ed., *Reichsbahn und Kraftwagenverkehr* (Berlin 1930); Pressedienst der Reichsbahn, ed., *Frage und Antwort zum Problem Gütertransport auf Eisenbahnen und Kraftwagen* (Berlin 1932); Eberhard Kolb, 'Die Reichsbahn vom Dawes-Plan bis zum Ende der Weimarer Republik', in Lothar Gall and Manfred Pohl, eds, *Die Eisenbahn in Deutschland. Von den Anfängen bis zur Gegenwart* (Munich 1999), 109–63.

9 Otto Ernst Sutter, 'Die Stadt der Straßen', in Hans Trumpler and Julius Ziehen, eds, *Jahrbuch der Frankfurter Bürgerschaft 1925* (Frankfurt am Main 1925), 127–9.

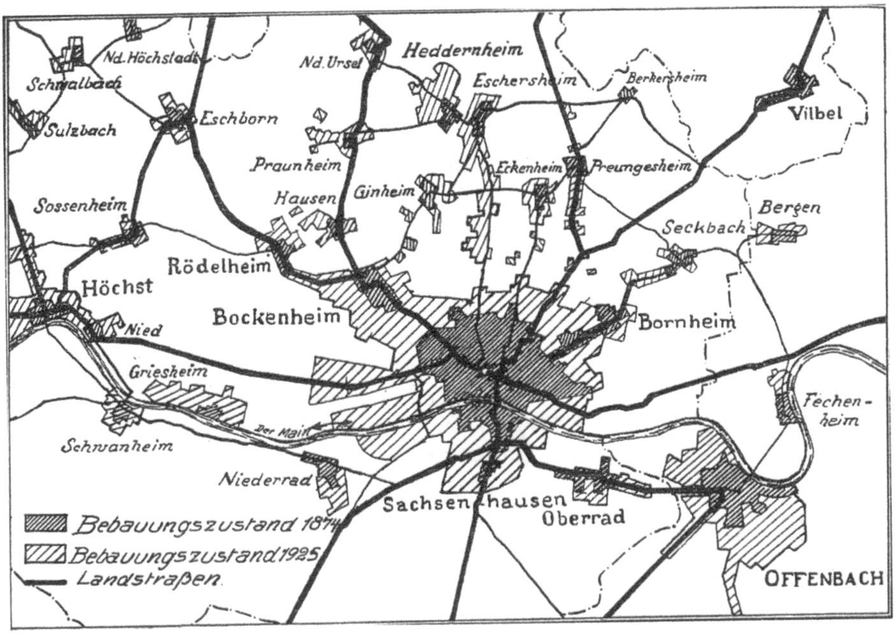

Figure 15.4 The city expansion of Frankfurt alongside the principal streets, 1874–1925

Source: Engel, 'Frankfurt am Main als Hauptknotenpunkt des Landstrassen-Netzes', in Ludwig Landmann and Hans Trumpler, eds, *Jahrbuch der Frankfurter Bürgerschaft 1926* (Frankfurt am Main 1926), 51–6, here 54.

Planning and Construction of the *Autobahn* Network in the Rhein-Main Region, 1926–37[10]

In 1926, Frankfurt councilmen, together with other counsellors of major cities and governmental representatives, founded a public-private partnership to study the feasibility of an expressway for motorised traffic between the German ports in the north and the Swiss border. The initiative had the vision to create a national artery for truck services and to tempt international motorised visitors to spend holidays in Germany. This proposal has to be seen in the light of a competing plan in France to connect the French channel ports with the Mediterranean Sea via a motorway. The German public-private partnership was named *Verein zur Vorbereitung*

10 For full details see Reiner Ruppmann, *Frankfurt und das Rhein-Main-Taunus-Gebiet – Schrittmacher für das Autobahn-Zeitalter* (Darmstadt 2011). A short cut presented Richard Vahenkamp, *Autobahnbau in Hessen bis 1943* (Darmstadt 2007). See also Richard Vahrenkamp, *The German Autobahn 1920–1945. Hafraba Visions and Mega Projects* (Lohmar 2010).

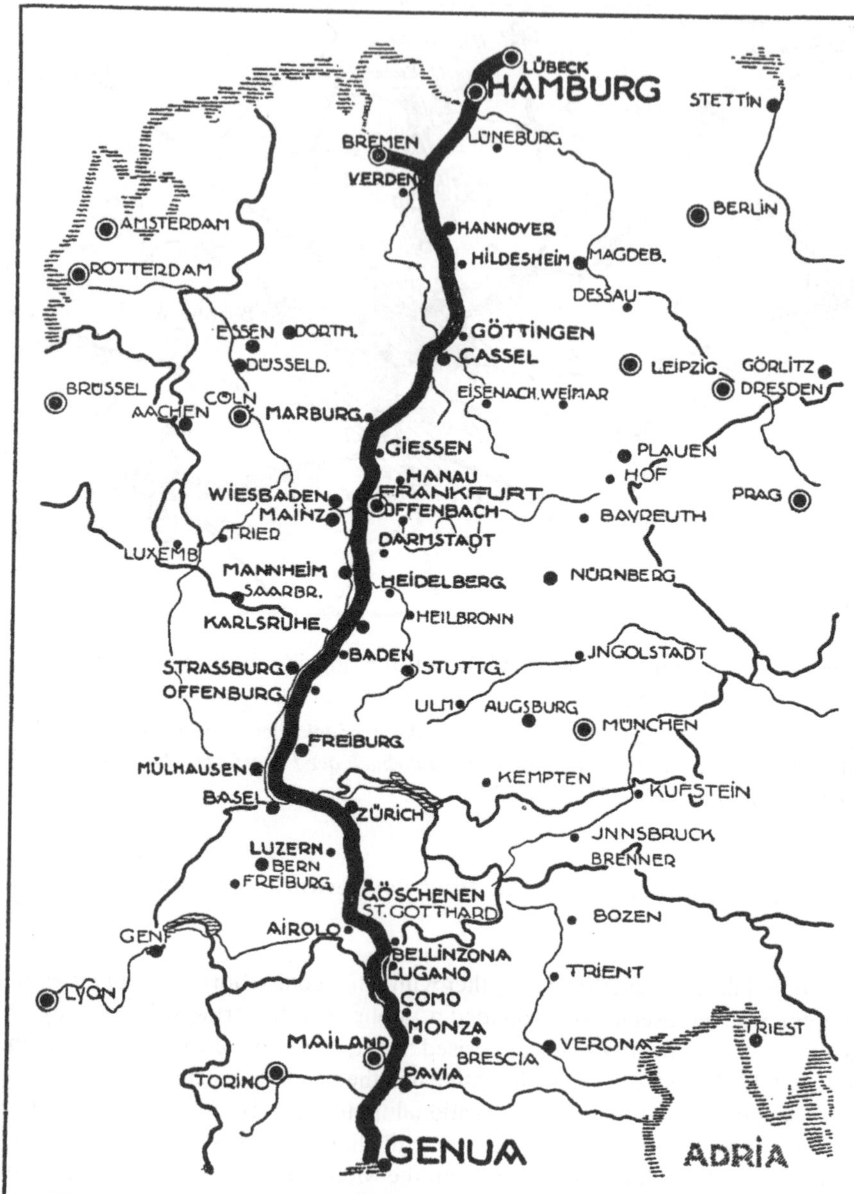

Figure 15.5 Principal layout of the three-to-four lane HaFraBa highway through Germany, 1926

Source: Robert Otzen, *Die Autostraße Hansestädte – Frankfurt – Basel. Erläuterungsbericht zum Entwurf der Autostraße* (Hannover 1927), 10 (image 5).

der Autostraße Hansestädte-Frankfurt-Basel (HaFraBa) (Association for the Preparation of the Motorway Hanseatic cities-Frankfurt-Basel). Planners intended that adjacent communes and more distant regions would join this central backbone via feeder roads. Frankfurt, located in the middle of the 880 kilometre-long route, saw itself as the main link between north-south and east-west long-range truck and car traffic.

The speaker of the HaFraBa executive board, Robert Otzen, and the HaFraBa members were all convinced that it was high time to promote the new transport facility, the *Autobahn*. They did not want to fight against railway or air transportation but sought a timely completion of German traffic routes. They felt the services of the three transport systems should be carefully coordinated with each other to maximise performance in favour of the German economy. To distinguish the new, innovative roads from all other public roads built with taxes and other public contributions, Otzen created the name *Autobahn*, derived from the term *Eisenbahn* (railway). In his opinion, the *Autobahn* was a mix between a railway track and a cross-country road. The objective was to make everybody understand that the expressway would be built with share capital and that users would have to pay a toll. Otzen also gave voice to the opinion of HaFraBa members that all main roads in Germany must be adapted to automotive traffic, otherwise the *Autobahn* would not be of the expected economic value.[11]

A small group of HaFraBa experts needed only one year to develop a first draft of the whole route and to design a detailed plan for the *Autobahn* section from Frankfurt to Mannheim and Heidelberg. But the HaFraBa society was not able to start construction of this first example of the *Autobahn* because German law prohibited all institutions from charging money for the use of a road. The HaFraBa sought to change the law or to obtain special permission from the government, but their efforts perished in the disorder of the political situation in Germany between 1930 and 1932.[12]

In the first months after Hitler was appointed Chancellor of the *Deutsche Reich*, the Nazi regime made various efforts to keep and to secure its sphere of influence by force. As Hitler had promised the implementation of a new political culture in favour of the voting masses instead of particular pressure groups, the Nazi government now had to proceed to action. It badly needed a highly visible popular symbol. To gain strength, Hitler picked up a comprehensible issue: the job creation scheme with which the Weimar government had tried to fight against unemployment. Following the recommendation of Fritz Todt, a persuasive and experienced road-building engineer and member of the NSDAP since 1923, the

---

11 Robert Otzen, *Die Autostraße Hansestädte – Frankfurt – Basel. Zweck und Ziele des Vereins 'Hafraba'* (Hannover 1927), and Robert Otzen, *Die Autostraße Hansestädte – Frankfurt – Basel. Erläuterungsbericht zum Entwurf der Autostraße* (Hannover 1927).

12 See Kurt Kaftan, *Der Kampf um die Autobahnen. Geschichte und Entwicklung des Autobahngedankens in Deutschland von 1907–1935 unter Berücksichtigung ähnlicher Pläne und Bestrebungen im übrigen Europa* (Berlin 1955), 124–50.

Führer obtained the HaFraBa documents as blueprints for the construction of a German *Autobahn* network.[13]

In the Weimar Parliament, Hitler's party, the NSDAP, had steadfastly voted together with the Communists against the 'road for the rich' whenever public measures against unemployment were put on the agenda of the legislative body. But now Hitler spent time and authority from March to June 1933 enacting the necessary laws as well as establishing the basic organisational structures for the *Autobahn* project. In particular he had to convince the hesitant General Director of the *Deutsche Reichsbahn-Gesellschaft*, Julius Dorpmüller, to expand his business into road transportation. From the time when Dorpmüller was appointed head of the *Reichsbahn*, he had fought hard against the competition of truck transportation, which he deemed harmful for the profit of his company. His position was strongly backed by the German Ministers of Transport, Finance and Economy, whose eyes were fixed upon the annual payment of reparations to the allies backed by the *Reichsbahn*.[14] But step by step Hitler ran Dorpmüller's blockade. In a conference on 1 June 1933, Dorpmüller agreed to start with the construction of the *Autobahn* sections from Frankfurt via Heidelberg and Mannheim, Munich, Salzburg and Berlin to Stettin and the Baltic Sea as soon as related laws are valid. To finance the stock of the new venture (*Unternehmen Reichsautobahn*, a sister company of the *Reichsbahn-Gesellschaft*) he provided 50 million Reichsmarks taken from the *Reichsbahn* employment program.[15]

The first main directorate for expressway construction, the *Oberste Bauleitung Kraftwagenbahnen/Reichsautobahnen* (OBK/OBR), was founded with the help of the *Reichsbahn* in Frankfurt on 26 June 1933.[16] The Frankfurt *Reichsbahndirektion* had to delegate railway engineers and employees as well as to grant rooms and office equipment. Four days later Hitler inaugurated Fritz Todt as Inspector-

---

13 In 1932, in response to an order from the NSDAP's department of economic policy, Todt had written a paper concerning road construction and road administration. Because the paper had a brown cover it was called the 'brown report' ('Brauner Bericht'). Bundesarchiv Berlin, R 4601/3001a, Fritz Todt, *Strassenbau und Strassenverwaltung*, unpublished typescript (Munich 1932).

14 Georg Walter, *Eisenbahn und Kraftwagen – ein dringendes Verkehrsproblem* (Berlin 1929). Some argue that this statement of defense was written by Dorpmüller himself under a pseudonym. See also Deutsche Reichsbahn-Gesellschaft, ed., *Reichsbahn und Kraftwagenverkehr* (Berlin 1930), and Alfred E. Gottwaldt, *Julius Dorpmüller, die Reichsbahn und die Autobahn. Verkehrspolitik und Leben des Verkehrsministers bis 1945* (Berlin 1995), 33–61.

15 See Konrad Repgen, Günter Hockerts, Hans Booms and Friedrich Kahlenberg, eds, *Akten der Reichskanzlei. Die Regierung Hitler*, ed. for Historische Kommission bei der Bayerischen Akademie der Wissenschaften und für das Bundesarchiv, part I: *1933/1934* (Boppard am Rhein 1983), vol. 1, document 153.

16 The field of activities included nearly the whole southwest of the *Deutsche Reich*. After Germany had won the war against France, a construction office was etstablished in Straßburg.

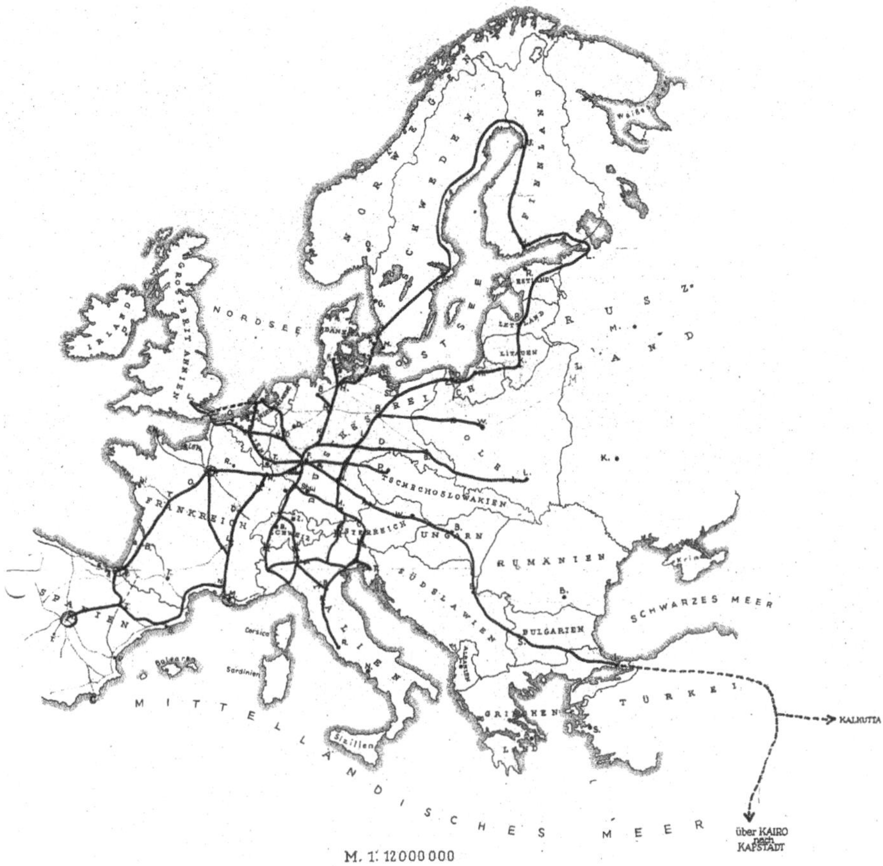

Figure 15.6 Frankfurt's depiction of its position in the European expressway system

Source: Institut für Stadtgeschichte Frankfurt am Main, Magistratssakte 6.286.

General of the German Roads. Todt also acted as *Generalinspektor* (principal) of the planning company *Gesellschaft zur Vorbereitung der Reichsautobahnen e. V.* (GEZUVOR), successor to the HaFraBa, and as supervisor of the federal *Gesellschaft Reichsautobahnen* (*Reichsautobahn* company); he reported directly to Hitler.

Todt chose Reinhold Niemeyer, head of the municipal planning office of Frankfurt, to lead the GEZUVOR's Rhein-Main department. Thus Niemeyer held a key position in process of planning the different *Autobahn* lines in the area and making them as close as possible to Frankfurt (Figure 15.6). With luck and the know-how of former HaFraBa engineers as well as the staff in the municipal planning office, he successfully intervened in the *Reichsautobahn* planning procedures in adjacent districts, working to put Frankfurt into the centre of the

German and European highway network. So Niemeyer created around the 'City of Roads', a network of expressways in the Rhein-Main area.

But Frankfurt never got the award it was so eager to receive from Hitler: the honour of adding the title 'City of Roads' to the city's name. Presumably Todt recommended that Hitler not do so, because the *Führer* was supposed to be the sole driving force behind the German *Autobahn* system, eclipsing any other individual or group. For the same reason, Todt had to extinguish the remembrance of the merits of the HaFraBa Association and the dominant role Frankfurt had played in it for more than five years. Although Todt knew that the *Reichsautobahn*'s construction in 1933 never would have made such enormous progress without the systematic groundwork of the HaFraBa engineers, he avoided saying so openly, because he needed Hitler's unreserved support to continue receiving financing for the *Autobahn* constructions. Todt had promised Hitler to have 1,000 kilometres of *Autobahn* per year ready for traffic. Todt called the new traffic network *Straßen des Führers* (Roads of the Leader) in texts and in speeches, and consistently fought any other designation for them.

For promotion, Todt published photos in his magazine *Die Straße* and in the Nazi newspapers *Völkische Beobachter* and *Hakenkreuzbanner*. In the early years, covers of *Die Straße* frequently showed Hitler in different poses on construction sites to underline that he was the 'Father of the *Autobahn*' and had brought employment back to German workforce.[17] Additionally, in the years 1936 to 1938 Todt published three well-designed books with the title *Drei (vier, fünf) Jahre Arbeit an den Straßen Adolf Hitlers*' (*Three, Four, Five Years of Work at the Roads of Adolf Hitler*) which contained a mixture of Nazi propaganda *ad maiorem gloriam ducis*, reports on road constructing technologies and impressive photos of monumental bridges, landscapes embellished with freeways and skilled labourers joyfully working for their motorised future.[18] Even today, these intentionally produced heroic pictures fascinate the public, as recent books have demonstrated. Most likely, the charm of these books is that they show how the *Autobahn* looked at its inception.[19]

---

17 *Die Straße*, vol. 1934–42.

18 Generalinspektor für das deutsche Straßenwesen, ed., *Drei Jahre Arbeit an den Straßen Adolf Hitlers* (Berlin 1936); ibid., *Vier Jahre Arbeit an den Straßen Adolf Hitlers* (Berlin 1937); ibid., *Fünf Jahre Arbeit an den Straßen Adolf Hitlers* (Berlin 1938). See also Charlotte Reitsam, *Reichsautobahn-Landschaften im Spannungsfeld von Natur und Technik. Transatlantische und interdisziplinäre Verflechtungen* (Saarbrücken 2009). See also Richard Vahrenkamp, 'Planning and Constructing the Autobahn Network in Germany During the Nazi-Period – Styles and Strategies', in Gijs Mom and Laurent Tissot, eds, *Road History, Planning, Building and Use* (Neuchâtel 2007), 87–98.

19 For example Berthold Flessa and Helmut Goller, *Die Geschichte der Autobahn 1934 bis 2000* (Münchberg 2000); Gero Fehlhauer *Die Geschichte der Reichsautobahn Chemnitz – Hof* (Reichenbach i. Vogtland 2006); Hans-Joachim Weise, *Vom Bau der Autobahn im Schleizer Oberland 1933 bis 1936* (n. l. 2006); Alfred Lambeck, *Die Bergisch-Märkische Autobahn Leverkusen-Kamen 1948–1958* (n. l. 2008).

Autobahn construction for the Frankfurt–Darmstadt section was started in the southwest periphery of Frankfurt in July 1933. The engineering staff used this first building site as an experimental and testing ground for future *Autobahn* constructions. Civil municipal road engineers in Frankfurt welcomed the opportunity to cooperate closely with the *Autobahn* construction staff. They took advantage of this exceptional situation by reinforcing their skills with regard to Frankfurt's special goal. The collaboration enabled Reinhold Niemeyer to give much technical input into Todt's numerous issuances of general regulations. Furthermore, the planning office of Frankfurt developed its own ideas for the construction of *Autobahn* access points and junctions with crossing roads, which turned out to be very helpful for the *Autobahn* works in progress.

A groundbreaking ceremony on the south bank of the River Main took place on 23 September 1933. On 19 May 1935 there was an inauguration for the first 20 kilometres. Hitler attended both of these events. With that kind of public staging, Nazi propaganda made people believe that the *Autobahn* works would solve the problem of unemployment in the whole *Deutsche Reich*. This was not the case, as many scholarly studies have proven.[20] The north-south *Autobahn* touching Frankfurt's western edge was built from the summer of 1933 to the fall of 1937. This was a segment of about 177 kilometres stretching from the city of Giessen, in the North, almost to the city of Karlsruhe, in the South. The east-west *Autobahn* from Cologne to Würzburg was under construction when Fritz Todt stopped the work in 1940. A short piece of around 16 kilometres between Wiesbaden and Frankfurt remained unfinished until 1956. Nevertheless, the contours around the City of Roads came into sight.

While the first *Autobahn* was built, Niemeyer, following an order from Todt, had to push major cities to prepare access roads to the drivable parts of the *Autobahn*. Unlike in the railway age, cities did not strive to build such links. When they looked at the patchwork of still-discontinuous *Reichsautobahn* lines, they could not see the need for an expensive investment into the infrastructure. Moreover, the volume of long distance traffic was quite low. Furthermore, the cities had no money to build new roads or upgrade existing ones to the level Todt demanded for access roads. Nevertheless, Niemeyer pondered how to lead the expressway traffic into city streets. He reflected on the mutual influence of through car and local traffic, and wondered how best to distribute this traffic inside cities without overloading the existing street network.[21]

---

20 Erhard Schütz and Eckhard Gruber, *Mythos Reichsautobahn – Bau und Inszenierung der 'Straßen des Führers' 1933–1941* (Berlin 1996); Benjamin Steininger, *Raum-Maschine Reichsautobahn. Zur Dynamik eines bekannt/unbekannten Bauwerks* (Berlin 2005).

21 Reinhold Niemeyer, *Großstadtprobleme*. Vorträge aus dem Haus der Technik, H. 13, unpublished typescript (Essen 1935); Reinhold Niemeyer, *Städtebau und Nahverkehr* (Leipzig 1941).

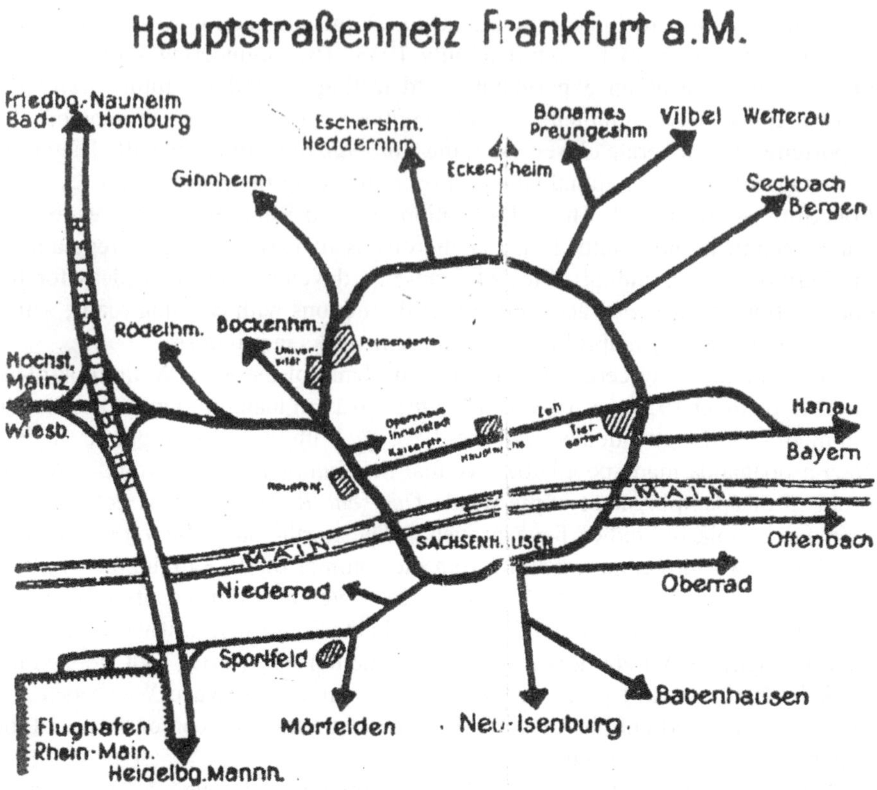

Figure 15.7 Scheme for distributing *Autobahn* traffic into the streets of Frankfurt, 1937

Source: Institut für Stadtgeschichte Frankfurt am Main, S3 F7461 (Frankfurter Zeitung of 24 January 1937).

Figure 15.7 shows the conception Niemeyer and the municipal planners proposed to link Frankfurt to the *Autobahn* and to channel the expected car traffic inside the city. He adapted the common solution from the railway age when he designed a ring avenue around the city centre. At that time the *Autobahn* junction in the south-west of Frankfurt had not yet been decided on but it was foreseen that the two main roads to Mörfelden and Neu-Isenburg would provide additional access points to the pending east-west *Autobahn*. Frankfurt city planners hoped to realise Niemeyer's plan until the 1960s, but never did so due to the enormous costs and the unfeasibility of razing several rows of houses in the southern quarter of the city.

Niemeyer himself had been unable to carry out his special mission. In 1936 he fell in disgrace when Nazi members of the Frankfurt City Council presented his disorderly life. Naturally he was removed from all management positions right away.[22]

[22] Institut für Stadtgeschichte Frankfurt am Main, MA 65.103: file Niemeyer.

Improvement of the *Autobahn* System in the Frankfurt Area, 1950–56

After the Second World War, mass motorisation in the Rhein-Main area started earlier than in other regions of West Germany. The headquarters of the United States Army in Europe was located here and played an important role; as a result, the first political structures of the new *Bundesrepublik Deutschland* took place in Frankfurt. At the same time, the geographical form of West Germany put the Rhein-Main region right in the middle of West Germany. Therefore governmental and local road authorities had to concentrate on the completion of the *Autobahn* network and the construction of new thoroughfares to match the soaring road transportation. Problems intensified with the decade of the so-called *Wirtschaftswunder*, the economic miracle of the 1950s and 1960s, that is, the growing industrial production and the increasing exchange of production material, parts and consumer goods. Then there was holiday traffic, which rose after 1960. This exploding traffic pressed Frankfurt into a bottleneck situation. As before, freight haulage and car traffic suffered from inadequate road capacities. Traffic engineers and mobility experts estimated the extension of the *Autobahn* system as possible solution. In consequence, six new routes were constructed in the Rhein-Main region, most of them according to the Niemeyer plans of the now-defunct GEZUVOR association.

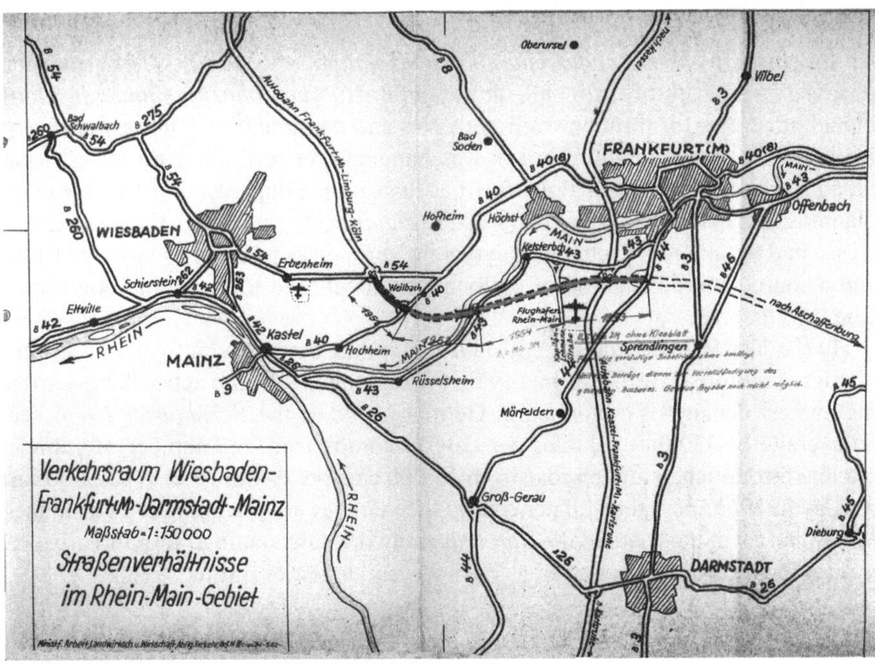

Figure 15.8 The *Autobahn* gap next to Frankfurt

Source: Hessian Main State Archive, Wiesbaden (Hessisches Hauptstaatsarchiv Wiesbaden), department 507, Nr. 8252a.

But first of all it was urgent to close the gap between the Cologne and Frankfurt *Autobahn* and the existing north-south route (Figure 15.8). Due to the uncertain financial situation – funds had to be raised legally by the Parliament year-to-year – work on the missing part lasted from 1952 to 1956. This *Autobahn* was built utilising the files and data of the former *Reichsautobahn* construction office. Even though the previously leading engineers had been let go under the country's denazification policy, most of the technical employees and some experts remained in the *Autobahn* Department of the Federal State of Hesse (*Hessisches Autobahnamt*).[23]

Without pomp and circumstances, the German Minister of Transport, Hans-Christoph Seebohm, held the ceremony for the opening of the Frankfurt *Autobahn* junction (*Frankfurter Autobahnkreuz*) close to the Frankfurt Rhein-Main airport on 15 July 1956. It was not the original HaFraBa plan of 1929 which came to fruition in this moment; still, the intersection realised the dream of former mayor Ludwig Landmann, promoter of the *Autobahn*, who had predicted the importance of expressways for traffic, transports and mobility in the future, and thus confidently supported measures to put Frankfurt in a key position.

Some Consequences of the *Autobahn* Network in the Frankfurt Area

At the birth of the *Bundesrepublik Deutschland*, the Ministry of Transport received responsibility for all thoroughfares (*Autobahnen*, *Bundesstraßen*), including streets for through-traffic in cities and communities. The responsibility for building and maintaining roads was handed over to the federal states. Even though in the Third Reich Frankfurt had lost its leading function for *Autobahn* planning and construction to Todt's *Reichsautobahn* organisation, the new state of Hesse had to take into account the city's importance as a hub of long-range traffic and a source and destination of regional and local road traffic in the polycentric Rhein-Main area.

In the last 50 years the Rhein-Main region has developed into an exceptional district of motorised traffic. Since 1950, the regional *Autobahn* network has carried the highest density of motorcars in Germany. Today, the *Frankfurter Kreuz* sees an average of 330,000 vehicles per day. In comparison: the number of vehicles passing through the junction rose from 46,000 cars per day in 1957 to 132,000 cars per day in 1965. Less than 20 per cent of the vehicles are travelling long distances. More than 80 of the users of the *Autobahn* network surrounding Frankfurt are local and regional commuters as well as business and logistics traffic.

---

[23] Reiner Ruppmann, 'Von der Obersten Bauleitung für Reichsautobahnen zum Amt für Straßen- und Verkehrswesen Frankfurt a. M'., *VSVI Journal*, 1, 2009, 24–34.

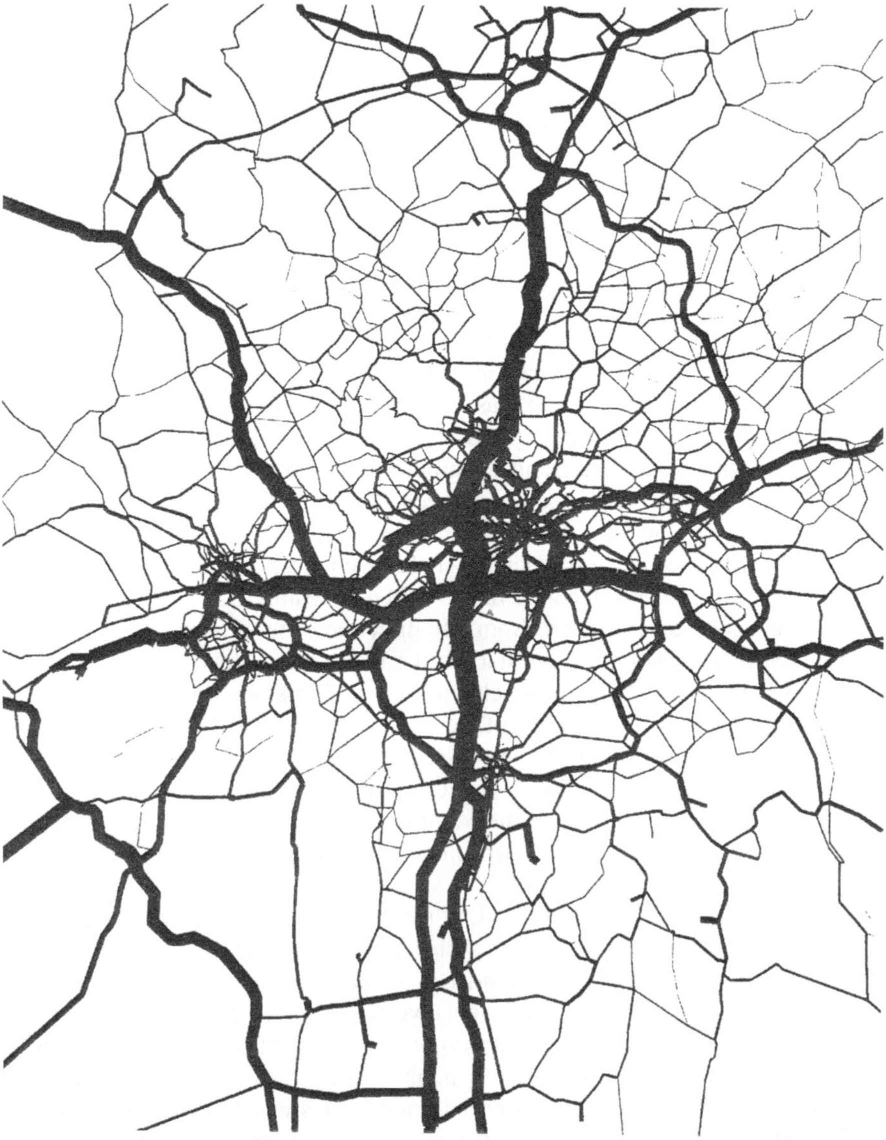

Figure 15.9 Road network for motorised traffic in the Rhein-Main region

Source: Planungsverband Ballungsraum Frankfurt/Rhein-Main, ed., *Verkehrsströme in der Region Frankfurt RheinMain. Die Bedeutung einer einheitlichen Basis für die Verkehrsplanung* (Frankfurt am Main 1999), 7.

The yearly increase of traffic volume still forces road engineers to widen existing *Autobahn* tracks and to close the last missing links. Figure 15.9 shows today's auto mobility and the density of motorised traffic on *Autobahn* routes and main roads in the Rhein-Main region. The thick lines represent the road traffic concentration on north-south and east-west *Autobahn* route that finds its centre of gravity in the *Frankfurter Kreuz*. *Autobahn* routes in the area continue to be a testing ground for adjustments of road capacities to the rising demand and for new methods of road paving and maintenance. In the 1960s the first *Autobahn* from Frankfurt to Darmstadt led the way to the construction of four-lane carriageways for each direction.

From 1995 to 2000, the *Frankfurter Kreuz* had to be totally reorganised to overcome daily traffic jams. Road engineers found an innovative solution, using a single bridge to transform the classic cloverleaf design of the crossing into a special drive-in and drive-out system without making use of much terrain. Around 2002, road authorities began using a computerised information and control system to keep traffic flowing to by-pass bottlenecks, and to activate the emergency lane on the right side of the three-lane carriageway as a fourth lane. The success of this innovation is impressive: traffic jams were reduced more than 60 per cent, and are expected to fall further in the near future with new features.

Traffic heads to Frankfurt from all directions; no priority is observable. Consequently a *circulus vitiosus* started: the better the motorways and four-lane main roads were that helped vehicles to access Frankfurt, the more motorised traffic used them. Until the middle of the 1970s, municipal authorities in Frankfurt made every effort to support the motorised traffic. For instance, in 1956 the first parking structure of Germany was opened in downtown Frankfurt. Companies also built parking lots for the cars of their employees. Department stores and private enterprises used the chance to earn money with overground and underground parking sites.

After the first oil crisis in 1974, a new traffic concept emerged, intended to develop better public transport systems to force back the cars that were overwhelming the cities and towns and to avoid the steady expansion of destructive urban sprawl. Large sums of money were invested to build the underground system, to extend express railway lines and to offer bus lines. Still, it was impossible to connect all settlements in the area to public transport facilities. Today, for that reason, the network of six- to eight-lane motorways and four-lane roads in the Rhein-Main region are much more important for the everyday mobility of people than railways, tramways or buses: 78 per cent of commuters come to Frankfurt by motor vehicle, while only 22 per cent use public transport. The percentage of car users in shopping and leisure time traffic is even higher.

Conclusion

Perhaps paradoxically, the *Autobahn* helped Frankfurt to remain a centre of the European railway network, and supported the development of the Rhein-Main airport into one of the busiest places in continental Europe. At the end of the day we see that neither cars nor airplanes really replaced railways: although the railway business declined dramatically in the 1950s and 1960s because the German government supported the supplementary traffic routes, at least the introduction of the high speed network brought people back to the trains. Today mobility experts aspire to find intelligent combinations of the three types of transportation facilities and to facilitate movement from one form of transportation to another – the so-called intermodal traffic.

In Frankfurt a very efficient three-modal traffic hub was implemented in 2000 when German railways completed the new Intercity Express station next to the Frankfurt Rhein-Main Airport and near the *Frankfurter Kreuz*. The seeds of this state-of-the-art solution had been planted about 70 years earlier when construction of the *Autobahn* and the airport started in 1933.

Further scholarly road traffic studies concerning the Rhein-Main area should examine more deeply the relationship between cities and the *Autobahn* network. Road structures inside cities and villages and peoples use of the different transportation modes can be understood and explained if the political, economic and social consequences of the regional *Autobahn* system are brought to mind.

References

Deutsche Reichsbahn-Gesellschaft, ed., *Reichsbahn und Kraftwagenverkehr* (Berlin 1930).

Engel, 'Frankfurt am Main als Hauptknotenpunkt des Landstrassen-Netzes', in Ludwig Landmann and Hans Trumpler, eds, *Jahrbuch der Frankfurter Bürgerschaft 1926* (Frankfurt am Main 1926), 51–6.

Fehlhauer, Gero, *Die Geschichte der Reichsautobahn Chemnitz – Hof* (Reichenbach i. Vogtland 2006).

Flessa, Berthold and Goller, Helmut, *Die Geschichte der Autobahn 1934 bis 2000* (Münchberg 2000).

Fremdling, Rainer, *Eisenbahnen und deutsches Wirtschaftswachstum 1840–1879. Ein Beitrag zur Entwicklungstheorie und zur Theorie der Infrastruktur* (Dortmund 1975).

Fremdling, Rainer, 'Industrialisierung und Eisenbahn. Der Anstoß zur Entwicklung der deutschen Schwerindustrie', in Harm-Hinrich Brandt et al., eds, *Zug der Zeit – Zeit der Züge. Deutsche Eisenbahn 1835–1985*, 2 vols (Berlin 1985), vol. 1, 121–33.

Generalinspektor für das deutsche Straßenwesen, ed., *Drei Jahre Arbeit an den Straßen Adolf Hitlers* (Berlin 1936).

Generalinspektor für das deutsche Straßenwesen, ed., *Vier Jahre Arbeit an den Straßen Adolf Hitlers* (Berlin 1937).

Generalinspektor für das deutsche Straßenwesen, ed., *Fünf Jahre Arbeit an den Straßen Adolf Hitlers* (Berlin 1938).

Gottwaldt, Alfred, *Julius Dorpmüller, die Reichsbahn und die Autobahn. Verkehrspolitik und Leben des Verkehrsministers bis 1945* (Berlin 1995).

Hein, Dieter, 'Vom Finanzplatz zur Industriestadt: Frankfurt 1871–1914', in Werner Plumpe and Dieter Rebentisch, eds, *'Dem Flor der hiesigen Handlung'. 200 Jahre Industrie- und Handelskammer Frankfurt am Main* (Frankfurt am Main 2008), 128–55.

Heinemeyer, Walter, *Das Werden Hessens* (Marburg 1986).

Kaftan, Kurt, *Der Kampf um die Autobahnen. Geschichte und Entwicklung des Autobahngedankens in Deutschland von 1907–1935 unter Berücksichtigung ähnlicher Pläne und Bestrebungen im übrigen Europa* (Berlin 1955).

Kammann, Georg, *Mit Autobahnen die Städte retten? Städtebauliche Ideen der Expressstrassenplanung in der Schweiz 1954–1964* (Zurich 1990).

Kolb, Eberhard, 'Die Reichsbahn vom Dawes-Plan bis zum Ende der Weimarer Republik', in Lothar Gall and Manfred Pohl, eds, *Die Eisenbahn in Deutschland. Von den Anfängen bis zur Gegenwart* (Munich 1999), 109–63.

Lambeck, Alfred, *Die Bergisch-Märkische Autobahn Leverkusen-Kamen 1948–1958* (n. l. 2008).

Mumford, Lewis, *The Highway and the City* (New York 1963).

Niemeyer, Reinhold, *Großstadtprobleme*, unpublished typoscript (Essen 1935).

Niemeyer, Reinhold, *Städtebau und Nahverkehr* (Leipzig 1941).

Otzen, Robert, *Die Autostraße Hansestädte–Frankfurt–Basel. Erläuterungsbericht zum Entwurf der Autostraße* (Hannover 1927).

Planungsverband Ballungsraum Frankfurt/Rhein-Main, ed., *Verkehrsströme in der Region Frankfurt RheinMain. Die Bedeutung einer einheitlichen Basis für die Verkehrsplanung* (Frankfurt am Main 1999).

Pressedienst der Reichsbahn, ed., *Frage und Antwort zum Problem Gütertransport auf Eisenbahnen und Kraftwagen* (Berlin 1932).

Rappaport, Philipp, and Heller, Karl, *Allgemeine Strassenplanung*, ed. by Hubert Hentrich (Halle a. d. Saale 1928).

Rebentisch, Dieter, 'Die kleine Stadt und der große Markt. Regionale und überregionale Zentralitäten der Stadt Frankfurt am Main 1866–1989', in Heinz Jürgen Priamus and Ralf Himmelmann, eds, *Stadt und Region – Region und Stadt. Stadtgeschichte, Urbanisierungsgeschichte, Regionalgeschichte* (Essen 1993), 51–70.

Reitsam, Charlotte, *Reichsautobahn-Landschaften im Spannungsfeld von Natur und Technik. Transatlantische und interdisziplinäre Verflechtungen* (Saarbrücken 2009).

Repgen, Konrad, Hockerts, Günter, Booms, Hans and Kahlenberg, Friedrich, eds, *Akten der Reichskanzlei. Die Regierung Hitler*, ed. for Historische Kommission bei der Bayerischen Akademie der Wissenschaften und für das Bundesarchiv, part I: 1933/34 (Boppard a. Rh. 1983).

Roth, Ralf, *Das Jahrhundert der Eisenbahn. Die Herrschaft über Raum und Zeit 1800–1914* (Ostfildern 2005).

Roth, Ralf, 'Von der Zollvereinsgründung bis zur Annexion der Stadt, 1834–1870', in Werner Plumpe and Dieter Rebentisch, eds, *'Dem Flor der hiesigen Handlung'. 200 Jahre Industrie- und Handelskammer Frankfurt am Main* (Frankfurt am Main 2008), 80–102.

Roth, Ralf, *Die Herausbildung einer modernen bürgerlichen Gesellschaft. Geschichte der Stadt Frankfurt am Main 1789–1866* (Ostfildern 2013).

Roth, Ralf and Polino, Marie-Noëlle, eds, *The City and the Railway in Europe* (Aldershot 2003).

Ruppmann, Reiner, 'Von der Obersten Bauleitung für Reichsautobahnen zum Amt für Straßen- und Verkehrswesen Frankfurt a. M'., *VSVI Journal*, 1, 2009, 24–34.

Ruppmann, Reiner, *Frankfurt und das Rhein-Main-Taunus-Gebiet – Schrittmacher für das Autobahn-Zeitalter* (Darmstadt 2011).

Schmucki, Barbara, 'Schneisen durch die Stadt – Sinnbild der "modernen" Stadt. Stadtautobahnen und amerikanisches Vorbild in Ost- und Westdeutschland 1925–1975', *WerkstattGeschichte*, 21, 1998, 43–63.

Schmucki, Barbara, *Der Traum vom Verkehrsfluß. Städtische Verkehrsplanung seit 1945 im deutsch-deutschen Vergleich* (Frankfurt am Main et al. 2001).

Schütz, Erhard and Gruber, Eckhard, *Mythos Reichsautobahn – Bau und Inszenierung der 'Straßen des Führers' 1933–1941* (Berlin 1996).

Steininger, Benjamin, *Raum-Maschine Reichsautobahn. Zur Dynamik eines bekannt/unbekannten Bauwerks* (Berlin 2005).

Sutter, Otto Ernst, 'Die Stadt der Straßen', in: Hans Trumpler and Julius Ziehen, eds, *Jahrbuch der Frankfurter Bürgerschaft 1925* (Frankfurt am Main 1925), 127–9.

Todt, Fritz, *Strassenbau und Strassenverwaltung*, unpublished Typoskript (Munich 1932).

Vahrenkamp, Richard, *Autobahnbau in Hessen bis 1943* (Darmstadt 2007).

Vahrenkamp, Richard, 'Planning and Costructing the Autobahn Network in Germany During the Nazi-Period – Styles and Strategies', in Gijs Mom and Laurent Tissot, eds, *Road History, Planning, Building and Use* (Neuchâtel 2007), 87–98.

Vahrenkamp, Richard, *The German Autobahn 1920–1945* (Lohmar 2010).

Walter, Georg, *Eisenbahn und Kraftwagen – ein dringendes Verkehrsproblem* (Berlin 1929).

Weise, Hans-Joachim, *Vom Bau der Autobahn im Schleizer Oberland 1933 bis 1936* (n. l. 2006).

Wirtschaftsamt Frankfurt, ed., *Der rhein-mainische Städtekranz mit seiner Zentrale Frankfurt am Main im südwestdeutschen Wirtschaftsgebiet* (Frankfurt am Main 1924).

Index

AA, see Automobile Association
Aachen 155, 290
AASHO, see American Association of State Highway Officials
Abercrombie, Patrick 320
Aberdeen 139
Ackermann, Michael 298
Adlerwerke 59
Administration des Ponts et Chaussées de Belgique 289
Advisory Committee on Traffic Signs for Motorways 326
air transport 23, 178
aircraft or -planes 23–4, 195
airports 220
Alexandria 9
Algeria 125
Allen, Geoffrey Freeman 137–8
Allen, Ralph 44
Allied Maritime Transport Council 123
Alweg train, see *Alwegbahn*
Alwegbahn 27, 29
America, see United States of America
American Association of State Highway Officials (AASHO) 236
American Automobile Association 6, 254
American Bureau of Public Roads (BPR) 21, 301
American Expeditionary Forces 175
American National Conference on City Planning 9
American Petroleum Institute 238
American Society of Civil Engineer's Outstanding Civil Engineering Achievement 262
Ames, Harry C. 199
Amsterdam 285
Amsterdam Treaty of 1999 301
Amtrak 25
Anaheim 25
Anhalter station 66
Antwerp 290
Argentina 224–5
Arrow, Tartan 141
Arroyo Seco Freeway 249, 261
Asia 133, 150, 221
Associated Container Transportation 143
Association for the Preparation of Highways Hanseatic cities-Frankfurt-Basel, see *Verein zur Vorbereitung der Autostraße Hansestädte-Frankfurt-Basel*
Association for the Study of Automobile Roads, see *Studiengesellschaft für Autostraßen*
Association of German Railway Administrations, see *Verein Deutscher Eisenbahnverwaltungen*
Assozazione Nationale Auto Strade (ANAS) 280
ATM, see *Azienda Tranvie Municipali*
Atterbury, William Wallace 195, 212
Augsburg 53
Austin, Texas 257
Australia 136, 225
Austria 21, 68, 111, 128, 277, 287–8, 302
Autobahn 10, 28, 155, 166, 223, 226, 250, 251, 278–9, 281, 283–8, 298–9, 318, 326, 373–4, 380–81, 383–4, 386–90, 392–3
Autobahn construction 386
Autobahn junction, see *Frankfurter Autobahnkreuz*
Autobahn network 166, 390
Autobahn planning 390
Autobahn routes 301, 392
Autobahn, Swiss 298–9
Autoestradas de Portugal, S.A. 296
autoestradas, Portuguese 296
Automatic Loading System 69, 71

Automobil-Verkehrs- und Übungsstraße (AVUS) 9
automobile, automobiles 14, 19, 23, 49, 57, 59, 62, 157, 161, 171–2, 175–6, 178–9, 182, 185, 220–21, 224–7, 229, 233, 235, 240–41, 247, 264, 278, 281, 286, 296, 303, 323, 339–2, 344, 355, 357, 365–8, 373, 379
automobile, American 347
Automobile Association (AA) 318, 329–31
automobile density 219, 224–6
automobile industry 1, 19, 59, 157, 165, 192, 220, 377
automobile industry, French 182
automobile producers, German 224
automobile traffic 378, 287, 289–91
automobile transport 217, 300, 360
Automobile Thoroughfare and Exercise Road, see *Automobil-Verkehrs- und Übungsstraße*
automobility 32, 357, 392
autopista 288, 297, 303
autoroute, autoroutes 289, 293–4, 298
autoroute de Normandie 287
autoroutes de penetration 290
autoroutes urbaines, see expressways
autosnelwegen 285–7, 289
autostrada 9, 278, 296, 298
autovias 297, 303
Avenue Champs Elysées 294
aviation 260
AVUS, see *Automobil-Verkehrs- und Übungsstraße*
Azienda Nazionale Autonoma delle Strade 9, 359
Azienda Tranvie Municipali (ATM) 358, 360–62, 364–9

B&O, see Baltimore and Ohio Railroad
Baader, Joseph von 43, 47–8, 50–51, 59
Bacon, Roger 45
Balfour Brown Committee 85
Baltimore and Ohio Railroad (B&O) 207–8
Baltimore and Philadelphia Railroad 207
Baltimore, Maryland 3, 195, 199, 205, 210
Banham, Reyner 327
Barber-Greene Company 245
Barcelona 125
Barker, Hugh 138
Barnes, Alfred 320
Barnett, Joseph 252
Barrett, Paul 8, 26
Bartolome, Charles de 82–3
Basle 111, 126, 283–4, 298–9
Bassett, Edward 9
Batavian Republic 285
Baudouin Highway 290
Becker, Frank 283
Bedouce, Albert 191
Beeching, Richard 138, 140–42, 323
Beharrell, George 86–8
Beijing-Guangzhou High-Speed Railway 25
Bel Geddes, Norman 249–50, 263
Belgian Bridge and Road Administration, see *Administration des Ponts et Chaussées de Belgique*
Belgium 21, 51, 109, 125, 277, 285, 289–91, 293, 301–3, 325–6
Belgrade 57
Bell, Robert 98
Bellefontaine 241
Ben Line 143
Berg, Geerke van den 136
Bergamo 279
Berkinshaw, John 44
Berliet 175, 182
Berlin 4–5, 9, 53–5, 65–6, 121, 134, 361, 377, 384
Berlin Industrial Exposition 55
Bern 298
Betjeman, John 327
Béziers 182
bicycle, bicycles 4, 291, 355, 379
bicycle industries 377
bicyclists 235
Bierbaum, Otto Julius 59
Birmingham 49, 139, 315–16, 319
Birmingham Motorway Express 331
Bismarck, Otto von 220
Bleasdale, Cyril 150
Blizard, George 316
Blois 181
Blue Ridge Parkway 248
Blum, Léon 191

Board of Trade Railway Department 79
Bonavia, Michael 88
Bonn 9, 155
Bontekoning, Y.M. 136
Bordeaux 180, 182
Bormann, Martin 166
Bortolotti, Lando 279
Boston 6, 55
Boston Route No. 128 6
Bott, Alan 138
box, boxes, see container
boxcar 204
boxcar freight 201
boxcar LCL transfer station 207
Boyd-Carpenter, John 322
BPR, see Bureau of Public Roads
BRB, see British Railways Board
Breda 285
Bremen 53, 70, 283
Brescia 279
BRF, see British Road Federation
Brides 173
BRISA, see *Autoestradas de Portugal, S.A.*
Bristol Corporation 294
Bristol Turnpike Trust 294
Britain, see Great Britain
Britannia 277
British Freight Transport 12
British Intelligence Service 22
British Rail 14, 136, 139, 141–3, 145–9
British Rail's Freightliner 137
British Railways Board (BRB) 138–41, 143, 145, 147–8
British Road Federation (BRF) 22, 315, 317–19, 322, 326
British Road Services 141, 145
Broek, G.J. van den 286
Bronx River Parkway 246
Brooklyn Bridge 255
Brooks, Tony 330–31
Browne, John Hutton Balfour 84, 89
Brüning, Heinrich 153–4, 162
Brunner, Christopher 320
Brussels 50, 289–91
Buckinghamshire 332
Buffalo 199
bulk cargo 158
bulk goods 164
bulk shipments 186
Bundesbahn, see *Deutsche Bundesbahn*
Bundesrepublik Deutschland 31, 157, 168, 226, 389–90
Bundesstraßen 390
Bureau of Public Roads (BPR) 17, 20, 234–6, 238, 241–2, 248, 250–53, 255–6, 329
Bureau voor de Waterstaat 285
Burgin, Leslie 319
Burnham, Daniel 7
Burnham plan of 1909 7
Burstall of Edinburgh 47
bus, buses 4, 15–16, 26–7, 60, 62, 154, 173, 177, 180–81, 195, 223, 247, 263, 323, 344, 347, 349, 357–8, 360, 362, 364–7, 369, 392
bus competition, see competition between rail and road
buses, horse-drawn 4, 62
business travel 53
Busseau-sur-Creuse 177
Butler, Joseph 110
Butterley Iron Works 121

Caen 180
Calais 57, 288
California High-Speed Rail 25
California 256, 263
Calvino, Italo 355
Camborne 47
Camphausen, Ludolf 47, 49–50, 57
Canada 3, 56, 225, 325
car, cars, see automobile
car density, see automobile density
car, flying 260
car industry, see automobile industry
car mobility, see automobility
car production, see automobile industry
car transport, see automobile transport
Carde 182
Cardozo, Benjamin 208
cargo container, see container
cargo freight, see freight
Carlisle (Kingmoor) 135
Carnforth 319
Caron, François 185
Carreteras Nacionales de España 297

Carriage of Goods at Sea Act 202
carriages, horse-drawn 171
carriageways 291, 392
Carter, Bruce 330
carts 4, 49, 174
Castle, Barbara 139
Caterpillar Tractor Company 244–5
Central Office of Information 329
Central Park in New York 8, 246
century of railways, see railway age
chambers of agriculture 189
chambers of commerce 160, 167, 189–90
chambers of industry and commerce 153, 156–7, 161–2
Channel Tunnel 148–9, 151, 222–3
Charlottenburg 9
Chautemps, Camille 191
Chemin de fer du Nord, see *Compagnie du chemin de fer du Nord*
Cherbourg 180
Chesapeake Bay 195
Chiasso 299
Chicago 7–8, 26, 29, 32, 55, 198, 210
Chicago and North Western Railway 198
Chicago, North Shore and Milwaukee Railroad 206
China 24–5, 150
Chivasso 368
Cincinnati 196
Cincinnati, Lawrenceburg and Aurora Interurban Railway 197
Citroën 182, 184
City and Ring Railway, see *Stadt- und Ringbahn*
city-beautiful planners 246
Clay, Lucius D. 17
Clermont-Ferrand 181
Cleveland 199, 250
coach, coaches 4, 48–9, 56, 60, 62–3, 65, 374
coach driver 62
Coalbrookdale 43
coastal shipping 105
Collins, Michael 138
Cologne 9, 153, 155, 165, 275, 387, 390
Colorado highway 262
Colvin, Brenda 327
combustion engine 77, 222, 233
Commercial and Motor Users' Federation 84
Commission for European Economy of the United Nations 276
Committee of Nuremberg 48, 57
Committee of the House of Lords on the Prevention of Road Accidents 319
commuters 5, 390, 392
Como 278
Compagnie de l'Est (Est) 176
Compagnie des chemins de fer de Paris à Orléans (PO) 176–7, 180
Compagnie des chemins de fer de Paris-Lyon-Méditerranée (PLM) 173–4, 176–9, 181, 185–6, 189–90, 192
Compagnie du chemin de fer du Nord (Nord) 125, 173, 176, 186
Compagnie du Midi 178
Compagnie du Nord, see *Compagnie du chemin de fer du Nord*
competition between rail and road 10, 13–15, 23, 28, 41, 86, 94, 101, 103, 121, 133, 151, 153, 156–7, 160–61, 163, 171, 176–8, 192, 198–9, 203, 206, 222–3, 317, 341–2, 355
concrete road 242
Conference on Rail and Road Transport 317
conflict between rail and road, see competition between rail and road
Congress on Public Transport by Motor Vehicle 175
Conseil national économique 186–7
Conseil supérieur des transports 186
container, containers 13, 16, 24, 69–70, 101, 109–11, 113, 116–20, 122–4, 126, 128–9, 133, 140, 143, 146–7, 159, 195–8, 200–217, 209–10
container shipment 199, 205
Container Terminal Altenwerder (CTA) 71
container terminals 70
container traffic 123, 125, 144
container trains 142
container trucks 115
containerisation 16, 69–70, 110, 112, 195–6, 199, 204, 210, 212
containers, British Rail's 141
containers, French 125

containers, London Midland and Scottish Railway 114
Conteno, Georges 348
Cook County, Illinois 250, 258
Corn, Joe 260
County of London Plan 320
Courtalain 180
Coutances 180
Crespi, Silvio 109, 121, 123
Crompton, Gerald 92
Crowe, Sylvia 327
Crowthorne, Berkshire 292
CTA, see Container Terminal Altenwerder
Cugnot, Josef 46
Culemeyer Street Roller, see *Culemeyer-Straßenroller*
Culemeyer, Johann 65
Culemeyer-Straßenroller 65–7
Curr, John 43–4

DAF, see *Deutsche Arbeitsfront*
Dardiff 139
Darlington 44
Darmstadt 153, 387, 392
Dautry, Raoul 186–8, 190–92
Davies, Russell 147
Dawes, Charles Gates 158
Dawes plan 158, 162, 167
De Ardense Autosnelwegen 290
Debon, Louis 173
Defense Highways 10
Delanghe, G. 175
Delft 286
Den Haag 287
Den Haag-Rotterdam Rijksweg 286
Denmark 325
Department of Transport by British Rail 145
Departmental Committee of the Board of Trade 79, 84
Deputy Head of Operations at PLM 175
Derby Canal Railway 44
Derby, UK 121–2
Derbyshire 110
deregulation 15, 104, 148, 168
Detroit, Michigan 242, 249, 253, 256
Deutsche Arbeitsfront 126
Deutsche Bundesbahn 4, 30, 70
Deutsche Reichsbahn-Gesellschaft (DRG) 4, 11, 14–15, 65–6, 123–4, 154, 157–8, 160–67, 223, 281, 379–80, 384
Deutscher Lloyd 70
Deutscher Straßenbau-Verband (German Road Construction Association) 379
Deutsches Reich 378–9, 383, 387
Dinard 180
Dirección General de Carreteras 297
docks 140
Dodgson, John 142–4
Doncaster 322
door-to-door service 65, 115, 124, 129, 164, 173, 380
Dorpmüller, Julius 11, 15, 164, 166, 384
Dortmund 165
Douarnenez-Tréboul 177
Doumergue, Gaston 186
DRG, see *Deutsche Reichsbahn-Gesellschaft*
Driver, Bryan 150
Droege, John 113
Duaner, D. 175
Duchy of Savoy 357
Duisburg 165
Duke of Bridgewater 222
Dunkirk 111
Durham 44
Dürrenberg 64–5, 67
Düsseldorf 155
Dutch Highway Association 289

E-roads, see road system, European
Earlestown Works 120
East Africa 123
Eastman, Joseph B. 195–6, 201, 211–12
École nationale des ponts et chaussées, see *L'École nationale des ponts et chausses*
Edinburgh 139
Eindhoven 126
Eisenbahnverkehrsordnung 164
Eisenhower, Dwight D. 17
Elbeuf 180
Electric Society of Northern Italy, Ltd. 358
Ellis Mills 3

Emmerich 286
England, see Great Britain
Enola yards 206
Erie and the New Haven railway 204
Esch, Lallange 293
Esslingen 53
estradas nacionais 296
Europe 13–14, 21–2, 24, 31, 42, 51–3, 55–9, 68–9, 95, 109, 112, 120–21, 128–9, 134–5, 157, 162, 221, 224, 230, 275–6, 296–7, 301–2, 332, 366, 389
European Commission 287, 301
European Ministers of Transport (CEMT) 300
European Union 134, 296–7
Evaux-les-Bains to Parsac-Gouzon line 177
Evreux 180
Expanded Road Programme 322
expressway, European 290, 385
expressways, express highways 20, 246, 250, 264, 290, 299, 379

Federal Aid Highway Act 17
Federal Coordinator of Transportation 195, 211
Federal German Railway, see *Deutsche Bundesbahn*
Federal Highway Administration (FHWA) 243, 261–3
Federal Republic of Germany, see *Bundesrepublik Deutschland*
Fédération nationale des transports français (FNTF) 191
Federation of British Industry 84
Felixstowe 136, 140, 151
Felixstowe road hauliers 147
Felletin 177
Fenwick fork lift trucks 123
FHWA, see Federal Highway Administration
Fiat 27–8
First World War 5–6, 14, 28, 57, 91, 94, 99, 111, 153, 155, 171, 173, 196–7, 200, 226, 229, 244, 341, 348, 356, 360, 377
Fitch, Benjamin 196
Flanders 291
Flandin, Pierre-Etienne 187
Florence 279, 357
Ford Company 225, 227
Ford, Henry 227, 283, 362, 369
Ford Model T 224
Ford tractor 126
Forshaw, J.H. 320
Forte, Charles 332
Fouga 182
France 3, 6, 13, 15, 21, 56, 110–11, 121, 124, 157–8, 171, 182, 225, 230, 257, 277, 287, 294–5, 302–3, 339, 381
Frankel, Marvin 140
Frankfurt am Main 26–31, 53, 55, 60–61, 123, 278, 283, 373–7, 380–81, 383–90, 392–3
Frankfurter Autobahnkreuz 390, 392–3
free roads 251
freeway, freeways 9, 20, 234, 240, 246, 250–53, 258–9, 261–4, 296, 303
freeway, American 19–20, 233–4
freeway construction 239
freeway network 297
freeway system, urban 248
freight 32, 48, 81, 91, 95, 113, 124, 159
freight business 128, 147
freight car 64–5
freight carriers 153
Freight Forwarder Act of 1942 211
freight haulage business 78, 87
freight locomotives 135
freight market 112, 135, 145
freight prices, pricing 92, 99
freight rates, see tariffs, freight
freight revenue 93
freight stations 70, 208
freight terminals 99, 115–16, 206
freight traffic 167, 186, 206
freight trains 70
freight vehicles 134, 172, 181, 323
Freightliner 133, 138–40, 142–7, 149–50
Freightliner Board 150
Freightliner business 14
Freightliner terminals 141
Freightliner train 137
French Automobile Club 172

Frola, Secondo 358
Fürth 44, 51
Futurama Highways and Horizons 10, 249–50, 253, 263

Gattie, Alfred 114
Gattie Scheme 114
Geary-Khamis dollar 229
Geddes, Norman Bel 10
Gélis, Louis 343
General Motors 10, 17, 249, 259
General Rates Classification 80
General Road Directorate, see *Dirección General de Carreteras*
General Road Plan of 1939–1941 297
Generalverkehrsplan (General Transport Plan) 30
Geneva 298–9
George Washington Memorial Parkway 8
German Democratic Republic 281
German Railway Company, see *Deutsche Reichsbahn-Gesellschaft*
German Reich, see Germany
German Roads Delegation 22, 315, 318–19, 326
Germany 3–4, 6, 11, 13–15, 21–2, 44–5, 47–8, 51–3, 55–6, 60, 63, 69, 116, 121, 123–4, 153–4, 156–9, 167, 182, 186, 222–3, 225–6, 230, 250, 277, 282–3, 285–6, 293, 300–302, 318–19, 325–6, 377, 382, 392
Gesellschaft für Oberbauforschung M.B.H. 121
Gesellschaft zur Vorbereitung der Reichsautobahnen e.V. (GEZUVOR) 385, 389
Gibb, George 145
Gibson, Thomas 92
Giessen 387
Giupponi, Luigi 360
Glasgow 138–9, 141
Glasgow's Gushetfaulds terminal 141
Glenwood Canyon, Colorado 262
Gloucester Carriage and Wagon Works 121
Gloucester, UK 121
Glünder, Friedrich 44
Godfernaux, Raymond 193
Good Roads Movement 226
Goods Clearing Scheme 114
Goods Managers Committee 113, 116
goods, see freight
goods coaches, see freight car
goods station, see freight stations
goods terminals, see freight terminals
goods traffic, see freight traffic
goods transport, see transport, freight
goods vehicle, see freight vehicles
Good-Year 329
Gordon, David 47
Gordon-England, Eric C. 323
Gotha 121
Gothaer Wagonfabrik A.G. 121, 124
Gotthard 68
Gotthard Railway Line 298
Göttingen 60
Grahame, C. 121
Grande Rocade 295
grands itineraries internationaux 295
Great Britain, see also United Kingdom 13–14, 21, 22–3, 44, 47, 95, 104, 109–10, 121, 125, 128, 133–5, 153, 156, 157–8, 164, 182, 186, 200, 218, 221–2, 225, 230, 291–2, 301–3, 322, 325, 332–3
Great Central Debating Society 98
Great Depression 171, 181, 200, 203, 206, 211, 220, 221, 229
Great Western Railway 93, 118
Greater London Plan of 1944 320
Greene, Sidney 141
Grenoble 173
Griffiths, Julius 47
Grimpret, Cyrille 185
Gruber, Eckhard 282
Gruppo Trasporti Torinesi (GTT) 369
Güterkraftverkehrsgesetz 167
Gurney, Goldsworthy 47

HaFraBa, see *Verein zur Vorbereitung der Autostraße Hansestädte-Frankfurt-Basel*
Hamburg 53, 71, 123, 283–4
Hancock, Walter 47
Hansard 114
Harrisburg 10, 206
Harrison, Anthony J. 142

Hartmannsgruber, Friedrich 282
Harwich 140
Hascher, Michael 111, 128
Haussmann's plans for Paris 7
Hautsch, Johann 45
Hays, Will H. 197
Hayuth, Yehuda 136
Healey Mills, Wakefield 135
Heidelberg 383–4
Hendon 138
Heysham 139
High Speed Ground Transportation Act of 1965 24
Higher Transport Committee, see *Conseil supérieur des transports*
highway, highways 8–9, 16–17, 20, 22, 28, 206, 210, 233, 249, 252, 254, 258, 262, 277–8, 280–82, 296–7
highway, American 235–6, 250, 253
highway, automatic 264
Highway Bill 251
highway building or highway construction 14, 22, 237, 278–80, 287, 291, 302
Highway Code Booklet 329
highway design 243, 246
highway engineers 250, 262
highway, federal 226
highway funding 240
highway, Italian 289
highway, German 289
highway network or system 8, 22, 223, 226, 288, 293, 297
highway network, Belgian 289
highway network, European 21–2, 275, 278, 299, 302, 386
highway planning 250
highway program 298
Highway Revenue Act of 1956 17
Hill, J. 47
Hitler, Adolf 21, 163–6, 223, 281, 283, 383–5
Hoboken, New Jersey 69
Hoch-Smith Resolution 203, 205–6
Höchst 381
Hof, Willy 283
Holland, see The Netherlands
Holyhead 49, 143
Hoover, Heribert 253
Hopkins, Valerie 328
Horniman, Roy 110, 114
House of Commons 78, 87
Houston 69
Huckepackverkehr 69
Hull 139
Hunterston 136
Huygens, Christiaan 45
hyperinflation of 1923 378

IBM 251
ICB, see International Container Bureau
ICC, see International Chamber of Commerce
ICC, see Interstate Commerce Commission
Illinois 239
Illinois Highway Department 243
Immingham 136
Imperial Chemical Industries 138
Imperial Federation of the Automobile Industry 161
India 3, 56
Indiana 239
Industrie- und Handelskammer, see chambers of industry and commerce
infrastructure 7, 14, 17, 19, 21, 27, 45, 48, 50, 69–70, 85, 111, 150–51, 154, 187, 220–21, 224, 226, 275, 283, 285, 296, 298–9, 301, 304, 355, 358, 364, 370, 374, 379, 387
inland navigation 105, 158
Institution of Civil Engineers 293
Institution of Highways and Transportation 293
Intermetro 368
intermodality 16, 62, 68, 72, 111, 115, 129, 136–7, 141, 147, 150, 195–7, 206
International Chamber of Commerce 70, 111, 186, 120
International Container Bureau (ICB) 66, 70, 122–6
International Container Committee (ICC) 112, 114, 120–23
International Container Competition 119
International Harvester 227
International Organisation for Standardisation (ISO) 111

International Road Federation (IRF) 22, 301
Interstate and Defense Highways 20, 239–40, 245, 252, 258, 263
Interstate Commerce Act of 1887 208
Interstate Commerce Commission (ICC) 196, 199–206, 209–12
Interstate Highway Act 239
Interstates, see Interstate and Defense Highways
Ireland 143
Irish Free State 125
Irun 288
ISO container 129, 133
Italian State Railways 123
Italy 13, 21–2, 26, 59, 111, 121, 123, 225, 230, 257, 277–8, 280, 283, 301–3, 325, 355, 357

Japan 18, 24
Javary, Paul-Emile 186
Jayot, Émile 344, 346
Johnson, Lady Bird 261
Joy, Stewart 140, 142, 144

Kaftan, Kurt Gustav 57–8, 283
Karlsruhe 387
Keynes, John Maynard 221, 283
Keystone Container Car Company 198, 209
Kirby, David 150
Kirchberg 293
Klink, Arjen van 136
Köln 123
Kondratiev cycle or Kondratiev wave 217, 221, 227, 229
Kornrumpf, Martin 283
Kraftverkehrs AG Westfalen 158
Kraftwagen-Betriebsverband (RKB) 165

L&Y, see Lancashire and Yorkshire Railway
L.C.L. Corporation 209
L'École nationale des ponts et chausses 241, 294–5
Lafayette, Indiana 347
Laffly 182, 184
Lancashire 110, 114
Lancashire and Yorkshire Railway (L&Y) 81, 115, 114
Lancaster 322
Lancia factory 368
Land, Edwin 260
Land, Peter 150
Landmann, Ludwig 377, 380
Lansing 256
Lärmer, Karl 281
Larroque, Dominique 350
Latour, Bruno 340
Lausanne 298
Lay, Maxwell G. 8, 20, 26
LCL, see less-than-carload-lot
Le Corbusier 26, 347
Le Croisic 177
Lebon, André 186–7
Leeds 134, 139
Lehigh Valley Railroad 199, 206, 210
Leipzig 64–5, 153
Lely, Cornelis 286
Lemon, Ernest J.H. 115
Lenzburg 298
Less Than Carload Lot Corporation 197
less-than-carload-lot (LCL) 196, 210
less-than-carload-lot (LCL) boxcars 198
less-than-carload-lot (LCL) business 197
less-than-carload-lot (LCL) rates or -tariffs 205, 208
less-than-carload-lot (LCL) shipments 207
LeTourneau machines 245
LeTourneau, Robert G. 244/245
lift vans 110, 115
Limoges 180
Lincoln Highway Association 254
Lings Colliery Line 110
Lippert, Frank 153
Lips, Michael Alexander 47–8, 50–51, 57, 59
Lisbon 296
List, Friedrich 62–3
Little Eaton Gangway 110
Liverpool 44, 50, 110, 139, 316
Liverpool and Manchester Railway (LMR) 3, 11, 110
Lloyd, Thomas Ifan 315, 322–3, 325
LMR, see Liverpool and Manchester Railway

LMS, see London Midland and Scottish Railway
LNER, see London and North Eastern Railway
LNWR, see London and North Western Railway
loading process 62
locomotives, English 45
locomotives, steam 45
London 12, 47, 49, 55, 92, 111, 114, 123, 126, 128, 139, 141, 158, 292–3, 315–16, 319, 322, 325–6
London and North Eastern Railway (LNER) 12, 91–4, 97–8, 101, 105, 118, 120
London and North Western Railway (LNWR) 78, 85–8
London and Paddington Steam Carriage Company 47
London Midland and Scottish Railway (LMS) 87, 92–3, 105, 111, 113–14, 116–18, 120, 126, 129, 138
London School of Economics 116
London-Yorkshire motorway 322
Long Island and West Chester Parkways 246
Long Island Motor Parkway 8–9
Long Island Parkway Commission 8
Looten. M. 347
lorries, see trucks
Los Angeles 9, 31, 249, 253
Lötschberg-Simplon axis 68
Louis XV 294
Louisville, Kentucky 347
Louviers 180
Lowe, David 138
Lübeck 283
Luca, Giuseppe de 279
Lucerne 298
Lucien Lainé 287/288
Luik (Lüttich/Liège) 290
Luxembourg 21, 277, 290, 293, 302–3
Lyon 192

MacAdam, John Loudon 48, 241, 294
macadamisation 48, 157, 241, 244, 294, 296
MacDonald, Thomas H. 235, 251, 254
Macmillan, Harold 291, 326
Maddison, Angus 229
Madrid 125, 288, 297
Magnat, Joseph 173
Main International Traffic Arteries 300
Maine 239
Mainz 60
Management Consortium Bid Ltd. 149
Manchester 44, 50, 139, 218, 222
Mannheim 165, 383–4
Margetts, Fred 138, 142
Mariage, André 344–5
Marples, Ernest 329
Marquett 140
Marseilles 125, 182
Marshal Plan 21, 301
Martin, Robert 330
mass motorisation 16–17, 19, 21–2, 27, 29, 227, 236, 280, 286, 303, 363, 370
mass transport 360, 369
Massachusetts 237
Massard, Émile 347
McCormick Warehouse 208–9
McKay, John P. 358
Mclean, Malcolm 69–70, 111, 195–6, 201, 212
Mechelen 51
Mellerowicz 161
Mer 181
Merchants Warehouse Company 208
Merritt Parkway 250, 261
Metro 342
Metropolitana Torino Ltd. 368
Mexico 325
Mexico City 255
Michelin 182, 345
Michigan 256
Michigan Highway Department 251
Midland Railway 78, 81, 85
Midlands 317
Milan 9, 121, 278–80, 301
Millbrook terminal 147
Ministero delle Communicazioni 361
Ministry of Public Works 188–9, 191
Ministry of Transport 12, 80
Minneapolis 198, 255
Minnesota 254, 262
Missouri Pacific Railroad 199

mobile steam engines 11
mobility 1, 18–19, 28, 32, 48, 72, 220, 233–4, 275–6, 356, 369
Moch, Jules 186
Modernisation Plan of 1955 135
monopoly 92, 128, 158, 160, 162–5, 167, 193
Montagu of Beaulieu, John 316
Mörfelden 388
Morocco 125
Morris Motor Company 112
Moses, Robert 8, 246, 248
motorbuses, see buses
motorcar, see automobile
motorcar manufacturer, see automobile industry
Motor Carrier Act of 1935 156, 211
motor lorries, see trucks
motor traffic, see traffic
motor transport, see transport
motor vehicle, see automobile
motorisation 1, 6–7, 19, 22, 26, 28, 32, 161, 224, 227, 355, 364, 368–9, 378, 390, 392
motorists 238
motorway, motorways 22, 220, 278, 289, 291, 296–7, 302, 315, 318, 320, 322–3, 325–6, 328, 330–31, 333, 355, 364, 392
Motorway Achievement Trust 293
motorway backbone, see motorway network
motorway construction 292
motorway network 13, 134–5, 292, 300, 320
motorway system, see motorway network
motorways, British 293, 315–16
Motorways Working Panel and Traffic Engineering Committee 327
Mount Vernon Memorial Highway 248
Moveable Connecting Rail 69
Mugniot, Eugène 192
Müller-Raemisch, Hans-Reiner 29–30
Mumford, Lewis 7
Munich 57, 153, 384
Municipal Tram Company, see *Azienda Tranvie Municipali*
Münster, Sebastian 43
Murdoch, William 47
Musnier, René 185–6
Mussolini, Benito 9, 278–9, 283
Myers, Geoffrey 150

Nairn, Ian 327
Nantes 180
Naples 279
Napoleon 285, 294
Nash, Phillip 81–2, 84, 89
Natchez Trace Parkway 248
National Alliance of Commercial Road Transport Associations and Federations 81, 84
National Carloading Corporation 209
National Economic Council, see *Conseil national économique*
National Environmental Policy Act of 1970 261–3
National Federation of Road Hauliers 184
National Freight Company 209
National Freight Corporation (NFC) 137, 139, 143, 145
National Interregional Highway Planning Committee 10, 17, 251
National Roadway Plan of 1946 296
National System of Interstate and Defense Highways 233, 253
National Union of Railwaymen (NUR) 141
Navy Seabees 245
Nebraska 257
Nederlandsche Vereeniging voor Autosnelwegen (NEVAS) 21, 286, 289
NER, see North Eastern Railway
Ness, James 139
Netherlands, see The Netherlands
Neu-Isenburg 388
Newcastle 139
New Deal 249, 283
New Haven 203
New Jersey Highway 247
New Jersey, Massachusetts 237, 239, 256, 259, 263
New Jersey Turnpike 253
New York 5, 8, 25, 46, 55, 69, 198, 205, 210, 239, 246, 248, 255, 347
New York Central Railroad (NYC) 196, 198–200, 202, 204–6, 209–10, 212

New York Railroad Company 16
New Zealand 225
Newton, Isaac 45
Nickel Plate Road 209
Niemeyer, Reinhold 385–8
Nogent 180
Nord, see *Compagnie du chemin de fer du Nord*
Normandy 287, 295
North Africa 125
North America 24, 52, 55, 224
North Dakota 257, 262
North Eastern Railway (NER) 12, 92–3, 97, 99
North London Line 151
North Rhine-Westphalia in Germany (*Ruhrgebiet*) 290
North Western & Midland Group 85
Northern and Western Motorway 316
Northern French Railway 111
Northern Ireland 126
Nottingham 143
NSDAP 383–4
Nuneaton 151
Nuremberg 44, 51
Nuremberg committee, see Committee of Nuremburg

Oakwood, Ohio 257
Ocean and Eastern Parkways 8
OCL, see Overseas Containers Ltd.
Offenbach 55, 380
Office of Road Inquiry (ORI) 20, 235
Officine Mechaniche Italiane 121
Ohio 239
Ohio Highway Department 245
oil crisis 27, 31, 143, 290–91, 356–7, 367, 369, 392
Oklahoma 239
Olmsted, Frederick Law 8, 246
omnibus, see bus, buses
Oostende 289–90
Orange, Maurice Prince of 46
Ord, Louis G. 115
Organisation for Standardization (ISO) 70
Ostia 279
Östreichische Bundesbahn (Austrian state Railway) 68
Otzen, Robert 278, 383
Outer Drive 249
Outram, Benjamin 110
Overseas Containers Ltd. (OCL) 138, 143
Owen Williams and Partners 327

Padua 279
Paganon, Joseph 172, 187
Palmer, William 47
Par, Cornwall 139
Paris 26–7, 29, 55, 57, 70, 120, 123, 125, 173, 176, 180–81, 192, 285, 287–8, 294, 339–40, 343, 347–8, 350, 368
Paris-Ivry 176
Parker, Peter 145
Parkinson & Cowan, Barker 138
parkway, parkways 8–9, 20, 246–7, 261
Parliamentary Road Group 318
Pasadena Freeway 9
Paterson, Carter 84
Paterson, Frank 150
pavement 41, 49, 240, 243
pedestrians 291, 379
Pennroad Corporation 209
Pennsylvania 237
Pennsylvania Railroad (PRR) 16, 195, 198–200, 202, 204–9, 212
Pennsylvania Turnpike 9, 250
Perronet, Jean Rodolphe 294
Peschaud, Marcel 185
Pevsner, Nikolaus 327
Peyron, Amedeo 368
Philadelphia 46, 199, 205, 208, 347
Pickfords 141
piggyback transport, see *Huckepackverkehr*
Pittsburgh 10, 46, 199
plan voisine 26, 347
PLM, see *Compagnie des chemins de fer de Paris-Lyon-Méditerranée*
Plummer, Alfred 112
Plymouth 47, 139
PO, see *Compagnie des chemins de fer de Paris à Orléans*
Poincaré, Raymond 177
Poitiers 180
Poland 125, 136
Pompeii 279
Pont, Francis du 17

Pontpierre 293
ponts et chausées, see *L'Ècole nationale des ponts et chausses*
Porto 296
Portsmouth, Virginia 255
Portugal 21, 277, 296, 302–3
post companies 41, 48
postal service 42, 60–61
Pouet, Lionel de Tinguy du 185
Pourcel, Auguste 175, 179
Pradel, Sylvia 282
Pralognan 173
Pratt, Major 47
Preston 322
Preston By-pass Motorway 291, 326, 328
privatisation 136, 149–50, 370
Providence 255
PRR, see Pennsylvania Railroad
Prussia 220
Pryke, Richard 142–4
Public Road Office 292
Public Works Administration (PWA) 247, 249
public-private partnership 240
Puerta del Sol 297
Puricelli, Piero 9, 278–80
Pybus, John 88

Quimper 177

RAC, see Royal Automobile Club
rail, rails 23, 32, 41, 43, 49, 57, 89, 105, 128, 133, 147, 186, 223, 355, 370
rail carrier 189
rail companies, see railway companies
rail containers, see railway containers
rail freight 14, 23, 99, 136, 138, 145–6, 199
Rail Freight Group 135
rail haulage, see railway haulage
rail network, see railway network
rail system, see railway system
rail terminal, see railway terminal
rail track, see railway tracks
Rail Transport Ordinance (*Eisenbahnverkehrsordnung*
rail transport, see railway transport
Railfreight Distribution (RfD) 147–9
Railfreight International 147
railroad, railroads, see railway, railways
Railroad Commission of Texas 199
railroad freight, see rail freight
railroad industry, see railway industry
rails, cast-iron 44
rails, wooden 44
railway, railways 10, 19, 23, 41, 43, 45, 48–50, 57, 62, 71, 80, 82, 85–8, 91–2, 95, 98–9, 104, 109, 111–12, 115, 119, 125, 129, 153, 157–9, 161–3, 166–7, 171–2, 175–80, 185–8, 192, 197, 203, 205, 209–12, 221–2, 224, 226, 233, 247, 280, 288, 303, 315, 317, 356, 364, 373–4, 376, 392–3
railway age 4, 59
Railway and Canal Commission 84
railway business 373
Railway C.O.D. 100
railway car 195
railway cargo 380
Railway Clearing House (RCH) 12, 78–9, 85, 96, 106, 113, 116
railway companies 11, 24, 59–60, 62, 80–83, 85, 89, 109, 113, 116–17, 128, 157, 171–2, 186, 188, 222, 369
Railway Companies Association 85
railway companies, British 100–101
railway construction 60, 285
railway containers 13, 119
Railway Conversion League (RCL) 22, 315, 322–4
Railway Country Lorry Service 101
railway, diesel 25
railway, double track 50
railway, Dutch 125
railway, electrical 4, 23, 31, 55–6, 358
Railway Executive Committee 79
railway freight, see rail freight
railway haulage 89
railway industry 203, 206, 211
Railway Information Bureau 116
railway, interurban 379
railway knot 60
railway line 10
railway manufacturers 182

railway modernisation 333
railway monopoly 84, 112
railway network 2, 7, 4, 24, 32, 52, 56, 59–62, 296, 299, 369
railway network, American 3
railway network, British 78
railway network, German 159
railway network, urban 29, 31
railway organisation 77
Railway Rates Tribunal 80
Railway reform 12
railway sector 53
railway station 61–2, 286
railway, Swiss 67, 126, 128
railway system 4, 11, 26, 31, 50, 55, 62–3, 363
railway technology 135
railway terminal 144
railway timetable 380
railway tracks 149, 355
railway transport 11, 13, 23, 32, 62, 77, 134, 142, 160, 184, 317, 360, 369
railway, wooden 43
railway workers 98, 102, 105
Railways Act of 1921 12–13, 77–80, 82, 85, 91–2, 113
railways, Austrian 67, 288
railways, British 12–13, 91, 102, 110–12, 116, 128, 135, 138–9, 150, 323
railways, European 3, 24, 393
railways, French 15, 125, 172
railways, German 67, 124, 155, 158, 393
railways, Hungarian 128
railways, Netherlands 126
railways, UK, see railways, British
railways, US 159, 226
Rates Advisory Committee 81, 83–4
RATP, see *Régie autonome des transports Parisiens*
Raymond, Stanley 139–40
RCH, see Railway Clearing House
RCL, see Railway Conversion League
Reading Railroad 207–8
Régneville 180
regulation 11–15, 68, 77–80, 83, 86, 88, 92, 103, 105, 111, 154, 156, 161–3, 167, 176, 188, 190, 210, 142, 263, 317, 325, 328, 362, 387
Reichenbach, Ritter von 47
Reichsautobahn, see *Autobahn*
Reichsbahn, *Reichsbahngesellschaft*, see *Deutsche Reichsbahn-Gesellschaft*
Reichs-Kraftwagen-Betriebsverband (RKB) 166
Reichskraftwagentarif, see tariff
Reichsverband des gewerblichen Kraftverkehrs und der Fuhrbetriebe Deutschlands e.V. 165
Reid, Bob 150
Régie autonome des transports Parisiens (RATP) 339–40
Renault 180, 182
Réseau Ouest-État 173
Reynolds, Joseph 47
RfD, see Railfreight Distribution
Rheinische Verkehrsgesellschaft 157
Richmond 205
Rijkswaterstaat (RWS) 21, 285–7
Rijkswegen 286
Rijkswegenplan of 1927 286–7
Rijswijk 285–6
Riotor, Léon 344
Ripley, William Z. 200
road, roads 21, 23, 32, 41, 89, 105, 128, 133, 147, 178–9, 186, 192, 233–4, 237, 241, 276, 295, 315, 323, 376, 379
Road and Rail Traffic Act of 1933 95
road builders 242, 244, 246, 248, 261–2
road competition, see competition between rail and road
road construction 6, 9, 17, 21–2, 27, 59, 225, 227, 239–40, 244, 286, 293, 378
road engineers 294
road haulage 11–15, 16, 80–85, 89, 91–3, 95, 99, 115, 128–9, 141, 144, 151, 153–7, 159, 161–7, 172
road hauliers 12–15, 81–2, 84, 101–2, 111, 115, 139, 141–2, 159, 165, 167, 172, 182, 187–8
road infrastructure, see road network
road investments 16, 20
road modernisation 2, 10, 14, 19, 21, 23, 26

road network 1, 17–19, 25, 50–51, 60, 62, 276, 285, 294, 323, 391
road network, British 22, 315
road network, Italian 9
road network, US 224
road planning 294
Road Powers for Railways 85
road programme 239
Road Research Laboratory 326–9
road services 83, 86, 189
road system 6, 11, 17, 19, 56, 62, 225
road system, American 235
road system, European 58, 276, 302
road terminals 144
road traffic 49, 55, 392
road transport 3, 11, 13, 15, 32, 41, 55, 62, 77, 80, 82, 112–13, 142, 157–8, 171, 178, 185–6, 191, 224, 317, 389
roads, British 332
Roads Campaign Council 322
roads, French 157
Roadside Beauty 262
roads, intercontinental 226
roads, multi-lane 240
roads, national 182, 296
roads, ordinary 333
road-user fees, see toll roads
roadway 71, 346
Robbins, Stanley C. 142
Rohde, Heidi 153
Rollende Landstraße (RoLa) 67–8
Romains, Jules 342
Rome 65, 112, 120, 279, 280
Romorantin 177
Roosevelt, Franklin Delano 10, 17, 211, 251–2, 283
RoSPA, see Royal Society for the Prevention of Accidents
Rostow, Walt Whitman 220, 227
Rotanks 118
Rotterdam 70–71
Rouen 180, 189
Rouen agreements 190
Rowland, Don 116
Royal Automobile Club (RAC) 318, 322, 329–30
Royal Commission on Transport 89
Royal Society for the Prevention of Accidents (RoSPA) 329
Rugby 134
Russia 3, 24, 56
RWS, see *Rijkswaterstaat*

S- and U-trains 7–8, 27, 30–31, 55, 62, 365, 367, 370
Saar Railways 124
St Albans 322
St Gallen 298
Saint-Nazaire 177
Salford 316
Salisbury, Maryland 195
Salzburg 384
Sampson, Anthony 332
San Antonio 257
San Diego, California 263
San Francisco 25
San Jose 25
Sanderson, Henry 150
SATAL, see *Société auxiliaire de transports d'Alsace et de Lorraine*
SATE, see *Société auxiliaire de transports automobiles de l'Est*
SATOS, see *Société auxiliaire de transports de l'Ouest et du Sud-Ouest*
SATTI, see *Società Anonima Tranvie Torinesi Intercomunali*
Sauvy, Alfred 340, 350
Scharrer, Johannes 47
Schenker 11, 14–15, 157, 163, 165, 223
Schimpff, Gustav 4–5, 7
Schivelbusch, Wolfgang 283
Schnellbahnen, see railway, electrical
Schumpeter, Alois 217, 221–3, 228–9
Schütz, Erhard 282
Scott, Peter 78, 92, 95, 105, 112
sea container 13, 133, 136, 140, 144, 146–7, 149–51
seaports 222, 226
Second World War 3, 13, 16–17, 19, 21–2, 27, 29, 57, 92, 104, 126, 133, 173, 221, 229, 238, 243, 245, 248, 257, 261, 280–82, 286–8, 295, 300–301, 315, 319, 339, 355, 362, 364–5, 389

Secretary of the Railway Research Bureau 110
Seebohm, Hans-Christoph 390
Sellier, Louis 344
Semmering 287
Sennigerberg 293
Service des Ponts et Chaussées 285
Sewell, A.S. 103–4
SGTD, see *Société générale des transports départementaux*
Sheffield 43–4, 139
Shell 329
Sherrington, Charles 110
ship transport 13
shipping 3, 23, 199
ships 133, 195
Sicily 280
Siegen 121
Siegener Eisen-Bahnbedarf Aktiengesellschaft 121
Siemens 55
Silesia 220
SNCF, see *Société nationale des chemins de fer français*
Società anonima elettricità Alta 358
Società anonima tranvie torinesi intercomunali (SATTI) 362, 365
Società Italiana Casse Mobile 123
Società torinese tranway e ferrovie economiche 358
Società tramways di Torino (Tramways Society of Turin) 358
Société anonyme des transports industriels et commerciaux 181
Société auxiliaire de transports automobiles de l'Est (SATE) 15, 179
Société auxiliaire de transports d'Alsace et de Lorraine (SATAL) 15, 179
Société auxiliaire de transports de l'Ouest et du Sud-Ouest (SATOS) 15, 179–180
Société auxiliaire de transports du réseau PLM (TPLM) 15, 179–181, 191
Société de l'autoroute ESCOTA 295
Société de transports auxiliaires de la région du Nord (STARN) 15, 179
Société de transports auxiliaires du réseau Paris-Orléans (STAPO) 15, 179–80
Société des messageries nationales 185
Société des transports auxiliaires des chemins de fer du Midi (STAM) 15, 179
Société des transports en commun de la région Parisienne (STCRP) 343–7, 350
Société générale des transports départementaux (SGTD) 176, 180
Société nationale des chemins de fer français (SNCF) 15–16, 125, 191, 193
Society of Economical Tramways and Railways 358
Society of Motor Manufacturers and Traders 322
South America 224
South Kearney, New Jersey 199
South Pacific 245
Southampton 136, 143, 147, 151
Southern Railway 118
Soviet regime 160
Spain 21, 125, 277, 297, 302–3
Special Roads Bill of 1948 320
Sprague, Frank J. 31
Stadt- und Ringbahn 5, 55
STAM, see *Société de transports auxiliaires des chemins de fer du Midi*
Stamp, Josiah 117
Standard Carloading Corporation 209
STAPO, see *Société de transports auxiliaires du réseau Paris-Orléans*
STARN, see *Société de transports auxiliaires de la région du Nord*
State Highway Department 20, 235, 239
STCRP, see *Société des transports en commun de la région Parisienne*
steam carriage 45–50, 59
steam coach, see steam carriage
steam mobile, see steam carriage
Steininger, Benjamin 283
Stettin 384
Stevens, John 47

Stevin, Simon 45–6
Stockton 44, 139
Stommer, Rainer 281
Stoneway 48
S-train, see S- and U-trains
Strasbourg 57
Straßen des Führers (Roads of the Leader) 386
Stratford 141
street network, see road network
street traffic, see road traffic
street transport, see road transport
streetcar, streetcars 26, 339–40, 345, 348–51
streetcar network or system 8, 26, 29, 350
Studiengesellschaft für Autostraßen 9
subterranean railways, see S- and U-trains
suburban rail network, see S- and U-trains
suburbia, suburbs 5–7, 47, 55, 173, 193, 220, 227, 262, 316, 332, 339, 341–3, 349–51, 360, 374
Swansea 143
Sweden 31, 128, 156, 325–6
Swedish State Railways 128
Switzerland 13, 21, 68, 111, 116, 121, 223, 277, 298, 302

Tait, Alec 150
Tardieu, André 179
tariff 11, 159–60, 162–3, 165, 198–200, 203, 210
tariff, carload 205
tariff, freight 166
tariff, LCL 205
tariff, railway 162
tariffs, freight 62, 166, 204
tax, taxes 24, 80, 178, 186, 188, 236–8, 383
tax, car 303
tax, gas 20, 237–40
tax, petrol 159
tax, road 236, 286
tax-payer 158
taxation 16, 144, 238, 317
taxation, fuel 363
Tea Room Plan of 1946 22, 320–22
Ted Taylor Four 330
terminal 140, 143
Texarkana 257
Texas & Pacific Railway 199
Texas Transportation Institute (TTI) 257–8
The Netherlands 13, 21, 41, 69–70, 127, 156, 257, 277–8, 285, 287, 301–2, 325–6
Thomas Telford Publishing 293
Thoumyre, Robert 191
Thurn and Taxis stagecoach company 374–5
Thwaite, B.H. 315–16
Tindall, Thomas 47
Tinsley, Sheffield 135
Todt, Fritz 14–15, 165, 383–5, 387
toll payment system 296
toll roads or toll motorways 239, 251, 316
Torino 279
tourism 53, 59, 62, 171, 227, 280, 369
tourists 180, 281, 325
TPLM, see *Société auxiliaire de transports du réseau PLM*
traffic 160, 275–6, 323, 333, 389
traffic congestion, see traffic jam
traffic, European 146
traffic jam 300, 316, 392
traffic policy 154
trains 24–5, 223, 351
trains, elevated 27, 29
tram, trams, see tramway, tramways
tram companies, see tramway companies
tram lines, see tramway network
tram network, see tramway network
tram services 181
tramway, tramways 27, 55, 110, 339–40, 347, 358, 360, 364–5, 370, 392
tramway companies 179, 358
tramway, electric 62
tramway, horse-drawn 62
tramway industry 358
tramway network 349, 359–60, 369
Trans-European Road Network (TERN) 301
Trans-European Transport Network (TEN-T) 301
transport 23, 50, 159, 223, 275–6, 339, 341, 373
Transport Act of 1947 77
Transport Act of 1968 139, 145

Transport Act of 1978 145
transport boxes 69
transport, freight 3, 7, 11, 13–14, 16, 53, 56–7, 60, 69, 77, 89, 112, 115, 133–4, 376
transport, goods 223
Transport Holding Co. 141
transport, individual 48, 56–7, 60, 302
transport industry 48
transport infrastructure 45, 355
transport networks 71–2
transport, passenger 5, 7, 16, 53, 56, 60, 160, 223
transport, personal 23
transport policies 6, 77–8, 81, 154, 160, 163, 165–6, 282, 300, 343, 356, 361, 367
transport, public 5, 26, 29, 339, 342, 357–8
Transport Research Laboratory 292
transport system 23, 47, 53
transport, urban 56
transport vehicles, see automobiles
transportation 221–2, 234, 281
Transportation Act of 1920 200–201, 203
Transportation Act of 1940 211
transportation, American 233
Tranvie Municipali (Municipal Tramways Company) 359
Treaty of Versailles 14, 158, 162
Trésaguet, Pierre 294
Trevithik, Richard 47
Trocquer, Yves Le 191
truck, trucks 13, 15, 20, 112, 126, 153–5, 157, 166–7, 171, 173, 184, 195, 199, 223, 226, 240, 242, 247, 303
truck company 165, 223
truck competition 201
truck traffic 14, 160, 297
truck transport 161
Trunk Road Act of 1936 291
trunk roads 294
Turin 26–9, 280, 355–9, 361–2, 365–70
Twenty-foot Equivalent Units (TEU) 70

U- and S-trains, see S- and U-trains
Uhlfelder, Hermann 278
UK, see United Kingdom
underground, see S- and U-trains
Union Internationale des chemins de fer (UIC) 24
United Kingdom 3, 11–15, 28, 52, 56, 69, 109–14, 120, 128–9, 133–4, 151, 161, 257, 379
United Nations Economic Commission for Europe 300
United States of America 3, 6, 8–9, 11, 16–17, 19, 21–2, 24, 28, 31, 56, 111, 116, 153–4, 156, 158, 161–4, 182, 195, 200, 202, 220–22, 224–8, 230, 283, 325–6, 379
United States Army 389
United States Mail 198
Universal Carloading & Distributing 210
Unternehmen Reichsautobahn 384
Unterpflasterstraßenbahn 29
urban mobility 26–7, 62, 355
urban sprawl 392
urbanisation 280
Urquhart, James 150
U-train, see S- and U-trains
Utrecht 285–7
USA, see United States of America

Van Doorne Aanhangwagenfabriek 126
Van Sweringen Lines 209
Vanderbilt Challenge Cup 8
vans, see trucks
Varese 9
Vaux, Calvert 8
vehicles 128, 182, 243, 390, 392
vehicles, horse-drawn 173, 176, 379
Venezuela 325
Venice 119, 121–2, 279
Verdun 155, 175
Verein Deutscher Eisenbahnverwaltungen 10
Verein zur Vorbereitung der Autostraße Hansestädte-Frankfurt-Basel (HaFraBa) 28, 226, 278, 283–4, 286, 298–9, 381–6
Versailles peace treaty, see Treaty of Versailles
Via Verde, see toll payment system
Viareggio 279
Vienna 186, 287
Villefranche-sur-Cher 177

Vinci, Leonardi da 45
Virginia 205, 262
Voies express, see *autoroutes*
Voisin Plan, see *plan voisine*

Walker, Gilbert 92, 95–6, 103–6
Wallonia 291
Warner, Bernard 142, 144
Warrington 319
Warsaw 57
Washington, DC 25, 347
water transport 133
waterway shipping, see waterways
waterways 71, 178, 221–2
Watford 134
Watt, James 45, 47
Wayne County, Michigan 242, 256
Wedgwood, Ralph 97, 99
Wegenfonds 286
Weimar 383
Weimarer Republic 378
Wenk, Gustav 298
West or Western Europe, see Europe
West or Western Germany, see *Bundesrepublik Deutschland*
West Virginia 239
White Motor Company 196
Wiesbaden 387
Willème-Coder 182–3
Williams, Owen 326
Williamson 118
Wilmington, Delaware 246
Wilson, Charles 17
Wilson, Lloyd 118
Wilson, Woodrow 196
Windisch-Hojnacki, Claudia 281
Wohl, Pau 110, 121
Wolkowitsch, Maurice 190
Woodburn, Allan 136
Works Progress Administration (WPA) 249
World Fair in New York 10, 249
World Motor Transport Congress 112, 120
Worsley 222
Würzburg 60, 387

Yago, Glenn 31
York Thruway 253
Yorkshire 93, 136, 292, 325–6

Zeitlin, Graham 137, 144–7
Zonder 285

Modern Economic and Social History Series

General Editor
Derek H. Aldcroft, University Fellow, Department of Economic and Social History, University of Leicester, UK

Derek H. Aldcroft
Studies in the Interwar European Economy
1 85928 360 8 (1997)

Michael J. Oliver
Whatever Happened to Monetarism?
Economic Policy Making and Social Learning in the United Kingdom Since 1979
1 85928 433 7 (1997)

R. Guerriero Wilson
Disillusionment or New Opportunities?
The Changing Nature of Work in Offices,Glasgow 1880–1914
1 84014 276 6 (1998)

Roger Lloyd-Jones and M.J. Lewis with the assistance of M. Eason
Raleigh and the British Bicycle Industry
An Economic and Business History, 1870–1960
1 85928 457 4 (2000)

Barry Stapleton and James H. Thomas
Gales
A Study in Brewing, Business and Family History
0 7546 0146 3 (2000)

Derek H. Aldcroft and Michael J. Oliver
Trade Unions and the Economy: 1870–2000
1 85928 370 5 (2000)

Ted Wilson
Battles for the Standard
Bimetallism and the Spread of the Gold Standard in the Nineteenth Century
1 85928 436 1 (2000)

Patrick Duffy
The Skilled Compositor, 1850–1914
An Aristocrat Among Working Men
0 7546 0255 9 (2000)

Robert Conlon and John Perkins
Wheels and Deals
The Automotive Industry in Twentieth-Century Australia
0 7546 0405 5 (2001)

Sam Mustafa
Merchants and Migrations
Germans and Americans in Connection, 1776–1835
0 7546 0590 6 (2001)

Bernard Cronin
Technology, Industrial Conflict and the Development of Technical Education in 19th-Century England
0 7546 0313 X (2001)

Andrew Popp
Business Structure, Business Culture and the Industrial District
The Potteries, c. 1850–1914
0 7546 0176 5 (2001)

Scott Kelly
The Myth of Mr Butskell
The Politics of British Economic Policy, 1950–55
0 7546 0604 X (2002)

Michael Ferguson
The Rise of Management Consulting in Britain
0 7546 0561 2 (2002)

Alan Fowler
Lancashire Cotton Operatives and Work, 1900–1950
A Social History of Lancashire Cotton Operatives in the Twentieth Century
0 7546 0116 1 (2003)

John F. Wilson and Andrew Popp (eds)
Industrial Clusters and Regional Business Networks in England, 1750–1970
0 7546 0761 5 (2003)

John Hassan
The Seaside, Health and the Environment in England and Wales since 1800
1 84014 265 0 (2003)

Marshall J. Bastable
Arms and the State
Sir William Armstrong and the Remaking of British Naval Power, 1854–1914
0 7546 3404 3 (2004)

Robin Pearson
Insuring the Industrial Revolution
Fire Insurance in Great Britain, 1700–1850
0 7546 3363 2 (2004)

Andrew Dawson
Lives of the Philadelphia Engineers
Capital, Class and Revolution, 1830–1890
0 7546 3396 9 (2004)

Lawrence Black and Hugh Pemberton (eds)
An Affluent Society?
Britain's Post-War 'Golden Age' Revisited
0 7546 3528 7 (2004)

Joseph Harrison and David Corkill
Spain
A Modern European Economy
0 7546 0145 5 (2004)

Ross E. Catterall and Derek H. Aldcroft (eds)
Exchange Rates and Economic Policy in the 20th Century
1 84014 264 2 (2004)

Armin Grünbacher
Reconstruction and Cold War in Germany
The Kreditanstalt für Wiederaufbau (1948–1961)
0 7546 3806 5 (2004)

Till Geiger
Britain and the Economic Problem of the Cold War
The Political Economy and the Economic Impact of the British Defence Effort, 1945–1955
0 7546 0287 7 (2004)

Anne Clendinning
Demons of Domesticity
Women and the English Gas Industry, 1889–1939
0 7546 0692 9 (2004)

Timothy Cuff
The Hidden Cost of Economic Development
The Biological Standard of Living in Antebellum Pennsylvania
0 7546 4119 8 (2005)

Julian Greaves
Industrial Reorganization and Government Policy in Interwar Britain
0 7546 0355 5 (2005)

Derek H. Aldcroft
Europe's Third World
The European Periphery in the Interwar Years
0 7546 0599 X (2006)

James P. Huzel
The Popularization of Malthus in Early Nineteenth-Century England
Martineau, Cobbett and the Pauper Press
0 7546 5427 3 (2006)

Richard Perren
Taste, Trade and Technology
The Development of the International Meat Industry since 1840
978 0 7546 3648 9 (2006)

Roger Lloyd-Jones and M.J. Lewis
Alfred Herbert Ltd and the British Machine Tool Industry, 1887–1983
978 0 7546 0523 2 (2006)

Anthony Howe and Simon Morgan (eds)
Rethinking Nineteenth-Century Liberalism
Richard Cobden Bicentenary Essays
978 0 7546 5572 5 (2006)

Espen Moe
Governance, Growth and Global Leadership
The Role of the State in Technological Progress, 1750–2000
978 0 7546 5743 9 (2007)

Peter Scott
Triumph of the South
A Regional Economic History of Early Twentieth Century Britain
978 1 84014 613 4 (2007)

David Turnock
Aspects of Independent Romania's Economic History with Particular Reference to Transition for EU Accession
978 0 7546 5892 4 (2007)

David Oldroyd
Estates, Enterprise and Investment at the Dawn of the Industrial Revolution
Estate Management and Accounting in the North-East of England, c.1700–1780
978 0 7546 3455 3 (2007)

Ralf Roth and Günter Dinhobl (eds)
Across the Borders
Financing the World's Railways in the Nineteenth and Twentieth Centuries
978 0 7546 6029 3 (2008)

Vincent Barnett and Joachim Zweynert (eds)
Economics in Russia
Studies in Intellectual History
978 0 7546 6149 8 (2008)

Raymond E. Dumett (ed.)
Mining Tycoons in the Age of Empire, 1870–1945
Entrepreneurship, High Finance, Politics and Territorial Expansion
978 0 7546 6303 4 (2009)

Peter Dorey
British Conservatism and Trade Unionism, 1945–1964
978 0 7546 6659 2 (2009)

Shigeru Akita and Nicholas J. White (eds)
The International Order of Asia in the 1930s and 1950s
978 0 7546 5341 7 (2010)

Myrddin John Lewis, Roger Lloyd-Jones, Josephine Maltby and Mark David Matthews
Personal Capitalism and Corporate Governance
British Manufacturing in the First Half of the Twentieth Century
978 0 7546 5587 9 (2010)

John Murphy
A Decent Provision
Australian Welfare Policy, 1870 to 1949
978 1 4094 0759 1 (2011)

Robert Lee (ed.)
Commerce and Culture
Nineteenth-Century Business Elites
978 0 7546 6398 0 (2011)

Martin Cohen
The Eclipse of 'Elegant Economy'
The Impact of the Second World War on Attitudes to Personal Finance in Britain
978 1 4094 3972 1 (2012)

Gordon M. Winder
The American Reaper
Harvesting Networks and Technology, 1830–1910
978 1 4094 2461 1 (2012)

Julie Marfany
Land, Proto-Industry and Population in Catalonia, c. 1680–1829
An Alternative Transition to Capitalism?
978 1 4094 4465 7 (2012)

Lucia Coppolaro
The Making of a World Trading Power
The European Economic Community (EEC) in the GATT Kennedy Round Negotiations (1963–67)
978 1 4094 3375 0 (2013)

Ralf Roth and Henry Jacolin (eds)
Eastern European Railways in Transition
Nineteenth to Twenty-first Centuries
978 1 4094 2782 7 (2013)

Manuel Pérez-García
Vicarious Consumers
Trans-National Meetings between the West and East in the Mediterranean World (1730–1808)
978 1 4094 5685 8 (2013)

Manuela Albertone
National Identity and the Agrarian Republic
The Transatlantic Commerce of Ideas between America and France (1750-1830)
978 1 4724 2136 4 (2014)

Leslie Rosenthal
The River Pollution Dilemma in Victorian England
Nuisance Law versus Economic Efficiency
978 1 4094 4182 3 (2014)

Robert E. Forrester
British Mail Steamers to South America, 1851-1965
A History of the Royal Mail Steam Packet Company and Royal Mail Lines
978 1 4724 1661 2 (2014)

John Woodland
Money Pits: British Mining Companies in the Californian and Australian Gold Rushes of the 1850s
978 1 4724 4279 6 (2014)

For Product Safety Concerns and Information please contact our
EU representative GPSR@taylorandfrancis.com Taylor & Francis
Verlag GmbH, Kaufingerstraße 24, 80331 München, Germany